SWEET HOME CHICAGO

FOURTH EDITION, REVISED AND EXPANDED

The Real City Guide

Edited by Amy Teschner

CHICAGO
REVIEW
PRESS

All photographs by Jim Alexander Newberry, except for the photo on page 194, which is by James Prinz © 1988.

Cover art: *Sweet Lorraine* by Joe Hindley, Chicago.

Published by Chicago Review Press, Incorporated
814 North Franklin Street,
Chicago, Illinois, 60610

Printed in the United States of America

ISBN: 1-55652-161-8

5 4 3 2 1

CONTENTS

FOREWORD

It has been almost twenty years since the first publication of *Sweet Home Chicago*. This city remains the most livable of big American cities. Twenty years later, architecture is flourishing, literature thrives, education is struggling for reform and rebirth, neighborhoods are booming, and there is as much or more good theater and dance than ever. Our mayor has a vision; gargantuan public works projects are planned to push the city into the next millennium. New waves of immigrants add even more color to the cultural tapestry of the city. At the same time, our slums are staggering, public transportation flounders, and black-white relations are a challenge to men and women of goodwill. The gap between rich and poor, privileged and underprivileged widens. The entrenched bureaucracies of the Board of Education and the city colleges get further and further out of touch with schools and students.

Our city is the best and worst of all worlds: a melting pot, a sleaze shop, a fertile delta into which flow innumerable hearty, creative, and desperate souls. Of all the cities in the country, Chicago remains the easiest one in which to open your new restaurant, find a cheap apartment, get involved in neighborhood politics, or find a job. Chicago is all around you. Wide open. Check it out.

Some notes about our original contributors: Dan Rose, author of our political chapter, has gone to work on numerous big-time political campaigns. Sally Banes has become a formidable writer on the performing arts. Don Moore has been instrumental in changing the educational system that he wrote about in the first edition. Steve Seliger has won major class-action suits that have ameliorated some of the legal injustices about which he wrote. With pessimism of reason and optimism of the heart, David Moberg continues to assail injustice and plump for revolution. Susan Gzesh no longer works with children but has become a prominent lawyer and activist.

To a new generation of Sweet Home Chicago writers, hipsters, movers and shakers, citizens in motion, *Sweet Home Chicago* is yours.

—*Tem Horwitz*

INTRODUCTION

Open a copy of the third edition of *Sweet Home Chicago*, written just six years ago, and you'll be transported to another place and time: Harold Washington is mayor, you can ride the bus for 90 cents, and the folks at the Belden Deli on Clark Street will serve you a bagel at 2 A.M.

Now we've got another Daley at the helm, the CTA "fare structure" is more ephemeral than a midwestern spring, and a mammoth CD store stands where the Belden used to be.

When my colleagues and I set out to revise *Sweet Home Chicago*, there was no doubt the book needed basic updating. The architecture chapter was missing important new buildings, many new restaurants, bars, and clubs deserved mention, and the art community had suffered and survived everything from a River North fire that destroyed nine galleries to severe threats of censorship and politically motivated NEA funding. Clearly we needed to refurbish the book for the nineties.

This effort to revise *Sweet Home Chicago* also sent me back to the book's first two editions, published in 1974 and 1977. I was fascinated to find chapters called "Body Awareness," "Occult," and "The Movement," and I began to see ways we could simultaneously update the book and stress its roots. *Sweet Home Chicago* has always been called "The Real City Guide." It has always been a book for people who want to know, enjoy, and participate in the city without spending a lot of money or glossing over pressing urban problems. It seeks to provide resources for Monday afternoon as well as Saturday night, for photocopying something at 4 A.M. as well as discovering the latest in local music. Much more than a guidebook, *Sweet Home Chicago* pays tribute to the city's diversity and size. It reaches beyond the expected listings to various alternative ways to explore a complex and vibrant place.

This acknowledgment of the *entire* Chicago has been our editorial guidepost. The contributors and I have tried to steer *Sweet Home Chicago* back to its original countercultural path by stressing community action. We have not pictured you as one big group of hippies or yuppies, but we have assumed that you associate urban life with the day-to-day realities of work as well as broad opportunities for play. We have tried to cover Chicago's particular twists on city life, from far-flung neighborhoods to an ambitious school reform program. We've tried to address a common interest in running uncomplicated errands, having a good time, and improving Chicago.

So this book is at once completely new (all the chapters have been rewritten) and grounded in a progressive view of city life. The "education" chapter is no longer confined to a listing of area schools and has a new title, "Chicago Schools," because we are in the midst of a crisis in our public education system. The other chapters new to this edition, all of them inspired by the original book, include "Secondhand Shopping," "Performance Art," "Crisis Intervention," "The Environment/Recycling," "Volunteering," and "Activism."

Readers familiar with the three previous editions will notice another change; we no longer have a chapter called "Women," not because we have jettisoned a feminist point of view, but because women comprise more than half the population of our city (and probably our readership). Thanks to two particularly active Chicago feminists, Linda Bubon and Ann Christopherson, who own and operate Women and Children First bookstore, programs and resources geared specifically to women are included in the appropriate chapters throughout the book.

Enthusiastic thanks also go to numerous others who fostered accuracy and variety on these pages, including John Gallagher, Cynthia Gordon, Joe Hindley, Kate Hinely, Tem Horwitz, Eunice Hoshizaki, Laura Larson, Fran Lee, Erin Lydon, Jim Magidson, Elizabeth Schulte, and the many other friends and colleagues who contributed ideas and resources to this fourth edition. I would also like to thank all the book's contributors for sharing their expertise and for writing about Chicago in all its entities, both flattering and stark. All of us believe Chicago deserves the attention we have tried to pay it on these pages. All of us believe it is an important and valuable city.

—Amy Teschner

SWEET HOME CHICAGO

Stuart McCarrell, cofounder and chair of The Nelson Algren Committee, in front of Algren's home.

The Real City

THE OTHER TOP TEN SIGHTS
NEIGHBORHOODS
CHICAGO POLITICS
CHICAGO SCHOOLS

THE OTHER TOP TEN SIGHTS

So you've been to the zoo, shopped on Michigan Avenue, strolled through the Art Institute, looked down from the top of Sears Tower, witnessed traders screaming and running around on the floor of the Board of Trade. What else is there to do in Chicago?

Lots. Now it's time for you to get off the beaten path, to head for the places you don't read about in most guidebooks, the *other* top ten sights.

BEST OF THE LAKEFRONT

The absolute best thing about Chicago is Lake Michigan. No, I'll rephrase that. The best thing about Chicago is the *accessibility* of Lake Michigan. Unlike other major American cities, Chicago has preserved almost all its shoreline as open space for the public. The lakefront is where Chicago plays, relaxes, and breathes. It's where you find the best views of the city, where you can go on a wintry day to be outdoors but totally alone, where you can escape the heat in the summer.

Every Chicagoan has a favorite lakefront spot. But singling out one site for this book proved to be an impossible task, not least because Chicago has a North Side and a South Side, two separate but equally important worlds. So I picked the *three* best lakefront spots—the best of the best, you might say.

The Point

At 55th Street, a large, open triangle of grassy land juts out into Lake Michigan to form Promontory Point. Stroll along the edge for a most spectacular view of Chicago's skyline some seven miles to the north, then plop down on your blanket to enjoy a peaceful afternoon. The Point is a relaxed place to barbecue, throw a Frisbee around, or lie in the sun, because there's no beach, just grass and rocks; the crowds go elsewhere. Swimming is forbidden here, but that doesn't stop the long-distance swimmers who gravitate to the deep, unpeopled stretch of water off the south edge of the Point. Windsurfers also find a haven in this part of the lakeshore. And the Point is perhaps the best place on the lakefront to watch the sun rise.

Cross back under Lake Shore Drive and you're in Hyde Park. This integrated, middle-class South Side community has a collegiate atmosphere (the sedate intellectual kind, not the frat-party kind) courtesy of the University of Chicago. Highlights include **57th Street Books** (1301 E. 57th), one of several excellent local bookstores; **Valois Cafeteria** (1500 E. 53rd) for good, cheap—and I mean *cheap*—home cooking (try the grits for breakfast, the corn muffins are wonderful, and their motto "See your food!" is nice); and the **parrots of Eastview Park** at 53rd and the lake. The large, bright green South American birds, escapees from a pet shop truck, have formed huge nests in this little park where they live, incongruously, year-round.

Olive Park

Directly east of the bustling Michigan Avenue shopping district, Olive Park is a quiet oasis in the heart of the city. This narrow strip of land just north of

Navy Pier is an urban anomaly. Because you have to walk under the Drive to get to it from the west, and because it's obscured from Navy Pier by the adjacent water filtration plant, few people even know of its existence. Its chief feature is a gracious promenade lined with leafy trees. There's also a grassy expanse of land, a fountain, and a memorial to Chicagoan Milton Olive, Pfc, who was awarded the Congressional Medal of Honor posthumously for falling on a grenade and saving his comrades in Vietnam. You can view the city skyline to the immediate west across a small inlet, or walk to the north edge of the park and stare out into the vastness of Lake Michigan. Picnic tables line the water's edge, and there's even a small beach.

Montrose Harbor and Montrose Beach

Enough of this relaxing stuff. If action is what you want, and lots of people do, the North Side's Montrose Beach area, around 4400 North, is for you. What kind of people? All kinds. Montrose has got to be the most diverse section of the lakefront. Wander around for an hour or so and you'll hear enough different languages to make you think you're on Ellis Island. You'll see organized soccer matches with intent Latino youths cheered on by crowds of picnicking family and friends. You may see Vietnamese boys tossing around a football, Russian couples strolling along the harbor, Filipinos playing volleyball, even rugby-playing yuppies chasing each other in the mud.

Dusk is a great time to be out here in summer. The barbecue grills have come out in full force, lending a succulent smoky haze to the scene. In the harbor, sailboat masts tap rhythmically to the gentle lapping of the water. The fishermen are still intent on their work along the pier, and the beach is starting to empty of families tuckered out after a long day of splashing in the water and baking in the sun. A lone windsurfer may still be gliding along just to the south, with a rose-tinged city skyline as a backdrop. It will strike you that Chicago's no melting pot—the different ethnic groups relaxing and playing here coexist separately, but peacefully. For a true urbanite, this patchwork of humanity is one of the great wonders of American city life.

THE RAVENSWOOD EL

You know those bright red double-decker London buses rumbling through the Loop with gawkers hanging out the top and sides snapping photos of the buildings?

Forget 'em. Who needs to pay tour fees when, for the price of a CTA fare (expensive enough, I admit) you can conduct your own tour of the city? We're talking about the Ravenswood Elevated line, which starts out on the North Side, circles the Loop, and takes you back to where you began. Riding around the city high up above street level, removed from all the traffic, you can see things that you couldn't see anywhere else—and especially not on a tour bus.

So pay your fee, grab a seat in the front car, and limber up for a little rubbernecking. Starting out at almost any station on the North Side you'll pass blocks of typical Chicago residential streets. Loop-bound between Belmont and Armitage the buildings get increasingly elegant; the view in both directions at the Armitage stop shows gracious two-flats with ornamentation just about at eye level. Looking forward you get a good glimpse of the approaching Chicago skyline, with the **John Hancock Building** off to the left and **Sears Tower** straight ahead. Between the Armitage and Sedgwick stops the track takes a few twists and turns, so you even get a little roller-coaster action along with the sightseeing experience.

The track straightens out and heads south after Sedgwick. As you approach the Chicago Avenue stop, the city pulls one of its urban contrast moves. You're aiming straight for the Sears Tower, with the River North gallery district immediately ahead, Old Town and the high-priced Gold Coast to your left, and **Cabrini-Green** to your right. This huge public housing project, with its eerily empty upper floors and gaping vacant lots, has gained notoriety simply because it isn't hidden away in poor South and West side neighborhoods like most other projects. It stands as an uncompromising reminder to commuters, tourists, and other passers-by that there's another Chicago beyond the gleaming skyscrapers, trendy cafés, and comfortable middle-class enclaves.

After the Chicago stop, the train makes a beeline for the **Merchandise Mart**. Above the broad brick expanse of the Mart you'll see a sliver of green glass, the **333 W. Wacker Building**, and on top of that hovers the Sears Tower. Three generations of Chicago architecture in a single slice—a great sight. The train stops right at the Mart, the Midwest's center for the marketing of furniture and furnishings, built by Joseph Kennedy in 1930.

Now comes the best part of the ride: crossing the **Chicago River** and heading into the urban canyons of the Loop. The view of the river is impressive, especially on a bright day with sunlight gleaming off the bridges and buildings. Look to the left for a good view of the twin towers of **Marina City**, one of the city's most distinctive landmarks. To the right, 333 Wacker elegantly reflects the river in its gentle curve. Pass over the river and you're into the Loop, heading south on Wells. Look east, where on weekdays the honking cars and purposeful pedestrians cry out to you, "Work! Work!" as they go about their business in the shadow of the hulking buildings. Note the station trappings at the Quincy stop; it's been restored to its original early 1900s style.

The train makes its turn east at Van Buren. As it turns look off to your right, where you'll see the space-age **River City** some distance away. Heading down Van Buren, continue looking to the right. You'll all but scrape up against a funny triangular building with narrow slits for windows. It looks like a piece of cheese but it's really a **federal prison**. You'll also pass right by the **Harold Washington Library**, where you'll get a good view of upper-story ornamentation. Note the cornstalks. The mysterious Latin phrase carved there, "*Urbs in horto*," happens to be Chicago's motto; it means "city in a garden," or something like that. To the left along Van Buren are some venerable old office buildings, the Fisher and the Monadnock.

The train turns back north on Wabash. Now's a good time to peek inside the office building windows. These old buildings have a lot of character to them; they seem like they should be filled with mysterious goings-on. As a matter of fact, famous fictional Chicago private eye V. I. Warshawski has her office here, according to her chronicler, Sara Paretsky. Heading back west on Lake Street you'll pass the **Chicago Theatre** on your left and then a rather squat glass structure, rounded on one side and looking somewhat like a blue and red igloo. It's the **State of Illinois Building**. Now it's back over the river to points north. You get a good view of the front of the Merchandise Mart; check out the disembodied heads facing the building.

For a more adventurous alternative (and a longer tour) you can hop off the train at Adams and Wabash, cross over the tracks, and jump on the Lake/Dan Ryan train going south. Major points of interest include the **Illinois Institute of Technology** (designed by Mies Van der Rohe) and **Comiskey Park** (where the White Sox play), and **Bridgeport**, home of the Daley clan. You can get off at Chinatown, have a great dim sum brunch, get back on the train going north, and pick up the Ravenswood again at Adams and Wabash. (Don't cross over the track this time.)

Have a great trip!

HAROLD WASHINGTON LIBRARY

On Sunday, September 29, 1991, Chicago's new central library at 400 S. State Street, between Van Buren and Congress, threw open its doors to the public. Thousands of people from all over the city streamed through the building—a mixed throng of black, white, Latino, Asian, young, old, rich, and poor that's usually seen in Chicago only during (extremely rare) celebrations of sports championships. The line to get in stretched halfway around the square-block edifice. The librarians had a funny sort of glow in their eyes, as if they just found out that their first novel won the Nobel Prize for Literature.

You wouldn't expect that something as cerebral as a library would excite Chicagoans, who consume vast quantities of green beer on St. Patrick's Day and bark raucously whenever Mike Ditka walks into a room. But this city can surprise you sometimes. Chicago had gone without a real central library since the 1960s, when the collection outgrew its space on Randolph and Michigan. It was split up and many of its books were either placed in storage or kept in a warehouse that, while open to the public, was hardly welcoming. From Mayor Daley the First through Bilandic and Byrne, the library was a political football, with proposals for a new site tossed around, approved, officially rejected, or mysteriously dumped. Finally, under Mayor Washington's guidance the current site was acquired, and plans for a new central library got officially under way.

A design competition for the new structure sparked tremendous public interest and debate, especially when architectural models of the five competitors were placed on display for the public to view and comment on. Architect Thomas Beeby won the contest with a somewhat conservative neoclassical structure. Many architecture critics gave his design a thumbs-down, but what do you know? Most of us ordinary folks, not knowing any better, seem to really like it. "It *looks* like a library," goes a typical comment. The newborn massive red brick edifice, trimmed with granite and topped with a green steel-and-glass roof, stands out boldly among its many architecturally famous older siblings. Inside, once you get past the rather confusing main lobby, the library's excellent soft lighting, comfortable seating areas, friendly decor, and spectacular skylighted "winter garden" will probably win you over.

Of course, Chicagoans now take pride in saying that the city has the largest circulating library in the world. It strives to cater to broad public needs as well as specialized interests, and a recent buying spree has helped rebuild its collection of books and other materials. Collections in the Civil War, Chicago history, Chicago theater, local authors, and popular music are particularly strong; the library holds the Chicago Blues Archive and plans are under way for a Jazz/Blues/Gospel Hall of Fame. The spacious second-floor children's library holds some 100,000 volumes in a bright, cheerful setting. Other features include reading materials in 90 foreign languages, a substantial audio collection, and a Film/Video Center. The computer catalog doesn't live up to its claim of user friendliness, but truly helpful librarians are on hand to come to your rescue.

You can find a lot going on at the library even if you never check out a book. Displayed throughout the building is a permanent art collection of paintings, sculpture, photography, mural, mosaic, and installation art. An exhibit hall on the lower level offers rotating exhibits. The children's library features puppet shows, storytelling, and other events. A monthly calendar lists a variety of films, lectures, readings, panel discussions, workshops, and concerts.

But if you're new to the library, you should probably start your visit at the top floor. Even the building's critics have acknowledged the stunning beauty of the spacious skylighted winter garden (it would be incredible during a storm). The exhibit on Harold Washington in an adjoining room will bring back strong memories if you're a Chicagoan or, if you're not, will help you understand the personality and significance of the city's first black mayor. This room will eventually house the Harold Washington Collection.

In its short life span the Harold Washington Library has already become an important part of civic life in Chicago. Even if you like to drink green beer, you should go and take a look. (Open Monday–Thursday, 9 A.M.–7 P.M.; Friday–Saturday, 9 A.M.–5 P.M.)

CHICAGO RIVER

Oh, so you're the outdoorsy type, are you? A nature lover? Consider yourself somewhat adventurous? Well, check this out: a canoe trip down the Chicago River, starting on the pastoral Northwest Side and ending up downtown, buffeted by tour boats and pointed at from bridges by incredulous pedestrians. Just don't fall in.

It may not be the Colorado River, but Chicago's other great waterway has enough intriguing features to make for a highly unusual and entertaining urban nature experience, whether you're in a canoe or a tour boat, on foot or bike. As every local schoolchild knows, one of America's great engineering feats was the reversal of the course of the Chicago River. It flows backward. Since I remember nothing else from that long-ago history lesson, I can't tell you why they did this, but they did it. For a while the river was a major trade route, with more traffic than any other waterway in America. The river helped make Chicago what it is today, yet for the most part it is sadly neglected as a natural resource and "point of interest."

Friends of the Chicago River (939-0490) is trying to change that by working to save the river from polluters and encroaching developers, increase open space along the banks, and generally promote the river as a vital Chicago landmark. The group offers walking tours on Saturday mornings from April to November. It also provides maps of the entire river within city limits with walking routes mapped out if you want to do it yourself. Although much of the area around the river is privately owned, there are plenty of publicly accessible routes, if you know where to look.

The Chicago River actually starts at Skokie Lagoon in the northern suburbs. The pleasant North Branch bike trail runs from the city's Caldwell Woods, around Devon Avenue, all the way north along the river, ending up at the Botanic Gardens. But for now let's focus on the river within city limits, where exploration involves confronting gritty urban reality as well as flora and fauna.

On the North Side the river features small parks broken up mostly by residential areas. You can walk or ride your bike along a river trail through almost uninterrupted woods from Caldwell Woods all the way south and east to Foster Avenue. Where the river meets the North Shore Channel you'll find Chicago's only "waterfall," a six-foot dam just below Foster. South Side points of interest involve industry and commerce, and you'll have to use the roads to see them. Between 18th and Cermak you can see five different types of bridges, including the historic Scherzer rolling lift bridge, more than 100 years old. From bridges at 35th or Archer you can get a good view of Bubbly Creek, a fork that originated in the old stockyards. The bubbles are caused by methane gas from past generations of . . . well, you get the picture.

Downtown, you can enjoy a little piece of nature amid all the high rises at Wolf Point, near the Apparel Center (go downstairs at Orleans). Because the whole city is raised up (another engineering feat), this small wooded area is the only place where the land is at its natural level. If you use your imagination you may get a sense of what Chicago was like before all the people came.

You can explore the downtown area from the river by taking a narrated river tour offered by the **Chicago Architecture Foundation** (922-3432) from May to October. Seeing and learning about Chicago's history and architectural heritage from this unique perspective will give you a deeper appreciation for the city. Did you know that Goose Island is so named because the Irish immigrants who lived there kept geese? The quaint old bridge houses and megalithic modern skyscrapers provide a fascinating contrast, and that 333 W. Wacker Building is really a knockout when viewed from the river. The more touristy Wendella and Mercury boat companies ply the river as far as Sears Tower. They're not quite as educational—more along the lines of corny but fun. They dock by the steps of the Wrigley building and offer frequent trips daily during warm months.

I wasn't kidding about that canoe ride, though. It can be done. Rent the canoe from **Chicagoland Canoe Base** (4019 N. Narragansett, 777-1489), where they're used to crazy ideas like this and can give you some helpful tips. They know just about everything there is to know about the Chicago River. You can put in just below that waterfall I mentioned, south of Foster. The key thing is to scope out in advance the best spot downtown to disembark (of course, you'll need two cars). Wolf Point is a good possibility; you can park pretty close to the river. You can go farther south, but you'll find it harder to find an accessible public spot. I recommend going on a Sunday when the crowds are down.

The trip will take a few hours (especially if you stop for lunch somewhere along the bank). At first, with the city hidden behind tall banks, you'll feel like you're out in the middle of nowhere. Gradually you'll start to see more and more signs of urban life, and by the time you're downtown you'll feel like you've traveled a lot farther in time and space than you actually have. And don't worry *too* much about falling in, because the river is no longer officially considered "toxic," merely "polluted." Because of the Deep Tunnel, constructed in the 1980s (yet a third engineering feat), raw sewage no longer finds its way into the river during storms, and stricter laws against dumping have enabled the river to gradually clean itself over the past several years. Let's hope that continued improvements give the Chicago River a more integral role in the city's life.

WICKER PARK/BUCKTOWN GALLERY DISTRICT

A working-class, primarily Polish and Latino neighborhood on the Near Northwest Side has witnessed an explosion in recent years: an explosion of the arts. More than a dozen galleries have sprung up, mostly featuring local artists. Coffeehouses and bars offer live poetry, artwork, and jazz. Alternative theaters present challenging works by local and international playwrights. A diverse, lively arts community now lives and works in the area, side by side with the original working-class residents.

For a stimulating journey of art exploration, head for the hub of activity, the intersection of Milwaukee, North, and Damen avenues. You'll find the **Abel Joseph Gallery** (1600 N. Milwaukee) on the ground floor of the landmark office tower (affectionately known as the Coyote building) on the northwest corner. Then cross over to the opposite corner to the other local landmark, the **Flatiron Building** (1579 N. Milwaukee). The **Space Gallery** is on the ground floor (enter on North Avenue). On the upper floors you'll find a maze of artists' studios, along with the **Near North West Arts Council**, a community-based arts advocacy and networking group. NNWAC has all kinds of information and maps of local galleries, but you might want to call ahead (278-7677); hours are somewhat erratic. Its own gallery is committed to exhibiting work by emerging artists. Other galleries around the intersection include **Ricky Renier Gallery** (1550 N. Milwaukee), **Gallery 1616** (1616 N. Damen), and **Gallery 1633** (1633 N. Damen), with many others located a little farther afield. Call NNWAC or check the *Reader* or *NewCity* (both are free weeklies) to find out about openings and gallery hours.

There's an energy to the scene that you won't find at the tonier, more establishment River North gallery district, and the atmosphere is casual and friendly. When your feet start to get weary, drop into one of the many coffeehouses where you can dawdle over coffee or lunch. Most provide more than food and drink: **Urbus Orbis** (1934 W. North), a popular gathering place, shows artwork and features performance artists. **Earwax Cafe** (1564 N. Milwaukee) offers food, records, and a unique selection of videos. Local bars also get into the artistic act. **Estelle's** (2013 W. North) and the **Borderline Tap** (1958 W. North) are among those that show art and offer weekly poetry nights. A vibrant alternative theater/performance scene includes the **Latino**

Chicago Theater; Guild Complex/Hothouse; Cabaret Teatro; and two multi-use spaces, the **Rudely Elegant Theater & Gallery** and **A Stage of One's Own**. To savor the full flavor of the neighborhood, head to the **Busy Bee** restaurant (1550 N. Damen) under the El, where locals of every stripe gather for delicious, reasonably priced down-home Polish food.

If Wicker Park/Bucktown is home to Chicago's alternative art world, then the **Around the Coyote Festival** is its annual open house. For one weekend in September the whole neighborhood is thrown open to inspection. Galleries, studios, even apartments of artists are on display. The event is a celebration of the incredible artistic and ethnic diversity of the local art community. A comprehensive program guide/map allows you to conduct your own walking tour of the neighborhood and gives you a chance to explore the area's historic buildings.

The invasion of the artists into this traditionally working-class neighborhood (home to Nelson Algren) has aroused fears of gentrification among the inhabitants. Less established artists and other locals may one day be priced out as developers take advantage of the neighborhood's new identity, and the area could be well on its way to becoming another Lincoln Park. (The rehabbers are already at work, particularly around Wicker Park.) But for now the scruffiness, the laid-back atmosphere, the experimental nature of the art scene, and (probably most important of all) the low rents make the Wicker Park/Bucktown Gallery District one of the most stimulating places in the city.

GARFIELD PARK CONSERVATORY

Chicago's West Side is known more for its tough neighborhoods than for its flora and fauna. But just as a tree grows in Brooklyn, thousands of plants from all over the world grow in Garfield Park Conservatory (300 N. Central Park), one of the planet's largest indoor botanical gardens.

If you lack the means to jet to Hawaii during a cold Chicago winter, step into the Conservatory to be transported, for a little while at least, into a tropical paradise. Graceful palms and other exotic plants fill the humid Palm House. The Fernery and the Aroid House also mimic tropical conditions with a wide collection of philodendrons, 100 different kinds of ferns, flowering tropical water lilies, and such oddities as the sea grape tree, devil ivy, the Dutchman's-pipe, and the bird of paradise tree. If you prefer the arid Southwest to the tropics, the Cactus House offers 400 species, from the tiny living stone to the giant saguaro. Other rooms contain citrus trees, spice plants, fig trees (including the giant banyan), and dozens of plants that you certainly never heard of before.

But the most dazzling display of fabulous flora can be found in the Horticultural Hall & Show House, the site of four major flower shows held throughout the year. The fall Chrysanthemum Show, the Azalea/Camellia Show in late winter, and the Christmas and Easter shows fill the exhibition space with a riot of colors, carefully arranged for maximum eye-pleasing effect. Everything on display is grown in the Conservatory's propagating houses. Call 533-1281 to find out if a flower show is currently taking place.

The Conservatory is housed in a landmark glass structure built in 1893 and covers more than four acres. Admission to this publicly owned resource is free. If you're really into learning about the Conservatory's collection, you can arrange a tour with the horticulturist by calling in advance. If you happen to be getting married and you're not into country clubs, you might even want to consider the Conservatory for a tasteful yet unconventional wedding site. The Chicago Park District operates the Conservatory as well as the smaller (but also beautiful) Lincoln Park Conservatory, next to the Lincoln Park Zoo, with similar seasonal flower shows.

SOUTH SHORE CULTURAL CENTER/ONE ARTIST ROW

The **South Shore Cultural Center** (71st and South Shore Drive) likes to call itself Chicago's "Palace on the Lake," and the boast is not too far off the mark. The grand, Spanish-style edifice features a huge ballroom, a bright solarium with doors opening onto the lakefront, and an elegant decor that harkens back to the 1920s. Built in 1906 as the ornate South Shore Country Club, the building fell into disrepair in the 1960s. It was saved from the wrecking ball by a coalition of determined neighbors and reemerged in 1985 as a multipurpose cultural center run by the Chicago Park District.

Restored to its former glory, the building itself is a sight to see, and numerous events, programs, and classes make it a beehive of activity as well. Its grounds, which occupy three-quarters of a mile of Lake Michigan shoreline, contain a nine-hole golf course, beachfront, and picnic areas, not to mention the Chicago Police Department's mounted patrol. An art gallery shows works primarily by African-American artists. A pleasant Music Recital Room offers frequent performances. "After Hours at the Studio" features a variety of acts and an open mike every Friday night.

There's also a seniors activity room and several classrooms filled with classes in music, drama, dance, aerobics, ceramics, woodcraft, and sewing. A monthly programming calendar lists concerts, art shows and fairs, outdoor festivals, special events, and theater and dance presentations (call 753-0640 for gallery hours and other programming information). The elegant reception rooms make the Cultural Center a popular spot for weddings, banquets, gatherings of all sorts, so you may want to book early.

The saga of the South Shore Cultural Center can be told about the surrounding community as well. Once a highly desirable neighborhood with gracious homes and apartment buildings, South Shore fell victim to disinvestment, neglect, and poverty in midcentury. But thanks to a strong coalition of local residents and businesses, the predominantly African-American community is rebounding as a vibrant, diverse area. Many of its buildings have been renovated at the impetus of South Shore Bank and its affiliates, City Lands, and the Neighborhood Institute, a nonprofit development company. Development of the 71st Street commercial strip has lagged behind the improvements in housing, but the Neighborhood Institute plans to change that.

It's made a great start with **One Artist Row** (1801 E. 71st), an "arts incubator" carved out of an abandoned, two-story, 16,000-square-foot building. Less than a mile west of the South Shore Cultural Center, One Artist Row is a cultural and commercial enterprise worth exploring. Storefronts on the ground floor hold African imports, the African-American Book Center, and specialty boutiques. Some stores display the work of artists whose studios are one flight up; plans are under way to create a permanent storefront gallery for their work. Wander up to the second floor to take a look—some of the studios may be open, and they're a diverse lot, including fabric collage, painting, jewelry making, set design, make-up design, and custom clothing design. Under the incubator concept the artists share services they might not be able to afford individually, such as computer, copier, conference room, marketing, and management services.

South Shore is home to a variety of cultural organizations, including the African-American Arts Alliance, ETA Theatre, Chicago Theatre Company, New Regal Theatre, and Association for the Advancement of Creative Musicians. The South Shore Cultural Center and One Artist Row fit the community like a glove.

CEMETERY SURPRISES

Graceland Cemetery

Mark Twain would have loved Graceland Cemetery (4001 N. Clark, 525-1105). The final resting place of Chicago's Gilded Age elite is filled with grandiose monuments to wealth and ego; the giants of Chicago business and industry did not stint when it came to erecting their own memorials. Imposing, often garish and tasteless, sometimes amusing—really, you'd never guess a visit to a cemetery could be so, well, entertaining. As well as historic.

Marshall Field, Cyrus McCormick, and Philip Armour are buried here, not to mention probably half the street names in Chicago. Legend has it that industrialist George Pullman was so hated by the working man that his family conducted his funeral at midnight to avoid a possible riot. Ironically, Pullman's giant Corinthian column is located beside the Palmer family's elaborate memorial. Civic and cultural leader Bertha Palmer, wife of hotel tycoon Potter, once tried to convince Pullman to adopt a more flexible attitude toward his workers, but to no avail. Don't miss the landmark Getty Tomb, resting place of lumber merchant George Getty. It is considered one of architect Louis Sullivan's finest works.

Capitalism isn't the only thing commemorated at Graceland. Sullivan himself is buried here, and his gravestone, erected years after his death, is a fitting tribute to the pioneer of the skyscraper. Daniel Burnham's grave site, prominently placed on a small island with a perfect view, mimics his central role in the design of Chicago. Mies van der Rohe and John Wellborn Root round out a who's who of Chicago architecture. Check out the monument to William Hulbert, founder of baseball's National League: it's a large granite baseball complete with stitching. Alan Pinkerton's monument boasts of his role as crime fighter and bodyguard to Lincoln (no mention of his work as a union buster). Also look for heavyweight hero Jack Johnson, progressive Governor John Peter Altgeld, publisher Joseph Medill, two amazing statues by Lorado Taft (the chilling "Death" and the gargantuan "Crusader"), and for some reason, Charles Dickens' brother Augustus.

The Chicago Architecture Foundation (326-1393) offers occasional tours of Graceland, or you can pick up a map and booklet at the office.

Rosehill Cemetery

If the imposing entrance to Rosehill Cemetery (5800 N. Ravenswood, 561-5940) looks vaguely familiar, it's because it was designed by William

Boyington, architect of the old Water Tower on North Michigan Avenue. The landmark castellated gateway was built in 1859, the year Rosehill opened for business—just in time for the Civil War.

And it's the Civil War that gives Rosehill its timeless quality. You get a sense here of the real history of real people. Unlike Graceland, where every grave seems to belong to some big leader, future street name, or at least a very rich person, Rosehill contains the graves of the foot soldiers of mid-19th-century Chicago—literally. More than 200 Union casualties occupy the section just inside the entrance, their graves marked in even rows of small rectangular stones. The monuments are filled with battle names: Shiloh, Fort Donelson, Vicksburg. A massive monument to the Chicago Board of Trade Battery proudly proclaims, "Miles traveled by rail, 1231. Marched, 5266." Another tribute to the ordinary citizen is the Volunteer Fireman's Monument, with a volunteer fireman perched atop a high column, holding a coiled hose and megaphone.

But the famous and important are here as well, including Civil War heroes (General George Thomas, known as the "Rock of Chickamauga"); businessmen, industrialists, and philanthropists (Schwinn, Richard Sears, Montgomery Ward, John Shedd, Julius Rosenwald, Avery Brundage); 12 mayors and a U.S. vice president. Other interesting graves include those of feminist-temperance leader Frances Willard, founder of the Women's Christian Temperance Union; Lincoln sculptor Leonard Volk, who designed many of the monuments including a highly idiosyncratic sculpture for his own grave site; and George Bangs, head of the Railway Mail Service (look for the large granite choo-choo disappearing into a tunnel). Then there's Leopold and Loeb victim Bobby Franks, the "girl in the glass case," and plenty of intriguing memorials to lesser known people.

Despite all the dead folks, Rosehill really seems more like a large, pleasant, beautifully landscaped park than a cemetery. Its 330 acres contain stately oaks and maples, winding paths, and small lakes filled year-round with geese and ducks. And needless to say, it's not one of your more crowded public spaces, unless you believe in ghosts. It's a great place to stroll, relax, think. Stop in at the office to pick up a map and booklet, or just wander around and make your own discoveries.

FRANK LLOYD WRIGHT'S OAK PARK

You don't have to be an architecture buff to develop a deep appreciation for Frank Lloyd Wright. All you have to do is take a trip to Oak Park and spend an afternoon exploring the world's largest collection of Frank Lloyd Wright architecture. Oak Park, due west of Chicago, was Wright's home from 1889 to 1909, the place where he developed his career and changed the face of architecture in America and throughout the world.

You won't find many guided tours promoted in this book because we believe the best way to discover and experience Chicago is to take the do-it-yourself approach (it's cheaper, too). But if you can afford it, take the **Frank Lloyd Wright Home and Studio Tour** (951 N. Chicago); you will not be disappointed. In fact, you'll be captivated by Wright's inventiveness and vision, the beauty of his creations, and the chaos of his life. This is where Wright created his renowned Prairie style of low, earth-hugging dwellings that would influence all of architecture. Check out the incredible furniture: who needs comfort when you have such wonders to behold? A suspended balcony highlights the octagonal, two-story drafting room. Other noteworthy features include the stained glass windows, intricate ceiling grilles, and innovative use of natural materials.

Before touring Wright's home, stop in at the **Visitors Center** (158 N. Forest, (708) 848-1500) around the corner. You can purchase tour tickets here and obtain maps and guidebooks. The **Ginkgo Tree Bookshop**, at the Wright home site, offers a nice selection of books and gift items. Tour tickets and maps can be found here as well.

After visiting the Wright home and studio, stroll around the neighborhood to see homes designed by Wright and his Prairie school disciples. Oak Park has 25 Wright structures, including Unity Temple, which he called his "little jewel." But other noted architects are well represented; in fact, Oak Park has more than 100 homes built in the Prairie style. This Japanese-influenced yet distinctively American architectural movement emphasized a close association with nature and a determination to turn away from European models to build houses suited to the Midwestern landscape. Interspersed with the Prairie style houses are venerable old Victorian homes, from Italianate to Queen Anne, making Oak Park a living representation of turn-of-the-century American design. All homes are privately owned, so resist the temptation to take a closer look.

Call the Visitors Center for hours, fees, and directions. Oak Park is easily accessible from downtown Chicago by car (take the Eisenhower Expressway, or I-290, west to Harlem Avenue and head north) or El (the Wright home is within easy walking distance of the last stop on the Lake Street El line). You'll find some nice little restaurants and stores in downtown Oak Park, which is a gracious older suburb known for its progressive, educated, and integrated population. It's also where Ernest Hemingway was born and raised, but that's a whole other story.

PULLMAN

Tucked between the Dan Ryan Expressway and heavy industry, way down at the southern edge of the city, lies a living museum of 19th-century urban and labor history: the company town of Pullman.

Railroad car magnate George Pullman built his "model town," America's first planned industrial community, in the 1880s. By offering his workers an alternative to crowded, disease-filled slums, he hoped to avoid the labor unrest that was so prevalent in those days. But despite the tidy facades and various amenities, Pullman's dream lasted less than 20 years, exploding in 1894 into one of America's most important—and acrimonious—labor strikes.

Today, walking the streets of this pleasant community, you'll see few signs of the town's turbulent past. What you will see is an architecturally unique neighborhood of row houses, homes, and mansions, anchored by the gracious Hotel Florence (named for Pullman's favorite daughter). The harmony and continuity of the facades attest to a unified design, yet each block has its own distinct features and character. Almost all the original buildings remain, making a stroll through Pullman feel something like a trip back to the turn of the century.

If George Pullman were alive today, he'd be the very definition of the term *control freak*. While he may have held some enlightened ideas about improving conditions for the lower classes, his own ideas were unfortunately the only ones he tolerated. He owned the whole town and allowed no other private ownership. There was only one bar, located out of reach of the masses in the Hotel Florence because Pullman didn't trust his workers with demon alcohol. There was only one church for a multiethnic population of 12,000 because Pullman was a Universalist and felt that one building could fill all the spiritual needs of the town. Inspectors roamed the town with the power to walk into anyone's home, at any time, to ensure that proper sanitary conditions were maintained. Unsurprisingly, Pullman referred to his workers as his children. Despite its modern trappings, his town resembled a feudal society rather than a utopia.

But Pullman was more an efficient capitalist than feudal lord, insisting that everything in the town turn a profit (even the lone church). And therein lay his downfall, because he slashed wages and laid off thousands during the Depression of 1893 but refused to lower his rents, causing hardship and anger among his workers-tenants. A strike broke out in May 1894, and it took on historic significance when railway workers across the country refused to move trains equipped with Pullman cars. President Cleveland sent in 14,000 federal troops against the wishes of Governor Altgeld and Chicago Mayor Hopkins, who both sided with the workers. Eventually union leader Eugene Debs went to prison and the workers lost. But the other big loser was George Pullman, whose reputation as an enlightened business leader was crushed. He died three years later.

The town of Pullman was incorporated into Chicago in 1889, and the Pullman Company was forced by the state supreme court to sell its nonindustrial properties by 1907. The residents, many of whom descended from the original Pullman workers, fought a plan in the 1960s to raze the entire community to make way for an industrial park. They won their battle and obtained city, state, and national historic landmark designation for Pullman. In 1974 they formed the Historic Pullman Foundation to encourage restoration of the buildings. The **Hotel Florence** (11111 S. Forestville) and many homes have since been restored.

The hotel, which serves lunch daily and a nice brunch on Sundays, is the starting point for a self-guided tour of Pullman. You can usually pick up maps and information there, and if you ask they'll give you a quick tour upstairs, where you'll see Pullman's suite, a typical hotel room, and various memorabilia. Highlights of the neighborhood include the **Greenstone Church** (it may be the only one, but it's a beauty), the **Market Hall**, and the **Arcade Row Houses**. To the north lies the site of the Pullman plant. If you want to discover Pullman from the workers' point of view, I highly recommend that you pick up *Touring Pullman*, a little booklet by William Adelman, before you go. It's available from the Chicago Architecture Foundation Shop and Tour Center (330 S. Dearborn) and contains fascinating tidbits about the town and the strike that you won't learn from the information available in Pullman itself.

From May to October the Historic Pullman Foundation offers guided walking tours the first Sunday of the month, starting at the **Historic Pullman**

Center (614 E. 113th). Group tours can also be arranged. The Annual House Tour, held in the fall, allows visitors inside some of the restored homes. Call the Historic Pullman Foundation at 785-8181 for tour times and fees. They'll also send you maps and information in advance if you plan to explore on your own.

—Deborah R. Weiner

NEIGHBORHOODS

The cliché endures: Chicago really is a city of neighborhoods—a vast mosaic of separate entities, each with its own history, personality, and particular landmarks and institutions. The neighborhoods originated most often as gleams in the eyes of ambitious land developers or as ethnic enclaves, which grew into towns that were in turn swallowed up by the swelling, 19th-century city. The result was and continues to be a diverse and colorful sprawl of traditional and newly hybrid communities and cultures. Less benign influences in these enclaves include both subtle and overt expressions of nationalism, xenophobia, and outright racism for which, unfortunately, Chicago also is known.

While the idea of "neighborhood" conjures up notions of time standing still in a place where "everybody knows your name," the truth is somewhere between that bucolic image and utter chaos. Chicago's neighborhoods have been most strongly characterized by two forces: people moving in and people moving out. It happens fast, in less than a generation. So, the West Side street populated exclusively by Poles and Jews that our Polish neighbor remembers fondly has vanished. She still likes it here, but it isn't the same. She shares the street now with extended Puerto Rican families, artists, and well-heeled whites. She figures if the gangs of the seventies didn't drive her out, the speculators of the nineties won't either.

The flux goes by different names: white flight, gentrification, and the neighborhood "changing," "going downhill," or "looking up." If you look at the history of your own particular neighborhood, you will discover that you and your current neighbors have moved in on someone else and that those people either chose to move on or were forced out. Whether running from something they perceive as bad or in search of something better, each new group papers over the world of its predecessors. So Operation PUSH, located in the South Side's Kenwood neighborhood, is housed in the former synagogue of the oldest Jewish congregation in Chicago.

This notion of neighborhood—apparently as old as the city of Pompeii—can also be construed as existing only in the fantasyland of real estate marketing copy and in the hopes and dreams of local merchants eager to lure customers to their strip or, in the case of Chicago, their crazy six-corner intersection. Laden over the whole geography is the ward map, which breaks the city into 50 aldermanic districts that were intended to reflect neighborhood boundaries but have not always changed apace. Aldermanic seats seem to change hands more slowly than churches and synagogues.

The idea of neighborhood is played out further in a powerful dichotomy between City Hall and the grassroots, a term that is used interchangeably with Neighborhoods (with a capital N). Grassroots is expressed in thousands of block clubs, church parishes, community associations, and independent political organizations fighting for causes such as safe streets, capital reinvestment, good public transit, and, of course, an ever-larger piece of the economic pie. Lest anyone despair, it's good to remember that though the City of Big Shoulders spawned the original Daley and his machine, it is also the birthplace of the eight-hour workday and Saul Alinsky's community organizing. Alinsky's brand of rabble-rousing and grassroots empowerment are copied all over the world, and his disciples are still "fighting the good fight" in Chicago's neighborhoods. It's also worth noting that Alinsky began his work in Chicago's Back of the Yards area (described later) adjacent to Daley's home turf, Bridgeport.

THE LOOP

All roads and El lines once lead to the Loop, which remains the seat of governmental power, finance, and business. Until the 1970s and the development of the Magnificent Mile, the Loop was also the heart of retail shopping in the city. The go-go Reagan years brought spectacular new shapes to the skyline: the AT&T building, the 311 S. Wacker building (the one with the lighted crown that makes it look like it ought to be the headquarters of White Castle), and the Harold Washington Library, to name a few. The current recession, with an office vacancy rate near 20 percent, brought new construction nearly to a halt and, as financing became elusive, put many projects on hold. The most obvious casualty is the Miglen-Beitler, building which, planned at 125 stories for the southwest corner of Wells and Madison, aimed to claim that much-coveted distinction of world's tallest building. Though undergoing major renovation, the current tallest building, **Sears Tower**, is also in limbo: with no buyer in sight, Sears has taken the building off the market though it still plans to move soon to its new headquarters in suburban Hoffman Estates. Another sign of the times is the loan default of Presidential Towers, the four taupe-colored luxury apartment buildings just west of the Chicago River. The complex was heavily subsidized by government money and then exempted from low-income housing requirements, thanks to our most powerful "representative" in Washington, Dan Rostenkowski. Meanwhile, City Block 37, at the corner of Dearborn and Madison, with construction on hold, has become **Gallery 37**, a showcase for the artwork of schoolchildren; in the winter it's an ice rink.

The magnificently refurbished **Chicago Theater** at 175 N. State represents both a victory for preservationists and the difficult task of demonstrating its feasibility and financial independence. Things may be looking up in this regard, as city plans to create a "Theater Row" in the North Loop are encouraged by the Goodman Theater's interest in relocating to the shuttered Harris and Selwyn theaters at 180 and 190 N. Dearborn. The move and purchase of the adjacent Garrick Garage and a building formerly occupied by the Woods Theater would vastly enlarge the Goodman's space, which since 1923 has been at the Art Institute.

Mayor Daley's latest plan for revitalizing retail shopping in the Loop seems dubious, calling for reopening the State Street Mall (built in 1978 to improve shopping) to auto traffic. At the same time, the banning of street parking in the Loop, which began during cleanup of the Great Chicago Flood of 1992, has made the Loop much less congested. Daley is also pressing for a new Downtown Area Circulator, a souped-up modern trolley with a price tag of as much as a billion dollars. Neighborhood groups are questioning transit priorities when the infrastructure of the CTA is falling apart.

Neighborhoods adjacent to the Loop are booming because of the revival of interest in living near the area's amenities. Streeterville, bounded by the lake,

Michigan Avenue, the Chicago River, and East Lake Shore Drive, is named after George Wellington Streeter who laid claim in 1886 to 150 acres of landfill, then fought vigorously for the next 35 years to obtain title. The area is a canyonland of high-priced high rises that are a stone's throw from the Loop, Michigan Avenue, and Oak Street Beach. Among the local amenities is the **Museum of Contemporary Art** (237 E. Ontario), which in 1995 plans to move to an expanded space with a sculpture garden on the site of the old armory on East Chicago Avenue. The recently renovated **North Pier Terminal** on East Illinois offers shops, restaurants, and nightclubs, and the Chicago Children's Museum. Plans are afoot, however, for the museum to move due east to Navy Pier, to anchor a family-oriented pavilion that might also include a theater and bicycle museum. Residents are increasingly concerned about congestion, which would be heightened by the Circulator and the threat of gambling boats off Navy Pier.

River North (Between Clark Street and the River on the west, from Kinzie north to Chicago Avenue)

River North, until the late 1970s a haven for frowsy warehouses, is now a well-established gallery district, and after work on Friday nights (particularly the first one of each month and especially the first Friday in September) the streets are full of gallery hoppers. "Arty" businesses—graphic design, photography, video production houses, and publishing houses—are ubiquitous here, as are shops selling upscale items for the home: lighting fixtures, gifts, leather furniture, and so on. Falling art prices and the current recession have taken a bit of a toll on the galleries, and the area still suffers psychic pain from a tragic fire that in 1989 destroyed the converted warehouse at 356 W. Huron, which housed eight galleries and the works of those artists they represented. Tourists and suburbanites head for the **Rock 'N' Roll McDonald's** (600 N. Clark) and the **Hard Rock Cafe** (63 W. Ontario) for rock memorabilia and burgers and **Ed Debevic's** for retro eats and a sassy wait staff. The area's working stiffs can't let a week go by without a lunch or two at **Brett's Kitchen** (233 W. Superior), which serves great deli sandwiches and good soups. Ask for Manuel.

River West (Chicago Avenue, Halsted Street, the Kennedy Expressway, and Grand Avenue)

The River West neighborhood, just west of Halsted and Milwaukee, is a brand-new loft neighborhood rising from warehouses and factories west of Halsted Street and Milwaukee Avenue. With remarkable speed, the area has seen factories and warehouses pushed out by rising rents, to be followed by galleries and businesses leaving River North in search of cheaper rents than those to be found in River North. Apartment construction and renovation of lofts is proceeding swiftly, as the area touts its image as the "cheaper cousin" to River North.

Unexpected tragedy came to River West in January 1992, when high-pressure natural gas caused 18 buildings to explode or burn, killing four people. **Kaboom** (770 N. Halsted), all jokes aside, is a megaclub decked out in postindustrial chic.

Near South Side, South Loop (From Congress Parkway south to Roosevelt Road, between Canal Street and Grant Park)

Printer's Row

Brand-new neighborhoods are rising south of the Loop. The magnificently restored Dearborn Station train depot, historic point of arrival for thousands of immigrants, provides the southern anchor for the Printer's Row neighborhood. Lofts in this area, which was once the center of Midwest publishing, attract affluent singles who walk to jobs in the Loop. Every June the Printer's Row Book Fair features the wares of local publishers and old, new, and antiquarian volumes from midwestern booksellers, as well as music and readings.

Dearborn Park

Due south, on the rubble of abandoned railroad yards and the city's earliest vice district, are the pricey Dearborn Park and Dearborn Park II developments. Amenities and neighborhood institutions are almost nonexistent for these luxurious, security-mad enclaves.

River City

Built in the late 1970s along the Chicago River to the west of Dearborn Park is River City, a self-proclaimed prototype for future urban communities. Visionary Bertrand Goldberg, also the architect of Marina City, designed River City to look from the air like a sinuous Mayan water snake. A glass brick atrium covers an internal street that runs the length of the development. Amenities include a health club, market, medical center, and an outdoor garden on the top floor. The down side is that River City remains quite isolated from the Loop, which recently prompted the Museum of Broadcast Communications to move from there to the Cultural Center.

NORTH SIDE

Gold Coast/Near North (From the Lakefront to LaSalle Street, between Chicago and North avenues)

Studs Terkel encapsulated the diversity and economic disparity of Chicago in the title of his book *Division Street, U.S.A.* The actual Division Street runs west from the hush of old money in the Gold Coast, past the tight clothing of the Rush Street nightclub scene, to the impoverished Cabrini Green housing projects.

Jewel grocery store on the corner of Clark and LaSalle is the mingling place for matrons in mink and poor blacks. The mere mention of notorious Cabrini Green, which sprawls over increasingly desirable real estate between Chicago Avenue and Division Street, does to developers what the bell did for Pavlov's dogs. (In other words, they wish they could get their hands on it.)

In the center of the Gold Coast/Near North area is **Sandburg Village**. In tried-and-true Chicago fashion, this gigantic complex, now home to 6,000 young professionals, was built with money originally intended for urban renewal in the 1960s. The **Newberry Library**, located on Washington Square Park between Clark and Dearborn, is one of the most important research libraries in the country specializing in niches as diverse as Americana, genealogy, and Renaissance manuscripts. The **Chicago Historical Society**, located at the south end of Lincoln Park near Clark Street and North Avenue, is an important and fascinating repository of Chicago and Illinois history. It sits on the site of the city's first cemetery.

Old Town (From Division Street north to Armitage Avenue, between LaSalle Street and Sheffield Avenue)

This once decayed old German neighborhood enjoyed a bohemian renaissance in the 1960s when artists, followed by white professionals, began rehabbing homes and former coach houses of Gold Coast mansions to the east. Many of the old haunts are now gone, including the Earl of Old Town, which launched the careers of folkies Steve Goodman and John Prine, and O'Rourke's, a wonderful, salty bar that was forced to move and unfortunately left behind those qualities that long made it a Chicago institution. Meanwhile, the Old Town Art Fair has grown into the largest juried art fair in the country, and Wells Street, once a strip of hippie head shops and boutiques, now offers upscale shops. Nearby on Halsted is the impressive new home of **Steppenwolf Theater**, the epitome of storefront or, specifically, church basement, theater all grown up. Like the new O'Rourke's across the street from the new Steppenwolf, Old Town is clean, quiet, and now solidly gentrified.

Lincoln Park/DePaul (From the Lakefront west to Clybourn Street and Ashland Avenue, between North and Diversey avenues)

Named for the city's largest park, which serves in a manner as the area's front yard, Lincoln Park is the flashiest of the gentrified Lakefront neighborhoods and a veritable yuppie mecca. The park itself boasts an excellent zoo, botanical conservatory, the recently renovated **Cafe Brauer** (2021 N. Stockton), and four of the city's most popular beaches. The south end of the park, from North Avenue to Wisconsin Street, was the city's first cemetary and was used to bury victims of an 1852 cholera epidemic as well as the remains of Confederate soldiers who died in prison camps on the city's South Side. Setting precedent for the area's future waves of gentrification, in 1864 most of the cemetery's estimated 20,000 bodies were relocated to make room for the park.

The fashionable and upscale area west of the park between Armitage and Diversey is home to white professionals increasingly of the married-with-children variety. As property values climb steadily, the abundance of thirty-something apartment dwellers is gradually and inevitably giving way to forty-something home and condominium owners. In metaphorical terms, Saturday morning breakfast with a stranger has given way to the near-religious significance of a trip to the local garden supply store, **Fertile Delta** (2760 N. Lincoln). This is not to say that the characteristic Big Ten Greeks are altogether gone but rather that the familiar fraternity-party atmosphere of the eighties has degenerated into a kind of interminable reunion or homecoming weekend. The area's legendary singles scene was dealt a sobering blow by AIDS awareness and continues to peter out as a result of the changing demographics and a consequent drop in hormone levels.

Replacing baser pursuits are the equally indulgent though safer occupations of dining and shopping. The Lincoln Park and DePaul neighborhoods are among the city's best for both. As of this writing, the area boasts no less than four **Starbucks** coffee franchises, the green-awninged Seattle import that has relegated the Braun to a state of disuse and threatens to make everyone forget about two folksy ice-cream makers from Vermont. Other neighborhood institutions include **Frances'** (2552 N. Clark), **Sole Mio** (917 W. Armitage), and **Melman's Cafe Ba-Ba-Reeba** (2024 N. Halsted) for dining; **Foodworks** (1002 W. Diversey) and **Sherwyn's** (645 W. Diversey) for healthy groceries; and the **The Great Ace** at Clark, Diversey, and Broadway for just about everything else. There are plenty of places to spend your money but almost nowhere to park. If possible, walk or take the CTA, which offers several options for getting in (and out) of the area.

Indicative of the area's intense gentrification and its resulting effects is the leafy and peaceful enclave surrounding **DePaul University**, a Catholic institution that has grown 25 percent in recent years and, as a result, has a new library and athletic facility on the way.

The south and west boundary for the Lincoln Park/DePaul neighborhood is the Clybourn corridor, which once formed a vital industrial district for the city. Because of development and spiraling property taxes, many of these manufacturers have been forced to close or relocate, taking with them the blue-collar jobs that had enabled the area to be somewhat racially and economically integrated. As a result of three geographically limited though significant Protected Manufacturing Districts (PMDs), the situation has been temporarily stabilized, and industry now sits cheek by jowl with yuppie shops and restaurants, furniture stores, baby boutiques, bookstores, and a colossal **Treasure Island** supermarket. The trendy **1800 North Clybourn** shopping mall is the new home of the **Remains Theater** and features an artist-designed miniature golf course, a Barbara's Bookstore, and the Goose Island Brewery, which makes its own beers and exceptional homemade potato chips.

Wrigleyville/New Town/Lakeview (From the Lakefront west to Ashland Avenue, between Diversey Street and Irving Park Road)

Located just north of Lincoln Park, Lakeview is trendy, culturally diverse, largely middle class, and still in most respects an affordable place to actually live. While Lincoln Park is gentrified—it's happened, not happening—Lakeview serves as an excellent place to study the process in action; every street features examples of the habbed, habbing, and habbed not (a.k.a. a property to be habbed later). At the heart of Lakeview is Wrigleyville, named for **Wrigley Field**, home of the Cubs. In 1988 (8-8-88 to be specific), after decades of controversy, lights went up over Wrigley Field, and night baseball was inaugurated. Thereafter, strict regulation of parking on game nights has helped smooth the ruffled feathers of residents who fought a bitter campaign against the change. (Once in a while you can still spot someone sporting a "No Lights" T-shirt.)

Wrigleyville boasts a wide array of restaurants, bookstores, fabulous vintage shops, and nightclubs, including **Lower Links** at Links Hall (3435 N. Sheffield), which offers a mix of avant-garde poetry, music, and performance art, and **Cabaret Metro** and the **Smart Bar** (3730 N. Clark), which cater to the black-leather crowd. Theaters abound and include the experimental **Live Bait** (3914 N. Clark) with adjoining **Nightcrawlers Cafe**; **Stage Left** (3244 N. Clark), featuring works of a sociopolitical bent; the **Theater Building** (1225 N. Belmont), which is home to several groups; and the venerable **Organic Theater** (3319 W. Clark). **Cafe Voltaire** (3231 N. Clark), a relative newcomer to the neighborhood, offers great coffees and desserts and occasional theater: a recent long run was Dylan Thomas's comedic verse *Under Milk Wood*, which got rave reviews. In the last few years, the thoroughfare Belmont Avenue has gotten less "edgy," while the flagship Swedish restaurant **Ann Sather's** (929 W. Belmont) still offers the best cinnamon rolls on the planet. The **Planet Cafe** (3923 N. Lincoln) is a funky eatery with astronomy decor offering 10 percent discounts to those who come to Sunday breakfast in their PJs. Specialty bookstores are many: **Season to Taste** (911 W. School) is a cook's fantasy, **People Like Us** (3321 N. Clark) offers gay and lesbian titles, and **Scenes Coffeehouse and Dramatist Bookstore** (3168 N. Clark) offers drama. Antique shops line Belmont west of Ravenswood.

A large portion of the city's gay community lives in New Town, located from the lake to Halsted. Halsted is a lively shopping district, with unique gift shops, vintage and antique furniture stores, and some great restaurants including the vegetarian **Chicago Diner** (3411 N. Halsted) and **Caffe Pergolesi** (3404 N. Halsted). The **Bread Shop** (3400 N. Halsted) sells health foods, fabulous goods, and tasty prepared vegetarian salads and entrees.

Ravenswood/Lincoln Square (From Ravenswood Avenue west to the Chicago River, between Montrose and Bryn Mawr avenues)

A truly continental neighborhood, Lincoln Square, a.k.a. Ravenswood, was once home to a large German population. Though much of that group has been dispersed or moved on to the suburbs, those that remain carry on the traditions.

Especially wonderful at Christmas time, but a treat all year round, **Meyer's Deli** in the square (4750 N. Lincoln) is an epicurean delight. The square itself (where Lincoln Avenue bends into Western Avenue) is home to **Merz Apothecary** (4716 N. Lincoln), the homeopathic pharmacy established in 1875. Its beveled glass door, hanging lamps, and wooden counters contribute to its Old World charm. Aside from the variety of herbal and natural medicines, there is a vast selection of European toiletries. Wonderful outdoor cafes and restaurants abound in this ever-changing and diverse hood. The **Grecian Taverna** in the square (4761 N. Lincoln) serves the freshest fish and meats available and is surprisingly inexpensive.

The Asian influence has steadily moved in from Uptown and areas to the west, resulting in many good Thai, Vietnamese, and Korean restaurants including **Vietnam Little Home** (4654 N. Damen). **King's Manor** (2122 W. Lawrence) is a bawdy dining hall reminiscent of the Middle Ages. A must to visit, the **Conrad Sulzer Library** (4455 N. Lincoln) is a gem of modern architecture and design with Swedish-style stenciled wooden chairs and a large jewellike skylight. The Ravenswood El winds conveniently through this area, and the rents are not as high as on the Lakefront. The lush tree-lined streets and neat lawns seem to lend a soft hush to this family-oriented neighborhood.

Roscoe Village (From Damen Avenue west to Western Avenue, between Addison and Belmont avenues)

This peaceful neighborhood—comprised primarily of post-WWII bungalows and two-family flats dating from the early 1900s—is decidedly less trendy than its eastern neighbor Lakeview. Mostly white working couples and families, many originally from Appalachia, mingle with a recent, albeit slow, influx of professionals, Latinos, and African-Americans. Among the local attractions are the **Village Tap** (2055 W. Roscoe), a basic neighborhood bar with an outdoor cafe and locally made Legacy on tap, and the **Beat Kitchen** (2100 W. Belmont), a happening place to hear folk, blues, and offbeat bands such as Maestro Subgum and the Whole, and a regular host of worthwhile benefits.

Uptown (From the Lakefront west to Ashland Avenue, between Irving Park Road and Foster Avenue)

Uptown is home to a huge assortment of ethnic groups. The area around Broadway and Argyle is sometimes called New Chinatown, and Chinese, Vietnamese, Thai, Cambodian, and Laotian people have carved out a number of lively communities there. Andersonville, located to the west on Clark between Foster and Bryn Mawr, is where the Swedes moved after they left the area around Clark and Belmont. There are lots of Swedish restaurants, furniture stores, and bakeries as well as a new Ann Sather's in the neighborhood. A large Middle Eastern population is also found in Andersonville and have established some excellent restaurants, one of which is **Beirut** (5204 N. Clark). Nearby **Maya** (5146 N. Clark) offers cheap and delicious Guatemalan food. **Women and Children First** bookstore (5233 N. Clark) is well worth a visit.

Starting in the seventies, with the move to remove patients from mental hospitals, Uptown near Broadway and Lawrence became a dumping ground for mentally ill people, many of whom were homeless. Halfway houses and shelters to serve them and others sprang up accordingly. Concurrently, real estate moguls and mogul wannabes began eyeing the deteriorating though sturdy and often magnificent housing stock in the neighborhood. Into the increasingly fractive atmosphere between haves and have nots stepped Alderman Helen Shiller, voted in as a champion of the poor and fierce advocate of affordable housing and social equity in general. Since then the tensions have subsided.

The **Riviera** nightclub (4746 N. Broadway) packs in music fans most weekends, and just north, the **Green Mill Lounge** (4802 N. Broadway) offers great jazz and the now nationally known Poetry Slam competitions. Next door to the Green Mill is the **Uptown Theater** (4816 N. Broadway), an enormous and ornate movie palace that has been vacant for many years though, economic conditions allowing, may yet be restored. Uptown's most famous resident is author Studs Terkel, whose oral histories give voice to the common men and women who populate this and similar areas of the city.

Edgewater (Between Foster and Devon avenues, from the Lakefront to Ravenswood Avenue)

Once billed as the "only electric-lighted suburb adjacent to the city," Edgewater reached a high tide of wealth in the 1920s when the **Edgewater Beach Hotel** (5333 N. Sheridan), now the Breakers home for independent seniors, was one of the hottest places in town. Changing times have seen a tremendous influx of diverse ethnic groups (nearby Senn High School educates students speaking 60 languages or dialects). A canyon of high-rise apartment buildings lines Sheridan Road from Bryn Mawr to Devon avenues, and remaining mansions have been razed or chopped into apartments. Thanks in large part to the active Edgewater Community Council, the blighted Winthrop-Kenmore corridor is seeing a slow rebirth, and two of the last remaining mansions on Sheridan Road have become a community center and a cultural center, respectively. The **Edgewater Beach Apartments**, a delightful pink elephant located at 5555 N. Sheridan, remains a prominent lakefront landmark.

East Rogers Park (From the Lakefront west to Ridge Avenue, between Devon Avenue and the Evanston border)

A crazy quilt of cultures and a bastion of independent political thinking, this last neighborhood south of Evanston also boasts the longest and arguably the least congested stretch of beach in the city. Once largely Jewish, the neighborhood is now home to college students from Loyola and Mundelein universities (recently merged) and Northwestern University, as well as Russians, Indians, Pakistanis, Poles, Jamaicans, and African-Americans. One of the strongest and most outspoken community organizations in the neighborhood is the Rogers Park Tenants Association, which began as a tenant advocacy group and now addresses an array of neighborhood concerns, including gangs.

Rogers Park accommodates many theater spaces, including the venerable though financially troubled **Wisdom Bridge** (1559 W. Howard), **Lifeline** (6912 N. Glenwood), and **Raven** (6931 N. Clark).

The social epicenter of the area is the sixties-style **Heartland Cafe** (7000 N. Glenwood), which serves vegetarian food that ranges from bland to wonderful and a vast array of beers in its Buffalo Bar. An adjoining shop offers political periodicals, including the *Heartland Journal* (the alternative tabloid published by owner Michael James), T-shirts, and natural products of all sorts. Heartland also schedules a line-up of music, poetry readings, and various benefits.

The neighborhood abounds with coffee shops, including the **No Exit Cafe** (6970 N. Glenwood), an authentic sixties coffeehouse with folk music, jazz, and great desserts, and **Ennui** (6981 N. Sheridan). Both have devoted followings. **Pusan House** (6928 N. Glenwood), a hole-in-the-wall Korean place, is much beloved by locals, as is **Elaine's** bakery (1414 W. Morse), which proclaims that "the sweetest people in the world pass through these doors."

West Rogers Park (From Devon Avenue north to the Evanston border, between Ridge Avenue and the Chicago River)

More stodgy and less densely built than its counterpart to the East, this neighborhood of frame and brick single-family domiciles, ranging in size from bungalows to behemoths, is home to a large Orthodox Jewish contingent, as well as more Indians and Russians. Along Devon Avenue look for Russian and Indian restaurants—**Viceroy** (2518 W. Devon) is a favorite—sari shops, and Jewish delis. **Indian Boundary Park** is a jewel of the park system and operates a small petting zoo. **Fluky's** (6821 N. Western), a hot dog stand and so much more, is a local favorite.

NORTHWEST/WEST SIDE

West Town (Between Grand and Division avenues, from the Kennedy expressway west to Western Avenue)

The small group of familiar West Town bars catering to artists —the **Rainbo Club** (1150 N. Damen), **Phyllis' Musical Inn** (1800 W. Division), the **Artful Dodger** (1734 W. Wabansia), and the **Lizard Lounge** (1824 W. Augusta)—now includes an important recent addition, the **Hothouse** (1569 N. Milwaukee), home to endless benefits and the place to hear some of the best jazz, salsa, and African music in the city. The **Bop Shop** (1807 W. Division) is a top-notch jazz club, and **Leo's Lunchroom** next door (1809 W. Division) is a funky restaurant owned by three locals. Leo's offers fabulous eats at low prices and features an airy back deck for summertime. Restaurants catering to a more well-heeled crowd have also appeared, notably **Jimo's** in what was once an all-night pharmacy on the corner of Milwaukee and North avenues, **Babaluci** (2152 N. Damen), **Gavroche** (1958 N. Damen) in Bucktown, and **Club Lucky** (1824 W. Wabansia), a 1940s-style Italian supper club that attracts the advertising crowd the way still water attracted Narcissus. Some things, however, never change, as the **Busy Bee** (1550 N. Damen) still serves delicious pierogies and potato pancakes for less than it costs to eat at home. (It's also the place where Hilary Clinton made her infamous campaign remark that she would rather work than stay home and bake cookies and have teas.)

Several theaters are now ensconced in the neighborhood: the nationally recognized **Latino Chicago Theater** (1625 N. Damen), in an old firehouse, as well as the **Curious Theatre Branch** (1900 W. North), the **Prop Theater** (1843 W. North), and the **Theater of the Reconstruction** (1853 W. North). Milwaukee Avenue, the diagonal street that gives the area much of its character, has changed little and remains a lively jumble of shops selling furniture and clothes, baby goods, bridal wear, wigs, linens, and religious objects (mostly cheap).

Ukrainian Village (Both sides of Chicago Avenue from Damen Avenue to beyond Western Avenue)

Ukrainian Village is a spirited ethnic enclave, a close-knit homogeneous community where distinctions of religion, language, and nationality play an important role. Churches plucked out of fairy tales are the center of community activity. The mosaic interior and large stained-glass windows of the majestic **St. Nicholas Cathedral** (2238 W. Rice) are well worth a visit. A few blocks away on Leavitt and Division is the chapel-sized **Holy Trinity Cathedral** designed by Louis Sullivan and modeled after the churches that dot the Ukrainian countryside. It is the only Russian Orthodox church he designed. Every Ukrainian Easter, just before midnight, the neighborhood residents gather to carry candles and baskets filled with elaborately painted eggs to Holy Trinity to witness the reenactment of Christ rising from the tomb.

Apart from the churches, locals gather at the delis and bakeries. **Kasia's** (2101 W. Chicago) is the most complete deli with kielbasa and fresh pierogis by the dozen. A block away, **Anne's Bakery** (2158 W. Chicago) slices your bread fresh. Their poppyseed and plum cakes are sensual delights. The streets are immaculate and most of the buildings date back to the twenties, creating a uniform line of three-flats with stone balconies. The lawns are impeccable, the gardens well tended, and the flowers that crowd many balconies are one of the city's true harbingers of spring.

Wicker Park (Between Division and North avenues, from the Kennedy Expressway to Western Avenue)

Wicker Park has always been a neighborhood of contrasts. A historic district today, it contains fabulous 1880s mansions on Beer Baron Row (Hoyne Street between Pierce and Schiller), and also the homes of several of the Haymarket martyrs, German anarchists sentenced to die in 1887 after a bomb of dubious origin killed seven policemen at a rally for the eight-hour work day. The incident is celebrated by socialists round the world as May Day.

In 1985 a ferocious political battle saw the victory of Luis Gutierrez for alderman, creating a City Council majority for Mayor Harold Washington. Once staunchly Polish and now largely Puerto Rican with lots of artists, Wicker Park is seeing a major incursion of yuppies attracted by the area's elegant homes and easy access to the Loop, via the northwest El line.

Bucktown (Between North and Fullerton avenues, from the Kennedy Expressway west to Western Avenue)

Just to the north of Wicker Park is Bucktown, a traditional working-class neighborhood with a bar on every corner. Once Polish and now Puerto Rican, Bucktown has also seen significant gentrification in recent years. Modest working-class cottages now sport skylights and decks, while mock Victorians are springing up on vacant lots.

Wicker Park and Bucktown contain several remarkable churches, the legacy of early immigrants to the area. At the corner of Wood and Cortland is **St. Mary of the Angels**, a magnificent copper-domed edifice that has been

The Chicago River.

called one of the country's finest examples of Roman Renaissance architecture. When high restoration costs threatened to close the church, neighborhood residents launched a vigorous and successful fund drive. **St. Stanislaus Kostka** on Noble Street near Division was the symbolic heart of the old Polish neighborhood. When Daley senior planned to bulldoze it to put in the Kennedy Expressway, outraged parishioners rose up and saved the church. You can see on any city map how the expressway is detoured around the site.

Logan Square (From the Kennedy Expressway west to Kimball Avenue, between Fullerton and Diversey avenues)

Perhaps the most striking intersection in the entire city, Logan Square proper is the site of a massive marble column celebrating the centennial of Illinois statehood. Logan Boulevard, which enters the square from the east, is suitably grand with huge, well-tended homes with sweeping lawns. Milwaukee Avenue cuts diagonally through the square and reflects the community's considerable ethnic diversity: Puerto Rican, Mexican, Cuban, as well as the older Polish community. The neighborhood is well cared for with street after street of elegant graystone two-flats sharing the neighborhood with solid apartment buildings built predominantly during the twenties.

Near West Side (From the Kennedy and Dan Ryan expressways to Western Avenue, between the Eisenhower Expressway and 15th Street)

In the past five years the area anchored firmly at its center by the **University of Illinois** and to the west by the medical facilities of the U of I, Rush-Presbyterian-St. Luke's, the massive Cook County Hospital, and the Chicago Technical Park has seen some of the most rapid change in the city. The latest ward remap may create a "Superward," joining this neighborhood with the Loop and the Magnificent Mile to fashion a new First Ward crammed with political and financial muscle.

Taylor Street

The old Italian neighborhood, which fought old man Daley to keep the university out, still hangs on tenaciously on Taylor Street, where some of the city's best Italian restaurants are located. Sadly, the restaurant Florence, a lovely establishment owned by Florence Scala (the activist who stood up to Daley) is closed. Taylor Street also now has most of the trappings of a university town—laundromats, coffee houses, fern bars, and the like. Upscale housing developments have popped up like mushrooms, and rental prices have climbed concurrently. There's even a place to put up mom and dad for the night: the suburban- looking Inn at University Village.

On the edges of these modern wonders are pieces of history, ethnicity, and some familiar Chicago institutions. Though the University bulldozed Jane Addams's original Hull House complex, the **Hull House** mansion (800 S. Halsted) is preserved on university grounds and contains a wonderful museum of the settlement house and immigrants who settled the area. **Maxwell Street** near Halsted Avenue and Roosevelt Road, a fabulous outdoor flea market that was begun more than 100 years ago by Jewish peddlers, still exists albeit under serious threat of being swallowed up by the expansionist University. The **South Water Market**, at 15th and Morgan streets, remains the city's wholesale vegetable market where those so inclined can purchase vegetables by the bushel basket. The prestigious **St. Ignatious Prep School** (1076 W. Roosevelt) sits alongside the soaring spire of Holy Family Church. The church, once the third largest Catholic church in the country, is undergoing a $4 million facelift to return it to its 19th-century splendor. Here also are the remnants of the old West Side Gold Coast, located north of the Eisenhower Expressway on Ashland Avenue; ironically, many of these mansions now house labor unions, more than 30 of which line the street.

Greektown

Along Halsted Street, just north of the Eisenhower Expressway, is Greektown, still the place to find the best Greek food in town. West of Greektown an area of warehouses and factories is—you guessed it—undergoing conversion to residential and business loft spaces, with snazzy bars and pricey restaurants to match. The gleaming studios of the **Chicago Access Corporation** (822 S. Green), where Chicago residents make public-access TV shows, is close to **Harpo Studios** (1058 W. Washington), where Oprah Winfrey has set up shop. The old **Fulton Market**, located along Fulton and Randolph streets just west of the Kennedy, still forms the core of the city's wholesale meat and fish markets. **Shelter** (564 W. Fulton), a down and dirty nightclub, and **At the Tracks** (325 N. Jefferson) are attracting a decidedly different crowd to the market area.

Lower West Side

Pilsen (Between Halsted and Western avenues from 16th Street on the north to Cermak and Blue Island avenues on the south)

The heart of the city's Mexican community, coexisting in general harmony with a large artist contingent, is found in Pilsen. Eighteenth Street in Pilsen looks for all the world like Mexico, with bright red, green, and yellow hues; terrific murals; salsa blaring from cars and music stores; and most signs in Spanish. The **Mexican Fine Arts Center** (1852 W. 19th) features the finest work being done by Latino artists locally and around the county, as well as seasonal shows. Their annual Day of the Dead exhibit in October is not to be missed, and neither is the wonderful gift shop. **Nuevo Leon** (1515 W. 18th) is a restaurant popular with locals and outsiders alike. Workers from the nearby UPS hub frequent **Paulie's** bar at 18th and Union streets. Artists have located primarily along Halsted Street near 18th Street, and their annual Pilsen Artists Walk provides the opportunity to visit artists in their homes and studios. The **Blue Rider** (1822 S. Halsted) offers some of the most unique theater in town.

Austin

Abutting Oak Park on the west, Austin is the largest community in the city, composed of several smaller neighborhoods. Austin Village is an integrated area of spectacular renovated Victorian and Prairie School homes that are opened for a tour every June. North Austin is predominantly white, and while though poorer and largely black South Austin has been plagued with housing abandonment, drugs, and crime, renovation of affordable housing has proceeded at a brisk pace. The South Austin Coalition is one of the most vital community groups in the city.

SOUTH SIDE

Hyde Park (From the Lakefront to Washington Park, between 51st and 59th streets)

Home to the **University of Chicago**, numerous seminaries, and a hefty number of Nobel laureates, Hyde Park probably has more bookstores per capita than just about anywhere in the nation. Favorites for new books are **57th Street Books** (1301 E. 57th) and **Seminary Coop Bookstore** (5757 S. University), which offers 10 percent membership discounts. The largest of the used bookstores is **Powell's** (1501 E. 57th).

Since urban renewal, which in the sixties and early seventies routed out a lot of the old bars and nightspots, the only decent place to get a beer has been the cavernous **Jimmy's Woodlawn Tap** (1172 E. 55th). At the **House of Tiki** (1612 E. 53rd), Hyde Park's only 4 A.M. bar, the owner-bartender refuses to serve tequila, warning gravely of its dangers. For eats, locals trek to **Valois** (1518 E. 53rd). This cafeteria, whose sign proclaims you can "See Your Food," serves classic pot roast and mashed potatoes, chicken pot pie, and terrific biscuits and eggs on Sunday mornings. **Ribs and Bibs** (5300 S. Dorchester) serves barbecued ribs and chicken and is another local favorite.

Washington Park, designed by Frederick Law Olmsted, is a green oasis, located to the west of Hyde Park. The **DuSable Museum of African-American History** (740 E. 56th) is one of the most important research museums of its kind in the country.

Kenwood

Hyde Park's recent history is linked with the Kenwood neighborhood directly to the north, where many U of C professors now live. This was once *the* most fashionable South Side neighborhood, with fabulous, rambling mansions and large yards, but the wealthy were driven away by the encroaching poor and the wafting fumes of the stockyards to the west. Aggressive housing tactics by neighborhood groups in Kenwood along with the University held off poor blacks, and the area is now middle-class and integrated. Drexel Boulevard, on the west edge of Kenwood, boasts elegant homes, and the corner of 50th and Drexel streets is the home of Operation PUSH.

The home of the late founder of the Nation of Islam, Elijah Muhammad, is located at the corner of 46th Street and Woodlawn Avenue. His stature and presence attracted other black luminaries to the area, including Louis Farakhan and Muhammad Ali.

South Shore (From the Lakefront to Stony Island, between Jackson Park Boulevard and 79th Street)

The original Irish residents were replaced by Jews, who, in turn, were replaced by blacks in the South Shore neighborhood. The area is now stabilizing as a predominantly middle-class black neighborhood with integrated pockets in the elegant Jackson Park Highlands area (former home of Jesse Jackson), the area just south of Jackson Park proper, and along the Lakefront. The **South Shore Cultural Center**, at 71st Street and South Shore, and its lakeside nine-hole golf course are a former country club that underwent an award-winning restoration. Community groups use its rooms for free, and Chicagoans from all over the city rent party rooms for weddings and other formal affairs.

Urban decay has a foe in South Shore Bank, which since 1972 has provided the financing necessary to restore a tremendous amount of housing and commercial properties in the neighborhood. The restored **Regal Theater** at 79th Street and Stony Island attracts a broad range of prominent black entertainers.

Pullman

Located at Cottage Grove and 111th Place, Pullman was billed as a model town for the workers at George Pullman's Palace Car Company, and it lasted from 1881 to 1894 when the infamous Pullman strike ended the experiment. Today this historic district, much restored, is largely Latino and ethnic white. A walking tour, written by labor historian William Adelman, gives a fascinating glimpse back at a failed capitalist utopia that in good times and bad was expected to earn its owner a 4 percent profit per year.

The better to preserve the moral fiber of his workers, Pullman allowed no bars in "his" town, prompting wily beer brewers to open huge drinking establishments just west of the area. Today working class Pullman's bars can be found in many corner bungalows: just look for the Old Style signs out front. **Hotel Florence** (11111 S. Forestville), named after Pullman's daughter, serves a wonderful Sunday brunch and showcases Pullman's restored personal suite.

Stockyard District

Back of the Yards

Made infamous in Upton Sinclair's *The Jungle*, the Back of the Yards supported thousands of working people in the packing houses and related industries until the closing of the stockyards in 1971. The neighborhood gained fame as the laboratory for the work of Saul Alinsky, the University of Chicago sociologist who invented grassroots organizing as we know it today. The Back of the Yards Council, which he helped found in the thirties, is still active, working to counter the loss of jobs brought by the closing of the stockyards. Succeeding waves of immigrants have changed the BOTY from an East European and Irish community to one that is largely Latino.

Bridgeport

Bridgeport, home of Mayor Richard M. Daley and his father before him, has been the heart of the Democratic machine since the 1930s. Bastion of the South Side Irish and home of the White Sox—now happily ensconced in palatial New Comiskey Park, near 35th Street and Shields Avenue—the working-class neighborhood remains an island of whites, infamous for its provincialism and racism. However, new immigrants include Asians and Latinos. If you're shopping for a house in Bridgeport, don't bother looking for "For Sale" signs—just about everything is word of mouth. **Healthy Food** (3236 S. Halsted), a Lithuanian restaurant, attracts diners from all over for its great breakfasts: blintzes, omelets, and heavy rye bread.

Chinatown (Between Canal Street and Lake Shore Drive, from the Stevenson Expressway north to the Santa Fe railroad yards)

Located near Archer and Cermak avenues on Wentworth, Chinatown is lively, colorful, and crowded. It's a great place to stop for authentic Chinese food and to watch the parade on Chinese New Year in early February. Plans for Chinatown Square, a 32-acre development going up now on old railroad yards north of Archer Avenue, include townhomes and senior housing, an Asian specialty shopping center, oriental theme gardens, and a hotel—the better to cater to the crowds from nearby **McCormick Place** and its expansion now on tap.

Marquette Park/Chicago Lawn (From 59th Street south to 75th Street, between Western Avenue and Central Park)

Marquette Park has long been a white, working-class neighborhood known elsewhere in the city largely for its racial tensions and sugary confections. Once headquarters to both the American Nazi Party and the Chicago chapter of Hell's Angels, things in the neighborhood have more recently quieted down. Sixty-third Street, the area's main drag, has undergone quite a metamorphosis in recent years, reflecting an influx of Latino and Middle Eastern residents.

The area's traditional residents are Lithuanians and Poles, which is evident along 69th Street from Western to California avenues where you'll find representative restaurants, food stores, and social clubs. Worth noting is **Neringa** (2632 W. 71st), an excellent Lithuanian restaurant in the area. **Marquette Park** itself is the largest park on the Southwest Side and includes a lagoon, a nine-hole golf course, and a beautiful rose garden.

The neighborhood's reputation as a paradise for sweet tooths is due largely to Dove Candies of Dove Bar fame, though the company recently relocated to Lockport, Illinois. **Gertie's Candies** (4231 S. Archer), which makes its own ice cream, and **Hoeffken's Busy Bakery** (3044 W. 63rd), reputed to be among the very best in the city, have not been spoiled by their successes and work to maintain their popular traditions.

Beverly (From 88th Street south to 107th Street, between Ashland, Beverly, and Vincennes avenues on the east and Western Avenue on the west)

Driving into Beverly, one has the distinct feeling of being in a small mid-western college town, the kind of place where the Cleavers might have lived. There was a brief period during the seventies when some homeowners were afraid of white flight, but, largely because of the efforts of the Beverly Area Planning Association (BAPA), things quickly settled down. BAPA put in a rumor hot line and sued a local realtor accused of blockbusting tactics. The area is now stable and integrated. Beverly includes some of the finest housing on the South Side and is a middle- and upper-class neighborhood, populated mostly by African-Americans and Irish Catholics.

Longwood Drive from 87th Street south is one of the most beautiful residential streets in the city. Longwood straddles an ancient geological ridge, and the surrounding area is rolling and even has, believe it or not, hills. The highest point in the city is the hill at the intersection of 111th and Lothair streets. If you drive or walk down Longwood, don't miss the replica of an Irish castle (now a Unitarian Church) at 103rd Street.

Hegewisch (From 115th to 138th streets from the Indiana border to Lake Calumet)

This tidy, modest, and tightly knit little community gained tremendous notice because it would have been virtually obliterated under Daley ad-ministration plans for a Lake Calumet airport. Most of Hegewisch's 8,000 people are lifelong residents, all white, and mostly Polish. The majority of the housing is two-story flats and bungalows. If the airport goes through (and at press time this appeared unlikely), Chicago will lose **St. Florian's Church** (13145 S. Houston), **Hegewisch United Methodist Church** (13501 S. Burley), and **Lebanon Lutheran Church** (13100 S. Manistee). **Mann Park**, which in-cludes extensive acreage, a large natatorium, a field house, and the Hegewisch public library (opened in November 1990) would also be con-spicuous fatalities of the proposed airport. The Daley administration promised to build a new Hegewisch to replace the one they hoped to bury in concrete, though the residents were predictably indignant.

SUGGESTED READING

For in-depth information about the history of Chicago neighborhoods, con-sult *Chicago: City of Neighborhoods* by Dominic Pacyga and Ellen Skerret (Loyola University Press). For current information about neighborhoods, check the "Neighborhood News" column of *The Reader*, a free weekly. For information on grassroots neighborhood organizing with a Chicago em-phasis, check *The Neighborhood Works* magazine published by the Center for Neighborhood Technology.

—Julie Johnson and Mark Noble with Cynthia Gordon

CHICAGO POLITICS

From today's perspective, Chicago's political history divides neatly into two volumes: the period up to and including the 21-year tenure of Mayor Richard J. Daley and everything since. The first volume's plot involves the creation and maturation of a great political machine; the second volume is about that machine's disintegration—by design, by accident, and by the forces of time. As in many major cities, for decades the history written in both volumes has been an almost exclusively Democratic one, though the lack of interparty competition hasn't made things boring.

VOLUME 1: "THE BOSS" AND HIS MACHINE

Should a Lake Calumet airport, downtown casinos, and other as yet unannounced grand plans for Chicago's future prosperity become reality—and live up to the promises made for them—it could be that at some future date Richard J. Daley will be remembered more as the father of Richard M. Daley than for the mark he left in his two decades as mayor. But for now, he is the beginning of Chicago politics as most Chicagoans know it, and his shadow still looms huge over the city. His tenure was the giddy climax of a period in Chicago's history when clout was king and politicians had names like "Bathhouse John" Coughlin and "Hinky Dink" Kenna. For many Richard J. Daley is and always will be "Da Mare," and every new city crisis (such as an underground flood) makes them long for the old days and "The City that Works."

Chicago's years under Richard J. Daley, 1955 to 1976, were a period in which patronage was what really worked and "ward guys" got the vote out. And the city grew. It grew expressways; a University of Illinois campus; McCormick Place not once, but when fire destroyed the first, twice; and the world's busiest airport in O'Hare. It lost its stockyards, but it grew the tallest buildings in the world. Richard J. was "The Boss," the unquestioned master of the city's Democratic machine, a political operation so powerful that it gave the mayor the ability not just to impose his will downstate on the Illinois legislature, but ultimately on the entire country when he delivered a presidential election in 1960 for John F. Kennedy. Perhaps it's the legacy of that latter event that to this day makes the city's Democratic torchlight parades preceding presidential elections events that any true Chicagoan must witness at least once to have any hope of understanding what this city is all about.

As his city grew, Mayor Richard J. Daley's political stature grew faster still, and no one dared issue a serious challenge to his reign.

But all that grew in the "City in a Garden" during the Richard J. Daley years wasn't pleasing to the eye. During his years Chicago also grew high-rise public housing, segregated neighborhoods, and an ugly image spawned in the late mayor's shoot-to-kill/shoot-to-maim orders to police with regard to arsonists and looters in the rioting following the Reverend Martin Luther King's slaying in April 1968. The city's image was tarnished further four months later by what a presidential commission would ultimately dub a "police riot" during the Democratic National Convention.

Perhaps because it was brought live via network television into homes from coast to coast, the events surrounding the 1968 Democratic convention linger to this day as part of the national image of Chicago served up during Richard J. Daley's years in office. Unfair, possibly, but nearly 25 years later it has still kept Chicago from ever being seriously considered to host another national political convention. The images of the clashes between antiwar protesters and Chicago police were too strong, too painful to young people, who could see themselves in the demonstrators being clubbed and gassed, and to their parents, who could easily see their children's faces on the bodies falling beneath the riot batons.

The events of 1968 may have been the first rumblings of a shift of the political continents in Chicago. Political phenomena of such a scope take time, and it would be more than a decade before Chicago saw a real move toward political reform. But as much as anything it was from this collection of weeds in Chicago's garden that the early spirit of an independent political movement grew, looking for a standard bearer to carry its flag.

VOLUME 2: THE MACHINE'S BREAKDOWN AND REPAIR

The first volume in Chicago's political history ended in the late 1970s. In essence, it closes with the death of Richard J. Daley in December 1976, though there was a bit of an afterword in the shape of the caretaker mayorship of Michael Bilandic. Bilandic was thrust into office by the city council when it was shocked to learn following Richard J. Daley's fatal heart attack that Chicago's parliamentary rules called for the mayor's office to pass to the city council President Pro-Tem Wilson Frost, a black. The closed-door city council machinations that resulted in Bilandic's being named interim mayor must have been as magnificent as any closed-door city council machinations can be. They also did a little bit more to nurture the growing political reform movement.

It's debatable whether Bilandic, never an inspiring media presence, lost his 1979 election bid to Jane Byrne or to the record snowfall that buried the city in January of that year, just months before the election. Whatever, city snow crews found it impossible to keep pace with the onslaught, and the transit system fared little better. When the snow cleared, there was Jane Byrne, a reformer out to tap that growing independent movement, who added to her base voters just plain angry that Mike Bilandic couldn't clear their way to work or a place for them to park when they got home. Her single term is the foreword in our second volume of the history of Chicago politics.

And Byrne did run as a reformer, drawing on a broad base of Chicagoans roused by her denunciation of the "evil cabal" that ran the city. Ultimately, though, there was little reform manifested in Mayor Jane's single term. There were, however, some excellent parties. Once in office, Byrne realized she needed the evil cabal more than the grassroots coalition that had elected her, and like her predecessors this mayor cut deals with the city council and did little for the black community. She had a sharp temper, was vindictive against those who crossed her, and briefly booted one of the city's daily newspapers from its space in the city hall press room. Many believe the photos of the mayor that paper chose to print over the rest of her term were its best revenge.

Aware, perhaps, that the bread her administration served up was unpalatable to many of Chicago's voters, Byrne did the logical thing—offered voters circuses instead. Festivals, fireworks, and everywhere the mayor's name, Chicago showed the world how to party with events like Chicagofest (boycotted by the city's black community in 1982) and Taste of Chicago. But, lo and behold, come election day 1983 the suburban teens so fond of collecting huge stacks of empty beer cups at Chicagofest couldn't vote, and Byrne found herself in trouble.

The 1983 Democratic primary contest set up as a three-way race featuring Byrne; Richard M. Daley, then Cook County state's attorney; and Harold Washington, a black congressman who'd run unsuccessfully in Bilandic's first reelection bid in 1977. Richard M. (not Rich Jr.) was seen by many as his father's rightful heir on the city throne, but Byrne instead perceived him (accurately it turns out, at least in 1983) as a spoiler who would split the white vote and hand the election to Washington. And so it was.

Despite the editorial backing of both the *Chicago Tribune* and the *Chicago Sun-Times*, in 1983 the younger Daley was unable to do anything more than split the white vote. In fact, though, Mr. Washington's victory resulted not only from his solid backing from Chicago's black voters, many of them voting for the first time, but also from the support of a sizeable portion of the city's white voters, the so-called "Lakefront Liberals." A true independent political coalition had come together behind a reform candidate, and the next volume of Chicago's political history began in earnest.

Where Byrne had quickly fallen in line with the evil cabal, Washington did no such thing. It's possible he wouldn't have been welcomed if he'd tried. For the last generation of the old Machine Democrats still active in the council drew up a new battle plan, one aimed at changing the base of power in Chicago from the city's executive branch to its legislative body. What ensued has become known as "Council Wars."

They were "The 29," the opposition city council members who took their marching orders from the "Two Eddies," Aldermen Vrdolyak, the leader, and Burke, his whip. Although Washington and his 21 council allies fought the good fight, for a time it seemed they were no match. No piece of legislation the mayor sent to council stood a chance before the 29. Just when the future of reform seemed hopeless in Chicago, however, to the rescue rode the courts, firing with one hand a decree barring patronage hiring and with the other a ruling that the city's gerrymandered council districts were illegal. When new districts were drawn and new elections held, Washington at last had a workable majority in the council and after nearly three years could begin serious work on his reform agenda.

As he worked to prune the political deadwood from city agencies and bring the city to a point of fiscal responsibility, Washington assembled a sort of municipal Rainbow Coalition, many of whom seemed as though they'd be more comfortable in front of a college classroom (where some of them are today) than walking the corridors of power. There were some, of course, whose only discernible previous experience—as well as their present employ—seemed to be activism, but over all it was a time of empowerment, of previously unrepresented constituencies coming to believe there was a place for them in Chicago's political scheme of things.

In the 1987 Democratic primary, Washington defeated former Mayor Byrne by 80,000 votes. In the general election he triumphed in what was, until its final days, a four-way race. The first Chicago mayor to win reelection since Richard J. Daley, the mayor's office appeared to be his as long as he chose to occupy it. And then, in November 1987, Washington died of a heart attack. The crowd that turned out in the Daley Center Plaza for a memorial service and filed past his body as it lay in state in City Hall was very much a reflection of the coalition that had put him in office. It was possibly the last time that coalition has come together.

Even as the mourning for Washington was going on, the city council was involved in machinations that made the events of the Wilson Frost–Michael Bilandic affair following Richard J. Daley's death look like a text on good taste and legislative restraint. Where most of the events of 11 years earlier had taken place discreetly behind closed doors, this battle was out there for everyone to see, culminating in a televised all-night council battle. A wager on what one single incident anyone who watched the proceedings remembers today is a sucker bet indeed—who could ever forget the sight of Alderman Richard Mell standing on his desktop demanding recognition from the chair, a twisted Chicago equivalent of Khrushchev's shoe banging at the United Nations. When a dazed Chicago regained its senses, there was, as in 1976, a caretaker mayor in office. Against the opposition of Washington's core council supporters, Alderman Eugene Sawyer had been chosen mayor, taking the reins from Alderman David Orr, Chicago's vice mayor, who had served as interim mayor for a matter of days until Sawyer's election by the council. Given the circumstances under which he won the office, it seemed likely Sawyer, a soft-spoken, well-intentioned 16-year alderman, would accomplish little as mayor. He didn't disappoint.

What Sawyer's brief stint as mayor did do was set the stage for Richard M. Daley's triumphant return to Chicago mayoral politics. In the spring of 1989 Daley defeated Sawyer in the Democratic primary, then handily won a three-way general election race against former Washington lieutenant Alderman Timothy Evans, the self-appointed heir to the late mayor's coalition now running as an independent, and former alderman and now former Democrat Vrdolyak, running as a Republican before fading from political sight altogether. In 1991 Daley solidified his hold on the mayor's office, breezing to victory in both the Democratic primary and the city's general election.

Regarded by his critics as something of an intellectual lightweight and ridiculed for his Bridgeport patois, Mayor Richard M. Daley has demonstrated he's not someone to be underestimated politically. He shocked everyone in early 1990 by delivering a full-blown proposal for an airport on Chicago's Southeast Side and followed that with a bigger shock still in the spring of 1992, when he unveiled a plan for a downtown casino gambling complex. The airport plan faltered in its first go before the Illinois Legislature—prompting an angry mayor to declare it "dead"—and the casino proposal's future is uncertain. But the legislative setback on the airport left Daley's opponents not so much flushed with victory as wary of the mayor's next airport maneuver, and though the casino plan may seem a longshot, few are willing to bet that the mayor lacks the political capital to turn the proposal into reality.

For those who've watched his career, it should come as no surprise if Richard M. Daley should prove a competent mayor; as state's attorney he acquired a reputation as a capable administrator of that office. His rep was one of surrounding himself with good people, people who ran the office effectively, and sure enough, he's now surrounded himself with many of the same people in City Hall.

But the way from here could be one fraught with peril. Like that of most older U.S. cities, Chicago's infrastructure—its roads, sewers, water lines, and other aspects of the city's physical plant—is desperately in need of maintenance, a situation highlighted by the subterranean flood of the Loop in April 1992. Meanwhile, the city's education system is in almost as serious need, and the public transportation system seemingly lost its way long ago. All this against a backdrop of ever scarcer financial resources for cities. The formula for success has become an ever more complicated equation, and that's the reason Daley has focused on grand plans—to provide the wherewithal for solving some of the serious problems in the future while stemming an ever-increasing burden on the residential property taxpayer. It's a tough game to win, a fact Daley seems to recognize with his indication that he has no desire to match the length of his father's residency on the fifth floor at City Hall.

These are far different times than when Richard J. Daley served as mayor, a fact of which Richard M. is well aware. With the second volume in Chicago's political history still in its opening pages, the current Mayor Daley has the opportunity to shape all that follows, and his role in Chicago politics may yet be as significant as his father's.

OTHER KEY PLAYERS

U.S. Representative Dan Rostenkowski, one of the most powerful politicians in the country, is "The Chairman." As head of the U.S. House of Representatives' Ways and Means Committee, any tax legislation has to go through him. Chicago politicians have long had a knack for going where the money is, but nobody's ever done it better than Dan Rostenkowski. His position lets him engage in political horse trading mere mortals can't possibly comprehend, but it's allowed him to look after his district, his city, and his state as well as anyone in Congress. The political architect of the Tax Reform Act of 1986, Rostenkowski talks of Mayor Richard J. Daley's skepticism when he indicated he wished to run for Congress in 1958 rather than shaping a political career in City Hall. He won that 1958 congressional race, and time has proven Rostenkowski's decision was a good one for all involved. A gerrymandered district that threw Lakefront precincts in with his usual Northwest Side electorate couldn't stop him in the 1992 Democratic primary. In the best tradition of Chicago politics, the office appears to be his as long as he chooses to hold it.

Born in Chicago of Puerto Rican parents, **Luis Gutierrez** ran against Mr. Rostenkowski in a race for ward committeeman in 1984. Now he's looking to his fellow Democrat to look after him in Washington as a member of the city's congressional delegation. First elected alderman in the special elections of 1986, he easily won reelection in 1987 and enjoyed similar support in his 1992 primary bid for the Democratic nomination for Chicago's newly created congressional "Hispanic district."

Edwin Eisendrath, the "yuppie alderman," may or may not prove to be a significant force on the city's political scene, though he does mirror the change many of the city's wards, particularly those on the Lakefront, are going through. Eisendrath represents the city's "independent" 43rd Ward, which traditionally has been made up of liberal Democrats, even while refusing to bow to the party machine. In recent years the ward has been increasingly populated with BMWs and cellular phones, however, and it has been known to vote Republican in gubernatorial and presidential races. The Harvard-educated former schoolteacher was elected alderman in 1987 claiming no ambition beyond bettering his city. Three years later, in 1990, he ran for Congress and was crushed in the Democratic primary by incumbent Sidney Yates. While some predicted his imminent aldermanic demise, he rebounded in the 1991 city council race, handily winning reelection. He may be the shape of things to come in city politics, though what that shape is isn't clear.

Appointed city treasurer by Mayor Richard M. Daley in 1989, **Miriam Santos** outdrew the mayor percentage-wise in 1991 election balloting as the most popular member of the Daley ticket. Not surprisingly, the former county prosecutor and Illinois Bell attorney was soon at odds with the mayor, squaring off over control of city pension funds. Santos won. One day soon she may be a candidate for Congress or, if Daley falters or chooses to leave office, a candidate for the mayor's job.

Television has become the most important force in politics, and **David Axelrod,** a former *Chicago Tribune* political reporter turned political strategist, has become the most important local political force in television. He's worked for mayoral candidates, congressional candidates, and presidential candidates. One of these days he'll put a client in the White House. Why not—it's a role that's part of Chicago's political history.

LOCAL RESOURCES

If you want to become involved in Chicago politics, here are some places to start:

Democratic Party of Cook County
134 N. LaSalle   263-0575

Republican Central Committee of Cook County
36 W. Randolph   855-0700

League of Women Voters
332 S. Michigan   939-5935

Independent Voters of Illinois—Independent Precinct Organization
202 S. State   663-4203

—*Rodd Zolkos*

CHICAGO SCHOOLS

Editor's Note: Previous editions of *Sweet Home Chicago* have included a chapter titled "Education"—a fairly lengthy list of schools in Chicago, from preschools to universities, both public and private. But since the third edition of *Sweet Home Chicago* was published in 1987, Chicago's public schools, like the public education systems in other U.S. cities, have become the focus of public concern, legislative efforts, and media attention. Currently Chicago is in the midst of a conspicuous school reform movement.

It now seems that a list of resources for the school shopper would fall far short of presenting Chicago education to the *Sweet Home* reader. After all, this book has long included a chapter on "Chicago Politics," which brings readers up-to-date on city hall shenanigans, and one called "Neighborhoods," which takes the reader through the myriad communities within the city at large. With this edition of *Sweet Home Chicago*, a book we are proud to call "The Real City Guide," it seems that our schools, no less than political schemes and distinctive neighborhoods, are defining us.

On the following pages, Dr. Judith Ponticell, a professor of education and longtime activist in Chicago's schools, guides us through the city's public school system and invites us to participate in its self-improvement.

THE CHICAGO SCHOOL REFORM ACT

The litany of statistics about Chicago's public schools are distressing and, at the same time, enlightening. For example:

- Of Chicago's 408,000 students, approximately 70 percent qualify for the federal free or reduced lunch program for poverty-level children and youth.

- In 1990, approximately 25 percent of first graders, 18 percent of fourth graders, and 30 percent of eighth graders scored at or above the national norm in reading.

- In 1990, approximately 38 percent of first graders, 26 percent of fourth graders, and 18 percent of eighth graders scored at or above the national norm in mathematics.

- Between 43 percent and 53 percent of students who enter Chicago public high schools never graduate.

- In 1989, approximately 3,300 employees were assigned to the central and district offices; none of them worked in the schools.

- Chicago spends more per pupil than 31 of the 50 largest school systems in the nation and $600 more per pupil than the statewide average.

For reform to succeed fully in urban public schools like Chicago's, the underlying beliefs, attitudes, values, and habits of the institution—the culture of the school—must be changed. This must occur not only at the classroom level but also at the organizational level, particularly in the ways decisions get made.

Local control of schools has been the norm, not the exception, in every Illinois district except Chicago. The Chicago School Reform Act of 1988 (PA

85-1418), adopted by the Illinois General Assembly to improve the quality of education in Chicago public schools, sets out to revitalize public education in Chicago by dramatically restructuring the system for making decisions about educational services. The act establishes "a process for placing the primary responsibility for school governance and improvement . . . in the hands of parents, community residents, teachers, and the school principal at the school level."

In 1989 this legislated reform disbanded Chicago's school board. A new school board was appointed by the mayor from a list of nominees submitted by a commission of parents and community members. Local school councils for each school are elected. The councils are comprised of six parents, two teachers, two community members, a nonvoting student representative, and the principal. The councils were charged with basically three duties:

1. *Selection and evaluation of the principal.* The Local School Council (LSC) and principal meet at least once annually for the purpose of preparing the principal evaluation. The LSC provides the principal with a written evaluation of performance by May 15 of each year of the contract. The principal is given the chance to respond, and there may be a subsequent revision of the evaluation. Criteria for the LSC's evaluation of the principal include: (a) progress in implementing the school improvement plan; (b) quality of instructional leadership provided by the principal; (c) progress toward a positive educational climate at the school; (d) progress in communication and human relations with parents, teachers, and the community; and (e) adequate performance in other mutually agreed upon expectations added to the contract.

2. *Monitoring and approving the school budget.* The principal prepares the school's budget; the LSC reviews, revises, and approves the budget. During the year, the LSC monitors the degree to which the budget effectively supports the implementation of the school improvement plan. Exactly how much control does the LSC have over the budget? The Basic/Personnel Budget determines how many teachers, administrators, and staff the school is entitled to, based on enrollment. It also provides money for instructional materials and supplies. It does not require LSC approval as it is created at the Central Office, but the LSC does have some options in the actual assignments of personnel that the budget provides.

The Program Funding Budget supports specific programs, generally those for which the school has submitted a special proposal. Program funding often supports federal Chapter I reading/math improvement for poverty-level students, early childhood education, vocational education, bilingual and special education, and the like.

State Chapter I Funding is the area over which LSCs have the greatest control. Under the Chicago School Reform Act, Chapter I funds are distributed to individual schools on the basis of low-income student enrollment. Funds can be spent on supplemental programs only, and principals, with the LSC's approval, develop spending plans. This area of the budget is virtually unrestricted as long as the use of funds is in support of the School Improvement Plan.

3. *Monitoring and approving the school improvement plan.* The School Improvement Plan projects the priorities and goals of each Chicago public school for a three-year period, within a framework of 24 systemwide goals (see Appendix A later in this chapter). It outlines how the goals will be achieved and indicates the activities and resources to be committed to each goal. The plan describes how parents and the community will be involved in the school and what steps will be taken to provide good working conditions and staff development opportunities for teachers and staff. The plan also explains how progress will be assessed and evaluated and how the LSC will monitor the plan.

The principal writes the School Improvement Plan in consultation with the LSC, parents, school faculty and staff, and community residents. He or she puts the plan into operation after the LSC approves it. The LSC is responsible, together with the principal, for monitoring the plan (i.e., for determining whether the school is meeting the expectations outlined).

The School Improvement Plan must give priority to (a) student proficiency in reading, writing, mathematics, science, and critical thinking skills; (b) student attendance and graduation rates; (c) transition to further education or employment; and (d) high expectations for all students. The School Improvement Plan is a public document.

In addition to the LSC, the reform law calls for teachers and other staff at each school to elect a Professional Personnel Advisory Council (PPAC) to advise the principal and LSC on curriculum, the School Improvement Plan, staff development, and other educational matters. Each school decides how the PPAC is organized and how many people are on it. In theory, the PPAC, LSC, and principal work together to improve the school.

WHAT IS GOING ON IN CHICAGO'S SCHOOLS?

The following vignettes are only illustrations of some of the efforts being made by individual Chicago schools. They reflect the efforts of principals, teachers, LSC members, parents, and community citizens to work together to find creative and comprehensive ways to address the dilemmas facing Chicago's schools. Many of these stories appeared in a promising new publication, *Catalyst: Voices of Chicago School Reform.* Published by the Community Renewal Society, *Catalyst* provides a long overdue opportunity for Chicagoans to find out what their schools are doing—what works, what doesn't, and what is being overlooked in the reform process.

Through training workshops and decision-making guidance, the **CANAL (Creating a New Approach to Learning) Project** (4071 S. Lake Park) is helping over 65 school communities identify, plan, and implement changes likely to increase student learning. CANAL Project schools developed School Improvement Plans a year before the Chicago School Reform Act legislated LSC elections. The project has initiated impressive new activity in schools aimed at changing urban minority and low-achieving students' school experiences (e.g., over 200 program designs, 100 new services and activities directly provided to students, and 20 pilot research projects initiated by teachers).

Key components of the CANAL program are vision creation, strategic planning, team building, consensus decision making, and comprehensive program evaluation. Through the project, schools have changed. **Frazier**

Elementary School (4027 W. Grenshaw) has become Frazier Humanities Center, with an emphasis on Junior Great Books and a fine arts partnership with Urban Gateways. **DuBois Elementary School** (330 E. 133rd) has created a high school and college visiting program to raise students' expectations for themselves. **Cooper Elementary School** (1624 W. 19th) has created a literature-based curriculum in its reading and language arts program. **Sumner Elementary School** (4320 W. 5th) has reached out to overcrowded Latino schools several miles away. The school has a Spanish language program for all students, a curriculum that embraces the Latino and African-American cultures, and a preschool fine arts program.

Through the **Illinois Alliance of Essential Schools Project**, schools are changing the ways they think about and work with adolescents. For example, **Sullivan High School** (6631 N. Bosworth) has created a paideia school within the traditional high school. The paideia school emphasizes critical thinking through the use of Socratic dialogue, a student-centered discussion strategy that places the responsibility for learning on collaboration among the students. The teacher assumes a facilitative and guiding role, rather than lecturing. **Steinmetz High School** (3030 N. Mobile) has created a Student Advocate Program to help troubled teens stay on track. Advocates are currently LSC members, police officers, counselors, parents of students not in the program, faculty, and staff. Advocates help the school keep better track of students' progress and provide more immediate assistance when in-school problems occur. Advocates donate time talking to students, checking their progress, and helping them through the reinstatement or discipline process when students run into trouble. **Englewood High School** (6201 S. Stewart) has piloted a peer coaching program for teachers, using videotaping to help colleagues analyze teaching effectiveness in the classroom. Both the coaching and videotaping strategies provide opportunities for teachers to visit each other's classrooms, talk about the effectiveness of their teaching strategies, learn and implement new teaching strategies together, and evaluate their performance.

Although both the CANAL Project and the Essential Schools Project have created opportunities for many schools to pursue planned change, individual schools and their LSCs have been making changes also. For example, at **Hope Academy** (5515 S. Lowe), the Invention Convention has proven to be a creative approach to teaching reading and problem-solving skills. First students read about inventors and their inventions. They then design and build their own inventions, which are showcased at the annual Invention Convention at the school. In some cases, students' inventions have had commercial potential. **The Beethoven School** (25 W. 47th) operates the Get Real Gift Center, which provides an opportunity for students, many of whom live in Robert Taylor Homes public housing, to see that mathematics has real-life meaning. The Merchants Association at the Chicago Merchandise Mart has donated items like candlesticks and vases to the center. Students do everything from accounting and inventory to shelf arrangement and sales. In addition to learning math in a real-life context, students have generated profits (more than $3,500) for the school.

A Full Inclusion Program for Special Education Students at **Reinberg Elementary School** (3425 N. Major) is providing an opportunity for faculty and parents to create an "inclusive," in the fullest sense of the word, school experience for students with disabilities. Faculty have completed leadership training workshops on inclusion and work collaboratively, often through team teaching, so that about 60 of Reinberg's 160 special needs students have been fully integrated into regular education classes. Reinberg has been recognized by the Inclusive Schools Project, a federally funded program aimed at providing grants to schools that are assuming leadership in integrating special education students into regular education classrooms.

Project Success at **Farragut Career Academy** (2345 S. Christiana) is an attempt to reduce the number of freshmen who fail courses and then drop out of school. Project Success pairs at-risk students with teachers and staff members who serve as surrogate parents. These surrogates identify students' problems, develop individual contracts outlining academic expectations, evaluate students' progress at the end of each marking period, and keep in touch with students' real parents.

College Tutors at **Gray Elementary School** (3730 N. Laramie) were made possible by using some of the school's Chapter I money to hire college students from local universities like the University of Illinois at Chicago, Northeastern, Loyola, and DePaul. The principal and LSC at Gray Elementary School created a program to help low-achieving students with reading. A seed fund of $20,000 enabled the school to pay $6 an hour to 17 college student tutors.

When teacher aides, clerks, or other nonteaching personnel are absent, Parents Serve as Substitutes at **Bass Elementary School** (1140 W. 66th). Through an agreement between the principal, teachers, and parents, parent substitutes are paid about $30 a day from discretionary funds. The program provides incentives to parents to get training and finish their GED, the high school equivalency exam. Parents are getting marketable skills while their service ensures that teachers will be supported in the classroom.

At **McKay Elementary School** (6901 S. Fairfield) students get a different look at parenthood through the Parenting Skills program of monthly visits by mothers with their babies and young children. Students have the opportunity to ask questions and see firsthand how children grow and how their needs, abilities, and responses change. In addition, they begin to learn how to care for infants and toddlers. The program is a joint project with Southwest Women Working Together, a nonprofit organization.

The LSC Babysitting Club at **Sawyer Elementary School** (5248 S. Sawyer) has provided the LSC with its own corps of babysitters to free parent members to attend meetings. Boys and girls in the sixth, seventh, and eighth grades with at least a C average are eligible to sign up for babysitting lessons and one- to two-hour assignments, which pay $10 each. Students get first-aid and CPR training from the local fire department.

At **Gompers Elementary School** (12303 S. State) LSC members have formed grade-level Parent-Teacher Teaching Teams to work with teachers on developing uniform standards and procedures, together with a curriculum guide for parents to use at home with their children.

Goodlow Magnet School (2040 W. 62nd) is Teaching New Teachers to Be Successful. Experienced and beginning teachers at Goodlow meet before the beginning of the school year and then monthly to talk about teaching and school policies and procedures. New instructors get help with everything from teaching more effectively and handling discipline problems, to working with parents and filling out school forms. The program encourages teacher collaboration and cooperation and supports beginning teachers in their critical first year.

Fridays are spent On Campus at **Harper High School** (6520 S. Wood). Part of the Adopt-a-School program at Harper sponsored by the Sara Lee Corporation, this project enables interested juniors and seniors to spend a day visiting local and out-of-state colleges and universities. Students sit in on college classes and talk to faculty members, financial aid counselors, and college students. The number of students enrolling in colleges has doubled.

Team-Teaching Bilingual Students at **Tilden High School** (4747 S. Union) prevents bilingual students from feeling isolated. Nonbilingual and bilingual teachers team up with mainstream Spanish-speaking students. In math and science particularly, English- and Spanish-speaking teachers teach classes that included both regular and bilingual students.

The Mothers Too Soon Program at **Fenger High School** (11220 S. Wallace) assists pregnant teens and young mothers in staying in school. During study halls, students are visited by a teacher who makes sure they are eating properly and seeing their doctors regularly. Linkages are made to social service agencies and school psychologists, in addition to low-cost babysitting services.

At **Healy Elementary School** (3010 S. Parnell) a $43,000 state grant to upgrade science in the primary grades enabled teachers to receive Hands-on Science training in 15 teacher workshops, together with the supplies and equipment needed to make student inquiry and problem solving possible. At **Dearborn Elementary School** (9025 S. Throop), seventh- and eighth-grade students have the opportunity to build solar-powered model cars as part of the national Junior Solar Sprint contest, sponsored by Argonne National Laboratory, the U.S. Department of Energy, and the Society of Automotive Engineers. Students learn firsthand about electricity, mechanics, and aerodynamics, as well as entrepreneurship, when they scavenge for materials to build the chassis of their cars.

The College-Career Counseling Center at **Curie High School** (4959 S. Archer) has succeeded in doubling the number of Curie students looking at college enrollment. The center, funded largely by $20,000 in state Chapter I funds, houses computers that help students explore interests and write letters of inquiry. A videotape library offers a look at about 70 colleges that have sent promotional videos, together with catalogs, brochures, and application forms. Student aides help run the center. In addition, the center sponsors an orientation for all juniors and facilitates college recruiting appointments.

At **Beaubien Elementary School** (5025 N. Laramie) teachers encourage positive behavior through on-the-spot rewards and consequences, using Assertive Discipline techniques. Money raised by the LSC provided two teachers with a week-long summer training course at Elmhurst College, together with training videotapes. The two teachers became in-house trainers who worked with the rest of the Beaubien staff. Discipline-related suspensions dropped from 93 to 30 in a year. At **Brenan Elementary School** (11411 S. Eggleston) $50,000 in Chapter I funds enabled the hiring of a second counselor and the expansion of a special program for troubled children. Teachers refer students with behavioral and personal problems to the counselors, who form small groups of students for weekly counseling sessions focusing on topics such as drugs, self-esteem, avoiding gangs, coping with family problems, or other topics generated by the children. In addition, some students with more severe problems are provided with individual counseling sessions.

Students Grade Themselves at **Irving Elementary School** (749 S. Oakley) to give children a larger stake in their own schooling and keep parents active in their children's education. A new report card provides space for children to record their accomplishments and rate their progress in reading and language arts, together with space for parents to report their children's behavior at home. The students use report card journals to keep careful track of their achievements as readers, writers, speakers, and listeners. Parents report on how often children talk about the school day, spend time reading or writing, and so on.

At **Phillips High School** (244 E. Pershing) Mentors and Black Role Models from the community work to keep students in school. As a component of Project Peace, a comprehensive safe-school program sponsored by the Phillips High School and the Chicago Housing Authority's Department of Resident Services and Programs, mentors visit the school each year to talk and listen to groups of students. Each mentor is paired with at least one student to provide support and encouragement during the year.

The LSC Safety Patrol at **Garvey Elementary School** (10309 S. Morgan) helps teachers fill in the gaps. Local School Council members at Garvey don red-and-white jackets and carry walkie-talkies as they patrol the school and playground before and after school hours and during lunchtime. They receive training from the local police department.

The Reading Aloud Program at **Reavis Elementary School** (834 E. 50th) was developed through a grant from the Heller Foundation. Beginning with a program for 140 children in the summer of 1989 and expanding with assistance from the Literacy Council of Chicago, Reavis uses parent volunteers to read to small groups of children two hours each day during the school year. In addition, parents are being helped to brush up on their own reading, writing, and critical thinking skills.

Bringing Community Ministers to **Chicago Vocational High School** (2100 E. 87th) is an attempt to provide support and counseling to troubled adolescents. Approximately 25 ministers are helping students with discipline and social problems at Chicago Vocational High School. Teachers refer students to the ministerial council, which talks to and advises these students. The program is providing positive role models for troubled African-American students, while enhancing community ministers' knowledge about the problems of urban youth.

Alumni Teachers at **Kipling Elementary School** (9351 S. Lowe) help the school meet the challenge of finding substitute teachers. Kipling encourages former students who have college degrees to return to substitute teach at their alma mater. Alumni are welcomed by students as well as faculty. Former students already know the school and community and serve as role models for the children.

Guggenheim's (7141 S. Morgan) Male Responsibility Program resulted from a unique partnership between the school and the community. When some men in the community wanted a place to play basketball and Guggenheim's principal wanted some fatherly counseling for the boys in his school, the Male Responsibility Program was born. Volunteer counselors are trained in a "circle of trust" technique to enable the development of an ongoing man-to-man discussion about the problems of growing up.

Year-Round Schooling

Several elementary schools have moved to year-round schooling to relieve severe overcrowding. At **Gale Community Academy** (1631 W. Jonquil) the school's students and faculty have been divided into four groups, with overlapping schedules of 60 days in school and 20 days off. The schedule has allowed Gale to reduce the average class size from 40 to 27. Student behavioral problems have decreased, and students have greater access to the school library, computer labs, gym, and support services. **Munoz Marin Elementary School** (3320 W. Evergreen), in addition to year-round schooling, has reconfigured its eight classrooms into learning centers (e.g., math, language arts, computer lab, etc.). Students and their teachers move from room to room depending on what they're studying. Other schools experimenting with year-round scheduling are **Curtis Elementary School** (32 E. 115th), **DuBois Elementary School** (330 E. 133rd), **Funston Elementary School** (2010 N. Central Park), and **Van Vlissingen** (137 W. 108th).

WHAT'S THE FUTURE FOR CHICAGO'S SCHOOLS?

Research on successful urban schools tells us that what is clearly needed to change students' learning experiences in urban schools is a different philosophy of instruction and decision making. A much needed goal is the building of a sense of collaboration and community, and a desire on the part of principals, teachers, students, and parents to belong to that community.

Stories of change and successes abound within the Chicago public schools. There are principals and LSCs working well together. There are more parents willing to help out. There are schools that are becoming more orderly. There are teachers who stress the importance and value of education and strive to help children develop a sense of worth and belonging. There are local businesses and community organizations getting involved in various ways with schools.

Ironically, many Chicago schools don't know of the successes of their colleagues. Widespread dissemination of information on what is succeeding and why is still a systemwide problem.

And, the system is still basically centralized. School budgets and program or supply approvals remain largely in the jurisdiction of central administration at Pershing Road. Financial problems still beset the entire system, deepening management problems and reducing supplies, equipment, and supplemental programs. In addition, overcrowding in Chicago public schools is getting worse.

In Chicago, the formal structures specified in the reform act have been put into place. Yet on the bottom-line issue—changing learning experiences for students in Chicago's schools—the jury is still out. On a recent survey of

Chicago elementary schoolteachers (Consortium on Chicago School Research, 1991), 57 percent of the respondents agreed that changes made since the implementation of the reform act had no effect on their classroom practices, and 55 percent believed that the School Improvement Plans would not change their instructional practices.

Effective urban schools research tells us that teachers must have fewer students and spend more time getting to know them. The curriculum must be narrower in scope so that students learn a few concepts well, learning how to learn in the process rather than trying to skim across a vast ocean of facts and fragments of ideas. More classes must be organized around student-centered opportunities for learning, and students must be taught and encouraged to take a greater responsibility for their own learning. The policies, structures, and resources needed to support teachers in making these changes in their classrooms are generally not controlled by the teachers themselves.

Most importantly, big cities like Chicago must recognize that the responsibility for providing quality education for urban youth lies only in part with the schools. The social deficits that many children in Chicago bring with them to school cannot be accepted as unquestioned givens. Many of the most exciting efforts in individual Chicago schools are based on a belief that all children can learn and that it is the school's responsibility to find out where to start within the knowledge, interests, skills, and goals of the children themselves. Even the best intentions of teachers and schools are likely to falter, however, when resources and public support of schools dwindle.

In the November 1991 issue of *Catalyst*, Susan Klonsky, editor of *Reform Watch*, a school reform newsletter published by the Chicago Donors Forum, reported that there are things that schools and their communities can, and are, doing to exercise initiative in planning and change. She noted the following points:

1. *Development*—Local School Council members, faculty, community, and local businesses are forming development groups to target long-term fundraising.

2. *Vision*—Schools are developing clear pictures of change to market for foundation and business grants.

3. *Networking*—Schools are linking up with other schools, both urban and suburban, to learn about and visit firsthand school improvement programs.

4. *Development specialists*—One or two members of the faculty and school community are receiving training to become grant proposal writers and funding locators. An important asset to schools interested in locating outside funding is the **Chicago Donors Forum Library** (53 W. Jackson). It is open free to the public.

5. *Leadership learning library*—Videotapes and guides published and sent to all schools in 1990 by **Leadership for Quality Education** (592-6532) and the Citywide Coalition for School Reform provide LSCs with information on the grant-seeking process.

6. *Business community*—There are business groups that assist in drawing schools and businesses closer together—for example, **Leadership for Quality**

Education (592-6532), the **Executive Service Corps** (580-1840), **Volunteer Network** (606-8240), and the **Chicago Association of Commerce** (580-6945).

7. *School adoption*—The Adopt-a-School Program provides guidelines for schools to seek out business and community organization partnerships for financial aid, goods, and in-kind assistance.

8. *Universities*—Colleges of Education in Chicago-area universities conduct numerous research projects related to education reform. By agreeing to become a research site or site for student teachers, schools may receive financial assistance, computer link-ups, consultation, and staff development assistance.

9. *Political action*—Work is under way with other schools and organizations to protect public funding gains, like Chapter I, and demand fiscal accountability from the Board of Education and Illinois legislature.

The process of changing schools is long and arduous. Studies of urban schools that have implemented large-scale reform or restructuring plans show that five to six years is a conservative estimate of the process of school change. There *is* change in Chicago public schools; much of it has resulted from the individual efforts of schools. But there remains much to be done. The question of equitable distribution of resources—what's fair to Chicago's youth—is the responsibility of policymakers, lawmakers, businesses, and taxpayers, not children, teachers, and schools.

SUGGESTED READING

Education Reform by S. Bacharach (Ed.).

Improving the Urban High School: What Works and Why by K. S. Louis and M. B. Miles.

The New Meaning of Educational Change by M. G. Fullan.

Restructuring America's Schools by A. Lewis.

Restructuring Schools by R. Elmore et al.

School Leadership: A Blueprint for Change by S. D. Thomson (Ed.).

School Reform, Chicago Style: How Citizens Organized to Change Public Policy by M. O'Connell.

School Restructuring, Chicago Style by G. A. Hess.

Students at Risk in At-Risk Schools by H. C. Waxman, J. W. de Felix, J. E. Anderson, and H. P. Baptiste.

APPENDIX A: CHICAGO'S GOALS AND OBJECTIVES

Under the provisions of the Chicago School Reform Act of 1988 (PA 85-1418), the Chicago public schools, like other Illinois public schools, are required to prepare a School Improvement Plan. The Systemwide Educational Reform Goals and Objectives Plan is approved by the Chicago School Finance Authority, an oversight committee that monitors the system's progress. The Chicago public schools' systemwide goals are as follows:

1. The annual four-year graduation rate will increase by 5 percent per year to 60 percent by June 1994.

2. Students will achieve increased proficiency in reading, writing, mathematics, science, and higher-order thinking at rates that will allow their achievement to equal or surpass national norms by the end of the 1993–94 school year.

3. Student attendance will improve by 1 percent annually.

4. The promotion of students advancing to the next grade will increase by 2 percent annually.

5. Teachers will continue their professional growth and improve their teaching ability.

6. The authority, responsibility, and accountability of principals will be increased.

7. The LSCs will be established and supported.

8. The performance of LSCs and district councils will be evaluated according to appropriate criteria.

9. Parents' involvement in the education of their children will increase.

10. The student-counselor ratio will be established at 250 to 1 in the high schools and at 500 to 1 in the elementary schools.

11. Schools will be organized to deliver appropriate instruction services effectively to meet the particular educational needs of their students.

12. A set of uniform curriculum objectives and standards will be established, with a multicultural and international emphasis.

13. High school students will have available all courses necessary to comply with the State of Illinois Board of Higher Education's college entrance criteria.

14. Class size will be reduced as near the statewide average as possible, with a priority placed on grades K–3, within available funds and other school priorities.

15. Short- and long-term policies and plans for improving physical facilities will be developed and implemented.

16. All eligible three- and four-year-old children will be provided with a preschool education, to the extent possible using available categorical funds.

17. Schools will use their categorical resources to serve students with special needs effectively.

18. Student awareness of, interest in, and exposure to journalism, drama, art, music, dance, visual arts, and athletics will be increased.

19. Students will be provided with opportunities to gain increased mastery of second languages and better understanding of international cultures.

20. Students will be provided programs and services that help them make the transition to higher education.

21. Students will be provided quality programs that prepare them for career employment.

22. Parents will be provided with increased options for selecting schools, consistent with the recommendations of the Illinois State Board of Education.

23. The relationship of the Board of Education and its administrative staff to local schools will be restructured so that there is less centralized control and more field-based assistance.

24. Funds budgeted by the Board of Education will be equitably distributed among schools and programs, in accordance with applicable laws, rules, and regulations.

—*Judith A. Ponticell, Ph.D.*

APPENDIX B: A LIST OF CHICAGO SCHOOLS

Illinois Department of Children and Family Services
1206 S. Damen, Chicago, 60612   793-2100
This office, which regulates and licenses day-care and night-care facilities, offers a brochure that tells you what to look for when selecting day care. Write to **Office of Communication/Community Relations, Department of Children and Family Services**, 406 E. Monroe, Springfield, 62701.

Day Care Action Council
4753 N. Broadway, Chicago, 60640   814-6800
This Cook County information service will refer you to up to three programs. The council also works with parents and day-care providers on affordability, insurance, licensing, funding, starting a center, and making formal complaints.

Evanston Committee for Community Coordinated Child Care
518 E. Davis, Evanston, 60201   475-2661
Child care referrals for Evanston and northern Cook County.

Hyde Park–Kenwood Community Conference
1376 E. 53rd, Chicago, 60615   288-8343
Publishes a directory of Hyde Park and Kenwood schools, including day-care facilities.

Jane Addams Center
3212 N. Broadway, Chicago, 60657   549-1631
Referrals for day-care centers and in-home child care.

National Association for the Education of Young Children
1834 Connecticut Ave., NW, Washington D.C. 20009
This national organization is a good resource for information on choosing a day-care program.

Elementary and High Schools

Public Schools

Chicago Board of Education
1819 W. Pershing, Chicago, 60632   535-8000
To find the public school in your district, call or write the Chicago School Board. People at the board's office can also give you the phone number for your district office and tell you about any special programs or schools that might be appropriate for your child.

Special Programs and Magnet Schools

Board of Education's Office of Equal Educational Opportunity   535-7790
This office runs many of the special programs and magnet schools in Chicago. Their booklet *Options for Knowledge* will tell you about the various special opportunities in Chicago's public schools, from magnet schools and voluntary transfer programs to schools with a particular emphasis such as the arts or technical education. To get the booklet, call 535-7790.

Some well-respected Chicago public high schools are not listed in the brochure, including **Lane Tech** (2501 W. Addison), which offers a technical and college prep curriculum; **Prosser** (2148 N. Long), which provides a vocational education, and Lane's South Side counterpart, **Lindblom** (6130 S. Wolcott).

Illinois Mathematics and Science Academy
1500 W. Sullivan, Aurora, 60506   (708) 801-6000
Admission to this three-year college prep academy is very selective—just 300 students per class. Students live on the premises. Tuition and room and board are free for Illinois residents.

For further information about the Chicago public schools, contact the following organizations:

Chicago Panel on Public School Finances
53 W. Jackson, Chicago, 60604   939-2202

Citizen's Schools Committee
36 S. Wabash, #1028, Chicago, 60602   726-4678

Designs for Change
220 S. State, #1900, Chicago, 60604   922-0317
This nonprofit research, advocacy, and training organization works for basic improvements in the day-to-day experiences of all Chicago public schoolchildren, especially those from poor neighborhoods.

Other groups involved with education advocacy are these:

Chicago Region Parent-Teacher Association (PTA)
53 W. Jackson, #1522, Chicago, 60604   786-1476

Teachers Advisory Council
161 W. Harrison, Chicago, 60605   341-0977

Parochial Schools

Catholic School Board
155 E. Superior, Chicago, 60611   751-5200

Jewish Board of Education
618 S. Michigan, Chicago, 60605   427-5570

Lutheran High School Association
333 W. Lake, Addison, 60101   (708) 628-6289

Private Schools

Independent Schools Association of Greater Chicago
1234 E. Madison Park, Chicago, 60615   971-3581

Chicago Academy for the Arts
1010 W. Chicago, Chicago, 60622   421-0202
This is a competitive school where students study music, dance, theater, and visual arts in preparation for a fine- arts career.

Marva Collins' Westside Preparatory School
4146 W. Chicago, Chicago, 60651   227-5995
Tuition at Marva Collins' is based on a sliding-fee scale.

Society of Montessori Schools
1985 Pfingsten, Northbrook, 60062   (708) 498-1105
Montessori schools are best known for preschool instruction, although they offer classes through the eighth grade. Call the above number for the name of a Montessori school in your area (city or suburbs).

These "Big Three" schools are prestigious, expensive, and competitive:

Francis W. Parker School
330 W. Webster, Chicago, 60614   549-0172
Kindergarten through 12th grade.

The Latin School of Chicago
59 W. North, Chicago, 60610   573-4500
Kindergarten through 12th grade.

University of Chicago Laboratory Schools
1362 E. 59th, Chicago, 60637   702-9451
Nursery school through 12th grade.

The following private schools offer kindergarten through 12th grade programs:

Chicago City Day School
541 W. Hawthorne, Chicago, 60657   327-0900

Harvard School
4731 S. Ellis, Chicago, 60615   624-0394

Morgan Park Academy
2153 W. 111th, Chicago, 60643   881-6700

North Shore Country Day School
310 Green Bay, Winnetka, 60093   (708) 446-0674

Roycemore School
640 Lincoln, Evanston, 60201   (708) 866-6055

Alternative Private Schools

Alternative schools tend to offer more freedom to students and vary in the amount of importance they place on traditional learning, such as reading and math skills. Tuition also varies greatly.

Alternative Schools Network
1150 W. Lawrence, Chicago, 60640   728-4030

Postsecondary Education

Junior Colleges

City Colleges of Chicago
226 W. Jackson, Chicago, 60608   641-2595
Chicago's junior college system is a good one, consisting of eight colleges and a technical institute, Dawson Skills Institute.

Daley College
7500 S. Pulaski, Chicago, 60652   735-3000

Dawson Technical Institute
3901 S. State, Chicago, 60609   451-2000

Harold Washington College
30 E. Lake, Chicago, 60601   781-9430

Kennedy-King College
6800 S. Wentworth, Chicago, 60621   962-3200

Malcolm X College
1900 W. Van Buren, Chicago, 60612   942-3000

Olive-Harvey College
10001 S. Woodlawn, Chicago, 60628   568-3700

Truman College
1145 W. Wilson, Chicago, 60640   878-1700

Wright College
3400 N. Austin, Chicago, 60634   777-7900

If you can't find the program you need at one of the city colleges, try one of the nearby suburban junior colleges:

Moraine Valley Community
10900 S. 88th, Palos Hills, 60465   (708) 974-4300
In-district tuition is $37 per credit hour.

Oakton Community College
Main campus:
1600 E. Golf, Des Plaines, 60016   (708) 635-1600
Skokie campus:
7701 Lincoln, Skokie, 60077   (708) 635-1600
In-district tuition is $25 per credit hour.

South Suburban College
15800 S. State, South Holland, 60473   (708) 596-2000
In-district tuition is $40.50 per credit hour.

Triton Community College
2000 Fifth, River Grove, 60171   (708) 456-0300
In-district tuition is $36.50 per credit hour.

Colleges and Universities

Chicago State University
9501 S. King, Chicago, 60628   995-2000
Offers bachelor's degrees and some master's degrees. Tuition for Illinois residents is $1,099 per semester for full- time study.

Columbia College
600 S. Michigan, Chicago, 60605   663-1600
Emphasizes the arts, media, and communications, along with comprehensive programs in liberal arts and sciences. Full- time undergraduate tuition is $3,282 per semester.

DePaul University
Loop campus:
25 E. Jackson, Chicago, 60604   341-8300
Lincoln Park campus:
2323 N. Seminary, Chicago, 60614   362-6710
Strong programs in music, theater, computer science, business (especially accounting), and law. Undergraduate tuition is $208 per credit hour; theater and music schools are higher.

Illinois Institute of Technology
3300 S. Federal, Chicago, 60616   567-3000
Best known for its programs in engineering, architecture, design, business, and law (Chicago-Kent College of Law is located downtown at 77 S. Wacker). Mies van der Rohe was dean of the architecture school for many years and designed much of the South Side campus. Tuition is $410 per credit hour.

Kendall College
2408 Orrington, Evanston, 60202   (708) 866-1300
This small liberal arts and business college offers a culinary and hospitality degree. Tuition is $152 per credit hour for students taking 16 credits or over, and $220 for students taking under 12 credits.

Loyola University
Main campus:
6525 N. Sheridan, Chicago, 60626   274-3000
Water Tower campus:
820 N. Michigan, Chicago, 60611   670-3000
A Jesuit institution with an emphasis on liberal arts and business curricula.
Undergraduate students can choose between the downtown and Rogers Park
campuses. Graduate business and law schools are located at the Water Tower
campus. Full-time tuition is $9,890 for an academic year.

Mundelein College
6363 N. Sheridan, Chicago, 60660   262-8100
A women's Catholic liberal arts college. Special programs for women return-
ing to school after a long absence. Also offers Weekend College, a degree
program that can be completed exclusively on weekends. Tuition is $233 per
credit hour.

National-Louis University
2840 Sheridan, Evanston, 60201   (708) 256-5150
Formerly known as the National College of Education, this university now
offers undergraduate and graduate degrees in education and administration,
business and management, and arts and sciences. There are also campuses in
the Loop, west suburban Lombard, and north suburban Wilmette and Elgin.
Undergraduate tuition is $190 per quarter hour; graduate tuition is $280 per
semester hour ($270 for arts and sciences, $150 for extension courses).

Northeastern Illinois University
5500 N. St. Louis, Chicago, 60625   583-4050
State-supported institution located on the far Northwest Side of the city.
In-state tuition is $1,146.25 per trimester for full-time study.

Northwestern University
Main campus:
180 Hinman, Evanston, 60201   (708) 491-3741
Chicago campus:
710 N. Lake Shore Drive, Chicago, 60611   908-8649
Major private university with an excellent national reputation. Full-time
undergraduate tuition is $15,075.

Roosevelt University
Main campus:
430 S. Michigan, Chicago, 60605   341-3500
Suburban campus:
2121 S. Goebbert, Arlington Heights, 60005   (708) 437-9200
Roosevelt was a pioneer in open admissions policy, enrolling students
without regard to sex, race, age, or economic class. Housed in the famous
Adler and Sullivan Auditorium Building. Undergraduate tuition is $274 per
credit hour.

Rosary College
7900 W. Division, River Forest, 60305   (708) 366-2490
This small liberal arts college is located in west suburban River Forest. Tuition
is $330 per semester hour.

St. Xavier College
3700 W. Division, River Forest, 60305   (708) 366-2490
Located southwest of the city, St. Xavier offers a weekend college program.
Undergraduate tuition is $318 per semester hour.

School of the Art Institute of Chicago
Columbus Avenue and Jackson Boulevard, Chicago, 60604   899-5100
Art education (with an emphasis on studio) in painting, design, filmmaking,
video, and time arts. Courses in art history, criticism, and liberal arts comple-
ment the undergraduate program. Strong national reputation. Undergraduate tuition is $6,225 for full-time study and $1,245 for one course.
Graduate tuition is $6,675 for full-time study and $1,335 for one course.

Spertus College of Judaica
618 S. Michigan, Chicago, 60605   922-9012
In cooperation with eight area colleges and universities, Spertus offers
degrees in liberal arts and Judaic studies. An excellent teaching museum and
research library are open to the public. Tuition for graduate courses is $150
per credit hour. Continuing education courses are also offered.

University of Chicago
5801 S. Ellis, Chicago, 60637   702-1234
The U of C is regarded as one of the top universities in the country. Undergraduate tuition is $17,061.

University of Illinois at Chicago
601 S. Morgan, P.O. Box 4348, Chicago, 60680   996-4350
Formed by the 1982 merger of the Medical Center and Chicago Circle campuses of the University of Illinois, UIC is the largest institution of higher
learning in the Chicago area, with a very wide range of majors and graduate
courses in many fields. Undergraduate tuition ranges from $826 to $1,750 per
semester, depending on the number of hours and course levels.

Commercial, Trade, and Correspondence Schools

Illinois Department of Registration and Education
100 W. Randolph, Chicago, 60610   814-4500
This office oversees the licensing of professions. Contact them if you question
the legitimacy of a program or suspect a school is making false advertising
claims. To find out if a school is approved for veterans, contact the **Veteran's
Administration Approving Section** (663-5510).

Continuing Education

Continuing education courses are offered at most colleges and universities,
and frequently at high schools, YMCAs, and YWCAs. The Latin School and
Francis W. Parker School publish catalogs of their noncredit courses. Usually
continuing education courses cost a lot less than regular degree-credit
courses at a college.

Discovery Center
2930 N. Lincoln, Chicago, 60657 348-8120
Monthly catalogs of course offerings are ubiquitous on downtown street corners and in the trendier neighborhoods. Subjects include aerobics, investments, the ever-popular flirting course, and much more. Classes range from one meeting to six weeks and cost from $25 to $139.

Cultural Exchange Organizations

Alliance Française
810 N. Dearborn, Chicago, 60610 337-1070

Chicago Council on Foreign Relations
116 S. Michigan, Chicago, 60603 726-3860

Crossroads Student Center
5621 S. Blackstone, Chicago, 60637 684-6060
Another cultural center in Hyde Park for foreign students. Crossroads is primarily a social center, with no housing space. English, French, and Spanish classes are also offered.

Goethe Institut
401 S. Michigan, Chicago, 60611 329-0915

International House
1414 E. 59th, Chicago, 60637 753-2270
Established in the 1930s as part of the University of Chicago, International House can house about 500 people. Residents (half American and half foreign) are mostly grad students. Housing fees for the academic year average $3,270 plus board. Single rooms can be rented for $28 per night, depending on availability. During the school year, reservations are usually necessary.

Institute of International Education
401 N. Wabash, #722, Chicago, 60611 644-1400
Offers information about scholarship opportunities for foreign students and general assistance to international students. They also have a reference section for Americans interested in study or work abroad. Open Monday–Friday from 9:30 A.M. to 4:30 P.M.

Japan America Society of Chicago
40 N. Dearborn, #910, Chicago, 60602 263-3049

Club Lucky.

Out and About

RESTAURANTS AND CAFES
NIGHTLIFE
LATE NIGHT AND ALL NIGHT
SECONDHAND SHOPPING

RESTAURANTS AND CAFES

We decided to keep this chapter simple: just an alphabetical list of our favorite places, garnered from a decade of living and eating out in Chicago. As long as we've lived here we've been determined to try many cuisines, happiest to pay only a little for wonderful food but willing to spend more for an occasional splurge on gourmet fare.

RESTAURANTS

Please keep in mind that restaurants close, change hours, increase prices, and play with their menus. It's probably a good idea to call and verify the information given below.

Angelina Ristorante
3561 N. Broadway   935-5933
Hours: Daily, 5:30 A.M.–11 P.M.
Southern Italian, Mid-North, Moderate
Cozy atmosphere with pretty, little tables and as strong an Italian menu as the city has to offer.

Ann Sather's
929 W. Belmont (Mid-North)   348-2378
5207 N. Clark (Andersonville)   271-6677
1329 E. 57th (Hyde Park)   947-9323
Hours: Daily, 7 A.M.–11 P.M.
Swedish, Inexpensive
A bread-lover's nirvana with extraordinary cinnamon rolls.

Arco de Cuchilleros
3445 N. Halsted   296-6046
Hours: Monday–Friday, 4 P.M.–midnight; Saturday, noon–midnight; Sunday, noon–10 P.M.
Spanish/Tapas, Mid-North, Moderate
Tapas are hot and cold Spanish dishes served in small quantities and great numbers. Order a few to start and then some more and then some more after that, from vegetables to potatoes to meaty taste treats, all the while munching on little pieces of bread. We like this tapas place because it's unpretentious, with good food, fruity sangria, and friendly service.

Athenian Room
807 W. Webster   348-5155
Hours: Monday–Saturday, 11 A.M.–10 P.M.; Sunday, noon–9 P.M.
Greek, North Side, Inexpensive
Standard Greek food.

Bangkok Restaurant
3542 N. Halsted   327-2870
Hours: Monday–Thursday, 11 A.M.–10:30 P.M.;
Friday and Saturday, 11 A.M.–11 P.M.; Sunday buffet, 11 A.M.–9:30 P.M.
Thai, Mid-North, Inexpensive
There are many places to eat Thai food in Chicago; Bangkok is one of the best.
Don't forget to start with satay (chicken or beef kabobs dipped in peanut
sauce).

Bar Louie
226 W. Chicago   337-3313
Hours: Monday–Friday, 11:30 A.M.–2 A.M.; Saturday, noon–2 A.M.;
closed Sunday
American, River North, Inexpensive
Delicious sandwiches, salads, calamari, and more in a bar atmosphere.

Batteries Not Included
2201 N. Clybourn   472-9920
Hours: Sunday–Thursday, 4 P.M.–10 P.M.; Friday and Saturday, 4 P.M.–11 P.M.
French Carribean, North Side, Moderate to Expensive
Should you have the sea scallops and shrimp with lobster sauce, or the
chicken and shrimp with oyster sauce, or one of the other tantalizing selections? We have good reason to suspect everything is good at this Carribean
bistro.

The Berghoff
17 W. Adams   427-3170
Monday–Thursday, 11 A.M.–9:30 P.M.; Friday and Saturday, 11 A.M.–10 P.M.;
closed Sunday
German, Loop, Moderate
Corned beef and cabbage, grilled fish, creamed spinach, a plate full of rye
bread on your table, and as strong a sense of 19th-century Chicago as you're
likely to find. Berghoff beer is mighty tasty, too.

Berghoff Brewery
436 W. Ontario   266-7771
Hours: Tuesday–Friday, 11:30 A.M.–2 P.M.; Tuesday–Thursday, 5 P.M.–10 P.M.;
Sunday, 4:30 P.M.–9 P.M.; closed Monday
German, Loop, Inexpensive
The brewery version of the Berghoff has some of the expected German fare as
well as light entrees and fresh grilled seafood. Among the beers you might
find fresh and on tap are Gold Lager, Bicycle Beer (berry flavored), and
Dunkel Lager.

Billy Goat Tavern
430 N. Michigan (lower level)   222-1525
Hours: Monday–Friday, 7 A.M.–2 A.M.; Saturday, 10 A.M.–3 A.M.;
Sunday, 11 A.M.–2 A.M.
Bar Food, Loop, Cheap
The inspiration for that "Saturday Night Live" skit ("cheezeborger,
cheezeborger, no fries, chips") back in the seventies, the Billy Goat is where
the old-school Chicago newspaper men and women hang (notice we didn't

say "journalists"). The cheeseburgers are as greasy as they are cheap, but fortunately, the beer is cold.

Bishop's
1958 W. 18th   829-6345
Hours: Monday–Friday, 11 A.M.–6 P.M.; Saturday, 11 A.M.–2:30 P.M.; closed Sunday
Chili, Cheap
Bishop's *is* chili in Chicago.

Brett's Kitchen
233 W. Superior   664-6354
Hours: Daily, 6 A.M.–4 P.M.
Deli, River North, Inexpensive
There are lots of deli sandwiches, great homemade soups, and big chocolate chip cookies at this corner lunch spot in River North. Fast but friendly service. Carry out or eat in.

Buona Fortuna
1540 N. Milwaukee   278-7797
Hours: Monday–Thursday, 5 P.M.–11 P.M.; Friday and Saturday, 5 P.M.–midnight; closed Sunday.
Italian, Wicker Park, Moderate to Expensive
This is a romantic place with delicious fish and pasta specials.

Burklee's
2153 N. Clybourn   549-7286
Hours: Tuesday–Thursday, 11 A.M.–9 P.M.; Friday, 11 A.M.–10 P.M.; Saturday, 9 A.M.–10 P.M.; Sunday, 9 A.M.–4 P.M.
Eclectic, North Side, Inexpensive
Many of the menu's offerings are Mexican, vegetarian, or both at this small and simple storefront restaurant. Friendly service. Good weekend breakfast.

Busy Bee
1546 N. Damen   772-4433
Hours: Monday–Friday, 6 A.M.–8 P.M.; Saturday, 7 A.M.–8 P.M.; Sunday, 7 A.M.–7:30 P.M.
Polish, Wicker Park, Inexpensive
A classic Chicago diner.

California Pizza Kitchen
414 N. Orleans (River North)   222-9030
Hours: Monday–Thursday, 11:30 A.M.–10 P.M.; Friday and Saturday, 11:30 A.M.–11 P.M.; Sunday, 1 P.M.–9 P.M.
Water Tower Place, 835 N. Michigan (Near North)   787-7300
Hours: Monday–Thursday, 11 A.M.–10 P.M.; Friday and Saturday, 11 A.M.–11 P.M.; Sunday, 11 A.M.–9 P.M.
Pizza, Inexpensive
Great mod individual pizzas (thin crust, fresh vegetables, basil, goat cheese, roasted red peppers, and the like). We recommend the cheeseless (yes, cheeseless) vegetable pizza.

Cape Cod Room
140 E. Walton   787-2200
Hours: Daily, noon–11 P.M.
Seafood, Near North, Expensive
Located in the Drake Hotel, where Lake Shore Drive winds around to Michigan Avenue, this is a classic place to celebrate with family or host out-of-towners. Ask for Shrimp Indiana, a curried shrimp not on the menu but worth a try.

Chicago Diner
3411 N. Halsted   935-6696
Hours: Monday–Friday, 11 A.M.–9:30 P.M.; Saturday, 10 A.M.–10 P.M.
Vegetarian, Mid-North, Inexpensive
Vegetarians who get curious about (or nostalgic for) the feel of a burger in the hand can find the perfect substitute at Chicago Diner, where the veggie burgers taste mighty good. Wonderful soups, specials, and fresh squeezed fruit and vegetable juices make Chicago Diner a great place to go for healthy "comfort food."

Club Lucky
1824 W. Wabansia   227-2300
Hours: Monday–Thursday, 5 P.M.–11 P.M.;
Friday and Saturday, 5 P.M.–midnight; Sunday, 4 P.M.–11 P.M.
Italian, Wicker Park, Moderate
A traditional, family style restaurant with daily specials, antipasta, and tasty grilled fish such as tuna and Florida grouper.

Cooking and Hospitality Institute of Chicago
351 W. Chestnut   944-0882
Hours: Monday–Friday, noon seating only
Gourmet, Near North, Moderate
Stop by and eat whatever the students are cooking (the menu changes every day). We doubt you'll be disappointed in either the taste or the presentation. Fledglings try harder.

Courtyards of Plaka
340 S. Halsted   263-0767
Hours: Sunday–Thursday, 11 A.M.–midnight;
Friday and Saturday, 11 A.M.–1 A.M.
Greek, Near West, Moderate
Plaka is a little more elegant than most of the other Greektown establishments. Standouts include the moussaka and red snapper.

Cozy Cafe
2819 N. Lincoln   549-9374
Hours: Daily, 7 A.M.–3 P.M.
Diner, Mid-North, Inexpensive
There's nothing fancy about the Cozy, but we like it. Nice outdoor seating for those rare warm-weather days.

Don Juan
6730 N. Northwest Highway
Hours: Monday–Thursday, 11 A.M.–10 P.M.;
Friday and Saturday, 11 A.M.–11 P.M.; Sunday, 12 P.M.–9 P.M.
Mexican, Far North, Moderate
As a rule the Mexican food in Chicago is mediocre at best. Don Juan is a welcome exception.

Edwardo's
1321 E. 57th (Mid-South) 241-7960
1937 W. Howard (Far North) 761-7040
1212 N. Dearborn (Near North) 337-4490
521 S. Dearborn (Near South) 939-3366
Hours: Sunday–Thursday, 11 A.M.–12:30 A.M.;
Friday and Saturday, noon–midnight
Pizza, Inexpensive
Of all the chains in our city that serve "Chicago-style" pizza, Edwardo's is our favorite because they use *fresh* ingredients. They have stuffed, pan, and thin-crust varieties—all of them good. For a new pizza experience try the tasty pesto pizza. We highly recommend the whole-wheat crust. The pasta dishes aren't bad, either.

Emilio's
4100 W. Roosevelt, Hillside (708) 547-7177
Hours: Monday–Thursday, 11:30 A.M.–10 P.M.; Friday, 11:30 A.M.–11 P.M.;
Saturday, 5 P.M.–11 P.M.; Sunday, 5 P.M.–10 P.M.
Spanish/Tapas, West Suburban, Moderate to Expensive
During peak hours there's usually a lengthy wait for a table at Emilio's, because it is one of the best places in the area to have sangria and paella. A festive place to go with a group and share lots and lots of different tapas.

La Fontanella
2414 S. Oakley 927-5249
Hours: Monday–Thursday, 11:30 A.M.–9:30 P.M.; Friday, 11:30 A.M.–11 P.M.;
Saturday, 2 P.M.–11 P.M.; Sunday, noon–9 P.M.; no lunch menu on weekends
Italian, Near Southwest, Moderate
A popular, *proven* Italian restaurant where meatballs and homemade pasta get rave reviews.

French Kitchen
3437 W. 63rd 776-6715
Hours: Daily, 5 P.M.–10 P.M.
French, Mid-Southwest, Moderate
Cute French country atmosphere with good food and service.

Frontera Grill
445 N. Clark 661-1434
Hours: Tuesday–Thursday, 11:30 A.M.–2:30 P.M., 5:30 P.M.–10 P.M.;
Friday, 11:30 A.M.–2:30 P.M., 5 P.M.–11 P.M.;
Saturday brunch, 10:30 A.M.–2:30 P.M., 5 P.M.–11 P.M.;
closed Sunday and Monday
Gourmet Mexican and Southwest, Near North, Expensive
Some of their specialties include grilled salmon, Swiss chard, and a delicious mole sauce.

Furama
4936 N. Broadway
Hours: Daily, 9:30 A.M.–9:30 P.M.
Chinese/Dim Sum, Far North, Moderate
Pluck your plate of steamed buns or dumplings from carts as they roll by. The large open dining room fills with the clatter of chopsticks and Chinese.

Galans
2210 W. Chicago 292-1000
Hours: Tuesday–Thursday, 11:30 A.M.–10 P.M.;
Friday and Saturday, 5 P.M.–11 P.M.; Sunday, 11:30 A.M.–9 P.M.; closed Monday
Ukrainian, Ukrainian Village, Moderate
Pierogy (stuffed dumplings), borscht, kartoplyanyk (potato pancakes), and much more will entice you at this Ukrainian Village institution.

Gandhi Indian
2601 W. Devon 761-8714
Hours: Daily, 11:30 A.M.–3:30 P.M.; Sunday–Thursday, 5 P.M.–10 P.M.;
Friday and Saturday, 5 P.M.–11 P.M.
East Indian, Far North, Inexpensive
Probably the best of the moderately priced Indian restaurants in Chicago.

Gavroche Wine Bar and Cafe
1958 N. Damen 276-7605
Hours: Sunday, Tuesday–Thursday, 5:30 P.M.–10:30 P.M.;
Friday and Saturday, 5:30 P.M.–11:30 P.M.; closed Monday
Eclectic, Bucktown, Moderate to Expensive
This small storefront restaurant excels in innovative appetizers and specials. The atmosphere is very simple, but the menu reflects genuine elegance. A quirky, creative place.

Gladys' Luncheonette
4527 S. Indiana 548-6848
Hours: Tuesday–Sunday, 7 A.M.–11:45 P.M.; closed Monday
Soul Food, Mid-South, Inexpensive
Eat a *real* breakfast (ham, eggs, grits, and biscuits) any time of day, or go to Gladys' for the best fried chicken you'll ever taste.

Gold Coast Dogs
418 N. State   527-1222
Hours: Monday–Thursday, 7:30 A.M.–midnight;
Friday and Saturday, 10:30 A.M.–8 P.M.; Sunday, 11 A.M.–8 P.M.
2100 N. Clark   327-8887
Hours: Sunday–Thursday, 10 A.M.–midnight;
Friday and Saturday, 10 A.M.–2 A.M.
325 S. Franklin   939-2624
Hours: Monday–Friday 10:30 A.M.–6 P.M.; Saturday, 11 A.M.–4 P.M.;
closed Sunday
Hotdogs and hamburgers, Near North, Cheap
Hot dogs, burgers, and sandwiches that many believe to be the best cheap
American food in the city. Cheese fries never tasted so good.

Golden Shell
10063 S. Avenue North   221-9876
Hours: Tuesday–Thursday, 6 A.M.–11 P.M.;
Friday and Saturday, 6 A.M.–midnight; Sunday, 6 A.M.–8 P.M.; closed Monday
Yugoslavian, Far South, Inexpensive
Lamb, eggplant, and seafood specialties as well as hearty breakfast food
make this large Yugoslavian restaurant very successful.

Goose Island Brewery
1800 N. Clybourn   915-0071
Hours: Kitchen open Monday–Thursday, 11 A.M.–11 P.M.;
Friday and Saturday, 11 A.M.–midnight; Sunday, 11 A.M.–10 P.M.
Bar open daily, 11 A.M.–1 A.M.
Bar Food, North Side, Inexpensive to Moderate
Various beers brewed on the premises (a porter and a stout, at the very least)
are always on tap. The most popular are Honker's Ale and Goose Island
Pilsner, but we like 'em all. The homemade potato chips are the perfect
accompaniment to the fresh beer. They serve a great mahi-mahi sandwich.

Gradley's Deli
3119 W. 111th   233-4004
Hours: Monday–Saturday, 11 A.M.–9 P.M.; closed Sunday
American, Far Southwest, Inexpensive
Walk through the liquor store to find home cooking you'll love at prices too
good to be true. Burgers and deli sandwiches.

Healthy Food
3236 S. Halsted   326-2724
Hours: Monday–Saturday, 6:30 A.M.–8 P.M.; Sunday, 8 A.M.–8 P.M.
Lithuanian, Mid-South, Inexpensive
Wonderful Lithuanian fare: hearty soups, apple strudel, and more.

Heartland Cafe
7000 N. Glenwood   465-8005
Hours: Monday–Friday, 8 A.M.–10 P.M.; Saturday, 8 A.M.–midnight;
Sunday, 9 A.M.–10 P.M.
Health Food/American, Rogers Park, Inexpensive
The Heartland has a laid-back homespun atmosphere and nice outdoor seating for warm days and nights, but the food is hit or miss. Does its quality depend on the chef's horoscope?

Heaven on Seven
111 N. Wabash (Garland Building)   263-6443
Hours: Monday–Friday, 7 A.M.–5 P.M.; Saturday, 7 A.M.–3 P.M.;
closed Sunday
Cajun, Loop, Inexpensive
Cajun creole food in a coffee shop atmosphere.

Iberico Cafe and Bar
739 N. LaSalle   573-1510
Hours: Monday–Thursday, 11 A.M.–11 P.M.; Friday, 11 A.M.–midnight;
Saturday, 5 P.M.–midnight; Sunday, 5 P.M.–11 P.M.
Spanish/Tapas, Near North, Moderate

Iggy's
700 N. Milwaukee   829-4449
Hours: Tuesday–Thursday, 7 P.M.–2 A.M.; Friday, 5 P.M.–4 A.M.;
Saturday, 7 P.M.–5 A.M.; Sunday, 8 P.M.–2 A.M.
Italian, Wicker Park, Moderate to Expensive

Italian Village
71 West Monroe   332-7005
Hours: Monday–Thursday, 11 A.M.–1 A.M.;
Friday and Saturday: 11 A.M.–2 A.M.; Sunday, noon–midnight
Italian, Loop, Moderate
Before Italian food got chic and "trattoria-ized" there was the Italian Village, replete with signed black-and-white photos of dining celebrities, a narrow steep staircase, small private alcoves for signing deals and enjoying trysts, good old-fashioned spaghetti and lasagna, ever-courteous service, and an utterly dependable house chianti. Fortunately, it's still there—one of the few good, affordable restaurants in the Loop. Just don't expect a postmodern dining experience.

Jerome's
2450 N. Clark   327-2207
Hours: Monday–Friday, 7 A.M.–11 P.M.;
Saturday and Sunday, 9 A.M.–11:30 P.M.
Gourmet, Near North, Moderate to Expensive
This is one of the best places in Lincoln Park to have an elegant but affordable meal. The specials are always interesting and usually very good. They serve a lovely, healthy breakfast, and fresh-baked whole-grain bread abounds.

Jimo's Diner
1576 N. Milwaukee   278-2424
Hours: Monday–Thursday, 5 P.M.–11 P.M.; Friday, 5 P.M.–2 A.M.;
Saturday, 10:30 A.M.–2 A.M.; Sunday, 10:30 A.M.–11 P.M.
Gourmet, Wicker Park, Moderate to Expensive
The appetizers alone are worth the trip. The menu ranges from inexpensive deli sandwiches to creative, higher-priced specials. Sometimes there's live entertainment, which can be overbearing. Interesting decor.

Kaz's
1154 S. Michigan   663-9318
Hours: Monday–Wednesday, 7 A.M.–9 P.M.;
Thursday–Saturday, 7 A.M.–10 P.M.; Sunday, 8 A.M.–8 P.M.
Lithuanian, Near South, Inexpensive
Big helpings of the good ol' fashioned meat-and-potatoes variety, just like June Cleaver used to make. A pleasant no-nonsense place handy after a Bears game.

Klay Oven
414 N. Orleans   527-3999
Hours: Sunday–Thursday, 5 P.M.–10:30 P.M.;
Friday and Saturday, 5 P.M.–11:30 P.M.
Indian, Near North, Moderate

Kotobuki
5547 N. Clark   275-6588
Hours: Tuesday–Friday, 11:30 A.M.–2 P.M., 5 P.M.–10 P.M.;
Friday and Saturday, 5 P.M.–10:30 P.M.; closed Monday
Japanese, Far North, Moderate
The sushi, tempura, and teriyaki are all good.

Leo's Lunchroom
1809 W. Division   276-6509
Hours: Sunday, Tuesday–Thursday, 8 A.M.–10 P.M.;
Friday and Saturday, 8 A.M.–11 P.M.; closed Monday
Eclectic, Wicker Park, Inexpensive
For breakfast they serve French toast and burritos, large meat and veggie sandwiches at lunch, and a diverse dinner menu that changes nightly and includes extravagant catch-of-the-day dinners and always a vegetarian dish.

Little Bucharest
3001 N. Ashland   929-8640
Hours: Daily, 4 P.M.–midnight
Romanian, Mid-North, Moderate
This place gets an A for effort in the ambiance department: pseudo-stained glass windows and wandering musicians in Romanian dress. The food is great, too (things like rabbit stew and spätzle), in generous portions.

Little Hunan
6144 N. Lincoln   583-7770
Hours: Daily, 11:30 A.M.–10 P.M.
Chinese, Far North, Moderate

La Llama
2666 N. Halsted   327-7756
Hours: Daily, 5 P.M.–10:30 P.M.
Peruvian, Mid-North, Expensive
The place for Peruvian food in Chicago. The appetizers are fabulous.

Lucky Platter
514 Main, Evanston   (708) 869-4064
Hours: Monday–Friday, 11 A.M.–10 P.M.;
Saturday and Sunday, 8:30 A.M.–10 P.M.
Eclectic American, North Suburban, Moderate
Platefuls of hot, healthy food.

Lutz's
2454 W. Montrose   478-7785
Hours: Tuesday–Thursday and Sunday, 7 A.M.–10 P.M.;
Friday and Saturday, 7 A.M.–11 P.M.; closed Monday
German, Mid-North, Inexpensive
Chicago's pastry heaven.

Maller Building Coffee Shop
5 S. Wabash, 3rd floor   263-7696
Hours: Monday–Friday, 6 A.M.–3:30 P.M.; closed Saturday and Sunday
Deli, Loop, Inexpensive
If you love deli food—lox, bagels, chopped liver, etc.—you'll enjoy hanging
with the crowd at Maller.

Mama Desta's Red Sea
3216 N. Clark   935-7561
Hours: Tuesday–Sunday, noon–midnight; Monday, 4 P.M.–midnight
Ethiopian, Mid-North, Inexpensive
Ethiopian food does not stress vegetarianism, but Mama Desta's offers great
meatless dishes, which in the Ethiopian tradition are served with thin,
spongy bread spread out over a platter. It's fun to rip off the bread and dip it
in the various dishes. Food this inexpensive is rarely this good—and good for
you.

Manny's Coffee Shop and Deli
1141 S. Jefferson   939-2855
Hours: Monday–Saturday, 5 A.M.–5 P.M.; closed Sunday
Deli, Near South, Inexpensive

Manny's Pancake House
3418 N. Sheffield   528-9890
Hours: Daily, 6 A.M.–4 P.M.
Diner, Mid-North, Inexpensive

Matsuya
3469 N. Clark   248-2677
Hours: Wednesday–Monday, noon–midnight; closed Tuesday
Japanese, Mid-North, Moderate
One of the best places in Chicago to enjoy sushi—delicious and elegantly
served.

Melrose
930 W. Belmont 404-7901
3233 N. Broadway 327-2060
Hours: Melrose *never* closes
Diner, North Side, Inexpensive
The Melrose serves straightforward fare, including fresh, ripe fruit, good sandwiches and fries, and a great Greek salad. If you crave grilled cheese and a piece of pie at 3 A.M., Melrose is your place.

Metropolis 1800
1800 N. Clybourn 642-6400
Hours: Tuesday–Thursday, 11:30 A.M.–2:30 P.M., 5:30 P.M.–10 P.M.;
Friday and Saturday, 11:30 A.M.–2:30 P.M.,5:30 P.M.–11 P.M.;
Sunday, 11:30 A.M.–2:30 P.M., 5:30 P.M.–10 P.M.; closed Monday
Gourmet, North Side, Moderate to Expensive
Wonderful appetizers and specials. We love the atmosphere, which is urban and polished but not cold. They have a great wine and yes, you should have dessert.

Metropolis Rotisseria
924 W. Armitage 868-9000
Hours: Daily, 11:30 A.M.–9:30 P.M.
Gourmet Deli, North Side, Inexpensive
People (like us) who don't have the time or money to eat at Metropolis 1800 every night can go to this corner carry-out version for delectable sandwiches, thin-crust pizzas, rotissery chicken (their specialty), wholesome soup, cracklin' home-baked bread, and gooey chocolate brownies. Carry out, eat in, or have your food delivered.

Mongolian House
3410 N. Clark (North Side) 935-1100
Hours: Monday–Thursday, 4:30 P.M.–10:30 P.M.; Friday, 4:30 P.M.–11:30 P.M.;
Saturday, 3 P.M.–11:30 P.M.; Sunday, 3 P.M.–10:30 P.M.
6345 N. Western (Far North) 338-6320
Hours: Daily, 11:30 A.M.–9:30 P.M.
Chinese, Inexpensive to Moderate
Our favorite dish is Buddah's Delight: tofu, vegetables, and crispy rice. It's not on the menu, but it's always available.

North Side Cafe
1635 N. Damen 384-3555
Hours: Sunday–Thursday, 11:30 A.M.–1 A.M.;
Friday and Saturday, 11:30 A.M.–2 A.M.
Eclectic, Bucktown, Inexpensive
A room with a bar, another with pool tables, and an outdoor patio make up this Bucktown eatery and bar. The appetizers, like salsa and chips and calamari, taste mighty good, and there are pizzas, sandwiches, burgers, and fish dishes to satisfy everyone at your table.

Not Just Pasta
2965 N. Lincoln   348-2842
Hours: Monday, 5 P.M.–midnight; Tuesday–Friday, 11 A.M.–midnight;
Saturday, 8 A.M.–1 A.M.; Sunday, 1 P.M.–midnight
Italian, Mid-North, Moderate
This place reminds us of similar restaurants in New York: a tight space,
colorful decor with moments of black and chrome, and a more expensive
menu than you'd expect. (For Saturday breakfast, you can expect to pay
about $2 more for an omelette than you would at the more dinerly spots.) The
food is very good, particularly the specials, which tend to include wonderful
combinations of fresh, fresh vegetables and tasty sauces.

O'Fame
750 W. Webster   929-5111
Hours: Sunday–Thursday; 11:30 A.M.–midnight;
Friday and Saturday, 11:30 A.M.–12:30 A.M.
Pizza, Lincoln Park, Moderate
Fresh ingredients grace the pizza at O'Fame—a very popular Lincoln Park
restaurant. We recommend the whole-wheat pizza crust, and they'll make
you a delicious cheeseless pizza if you ask for one. The pasta dishes are great,
too.

Old Jerusalem
1411 N. Wells   944-0459
Hours: Daily, 11 A.M.–11 P.M.
Lebanese and Middle Eastern, Old Town, Inexpensive
For delicious falafel, taboulleh, hummus, and more, go to OJ. Bring your own
wine or beer or have a glass of fresh-squeezed carrot juice.

A 1,000 Nights Cafe
1612 N. Sedgwick   944-4811
Hours: Sunday and Monday–Thursday, 11 A.M.–10:30 P.M.;
Friday and Saturday, 11 A.M.–midnight
Middle Eastern, North Side, Inexpensive
A quiet, calm atmosphere prevails at this little Middle Eastern restaurant,
where the food is good and the service is friendly. Try the mint tea.

La Paella
2920 N. Clark   528-0757
Hours: Tuesday–Saturday, 5:30 P.M.–11 P.M.; Sunday, 5:30 P.M.–10 P.M.;
closed Monday
Spanish, Mid-North, Expensive
This is a very romantic, albeit expensive, restaurant with delicious seafood
and, yes, wonderful paella. The menu also includes some daring dishes like
fish cheeks.

Las Palmas
1773 W. Howard   262-7446
Hours: Monday–Friday, 11 A.M.–10 P.M.; Saturday and Sunday, 11A.M.–11 P.M.
Mexican, Rogers Park, Moderate
A cheery family-run place that consistently serves unusually good Mexican
fare, including seafood. The jumbo margaritas pack a pleasant punch, too.

Pars Cove
435 W. Diversey   549-1515
Hours: Daily, 11 A.M.–midnight
Persian, Mid-North, Moderate
Charbroiled salmon, chicken, beef, and lamb kabobs, as well as other Persian dishes, including vegetarian options.

Pasteur
4759 N. Sheridan   271-6673
Hours: Monday–Thursday, noon–2:30 P.M., 5 P.M.–10 P.M.;
Friday and Saturday, noon–2:30 P.M., 5 P.M.–11 P.M.;
Sunday, noon–2:30 P.M., 5 P.M.–9:30 P.M.
Vietnamese, Far North, Inexpensive

Penny's Noodle Shop
3400 N. Sheffield   281-8222
Hours: Monday–Thursday, 11 A.M.–9:30 P.M.;
Friday and Saturday, 11 A.M.–10:30 P.M.; Sunday, noon–9:30 P.M.
Thai, Mid-North, Inexpensive
There's usually a wait at Penny's because the food is wonderful and cheap. Bright, cheerful atmosphere.

Pilsner
6725 W. Cermak, Berwyn   (708) 484-2294
Hours: Sunday, 11 A.M.–8:30 P.M.; Tuesday–Saturday, 11 A.M.–9 P.M.;
closed Monday
Czechoslovakian, West Suburban, Inexpensive

Pizza Capri
716 W. Diversey (Mid-North)   296-6000
1733 N. Halsted (North Side)   280-5700
Hours: Monday–Thursday, 11 A.M.–midnight;
Friday and Saturday, 11 A.M.–1 A.M.; Sunday, noon–midnight
Pizza, Inexpensive to Moderate
Darn good pizza.

Planet Cafe
3923 N. Lincoln   348-6933
Hours: Sunday–Thursday, 8 A.M.–10 P.M.; Friday and Saturday, 8 A.M.–11 P.M.
Diner, North Side, Inexpensive
Great beer selection and familiar food. Burgers are a specialty.

Raj Darbar
2350 N. Clark   348-1010
Hours: Friday–Sunday, 11:30 A.M.–2:30 P.M.;
Sunday–Thursday, 5 P.M.–10 P.M.; Friday and Saturday, 5 P.M.–11 P.M.
Indian, Lincoln Park, Inexpensive to Moderate
They'll cook your dish "mild, medium, or hot" at this inviting Lincoln Park Indian restaurant, which offers a wide selection of vegetarian, chicken, lamb, beef, and seafood dishes, including excellent curries.

Red Apple
3123 N. Milwaukee   588-5781
Hours: Daily, 11 A.M.–10 P.M.
Polish, Mid-North, Inexpensive
The food is outstanding and the prices even better at this all-you-can-eat buffet. You'll think you've died and gone to Polska Paradise!

Red Rooster Wine Bar and Cafe
2100 N. Halsted (entrance on Dickens) 929-7660
Hours: Sunday and Monday–Thursday, 5 P.M.–10:30 P.M.;
Friday and Saturday, 5 P.M.–11:30 P.M.
Country French, North Side, Moderate
This small romantic restaurant in the back of pricey Cafe Bernard offers delicious, elegant specials, many of them fish or pasta at great prices. Nice affordable wine list, too.

Red Tomato
3417 N. Southport   472-5300
Hours: Monday–Thursday, 11:30 A.M.–2 P.M., 5 P.M.–10:30 P.M.;
Friday and Saturday, 11:30 A.M.–11 P.M.; Sunday, 4 P.M.–9:30 P.M.
Italian, Mid-North, Moderate
One weekly special frequently cooked with mushrooms, shrimp, or salmon. Tasty gourmet pastas.

RoseAngelis
1314 Wrightwood   296-0081
Hours: Sunday–Thursday, 5 P.M.–10 P.M.; Friday and Saturday, 5 P.M.–11 P.M.
Italian, North Side, Moderate
We like the pizza appetizer and all the sublime pasta dishes.

Rosebud
1500 W. Taylor   942-1117
Hours: Monday–Friday, 11 A.M.–3 P.M.; Monday–Thursday, 5 P.M.–10:30 P.M.;
Friday and Saturday, 5 P.M.–11:30 P.M.; Sunday, 4 P.M.–9:30 P.M.
Italian, West Side, Moderate to Expensive
Our favorite of the Taylor Street Italian restaurants. The Chicken Vesuvio will enchant you, unless you'd rather be charmed by the cavatelli. Save room for tiramisu!

Santorini
138 S. Halsted   829-8820
Hours: Sunday–Thursday, 11 A.M.–midnight;
Friday and Saturday, 11 A.M.–1 A.M.
Greek/Seafood, Near West, Moderate
One of the better atmospheres among the Greektown establishments. The tzatziki is particularly tasty, and they help you enjoy it by keeping the bread basket full.

Scoozi
410 W. Huron   943-5900
Hours: Monday–Friday, 11:30 A.M.–2 P.M.;
Monday–Thursday, 5 P.M.–10:30 P.M.; Friday and Saturday, 5 P.M.–11:30 P.M.;
Sunday, 5 P.M.–9 P.M.
Italian, River North, Moderate to Expensive
Faux Italian patina in an old loft building makes for a novel dining experience. We love the food—from the margerite pizza appetizer to the tiramisu.

Shaw's Crab House
21 E. Hubbard   527-2722
Hours: Monday–Thursday, 11:30 A.M.–2 P.M., 5:30 P.M.–10 P.M.; Friday, 11:30
A.M.–2 P.M., 5:30 P.M.–11 P.M.; Saturday, 5 P.M.–11 P.M.; Sunday, 5 P.M.–10 P.M.
Seafood, Near North, Expensive
Outstanding seafood with prices to match. Both the clam chowder and crab cakes are worthy specialties.

Six Corner Coffee Shop
2753 N. Western   HU6-9597 or HU6-9682 (HU=48)
Hours: Daily, 4:30 A.M.–4 P.M.
Diner, Northwest Side, Inexpensive
Where Diversey, Elston, and Western meet, there sits this basic diner, where the service is good, the food is cheap, and the orange juice is fresh squeezed.

Sole Mio
917 W. Armitage   477-5858
Hours: Monday–Thursday, 5 P.M.–10:30 P.M.; Friday and Saturday, 5 P.M.–11
P.M.; Sunday, 5:30 P.M.–10 P.M.
Italian, North Side, Expensive
When you're in Sole Mio, you feel like you're in someone's house. Chicago has plenty of less expensive Italian bistros with comparable food, but at Sole Mio you get intimate elegance with the creative pasta dishes. Rumour has it Robert De Niro dined at Sole Mio on two consecutive nights when he was in town filming *Backdraft*.

Svea Restaurant
5238 N. Clark   275-7738
Hours: Daily, 7 A.M.–4 P.M.
Swedish, Far North, Inexpensive
A great Andersonville restaurant, especially for breakfast. Swedish pancakes, French toast, tasty eggs. Very good and medium priced.

Sweet Bean Cafe
111 N. State   642-5999
Hours: Monday–Thursday, 11 A.M.–10 P.M.; Friday, 11 A.M.–11 P.M.; Saturday,
9 A.M.–11 P.M.; Sunday, 9 A.M.–9 P.M.
American, Near North, Moderate
Cute but hip. Soup and sandwiches and pasta—all quite good.

Three Happiness
2130 S. Wentworth   791-1228
Hours: Daily, 10 A.M.–2 P.M.
Chinese, Near South, Inexpensive
The Dim Sum of your dreams.

Tucci Milan
6 W. Hubbard   222-0044
Hours: Monday–Thursday, 11:30 A.M.–10 P.M.; Friday, 11:30 A.M.–11 P.M.;
Saturday, noon–11 P.M.; Sunday, 5 P.M.–9 P.M.
Italian, Loop, Moderate to Expensive
Like many of Chicago's hippest and most reliable restaurants, Tucci Milan is
owned and operated by the Lettuce Entertain You company. Dip your bread
in olive oil, savor your wine, enjoy a fresh salad with a lot of greens you've
never seen before, order a well-conceived pasta special, and relax in this truly
urban Italian restaurant. The "Heart Healthy" entrees don't sacrifice taste for
low cholesterol.

Tuttaposto
646 N. Franklin   943-6262
Hours: Monday–Thursday, 11:30 A.M.–2 P.M., 5 P.M.–10 P.M.;
Friday, 11:30 A.M.–2 P.M., 5 P.M.–11 P.M.; Saturday, 5 P.M.–11 P.M.;
Sunday, 5 P.M.–9 P.M.
Mediterranean, River North, Moderate to Expensive
Tuttaposto gets high marks for its presentation. The pizzas are always good
(especially the double-decker mushroom), and we like the innovative salads
and pasta dishes. Pleasant atmosphere.

Twin Anchors
1655 N. Sedgwick   266-1616
American, Old Town, Inexpensive
Hours: Monday–Friday, 5 P.M.–11:30 P.M.;
Saturday and Sunday, noon–11:30 P.M.
This is a corner neighborhood bar that serves very, very popular barbecued
ribs.

Valois
1518 E. 53rd   667-0647
Hours: Daily, 6 A.M.–10 P.M.
American, Hyde Park, Inexpensive
At this popular Hyde Park hangout you'll find good food and good prices,
especially for breakfast.

Vinci
1732 N. Halsted   266-1199
Hours: Monday–Thursday, 5:30 P.M.–10:30 P.M.;
Friday and Saturday, 5:30 P.M.–11:30 P.M.; Sunday, 4:30 P.M.–9:30 P.M.
Italian, North Side, Moderate to Expensive
We know we've already listed a lot of romantic, postmodern Italian res-
taurants, but this one deserves a try. The grilled vegetable pizza appetizer is
fabulous; they do amazing things with goat cheese and basil and sun-dried

tomatoes, and mozzarella, and mushrooms, and seafood, and more. And the tiramisu deserves a medal.

Wishbone
1800 W. Grand   829-3597
Hours: Tuesday–Friday, 7 A.M.–11 A.M.;
Saturday and Sunday, 8 A.M.–2:30 P.M.; Tuesday–Friday, 11:30 A.M.–3 P.M.;
no dinner
Southern, East Ukrainian Village, Inexpensive
One of the more pleasant "problems" that one might face on any morning in Chicago is the difficult choice between a cinnamon role at Ann Sather's and a corn biscuit at the Wishbone. Then, if you should happen to decide on the Wishbone you face the additional problem of choosing your side dish: Should it be the potatoes or the cheese grits? The Wishbone offers Southern, New Orleans fare: shrimp etouffee, black-eyed peas, and the like. Our favorite breakfast item is the Wishbone omelette: three eggs, salsa, and cheese.

Wishbone II Restaurant and Cafeteria
1001 Washington   850-2663
Hours: Monday, 6 A.M.–3:00 P.M.; Tuesday–Friday, 6 A.M.–3:00 P.M.
and 5 P.M.–10:30 P.M.; Saturday, 8 A.M.–2:30 P.M. and 5 P.M.–10:30 P.M.;
Sunday, 8 A.M.– 2:30 P.M.
Southern, River West, Inexpensive to Moderate

Yugo Inn
2824 N. Ashland   348-6444
Hours: Wednesday–Sunday, 5 P.M.–midnight; closed Monday and Tuesday
Yugoslavian, Mid-North, Moderate
A lot of different Serbian meat dishes using grilled beef, pork, and veal can be enjoyed at Yugo Inn.

CAFES

Over the past few years Chicago's cafe scene has really blossomed. We're talking little cozy places with all kinds of coffee drinks and varieties of tea; moist fruity muffins, golden scones, delectable pastries, provocative publications lying about on hip retro furniture, the melodic hum of conversation, intriguing art on the walls, and long hours. But there are a lot of imposters, too. Among the legions of new cafes, some have great atmosphere and wonderful fare; others seem thrown together and, well, insincere, which proves that cafes can't be mass produced. Chicago isn't Paris, but we've got some places where geniuses must be meeting and movements (both literary and political) might be launched. Here are some of our favorites. (Remember the motto "Drink coffee and wear black.")

Cafe Aroma
1202 W. Webster   404-6070
Hours: Sunday–Thursday, 8 A.M.–11 P.M.; Friday and Saturday, 8 A.M.–1 A.M.
Have your tarot cards read on Tuesday or Thursday. Hear live music on Friday.

Cafe Ennui
6981 N. Sheridan   973-2233
Hours: Monday–Thursday, 7:30 A.M.–10:30 P.M.; Friday, 7:30 A.M.–midnight;
Saturday, 8 A.M.–midnight; Sunday, 8 A.M.–10:30 P.M.
Displays local art.

Cafe Express
615 Dempster, Evanston   (708) 864-1868
500 Main, Evanston   (708) 328-7940
Hours: Monday–Friday, 7 A.M.–11 P.M.; Saturday, 8:30 A.M.–11 P.M.;
Sunday, 9 A.M.–4 P.M.
The Dempster Street location is near Northwestern and has a slightly funkier
atmosphere than its newer branch on Main Street, but both offer outdoor
seating and great snacks.

Cafe Selmarie
2327 W. Giddings   989-5595
Hours: Sunday and Tuesday–Thursday, 10 A.M.–10 P.M.;
Friday and Saturday, 10 A.M.–11 P.M.
BYOB.

Cafe Voltaire
3231 N. Clark   528-3136
Hours: Sunday–Thursday, 11 A.M.–1 A.M.;
Friday and Saturday, 11 A.M.–3 A.M.
Live entertainment seven days a week: theater, music, poetry readings, per-
formance art. Exhibits local art. Serves beer and wine.

Caffe Pergolesi
3404 N. Halsted   472-8602
Hours: Monday–Thursday, 4 P.M.–11 P.M.;
Friday and Saturday, 3 P.M.–11 P.M.; Sunday, 9:30 A.M.–9 P.M.
Before cafes were *au courant* and on every corner, we had Pergolesi, which
happens to be the oldest coffeehouse in Chicago. A great beatnik cafe, not to
be bypassed for the newer models. Displays local art. BYOB.

Coffee Chicago
801 N. Wabash   664-6415
Hours: Monday–Thursday, 7:30 A.M.–10 P.M.; Friday, 7:30 A.M.–midnight;
Saturday, 8:30 A.M.–midnight; Sunday, 10 A.M.–6 P.M.
2922 N. Clark   327-3228
Hours: Monday–Thursday, 7:30 A.M.–11 P.M.; Friday, 7:30 A.M–midnight;
Saturday, 8 A.M.–12:30 A.M.; Sunday, 8 A.M.–10 P.M.
3323 N. Clark   477-3323
Hours: Monday–Thursday, 8 A.M.–11 P.M.;
Friday and Saturday, 8 A.M.–midnight; Sunday, 9 A.M.–10 P.M.
Serves beer and wine.
6744 N. Sheridan   274-1880
Hours: Monday–Thursday, 8 A.M.–11 P.M.;
Friday and Saturday, 8 A.M.–midnight; Sunday, 8 A.M.–10 P.M.

1561 N. Wells   787-1211
Hours: Monday–Friday, 7:30 A.M.–midnight;
Saturday, 8 A.M.–12:30 A.M.; Sunday, 9 A.M.–11 P.M.
828 N. State   335-0625
Hours: Monday–Thursday, 7:30 A.M.–11 P.M.;
Friday and Saturday, 7:30 A.M.–midnight; Sunday, 7:30 A.M.–10 P.M.

Earwax
1564 N. Milwaukee   772-4019
Hours: Monday–Thursday, 11 A.M.–midnight; Friday, 11 A.M.–1 A.M.;
Saturday, 9 A.M.–1 A.M.; Sunday, 9 A.M.–11 P.M.
This Wicker Park cafe is attached to a record store, so they play their own
CDs. Sometimes local art is on display.

Java Jive
909 W. School   549-3500
Hours: Daily, 8:30 A.M.–midnight
Live jazz on Sunday, noon–2 P.M.; live Brazilian jazz on Wednesday evening;
and classical guitar every Friday evening. Exhibits different local art each
month.

Kava Kane
1013 W. Webster   404-5282
Hours: Sunday–Friday, 9 A.M.–11 P.M.; Saturday, 10 A.M.–midnight
Displays local art.

Nightcrawler Cafe
3912 N. Clark   871-4062
Hours: Sunday, Monday, Wednesday, Thursday, 5 P.M.–midnight;
Friday and Saturday, 5 P.M.–2 A.M.
Nightcrawler has a cafe atmosphere, but the menu is extensive, with hearty
soups and a full bar. Attached to Live Bait Theatre.

Scenes Coffeehouse and Dramatist Bookstore
3168 N. Clark   525-1007
Hours: Monday–Thursday, 9:30 A.M.–midnight; Friday, 9:30 A.M.–1 A.M.; Saturday, 9 A.M.–1 A.M.; Sunday, 9 A.M.–6 P.M.
Specializes in theater and film books—and people sipping coffee and looking
"intense."

Starbucks Coffee
Many locations in the Loop and North Side
Hours: Vary by location, but North Side neighborhood Starbucks tend to be
open Monday–Thursday, 6 A.M.–10 P.M.; Friday, 6 A.M.–11 P.M.;
Saturday, 7 A.M.–11 P.M.; Sunday, 7 A.M.–10 P.M.
Loop locations close much earlier.
OK, Starbucks are more coffee boutiques than genuine cafes, but they do
have four-star java served every imaginable way. More yuppie than arty,
more carry-out or short visit than sit all day, Starbucks is worth mentioning
because those green awnings are getting ubiquitous in Chicago, due to superb coffee and pastries. We're addicted.

Third Coast Coffee House and Winebar
888 N. Wabash   664-7225
Hours: Daily, 7 A.M.–2 A.M.
Offers a nice selection of beer, wine, port, and brandy. There's live music on
Thursday evening. The art exhibit changes monthly. This one is nice because
it has outdoor seating, but we prefer the Dearborn Street version:
1260 N. Dearborn   649-0730
Hours: Sunday and Monday, 7:30 A.M.–midnight;
Tuesday–Saturday, open 24 hours
Full bar with acoustic guitar performances on Tuesday and Thursday. A great
place to go to continue a stimulating dinner conversation that seems destined
to last for hours.

Uncommon Ground
1214 W. Grace   929-3680
Hours: Monday–Thursday, 8 A.M.–11 P.M.; Friday, 8 A.M.–midnight;
Saturday, 9 A.M.–midnight; Sunday, 9 A.M.–10 P.M.
Folk and pop singers on Friday and Saturday evening and live jazz on
Sunday. A very inviting place.

Urbus Orbis
1934 W. North   252-4446
Hours: Monday–Thursday, 9 A.M.–midnight;
Friday and Saturday, 9 A.M.–1 A.M.; Sunday, 9 A.M.–10 P.M.
Urbos Orbis is attached to a theater, where there are several performances
every week.

—Amy Teschner and Anthony Hurtig

NIGHTLIFE

Fortunately Nancy Reagan doesn't live in Chicago, because almost everything to do at night in this town involves that ubiquitous drug: alcohol. We admit this chapter is mostly a list of bars and clubs, with some quieter alternatives. Please keep in mind, however, that a truly great night in Chicago often includes one of our city's many eating establishments. For a list of worthy restaurants, see the "Eating" chapter. For a list of where to drink, dance, talk, and laugh the night away, keep reading here.

What follows is an assortment of bars, clubs, coffeehouses, and other fun places to go at night. While using this chapter to plan your night out, don't forget that Chicago nightlife is ever changing. Cool clubs close, bad bars open, clienteles shift, ownership changes. What we've set forth here are merely some guidelines, a listing of places that we really like, or at least wouldn't be embarrassed to be seen in. What we haven't included are obvious places such as Rush Street, Division Street, and the Excalibur because we feel true Chicagoans wouldn't be caught dead there. We also haven't included places that might be unsafe for the general public or that are in unsafe neighborhoods. To our regret, we may have inadvertently overlooked some great little places. So we suggest you talk to the people at the places we do list; they may tell you about some undiscovered or new places for your nocturnal enjoyment.

We have assumed that our audience is much like ourselves—people looking for a true urban experience, not always the same old thing, a little excitement, a friendly atmosphere. The great thing about Chicago is that it does offer something for everyone, and if you don't want to drink or dance, there are other options.

This chapter is organized by category of entertainment (tavern/pubs, dance clubs, cafes, live music, and other) and by general neighborhood. Places marked with a Ⅲ➡ are open really late (till 4 or 5 A.M.) for you true late-night types and insomniacs. Also, if you are a devoted night person and conduct most of your life between midnight and dawn, you'll find some useful information in the chapter "Late Night and All Night."

TAVERNS/PUBS

These are places to meet friends, drink, relax, maybe play a few games. Music is usually just for atmosphere.

Lincoln Park/Near North/Old Town/Clybourn Corridor

The Blue Room Ⅲ➡
1400 N. Wells   951-6441
The Blue Room looks good. So do the people in it. It's an indigo-hued, couch-and armchair-strewn hangout for the young and self-conscious. And we'll tell you something, it's a darned good thing the walls are blue in here and not, say, lined with mirrors. If they were, no one would ever look at anyone else. But let's be fair, they do book some decent musicians in here, the staff is friendly, and Old Town doesn't have many decent places to drink.

The Bluebird Lounge
1637 N. Clybourn 642-3449

What does the Bluebird Lounge have in common with the University of Chicago football team? Neither one has any jocks. Which means that if you liked the crowd in Maxtavern or Sheffield's a few years back, you'll probably be happy in the Bluebird. The drinks are fairly cheap, the bartenders are cool, and they have good taste in music, too. So check it out for a low-key, frat-free time.

Deja Vu ⅢⅢ➤
2624 N. Lincoln 871-0205

Just an average bar that gets pretty crowded late at night. What makes it special are the Big Band nights (Tuesday) and Turtle Races (Wednesday)— something fun and different when the whole club/bar scene gets too tiresome.

O'Rourkes
1625 N. Halsted 335-1806

Popular with the "literary" crowd, this bar has survived its recent move to a more yuppie neighborhood (for a dissenting opinion see the "Neighborhoods" chapter). Enjoy a drink with such Irish laureates as Wilde, Yeats, and Joyce. Across the street from the Steppenwolf, it's a good place to go before or after the theater.

Red Lion Pub
2446 N. Lincoln 348-2695

This is an authentic British pub, complete with British ales, ciders, fish and chips, shepherd's pie, and a surly British waiter. A strolling minstrel on Friday and Saturday and a small theater are extra added attractions. This is a good place to toast Shakespeare on his birthday.

Weeds
1555 N. Dayton 943-7815

If you're looking for a bar with old jockstraps, brassieres, and women's shoes dangling from its ceiling, try Weeds on for size. It's a funky little place, located at the end of a funky little North Side street, run as a private fiefdom by its legendary owner Sergio. Now, if Sergio likes you, knows you, or is being highly tipped by you, he'll take care of you. Otherwise, you may be left feeling like a party crasher. But hey, the drinks are cheap, and there's a poetry slam every Monday and live music every Friday and Saturday. Now, if we can just get that Sergio guy to like us. . . .

Lakeview

Crash Palace
2771 N. Lincoln 327-7253

The Crash Palace is dark. The people wear black. The music is hip. The music is loud. The drinks are cheap. The men's restroom is dirty. The Psychotronic Film Society presents B movies here once a week. There is no one here on weekdays until late. There is no cover any day of the week. There are images of Jesus on the red walls. You'll probably either really like this place or dislike it intensely.

Gingerman
3740 N. Clark   549-2050
A very laid-back, comfortable place that features a wide variety of beer and good pool tables. Despite the part-time punkers and pony-tail guys, the atmosphere is convivial. They feature classical music after Cubs games, so there's no real danger of the place filling up with fluorescent pink baseball caps.

Maxtavern
2856 N. Racine   348-5055
What was once a really cool neighborhood bar has been discovered by yuppies. The place is *packed* on weekends, as frat boys mingle with the old regulars. Give it a try on a weeknight to check out the numerous globes, photo booth, and beer specials. The music is usually pretty good, depending on the album selection of the bartender. Maxtavern also has one of the best ladies' restrooms (public) in the city.

Sheffield's
3258 N. Sheffield   281-4989
This is another great neighborhood bar that is infiltrated by way too many jocks and sorority girls on the weekends. However, friendly bartenders, great drinks (winter and summer specials), good music, and pool tables inside and out make this a fun place to hang during the week. In the summer enjoy a pitcher of beer in one of the nicest gardens in the city; in the winter have a hot toddy with the kitty next to the fireplace.

Ugly Bar ⅢⅢ➡
2944 N. Lincoln   248-4598 (248-UGLY)
The Ugly Bar? Who are they kidding? This place is filled with the "beautiful people"—as well as lots of attitude, a chi-chi atmosphere, and a pretentious staff. The decor features upside-down black-and-white TVs as lamps (clever idea that gets annoying). The Ugly Bar does, however, feature food late at night and a nice outdoor patio with bocce ball. It's also located right next door to the Discovery Center, so you can cruise on over after class and put those "Learn to Flirt" lessons to work.

Wrigleyville Tap
3724 N. Clark   528-4422
Similar to the Gingerman and just a few doors south, this place is a little rougher around the edges and has a little more attitude. It features pool tables and a basketball game and sports paraphernalia that is ignored by the black T-shirted, pony-tailed regulars. The music here is good, thanks to a great jukebox that has everything from Patsy Cline to the Ramones.

River North/West

Green Door
678 N. Orleans   664-5496
This cozy tavern is so close to the gallery district that burning planks from the great fire of 1989 fell on its roof. But it survived to remain one of the best places to grab a brew or have some good eats after looking at art. But don't let that fool you. The crowd is very mixed and very unpretentious.

North

Augenblick
3907 N. Damen   929-0994
OK, so if you had a bar with a nice German name like Augenblick, what kind of music would you naturally feature? Why, Irish music, of course. But, hey, walk into this place on a Tuesday night, and the combination works just fine. You'll see traditional Irish music being blasted out by a variety of talented instrumentalists, jamming so enthusiastically they'll be needin' to wash up with some Irish Spring after. The crowd here is laid-back, relatively hip, and there are many good brews available. We kinda like this place.

Planet Cafe
3923 N. Lincoln   348-6933
At its former location on Damen Avenue, the Planet Cafe used to be just that—a cafe-restaurant that served a particularly good breakfast amid decorations evoking an episode of "The Jetsons." Well, Saturday morning can still be utterly nostalgic at the new location on north Lincoln Avenue, only now there's a bar attached. The bar serves a great selection of beers and offers a Bloody Mary special on the weekends. (George Jetson would be so proud.) Open Saturday until 3 A.M., which doesn't earn it a ⏴, but isn't too bad.

Ten Cat Club
3931 N. Ashland   935-5377
The Ten Cat is a hip neighborhood bar in a neighborhood that needed one. Nope, there aren't a lot of entertainment options up here on this stretch of Ashland. But walk into the Ten Cat, and you've got pool, good music, and a decent mix of locals and hipsters. It's worth a visit, if you can tear yourself away from the rest of the Great White Way outside the door, that is.

Bucktown/Wicker Park/ Ukrainian Village

Charleston
2076 N. Hoyne   489-4757
The Charleston is a microcosm of the sweeping change that has taken place in its Bucktown neighborhood. The earthy, laid-back clientele of yore has been replaced (on weekends, at least) by people with Jeeps parked out front and lots of cash. But the place still manages to have some charm. The free live music on weekends is usually pretty decent, and the old place just looks good. Like a bar should, you know? So check it out on a weeknight.

Danny's
1951 W. Dickens   489-6457
Two big lumbering dogs greet you as you enter Danny's, giving it a very homey feel. Originally a house, none of the original walls were torn down, so there are lots of little rooms in which to lounge. The music is loud but good, the crowd of artists and advertising people is friendly. Supposedly this is a great pick-up place, but no one has ever hit on either of us here, so we refuse to believe it. Danny's also features some of the best art you'll see in Chicago. (That is not to say that all of it is good—it's just that there's so much bad art on the walls of Chicago bars and coffeehouses.)

The Gallery Cabaret
2020 N. Oakley   489-5471
The Gallery is one of the few places in Bucktown not yet popular with advertising agency art directors. Maybe it's because the art in here is so, well, interesting. And omnipresent. You see, this low-key tavern cum live music showplace is literally festooned with art. That's why they call it the Gallery. But you know what, the drinks are sure priced right in here. We like that. And we've enjoyed some of the bands that have played in here. Plus, the bartender is a very nice fellow. There's a weekly poetry slam, too.

Rainbo Club
1150 N. Damen   489-5999
The Rainbo Club is a big square room with no squares in it. People, that is. Because this is the playground of the Wicker Park artist. There's cool art on the walls, cool music on the stereo, and cool people checking it out. Even on weeknights, this place draws a good-sized crowd of hipsters. So put on a T-shirt, splash some paint on those work boots, and don't check your attitude at the door.

Rip Tide Lounge ➠
1745 W. Armitage
Rip Tide is definitely a very *late*-night place; don't bother showing up much before 2 A.M. The crowd is typical Bucker Park types who wander over after Danny's or the North Side closes. This is a tiny place, but the very cool art deco bar and year-round Christmas decorations make it festive. Much of the atmosphere is supplied by the Elvis on the jukebox and the tough, middle-aged women bartenders who are ready to join you in a couple shots of Jagermeister.

DANCE CLUBS

Dancing and loud, lively (but not live) music are the primary functions of these places. Have fun, but don't expect to carry on a conversation.

Lincoln Park/Near North/Old Town/Clybourn Corridor

950 Club
950 W. Wrightwood   928-8955
The 950 is as dependable as McDonald's. If you were there five years ago, you know you can expect the same thing today. In fact, the same group of regulars is still hanging out there. The music is alternative—both old and new. The Cure, Echo & the Bunnymen, Nitzer Ebb are still favorites. The crowd is a little straight, but not offensively yuppie.

Exit ➠
1653 N. Wells   440-0535
If there's still a guy with a Mohawk in the city of Chicago, this is where you can find him. Exit is a weird combination of South Side big-hair types, leather jacket punkers, and night owls who come here after the other bars close. The music selection is still pretty good, however, and some exhilarating dancing can be had here on the sunken dance floor. Exit also features the occasional

live band, performance artist, and pseudonotorious "Bondage Nights" on Wednesday.

Neo ⮕
2350 N. Clark   528-2622
Once one of the "wildest" places to go in Chicago, this small, dark dance club has become just another place for yuppies looking for late-night action and a little life-on-the-edge. But if, per chance, you're looking for fun on a Monday night, Neo's the place. Hipsters and urbanites only, please.

Outtakes
16 W. Ontario   951-7979
This small bar/dance club is famous for its aquarium bar. If you're nuts about fish, check this place out. There's a small dance floor and outdoor patio. The crowd tends to be a little stiff because of its bad locale close to Excalibur and the Rush/Division street bars. Then again, you can think of it as an island refuge.

Lakeview

Avalon
959 W. Belmont   472-3020
Located in the heart of the seedy city action (next to the Belmont El stop, across the street from Berlin, around the corner from the Vic), Avalon attracts a diverse yet surprisingly tame crowd. Three clubs in one, the first room you hit as you reach the top of the stairs is the dance floor, where young, not-too-hip urbanites dance to a mix of the latest dance and alternative tunes. To the right is the main room, which features bands, usually of the local rock 'n' roll variety. The band dictates what the crowd will be like. Down the hall is a smaller cabaret-type room, which features lesser-known bands, acoustic or experimental music. This could be a good place to escape for a few minutes, but the music in here is usually pretty awful.

Berlin ⮕
954 W. Belmont   348-4975
Berlin is probably Chicago's best-known gay bar. On weekends the trendiest gay boys mingle with curious heterosexuals, as the place fills up with people looking for a fun, late-night dance spot. The place is tiny and usually packed; the music is contemporary dance, but don't be surprised if you hear the occasional Donna Summer tune. Exhibitionists are provided with two platforms on which to dance. Video screens show cartoons or porn flicks. The decor has a "theme" that changes every couple of months. Obsession Wednesday themes vary, but Disco Obsession is the last Wednesday of every month. Berlin is also famous for its wild Halloween and New Year's Eve parties.

Smart Bar ⮕
3730 N. Clark   549-0203
Downstairs from the Metro is the Smart Bar—a dungeonesque, low-ceilinged dance club. The music is a good mix of house, industrial, thrash, and alternative. You'll also hear the occasional AC/DC tune. The weekend crowd is going to depend on what band is playing upstairs, but suburbanites and bad

dancers on dates tend to flock in. Wednesday and Sunday are the best nights for urbanites, and the music is usually best on these nights. Drink specials for the ladies on Wednesday and shot and beer specials on Sunday bring in a big crowd. The place is usually *packed* by 1 A.M. and stays that way until closing (5 A.M.). One caution on Sunday: dudes who have struck out all weekend see this as their last opportunity to score.

River North/West

China Club ⅢⅢ➡
616 W. Fulton   466-0812
The hottest club in New York and L.A. has fallen flat in Chicago. Despite the crowds of big hair, microminis, and high heels outside, a recent report in the *Tribune* said the place just isn't filling up. Could this shopping mall of a club (yes, there is a China Club store inside) be just too big? And if it's celeb watching you want, go down the street to Shelter. (One of us once touched Billy Baldwin's stomach there.) What does make this club almost worthwhile is the large room off to the side where they feature live dance, blues, rock 'n' roll bands. If they focus on this aspect, this club just might make it in Chicago.

Industry
640 W. Hubbard   226-7598
This cavernous dance club never really caught on. The place is usually pretty empty, which means there's plenty of room to dance. Unfortunately, the music is mediocre, but the DJs are willing to play requests. The decor is pretty cheap.

Kaboom ⅢⅢ➡
747 N. Green   243-8600
Less hip than Shelter, this mega dance club deserves at least one visit to check out the great space and incredible decor. It's very chic without being pretentious. Check out the huge Lichtenstein-wannabe painting over the dance floor. The Cabaret room is reminiscent of Ricky Ricardo's club with its live music and oversize, oval cushy booths. Porn movies are shown in here on Sunday (gay night). Upstairs there's a roomy pool/game area. The crowd here tends toward the suburban and less hip urbanites. Suits, big hair, and nose jobs are not unusual. The music is pretty good—of the basic dance variety, but not too adventuresome.

Shelter ⅢⅢ➡
564 W. Fulton   648-5500
This is undoubtedly the hippest, hottest dance club in Chicago. Be prepared to stand in line to get in and be humiliated by the doorman. Once inside, it's pretty dark (except for the illumination of hundreds of lava lamps), the space is raw, and the decor is a mix of thrift-store Victorian and sixties mod. The main bar area flanks a spacious dance floor where you can quickly work up a sweat to some of the best house music mixed in Chicago. The Paramount Room is reserved for private parties and so-called VIPs, but a smile will often get you past the doorman. Sofas and jazz set the mood. The crowd here is ethnically diverse and a little young. Dress well, as see and be seen is the game here, and fashion first is the rule. Always packed on weekends,

Thursday is most popular for urbanites, and Sunday is big with the gay crowd.

Bucktown/Wicker Park/Ukrainian Village

Artful Dodger
1734 W. Wabansia   227-6859
Have you ever tried to dance to Led Zeppelin's "Communication Breakdown" in front of other human beings? Well, it could happen to you here. But don't worry, the dance floor at the Dodger is dark. Even better, the folks here serve a wide variety of colorful and potent novelty drinks, like French aphrodisiac "love beer" and some pretty cool glow-in-the-dark margarita stuff, too. So after a while, you won't be worrying about how stupid you look dancing to sixties garage rock—you'll be wondering why they have to close so damn early.

Lizard Lounge
1824 W. Augusta   489-0379
As you're cruising down Augusta, the only way to find the Lizard is by the throbbing strobe light in the window. A small, low-profile, laid-back dance club, it is loved by both artsy locals and daring suburbanites alike. The music is eclectic—a strong mix of house, funk, and punk. If the DJ plays a really great song, he won't hesitate to join you on the packed dance floor. They love Elvis here and feature one of his favorite snacks every week (Ho Ho's and PB & J). The crowd is a little older (25+) than you'll find at some other dance clubs.

LIVE MUSIC

These are some of our favorite places to hear live music. For a more complete discussion (with listings) on the Chicago music scene, see the various music chapters.

Lincoln Park/Near North/Old Town/Clybourn Corridor

Batteries Not Included
2201 N. Clybourn   472-9920
Up front is an unassuming bar that's an OK place to kill time before or after a movie. (Batteries is right across from Webster Place cinemas.) The back room, which looks exactly like a suburban basement rec room, features local bands. Pick and choose; sometimes they're great up-and-coming local acts, sometimes they're local acts that suck.

Lakeview

Beat Kitchen
2100 W. Belmont   281-4444
The Beat Kitchen will remind you of the Elbo Room. Because a lot of the bands that play here are cool, but a lot of the patrons aren't. Not that they're going to beat you up or anything, just that they're likely to have been members, at one time or another, of some fraternity or sorority. Still, how many places do you know that have a good live band playing just steps away from some pretty decent homemade mini pizzas? That's right, the Beat Kitchen actually does have a kitchen. Live music is on offer here pretty much seven nights a week. Cover charges range from about $3 to $8.

Cabaret Metro ⮕
3730 N. Clark   549-0203
Upstairs from the Smart Bar, the Metro features local and national bands, usually of the alternative variety. This is a great place to see a band. Small enough to be considered intimate, big enough to handle all that metal. If the main floor gets too raucous for you, check out the balcony. By the way, the bands are usually pretty good. We've stumbled across some great acts quite by accident here. Wednesday they feature three bands for four bucks (ladies free).

Elbo Room
2871 N. Lincoln   549-7700
The only thing underground about this live music showcase is its location. Here yuppies reign, but even that doesn't make it an altogether unpleasant experience. Because if you like the band that's playing, this is a great place to get close to the musicians. The sound system is first-rate, also. And the owners even try to put up some decent art on the walls. On nonweekend nights, you'll find nonrock entertainment from improv to big band jazz. Upstairs, there's a good restaurant that truly could use a little more elbow room.

Lincoln Tap Room
3010 N. Lincoln   868-0060
Another nice, simple little place to see local acts. This place hasn't developed much of a crowd yet, but we hope it will. A dance floor in front of the stage (where people actually dance to live music) and cozy booths along the wall make the Tap Room special.

Lounge Ax
2438 N. Lincoln   525-6620
Lounge Ax is one of the few *really* small places in the city where you can still see big-name acts (as well as local bands). This is a great place to hear a band; get there early so you can get a good spot up front—and be prepared to sweat.

Oz
2917 N. Sheffield   975-8100
Just as in the beloved film, the head guy in this Oz is a little bald dude in a robe. His name is Oz, and he's actually set up a pretty decent place to see live jazz. He's a pretty friendly fellow, too, and has many varieties of beer and cognac on hand. The cover charges usually average around five bucks, and the jazz is usually of the fusion-ish variety. It's also entertaining to sit near the restrooms and watch both men and women try to remember their gender symbols so that they won't walk into the wrong room.

Wild Hare ▥➡
3520 N. Clark   327-0800
Touting itself as the "Reggae Capitol of America," the Wild Hare features great bands (all reggae, only reggae) and extremely limited seating, and there's always a crowd, which tends to be a little mainstream. If you really like reggae, you might also try **Exedus II,** which is right across the street.

North

Biddy Mulligan's
7644 N. Sheridan   761-6532
Old rock 'n' roll stars never die; they just end up playing at Biddy Mulligan's a couple times a year. Yes, it's true; all your favorite seventies superstars can be seen playing at this Rogers Park roadside attraction on their current low-budget "We couldn't afford the Holiday Inn this time" tour. So check *The Reader,* and if you like the band that's playing, this isn't a bad place to see 'em up close for around 10 bucks.

Clearwater Saloon
3937 N. Lincoln   549-5599
The Clearwater is a live music place that's, well, a little bit country and, yes, a little bit rock 'n' roll. They feature local and national music, local and foreign beer and spirits, and lots of those promotional mirror things on the walls. Cover charges are pretty reasonable here, and all in all, it's a decent medium- to low-key spot to hear music.

Bucktown/Wicker Park/Ukrainian Village

Bop Shop
1807 W. Division 235-3232
The name says it all. This jazz club is way too big to have that nice, cozy feel, but the living room seating in the back room has its advantages. If you like jazz but hate an uptight, stuffy atmosphere, this is your place.

Dreamerz Ⅲ➡
1516 N. Milwaukee 252-1155
OK dude, so like, what if all the leather punks who hang at Dreamerz had like this ultimate rumble with the dudes who hang at Exit? Well, it would be one heck of a bitching cataclysm. One of us (we won't say which) was up till five last night doing Jagermeister shots at Dreamerz. And they had this great band upstairs for two bucks, with this wasted lead singer banging a tire iron on an anvil in time to the drums. And the drinks were real cheap, and the DJ kept spinning one classic death metal/hardcore/thrash opus after another. And then afterward, we all went across the street for a veggie taco, and looked at each other under those bright fluorescent lights, and we all had like, you know, the pallor of death. In other words, we recommend that you visit Dreamerz, but not before at least 1:30 in the morning.

Get Me High Lounge
1758 N. Honore 252-4090
Here's a place that must have been named before all the "Just Say No" stuff got started. But, you know what, you'd have to be stoned to be uncomfortable here. It's a hip little hideaway tucked under a bridge on a quiet Bucktown street. Inside, you'll find funky stuff covering every inch of wall space and live jazz filling the air. Cover charges average around four bucks, and the whole place can only hold about one good-size extended family.

Phyllis' Musical Inn
1800 W. Division 486-9862
Live music, live music, and more live music. The best of the local bands play here (Stump the Host, Shrimp Boat), much to the delight of the local artists who hang here. Without a band there's really not much to this place.

CAFES

Similar to taverns and bars, these are nice places to gather and meet friends. Unlike bars, however, they are generally well lit and serve food, but not necessarily alcohol.

Lincoln Park/Near North/Old Town/Clybourn Corridor

The Third Coast Ⅲ➡
888 N. Wabash 640-0730
1260 N. Dearborn 649-0730
Let me tell you a true story about the Third Coast (the one on Wabash). I (Michael) was meeting a blind date there once, and she asked me how she would recognize me. "Why, I'll be the guy with the black turtleneck and the long hair," I told her. Well, she gets there, and every single dude in the place

has a turtleneck and a "do"! I guess the moral of my story is that the people here have a certain look I like to call chic. They're here to see. They're here to be seen. They're here to sip coffee and booze and Italian sodas under the stars in the summertime—and under each other's gaze in the other months. The food here can be pretty good, too, but it will not arrive promptly at your table, I wager. So, check out this Third Coast if you're having a good hair day, or, if you want something a little more low-key (less self-conscious), check out the other Third Coast on Dearborn.

Espial
948 W. Armitage   871-8123

Why, in the name of all that's holy, would someone take a hip little cafe like Espial and put it smack dab in the center of Armitage Avenue's 24-hour-a-day frat party? We don't know, but, believe us, you'll be glad they did. Because here you can quaff a Latte or an aperitif in a very pleasant atmosphere, while just outside rage the hormones of Lincoln Park's ubiquitous "white sneaker dudes." By the way, Espial also features some pretty good food and weekend entertainment in the cozy back room.

Lakeview

Cafe Voltaire
3231 N. Clark   528-3136

A comfortable place to sit and sip coffee or enjoy delicious vegetarian dishes. Once famous for its snotty waitstaff, the service is now rather friendly. The art on the walls is sometimes worth seeing, and there are various plays and performances in the basement.

Nightcrawlers
3912 N. Clark   871-4062

Conveniently located next to the Live Bait theater, up the street from the Metro, and across from Graceland Cemetery, Nightcrawlers offers light fare, but the focus is on coffee drinks and fine wines. Usually the service is typical of most too-cool cafes—slow and with an attitude. Try the key lime pie.

The Torchlight Cafe
3358 N. Paulina   404-9588

The Torchlight is a luminous addition to Chicago's coffeehouse scene. It's got a full bar, some decent patisserie- style grub, and live entertainment to boot. Plus, the look of the place, with its mosaics, hand-painted tables, and rich woods, is easy on the old peepers. What's more, there isn't exactly a plethora of other nocturnal hangouts in this hood.

Bucktown/Wicker Park/Ukrainian Village

Urbis Orbis
1934 W. North   252-4446

You probably never will be the hippest person in Urbis Orbis, but, if you can live with that, you can have a great time in here. It's a big, airy Wicker Park coffeehouse with a terrific looking handmade 50-foot bar, and some of the more interesting denizens of Wicker Park populating it. Yes, the people watching in here can be quite cinematic. The food and coffee (no alcohol is served) is decent, if uninspired. The art on the walls is also a notch above most such repositories. Check this place out some night with one of your hipper friends or, even better, a copy of Camus in the original French.

OTHER

That is, other things to do besides stand around and drink.

Lakeview

Annoyance Theatre
3153 N. Broadway   929-6200
A perfect name for this place, because many of their performances are just plain annoying. A good change if you're tired of doing the bar thing, although it's probably a good idea to be wasted when you see such satirical musicals as "Co-ed Prison Sluts" and "Your Butt." Call for specific plays and times.

Live Bait Theatre
3914 N. Clark   275-5255
Thirty plays performed in 60 minutes, Too Much Light Makes the Baby Go Blind, makes this a fun-filled, fast-paced late night at the theater. The cast has hundreds of plays from which to choose, so you can go back many times and never be bored. You won't like every play you see, but most will make you laugh or cry or at least think. Reasonably priced, a roll of the die determines your admission fee. The fun starts at 11:30 P.M. Friday and Saturday, but the theater is small, so get there early.

Lower Links
954 W. Newport   248-5238
How cool is Lower Links? So cool, they refuse to open on any night when the Cubs are playing a home game. But the folks here don't really have to worry. After all, how many Cub fans do you know who love performance art, experimental music, and bohemian surroundings? If you're into these things, however, Lower Links is a treasure. Step into this subterranean, darkened club any Thursday, Friday, or Saturday night, and you'll see some of the most adventurous entertainment this town has to offer. Sunday through Wednesday you'll have to settle for world music spun by DJs. This is one of our favorite places. Support it.

Southport Lanes
3325 N. Southport   472-1601
One of the few bowling alleys, probably in the country, that still has young, muscular men reset the pins for you. There are only three lanes, so call ahead to make sure they're not going to be taken by leagues. Even if you can't get a lane, it's fun to watch other people bowl.

—Michael Hush and Ellen Snook

LATE NIGHT AND ALL NIGHT

The main character in the movie *After Hours* is a straitlaced young man suddenly subjected to the wild and wacky late-night life of New York. He sits in the back seat of a taxi and helplessly watches his cab fare fly out the window. Then the night claims him.

I thought of the movie as I began to write about Chicago's late-night netherworld. Here in the Second City, whether you're straitlaced or curious, need to send a fax, or crave a banana split, the late night has plenty to offer anyone at any speed.

One thing is certain: when you stumble into your work cubicle or fall into your bed as the sun reaches across Lake Michigan, you'll eventually want to tell someone about the time you had, the food you ate, and the Chicagoans you met. Or maybe make a movie about it. Enjoy.

ANSWERING SERVICES

24 Hours Answering
520 N. Michigan   644-1995

BAKERIES

Heinemann's Bakery Outlet
3925 W. 43rd   523-5000
Heinemann's, open 24 hours, is a Chicago institution for my family and many others. I highly recommend the cream-filled crumb coffeecake (mmmmm).

Jewel Bakeries
Throughout the Chicago area
While lacking the neighborhood-bakery feeling, the bakeries attached to the ubiquitous Jewel grocery stores whip up some treats that smell delectable. Some bakeries attached to the 24-hour Jewel grocery stores are expanding their hours. Check the yellow pages under "Bakeries" and phone first.

Melrose Bakery
930 W. Belmont   404-7901
I've found the selections get pretty slim (and are a little stale) around 3, 4, and 5 A.M., but come the (later) early morning, the oven is on and the stuff is fresh. Open 24 hours.

BOWLING ALLEYS

I had a good time bowling at childhood birthday parties, but in my adulthood I have learned that the later the hour, the more fun the bowling experience. These places not only have lanes galore for the less-than-serious bowler, they provide a variety of action, such as dancing, drinking, and the occasional pool room.

Marzano's Miami Bowl
5023 S. Archer at Pulaski   585-8787
Features 80 lanes, 24 hours.

Rock 'N' Bowl
Until 5 A.M. on Fridays and Saturdays at two locations:
Diversey-River Bowl
2211 W. Diversey   227-5800
Additional attractions: dance floor, restaurant, pool.
Gateway Bowl
6432 W. North   637-1400

Waveland Bowl
3700 N. Western   472-5900
Offers 40 lanes, 24 hours.

Marigold Arcade
828 W. Grace   935-8183
Open 24 hours on weekends, 32 lanes.

CARRIAGES

For the romantic couple or the out-of-town tourist, the carriage rides that take place along Michigan Avenue and near Lake Shore Drive offer a different, slow look at the city. Pick up a late-night ride on the corner of Michigan Avenue and Pearson Street, across the street from Water Tower Place.

The Noble Horse   266-7878

Chicago Horse and Carriage Co.   280-8535

CITYWIDE SERVICES

Jewel Grocery Stores
Some are open 24 hours, until midnight on Sundays.

White Castle
A Chicago tradition, the out-of-towner might want to try several "sliders," because one of the small, square burgers is never enough (though in the morning, your digestive system might argue that one is too much).

White Hen and/or 7-Eleven Convenience Stores
One of these is on many a corner in Chicago. They're always open, the coffee is hot, and the packaged junk foods are in plentiful supply.

Dunkin' Donuts
My favorite Dunkin' Donuts is on the corner of Belmont and Clark, where rebellious teens gather on weekends before trying to find somewhere else to go. Until Starbucks and the other coffee boutiques came along, Dunkin' Donuts was Chicago's best carry-out coffee from a franchise. (And it's still very good.)

CURRENCY EXCHANGES

Most currency exchanges offer the same things: money orders, checks cashed, CTA tokens and passes, stamps, sometimes copy services and maps. Here are some 24-hour locations:

Zenith Currency Exchange
1938 W. North   227-6656

69th Street Currency Exchange
6858 S. Ashland   436-7300

Chicago and LaSalle Currency Exchange
770 N. LaSalle   642-0220

DENTISTS

Always There Dental Care
2200 N. Halsted   348-0565
3701 N. Southport   348-0565
This place has a great sign. Toothbrush in hand, the superhero-dentist goes forth to fight tooth decay and fix your emergency tooth problems.

Augusta Dental Center, Ltd.
3460 N. Lincoln   549-2800
Emergency services 24 hours.

EARLY A.M.

Starbucks Coffee stores expanded from Seattle to Chicago, though I can't find much logic in that. They provide a relaxed, warm, wonderful-smelling atmosphere beginning early, usually around 6:30 A.M. for commuters who want the first cup of coffee before they get to work. All that caffeine gives Chicagoans the energy to argue endlessly over which Starbucks drink is the best and how to order them correctly (as in "I'll have a grande iced skim latte with hazelnut and a tall cappuccino with an extra shot"). The pastries are good, too. Popular locations include:
1533 N. Wells   337-8899
1001 W. Armitage   528-1340
3358 N. Broadway   528-0343
2200 N. Halsted   935-2622
619 W. Diversey   880-5172

Reva's Place
1754 W. Balmoral   275-1202
A friend of mine discovered Reva's some time ago; it's noticeable because it's the only bright pink building on the block, and is surrounded by bungalows and other Chicago brick constructions. Good food, friendly service.

Mary's Kitchen
1775 W. Sunnyside   334-0101
Only a few blocks away from Reva's is Mary's, offering the same kind of early-morning, stick-to-your-ribs breakfast food for a different round of regulars.

Busy Bee
1550 N. Damen   772-4433
Over in the Wicker Park neighborhood, "The Bee," as some regulars call it, opens early for the late- nighters coming home on the El overhead. The Busy Bee also has the distinction of being the restaurant mentioned in the most chapters of this book.

Chicago Bagel Authority
953 W. Armitage 248-9606
Bagels galore! Open at 6 A.M. on weekdays.

FLORISTS

CityScents
1331 W. Fullerton 549-1900
211 E. Ohio 836-0211
Offers 24-hour service.

FOOD

I'd call them restaurants, but there's a character to these places that more
formal restaurants lack. These places are joints: the cups of coffee are bottom-
less, the food is plentiful, the booths are packed, and the waitresses know the
late-night reveler-regulars. All are open 24 hours except Clarke's on Sundays,
open 'til midnight then.

Clarke's Pancake House
2441 N. Lincoln 472-3505

Fielos
10352 S. Western 238-3125

Golden Nugget
4747 N. Ravenswood 769-6700
2720 N. Clark 929-0724

Lazo's Tacos
2009 N. Western 486-3303

Melrose Restaurant
3233 N. Broadway 327-2060
930 W. Belmont 404-7901
Better-than-average diner food.

Snow White Grill
2572 N. Clark 871-1131

White Palace Grills
1159 S. Canal 939-7167

HEALTH CLUBS

Some health clubs are so ruthless they never (or almost never) close.

Charlie Club and Resort
112 S. Michigan 726-0510
Open 24 hours.

Nautilus and Aerobics on Broadway
3221 N. Broadway 248-3939
Monday–Thursday until midnight. If you can stand the close quarters of this
rather small club, then exercise away.

Lakeshore Athletic Club
1320 W. Fullerton   348-6377
This full-service club opens earlier than most (4:30 A.M. during the week, 6 A.M. on weekends) and stays open until midnight (until 11 P.M. on weekends). The weight room closes earlier.

LAUNDRIES

Keep in mind that most laundromats have run their last wash an hour before closing. Even so, these places offer a little more time for those in dire need of clean underwear.

Harlem Laundromat and Cleaners
5741 S. Harlem   586-5757
Open seven days until midnight.

Riverpoint Coin Laundry and Drop Off
1730 W. Fullerton   549-5080
Open 24 hours.

LOCKSMITHS

When I locked my keys in my car, with the car still running, and left for four hours, I was able to get help at 3 A.M. when I returned. But I haven't lived it down.

ABAL Lock
500 N. Michigan   527-2728 or 266-0189
Auto and home, 24 hours.

Amazing Lock Service
739 W. Belmont   935-8900
Available 24 hours.

Armitage Citywide
3004 N. Cicero   777-0772
6272 W. North   889-4535

AAA Chicago Metropolitan Area
1-800-262-6327

MESSENGER

These messenger services are quick, friendly, and will call back to let you know if they have problems delivering your package. Prices and delivery times vary, depending on distance, package size, and number.

Arrow Messenger
1322 W. Walton   489-6688

Cannonball, Inc.
875 W. Huron   829-1234 or 829-1200

MOVIES

These Chicago institutions offer alternative shows late at night.

Music Box Theater
3733 N. Southport 871-6604
One of Chicago's finest vintage movie houses, their midnight showings change every few weeks. It's especially comforting for insomniacs, as stars twinkle and clouds float on the ceiling.

400
6746 N. Sheridan 764-9100
A haunt for Loyola students, this place has been picking up some other fans with the midnight showing of *Rocky Horror Picture Show*.

MUSIC

Like so many of the categories in this chapter, music receives far greater attention elsewhere in this book. Still, I feel compelled to recommend the late-night atmospheres of two music clubs: the Green Mill and Deja Vu. Not places for the soft-hearted jazz or blues fans, the music lasts and lasts long and late on the weekends at both places. I recommend Ed Petersen's saxophone quintet or the Sunday night poetry slam at the Green Mill, and Big Band night or the turtle races ($1 cover, come on!) at "The Vu."

The Green Mill
Lawrence Avenue and Broadway (4800 N.) 878-5552

Deja Vu
2624 N. Lincoln 871-0205
Other places I'm merely suggesting after-hours are:

Kingston Mines
2548 N. Halsted 477-4646

Wise Fools Pub
2270 N. Lincoln 929-1510

Dreamerz
1516 N. Milwaukee 252-1155

PAWNSHOPS

I got a great deal on a secondhand saxophone from a pawnshop (the previous owner's name was even stenciled into the piece), so pawnshops have a special place in my heart.

State Pawners and Jewelers
160 N. State 726-1163
Open 24 hours every day, this one is quite a spectacle all by its lonesome when the commuters and shoppers have gone home for the evening or weekend.

PHARMACIES: PRESCRIPTIONS ONLY

If you're in pain, it helps to know where to go. Remember to call first, but these Chicago area stores are usually quick and efficient in filling your prescriptions.

Cosmopolitan Drug Co.
754 N. Clark (corner of Chicago and Clark)   787-2152
Many favor this pharmacy for its slogan, "I get my drugs at Cosmo" (they even sell T-shirts). It's open 365 days a year until midnight and will deliver your prescription at no extra charge.

Osco Drug
For the location nearest you, call 1-800-654-6726.

Walgreens
757 N. Michigan   664-8686
740 W. Diversey   929-1097
1601 N. Wells   642-4008
Howard Street and Western Avenue   764-1765
3302 W. Belmont   267-2328
75th and State   224-1211
6310 N. Nagle   774-2225
1554 E. 58th   667-1177
3405 S. Martin Luther King   326-4058
Like the Osco stores, Walgreens pharmacies are located throughout Chicago and many are open 24 hours. *Sweet Home Chicago* readers should know, however, that Walgreens recently refused to carry *What You Can Do To Avoid Aids* by Magic Johnson.

PHOTOCOPIES

Kinko's
3001 N. Clark   528-0500
2451 N. Lincoln   327-7770
444 N. Wells   670-4460
6548 N. Sheridan   761-2777
1309 E. 57th   643-2424
84 W. Van Buren   421-7373
Offering help and solace to the almost-desperate student or professional, Kinko's also provides computer service at most locations; call to find out if it's Apple or IBM. Full-service 24-hour branches are cited here.

American Reprographics Management, Inc.
10 N. Dearborn   332-2764
Open 24 hours.

Original Instant Printing Centers
200 S. Clark   726-6275
Until 1 A.M. on Saturday.

PHOTO DEVELOPERS

Most photo developers are drop in the morning, pick up the next day or one-hour places. However, **Sentury 1 Hour Photo** is open Monday–Friday until 10 P.M. at 2802 N. Clark (Clark and Diversey), 404-8756.

PLEASURE

Interesting finds for the curious.

Pleasure Chest
3143 N. Broadway   525-7151 or 525-7152
The boutique for today's lovers, open seven days, noon until midnight.

Cupid's Treasures
3519 N. Halsted   348-3884
A love boutique, open seven days from noon to midnight.

POSTAGE

MailBoxes Etc.

858 W. Armitage 528-0011	3023 N. Clark 281-8988
3712 N. Broadway 975-7100	1730 W. Fullerton 248-2121
60 E. Chestnut 787-7277	7144 N. Harlem 792-9595
2568 N. Clark 935-7755	1507 E. 53rd 288-3173

What is there to be said? When it needs to go, it needs to go. MailBoxes, Etc., provides a little extra besides postage, including packaging, copying, and fax services. Locations above have 24-hour copying and fax services.

PUBLIC NOTARIES

Around the Clock Notary
477-2400 (house calls, too)

RECORDS

Tower Records and Video
2301 N. Clark   477-5994
Open until midnight.

Pravda Records
3729 N. Southport   296-0744
Next to Cabaret Metro/Smart Bar, this alternative music shop sells just about any group on the nontraditional scene; the store sometimes is open selling records after a band performs at the Metro.

SERVICE STATIONS

D'Agostino Standard
841 W. Irving Park   24-hour towing: 477-2210, 528-1950, or 549-8686
Mechanic always on duty.

Loop Service Amoco
600 W. Randolph   782-1282
24 hours. Road service.

Passaglia Auto Repair
520 N. Wells   337-4884

SHOWS

My theory on live shows is the smaller the theater, the better the chances it will move around. Check the paper or call these places to see if they're still offering late-night shows. And check the theater chapter in this book for a more complete list of companies, any of which might offer a late-night performance.

Second City Theatre
1616 N. Wells   337-3992
SC's free after-show improv sessions last about 30 minutes on Sunday and Tuesday–Thursday. It's a chance to see potential "Saturday Night Live" stars on their way up working with humor on the spur of the moment.

Annoyance Theater
3153 N. Broadway   929-6900
Noted for its "Brady Bunch" spoof that took them off-Broadway and away from us, Annoyance Theater offers a variety of shows each week, starting around 7 or 8 P.M. and going for the occasional 10 or 11 P.M. show. Call for show days and times.

Live Bait Theater
3914 N. Clark   275-5255
Again, chances are they'll have a show around 10 or 11 P.M.

Lower Links
954 W. Newport   248-5238
Noted mostly for performance art, sometimes music and poetry/prose readings, Lower Links lies behind an unassuming door and feels (and looks) like someone's basement. Kerouac and Ginsberg would like this place.

Other alternative theaters with sometimes late-night offerings:

Kill the Poets
1803 W. Division   296-4046

Shattered Globe Theater
2856 N. Halsted   486-7915

Mary Archie Theater
Angel Island, 731 W. Sheridan   871-0442

Cafe Voltaire
3231 N. Clark   651-9536

STORAGE

Who knows what you would want to store at 2 A.M., but I'm just suggesting if you need it, since you might want 24-hour access to your own stuff.

East Bank Self Storage
429 W. Ohio   644-2002

Chicago Lock Stock and Storage
2001 N. Elston   227-2448

TATTOOS

While it's a step I'm still considering, if you've decided on a design and there's no turning back, here are two places that will welcome you.

Custom Tattooing
3817 N. Lincoln   248-0242
On Friday and Saturday until midnight.

Jade Dragon Tattoos Studio
5331 W. Belmont   736-6960
Open until midnight.

VETS/ANIMAL CARE

Chicago's Anti-Cruelty Society has emergency numbers for centers on the North and South Sides. To get the numbers call the headquarters on 501 N. LaSalle at 644-8338.

Beverly Hills Animal Hospital
11012 S. Western   779-7790

Chicago Vet Emergency Services
3123 N. Clybourn   281-7110
Monday–Friday, 7 P.M.–8 A.M.; Wednesday, noon–8 A.M.;
Saturday, noon–Monday at 8 A.M.

South Shore Animal Clinic
2320 E. 79th   388-3771

VIDEOS

Tower Records
2301 N. Clark   477-1399
Open until midnight.

Blockbuster Video
11047 S. Western   238-5544
1201 N. Clark   664-1225
3120 N. Clark   525-5757
9110 Stony Island   933-7474
2301 W. Lawrence   769-6699
These video stores can be found throughout Chicago and will act promptly to get any films you cannot find. Remember that membership cards are not transferable; where the card was issued is where it's valid. The stores are open until midnight. One final, political note about Blockbuster: the chain requires its employees to take a drug test.

—Genevieve Sedlack

SECONDHAND SHOPPING

When I was a teenager, my secondhand shopping trips were all about discovery. I would head north from the distant South Side ready to meet the challenge: to find—from a large selection of previously used, frequently gross things—some really funky stuff with a lot of character and several secret past lives.

While touring Chicago's vast supply of secondhand, resale, and vintage stores, it is important you remember there's more to it than looking at (and wandering through) old stuff. If you're reading this chapter, chances are I'm telling you something you already know, but I wanted to remind you that most of these places require patience and interest. It takes a certain person in a certain mood to find a cache among the cast-offs. But you know that, too.

I think we'll agree that the search is half the fun, and the surprises and treasures of a day spent secondhand shopping are well worth the time, energy, and money. Enjoy the hunt!

CLOTHES, JEWELRY, ACCESSORIES

The Alley
858 W. Belmont   883-1800
Hours: Monday–Thursday, 10 A.M.–10 P.M.;
Friday and Saturday, 10 A.M.–12 P.M.; Sunday, 10 A.M.–9 P.M.
The Alley is one of the stores in the Alternative Shopping complex at the corner of Belmont Avenue and Clark Street. Their stock ranges from cotton T-shirts to leather jackets, so if you're not sure what your buying mood is, this might be a great place to begin.

Bewitched
4003 N. Southport   525-5807
Hours: Wednesday, Friday, Saturday, 12 P.M.–6 P.M.; Thursday, 12 P.M.–8 P.M.;
Sunday, 12 P.M.–5 P.M.

Brown Elephant for the Howard Brown Memorial Clinic
3641 Halsted   549-3549
Hours: Daily, 12 P.M.–6 P.M.
My roommate swears by this place; she's come home with at least three new outfits on several different occasions, all for around $20. You have to look hard here, from furniture to fashion, but the finds are worth it.

Dreamland
3317 N. Broadway   248-5558
Hours: Monday, 12 P.M.–8 P.M.; Thursday, 12 P.M.–7 P.M.;
Saturday, 12 P.M.–6 P.M.; Sunday, 12 P.M.–5 P.M.
Don't let the boas and feathered hats on display fool you. This store carries lots of men's fashions—shirts, suit jackets, ties, and hats (fedoras, even!). The women's things aren't so bad, either, as there is a large selection of dressy dresses spanning the ages, from prom to cocktail parties.

Entre-nous
21 E. Delaware   337-2919
Hours: Monday–Friday, 11 A.M.–6 P.M.; Saturday, 12 P.M.–5 P.M.
Sells "previously owned" designer fashions.

Flashy Trash
3524 N. Halsted   327-6900
Hours: Monday–Wednesday, 12 P.M.–7 P.M.; Friday, 12 P.M.–8 P.M.;
Saturday, 11 A.M.–7 P.M.; Sunday, 12 P.M.–6 P.M.
I had my reservations when they had a blowout sale on bell-bottoms, but hey, the past is the past. The wide selections of other fashions from other ages, as well as the accessories of the times, span many eras and make an easy task of finding something to buy. If you need a tuxedo shirt, this is your place.

Hubba-Hubba
3338 N. Clark   477-1414
Hours: Monday–Saturday, 11 A.M.–6:30 P.M.;
Sunday, 12 P.M.–5 P.M.; and by appointment
Vintage clothes are mixed in with brand-new stuff, and the prices can run rather high, but this is a very reliable source of dress-up and festive casual attire. There are odds and ends and bits and pieces of pretty, pretty things.

Hurricane Rochelle
2153 W. Division   384-7087
Hours: Saturday, 12 P.M.–7 P.M.;
Sunday, 12 P.M.–6 P.M.; and by appointment

Jazz 'E Junque
3831 N. Lincoln   472-1500
Hours: Monday, 10 A.M.–2 P.M.; Tuesday and Thursday, 10 A.M.–5:30 P.M.; Friday–Saturday, 11 A.M.–4:30 P.M.
Their pride and joy is the wide collection of vintage cookie jars they buy and sell.

Jungle Red
3420 N. Halsted   525-5620
Hours: Monday–Friday, 12 P.M.–9 P.M.; Saturday, 10 A.M.–6 P.M.;
Sunday, 12 P.M.–5 P.M.
The eye-catching dummy dolled up in a red-and-white polka-dotted dress cuts a very inviting figure. Walk in and peruse the place for both furniture and clothes.

Just Vintage Clothing
2935 N. Clark   549-7787
Hours: Monday–Friday, 12 P.M.–7 P.M.; Saturday, 11 A.M.–6 P.M.;
Sunday, 12 P.M.–6 P.M.
I got the beaded top of a lifetime at this place; it waited two months for me while I made up my mind to buy it. Deep down I knew I had to have it. Much to my surprise, the beaded top knew it too. They carry some dapper men's fashions as well.

Mad Max's
858 W. Clark   348-8738
Hours: Friday–Sunday, 12 P.M.–7 P.M.
Also part of the Alternative Shopping Complex, same idea as the Alley.

Mirror Mirror
2961 N. Lincoln   929-8899
Hours: Wednesday–Thursday, 6 P.M.–9 P.M.; Saturday, 12 P.M.–5 P.M.;
Sunday, 12 P.M.–3 P.M.
Gotta have a vintage wedding dress, complete with vintage accessories? This store specializes in them and also offers a very limited supply of men's fashions.

Silver Moon
3337 N. Halsted   883-0222
Hours: Daily, 12 P.M.–6 P.M.
Classic window displays of clothes, heels, and top hats decorate the windows here with elegant and understated simplicity. They offer two rooms of furniture and clothes/accessories to pick through, and both Fred Astaire and David Byrne would be pleased with the tuxedo offerings.

Strange Cargo
3448 Clark   327-8090
Hours: Monday–Friday, 12 P.M.–7 P.M.; Saturday, 11 A.M.–7 P.M.;
Sunday, 12 P.M.–6 P.M.
According to their pitch, they offer "plunder from the thirties and forties." Men's fashions and Hawaiian shirts galore.

Wacky Cats
3109 N. Lincoln   929-6701
Hours: Monday–Friday, 12 P.M.–7 P.M.; Saturday, 12 P.M.–6 P.M.;
Sunday, 12 P.M.–5 P.M.
Stuff from the 1940s through the 1990s, so understand you'll have to *look*.

FURNITURE/ANTIQUES

Although my antiquing experience is pretty limited, I can recommend that if you want to make a full day of it, you call these places first to double-check their hours. Several suggestions: it's safe to say that most places are definitely open after noon; Monday is usually "we're closed" day, and since many of the dealers are small businesses in a not-so-healthy economy in a not-so-essential business, they struggle. Some nights (or days) they call it quits early or decide to put off opening. What's best, and you can tell here by the addresses, is just walking along an area filled with stores and going in as you pass by. Halsted and Belmont avenues are ideal for this activity, and both offer other secondhand stores as well.

Affordable Antiques
1832 W. Belmont   327-0707
Hours: Thursday, 2:30 P.M.–5 P.M.; Saturday and Sunday, 2:30 P.M.–4:30 P.M.

Aged Experience Antiques
2034 N. Halsted   975-9790
Hours: Tuesday–Saturday, 12 P.M.–6 P.M.; Sunday, 12 P.M.–5 P.M.

Americana
3924 N. Southport   935-4204
Hours by appointment
Mostly political memorabilia, period pieces.

Antique Palace
3020 N. Lincoln   477-6700
Hours: Monday–Friday, 9 A.M.–6 P.M.; Saturday, 11 A.M.–6 P.M.;
Sunday, 12 P.M.–6 P.M.

The Antique Warehouse
2050 N. Halsted   528-0545
Call for hours.

Athenee, Inc.
3457 N. Halsted   404-2104
Hours: Tuesday–Saturday, 10 A.M.–6 P.M.; Sunday, 12 P.M.–5 P.M.
Very ornate furniture and art, probably a bit pricey but nice to view if you
hope to move to Versailles some day.

Betty's Resale Shop
3439 N. Lincoln   929-6143
Hours: Daily, 10 A.M.–8 P.M., but call to make certain

Boomerang
641 W. Buckingham   348-7755
Hours by appointment

The Brass Works
2142 N. Halsted   935-1800
Hours: Friday, 10 P.M.–6 P.M.; Saturday, 11 A.M.–5 P.M.

The Brokerage
3444 N. Halsted   248-1644
Hours: Wednesday–Sunday, 1 P.M.–6 P.M.
They have everything from campaign buttons to full vanity sets.

Buckingham Antiques
1901 W. Belmont   281-7374
Hours by appointment

Bygone Treasures
2155 W. Belmont   549-2388
Call for hours.

Chez Garbage
3336 N. Clark   281-2611

Collectique
2127 W. Belmont   525-2300
Hours: Saturday and Sunday, 12 P.M.–5 P.M.

Cracker Barrel Antiques
2120 W. Belmont   296-2030
Hours: Tuesday–Saturday, 12 P.M.–5 P.M.

Formerly Yours
3443 N. Halsted   248-7766
Hours: Daily, 12 P.M.–6 P.M.
One of my favorites! As I mentioned, I don't profess to know anything about antiquing, but they have wide and extensive collections of gorgeous furniture, beautiful old jewelry and picture frames, stained glass from old bungalows and buildings, and period piece lamps. The prices really aren't bad.

The Good Old Days
2138 W. Belmont   472-8837
Call for hours.

Gracie's Antiques
1919 W. Belmont   472-2445
Call for hours.

International Antiques Center
2300 W. Diversey   227-2400
Hours: Wednesday–Sunday, 11 A.M.–6 P.M.

Josie's
3323 N. Broadway   871-3750
Hours: Monday–Friday, 12 P.M.–7 P.M.; Saturday, 12 P.M.–6 P.M.;
Sunday, 12 P.M.–5 P.M.
A small store, they sell smaller items such as jewelry, a few lamps, pictures, and some furniture. I get the feeling they know what they're dealing.

Miscellania
1800 W. Belmont   348-9647
Hours: Wednesday–Sunday, 12 P.M.–5 P.M.

Mixed Emotions Antiques & Collectibles
1909 W. Belmont   929-9867
Hours: Monday–Sunday, 12 P.M.–5 P.M.

New City Enterprises
3020 N. Lincoln   327-7601
Hours: Monday–Friday, 12 P.M.–6 P.M.; Saturday, 11 A.M.–6 P.M.;
Sunday, 12 P.M.–6 P.M.

Nineteen Thirteen
1913 W. Belmont   404-9522
Hours: Thursday–Sunday, 12 P.M.–5 P.M.

Portobello Road
3313 N. Broadway   472-6762
Hours: Tuesday–Thursday, 12 P.M.–7 P.M.; Friday–Sunday, 11 A.M.–6 P.M.
What happened to the things owned by June Cleaver's friends when they all moved into condos? To Portobello Road. This place carries kitchen-fulls of "historic" dining ware: pots, pans, shakers, glasses. There's lots of glass and china, some plastic, but all of it makes spending time in the kitchen look like fun.

Roscoe Village Antiques
2252 W. Belmont   281-2522
Call for hours.

Thru-a-Glass
2255 W. Belmont   528-1617
Hours: Daily, 1 P.M.–7 P.M., but call first

Time Well
2780 N. Lincoln   549-2113
Hours: Monday, 12 P.M.–7 P.M.; Wednesday–Friday, 3 P.M.–8 P.M.;
Saturday and Sunday, 12 P.M.–5 P.M.

Twentieth Century Revue
1903 W. Belmont   472-8890
Hours: Wednesday–Sunday, 12 P.M.–5 P.M.

Unforgettables
5357 N. Clark   561-4141

Urban Artifacts
2928 N. Lincoln   404-1008

Used to Be Yours
3450 N. Clark   871-5505

What's New What's Not
4613 N. Lincoln   728-7134

RECORDS

The Discover Cafe
2436 N. Lincoln   868-DISC
Hours: Sunday, 9 A.M.–12 A.M.; Monday–Thursday, 10 A.M.–2 A.M.;
Friday, 10 A.M.–1 A.M.; Saturday, 9 A.M.–2 A.M.
Each table has a Discman on it so you can BYOD or sample their selection.
About four months old, the Discover Cafe is ready to become a fixture in the
neighborhood, next to the Three Penny moviehouse. The staff is friendly and
the hours—all right!

Dr. Wax
2529 N. Clark   549-3377
Hours: Monday–Saturday, 11:30 A.M.–9 P.M.; Sunday, 12 P.M.–6 P.M.

Rave Records
3730 N. Clark   549-2325
Hours: Thursday–Saturday, 12 P.M.–2 A.M.
If you're anywhere near Cabaret Metro, there's no reason not to stop in before
or after a Metro show.

Reckless
3157 N. Broadway   404-5080
Hours: Monday–Saturday, 10 A.M.–10 P.M.; Sunday, 10 A.M.–8 P.M.
From run-of-the-mill soundtracks to imports from England Reckless is what
an independent record store is all about. You bring a card (much like the back
of the book card from the old library book check system) to the counter and

the people get what you want. If you want to browse, listen to the tracks of comedy and music they play. I don't think the FCC would like it.

Record Exchange
1041 W. Belmont 975-9285
Hours: Monday–Saturday, 12 P.M.–9 P.M.

Record Hunt
3149½ N. Broadway 929-9607
Hours: Daily, 12 P.M.–8 P.M.
Want to see what album covers were like before Tipper Gore had her way? Here's your chance to relive some of the worst music of the seventies or locate elusive albums (remember those round things made of vinyl?).

2nd Hand Tunes
2604 N. Clark 929-6325

Wax Trax
2449 N. Lincoln 929-0221
Hours: Monday–Saturday, 11 A.M.–10 P.M.; Sunday, 12 P.M.–8 P.M.
Another independent record store (and Ministry's original label), this place fits less and less into the trendy Lincoln Avenue strip of stores and shops in Lincoln Park. Where have all the angry young teens gone? As the memories of punks hanging out in the park on Fullerton and Halsted continue to fade, its nice to know they can be safe and angst-y for a little while inside Wax Trax.

USED BOOKS

I appreciate several things about used bookstores: the must, the dust, the time to browse, the already-cracked bindings and already-written-in books, the occasional sleeping cat or kitty lurking around, nooks and crannies and places to sit, and the interested, usually bespectacled owner who knows the place inside out and can tell you exactly where everything is. These are a few of my favorite things.

Abraham Lincoln Book Shop
357 W. Chicago 944-3085
Hours: Monday–Saturday, 9 A.M.–5 P.M.
Shelby Foote would have a field day, and I'm sure Lincoln would be interested in the paintings of himself.

Act I Bookstore
2632 N. Lincoln 348-6757
Hours: Monday–Thursday, 10 A.M.–8 P.M.;
Friday and Saturday, 10 A.M.–6 P.M.; Sunday, 12 P.M.–6 P.M.
Actors of the World Unite! Here is a place to find your hearts' desire: perfect roles. Scripts galore.

Aspidistra Bookshop
2630 N. Clark 549-3129
Hours: Monday–Saturday, 11 A.M.–9:30 P.M.; Sunday, 12 P.M.–7:30 P.M.
Perfect example of what I meant by employees and owners who know where everything is while you browse and browse and browse through piles of a wide range of topics and likeable prices. Check out their sidewalk sales, too.

Black Star Bookstore
6544 N. Sheridan 743-6685
Hours: Daily, 12 P.M.–9 P.M.
Occult, anyone?

Book Adventure
3705 N. Southport 477-4725
Books and baseball cards.

Bookleggers Used Books
2935 N. Broadway 404-8780
Hours: Daily, 12 P.M.–7 P.M.

Books on Belmont
614 W. Belmont 528-2665
Call for hours.
Cat in the window (probably not for sale), stacks, and shelves—and this place makes *house calls*.

Booksellers Row
2445 N. Lincoln 348-1170
Hours: Daily, 11 A.M.–10:30 P.M.
408 S. Michigan 427-4242
Hours: Monday–Saturday, 10:30 A.M.–10:30 P.M.; Sunday, 12 P.M.–10:30 P.M.

Everybody's Bookstore
2120 W. Devon 764-0929
Hours: Monday–Saturday, 12 P.M.–6 P.M.

Fiery Clock Face
5311 N. Clark 728-4227
Hours: Tuesday–Sunday, 10–6 P.M.

Powell's
2850 N. Lincoln 248-1444
Hours: Sunday–Friday, 11 A.M.–9 P.M.; Saturday, 10 A.M.–10 P.M.
1501 E. 57th 955-7780
Hours: Daily, 9 A.M.–11 P.M.
828 S. Wabash 341-0748
Hours: Monday–Friday, 10:30 A.M.–8:30 P.M.; Saturday, 10 A.M.–10 P.M.; Sunday, 12 P.M.–8 P.M.

Puddinhead Books
1446 N. Milwaukee 486-0865

Selected Works
3510 Broadway 975-0002
Hours: Daily, 12 P.M.–9 P.M.
Nooks and crannies for the whole family, plus sheet music, a little art, and an owner who's ready to converse.

Shake Rattle & Read Book Box
4812 N. Broadway 334-5311
Hours: Monday–Thursday, 12 P.M.–6 P.M.; Friday and Saturday, 12 P.M.–7 P.M.

VARIOUS OTHER MENTIONABLES

The Ark
3345 N. Lincoln   275-0062
Hours: Monday–Wednesday, 10 A.M.–5:30 P.M.; Tuesday, 10 A.M.–7 P.M.;
Friday, 9:30 A.M.–3 P.M.; Sunday, 11 A.M.–5 P.M.
Three floors overflow with furniture, pictures, clothes, and other collectibles.

Gently Used Office Furniture
934 W. North   649-6688
Hours: Monday–Friday, 10 A.M.–6 P.M.; Saturday, 10 A.M.–4 P.M.

Interiors on Consignment
2150 N. Clybourn   868-0797
Hours: Thursday, 11 A.M.–7 P.M.; Friday and Saturday, 10 A.M.–6 P.M.;
Sunday, 10 A.M.–5 P.M.

Metro Golden Memories
5425 W. Addison   736-4133
Hours: Monday–Saturday, 10 A.M.–6 P.M.; Sunday, 12 P.M.–5 P.M.
Ah, the stars and their films of yesteryear. Ask and they will do their best to find.

Moondog's
2301 N. Clark   248-6060
Hours: Monday–Friday, 10 A.M.–9 P.M.; Saturday, 10 A.M.–11 P.M.;
Sunday, 11 A.M.–6 P.M.
Get the Spidey senses tingling. Moondog's offers a wide array of comics old and new for the die-hard doodle lover.

Vintage Posters International, Ltd.
1551 N. Wells   951-6681
Hours: Tuesday–Friday, 11 A.M.–7 P.M.; Saturday, 11 A.M.–6 P.M.;
Sunday, 12 P.M.–5 P.M.
Posters to me are as beautiful as some paintings; this gallery holds showings and sells such wonderful work.

—Genevieve Sedlack

Arts and Culture

MUSIC
CLASSICAL MUSIC
JAZZ, BLUES, AND THE AVANT-GARDE
FOLK MUSIC
ROCK
COUNTRY, GOSPEL, ETHNIC, AND MORE

DANCE
THEATER
FILM
ART
PERFORMANCE ART
PHOTOGRAPHY
LITERARY LIFE
ARCHITECTURE
MUSEUMS

MUSIC

Chicago has an extensive and varied musical life with a wealth of activities and a rich history in every area. The flagship is an orchestra that has an unbroken record of a century of the highest-quality music making; parallel to it, but not unbroken, is a history of opera going back 80 years. Creative activity goes back as far and in the past has produced John Alden Carpenter, Leo Sowerby, and Ruth Crawford Seeger. At the popular end, 19th-century Chicago was the home of George ("Tramp, Tramp, Tramp") Root and Henry Clay ("Marching through Georgia") Work. Today, the nationally known composers making Chicago their home include Easley Blackwood, George Flynn, M. William Karlins, Robert Lombardo, William Russo, Howard Sandroff, Ralph Shapey, Alan Stout, and the author of many of the music chapters in this book, Ray Wilding-White.

After New Orleans, Chicago is the most important city in the history of jazz. Urban blues grew up in Chicago (the style is nearly synonymous with the city), and its influence on rock music is immense. Gospel music was practically created here.

Today there is an active concert life led by Chicago's world-class orchestra and opera company. As befits their proud local history, jazz, blues, and gospel music are thriving; to this must be added a rich ethnic and folk heritage, to say nothing of a healthy and humming rock/pop scene. Chicago can provide for every taste.

119

CLASSICAL MUSIC

CONCERT MUSIC

The flagship of the Chicago concert world is the Chicago Symphony Orchestra, an undeniably world-class orchestra with a distinguished, century-old history. Its founder, Theodore Thomas, was an extraordinary man to whose crusading career we owe the inspiration for all the major orchestras in America. His last dream was for a hall of his own, which he got and which he survived only by weeks. Theodore Thomas Orchestra Hall (look up at the front of the building) is now referred to as Orchestra Hall.

The CSO, as it is usually abbreviated, is very good but also expensive. Fortunately, there are less pocket-clearing alternatives, and it is worth remembering that the musical (or any form of artistic) vitality of a city is not only due to a few large groups but also to the many smaller ones.

Major Orchestras

(Note: When a number of concerts/programs is given, this does not include repetitions at the same or different locations.)

Chicago Symphony Orchestra
Daniel Barenboim, Musical Director;
Sir Georg Solti, Laureate Musical Director
Orchestra Hall
200 S. Michigan 435-6666 (for tickets and information);
435-8122 (business office)
Runs from September to early June; tickets sell for $5- $54. Students and seniors can get tickets for $10 or less after 5 P.M. on the day of the performance (after 12 noon for matinees).

A CSO offshoot is the **Civic Orchestra** (435-8159), a training orchestra for young professionals that gives six free concerts a year. Tickets can be ordered by mail from Orchestra Hall (see CSO, above) or obtained at the door at concert time. The CSO also sponsors chamber music, piano, and jazz/pop concerts (see "Chamber Music," below).

In the summer the CSO moves to its lovely summer quarters wherein are provided food and music al fresco with an occasional diesel train obbligato:

Ravinia Festival
Green Bay and Lake Cook Roads, Highland Park, 60035 (708) 728-4642 (RAVINIA)
Several series—including the Chicago Symphony Orchestra, chamber music, dance, Musica Viva (a contemporary music), jazz/pop series, and children's—run from June to early September. Prices vary widely according to the event. There is also a winter series called "Rising Stars at Ravinia," which features international artists under 30 years old in three sub-series: violin, piano, and chamber music. Concerts take place weekly November–May.

Grant Park Concerts (Grant Park Symphony Orchestra and Chorus)
P.O. Box 94291, Chicago, 60691   819-0614
Free concerts are given at the Petrillo Music Shell in Grant Park June–August
on an average of four nights a week; the orchestra and guests are excellent. A
donation of at least $45 for two gets you a membership in the Grant Park
Concert Society and seats in the reserved section. Otherwise come early or
bring a blanket, soda pop, and good company and sit on the grass.

Symphony II
1123 Emerson, Evanston, 60201   (708) 866-6886
Three concerts in the Pick-Staiger Auditorium of Northwestern University,
two for full orchestra and one for chamber orchestra. Prices are $13.50–$27.50.

Smaller Orchestras

The Chicago Chamber Orchestra
Dieter Kober, Music Director
410 S. Michigan, #631, Chicago, 60605   922-5570
Thirty-piece orchestra giving some 20 free concerts (Holiday Special excepted) at various locations.

Chicago Sinfonietta
Paul Freeman, Music Director
7900 W. Division, River Forest, 60305   (708) 366-1062
Its mission is "to offer minority musicians an opportunity to develop their
talents."

Chicago String Ensemble
Alan Heatherington, Music Director
3524 W. Belmont, Chicago, 60618   332-0567
Superb ensemble dedicated, as the name indicates, to the literature of music
for strings. Five concerts, $13–$16; students and seniors, $10.

Concertanti di Chicago
30 S. Wacker, #1300, Chicago, 60606   993-7887
Thirty-piece chamber orchestra that gives a series of five concerts. Tickets cost
$22.50; students and seniors, $17.50.

Northwest Indiana Symphony
1040 Ridge, Munster, Indiana, 46321   (219) 836-0525

Suburban Orchestras

There are quite a few orchestras in the greater Chicago area. Some, with a
combination of qualified nonprofessionals and "ringers," put on some very
good concerts, others are more for fun. If you live in the area, it is worth
checking the nearby ones out. For more details call the Chicago Music Alliance (987-9296).

Elgin Symphony Orchestra
1700 Spartan, Elgin, 60123-7193   (708) 888-7389
The **Elgin Choral Union** ([708] 697-1000, ext. 7225) works with this orchestra.

Fox River Valley Symphony
5 E. Galena, Aurora, 60506   (708) 896-1133

Illinois Philharmonic Orchestra
210 Illinois, Park Forest, 60466   (708) 481-7774
This orchestra covers the far South Side.

Lake Forest Symphony Association
700 E. Westleigh, Lake Forest, 60045   (708) 295-2135

Northbrook Symphony Orchestra
707 Skokie, #600, Northbrook, 60062   (708) 272-0755

OPERA

Like the CSO, the Lyric Opera is a world-class organization. Not counting traveling companies that go back a century and a half, opera in Chicago started in 1910 when it achieved two golden decades with the golden artistic touch of Mary Garden and the golden coffers of two tycoons, first McCormick and then Insull. This age and the nation both crashed in 1932, but opera tottered along on uncertain legs until after World War II, when it finally crashed for good. It was brought back to life in 1954 by the indomitable and controversial Carol Fox whose successor, Ardis Krainik, has made it one of the world's major opera companies. The repertoire has gone beyond the usual war horses and includes contemporary and American works. The productions are spectacular, and, of course, there are the stars. But it comes at a price; if you want to impress a date with dinner and the best seats you can easily blow a week's salary.

Chamber Opera Chicago
500 N. Orleans, Chicago, 60610   822-0770

Chicago Opera Theatre
20 E. Jackson, #1400, Chicago, 60604   663-0555
The brainchild of Alan Stone, the Chicago Opera Theatre is the other opera company in Chicago, and the quality is good. There are three productions a year, one of them an American opera. Two of the annual productions are at the Athenaeum Theatre and one appears at a variable location. Productions fall between February and June and cost $13.50–$46.50.

Light Opera Works
927 Noyes, Evanston, 60201   (708) 869-6300
If you have a sweet tooth for the Kafe mit Schlag of Lehar, Herbert, et al., check out this company. Three productions: June, August, and December, at prices of $15–$36.

Lithuanian Opera Company
5620 S. Claremont, Chicago, 60629   737-0235
Have you ever heard *La Traviata* in Lithuanian? This opera company does the standards in Lithuanian, Lithuanian operas, and relevant works such as (La Gioconda) Ponchielli's *I Lituani*. One production repeated at various locations, $15–$40.

Lyric Opera of Chicago
20 N. Wacker, Chicago, 60606   332-2244
Eight productions from mid-September to early February, $16–$89.

Lyric Opera Center for American Artists 332-2244
Like the Civic Orchestra, this is a training ground for young professionals.
There are two public performances a year at different locations and with
varying prices.

The Opera Factory
6161 N. Hamilton, Chicago, 60659 761-1334
The Spanish equivalent of operetta is Zarzuela, a genre tackled, among other
Latin offerings, by the Opera Factory. Tickets run $15–$18.

CHORUSES

Among the inalienable rights of man is the right to bellow like a bull (or like
a cow, as the case may be); and throughout the land this need is filled by
choruses of every size, singing in every style and covering the full range of
musical and vocal ability. Unlike instrumental ensembles, choruses are nearly
always volunteer, and membership is by audition. Requirements, of course,
vary considerably. The CSO maintains a large chorus directed by Margaret
Hillis that performs only with the orchestra. A set number of singers is paid,
and the rest are chosen by open auditions held each spring; there are an-
nouncements on WFMT and in the papers, or call 435-8172. Hillis also conducts the largest of the plethora of Christmas season **Do-It-Yourself
Messiahs**. This one is sponsored by Talman Home Federal (434-3322), which
rents Orchestra Hall for the occasion.

Large Choruses

The **Lyric Opera** maintains a paid chorus for its productions. Open auditions
are held in December and January. Call 332-2244.

Apollo Chorus
Thomas Hoekstra, Music Director
P.O. Box 9722, Downers Grove, 60515 (708) 960-2251
The oldest chorus in Chicago, the Apollo has 200 voices. Membership is by
audition. Three concerts at $9–$27.

Music of the Baroque
Tom Wickman, Music Director
343 S. Dearborn, #1716, Chicago, 60604 663-1900
This midsize chorus is also an orchestra, and some concerts do not use the
chorus; also, some concerts are not baroque. The genre may be hard to
pigeonhole but not the quality, which is superb. Membership is by audition.
Eight concerts, priced at $17.50–$34.50; students and seniors, $13.

North Shore Choral Society
P.O. Box 103, Evanston, 60204 (708) 303-5746
This is the most established suburban chorus, with 100 voices.

William Ferris Chorale
William Ferris, Music Director
100 W. Grand, #200, Chicago, 60610 622-2070
This is an established 50-voice chorus with a repertoire that includes some
20th-century American. Membership is by audition. Four concerts at $18–$25.

Windy City Gay Chorus
606 W. Barry, #216, Chicago, 60657   404-9242

Smaller Choruses

Choral Ensemble of Chicago
George Estevez, Music Director
2335 N. Orchard, Chicago, 60614   935-3800

Fleur de Lys Chorale
Dennis Northway, Conductor
644 W. Aldine, Chicago, 60657   281-2107
Sixteen voices; four concerts at $10.

Halevi Choral Society
3480 N. Lake Shore Drive, Chicago, 60657   761-1382
Specializes in Jewish music.

His Majestie's Clerkes
Anne Heider, Music Director
P.O. Box 1001, Evanston, 60204   (708) 866-7464
Twenty-four voices performing a cappella Renaissance and baroque reper-
toire. Eight concerts at $15; students and seniors, $7.

James Chorale
James Rogner, Conductor
4753 N. Broadway, #918, Chicago, 60640   907-2189
Eclectic repertoire. Tickets are $14; students and seniors, $10. Performs only in
buildings designated as landmarks.

Oriana Singers
William Chin, Conductor
3750 W. Peterson, Chicago, 60659   262-4558
With only six voices, this is more of a madrigal group. Four concerts, $15.

Children's Choirs

Chicago Children's Choir
1720 E. 54th, Chicago, 60615   324-8300
This group is very strong.

Glen Ellyn Children's Chorus
Sandra Prodan, Director
586 Duane, Glen Ellyn, 60137   (708) 858-2471
The best children's chorus in the Chicago area, this excellent group has 200
voices, ages 8–16. Membership is by audition. Three concerts, $8.

John Work Chorale
500 E. 33rd, #1714, Chicago, 60616   534-6486 or 842- 4627
This 16-voice chorale is named for the famous black composer and choral
arranger, Delanor O'Bannion. One of his students went on to found and
conduct this a cappella black chorus, which has been performing spirituals
and classical repertoire (but no gospel) for 30 years.

Jubilate! Children's Choir
300 Green Bay, Winnetka, 60093   (708) 446-3822
   (See also the spectacular **Soul Children of Chicago**, listed in the "Gospel" chapter.)

CHAMBER MUSIC

(See also "Music You Don't Have to Pay For" in the chapter titled "Country, Gospel, Ethnic, and More.")

Performing Arts Chicago
410 S. Michigan, #911, Chicago, 60605   242-6237
Time was when chamber music suggested four bored men in tuxedos, but no more since the leadership of Susan Lipman has brought imaginative programming to Performing Arts Chicago, covering everything from the Beaux Arts Trio to Diamanta Galas. Tickets run $24–$35.

   The CSO has acquired the **Allied Arts Concerts**, which sponsor two series of name performers at Orchestra Hall: the "Piano Series" of 12 concerts, $5–$30, and the "Pop Series" (jazz/pop) of 10 concerts, $5–$36. Call 435-6666.

   The orchestra also sponsors the **Nakamichi-CSO Chamber Music Series**, 15 concerts by different groups made up of members of the orchestra; some are permanent groups and some ad hoc. All concerts are in the Orchestra Hall Ballroom at $8. Call 435-6666.

   Several universities sponsor concert series besides their usual in-house concerts.

Arts at Argonne
Argonne National Lab/Building 221.C244, Argonne, 60439   (708) 972-7160

Chamber Music Society of the North Shore
670 Longwood, Glencoe, 60022   (708) 835-5084

Contemporary Chamber Players
Ralph Shapey, Conductor
Concert Office, Department of Music
5845 S. Ellis, Chicago, 60637   702-8068
The University of Chicago presents various concert series and also sponsors this group. Local musicians play recent music, and most events are at Mandel Hall.

North Park College
3225 W. Foster, Chicago, 60625   583-2700

Pick-Staiger Auditorium
Northwestern University
1977 Sheridan, Evanston, 60201   (708) 491-5441
Various series are presented here.

Wheaton College Artists Series
Edman Chapel
Franklin and Washington, Wheaton, 60187   (708) 752-5818
This series includes larger ensembles. Five concerts at Edman Chapel, $12–$20; students, $8–$14; seniors, $10–$17.

ENSEMBLES
General Repertoire

Chicago Chamber Musicians
1301 W. Arthur, Chicago, 60626   973-4513
Most concerts are at the Cultural Center.

The Chicago Ensemble
2929 N. Campbell, Chicago, 60618   509-9031
Five concerts, $15.

Rembrandt Chamber Players
P.O. Box 775, Evanston, 60204   (708) 328-2492

Period Repertoire

The Bach Society
550 Frontage, #2025, Northfield, 60093   (708) 470- 1154

Basically Bach
P.O. Box 479, Chicago, 60690   334-2800
Period instruments; tickets at $9–$30.

Specialized Repertoire

American Women Composers
6437 N. Greenview, #1, Chicago, 60626   764-7360

Small Groups

Chicago Brass Quintet
410 S. Michigan, #809, Chicago, 60605   663-4730
Where the quartet was once the favored format, the trio now seems to have taken over. Chicago has the **Trio Elan** and the **Exultate, Kimbark,** and **Leonardi** trios.

Early Music

Ars Musica Chicago
9332 S. Moody, Oak Lawn, 60453   (708) 599-8690

Early Music at the Newberry
60 E. Walton, Chicago, 60610-9762   943-9090
This is Mary Springfel's outstanding series, offering five concerts at **Scottish Rite Cathedral** (935 N. Dearborn). Prices are $18, students and seniors, $9.

Orpheus Band
3543 N. Greenview, #1, Chicago, 60657   549-2969

Scholars of Cambrai
Gail Gillespie, Music Director
4919 S. Dorchester, Chicago, 60615   268-9879
Vocal and instrumental music.

—Ray Wilding-White

JAZZ, BLUES, AND THE AVANT-GARDE

JAZZ

The Mississippi Valley pianists—Tony Jackson, Glover Compton, Jelly Roll Morton, et al.—were here before World War I playing a music that Chicago had dubbed "ragtime" at the turn of the century. Then, as the war ended, a new band sound came up from New Orleans: Tom Brown, the great Freddie Keppard, and what became known as the Original Dixieland Jazz Band were brought up by clubs or vaudeville and once again Chicago gave it a name: jas, jass, jaz, jasz, and finally jazz.

When King Oliver's Creole Jazz Band with New Orleans greats like the Dodds Brothers, Kid Ory, and, above all, Louis Armstrong, moved into the Lincoln Gardens in 1922, a standard was set. "The Stroll," as State Street in the south 30s was called (now IIT), it became a jazz beehive with the likes of Oliver, Morton, Hines, and more. "If you put a trumpet in the street it would blow itself," said Eddie Condon. This attracted a group of youths from western Chicago—the legendary Austin Gang: McPartland, Freeman, Tough, Teschmaker, etc.—who took what they learned and made of it the Chicago Style.

Since then Chicago has produced any number of jazz greats: Benny Goodman, Gene Krupa, King Cole, Gene Ammons, Milt Hinton, Lee Konitz, Lennie Tristano, and on down to the brilliant innovators of the AACM (Association for the Advancement of Creative Music) such as Anthony Braxton or Muhal Richard Abrams who turned things upside down in the 1960s.

There have been peaks and there have been valleys, but there has always been jazz, and the last decade has seen a steady rise in activity; today there are a lot of jazz spots and an abundance of great talent. Look for older names such as E. Parker McDougal, Von Freeman, Jodie Christian, Willie Pickens, Bobby Lewis, John Young, and Eddie Johnson, or AACM graduates Mwata Bowden, Douglas Ewart, and Henry Threadgill.

And if these musicians aren't looking behind them, it's because gaining on them are the likes of guitarist Fareed Haque; saxophonists Ed Peterson, Lin Halliday, and Jim Gailloretto; drummers Paul Wertico, and Jeff Stitely; and trumpeter Brad Goode. The newest does not necessarily come from the youngest; the medal for creativity on the cutting edge linked with endurance goes to Hal Russell and NRG, which has uncompromisingly been leading the charge for over two decades.

Major Jazz Venues

Andy's
11 E. Hubbard   642-6805
The present jazz resurgence pretty much started here with the experiment, in 1978, of "Jazz at Five" in an old pressmen's bar; it caught on and now the pressmen are gone, the yuppies are there in crowds, and there is also "Jazz at Noon" and "Jazz at Nine." This is the place to go to find the old established names: Bobby Lewis, the eternal Franz Jackson, Cy Touff, Barrett Deems, and, not to be missed, Chicago's best trad pianist, Erwin Helfer.

The Bop Shop
1807 W. Division   235-3232
A great jazz venue. (Note: the jazz stops for a poetry slam once a week.) This is a relatively new club with strong bookings.

Get Me High
1758 N. Honore   252-4090

The Green Mill
4802 N. Broadway   878-5552
For years this has been the main outlet for top young Chicago talent. (The Green Mill also hosts the poetry slam on Sunday nights.)

The Jazz Institute of Chicago
410 S. Michigan, #716   427-1676
This organization sponsors special events, notably the winter **Jazz Fair**. It also maintains the **Jazz Hot Line** (427-3300), which has the latest in what's happening 24 hours a day.

Joe Segal's Jazz Showcase
Blackstone Hotel
636 S. Michigan   427-4300
This is the place for the big national names.

Other Venues

The Backroom
1007 N. Rush   751-2433

The Bulls
1916 N. Lincoln Park West 337-3000
The grotto effect decor is peculiar.

The Cotton Club
1710 S. Michigan   341-9787
Some national acts show up here (e.g., Cassandra Wilson).

Dick's Last Resort
435 E. Illinois   836-7870
This is where good musicians have to battle a lamentably hokey atmosphere. Some blues and, believe it or not, a Sunday gospel music brunch.

The Moosehead Bar and Grill
240 E. Ontario   649-9113

Oz
2917 N. Sheffield   975-8100

Pops for Champagne
2934 N. Sheffield   472-1000
Both of these last two are upscale spots. Pops has Sunday jazz brunches.

Small Jazz Spots

Smaller places often have some good performers on a one- or two-nights-a-week basis. Two South Side spots of long standing are near each other.

The New Apartment
504 E. 75th   483-7728
Von Freeman hangs out here on Tuesday.

The Other Place
377 E. 75th   874-5476
Music Monday and Tuesday.

The Velvet Lounge
2128½ S. Indiana   791-9050
The lounge is run by AACM graduate Fred Anderson and has been a meeting ground for members of that fraternity. Jam sessions on alternate Sundays, 5 P.M.–9 P.M.

Other smaller places, where it is a good idea to check what the act is first, include these (see also "Eclectic Clubs" below):

Alexander's Steak House
3010 E. 79th   768-6555

The Blue Milan
Papa Milano's   1400 N. Wells   951-6441

Lonie Walker's Underground WonderBar
10 E. Walton   266-7761
Bobby Broom's Big Deal Trio plays Sunday night. (Broom was Miles Davis's guitarist.)

MacGyver's
5355 N. Clark   271-2531

Weeds
1555 N. Dayton   943-7815

Yvette
1206 N. State   280-1700

Lounges/Clubs

Not all the good jazz is found in jazz spots; some players frequent those cozy little watering holes (everybody has a favorite) that are more often the habitat of that elegant and, until Bobby Short, often ignored fraternity, the club or lounge singer (and/or pianist). There are quite a few fine club performers in Chicago; some move around to a few clubs and some stay put.

Biasetti's Steak House
1525 W. Irving Park   549-9767
For longevity, 76-year-old Lonnie Simmons takes the prize with 23 years at Biasetti's.

The Coctails.

Mnemio.

Coque D'Or
The Drake Hotel
140 E. Walton 787-2200
The irrepressible Buddy Charles is a one-man piano show at the Coque d'Or Tuesday–Saturday.

Gold Star Sardine Bar
680 N. Lake Shore Drive 664-4215
Patricia Barber is as good a jazz singer as she is a jazz pianist; she's a fixture at the Sardine Bar.

Hanna Lounge
Hotel Nikko
370 N. Dearborn 744-1900
Kelly Brand plays nice piano here Wednesday, Thursday, and Saturday.

Milt Trenier
610 N. Franklin 266-6226
Trenier is the quintessential lounge player, and he has had his own place at various locations for years. This is his current venue.

Some other interesting people to look for are Chicago's premier jazz violinist, Johnny Frigo, song stylist Audrey Morris, singer-guitarist Frank D'Rone, jazz singers Jeannie Lambert, Kimberly Gordon, and Jo Bell, and jazz pianist-vocalist Judy Roberts. Some nice places to hear such talent are these:

Christopher's on Halsted
1633 N. Halsted 642-8484

Toulouse
49 W. Division 944-2606

Yvette Wintergarden
311 S. Wacker 408-1242

Eclectic Clubs

There's quite an education to be had from being a patron of one of the clubs that books a wide variety of acts. Since they don't pigeonhole, they are here grouped separately. Check *The Reader* or call first to see if they are doing your kind of thing, or better yet, take a chance and just go.

At the Tracks
325 N. Jefferson 332-1124
Very attractive upscale decor, good food, and a variety of acts.

Biddy Mulligan's
7644 N. Sheridan 761-6532
Lots of good acts that play on a peculiarly placed bandstand. Weekends tend to draw a college/beer type of crowd.

Bub City
901 W. Weed 266-1200
New and slightly trendy.

Club Equinox
2300 N. Lincoln 477-5126

The latest incarnation of a location that has been all kinds of things through the years.

Cubby Bear
1059 W. Addison   327-1662
Some surprising acts, local and national, show up here (Sun Ra and his Arkastra to Chuck Berry). The listening area is open to the bar, whose crowd thinks it's still in the Wrigley Field bleachers across the street.

Deja Vu Bar and Grill (The Vu)
2624 N. Lincoln   971-0205
Straight-ahead R & B, and some jazz, in this straight- ahead uncostly bar. The 17-piece house band plays big band jazz Tuesday night for $1 cover.

Elbo Room
2871 N. Lincoln   549-7700
Good food in an intimate little place with a strange shape and even stranger sight lines. Groups musical and theatrical of every ilk.

Fitzgerald's
6615 Roosevelt, Berwyn   (708) 788-2118
Pleasant environment with attentive audiences. Blues, jazz, rock, Cajun, poetry, you name it.

Hot House
1565 N. Milwaukee   235-2334
Nice stripped-down place with outrageous art on the walls. Hi-tek, Near Eastern, avant-garde jazz, and, once a month, poetry to music with David Hernandez and Street Sounds.

Schuba's
3159 N. Southport   525-2508
Ranges from folk to rock. Lots of good local names play in a separate but noisy back room.

Two suburban venues besides Fitzgerald's are these:

Durty Nellies
55 N. Bothwell, Palatine   (708) 358-9150

Shades
21860 N. Milwaukee, Deerfield   (708) 634-2583

BLUES

As jazz flourished and faded on "The Stroll," blues pianists came into their own at the South Side "rent parties"—Pine Top Smith, who popularized the term *boogie woogie*, Little Brother Montgomery, and the legendary, indestructible Sunnyland Slim.

Then came the bluesmen, scuffling for small change in the once colorful but now doomed **Maxwell Street Market** (starts south of Halsted Avenue and Roosevelt Road, and there is still music there on weekends). Then they took over the South and later the West side taverns, and here the moody, introspective rural sound became brash and urban—the classic Chicago Style with harmonica, electric guitars, drum set, and a loud driving beat. Chicago blues and the recording companies were inextricably connected from Paramount in the 1920s to Chess in the 1950s and now to Alligator, whose set *Living Chicago Blues* is a good primer (4 CDs or cassettes).

The history-making men have been legion: Big Bill Broonzy, the Sonny Boy Williamsons I and II, Little Walter, Willie Dixon, Magic Sam, Buddy Guy, Junior Wells, and the star names of Howlin' Wolf and Muddy Waters. From Muddy's 1958 English tour sprang English rock: Mayall's Bluesbreakers, Eric Clapton, the Rolling Stones (named after a Muddy tune.)

Chicago blues is now big and international, but it is almost all gone from the South and West sides. Clubs are mostly on the North Side and cater to a mostly white, upscale, or tourist trade. The atmosphere varies from club to club, but the artists are great and tend to do a circuit. There is no end of talent: Billy Branch, Son Seals, the Kinsey Report, Willie Kent, Magic Slim, Otis Clay, Lonnie Brooks, Dion Payton, Koko Taylor, Sugar Blue, Valerie Wellington, and lots more.

South Side Spots

Despite what I said earlier, there is still some blues life left on the South Side.

Artis's
1249 E. 87th   734-0491
Music Sunday and Monday.

The Cuddle Inn
5317 S. Ashland   778-1999
Music Friday and Saturday.

Lee's Unleaded Blues
7401 S. Chicago   493-3477
Under different names, this club has been here, it seems, forever.

The New Checkerboard Lounge
432 E. 43rd   624-3240
Time was when this and Theresa's were *the* famous South Side blues spots. Theresa's is gone, and more's the pity.

North Side Spots

B.L.U.E.S.
2519 N. Halsted   528-1012
A small club that maintains a nice funky atmosphere. Its Belmont Avenue cousin is more upscale.

B.L.U.E.S. etcetera
1124 W. Belmont   525-8989

Kingston Mines
2548 N. Halsted   477-4646
The oldest of the North Side clubs.

Lilly's
2513 N. Lincoln   525-2422
A small club with a pleasant atmosphere if peculiar sight lines.

Wise Fools Pub
2270 N. Lincoln   929-1510

West Side

Rosa's
3420 W. Armitage   342-0452
Slightly off the beaten track is a club started by two Italian blues buffs who crossed the ocean to open a blues club in a Hispanic neighborhood of Chicago. The atmosphere is about as close to what a blues club should be as any in town.

Nearer the Loop

Blue Chicago
937 N. State   642-6261

Blue Chicago on Clark
536 N. Clark   661-0100
Home bases for some blueswomen: Gloria Hardiman, Ditra Farr, Gloria Shannon.

River West
1860 N. Elston   276-4846

South of the Loop

Buddy Guy's Legends
754 S. Wabash   427-1190
Large, nice place with excellent sight lines. Buddy himself is, of course, a legend.

Suburban Spots

Hugh's Too
720 S. Barrington, Streamwood   (708) 213-1456

Slice of Chicago
36 N. Northwest Hwy., Palatine   (708) 991-2150

AVANT-GARDE VENUES

Avant-garde is a pretty flexible word, and the boundaries start crossing over into jazz/rock, dance, performance art, and theater; not knowing quite where you're at is part of the fun.

Club Lower Links
954 W. Newport   248-5238 (office) or 248-9496
In the basement of Links Hall, where the decor suggests Bela Lugosi working out of a resale store, all sorts of events take place, from poetic music to musical poetry and more. See *The Reader*.

Links Hall
3435 N. Sheffield   281-0824
The oldest venue for all kinds of nearly ineffable entertainment is this suitably frowzy old meeting hall where the performances are punctuated by the passing El trains just outside the windows. Cover is $7 at the door, or call for reserved admission.

Randolph Street Gallery
756 N. Milwaukee   666-7737
The sort of events that you can enjoy at Lower Links also pop up weekly at Randolph Street Gallery.

Southend Musicworks
1313 S. Wabash   939-2848
The best musical acts, many national and international, come to these spartan quarters. There are two seasons, March–June and September–December. Depending on the act, $5–$15 at the door.

You can also check out coffeehouses and art galleries, particularly in the Bucktown and Wicker Park areas, for sporadic events.

MUSIC STORES

Jazz Record Mart
11 W. Grand   222-1467

For alternative rock (there are various schools within this term; stores tend to point in different directions), check out these stores. (The "Secondhand Shopping" chapter has a section on used record stores, too, for hard-to-find or older albums.)

Dr. Wax
2529 N. Clark   549-3377
Strong on world music.

Pravda Records
3729 N. Southport   296-0744
Strong on Chicago bands and independent labels. Lots of house and industrial.

Wax Trax
2449 N. Lincoln   929-0221

For jazz, blues, and other styles on Chicago radio, see the "Radio" chapter for specific programming details.

—Ray Wilding-White

FOLK MUSIC

Folk is out, acoustic is in. Ethnocentrism is out, world music is in. That, in a semantic if simplified nutshell, summarizes the current folk scene. Fair-weather folkies may have dropped by the wayside years ago, but the core of the folk community—those few and hardy souls—remain as solid and as devoted as ever. If Chicago no longer has the sheer number of folk clubs that it had 20 or even 10 years ago, that doesn't mean that the music has died out. On the contrary, folk music, if anything, has returned to its roots—to the coffeehouses, living rooms, and church basements where it started. The difference between past folkies and modern folkies is one of lower expectations. Economic necessity has forced the current generation to accept humbler ambitions and secure more modest means to accomplish their goals.

But there's still plenty of activity going on about town. In recent years, there has been a movement toward using smaller venues and presenting concerts in people's homes. Meanwhile, coffeehouses such as Uncommon Ground in Wrigleyville or Kopi Cafe in Andersonville and, of course, the time-defying No Exit in Rogers Park prove that coffee and acoustic music go hand in hand, that somehow a brewing espresso machine and a strumming guitar remain inseparable.

In addition to the **Old Town School of Folk Music** and a number of smaller spots, many in the suburbs, several churches in the area (notably the **Second Unitarian** on the North Side, the **Mont Clare Church** on the far Northwest Side, and the **Unitarian Church** in Evanston), present folk music on a regular basis. That's not to mention the various storytelling and folk dance groups scattered throughout the Chicago metropolitan area.

As we approach the end of the 20th century, folk music enters a transitional phase. The boundaries have been redrawn and the definition of what constitutes folk has been rewritten. Now such diverse styles as klezmer, Celtic, bluegrass, old timey, salsa, Cajun, reggae, and African music can be included under the banner of "folk." In Chicago, like the rest of the nation, the best of folk music has come to encompass a healthy and vibrant eclecticism.

FOLK VENUES

The following are clubs, coffeehouses, and churches that frequently feature folk or acoustic acts.

In the City

Beat Kitchen
2100 W. Belmont 281-4444
Occasional folk acts in this comfortable North Side venue run by the same people who operated that once popular Lincoln Avenue night spot, Orphans.

The Blue Room
1400 N. Wells 951-6441
Mostly jazz but also acoustic music in a smoky, sophisticated setting located above the upscale Mirador restaurant.

Cafe Voltaire
3231 N. Clark   528-3136
Acoustic music is occasionally presented in the basement of this avant-garde coffeehouse, much of it with a decidedly aggressive edge.

Earl's Pub
2470 N. Lincoln   929-0660
Modest Lincoln Avenue tavern, run by the indefatigible Earl Pionke of Earl of Old Town fame, that features an open stage and occasional folk acts.

Heartland Cafe
7000 N. Glenwood   465-8005
It's hard to pin down this rambling, ramshackle, Rogers Park institution. It's part health food restaurant, general store, and laidback nightclub with just the right touch of sixties/seventies angst and an eclectic musical lineup to boot.

Kopi Cafe
5317 N. Clark   989-KOPI
Acoustic music on Thursday nights in this combination coffeehouse, travel bookstore, boutique, and art gallery.

Mont Clare Coffeehouse
6935 W. Medill   714-0328
Not-for-profit coffeehouse sponsored by the Mont Clare Congregational Church. Open September–June with concerts, by mostly local talent, presented on the second Saturday of each month. Mont Clare is organized by Tom and Chris Kastle, a husband-and-wife team who specialize in the music of the Great Lakes. Admission to concerts is $4, $1 for children 12 and under; singarounds, $2 per adult, children free.

Mr. Coffeehouse
Old Town School of Folk Music
909 W. Armitage   525-7793
Mr. Coffeehouse is a weekly informal gathering of Old Town students, teachers, local musicians, and other guests. The evening consists of two parts. The song circle begins at 6:30 P.M. Here people can sing, request a song, or swap songs. Then featured guests are invited to perform at 8:30 P.M. At least one Friday a month, Mr. Coffeehouse presents a student concert. This gives Old Town students an opportunity to show off their skills. Occasionally, Mr. Coffeehouse also sponsors special events such as the "Tribute to Big Bill Broonzy" or "Woody Guthrie's Birthday" celebration.

No Exit Cafe and Gallery
6970 N. Glenwood   743-3355
The granddaddy of the Chicago folk/coffeehouse scene, the No Exit has been around in one form or another for over 30 years. With its wooden tables and beat-era ambiance, it remains the quintessential Chicago coffeehouse. It's a great place to relax, hear some music, enjoy a cup of cappuccino, or munch on the goodies from the kitchen. No Exit regulars include Jim Craig, Brian Gill, Phil Cooper and Margaret Nelson, and Jim McCandless. Open stage on Monday.

None of the Above Coffeehouse
Second Unitarian Church
656 W. Barry   929-4852
Presents Chicago-area musicians, storytellers, and poets on the third Satur-
day of each month September–November and on the second Saturday in
December and on the third Saturday January–June in the church basement.

Oasis Center
7463 N. Sheridan   274-6777
Sing-along held on the third Saturday of each month.

Old Town School of Folk Music
909 W. Armitage   525-7793
Venerable institution, established in 1957, that gained a new lease in life with
the arrival of Jim Hirsch as executive director in the mid-eighties. The school
has expanded its previously narrow range of music to include various types
of indigenous music from around the world. Under the new definition of the
school's vocabulary, folk has come to mean anything from Celtic music to
bluegrass to Latin rhythms. Presents concerts by major national and international talent. In recent years, the venue's diversification has assured not only
its survival but has cemented its reputation as arguably the best venue in the
city to hear folk music. Among its programs: eight-week classes in vocal
techniques, chorus, sea shanties, fiddle, banjo, dulcimer, harmonica, and
traditional dance; four-week classes in guitar, shapenote singing, bluegrass
banjo, and world music; the eight-week Blues School is an intermediate to
advanced program for the more serious student; summer weekend program
in country blues, harmony, and music theory; also private instruction and
children's programming. The Resource Center, which is open to the public,
contains over 10,000 recordings, books, and magazines. Membership: individual, $25; family, $40.

Uncommon Ground Coffeehouse
1214 W. Grace 929-3680
Pleasant Wrigleyville coffeehouse that presents music, usually acoustic or
light jazz, on Friday and Saturday nights and Sunday evenings.

In the Suburbs

The Beacon Coffee House
The Unitarian Church
1330 Ridge, Evanston   (708) 328-2893
Concerts usually held once a month. Recent performers have included Chris
Farrell, Jim Craig, Catherine Hall, and Lee Murdock. At Beacon, you can hear
everything from sea shanties and cowboy songs to Celtic music and finger-
picking guitar.

Cafe Kismet
131 N. Genesee, Waukegan   (708) 244-1111
One of the more recent additions to the Chicagoland folk scene. Regulars at
this north suburban club include performers such as Andrew Calhoun, John
Awsumb, and Karen Jordan. There's an open mike on Monday.

The College of DuPage Arts Center
22nd Street and Lambert Boulevard, Glen Ellyn   (708) 858-3110
Big names presented in modern, auditorium-style seating.

David Adler Cultural Center
1700 N. Milwaukee, Libertyville   (708) 367-0707
This west suburban venue attracts big names in the folk and country genres.
Open stage and jam sessions, too.

Fitzgerald's
6615 Roosevelt, Berwyn   (708) 788-6670
One of the best places in the city to hear any music, period. Fitzgerald's
specializes in American roots music, which could mean anything from Cajun
to country to acoustic in an informal, roadhouse atmosphere.

Michelangelo's
329 E. Indian Trail, Aurora   (708) 897-3655
Pizzeria that doubles as the home base for the west suburban Fox Valley
Folklore Society.

Prairie Star Cafe
538 Crescent, Glen Ellyn   (708) 790-1993
Another addition to the metropolitan folk scene, the Prairie Star presents an
open stage on the first and third Tuesday of each month as well as a busy
lineup of local talent.

Two Way Street Coffeehouse
1047 Curtiss, Downers Grove   (708) 969-9720
Other places come and go, but the west suburban Two Way Street remains.
This amiable coffeehouse, located in a church basement, has managed to
survive for almost three decades. The secret of its success is simple: the
owners keep the prices down, and the entertainment is of a consistently high
caliber.

FOLK FESTIVALS

Fox Valley Folklore Festival
755 N. Evanslawn, Aurora   (708) 844-3655
Early September fest that features singers, musicians, storytellers, folk dancing, concerts, and workshops, barn dances, ghost stories, folk arts, and food
vendors.

Mont Clare Folk Festival
6935 W. Medill   714-0328
Usually held in June, this festival presents performances, workshops,
children's activities, singarounds, and crafts.

University of Chicago Folk Festival
Mandel and Ida Noyes Halls
5801 S. Ellis   702-4300
For more than 30 years, the University of Chicago Folk Festival, held in
January or February, has been presenting traditional folk music. The
programmers tend to lean toward obscure performers and other unsung

heroes of the folk genre. Also free workshops, dancing, food, and folk-related paraphernalia on sale.

SOCIETIES AND ORGANIZATIONS

Aural Tradition
P.O. Box 14407, Chicago, 60614-0407   728-7409
This Chicago organization emphasizes the traditional vocal and instrumental music, dance, and stories of the United States and the British Isles and publishes a newsletter. Membership: $7; with first-class postage, $10.

Chicago Sacred Harp Singers
1807 W. North, Chicago, 60622   486-7400
Sacred harp singing, or "shape note" singing (so called because of its unique system of notation), consists of unaccompanied, four-part harmony singing, usually of a religious or patriotic nature. Shape note singing originated in England in the 18th century and spread to New England and later to the southern states and the American heartland. The Chicago Sacred Harp Singers sponsor potluck dinners and sing-alongs and publish a newsletter eight times a year (the subscription is $10). There's also an annual Midwestern convention in May. Amateurs are always encouraged to attend the group's activities.

Ed Holstein Presents!   951-1987
The Holstein brothers' Lincoln Avenue folk club—the late and lamentable Holstein's—may be history, but longtime folkie and promoter of folk music Ed Holstein is still in the business. He now sponsors national and international folk talent such as Tom Rush and Tom Paxton. Concerts are usually held at the Old Town School of Folk Music.

Fox Valley Folklore Society
755 N. Evanslawn, Aurora   (708) 897-3655
Organization that has been supporting and promoting folk music in the Fox Valley area since 1975. Sponsors open mikes on the first Wednesday of each month; singarounds on other Wednesdays; a cappella session on the second Wednesday; and songwriting sessions on the fourth Wednesday. All presented at Michelangelo's (see above). Also sponsors the **Folk Music Information Phone** ([708] 844-3655), which is updated weekly.

Plank Road Folk Music Society
P.O. Box 283, Brookfield, 60513   (708) 387-9312 or (708) 450-9152
Promotes and preserves traditional and acoustic music in the Chicago area. Sponsors a singaround once a month at 2 P.M., usually on the third Saturday of each month (call for location) and publishes a quarterly newsletter, the *Plank Road News*.

Real People's Music
1825 W. Larchmont   281-4234
Operated by veteran folk music writer Josh Dunson, Real People's Music specializes in multicultural programming, especially the traditional music of working people. Clients include Si Kahn and Guy Carawan.

PUBLICATIONS

Common Times
6935 W. Medill, Chicago, 60635   714-0328
Quarterly magazine published by the folks who run the Mont Clare Coffeehouse. Extensive folk music, dance, and storytelling listings, articles, and reviews. Subscription: $5.

Popular Folk Music Today
705 S. Washington, Naperville, 60540   (708) 305-0770
Quarterly newspaper that specializes in the folk music of the Kingston Trio past and present as well as other folk news. Subscription: $10.

The Reader, *The Illinois Entertainer*, *Chicago* magazine, the *Chicago Tribune*, and the *Chicago Sun-Times* occasionally present feature articles on folk music and folk artists. Both the *Reader* and *Chicago* magazine offer detailed calendar listings and, in the case of the latter, cogent and thoughtful descriptions of upcoming acts.

FOLK RADIO

WBEZ-FM (91.5)

"Passport" with Chris Heim
Saturday: 7 P.M.–9:30 P.M.
World music.

"Earth Club" with Stuart Rosenberg
Sunday: 5 P.M.–7 P.M.
All types of music in the folk tradition and beyond.

"The Thistle and Shamrock" with Fiona Ritchie
Sunday: 8 P.M.–9 P.M.
Celtic.

"The Folk Sampler" with Mike Flynn
Sunday: 9 P.M.–10 P.M.
American folk and country.

"The Song Bag" with Bill Munger
Sunday: 10 P.M.–11 P.M.
Songs and songwriters.

WDCB-FM (90.9)

"River City Folk" with Tom May
Monday: 4 P.M.–5 P.M.
Folk.

"More Than Music" with Sid Fryer
Thursday: 3 P.M.–5 P.M.
Folk but also country and western, zydeco, rockabilly, and more.

"Folk Festival" with Scot Witt
Friday: 3 P.M.–5 P.M.

"Treasures from the Isles" with Mike Fleischer
Sunday: 3 P.M.–4 P.M.
Celtic.

WFMT-FM (98.7)

"The Midnight Special" with Rich Warren, Ray Nordstrand, or Norm Pellegrini
Saturday: 10 P.M.–midnight
Eclectic folk.

WNUR-FM (89.3)

"The Folk Show" with Jonathan Andrew
Sunday: 7 A.M.–11 A.M.
Eclectic.

RECORD COMPANIES

Flying Fish Records
1304 W. Schubert   394-3474
Traditional and contemporary folk, world music, blues, old time, New Age, jazz, Celtic, country, and bluegrass. Also distributes Bling Pig (blues), Atomic Theory (alternative), and Temple (Celtic), among other labels.

RECORD AND INSTRUMENT STORES

Different Strummer
909 W. Armitage   525-6165
Hours: Monday–Thursday, 10 A.M.–10 P.M.;
Friday and Saturday, 10 A.M.–5 P.M.
The music store of the Old Town School of Folk Music. Stocks guitars, banjos, mandolins, dulcimers, autoharps, fiddles, harmonicas, concertinas, bodhrans, ukes, and world percussion instruments; a large and diverse selection of cassettes, CDs, and records; musicians' supplies; music instruction books; handles repairs, rentals, and special orders. The Different Strummer also presents a series of free workshops on guitar and banjo maintenance at 1 P.M. on Saturday throughout the year.

Hogeye Music and Hogeye Folk Arts
1920 Central, Evanston   (708) 475-0260
Carries instruments, instructional books, and recordings. Hogeye also presents in-house concerts and offers private lessons in guitar, mandolin, fiddle, banjo, and hammered and Appalachian dulcimer.

Rose Records
214 S. Wabash (and various locations)   987-9044
A record lover's haven, Rose Records stocks the latest folk releases as well as many ethnic and hard-to-find folk recordings and anthologies.

Tobias Music
5013 Fairview, Downers Grove   (708) 960-2455
Music shop run by musicians for musicians. Specializes in fine guitars in all price ranges.

Tower Records
2301 N. Clark   477-5994
Huge, all-purpose record/cassette/CD store that stocks the latest in folk and folk-related recordings.

Val's Halla Records
723½ South, Oak Park   (708) 524-1004
An Oak Park fixture that carries a large selection of new and used folk recordings.

SUGGESTED READING

Folk Music: More Than a Song by Kristin Baggelaar and Donald Milton.

Folk Song America: A 20th Century Revival by Norm Cohen.

"The Exit" in *The Reader*, **September 30, 1983, by Richard Lee.**

The Listener's Guide to Folk Music by Sarah Lifton.

The Old Town School of Folk Music Its First Ten Years, or The Biography of a Hunch by Win Stracke.

—June Skinner Sawyers

ROCK

THE MUSICIAN'S VIEWPOINT

Rock music is big business these days, and the business centers for the music industry remain entrenched in Los Angeles and New York. Surprisingly, however, rock communities in smaller metropolitan areas have managed to promote and distribute their local music effectively: Minneapolis and Athens, Georgia, have made big splashes in the past decade, with Seattle and Boise poised to make their marks, while the perennial dark-horse towns—Memphis, New Orleans, and Austin—continue to enjoy vibrant and important local rock scenes.

Which brings us to Chicago. Considering the great musical heritage of the Second City (or do we call it the "third" now?) and its status as Blues Capital of North America, one would assume that a local rock scene would be flourishing here—making a national impression, creating constantly, sweating out a new world rock order, making lesser cities stand up and take notice, and forcing garage bands nationwide to consider moving here just to be a part of it all!

Unfortunately, Chicago suffers from what could be referred to as "the Nashville Syndrome." Nashville has a thriving music scene with plenty of venues, national distribution networks, radio coverage, even a local TV show that spawned a cable network—dadburn, it spawned a lifestyle! Yep, Nashville has a wonderful music scene, if country and western suits you, pardner. But there can't be a seminal rock scene in Nashville; there's no room for it, no respect for it.

Now, do you play the blues? Chicago is the place you ought to be. Do you want to be a rock player in Chicago? Well, OK, but you're on your own. Don't expect to become a member of any Rock and Roll Society or anything. Don't expect any regular local airplay. Don't expect club owners to want anything other than for you and your band to fill their rooms with all your thirsty friends and their thirsty friends. And for starters, let's try to fill that room on a Monday night at 11:00 P.M., shall we? If it works out, maybe you can have a Thursday. . . .

Enough, already. Recently, a few local acts have managed to break through nationally. Material Issue has enjoyed a successful initial CD release, and the accompanying video was on regular MTV rotation for a time. Big Shoulders, Eleventh Dream Day, and Smashing Pumpkins all signed major label deals and are experiencing varying degrees of success and nationwide recognition. Ministry/Al Jourgensen continues to produce superior EPs via the Wax Trax label, which is the only rock label in Chicago with a semblance of a distribution network. Pegboy, an up-and-coming "in your face" postpunk outfit, signed with Caroline records out of New York. So there. Rock does exist in Chicago, and who knows? Maybe Chicago is on the verge of coalescing into a cohesive rock force. Yeah, that's it.

THE LISTENER'S VIEWPOINT

Now that you're more aware of some of the obstacles facing local talent in Chicago, your appreciation of live music should and will increase accordingly. Rock clubs in Chicago fall into three basic categories: big national acts, medium national/local acts, and small occasionally national/mostly local acts.

Clubs Highlighting the Big Nationals

Aragon Ballroom
1106 W. Lawrence   561-9500
The Aragon Ballroom is a Chicago institution, providing rock entertainment since the mid-1960s and live entertainment dating back to the 1920s. They book major rap, funk-rock, metal, etc. Plan on standing, dancing, or moshing throughout the show; there's also a nice balcony for a unique viewing perspective.

Cabaret Metro
3730 N. Clark   549-0203
The Metro handles, but does not limit itself to, the best of the alternative and thrash bands passing through town Thursday–Sunday, sometimes with early all-ages shows and sometimes with late shows. Keep in mind, however, that I'm using the word *alternative* somewhat loosely. It's getting to be a bit of a misnomer, as the mainstream claims it and more and more pop music fans drop it into their conversation. Anyway, chances are good that the band you're just hearing about played at Metro last month. They also give the locals a chance, with four bands for the price of one on Wednesday nights. The industrial dance party takes place downstairs at Smart Bar; one admission covers it all.

Oak Theater
2000 N. Western   235-0088
At this writing the Oak Theater is pretty new. They seem to be concentrating on country- and roots-rock bookings.

Park West
322 W. Armitage   929-1322
The Park West handles more mainstream adult-type rock as a rule, with a nice, comfortable room in which to listen and enjoy.

Riviera Night Club
4746 N. Racine   769-6300
The Vic and the Riviera book a variety of acts. Get there early for your own table!

The Vic Theater
3145 N. Sheffield   472-0449

Medium-Sized Venues

Biddy Mulligan's
7644 N. Sheridan 761-6532
Biddy Mulligan's showcases a rather eclectic mix of blues-rock and metal with a reunion tour or three thrown in. The only place in town you'll get to see Foghat again, if you so desire.

The Cubby Bear
1059 W. Addison 327-1662
Across from Wrigley Field, the Cubby Bear books national tours as well as local bands, with a leaning toward country rock.

Fitzgerald's
6615 W. Roosevelt, Oak Park (708) 788-2118
Though not within the city limits, Fitzgerald's must be included on this list on the strength of their year-round roots-rock bookings and excellent American Music Festival each July. Not to be missed!

Lounge Ax
2438 N. Lincoln 525-6620
Lounge Ax books national tours, often with an alternative slant. Like the Cubby Bear, Lounge Ax has undergone a recent interior facelift to improve sight lines.

Where to See Local and Regional Acts

Smaller clubs dot the city and book local and regional acts with an almost infinite variety of styles. Pick up the free weekly *The Reader* to see who's playing where.

Avalon
959 W. Belmont 472-3020
Two stages plus a dance room to keep your interest.

Beat Kitchen
2100 W. Belmont 281-4444
This place used to be Orphan's on Lincoln Avenue. The sound system didn't make the move, however (the new one is excellent).

Clearwater Saloon
3937 N. Lincoln 549-5599

Club Dreamerz
1516 N. Milwaukee 252-1155
Inhabited by the denizens of the night, with the thrash heaven room upstairs.

Elbo Room
2871 N. Lincoln (in the basement) 549-7700

Lincoln Tap Room
3010 N. Lincoln 868-0060
Newly renovated!

Phyllis' Musical Inn
1800 W. Division 486-9862
This is the place that draws the Art Institute music lovers.

Schuba's
3159 N. Southport 525-2508
Schuba's books a combination of good local acts and various new country coming through town.

VooDoo
1248 W. George 975-8330
Across the street from Elbo Room.

DANCE CLUBS

In addition to the excellent variety listed above, a few of the dance clubs should be mentioned here, since they will occasionally feature live performances (see also the "Nightlife" chapter). These clubs seem to have the shortest life expectancies, since they rely on the trendiest of the trendy customers—a somewhat fickle constituency. Exit is the exception to this rule. The rest book dance-oriented music and exist as of this writing.

China Club
616 W. Fulton 466-0812
A roomy place.

Excalibur
632 N. Dearborn 266-1944
Formerly Limelight.

Exit
1653 N. Wells 440-0535
Exit has served the underground postpunk and thrash community well for a number of years and will stage infrequent live appropriate "events."

Ka-boom!
747 N. Green 243-8600

Shelter
564 W. Fulton 648-5500

—Lee Swets

COUNTRY, GOSPEL, ETHNIC, AND MORE

COUNTRY

Chicago's country music scene is a welcome respite from the overcrowded North Side blues clubs. It isn't Nashville, but there is definitely a colorful subculture happening in this town spanning generations and classes. Whether you're looking for a redneck girl or just want to do some two-stepping, be sure to check out the following clubs.

Bub City
901 W. Weed   266-1200
A place to show off your cowboy boots. They have live music Wednesday–Saturday. A young and lively place adding a bit of twang to the ultra urban Lincoln Park and Bucktown crowds.

Cadillac Ranch
1175 W. Lake, Bartlett   (708) 830-7200

Carol's Pub
4659 N. Clark   334-2402
Gritty atmosphere, more seriously country. Not a place for Izods.

Clearwater Saloon
3937 N. Lincoln   549-5599

Dixie Que
2001 W. Fullerton   252-5600
A restaurant with live music on the weekends. They serve Blackened Voodoo beer, and you can eat and listen to music outside.

Lakeview Lounge
5110 N. Broadway   769-0994

Main Street Pub
1572 N. Milwaukee   489-3160
Some know it as the Double Door. A Wicker Park bar that features live country music regularly. Very much a neighborhood place with a colorful cast of regulars. Check out the unique Elvis collection.

Nashville North
101 E. Irving Park, Bensenville   (708) 595-0170

Sundowner's Ranch
3040 N. Mannheim, Franklin Park   (708) 451-6033
Originally the Bar RR Ranch downtown on Randolph, the Ranch hosts the Sundowners, who have been playing together for 40 years. Everyone is on a first-name basis. They have 30 different kinds of chili. Free dance lessons on Monday and Tuesday night and Saturday afternoon for line dancing and other fancy footwork. A place country legends call home and well worth a trip to the burbs.

—Cynthia Gordon

GOSPEL

If David had any place in mind when he wrote, "Sing him a new song. Praise him with the trumpets, with the drums, with the stringed instruments and horns and loud clanging cymbals," it must have been Chicago, for that is what you can hear, in one way or another, in the estimated 2,000 churches that pepper the African-American neighborhoods.

It was in Chicago around 1930 that "Georgia Tom" Dorsey, the pianist for Ma Rainey and Tampa Red, left hokum and blues for the church. Dr. Thomas Dorsey, as he became, brought the earthy touch of his background to the world of the spirituals and gave them a strong beat and popular touch. To this were added the business and promotional acumen of his partner Sallie Martin and the musical refinement of Roberta Martin. With this, gospel music as we know it was born. Many of Dorsey's gospel songs have become classics, but among them, "Take My Hand, Precious Lord," sung by Mahalia Jackson at Dr. Martin Luther King's funeral, has acquired the status of "A Mighty Fortress" or "Rock of Ages."

The decades that followed produced a string of stars: the Caravans, arguably the most exciting group ever; the Soul Stirrers, from whence came the crossover star Sam Cooke; Alex Bradford, who took gospel onstage with Black Nativity; James Cleveland; Shirley Caesar; and Mahalia Jackson. Still going strong in a sea of new faces are the Barrett Sisters, Albertina Walker, Inez Andrews, and the Pilgrim Jubilees. Watch for church concerts called "benefits" and various special events.

From 1963 to 1984 Sid Ordower produced the program "Jubilee Showcase" on WLS-TV on which many important artists appeared. A hundred of these shows, digitally transcribed to tape, are now available for viewing at the Chicago Public Library Music Information Center of the Harold Washington Library Center (400 S. State).

The best place to hear gospel music is in its natural habitat:

First Church of Deliverance Spiritual
Ralph Goodpasteur, Minister of Music
4315 S. Wabash   373-7700
A major force in Chicago. The somewhat conservative music mixes gospel and classics.

A couple of major churches with pastors who are famous both as such and as recording artists are the first two here:

Christian Tabernacle Baptist
Rev. Maceo Woods
4712 S. Prairie   548-2500

Fellowship Missionary Baptist Church ("The Ship")
Rev. Clay Evans
45th Place and Princeton Avenue   924-3232

Cosmopolitan Church of Prayer
842 E. 65th   324-5400
The redecorated church they have recently moved into is spacious, and the choir is excellent.

Maywood Progressive Cogic
431 S. 13th, Maywood   (708) 344-4673
About as hip musically as you can get. The tight 50-voice choir is backed by a group that looks, and often sounds, like the Basie band.

New Hope MBC
4255 W. Division   772-1515
The choir is good, but the interest is the preacher, Rev. "Singing Sammy" Lewis, a one-time Chess Records artist who delivers as good a "hootin'" sermon as can be found.

There are also some community choruses that give very good concerts, usually in churches.

Olivet Baptist
405 E. 31st   842-1081
This older and more conservative church is the home of the Norfleet Singers, who hold more to the spiritual tradition.

The Jessy Dixon Singers
This traveling group gives occasional Chicago concerts. Two a year are at Dixon's home base, **Faith Tabernacle** (3750 N. Halsted). For information call **Dixon Ministries** at (708) 677-9211.

Soul Children of Chicago
Walt Whitman, Director
7801 S. Throop   846-0404
A fascinating group of 110 voices, ages 7-16, who sing a variety of music but mostly gospel.

Thompson Community Singers ("The Tommies")
Rev. Milton Brunson, Director
815 N. Central   921-2554
The concert on the last Sunday of each month held in **Christ Tabernacle Missionary Baptist** (854 N. Central) is a real barn burner.

ETHNIC

The fact that Chicago is a city of neighborhoods is intrinsic to the music here. The neighborhoods have been, and continue to be, shaped by the ethnic groups that have made Chicago and given it its color. The many groups have built communities for themselves, which have helped to preserve and celebrate their cultural heritage. In music, some ethnic groups can point to an outstanding name (or names) that act as a beacon in their history.

Irish

The Irish recall with pride the name of Francis O'Neill, Chicago's superintendent of police at the turn of the century, whose collections of Irish melodies are the classics in the field. From his time down, one can call to mind a long list of great players from the legendary Patsy Touhey to the present-day Liz Carroll and Marty Fahey. The heart of Irish music is the "sessions" where musicians gather informally and jam, as it were; sessions are, happily, alive and well.

Augenblick
3907 N. Damen   929-0994
Music on Tuesday.

Chicago Gaelic Park (The Lounge)
6119 W. 147th, Tinley Park   (708) 687-9323
Music Friday and Saturday evenings and Sunday afternoon.

Tommy Nevins'
1450 Sherman, Evanston   (708) 869-0450
Sessions every other Sunday at 2 P.M. The players then often move to . . .

The Abbey Pub
3420 W. Grace   478-4408
The listening room books local and touring groups. Sessions in the bar on Sunday evenings. Nice atmosphere. The Irish food and Guinness and hard cider on tap don't hurt the place.

Irish American Heritage Center
4626 N. Knox   282-7035
Varied activities; call for information or look in the Irish papers found in the Irish stores.

6511 Club
6511 S. Kedzie   737-6703
Music Friday and Saturday; sessions on the second Sunday evening of the month.

Serbo-Croatian

The **Serbo-Croatian** community (it continues this way in spite of the recent upheavals) also has its legendary figures. Honored by the NEA, the **Popovich Brothers** have been performing the traditional tamburitza repertoire since 1928 and are the musical inspiration of this far South Side community. Originally five brothers, Adam and Ted are still going strong and can be heard on occasion at . . .

The Rafters
9757 S. Commercial   731-0288
Across the street is **St. Archangel Michael Church** (9805 S. Commercial, 375-3848), where Adam Popovich leads the Svoboda Singing Choir and massed tamburitza on special occasions.

The Golden Shell
10063 S. Avenue N   221-9876
Music on Friday and Saturday, and the food is good.

Greek

Greek music, both here and in the homeland, has added the whole paraphernalia of drum sets, electronic keyboards, amplified bouzoukis, etc., and it is hard to find any traditional "village music." You might try the many summer festivals held by the numerous Greek churches in town.

Deni's Den
2941 N. Clark   348-8888
Good food and a very good band. This is also the home of the well-known singer-personality Vasilios Gaitanos.

The traditional male chants of the Greek Church are still well preserved in the local churches, and the best place to hear them is here:

Greek Orthodox Church of the Assumption
601 S. Central   626-3114
Catch the 10 A.M. service for the real thing.

Jewish

Similarly, Jewish cantorials can be heard in the synagogues, but the lesser-known, fun Klezmer street music is only now making a comeback.

Cafe Continental
5515 N. Lincoln   878-7077
The Maxwell Street Klezmer Band (named after the old Jewish neighborhood) plays here once a week; at other times there are balalaika bands and so forth.

Polkas

The polka, contrary to popular myth, is not Polish, but Czech. Chicago is a center for the polka, has its own style, and has produced such stars as Eddie Blazonczyk and Lenny Gomulka.

Some real Polish music, nicely arranged for chorus, along with works by Polish composers, is presented at the following spots:

International Polka Association and Museum
4145 S. Kedzie   254-7771
Call first since this association is not open on a regular basis.

Baby Doll Club
6102 S. Central   582-9706
You can dance to the Cleveland-style polkas of Eddie Korosa's Merrymakers at the Baby Doll on Friday and Saturday from 9:30 P.M. and Sunday from 5:30 P.M.

Polish

Some real Polish music, nicely arranged for chorus, along with works by Polish composers, is presented at the following spots:

Lira Singers
Lucyna Migala, Director
3750 W. Peterson   539-4900
Performances at various locations.

Andrej Tokarz
P.O. Box 4611, Oak Brook, 60521   (708) 646-2045 or 561-9310
The very traditional Polish highlander music from the Tatra mountains is performed by a group led by the dedicated Tokarz, at various locations.

Other

The Ukrainian bandura can still be heard on Saturdays at

Galans
221 W. Chicago   292-1000

Gypsy music, along with show tunes, is played by Alex Udvary, Chicago's lone cembalum player, at:

Kenessey's International
403 W. Belmont   929-7500
Friday and Saturday, 7 P.M.–midnight.

Chicago has plenty of **Mexican** mariachi bands, but they usually play weddings and the like. If you don't want to marry a Mexican just to hear the music, try

Hacienda de los Gutierrez
3434 W. 26th   762-1240
Wednesday–Sunday evenings. And watch for performances at various places by the fine Mexican plucked string ensemble called Las Cuerdas Classicas.

Jibarro music, the get-down music of **Puerto Rico**, can be heard Sundays at 6 P.M. at the

Club Lumuri
1944 W. Division   252-9250
The singers are off the floor; live with them just to hear the wonderful quatro playing of Gilberto Avilez.

Assorted **Latin American** music with an emphasis on **Brazil** can be heard at two places that share a guitar player:

Lisboa Antigua
1640 N. Wells   266-2021
Friday and Saturday

Rio's Casa Iberia
4611 N. Kedzie   588-7800
Monday–Saturday

Oddly enough, considering the size of the colony, there is no venue and little support for **Indian/Pakistani** music. The excellent dance company of Hema Rajagopalan brings in musicians. Call (708) 323-7835.

By contrast, the **Chinese** community gives strong support to the touring, professional Chinese Classical Orchestra. For information, write or call the Chinese Music Society of North America (P.O. Box 5275, Woodridge, 60517-0275, [708] 910-1561).

The Friends of the Gamelan own their own gamelan (the word means both an orchestra and its instruments). They play a traditional and contemporary **Javanese** repertoire and give one or two concerts a year. The group is always looking for enthusiasts and potential performers, and they provide on-the-job training. Contact the Department of Music, University of Chicago (5845 S. Ellis, Chicago, 60637, 363-7395).

Jessie Jones and Liz Torres, owners of Streetside Music record store and collaborating recording artists.

LISTINGS

With so much happening there is no such thing as a *complete* listing of events. The most comprehensive listing is found weekly in *The Reader*, which is distributed free on Thursday in many locations. Fairly extensive listings appear monthly in *Chicago* magazine, sold at magazine stands. Any number of small, free periodicals can be found in bookstores, coffeehouses, etc.; listings are limited, but they sometimes cover specialized areas (e.g., poetry slams in *Strong Coffee*.)

For general information about concert music, contact the **Chicago Music Alliance** (410 S. Michigan, #819, Chicago, 60605, 987-9296). For general music information, call **CONTACT, the Illinois Music Network** (Music Information Center of the Harold Washington Library, 747-4850. See also other sources of information in the "Jazz" and "Folk Music" chapters.

MUSIC YOU DON'T HAVE TO PAY FOR

Considering how pricey concerts and clubs are getting, it is good news that there is a great deal of music, some of it very good indeed, that doesn't cost a thin dime.

Festivals

Not to be ignored are the festivals run by the City of Chicago, usually with some commercial cosponsorship. The four big ones are the **Blues Festival** held on the first weekend in June, the **Gospel Festival** held on the second weekend in June, the **Jazz Festival** held during the week of Labor Day, and **Viva Chicago!** (Latin-American music) held in late September. All of these are held at the Petrillo Music Shell in Grant Park and, sometimes, some adjacent areas. There is also the **Country Music Festival**, which is held in conjunction with **A Taste of Chicago**, and there are the 80 neighborhood festivals that are sponsored throughout the city from May through September. Information and fliers for all of the above can be obtained from the **Mayor's Office of Special Events** (744-3370; TDD: 744-2964).

Each spring **New Music Chicago** holds a festival at the Cultural Center. For information on the **University of Chicago Folk Festival**, see the chapter on "Folk Music."

Free Concert Series and Special Events

For a really great lunchtime break, listen to soloists and chamber groups from around the world perform weekly on the **Dame Myra Hess Memorial Concerts**. These concerts are performed Wednesday at 12:15 P.M. at the Chicago Public Library Cultural Center (78 E. Washington, 346-3278 [FINEART]) and are broadcast live on WFMT (98.6 FM). For information, call the **International Music Foundation** (670-6888). The Cultural Center also presents a wide variety of concerts, concert series, and other events; call for details.

Harold Washington Library Center
400 S. State 747-4850
The library presents the **Great Music at the HWLC** series of daytime chamber music concerts. These are presently biweekly but may expand. There is also a hear-and-meet-the-artist series called **Speakin' of the Blues**, and an ethnic series is in the works. Call for details about these and about special events.

See also Grant Park concerts and Chicago Chamber Orchestra under "Orchestras" in the "Classical Music" chapter.

Finally, in summer don't miss all the buskers who toot and pick and holler and thump on the streets and in the parks and subways. For example, at this writing there is a nifty blues duet called Brother & Sister that plays State Street.

SERVICES
Schools
Full-degree Program
American Conservatory of Music
16 N. Wabash, #1850, Chicago, 60602 263-4161

Northwestern University School of Music
711 Elgin, Evanston, 60208 (708) 491-7575

Bachelor's and Master's Degrees Only
Chicago Musical College of Roosevelt University
430 S. Michigan, Chicago, 60605 341-3780

DePaul University School of Music
804 W. Belden, Chicago, 60614 362-8373

Undergraduate Program Only

Columbia College
Music Department
600 S. Michigan, Chicago, 60605 663-9462

Triton College
2000 Fifth, River Grove, 60171 (708) 456-0300; Admissions, ext. 252

University of Illinois at Chicago
1040 W. Harrison, Chicago, 60607 996-2978
Associate degree in arts; two-year college.

Courses Only

Sherwood Conservatory of Music
1014 S. Michigan, Chicago, 60605 427-6267
   (See also "Violin Makers," below.)

Stores

General Music Supplies

Biasco Musical Instrument Co.
5535 W. Belmont, Chicago, 60641 286-5900
   (See also A Different Strummer [OTS] and Hogeye Music in the "Folk Music" chapter.)

Sheet Music and Scores

Carl Fisher of Chicago
312 S. Wabash, Chicago, 60601 427-6652

Makers and Repairs

The makers listed have a reputation for high-quality work.

General Repairs, Wind and String

Duane Smeltekop
6920 Roosevelt, Oak Park (708) 848-1075

Violin Makers

It may come as a surprise to some to learn that Chicago has become a major violin maker's center. Included here also are makers of violas and cellos.

Bernard Gutterman
3252 S. Halsted, Chicago, 60608 225-6463
No repairs. By appointment.

Carl F. Becker
1416 W. Belmont, Chicago, 60657   348-5698
Also repairs. By appointment.

Fritz Reuter & Sons
1565 W. Howard, Chicago, 60626   764-2766
Also repairs.

Kenneth Stein
1320 Sherman, Evanston, 60201   (708) 491-9550
Maker and full-service store.

Michael Becker Fine Violins
28 S. Third, Park Ridge, 60068   (708) 823-5491

Park and March
3446 N. Albany, Chicago, 60618   463-7101
Located in and graduates of the Chicago School of Violin Making, listed below. Repairs.

Tshu Ho Lee
3446 N. Albany, Chicago, 60618   478-0505

W. H. Lee & Co.
410 S. Michigan, Chicago, 60611   786-0459
All grades of violins. No repairs.

Violin Dealers and Repair Only

Bein & Fushi Rare Violins
410 S. Michigan, Chicago, 60611   663-0150

Kenneth Warren & Son Ltd.
407 S. Dearborn, 11th floor, Chicago, 60610   427-7475
Also handle violas and cellos.

Violin-Making School

Chicago School of Violin Making
Tshu Ho Lee, Director
3446 N. Albany, Chicago, 60618   478-0505

Guitar Maker

Richard Brune
800 Greenwood, Evanston, 60201   (708) 864-7730
Classical guitars and lutes.

Harpsichords and Clavichords

Gerhart Smeltekop
1045 Garfield, Oak Park, 60302   (708) 848-5406
Repairs only.

Trumpets

Schilke Music Products Inc.
4520 James, Melrose Park, 60160   (708) 343-8858 or (312) 922-0570

French Horns

Lewis Orchestral Horns
1770 W. Berteau, Chicago, 60613   348-1112

Drums

Drums Ltd.
222 S. Jefferson, Chicago, 60606   606-0707
Absorbed the legendary Frank's Drum Shop. Sales and service only.

Accordions

Italian-American Accordion Mfg. Co.
3137 W. 51st, Chicago, 60632   776-2992

Records

Companies

Alligator
1441 W. Devon, Chicago, 60660   973-7732
A leading contemporary blues label.

Delmark Records
Jazz Record Mart
11 W. Grand, Chicago, 60611   222-1467
Jazz and blues, some important issues.

D.J. International
727 W. Randolph, Chicago, 60606   559-1845
House music.

Flying Fish
1303 W. Schubert, Chicago, 60614   528-5455
A major folk label that also distributes many smaller labels.

Jive
1932 S. Halsted, Chicago, 60608   226-2522
Various popular styles.

Pravda Records
3729 N. Southport, Chicago, 60613   296-0744
Alternative rock.

Wax Trax Records
1659 N. Damen, Chicago, 60647   252-1000
Alternative rock.

Stores

Rose Records, the largest chain of record stores, has nine outlets in Chicago proper and many more in the suburbs and other towns.

Home store: 214 S. Wabash   987-9044

Chicago area branches:
3259 N. Ashland   880-0280
3155 N. Broadway   472-2114
7601 S. Cicero (Ford City)   585-3201
6525 W. Diversey (The Brickyard)   745-8188
9600 S. Evergreen Plaza, Evergreen Park   (708) 422-7767
1634 E. 53rd   752-7300
820 W. North   482-8228
300 W. Washington   629-1802

Gramaphone
2663 N. Clark   472-3683
Emphasis on music to dance to.

Jimmy's Records and Variety
1613 W. 87th   239-0328
Jazz, blues, soul, etc.

Rolling Stone Records
7300 W. Irving Park, Norridge   (708) 456-0861
Known for cut-outs and bargains.

Used Records

Many of these stores also carry new albums.

Beverly Rare Records
11612 S. Western   779-0066
5608 Cermak, Cicero   (708) 656-7151
If you have to find that old 45 of the Rivingtons doing "Pa Pa Oom Mau Mau," here's where you look.

Out of the Past
3948 W. Madison   722-8901
4407 W. Madison   626-3878
Used soul, R & B, etc.; the 4407 store has a particularly large inventory.

Record Exchange
1505 W. Morse   973-0452
1041 W. Belmont   975-9285
609 Dempster, Evanston   (708) 475-8848
Large inventory.

Remember When Records
313 Ogden, Downers Grove   (708) 963-1968
Rock/pop new and used. Strong on out-of-print items.

Second Hand Tunes
2250 N. Clark   281-8813
2604 N. Clark   929-6325
1375 E. 53rd   684-3375
800 Dempster and 818 Dempster, Evanston   (708) 491-1690
(which store answers has something to do with quantum mechanics)
179 S. Oak Park, Oak Park   (708) 524-2880

Gospel

New Sound Gospel Distributors
5958 W. Lake   261-1115
Wonderful little store that stocks only gospel, run by the knowledgeable and
friendly Lee Johnson.

French

Quisqueye Transfer Imports
335 Howard, Evanston   (708) 864-8384

Greek

Nikos Imports
330 S. Halsted   263-6342

Irish

The Irish Boutique
434 Coffin (& 238 Coffin), Long Grove   (708) 634-0339

Italian

Italian Records and Video
7179 W. Grand   637-5300

Latin-American

La-Voz-De-America Record Shop
4628 N. Broadway

Polish

Polish Record and Video Center
2942 N. Milwaukee   486-6700

Ukrainian

Delta Import Company
2242 W. Chicago   235-7788

Radio

Check out the "Radio" chapter for more detailed information, including specific programming.

WFMT 98.7 FM 565-5000

This is the flagship of good music broadcasting in America and, in spite of many troubles, has maintained high standards for more than 40 years. It broadcasts the CSO, the Lyric Opera, and the Dame Myra Hess concerts live, as well as many local artists and a variety of folk, drama, commentary, and other literary programs.

WNIB 97.1 FM 633-9700

The only other concert music station now left in Chicago; its programming tends to be very conservative.

WBEZ 91.5 FM 890-8225

This local PBS outlet is primarily a current events station but also carries substantial jazz programming and some blues, folk, and ethnic.

WDCB 90.9 FM (708) 858-5196

Substantial jazz programming from the College of Du Page County along with concert music, blues, etc.

WXRT 93.1 FM 777-7771

This maverick of the rock scene steadfastly refuses to go into the format straitjacket. Various styles of rock, old and new, along with some blues and jazz. It plays and sponsors concerts by local talent.

Concert music is also heard on these stations:

WMWA 88.5 FM (708) 998-9556

WNIU 89.5 FM (De Kalb) (815) 953-9648

—Ray Wilding-White

DANCE

So you're interested in the Chicago dance scene . . . you will be disappointed if you are looking for an electric dance environment to compare to New York City's. However, whether you want to see, learn, perform, or create dance, there are plenty of opportunities in Chicago for those who are eager and willing to shop around.

There are currently 38 performing companies in Chicago. Together they offer enough variety to please most tastes, from modern, jazz, ballet, and tap to traditional African, East Indian, American Indian, Spanish, Latino, and sacred dance forms. Many of these companies provide training in their respective dance forms, and companies such as Muntu, Joseph Holmes, Akasha, Mordine and Company, and the Chicago Moving Company participate in in-school residencies. If you are, or are aspiring to be, a professional dancer, you can choose from a number of excellent independent teachers in Chicago. Among them you will find Warren Conover, Larry Long, and Anna Paskevska for ballet; Randy Duncan, Gus Giordano, and Joel Hall for jazz; Jan Erkert, Nana Shineflug, and Shirley Mordine for modern. If you are interested in earning a B.A. in dance, Columbia College provides an excellent program that also exposes its students to nationally and internationally renowned artists through performances and residencies.

Funding for the arts, and dance in particular, has declined significantly in recent years. Funding in Chicago has historically been "safe," favoring work with commercial or popular appeal. As a result it is increasingly difficult for small, less mainstream companies and performance venues to sustain themselves. A clear indication of this in Chicago is the recent loss of MoMing Dance and Arts Center. Founded in 1973, MoMing provided a home and midsize production venue for independent teachers, dancers, and choreographers. This was a great loss of an important community resource; however, there are opportunities to produce work and perform with independent choreographers at a number of more alternative spaces including the Blue Rider Theatre, the Dancespace, Links Hall, Puszh Studios, Randolph Street Gallery, and Beacon Street Gallery. The Dance Center of Columbia College also offers a summer session that includes a choreographic workshop and culminates in a fully produced concert. Productions at these venues offer dancers and choreographers the opportunity to perform and create work, as well as provide audiences exciting new work, often for less than the cost of a movie.

Another obstacle to the Chicago dance scene is the limited media coverage of dance events. Dance reviews tend to appear after a concert has come and gone. The space allotted to dance by Chicago publications is minimal, and there is a lack of informed, informative, and supportive dance critics in the city. Ultimately, the development of media support for dance in Chicago has the potential to generate more informed and enthusiastic audiences, affect funding, and improve the vitality of the Chicago dance community. In the meantime, as you search to discover, learn about, and appreciate dance in Chicago, you are better off making use of the **Chicago Dance Coalition** (CDC). CDC has a 24-hour telephone service listing area dance performances and events (419-8384), a monthly performance calendar, an annual dance instruction directory, and publishes the semiannual *Chicago Dance Magazine*.

Despite the various difficulties confronting dance in Chicago, there are encouraging recent developments. The **Dance Center of Columbia College** is a dedicated presenter of local, national, and international dance artists. In its presenting season of 1991–92 the Dance Center and the national organization of Dancing in the Streets coproduced "Dancing in the State," a free public event featuring site-specific work by local artists Shirley Mordine and Timothy Buckley and New York artists Elizabeth Strebb, Stephan Koplowitz, and Christopher Janny. It also presented a week-long festival of Dance-Africa/Chicago featuring the African American Dance Ensemble from Durham, North Carolina, Muntu Dance Theatre from Chicago, and Ko-Thi Dance Company from Milwaukee.

The new **Harold Washington Library** has a theater designed specifically for dance. In its first season the library, in conjunction with the Dance Center, presented performances and free lecture demonstrations by nationally and internationally renowned artists Suzanne Linke, Muna Tseng, Margaret Jenkins, Trisha Brown, and its own resident company directed by Shirley Mordine. Each of these events received a relatively significant amount of media attention and were important in attracting broader, more diverse audiences and expanding the visibility and strength of the Chicago community.

Larger performance venues include the **Civic Stages Chicago**, which presents national touring companies such as American Ballet Theatre, the Joffrey Ballet, Pilobolus, Bill T. Jones, and local companies such as Hubbard Street Dance Company and Joseph Holmes Chicago Dance Theatre. The **Auditorium Theatre** also presents national and international dance companies in venues such as the Chicago Theatre, Arie Crown Theatre, and the Civic Stages Chicago.

Dance in Chicago struggles against an ongoing series of obstacles. Although there are many companies that represent a broad range of styles, only a handful of companies are truly thriving and can offer a dancer actual employment. Yet, Chicago's community remains strong in many respects. If you are interested in seeing dance, there is a wealth of performances by national, international, and local artists to please most audiences. You can find high-quality professional training in Chicago, as well as production venues or alternative spaces to produce your own work. Furthermore, Chicago is a relatively affordable city. This in conjunction with the opportunities it provides makes it an attractive choice for many dancers and choreographers and a city with great potential to develop that more "electric" dance scene.

RESOURCES

By no means is the following a complete listing of dance resources in Chicago, but it's a start.

Performance Venues

Small (less than 100 seats)

Beacon Street Gallery
4520 N. Beacon   528-4526

Blue Rider Theatre
1822 S. Halsted   738-2086

Chicago Public Library Cultural Center Theater
78 E. Washington   744-6630

The Dancespace
410 S. Michigan, #833   939-0181

Links Hall
3435 N. Sheffield   281-0824

Puszh Studios
3829 N. Broadway   327-1567

Randolph Street Gallery
756 N. Milwaukee   666-7737

Other (250–3,600 seats)

Auditorium Theatre
50 E. Congress   922-4046

Civic Stages Chicago
20 N. Wacker   346-0270

Dance Center of Columbia College
4730 N. Sheridan   271-7804

Harold Washington Library Center
400 S. State   747-4800

Dance Instruction

Chicago Moving Company (modern)
1225 W. School   880-5402

Dance Center of Columbia College (ballet, modern, jazz)
4730 N. Sheridan   271-7804

The Dancespace (modern, ballet, jazz)
410 S. Michigan, #833   939-0181

Gus Giordano Jazz Dance Center (ballet, modern, jazz)
614 Davis, Evanston, 60201   (708) 866-9442

Joel Hall Dance Studio (ballet, modern, jazz)
1225 W. School   880-1002

Joseph Holmes Chicago Dance Theatre Studio (ballet, modern, jazz)
1935 S. Halsted   942-0881

Lou Conte Dance Studio (ballet, jazz)
218 S. Wabash, 3rd floor   461-0892

Muntu Dance Theatre (African)
6800 S. Wentworth, #396E   602-1135

Ruth Page Foundation School of Dance (ballet, jazz)
1016 N. Dearborn   337-6543

Dancewear

Capezio Dance Fitness Shop
2828 N. Clark   929-0385

Leo's Dancewear Inc.
1900 N. Narragansett   745-5600

Motion Unlimited
218 S. Wabash   922-3330

Other Resources

The Dance Center of Columbia College
4730 N. Sheridan   271-7804
Video collection.

Harold Washington Library Center
400 S. State   747-4800
Dance-related reading.

The Newberry Library
60 W. Walton   943-9090, ext. 210
Dance-related reading, video collection.

SUGGESTED READING

Here is a random sampling of good reading in the field.

The Art of Making Dances by Doris Humphrey

The Black Tradition in American Dance by Richard A. Long

Dance Injuries—Their Prevention and Care by Daniel Arnheim

Dance Kinesiology by Sally Fitt

First Steps in Teaching Creative Dance to Children by Mary Joyce

How to Dance Forever: Surviving Against the Odds by Daniel Nagrin

Inside Dance by Murray Louis

Prime Movers by Joseph Mazo

Reading Dancing by Susan Leigh Foster

Terpsichore in Sneakers by Sally Baines

—Ann Boyd

THEATER

Half of Chicago's new arrivals seem to be fresh-out-of-school actors. They're drawn by some mysterious magnetism to the musty lofts and storefronts, urban equivalents of Andy Hardy's barn, that house Chicago's panoply of small theater companies. Some theater folk hope to recapitulate the cosmic success story of the Steppenwolf group—a gang of Illinois State grads who rose in what seemed like minutes from Highland Park basement to bicoastal fame. Others come simply because they know that this is a city that rewards impatience, that will let them do their thing *right now*, if they're willing to do it all themselves. They come to make theater in a peculiarly Chicago manner: not by waiting to be cast in somebody else's play, but by gathering together in ensembles and taking on producing responsibilities themselves. It's this unceasing stream of young people that gives Chicago theater its character and vitality.

But it's easy to oversimplify. The storefront nonprofit troupe may be Chicago's trademark, but it's just one element in a bigger picture. Theater didn't start here in the mid-seventies, with the Steppenwolf onslaught, or in the late sixties, when the Body Politic began to shelter a host of countercultural arts groups under its institutional umbrella.

There has been theater here as long as there's been a "here" here, and every epoch in the city's evolution has produced its own dramatic expression. Exploring the totality of local theater is like scraping away the multiple layers of pigment on a canvas, revealing older, once-dominant designs—what painters call *pentimento*.

So let us take a pentimental journey, stopping to see what remains of every stage in the development of Chicago's most significant cultural resource. (A complete listing of the city's theaters and theater companies, with addresses and phone numbers, appears at the end of the chapter.)

COMMERCIAL THEATER

> *The art of the theatre . . . is only half an art and*
> *half a get-rich-quick operation.* —Ben Hecht

In the beginning was the commercial theater, and to this day, many a local burgher associates "theater" not with off-Loop shopfronts but with imported East Coast productions staged in hangar-sized downtown houses. In fact, after a shaky quarter century or so, theater-as-business has reasserted itself here in forms new and old.

For-profit theater comes in three basic flavors: the touring Big Show; dinner theater; and a recent innovation, the locally produced off-Loop presentation.

The Broadway Shows

The musical extravaganza, once considered a dinosaur, has lately fought a surprisingly successful battle against extinction. For years, few Broadway musicals came to Chicago, home of hostile critics and indifferent audiences. Now, New York producers have only to chant three magic words—"Andrew

166

Lloyd Webber"—to invoke massive, turnaway crowds. Entire suburbs empty in the rush to experience the hydraulic sets and nifty costumes.

One shouldn't complain. The revival of the Big Show has saved several historic Loop theater spaces from mothballdom: Louis Sullivan's magnificent **Auditorium**; the archetypal movie palace, the **Chicago Theater**; and the **Shubert**, a red-plush proscenium theater of the old school. This last-named space has recently been purchased by Sam Shubert's arch-rival, the Nederlander organization of New York, which is scheduling a whole season of Broadway transplants. A promising development: It means, first of all, that we have a steady pipeline to recent New York productions; second, that some lights will still be burning in the Loop even after the nightly 5 P.M. exodus.

Ticket costs for these shows are reasonable . . . if you're a hotshot commodities broker or have recently won the lottery. It's way beyond the average mortal's price range: the best seats will set you back $60, just like on Broadway (so much for our second-city complex). Working stiffs have a few options: buying the $15 cheap seats, located somewhere outside the ozone layer; getting two-for-ones at one of several Hot Tix booths (more on this later); or, in the worst-case scenario, becoming a theater critic.

Dinner Theater

If the touring New York show is a phenomenon with roots in the forties and earlier, when the Loop constituted a formidable theater and nightlife district, then dinner theater, with its suburban milieu and air of cultural homogeneity, plunks us down firmly in the late fifties and early sixties.

This form, widely considered a joke elsewhere, has prospered here not only financially but artistically. High production values, good direction, top performing talent are all reasons why, if you've got a car, you might want to give these theaters a try. Their stock-in-trade is musicals, of course, and in the old days they stuck to the chestnuts, presenting umpteen *Fiddlers on the Roof* and *Oklahoma*s. Now the **Candlelight, Lincolnshire, Pheasant Run,** and **Drury Lane** theaters have gained so much respect they're occasionally used as try-out houses for new New York–bound musicals—a nice reversal of the old pattern. One more thing to be said in their favor: because they have a different contract with the Actors Equity union than the nonprofit theaters, they actually pay their performers close to a living wage—a rarity hereabouts.

Other variations on the dinner-theater theme include the **Cafe Mystery Dinner Theatre** at the Loop's Bismarck Hotel, in which diners experience a midmeal homicide and postprandial denouement, and the **Kings Manor** and **Dry Gulch,** which offer "theme" dinners (medieval and Wild West, respectively) featuring singing waiters and other hokey delights. They're about the final surviving instance of live low-brow theater, vaudeville's touristy last gasp. But I speak too soon. There are plans afoot to launch a neovaudevillian cabaret, offering several musical and comedy acts each night. To be called the **New Variety Theatre,** the nightclub gives proof that no variety of theater ever dies—it's just recycled into something hip and "new."

Off-Loop Commercial Theater

The newest species of for-profit performance. It's a sign of Chicago's development that a handful of producers (conspicuous among them the three
Michaels: Cullen, Frazier, and Leavitt) have gone into the business full-time
and have been able to find financial backers for their projects. Most of the
shows they mount originate in New York; a significant minority are local
nonprofit productions deemed worthy of a larger venue. Some commercial
productions are strange hybrids of local and imported: Wendy Wasserstein's
The Heidi Chronicles, for instance, was legitimized by Broadway, produced
with a Chicago cast by the nonprofit National Jewish Theater, and then
commercially remounted with the same cast in a bigger space at higher
prices.

The 250–500 seat theaters that house these productions are located on or
near Halsted Street, from North Avenue to about Belmont Avenue. This
two-mile stretch has over the last 10 years become Chicago's Little Broadway.
It takes in the **Royal-George, Apollo, Halsted, Wellington,** and **Briar Street**
theaters, as well as the new and old Steppenwolf spaces and the **Organic
Theater.** The three-stage **Theater Building** on Belmont is used for smaller-
scale commercial ventures; it also houses several nonprofit troupes.

Theater-goers can expect high production values, strong Equity casts composed mostly of Chicago talent, and fairly high ticket prices, generally between $25 and $35.

Improvisational Comedy

We shouldn't leave the world of commercial theater without mentioning
Second City, the nation's most famous comedy club. Second City has so long
been "not what it used to be" that hardly anybody remembers what that was.
This birthplace of Chicago-style improvisational comedy has lost the subver-
sive, satirical edge it had decades ago and has settled into a prosperous
complacency.

You can catch sharper, hungrier improv shows at Second City's junior
companies: **Second City ETC,** which performs next door to the main stage,
and **Second City Northwest,** in Rolling Meadows. Other improv groups to
watch for include **Avante-Garfielde** in Hyde Park, the **Harold,** the **Improv
Institute,** and **Sarantos Studios.**

THE NONPROFIT ESTABLISHMENT

(Since) the early sixties Chicago theater has been a community not of *aspirants*
but of *citizens*. Its progress and development . . . has been the progress of
groups—of individuals dedicated to the progress of a performance group.
—David Mamet

Nonprofit theater has existed in Chicago since the teens, but the off-Loop
movement began in earnest only in the mid-seventies. The scene then seemed
youthful and unfettered; it's tamer now, with mouths to feed and houses to
keep up. It's hard not to become preoccupied with the nonartistic considerations—grantsmanship, marketing, administration—that arise whenever creative impulse hardens into permanent institution. These theaters produce
plenty of high-quality work, but most of the older ones hew closer to public

taste than they once did and furnish a more predictable product. Most depend upon subscribers for much of their revenue; careful planning and budgeting rather than spontaneous energy is the order of the day.

Here's a listing of what I consider the nonprofit elite. All but one of these theaters have a contract with Actors Equity; all have permanent performance spaces with more than 150 seats; all but two have subscription seasons. These Big 13 take in about 80 percent of all revenue that flows into nonprofit theater; the other 100 or so theaters split what's left.

By far the largest and richest theater in Chicago, the **Goodman Theater** is part (along with the Chicago Symphony and Lyric Opera) of Chicago's holy trinity of performing arts. It's been around since 1925, but don't let that fool you: this theater, located within the Art Institute complex, is no staid old dame. It has surrendered to the off-Loop movement, drawing from the same talent pool (occasional imported director excepted) and expressing the adventurous spirit that once characterized the movement as a whole. Indeed, its artistic director (Robert Falls) came to the Goodman from Wisdom Bridge, one of the leading off-Loop theaters. Goodman productions may scandalize the critics (an example is the 1992 *Twelfth Night*, which gave a *Cage aux Folles* overkill to Shakepeare's gender-bending comedy), but they rarely bore anyone. Tickets are $20–$33.

Steppenwolf Theatre needs little introduction. It is at this writing certainly the Midwest's most famous ensemble, and, particularly since winning a Tony in 1990 for its spellbinding adaptation of *The Grapes of Wrath*, perhaps the nation's. Many of its first- and second-generation players (John Malkovich, Laurie Metcalfe, and John Mahoney, to name a few) have been launched out of Chicago's relatively small orbit into stardom. But the ensemble chugs along, endlessly replacing old, gone-to-the-coast personnel with fresh and talented faces, and the big names do return periodically. The troupe is blessed with a huge subscriber base and piles of money, which allowed it to move south in 1991 from its old Lakeview space to a brand-new, cutting-edge theater that seats hundreds more. But the move, alas, has had its downside: it has made Steppenwolf cautious. Few who saw the troupe's landmark production of Lanford Wilson's *Balm in Gilead* in the early eighties—a punishing trip to the urban heart of darkness—would believe that the group would mount *Harvey*, the rabbit play, a few years later. That's what investing millions in a new house will do to you: you can't afford to turn anybody off. Whether the company will recapture the on-the-edge intensity that made it famous remains to be seen. Ticket prices are high, in the $25–$30 range.

Around since 1954, the **Court Theatre** is the city's second-oldest repertory company. Ensconced in a handsome, well-designed theater space near the University of Chicago campus, the Court reflects the cultural ambience of the neighborhood. Classics are the specialty here, and they're performed in deluxe fashion under the artistic direction of Nicholas Rudall. The atmosphere is pure Hyde Park: occasionally professors lead discussions after the performance. Because of the Court's university affiliation, U of C students can attend quite cheaply; less favored folk must pay $14–$25.

The Court dominated the classics field for many seasons, but it now has a worthy rival: Barbara Gaines' **Shakespeare Repertory**. This young company has become an important part of the scene: its well-acted, beautifully designed productions give even Washington's venerable Folger Shakespeare Theater a run for its money. The company produces two plays per year at the Ruth Page Auditorium in the Gold Coast. Prices are $20–$25. Serious Shakespeare lovers can practice their bardolatry in the summer, too, thanks to the **Oak Park Festival Theatre**. The Festival performs one Shakespeare work a year outdoors, in the suburb's handsome Austin Gardens.

Evanston, Chicago's other culturally enlightened suburb, boasts two Equity theaters. **Northlight** is the older and larger of the two and puts out a quite varied schedule, ranging from Shaw to Athol Fugard to world premieres by local playwrights. Performances are in the Coronet Theatre, a former cinema. Large and somewhat awkward, the proscenium space lacks the intimacy of most off-Loop houses. Prices: $21–$25. **Next Theatre** is a younger and more exciting, if less reliable, theater. Founder Harriet Spizziri has made it something of a pipeline for recent Northwestern theater grads, whose directing work can be immensely stimulating and original—or cartoonish and jejune. If you like theater emphasizing the director's touch, Next is for you. Tickets are $16–$22.

The other suburban member of the 13 is the young **National Jewish Theater**, handsomely housed in Skokie's Mayer Kaplan JCC. Play selection isn't the strength here (works range from profound meditations on the Jewish experience to sitcom piffle), but NJT has the money and savvy to put on some outstanding shows. Leader Arnold Aprill is a Chicago theater hand from way back and can draw on top-notch talent, such as Chicago's ace director, Terry McCabe. If you're in Skokie and bored to tears, there's now a place to go. Tickets are $17–$24.

The three theaters closest to the heart of the off-Loop movement are the **Body Politic**, **Victory Gardens**, and **Wisdom Bridge**. Their formative period was the mid-seventies, when the world was young and Lincoln Avenue had aspirations to hipness. Now Lincoln is a yuppie wasteland, and Body Politic and Victory Gardens, which share a building on the avenue, seem to lack fire in the belly. Their plays make use of top Equity talent and skilled directors and designers, but nobody's taking risks. Wisdom Bridge, situated on Chicago's northern fringe in a converted karate studio, also has settled into a docile respectability. For a while one of the most progressive companies in the city, Wisdom Bridge has struggled to find an identity since Artistic Director Robert Falls moved downtown to take the Goodman's helm. Body Politic and Wisdom Bridge are going through life-threatening financial woes in the recessionary nineties. Victory Gardens is faring better; its emphasis on locally written original plays gives it a tighter niche. But little distinguishes these companies from the regional theaters in a dozen other cities. Tickets range from $19–$28.

Pegasus Players is a shining example of a nonprofit theater not mired in midlife crisis. Founder Arlene Crewdson hews nobly to her purpose: providing first-class theater to a wide audience, one that includes the city's poorer residents. The goals of public service and artistic excellence don't collide. The theater manages to showcase intriguing scripts (in 1991, for example, Pegasus resurrected a long-buried Duke Ellington musical), get sterling performances out of its non-Equity talent, and keep ticket prices relatively low ($16–$20). Pegasus sponsors an annual Young Playwrights Festival, which gives high school dramatists the rare chance to see their works staged. It's one of the programs that makes this theater a ray of light in the benighted Uptown neighborhood.

The **Organic Theater Company** has been so confused for so long about its identity, it's gotten used to the situation. Founder Stuart Gordon (who would head for Hollywood in 1985) gave the troupe the anarchic flavor that would mark it as Chicago's quintessential sixties company. The point in the early days was to create theater, campily extravagant or hyperrealistic, that engaged the senses and emotions more than the cerebrum. In the early 1980s, the theater moved into a cavernous former movie theater; the point now is to somehow fill those acres of seats. The Organic is now not so much a theater company as it is a producing organization and landlord, meaning its shows lack a consistent tone or personality. It scores when it stages plays with a political bite (such as the long-running *Do the White Thing*), which at least bring in the ex-sixties types; it falters when it aims for the mass audience. Chicago still waits for the Organic to reclaim its place as an important avant-garde theater. What creative energy the troupe does have is focused on the Greenhouse, a smaller upstairs studio theater used for the staging of new—and sometimes very exciting—works by up-and-coming directors and playwrights. The Organic has no season subscriptions. Main-stage tickets are in the $20–$25 range; Greenhouse tickets run from a couple of bucks to $15.

Remains Theater is one of the success stories of Chicago theater: a tiny group leading a gypsy existence that made good and didn't get a big head about it. For a decade, the Remains ensemble would put on perhaps one show a year in other people's spaces, and that show would as often as not be the year's blockbuster. Since 1990, the group has possessed a big, flexible space of its own in the nouveau riche Clybourn Corridor. Yet it still has a knack for the offbeat and the daring, such as its ambitious 1991 hit, *The Chicago Conspiracy Trial*, about the Chicago Seven trial/carnival. Its corps of performers is among the city's best: William Petersen, Gary Cole, and Amy Morton all call Remains home. And you don't have to take out a second mortgage to see this parade of talent—the theater sells a good number of $10 tickets for every performance.

All of these theaters need volunteer ushers; if you'd like to see a play free, call the box office and try to set up a date. But act quickly: there's an informal network of ushers in Chicago who tend to snap up the best shows.

THE LITTLE THEATERS

This section takes us to the present. For the small storefront theaters, having little institutional history to draw upon, must engage their audiences by hitting them where they live. The successful troupes survive by sticking to their idiosyncrasies. In an ever more fragmented society, the secret to developing audience loyalty is finding one's niche.

What we have is an embarrassment of riches, a proliferation of small ensembles far too numerous to name, let alone do justice to. All I can offer is a sampling. Ticket prices are quite a bit lower than for the biggies; expect to pay $5–$12 at these minute, unadorned theater spaces. So go ahead; take a chance. Many of these storefront productions will be ordinary, or worse; and a bad play in an un-air-conditioned theater is not one of life's peak moments.

But once in a while you'll discover a hidden gem—a production possessing an originality and intensity of vision that the larger players can't match.

Moving from north to south, we begin in Rogers Park, home of several small theaters. Worth investigating are the **Raven Theatre**, which offers both a strong main-stage series as well as interesting (and inexpensive) off-night offerings; **Cardiff Giant**, which develops its unique, perversely comic works through a process of group improvisation; **Lifeline Theater**, which produces both adult plays (especially adaptations of 19th-century classics) and very fine children's drama; and **Center Theater**, which stages a fair number of world and local premieres in its main and studio spaces.

Footsteps Theater Company in Andersonville is theater from a woman's point of view. They have presented lesbian plays by Jane Chambers, plays on subjects important to women like breast cancer and incest, and classical pieces with all-women casts.

Edgewater and Uptown are economically and ethnically mixed neighborhoods with their share of urban problems; area theaters tend to have a political edge. **Commons Theatre**, for example, gravitates toward socially relevant plays, and it has staged Brecht with notable success. Then there are the **Neo-Futurists** (inspired by the turn-of-the-century Italian Futurists) whose *Too Much Light Makes the Baby Go Blind* has been running for years. The ever-changing *Baby* is one of the most entertaining shows in town (admission is decided by the roll of a die), but its fun is married to a social message. **Chicago Actors Ensemble** calls Uptown home; a politically committed, avant-garde theater, CAE's work (such as the 1990 *Red Tango*) challenges and provokes.

Young, relatively affluent Lakeview probably houses more performance spaces than any other neighborhood in the city. Theater here may be less overtly political, but it doesn't lack attitude. Take **Metraform**—more widely known by its space, the Annoyance Theatre. This group produced the monstrously successful (as I write this, it's playing in New York *and* Los Angeles) *Real Live Brady Bunch*, based on real live TV scripts, and a host of other absurdist takes on pop culture. Then there's **Torso Theatre**, presenter of the gross-out comedy of nihilism, *Cannibal Cheerleaders on Crack*. The general feeling behind these blackly campy productions is that perhaps one can no longer dream of changing the world, but one can still give it the finger. Other notable neighborhood groups include **Bailiwick Repertory**, which in addition to its main-stage productions sponsors an annual Directors Festival of one-acters; **City Lit**, which excels at adapting classic and contemporary fiction; **Live Bait**, which mixes performance art elements into its well-designed if uncertainly scripted productions; and the socially conscious (but never dogmatic) **Stage Left**.

Strawdog Theatre Company has made a name for itself with its stylized Sam Shepard interpretations, while **Lookingglass** has garnered attention and praise for its startling visual effects and rejection of traditional narrative patterns. Chicago theater has always privileged word over image; the avant-garde Lookingglass provides a healthful corrective. Theater mavens who want to be one step ahead of the crowd should also check out the dank basement of **Cafe Voltaire**. This tiny space has recently become an important incubator of independently produced plays. Dylan Thomas' *Under Milkwood* began an immensely successful run here in 1991, and so have many other more transient but equally engaging works. The Cafe has a beatnik feel, as do many of the plays here: Beckett and Ionesco productions abound.

The Near Northwest Side has become the focal point of Chicago's bohemia, and the local theater scene shows it. Drop in at cramped North Avenue spaces such as **The Garage**, the **Rudely Elegant Theatre**, or the **Curious Theatre Branch**, and you'll find an unorthodox style of drama inspired by the audience-provoking aesthetic of performance art. One group to watch for is the **New Criminals**, whose masked, theatrical style blends Italian *commedia dell'arte* and German Expressionism. They're led by movie star John Cusack—Hollywood heartthrob, Bucktown bad boy. Two other significant companies are **Synergy**, which performs solid productions of better-known contemporary plays, and the somewhat more adventurous **Griffin**, which boasts a late-night series on top of its prime-time offerings.

The decidedly ungentrified neighborhood of Pilsen houses two theater companies worth the trip. **Interplay** presents high-quality Equity productions of newer works, while the **Blue Rider** provides a platform for flamboyant theater personality Donna Blue Lachman's one-woman shows.

ETHNIC/MINORITY THEATER

Chicago is blessed with a rich supply of minority talent and with several theaters that focus on minority concerns. The South Side hosts the Equity-affiliated **Chicago Theatre Company**, which put on the well-received *The Meeting* (recounting a fictitious encounter between Martin Luther King and Malcolm X) a couple of years ago, and **ETA Creative Arts Foundation**, which for 20 years has combined professional theater with a very full roster of classes, school presentations, and workshops. On the North Side, the **Black Ensemble Theater** presents new work on African-American themes; their specialty is politics and biography put to music. Wicker Park's **Latino Chicago Theater** offers sometimes raw but always innovative theater in English and Spanish. **Gadfly Theatre**, **Chameleon Productions**, and **A Stage of One's Own** concentrate on feminist drama, while Marlene Zuccaro's politically engaged **Zebra Crossing Theatre** has a strong (and sometimes excessive) commitment to color-blind casting. Bailiwick Repertory sponsors a summer series dedicated to gay and lesbian plays, and many of the works produced by the young **Cloud 42** troupe seem to have a gay theme.

PUPPETRY

Chicago has always been a good city for puppets—just look at the relationship between aldermen and developers. The city that gave the world the Kungsholm Puppet Opera and Kukla, Fran, and Ollie is experiencing an adult puppet renaissance. **Hystopolis Puppet Theatre** is definitely worth watching; its 1990 rod-marionette production of Elmer Rice's *The Adding Machine* was a revelation. Blair Thomas, founder of the **Red Moon Theater** puppet company, is also gifted with a highly original design sense; his expressive, often larger-than-life creations enact his own poignant, metaphorical dramas. And then there's Michael and Laura Montenegro's **Zapato Puppets**, a group held in the highest esteem by other puppeteers. Unfortunately, the Evanston-based troupe rarely performs these days. Call them to find out their schedule.

THEATER FESTIVALS

One way to experience a wide range of theater offerings it to attend one of Chicago's several festivals. The glitziest is the **International Theatre Festival,** a biannual event (even years) that brings together theater companies from the world's four corners. The month-long fest takes place at the downtown Blackstone Theater (60 E. Balbo) as well as such other large spaces as the Steppenwolf (1650 N. Halsted) and UIC Theatre (1040 W. Harrison). Tickets are steep—$20–$40—but they're cheaper than plane fare to, say, Venezuela or Siberia. Call the festival office at 644-FEST.

Another, more modest festival (but at least as much fun) is the Bucktown Rhinoceros Fest, featuring smaller Northwest Side theater groups, which takes place in August at various spaces close to the intersection of North and Milwaukee avenues. Complete schedules are printed in the weekly *NewCity.*

Sick of the city? Rent a car and drive out to the Shakespeare festival given by the **American Players Theater,** in pretty Spring Green, Wisconsin (about 30 miles west of Madison). The outdoor productions are so good you'll hardly notice the mosquitoes. Call (608) 588-2361. And don't forget: we're a day's drive from the big Ontario fests—the Shakespeare season in Stratford, and the George Bernard Shaw festival in quaint Niagara-on-the-Lake.

PARTICIPATION

Chicago abounds with community theater. Many field houses in city and suburbs have their own tiny stage, ideal for enthusiastic productions of popular musicals. During the summer, some of these neighborhood groups have their moment of glory, putting on brief runs at the **Theater on the Lake,** a tattered but still charming facility on Lake Shore Drive at Fullerton Avenue (348-7075). For information about theater groups and classes, call the Park District's Recreation Department at 294-2320.

For those with a professional interest in theater, the following institutions offer training for actors:

The Actors' Center 549-3303

Center Theatre's Training Center for the Working Actor 508-0200

Lifeline Theatre 761-4477

Piven Theatre Workshop (708) 866-6597

Raven Theatre Workshop Program 338-2177

Sarantos Studios 528-7114

Victory Gardens 549-5788

Aspiring playwrights should check out these resources:

Chicago Dramatists Workshop 663-0630

The Playwright's Center 334-9982

The strongest college theater departments are these:

The Theatre School, DePaul University
2135 N. Kenmore   341-8375
DePaul stages its productions at the fine old Blackstone Theater at 60 E. Balbo.

Northwestern University Theatre and Interpretation Center
1979 Sheridan, Evanston   (708) 491-5146

Columbia College
62 E. 11th   663-9465
The renovated Getz Theater is its venue.

(P.S. Student productions at these theaters represent about the best bargains in town. For information, call the various box offices: DePaul at 341-8455, Northwestern at [708] 491-7285, and Columbia at 663-9465.)

The best way to situate yourself in the theater scene is to hang out with other theater folk, and the best place to find actors is in cafes, especially cafes in the theater-heavy Lakeview area. You'll find few but fellow thespians at **Scenes bookstore/cafe** (3168 N. Clark), where you can simultaneously browse for scripts, catch up on theater gossip, and sip espresso. Also worth investigating is **Act I Bookstore** (2632 N. Lincoln), which stocks a large collection of dramatic literature, prints its own line of scripts by Chicago playwrights, and publishes *PerformInk*, an interesting theater newspaper for and by theater people. *PerformInk* is one important source of audition information; another is **Casting Call**, a phone hot line listing non-Equity parts in the Chicago area. The service costs $.50 per minute; call 976-CAST.

THEATER ON THE CHEAP

The League of Chicago Theatres sponsors an elaborate reduced-price ticket program called **Hot Tix**. LCT member theaters (there are over 100 of them) generally prefer half-price tickets to unoccupied seats and so, depending on ticket sales, release some day-of-performance tickets to Hot Tix. Lucky you: this enables the theatergoer to buy two tickets for the price of one (plus a service charge).

Hot Tix booths
108 N. State
1616 Sherman, Evanston
158 Forest, Oak Park
The booths are open Monday–Saturday and now take Visa and MasterCard as well as cash. You can also buy Hot Tix tickets (cash only) at Rose Records stores in Hyde Park, on Clybourn, and in several suburbs. It's even possible to charge discount day-of-performance tickets by phone and pick them up at the theater; call HOT-TIXX.

INFORMATION ABOUT THEATER

Chicago artists have never been given their due by the Chicago media, and theater is no exception. We still have a second-banana complex, preventing us from taking our own to heart until they've been recognized by (and probably fled to) the coasts. While the two major dailies (as well as smaller papers such as the *Daily Herald* and *Southtown Economist*) do review shows as they open, they don't exactly lavish space on them. You'll rarely find in the *Tribune* or *Sun-Times* the sort of lengthy analysis of plays or the theatrical climate that Frank Rich writes for *The New York Times*. *Tribune* critic Richard Christiansen is the dean of the daily reviewers; while his aesthetic criteria are on the conservative side, his views are strongly put and worth considering. Both the *Trib* and *Sun-Times* print exhaustive theater listings in the Friday editions. However, the papers' arts coverage is skewed toward the latest rock act, movie, or Broadway hit to roll through town. The locally conceived is neglected in favor of the globally hyped.

Local television and radio are no better in their coverage of theater. The only exception is public radio station WBEZ 91.5 FM, which carries Friday evening and Saturday afternoon talk shows ("Backstage Pass" and "Artistic License," respectively) devoted to the local performing arts scene.

Theater fans must resort to the alternative press for a deeper look at Chicago theater. The weekly *Reader* is the single best source of information. *Reader* reviews can be formulaic and self-involved, and the various critics vary in terms of sensitivity and basic writing skills. Nevertheless, the reviews are the most ample, useful, and thought-provoking.

Chicago's other free weekly, *NewCity*, used to print complete reviews but now sticks to one-paragraph notices—the critical equivalent of sound bites. *NewCity*'s theater section is worth reading for its profiles and feature stories, which are almost unique in taking local performers seriously.

SUGGESTED READING

The shelves are strangely empty of books on Chicago theater—evidence that the New York–based book publishing industry (like the New York–based "national" media) believes that American theater remains a Manhattan phenomenon. There are no institutional histories of the Goodman, Steppenwolf, or Organic theaters, or of David Mamet's old St. Nicholas troupe.

Lacking a standard text, the theater buff's best resource is a slim booklet called *Resetting the Stage: Theater beyond the Loop 1960–1990*. Edited by theater historian Scott Fosdick, *Resetting the Stage* is a series of informative essays and eye-witness chronicles of the growth of the off-Loop movement. It originally accompanied a 1990 exhibit based on the Chicago Public Library's extensive theater archives, which are housed in the Harold Washington Library's 10th-floor Special Collections area. If you're interested in the theater collection (which includes many videotaped performances), talk to library archivist Lauren Bufferd.

To judge by the literature, our only theatrical institution of any importance is Second City. Several books have been written on this source of "Chicago-style" improvisational comedy: *Something Wonderful Right Away*, by playwright Jeffrey Sweet (Avon, 1978); the chatty, anecdotal *The Second City*, by Donna McCrohan (Perigee, 1987); and *The Compass*, by Janet Coleman, an in-depth study of the Compass Players, Second City's fifties predecessors (Knopf, 1990).

The League of Chicago Theaters used to publish a theatrical yearbook, giving the vital statistics of each member company. Unfortunately, the funding dried up a few years ago. The 1989 yearbook (the last published) is the most valuable profile of local theater available; let's hope the organization can update it soon. The book is available at the LCT office (67 E. Madison, 977-1730).

CHICAGO THEATERS AND THEATER COMPANIES

A Stage of One's Own Theatre Company
2051 W. North, Chicago, 60647   276-4006

Apollo Theatre
2540 N. Lincoln, Chicago, 60614   935-6100

Auditorium Theatre
50 E. Congress, Chicago, 60605   922-2110

Avante-Garfielde
Jimmy's Woodlawn Tap
1172 E. 55th, Chicago, 60615

Bailiwick Repertory
Theatre Building
1225 W. Belmont, Chicago, 60657-3205   327-5252

Black Ensemble Theatre
4520 N. Beacon, Chicago, 60640   769-4451

The Blue Rider Theatre
1822 S. Halsted, Chicago, 60608   733-4668

Body Politic Theatre
2261 N. Lincoln, Chicago, 60614   871-3000

Briar Street Theatre
3133 N. Halsted, Chicago, 60657   348-4000

Cafe Voltaire
3231 N. Clark, Chicago, 60657   528-3136

Cafe Mystery Dinner Theatre
Bismarck Hotel
171 W. Randolph, Chicago, 60601   236-0123

Candlelight Dinner Playhouse
5620 S. Harlem, Summit, 60501   (708) 496-3000

Cardiff Giant
1257 W. Loyola, Chicago, 60626   262-9544

Center Theater
1346 W. Devon, Chicago, 60660   508-5422

Chameleon Productions
4753 N. Broadway, #918, Chicago, 60640   878-8458

Chicago Actors Ensemble
Preston Bradley Community Center
941 W. Lawrence, Chicago, 60640   275-4463

Chicago Theater
175 N. State, Chicago, 60601   443-1130

Chicago Theatre Company
1801 E. 71st, Chicago, 60637   493-1305

City Lit Theater Company
Live Bait Theatre
3914 N. Clark, Chicago, 60613   271-1100

Cloud 42
Theater Building
1225 W. Belmont, Chicago, 60657-3205   327-5252

The Commons Theatre
1020 W. Bryn Mawr, Chicago, 60660   769-5009

Court Theatre
5535 S. Ellis, Chicago, 60637   753-4472

Curious Theatre Branch
1900 W. North, Chicago, 60622   276-1147

Drury Lane Dinner Theatre
2500 W. 95th, Evergreen Park, 60642   (708) 422-0404

Dry Gulch Dinner Theatre
9351 Irving Park, Schiller Park, 60176   (708) 671- 6644

ETA Creative Arts Foundation
7558 S. Chicago, Chicago, 60619   752-3955

Footsteps Theatre Company
6968 N. Clark, Chicago, 60626   465-8323

Garage Theatre
1843 W. North, Chicago, 60622   989-4756

The Goodman Theatre
200 S. Columbus, Chicago, 60603   443-3800

Griffin Theatre Company
2700 N. Elston, Chicago, 60647   278-2494

The Harold
ImprovOlympia at Wrigley Side
3527 N. Clark, Chicago, 60657   880-0199

Hystopolis Puppet Theater
Free Street Community Arts Center
441 W. North, Chicago, 60610   787-7387

The Improv Institute
2319 W. Belmont, Chicago, 60618   929-2323

Interplay
1935 S. Halsted, Chicago, 60608   243-6240

King's Manor Dinner Theatre
2122 W. Lawrence, Chicago, 60625   275-8400

Latino Chicago Theatre Company
The Firehouse
1625 N. Damen, Chicago, 60647   486-5120

Lifeline Theatre
6912 N. Glenwood, Chicago, 60626   761-4477

Live Bait Theatrical Company
3914 N. Clark, Chicago, 60613   871-1212

Lookingglass Theatre Company
Chicago Filmmakers
1229 W. Belmont, Chicago, 60657   477-7010

Marriott's Lincolnshire Theatre
10 Marriott, Lincolnshire, 60069   (708) 634-0200

Metraform
Annoyance Theatre
3153 N. Broadway, Chicago, 60657   929-6200

National Jewish Theater
Horwich/Kaplan JCC
5050 W. Church, Skokie, 60077   (708) 675-5070

Neo-Futurists
Neo-Futurarium (a.k.a. Nelson Funeral Home)
5153 N. Ashland, Chicago, 60640   275-5255

New Variety Theatre
400 N. Clark, Chicago, 60605   329-0101

Next Theatre Company
927 Noyes, Evanston, 60201 (708) 475-1875

Northlight Theatre
600 Davis, Evanston, 60201   (708) 869-7278

Oak Park Festival Theatre
Austin Gardens
P.O. Box 4114, Oak Park, 60303   (708) 524-2050

Organic Theater Company
3319 N. Clark, Chicago, 60657   327-5588

Pegasus Players
O'Rourke Center for Performing Arts
Truman College
1145 W. Wilson, Chicago, 60640   271-2638

Pheasant Run Dinner Theatre
Route 64 (North Avenue), St. Charles, 60174   (708) 584-6342

Raven Theatre Company
6931 N. Clark, Chicago, 60626   338-2177

Red Moon Theater Studio
2001 N. Point, Chicago, 60647   772-9069

Remains Theatre
1800 N. Clybourn, Chicago, 60614   335-9800

Royal-George Theatre
1641 N. Halsted, Chicago, 60614   988-9000

Rudely Elegant Theatre
1934 W. North, Chicago, 60622   489-9848

Sarantos Studios
2857 N. Halsted, Chicago, 60657   528-7114

Second City
1616 N. Wells, Chicago, 60614   337-3992

Second City ETC
1608 N. Wells, Chicago, 60614   642-8189

Second City Northwest
1701 W. Golf, Continental Towers, Rolling Meadows, 60008   (708) 806-1555

Shakespeare Repertory
Ruth Page Auditorium
1016 N. Dearborn, Chicago, 60610   281-1878

Shubert Theatre
22 W. Monroe, Chicago, 60603   902-1500

Stage Left Theatre
3244 N. Clark, Chicago, 60657   883-8830

Steppenwolf North
(Steppenwolf's old space)
2851 N. Halsted, Chicago, 60657   472-1919

Steppenwolf Theatre
(Steppenwolf's main space)
1650 N. Halsted, Chicago, 60657   335-1650

Strawdog Theatre Company
3829 N. Broadway, Chicago, 60613   528-9889

Synergy Theatre Company
1753 N. Damen, Chicago, 60647   975-1703

Torso Theatre
2827 N. Broadway, 2nd floor, Chicago, 60657   549-3330

Victory Gardens Theater
2257 N. Lincoln, Chicago, 60614   871-3000

Wellington Theater
750 W. Wellington, Chicago, 60657   975-7171

Wisdom Bridge Theatre
1559 W. Howard, Chicago, 60626   743-6000

Zapato Puppets
Noyes Cultural Center
927 Noyes, Evanston, 60201   (708) 328-4175

Zebra Crossing Theatre
4437 N. Ravenswood, Chicago, 60640   728-0082

—Hugh Iglarsh

FILM

THE "REEL" CITY GUIDE

It's not surprising that some would call Chicago the "Hollywood of the Midwest." After all, in the past 10 years more than 100 films, including documentaries, were shot in the Chicago area. *The Blues Brothers, Thief, Child's Play* and *Child's Play II, When Harry Met Sally, Backdraft, The Untouchables,* and others put hundreds of locals to work as extras, grips, assistants, stylists, and so forth. They also tied up local traffic, upset local businesspeople, and confounded star gazers who were constantly on the lookout for the elusive Robert DeNiro, Madonna, and others. The Illinois Film Office is quick to point out that this invasion of Hollywood hunks, hucksters, and hangers-on translates into big bucks for Chicago and the Land of Lincoln. In 1990 alone more than $30 million was generated by the filming of feature-length movies as well as some television productions. More important, the recognition of Chicago and its environs as an acceptable and exciting place to make movies has added another dimension to this sweet home of ours.

At the same time producers have opted to locate here, city and suburban folks continue to support Hollywood's efforts at the movie theaters. Boasting more than 300 first-run screens, offered by four major theater chains as well as some independents, the Chicago area houses more than 90 movie theaters at a time when video stores are popping up on almost every street corner, offering $.99 rentals and free popcorn to entice their customers.

Support for the big screen is nothing new to Chicagoans, who first attended theaters at the turn of the century. Palaces were built here to keep film fans comfortable as well as to make going to the movies a special and memorable occasion. The Uptown, the Granada, and the Chicago Theatre are just some of the huge, ornate structures that attracted moviegoers of all ages.

Film viewing in Chicago started in little storefront operations that showed short "experimental" films on walls and sheets. From 1897 to 1917 Chicago exhibitors needed products to bring customers into their storefront theaters. Carl Laemmle, William Selig, George K. Spoor, and Gilbert M. Anderson produced miles and miles of these "shorts." Selig's company went into business in 1897, filming three- to five-minute stories that simply showed a single actor or two arguing, fighting, running, being chased, or other simple ideas. In 1907 Spoor and Anderson formed Essanay Studios at 435 N. Clark and then 1333 W. Argyle, busing in stars of the day including Francis X. Bushman, Wallace Beery, Ben Turpin, Tom Mix, and a comic star named Charlie Chaplin.

However, by 1918 Essanay turned west for some of their productions, thanks to cold and snowy Chicago winters. Chicago's "Film Row" (on Wabash from 800 south to 15th Street) continued to be the center of film distribution for the Midwest as theater owners could find their features, shorts, trailers, posters, and advertising materials from two dozen or more major studio and independent exchanges. MGM, Columbia, Paramount, Warner's, Republic, Fox, Universal, RKO, Disney, Monogram, American International, Allied Artist, and others all kept offices on Film Row. In addition owners could buy theater seats, bulbs, candy, popcorn, giveaways (plates and dishes, etc.), carpeting, and much more as the street catered to the needs of the important film exhibition business. Back in the twenties, thirties, forties, and fifties, there were more than a million seats in the Chicago area and more than 100 theaters, from Rockford to Alton, from Racine to South Bend. Tickets were priced from $.25 to a dollar.

Eventually, Chicago lost all of its production facilities and companies to Hollywood, and the federal government broke up the monopoly that had kept the manufacturing and distribution of film-related equipment centered in the Windy City. Even when companies approached the city later on in the fifties and sixties, Mayor Richard J. Daley rarely allowed shooting within the city limits. That's why films that were supposed to be based in Chicago, like *The Benny Goodman Story*, *In Old Chicago*, *The Gene Krupa Story*, and the classic *St. Valentine's Day Massacre*, were filmed in Hollywood.

Thanks to the efforts of the Illinois Film Office and the Chicago Film Office, production has sprouted once again. Actors and crews have never been busier, allowing hundreds of talented Chicagoans the chance to show their stuff on big and small productions alike. Even the "little people" of film, the extras, are finding more and more days of work as directors find Chicago locations interesting and exciting for their productions. The **Illinois Film Office** (427-3456) operates a casting hot line for those interested in work, though the number tends to be busy.

THEATERS

As for the film-viewing experience, the theaters and the screens have gotten smaller, and the term *multiplex* has become an integral part of the theater owner's language. The Esquire Theatre, the McClurg Court Theatre, the Davis, the Broadway, and others now boast of their multiple screens where once a single screen sufficed. The reasons were economic and, as some movie-goers are quick to point out, it's better to have multiple screens than no screen at all. Along with this growth of commercial movie exhibitions, specialty theaters and societies have sprouted and continued to blossom in and around Chicago, all supported by various Chicagoans who value the experience of watching a movie on the big screen. Here are some of the more interesting places to settle back with a box of buttered popcorn and watch a movie.

First-Run Houses

Music Box Theatre
3733 N. Southport   871-6604
This old movie house is a shining beacon on the North Side for film fans. Sitting modestly on a relatively quiet neighborhood street only a few blocks from Wrigley Field, the folks that run this refurbished theater offer plenty for your money: a five-times-a-year film calendar listing all of their films with show times and descriptions, an eclectic mix of classic films, new foreign and independent releases as well as weird midnight movies, plus an elegant presentation. The star-and-cloud machine that lights the twinkling lights in the theater works, and the owners have been known to spell intermissions with organ instrumentals on the beautiful Music Box Theatre organ. Discount

pricing for ticket packages and a yummy concession stand round out what should be your favorite movie house.

Fine Arts Theatres
418 S. Michigan   939-3700

M&R Loews operates this multiplex theater, filling its four screens with first-run foreign and independent films. The Fine Arts Building that houses the theaters is unique, converted into an arts building back in 1898.

Biograph Theatre
2433 N. Lincoln   348-4123

Probably Chicago's most famous theater, the Biograph has been a triplex now for a few years. Programming, supplied by the folks at Cineplex Odeon, is no longer as challenging as it was when it was an independent, but the big theater, as opposed to the two smaller screens upstairs, is still one of the best places to view a movie.

McClurg Court Theatre
330 E. Ohio   642-0723

Cineplex Odeon took this monument to proper theater projecting and almost ruined it. They added two screens and got rid of the balcony to make this a triplex. Fortunately, the main floor is still whole, complete with its curved screen and multitrack THX audio system.

Omnimax Theatre
57th Street and Lake Shore Drive   684-1414

This is not to be missed. Large-screen spectacular films shot with multiple cameras and recorded with multitrack audio fill the five-story screen housed at the Museum of Science and Industry at the Henry Crown Space Center.

Second-Run Houses

First-run films tend to draw the biggest crowds, but for your best bargain, if you're willing to wait until a film has lost its place among the big box-office draws, check out these second-run houses for single and double features.

The Cheap Seats

Adelphi
7074 N. Clark   764-3656

Its Art Deco marquee was replaced and the name changed to the North Shore Cinema, but recently it has reverted back to the Adelphi, a theater built in 1917, showing double features for $2.

Bensenville I and II
9 S. Center, Bensenville   (708) 860-7774

Double features for only $1.50.

Bremen Theatre
159th Street and Oak Park Avenue, Tinley Park   (708) 429-1010

A four-plex theater priced at $1.50 per screen.

Brighton
4223 S. Archer   927-9090
One of the few theaters in this part of the city that offers double features.

Davis Theatre
4614 N. Lincoln   784-0893
The Davis was once a huge theater but has since been divided into four screens. The atmosphere is worse than typical for budget theaters. Noisy crowds and sticky floors occasionally get in the way of enjoying your $2 worth of viewing entertainment.

Des Plaines
1467 Miner, Des Plaines   (708) 298-6715
It's only a dollar to get into this twin theater.

Diana Theatre
17735 S. Halsted, Homewood   (708) 798-1140
Cineplex Odeon owns this four-plex, priced at $1.75.

Dolton Theatre
14112 Chicago, Dolton   (708) 841-8850
Single features for only a single!

Forest Park
7600 W. Roosevelt, Forest Park   (708) 771-4337
The giant Cineplex Odeon chain owns this budget triplex house, with features priced at only $1.

400 Theatre
6746 N. Sheridan   764-9100
Before its last renovation, this budget-minded theater was home to "Loveseats," extrawide seats that could serve as romantic hot spots for couples. Double features for $2.

Glen Theatre
On Clifton Boulevard, Glen Ellyn   (708) 469-0780
Four screens of single features priced at $1.50.

Glenwood Theatre
183rd Street and Halsted Street, Glenwood   (708) 754-7469
Single features priced at $2, with $1 admission on Wednesdays.

Harlem Corners
87th Street at Harlem Avenue   (708) 598-5559
Six screens are housed here on the far Southwest Side with $1 admission price before 6 P.M. and only $.50 more after 6. Some double features offered as well!

Highland Park Theatre
445 Central, Highland Park   (708) 432-3300
Highland Park's only movie theater is a budget one with four screens and a price of $1.50.

Hinsdale Theatre
29 E. 1st, Hinsdale   (708) 986-1203
Single features at a price of $2.50.

The Hub Theatre
1746 W. Chicago   226-0313
Chicago's newest sub-run theater boasts a $2 admission price for its double feature.

Lake Theatre
Lake Street between Harlem and Marion, Oak Park   (708) 848-9088
Four screens in the heart of Oak Park. One of a group of "classic" cinemas that includes the Elk Grove, the Tivoli, the Tivoli South, the Tradewinds, and the York Theater in Elmhurst. Most are $1.50 to $2 for single features.

Logan Theatre
2646 N. Milwaukee   252-0627
Four screens of subsequent run films, each priced at $2.

Morton Grove
7300 W. Dempster, Morton Grove   (708) 967-6010
A typical suburban theater, clean and well run, that offers four screens of film fun, each priced at $1.50.

Olympic
6134 W. Cermak, Cicero   (708) 652-5919
On the West Side, double features for $2.00.

Centre
120 Plaza, Park Forest   (708) 503-0707
Three screens of films. Admission $1.50.

The Patio
6008 W. Irving Park   545-2006
A neat place to watch movies. Single features here are priced at $1.50.

The Pickwick
18 S. Main, Park Ridge   (708) 825-5800
A beautiful art deco movie palace that is almost as much fun to look at as the movies they show on three screens for $1.50 each.

The Portage Theatre
4050 N. Milwaukee   202-8000
Double your pleasure here as the Portage offers two screens of double features, $2 each.

Skokie Theatre
7924 N. Lincoln, Skokie   (708) 673-4214
You'll spend just $1.50 for the weekly showing of a single feature.

Three Penny
2424 N. Lincoln   935-5744
Across from the first-run Biograph Theatre, the Three Penny has always battled its nearby neighbor for crowds. Some first-run showings, especially of foreign flicks, and exceptional second-run showings make this a theater to keep track of. Currently, they publish a schedule of upcoming films.

Tivoli
5021 Highland, Downers Grove   (708) 968-0219
One of the "classic" cinemas.

Villa Park   (708) 279-7922
Four screens of single features priced at $1.50.

Village Theatre
1548 N. Clark   642-2403
Once one of the great bargains in the city with quite interesting double features, the Village has been plexed and now boasts four screens and single features for $2.50.

Wheaton Theatre
Glen Ellyn   (708) 668-1680
Four screens of single features priced at $1.50.

FILM RESOURCES
Groups and Offbeat Venues

In spite of million-dollar budgets and big-name stars, the movie industry still struggles with lousy box-office action, failed flicks up on the silver screen, and an audience that typically finds itself being talked down to instead of respected by the powers that be in Hollywood. As a result, customers that were once willing to shell out a few bucks for a couple of hours of entertainment based on the stars or the story involved now admit that it takes more than a big name to get them back into the theaters. While this new attitude has hurt commercial film showings, it has helped attendance at specialized screenings offered by a variety of film organizations. Chicago also boasts a few unique film festivals, offered annually by a variety of groups.

Chicago Filmmakers
1229 W. Belmont   281-8788
Chicago Filmmakers started in 1973 organizing screenings of experimental films on Saturday nights at N.A.M.E. Gallery. Some nights anyone could bring in a self-produced film. Most nights were dedicated to themed premieres and special showings of efforts by local filmmakers. Their new location at the Theatre Building has given them a better space and better exposure for their always interesting and ever-expanding schedule of events.

Chicago Film Critics
1152 North LaSalle, Building B, Chicago, 60610-2695
This noted organization, much like the New York and Los Angeles groups, presents an annual ceremony each March to announce the winners of the Flame Awards, as voted on by a collection of more than 40 Chicago film critics. Also, they have started "The Friends of the Critics" group. For $75 a year, members receive eight screening passes for two, an invitation to an exclusive gathering the with the critics, deals on travel packages for film festivals, and more. Write to the above address for more information.

Chicago Lesbian and Gay International Film Festival   281-1981
Started in 1980, this group imports films from all over the world and the
United States for 7 to 10 days and nights of screenings and sometimes discussions, usually at Chicago Filmmakers and the Music Box Theatre. The festival
draws largely mixed audiences—gay and straight—to its shows.

Chicago Women in Film
30 N. Michigan, #508   372-2376, hot line: 236-3618
This organization is devoted to enhancing women's skills and status in the
film and video community.

Chicago Public Library
400 S. State   747-4300
The new Harold Washington Library in downtown Chicago hosts a series of
weekly screenings of various commercial and theme-oriented films, all
provided free of charge. Formerly, the Cultural Center at 78 E. Washington
was home to these screenings and may continue to feature films. In any case,
be on the lookout for advance word about these free events. Also, various
library branches offer occasional screenings in the different neighborhoods
around town. You'll have to check with each branch to find out what they're
up to.

Chicago Latino Cinema
Columbia College
600 S. Michigan   431-1330
This film group recently celebrated its seventh Annual Chicago Latino Film
Festival, featuring films from Brazil, Colombia, Chile, Ecuador, Venezuela,
Spain, Peru, Jamaica, Nicaragua, Panama, Costa Rica, Cuba, Portugal,
Mexico, Puerto Rico, and the United States. Based at Columbia College, a
school known for its film production courses, the organization offers year-
round screenings and special events for its members.

Cinema Chicago
415 N. Dearborn   644-3400, hot line: 644-FILM
As host of the Chicago International Film Festival, Cinema Chicago attempts
to bring relatively unknown foreign and independent films to Chicago every
fall. World premieres are also held at the same time, though the competition
from other fests for premieres is greater now than ever. Members of this
organization are also invited monthly to special screenings of new releases.

Doc Films
Max Palevsky Cinema, Ida Noyes Hall
1212 E. 59th   702-8575
This organization at the University of Chicago boasts of being the first film
"society" in the United States. Regardless, the creative minds involved in the
programming are usually on the money, offering interesting and entertaining
movies nightly on the South Side.

Left to right: Tony Fitzpatrick, Jim Sikora, and Ann Host. Sikora, Chicago's "King of Super-8," films Fitzpatrick in *Love, After the Walls Close In.*

Facets Multimedia
1517 W. Fullerton   281-9075
Daily films on a couple of screens including premieres of foreign and independent films, documentaries, and retrospectives. Occasional appearances by directors and writers are scheduled throughout the year. Facets is host to the Chicago Children's Film Festival, adding to its reputation for regularly showing some of the finest film fare for kids. For those willing to watch films on tape, Facets houses a video rental outlet that offers a fantastic collection of hard-to-find videos. You won't believe the selection.

Film Center of the Art Institute
Columbus Drive at Jackson Boulevard   443-3733
As a downtown location for film showings, the Film Center could rightly be called Chicago's best example of film appreciation. Promoted to its members and the rest of the city by its own publication, *The Film Center Gazette*, the Center arranges retrospectives, screenings of recently completed independent films, lectures, and free showings from the school's extensive library. Directors sometimes appear at premieres of their latest work. Members are regularly invited to free preview screenings of new commercial releases.

International House Film Society
1414 E. 59th   753-2254
The University of Chicago's second film group with showings during the week.

Psychotronic Film Society 346-0270
The name is a combination of *psycho* (horror) and *tronic*, or electronic. Started by Michael Flores in 1986 to celebrate some of the forgotten films of Hollywood, Los Angeles, and other locales, this group is legendary for its showings. Some of them include *Deranged, School Girl Ninjas, Rock and Rule*, and other assorted "classics" that never seemed to play the regular theaters in town. Though most screenings take place in various clubs around town, Flores has taken that first step toward commercialism by opening on weekends a long, dark screening room at the Civic Studio Theatre above the Civic Opera House (20 N. Wacker, downtown). It's Chicago's only regularly operating movie theater with a bar!

Talman Classic Film Series
Talman Theatre
4901 W. Irving Park   726-8915
One of Chicago's oft-publicized and oft-promoted banks, Talman offers Saturday screenings of classic films.

University of Illinois at Chicago Films 413-5070
This campus features weekend showings of commercial and classic films at various locations, for students and nonstudents alike.

Women in the Director's Chair
3435 N. Sheffield   281-4988
This organization promotes various women, both local and national, who are working in film and video.

Essential Sources of Information

The Reader
As Chicago's premiere free weekly, this paper welcomes the traditional weekend with listings of just about every movie playing in the Chicago area. Though show times can be found only for the offerings at commercial theaters, the capsule reviews are an immense step above the typical newspaper theater listings.

Chicago Tribune
Friday's edition contains a separate pullout section entitled "Take 2," offering the latest reviews, ads, and even a panel of high school movie critics aimed at convincing teens to start reading the paper. With critic Dave Kehr penning some of the city's best critiques on Fridays as well as during the week and veteran Gene Siskel writing a column for each Friday edition plus a lengthy listing of most current releases and reviews, the *Chicago Tribune* is an excellent source for moviegoers.

Chicago Sun-Times
Roger Ebert and a host of other critics take care of the reviews for this daily, offering page after page of reviews, ads, and more on Fridays. But they beat the *Tribune* by one step with a special listing on Sundays of the films that are scheduled to open the following week. Occasional interviews with directors and megastars also find themselves popping up in the Sunday edition.

NewCity

Based in the south Loop area but aiming for the entire city, this free weekly offers complete listings of films ("film clips") along with reviews ("short takes") and a film calendar ("film calendar"). New editions come out every Thursday.

If you're without a newspaper but near a phone, there is a new recorded information telephone service that can tell you where and when your favorite current film is playing in and around Chicago. Callers to (312) 444-FILM can use their touchtone phones to buy film or theater tickets and then hear show times and locations.

—Mark Guncheon

ART

CHICAGO SCANDALS

Censorship and funding have become the central issues for the arts in America since the late 1980s. Willard Boyd, president of the Chicago Field Museum, recently stated, "This is a period of cultural misunderstanding and disrespect through the arts." Despite the threatened certainty of this nation's leader in art support, the National Endowment for the Arts (NEA), art in Chicago has continued to provoke. In response to the pressures from the Right, the result has been, as in any state where one's rights are being threatened, a resurgence of sociopolitical art and an insistence on freedom of expression. A number of recent events in Chicago's art world have had a profound impact on the community at large.

Mirth & Girth (1988) brought nine aldermen and 17 bomb threats to the School of the Art Institute (SAIC). The painting, graduating senior David Nelson's entry in a fellowship competition, portrayed the late Mayor Harold Washington in frilly women's lingerie (apparently based on a rumor the artist heard regarding Washington's appearance as he arrived at the hospital following his fatal heart attack). The Chicago City Council asked that all funds and contributions to the Art Institute be withheld until the painting was removed from public view. Within four hours, the painting had been seized by nine aldermen under the local statute of incitement to riot (the painting was later returned, damaged). In the following days, Art Institute Chairman of the Board of Trustees Marshall Field made $16,000 worth of apologies in ads in the *Chicago Tribune*.

The second public controversy, directly on the tails of the "Harold Washington Scandal," reached the chambers of Congress: the "Flag Incident." In late February 1989 during an SAIC juried exhibition of 72 minority artists, a Vietnam veteran was confronted with an entry labeled "What Is the Proper Way to Display the U.S. Flag?" The installation by "Dread" Scott Tyler was a photomontage depicting a flag-burning demonstration and coffins of veterans draped with the U.S. flag. Next to the photos a shelf held a notebook asking viewers to indicate their responses; directly under the shelf was a U.S. flag, which apparently invited participants to step on the flag. The hype on this event was so accelerated that within days and for a month the steps outside the Art Institute were the site of hundreds of protestors, from Vietnam vets to all-American citizens taunting visitors, waving "Honk If You Love the Flag" signs. Television reported police arrests, minor assaults, and death threats; veterans filed suit. Memberships were canceled; donors pulled their support. Next to the installation a sign was posted indicating that stepping on the flag is a #4 felony and punishable by up to three years in jail and a $10,000 fine.

Worse still were the subsequent financial menaces. Targeting the Art Institute, the Chicago Park District threatened to cut off $28 million in annual funds to eight museums on Park District land, but later it agreed to continue funding, as the Art Institute and the School of the Art Institute are largely independent. In the end, federal funding was indeed cut, to $1.00 per year for both the SAIC and the Illinois Arts Alliance Foundation for having issued a statement of support during the incidents surrounding the exhibit. The estimated loss for the SAIC for fiscal year 1992 was $65,000.

The fact that these indignant works were created by students could have been dismissed as youthful exhibitionism, yet in both cases the issue and anger shifted from the works of art to the institution that attempted to support freedom of expression. The public outrage at these events has had the most injurious government response of "If you don't do it our way, you won't get our money."

What's the Big Deal over NEA Funding?

The Endowment is a source of revenue that supports groups and individuals in theater, music (symphonies, opera), dance, photography, painting, and sculpture. Initiated in 1967, it has allowed people to pursue forms in art that are not supported solely by private donations. An NEA endorsement of a project also gives corporate donors a sense of safety concerning government tax deductions, as well as providing substantial gains from matching grants. (For example, the $119 million in 1988 NEA grants, each a few thousand dollars, produced $1.3 billion in matching money for artists to complete their projects.) The federal monies service individuals, groups, and all states, and each state in turn has a funding institution that assists artists and arts organizations through grants and programs; Illinois's is the Illinois Arts Council. The state appropriations are then distributed locally, here through the Chicago Office of Fine Arts.

In 1991 the NEA received a total of $175.6 million to distribute; this amounts to an approximate total of *$.69 per person per year for the arts* (meanwhile the 1991 defense budget was $308 billion). Because society considers the arts secondary, in this time of budget cutting the 25-year commitment to federal funding for the arts is being jeopardized. At home, Governor Jim Edgar has reduced monies for the Illinois Arts Council 27 percent over the past three years.

Principal arts foe Jesse Helms, a Republican senator from North Carolina, has aggressively fought to forbid funding of "that type of art that turns the stomach of any normal person." With the 1989 "Helms Amendment" he was joined by a growing campaign against government support of art, claiming that certain works funded by the NEA were "indecent or obscene." Arts supporters and lobbyists fought to defeat the amendment and create a compromise bill that would allow legislators to disapprove of "offensive" and "blasphemous" art without damaging the NEA and its programs. An outside panel of 12 (including not one artist, arts administrator, writer, critic, or curator) was appointed to monitor NEA grant procedures, prohibit funding of "obscene" art, and sponsor only art that is "within the general standards of decency." This was the first demonstration of content restrictions in the history of the NEA. Today, each of the thousands of grant recipients must sign a form agreeing to the terms and rules dictated by politicians, under the threat of not receiving funds. Art funding can be risky because art is risky, but censorship makes it pointless. Neutral, apolitical, inoffensive art is guaranteed to be forgotten.

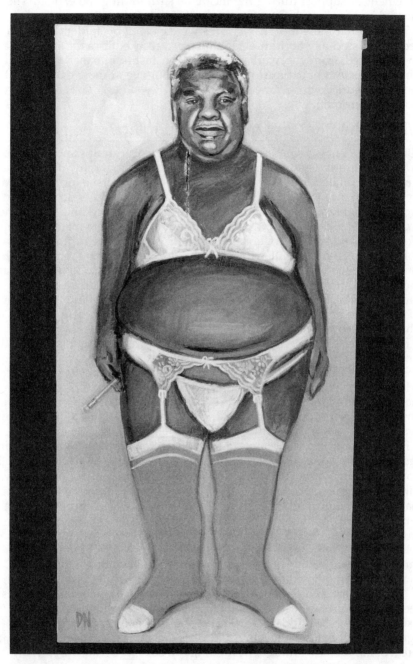

David Nelson's *Mirth and Girth*. Photo by James Prinz, © 1988.

CHICAGO ART

Chicago has the nation's third-highest concentration of artists. Many of the artists exhibit in Chicago galleries; some show nationally and internationally; some just show their friends. Two areas in the city are considered "artist" neighborhoods: the Wicker Park/Bucktown district and Pilsen, south of the Loop around 18th Street. Yet in answer to the question "What is Chicago art?" today, unanimously it is about diversity and not wanting to be grouped in a single definition. The 1950s Chicago "Monster Roster" and the sixties/seventies "Imagists" put Chicago on the art map, and the artists associated with these schools (e.g., Leon Golub, Ed Paschke, Roger Brown, Jim Nutt) have asserted their historic importance and continue to be highly regarded worldwide. The art history of Chicago is linked to the development of the city itself—its diverging ethnic cultures and attitudes, pride and satisfaction in work, independence and self- sufficiency. Artists today produce idiosyncratic, individualized styles. Maintaining their differences, however, a closely woven group of young Chicago artists with a postmodern bent does exist: Tony Tasset, Gaylen Gerber, Jeanne Dunning, Judy Ledgerwood, Mitchell Kane, Hirsh Perlman, Vincent Shine, and Mike Hill. (Buy now!)

ART MUSEUMS

The Art Institute
Michigan Avenue and Adams Street   443-3600
Hours: Monday–Friday, 10:30 A.M.–4:30 P.M.;
Tuesday (free admission), 10:30 A.M.–8 P.M.;
Saturday, Sunday, and holidays, 10 A.M.–5 P.M.
Founded in 1879 as the Chicago Academy of Fine Arts, the Art Institute of Chicago functioned primarily as a school and exhibition hall until the 1893 World's Fair, which opened the eyes of all to "a never-ending wild excitement" (artist-collector Frederic Bartlett later donated many important works including Seurat's *Grand Jatte* and Picasso's *The Old Guitarist*). Then, the advent of the Armory Show in 1913 brought Chicago its first exposure to European modernism; almost 200,000 visitors came to the museum, mostly to laugh and mock. By 1934 the museum's dedication to collecting and exhibiting 20th-century art was obvious, with its first Braque, Matisse, Leger, Brancusi, and four Kandinskys.

Acceptance of the *au courant* was not, however, the status quo, and in 1936 a censorship group came forth at the Art Institute called "Sanity in Art." Founded by a the wife of a trustee and backed by the press, their mission was to prevent vulgarity in the museum's exhibitions. "Painting has gone mad," they insisted. "The trash now on exhibit at the Art Institute has no right to occupy wall space." The group would regularly storm Katherine Kuh's contemporary gallery where they would insult the artwork and customers and smash windows, only to be stopped by the police. Years later Kuh was appointed by the Institute, first as a publicist, educator, reformer, and finally as a curator. She is responsible for bringing the first Surrealist show, in 1947, and writing the first major catalog published by a museum. Still, by 1949, Rep. George Dondero of Michigan approached Congress accusing her and director Daniel Rich of "encouraging Communism" through the Institute's exhibitions.

The museum today boasts 10 curatorial departments and more than 300,000 works covering 40 centuries of art. It is home of America's greatest collection of French Impressionist and Post-Impressionist painting; a substantial, distinguished, and newly reopened collection of 20th-century art; and important architecture, photography, and textile collections. The Art Institute continues to expand, physically and in terms of acquisitions. The elegant Daniel F. and Ada L. Rice wing brings rotating modern and contemporary exhibitions, and the most recent and very significant addition is the Mrs. Edwin A. (Lindy) Bergman collection of Surrealist art. Seventy-seven major Dada and Surrealist works mount the Bergman total museum donations to 118 works. And with the generous contributions from the estate of artist and collector Claire Zeisler, the Institute is now regarded as a major center, a virtual who's who in Surrealist art including works by Max Ernst, Yves Tanguy, Magritte, Balthus, Dubuffet, Miro, Klee, and others. Be sure not to miss the newly reopened galleries of Chinese, Japanese, and Korean art.

The Art Institute has the second largest museum library in the country, and the School of the Art Institute is one of few schools affiliated with a major U.S. museum. Alumni include Georgia O'Keefe, Ivan Albright, and Ed Paschke.

The Museum of Contemporary Art
237 E. Ontario   280-5161
Hours: Tuesday–Saturday, 10 A.M.–5 P.M.; Sunday, 12–5 P.M.;
closed Monday; free on Tuesday
By the 1960s the Art Institute had become the fortress of Chicago's old-monied families and functioned somewhat like a private club. Not welcome were the nouveau riche, contemporary collectors, and especially Jews. Thus began the Museum of Contemporary Art, with a significant number of $50,000 individual pledges as start-up funds. In a former bakery on Ontario Street, the MCA first opened its doors in 1967. The late sixties and early seventies established the MCA as a precursor to performance art; the building was wrapped by Christo (1969), which resulted in the firing of the museum's first director, Jan van der Marck, and in 1975 Chris Burden lay under a sheet of glass for 45 hours, an act that received international news coverage. Other historic events include an Imagist show (1972), an Yves Klein retrospective (1982), and Anselm Kiefer and Georg Baselitz shows (1984).

By this time the Museum was obsessed with the critical need for a larger facility and started the ball rolling. A site at the right price ($1.00/square foot) was decided upon, and by 1991 trustees of the board of directors had committed $37.5 million toward a $55 million goal. In the fall of 1995 at the Illinois National Guard Armory (next to the Water Tower pumping station and overlooking Lake Michigan) will be a 125,000-square-foot aluminum and glass structure, the first American commission for Berlin architect Josef Paul Kleiheus. The new museum will be "an instrument for the presentation, interpretation, study, and research of contemporary art," according to Director Kevin Consey, with four times the existing formal exhibit space, adjustable walls and ceilings, multipurpose spaces for electronic media, new music, performance art, video, and film. Also included will be an in-house education center with a 350-seat auditorium and classrooms. The museum and one-acre sculpture garden will sit on a base of Indiana limestone, maintaining an aesthetic link to the surrounding buildings. Now the diverse permanent collection has room to expand, as does membership and frequency of visits. Exhibitions always have related lectures; artists' talks, discussions, and guided tours are available.

OTHER MUSEUMS

Terra Museum of American Art
666 N. Michigan   664-3939
Hours: Tuesday, 12–8 P.M.; Wednesday–Saturday, 10 A.M.–5 P.M.;
Sunday, 12–5 P.M.; closed Monday
The Terra Museum houses one of the country's preeminent collections of 18th- to 20th-century American art. In 1981, Daniel J. Terra was appointed ambassador at large for cultural affairs by Ronald Reagan. Terra has collected over 500 of the finest examples of American art, especially American Impressionism. The permanent collection features work by John Singer Sargent, William Merritt Chase, Mary Cassatt, Winslow Homer, Edward Hopper, and Andrew Wyeth. The museum also hosts curated, touring, and special exhibitions. Terra's fondness of the Impressionist movement has prompted his opening of the Terra Museum in Giverny, France, in the fall of 1992.

David and Alfred Smart Museum of Art
5550 S. Greenwood   702-0200
Hours: Tuesday–Friday, 10 A.M.–4 P.M.; Saturday, 10 A.M.–6 P.M.;
Sunday, 12–6 P.M.; closed Monday and all major holidays
The University of Chicago's David and Alfred Smart Museum holds the finest permanent collection of classical antiquities, painting, and sculpture from the Middle Ages to contemporary, as well as art from East Asia—all purchases of the Smart Family Foundation, established in 1974. Each year four major exhibitions are mounted, which usually examine a period or a premise in depth. The museum also sponsors a lecture series and guided tours.

The Renaissance Society
The University of Chicago
5811 S. Ellis   702-8670
Hours: Tuesday–Friday, 10 A.M.–4 P.M.; Saturday and Sunday, 12–4 P.M.;
closed Monday
Founded in 1915, the Renaissance Society maintains an international reputation as one of the finest resources for contemporary art. This American version of a *Kunsthalle* has been committed to bold, early responses to the most challenging and provocative European and American art. Openings are held Sunday afternoons, and everybody who's anybody attends. Concerts, performances, film and video screenings, and talks by noted contemporary artists and critics are definitely worth following.

On April 15, 1989, a fire in River North destroyed nine art galleries.

GALLERIES

A beautifully paved parking lot at the corner of Huron and Orleans sits without a suggestion of the former six- story Adler & Sullivan building, up for landmark designation, referred to as "Gallery Place" and considered the heart of art in Chicago. On April 15, 1989, it burned with the contents of nine galleries: thousands of artworks with an estimated total value of $50 million. (The contractors were working on the building without a permit; the city had issued three "stop" orders, there had been two previous small fires, the sprinkler system was disconnected, and fire doors were not in place.) Some of the galleries managed to quickly reopen in the Merchandise Mart for the May International Art Exposition and have since resumed business at other locations. The artists were protected under the Illinois Art Consignment Act, which legally holds gallery owners responsible for artwork on display and in storage.

Today over 100 Chicago galleries continue to exhibit and sometimes sell art. The season begins each fall, the first Friday after Labor Day, with "Gallery Night" when plastic cupfuls of questionable (but free) wine and designer water are offered to all, and many do appear. Perhaps artistic inspiration is secondary to finding that artsy woman or man; the people watching is great!

Chicago galleries make a concerted effort to coordinate their opening nights, every four to six weeks, to stimulate an "art scene" and anticipate a genuine interest in what artists are doing today. Those more serious about collecting come on Saturdays. The Chicago galleries, unlike those in New York or Europe, are not hostile places; staffpeople are generally very friendly and pleased to discuss the art or the market. There is, however, a growing animosity among dealers toward collectors who are introduced to art in Chicago and subsequently go to New York, for affirmation and perhaps a more significant discount, and buy there. Activity in the galleries has certainly slowed since the roaring eighties, and the Gulf War and aftermath have reduced sales to a trickle. Many galleries have closed.

A complete list of Chicago's commercial and alternative galleries can be found in the free monthly *Gallery Guide* and in the locally published *Chicago Gallery News*. Both have detailed maps and can be found in any gallery.

Selective Gallery Listing

Roy Boyd Gallery
739 N. Wells 642-1606
Hours: Monday–Wednesday, Friday and Saturday, 10 A.M.–5:30 P.M.;
Thursday, 10 A.M.–7 P.M.; closed Monday June–August
Contemporary abstract painting and sculpture. Mostly Chicagoans; Roy and Anne Boyd have a gallery in Santa Monica as well.

Feigen
325 W. Huron, #204 787-0500
Hours: Tuesday–Wednesday and Friday, 10 A.M.–5:30 P.M.;
Thursday, 10 A.M.–7 P.M.; Saturday, 10:30 A.M.–5:30 P.M.
Since 1989 Feigen has been competitive with Robbin Lockett and Rhona Hoffman in showing the most cutting-edge contemporary American and European artists. Very slick presentation, despite the lack of sales.

Oskar Friedl
750 N. Orleans, #302   337-7550
Hours: Tuesday–Saturday, 11 A.M.–5:30 P.M.
Oskar has a very talented stable of mostly European painters and sculptors; he's in a tiny space, but it's definitely worth a visit.

Richard Gray
620 N. Michigan   642-8877
Hours: Tuesday–Saturday, 10 A.M.–5:30 P.M.
Chicago's most well-reputed European and American modern and contemporary master dealer.

Carl Hammer
200 W. Superior   266-8512
Hours: Tuesday–Friday, 10 A.M.–6 P.M.; Saturday, 10 A.M.–5:30 P.M.;
Sunday and Monday, by appointment.
Exhibitions include self-taught and "Outsider" artists, including Vonn Bruenchenheim, Bill Traylor, Lee Godie, Mr. Imagination, and other contemporary artists.

Rhona Hoffman
215 W. Superior   951-8828
Hours: Tuesday, Wednesday, and Friday, 10 A.M.–5:30 P.M.;
Thursday, 10 A.M.–7 P.M.; Saturday, 11 A.M.–5:30 P.M.
Indisputably the "big-name" contemporary art gallery in Chicago, with most provocative work. Rhona, formerly in partnership with the now Seattle-based Donald Young, has a long- standing commitment to the best in contemporary.

R. S. Johnson
645 N. Michigan   943-1661
Hours: Monday–Saturday, 9 A.M.–5:30 P.M.
Mr. and Mrs. Johnson are authorities on and collectors and exhibitors of 19th- and 20th-century master paintings and sculpture and Old Master paintings. Even if Goya is not your bag, go in for a chat—you're sure to learn much.

Phyllis Kind
313 W. Superior   642-6302
Hours: Tuesday–Saturday, 10 A.M.–5:30 P.M.; Thursday, 10 A.M.–8 P.M.
Represents Chicago "Imagists" including Ed Paschke, Roger Brown, and Jim Nutt; also has a New York gallery.

Klein
400 N. Morgan   243-0400
Hours: Tuesday–Saturday, 10 A.M.–5:30 P.M.; Sunday, 12–4 P.M.
This stunning gallery is a bit off the gallery district path but absolutely worth the trip. Contemporary abstract painting, sculpture, and works on paper.

Robbin Lockett
703 N. Wells   649-1230
Hours: Tuesday–Saturday, 10 A.M.–6 P.M.
This small space presents the most challenging work being made today, by
Europeans and Americans. Watched by European galleries to determine the
state of the U.S. art market.

Isobel Neal
200 W. Superior, #200   944-1570
Hours: Wednesday–Saturday, 11 A.M.–6 P.M.; by appointment other times
Shows a variety of talented African-American painters and sculptors.

Roger Ramsay Gallery
325 W. Huron   337-4678
Hours: Tuesday–Saturday, 10 A.M.–6 P.M.
Contemporary American and European photography, painting, and sculpture.

Ricky Renier Gallery
1550 N. Milwaukee   227-3090
Hours: Tuesday–Friday, 3–6 P.M.; Saturday, 1–6 P.M.; and by appointment.
A precursor to the Wicker Park "artist's district," Ricky shows clean contemporary American and European paintings, sculpture, and installations.

Sazama
300 W. Superior   951-0004
Hours: Tuesday–Friday, 10 A.M.–5 P.M.; Saturday, 11 A.M.–5 P.M.
A gallery to watch: environmental installations, contemporary painting and
sculpture. Some Latin-American art.

Zolla/Lieberman
325 W. Huron   944-1990
Hours: Tuesday–Saturday, 10 A.M.–5:30 P.M.; Thursday, 10 A.M.–7 P.M.
Probably the strongest contemporary painting gallery in the city, Roberta and
Bill have been selling quality art for over 15 years in Chicago.

Alternative Galleries

Alternative and not-for-profit galleries are always popping up, so check the
monthly *Gallery Guide* or *Tribune* "Friday" section for accurate listings of
openings and events.

N.A.M.E. Gallery
700 N. Carpenter   226-0671
Hours: Tuesday–Saturday, 12–6 P.M.
Chicago's first alternative gallery, a not-for-profit offering a variety of
regional and national visual and performance art. Be sure to attend the
annual St. Valentine's Day Benefit Auction with fun art, dining, and dancing.

Randolph Street Gallery
756 N. Milwaukee   666-7737
Hours: Tuesday–Saturday, 12–6 P.M.
Multimedia, community-oriented art, dance, performance, poetry, artists
talks, readings. Don't miss the annual multiples benefit.

John David Mooney, sculptor.

World Tatoo Gallery
1255 S. Wabash, 3rd floor, north   939-2222
Hours: Monday–Saturday, 12–5 P.M.
Situated in a huge loft, this is a great place for a party, and many are hosted here. Multimedia nights include lesser-known painters with performance, poetry readings, disc jockeys, and dancing.

PRESS

Chicago has many art critics, most are free-lance writers for local, national, and international magazines; there are two full-time *Chicago Tribune* critics. The *Tribune* features gallery and museum reviews Fridays and Sundays; the *Sun-Times* has not had an art journalist since 1990. Watch for insightful articles in *NewCity* and especially in *The New Art Examiner*.

ART EVENTS

The **Chicago International Art Exposition** (CIAE) has been the largest and most important exposition of 20th-century and contemporary art in the United States. Organized since 1980 by the Lakeside Group, the mid-May fair runs for four days and attracts dealers, collectors, artists, and viewers from all over the world. The primary location had been stunningly situated at Navy Pier, hosting the most reputable galleries in the "rotunda" space, which juts out into Lake Michigan. As of 1991, the much-needed renovation of Navy Pier has resulted in the unfortunate "next to McCormick Place" locale south of the Loop, where all standard conventions take place. Still, the event is a spectacular one, with close to 200 galleries from 20 countries, each selected by a committee as outstanding in the field of contemporary art. Try to get in on the dealer/artist/collector after-fair parties—Art Expo time is when the art scene truly hops.

Initiated in Chicago in 1990, **Around the Coyote** generates a Mardi Gras–like atmosphere each September in Wicker Park. From all over the city, more than 500 emerging and established artists—painters, sculptors, actors, poets (Gwendolyn Brooks read in 1991), photographers, performance artists, filmmakers, computer artists, writers, musicians, and dancers—open their studios and share their talent with the public. The organizer, Frenchman Jim Happy-Delpech, was previously involved with a similar event in the Paris Bastille area and foresaw the possibilities of re-creating it here. The Coyote, a nickname for the tallest tower at the intersection of Damen, North, and Milwaukee avenues, brings over 15,000 curious and collecting visitors; last year over $40,000 worth of painting and sculpture were sold. Around the Coyote operates year-round in establishing Chicago as a world-class cultural center. All events are free; just follow the painted coyotes. For more information call 342-6777.

ADVOCACY

Local renaissance man Frank Galati announced at a recent conference, "Society is created by art and lives through art. . . . The arts are a government responsibility and a national need. A government that doesn't support art is a government that doesn't value it or see virtue in it. Arts should be endowed and encouraged by congress, not punished."

Many people realize that the arts are important, yet they don't see that the arts are important to them. In the currently challenging political environment, art advocacy must become more personal to succeed. Now it is especially important to promote awareness of the arts, to work toward consciousness-raising in addressing the value of the arts and culture. The number of art groups is up, as are audiences; we must not disconnect art from its vibrant social milieu.

Chicago Artists Coalition
5 W. Grand   670-2060
Hours: Monday–Friday, 10 A.M.–5 P.M.
Their monthly newsletter provides information on local and national art issues and articles and listings of interest to artists. A membership organization, the CAC maintains a slide registry (available by appointment only) of over 800 artists available for galleries, publishers, buyers, curators, and designers; also has a job referral service.

Greater Chicago Citizens for the Arts
1150 N. Lake Shore Drive   280-1025
This volunteer group is dedicated to endorsing and supporting pro-arts candidates on a local, state, and federal level. Started in 1990 and modeled after the San Francisco Democratic Arts League (after many artist's rallies, political speeches, etc.), it has over 500 members.

Illinois Arts Alliance (IAA)
67 E. Madison   855-3105
Founded to advocate for favorable public policy and funding for the arts, IAA offers recommendations on how to take action in favorably influencing art-related legislation. It is establishing governmental affairs committees on all art boards across the state and working with art organizations in making advocacy a regular agenda item. IAA represents every art discipline in Illinois.

Lawyers for the Creative Arts
213 W. Institute   944-2787
This group offers free legal assistance and educational services to artists and art organizations. Founded in 1972 and supported by grants from the Illinois Arts Council, the Chicago Office of Fine Arts, and foundation and corporate contributions, LCA is comprised of over 325 lawyers who volunteer professional services to the arts in Illinois. They offer advice on contractual rights, assist with claims and registration of copyright protection, help groups incorporate as not-for-profit organizations, and assist with tax-exempt status.

Near Northwest Arts Council
1579 N. Milwaukee   278-7677
NNWAC was founded in 1985 as a nonprofit community-based organization providing resources for education, employment, exhibition, work and performing space, funding, and vital services essential to the cultivation of the arts and artists. NNWAC promotes and encourages participation in com-

munity art projects in order to create an environment conducive to artistic growth.

THE WOMEN'S ART SCENE

Women have long been patrons of the arts, supporting the work of artists by providing gallery space, purchasing paintings and sculptures, and guiding aesthetic development with their taste and judgment. They have also been artists themselves, although sexist attitudes and conditions have, historically, failed to nurture and recognize their talents and contributions. In Chicago, several galleries and organizations have been created to highlight and support women's artistic thought and work.

The Chicago Women's Caucus for the Arts
700 N. Carpenter   226-7323
This membership organization (with a sliding-fee schedule) holds monthly meetings, sponsors programs, conducts studio visits, and generally exists to promote women's art.

Sister Serpents
P.O. Box 578145, Chicago, 60657   539-3049 (contact Mary Ellen Croteau)
Sister Serpents is a radical feminist art collective that displays both in galleries and on the streets. The group's artistic mission is to use the vision of its members to attack misogyny in the culture.

Two women-run art cooperatives play an important role in the Chicago art community:

ARC
1040 W. Huron   733-2787
ARC's mission since it was founded in 1973 has been to provide alternative space for emerging artists. It continues to serve that purpose and often hosts experimental shows like "Woman as Survivor," which featured the work of 40 women artists from across the country.

Artemisia
700 N. Carpenter   226-7323
Hours: Tuesday–Saturday, 11 A.M.–5 P.M.
Artemisia also supports emerging and alternative artists. In addition, it features the work of gallery members and showcases major women artists who have not had the opportunity to exhibit in Chicago.

Two relative newcomers to the scene are unique galleries featuring women-made and/or woman-inspired jewelry and art.

WomanWild
5237 N. Clark   878-0300
An art/gift gallery carrying items from quilted greeting cards to bronze sculpture and art deco stained-glass pieces, crafted by nearly 100 different women artists.

Ancient Echoes
1800 N. Clybourn   337-7733
A stunning collection of contemporary jewelry and art inspired by mythic and ancient images, feminine spirituality, and matriarchy, with a price range of $5 to $5,000.

OTHER IMPORTANT ART ADDRESSES

Arts Club of Chicago
101 E. Ontario   787-3997
Hours: Monday–Saturday, 10 A.M.–5:30 P.M.
Established in 1916, the Arts Club has always maintained close ties to the Art Institute but with more challenging, always contemporary art. The first exhibitions of Sheeler, Stella, and Demuth were mounted here, and one was introduced to the music of Prokofiev and Stravinsky as well as the dance of Martha Graham. This was the only place in Chicago that would exhibit Mondrian or Klee in the thirties.

Betty Rymer Gallery
Columbus Avenue and Jackson Boulevard   443-3703
Hours: Monday–Friday, 10 A.M.–5 P.M.

Gallery 2
1040 W. Huron   226-1449
Hours: Tuesday–Saturday, 11 A.M.–6 P.M.
Both showcase the strength and diversity of students of the School of the Art Institute.

The Chicago Cultural Center
78 E. Washington   744-6630
Office on Fine Arts hot line: 346-3278
Hours: Monday–Thursday, 9 A.M.–7 P.M.; Friday, 9 A.M.–6 P.M.;
Saturday, 9 A.M.–5 P.M.; Sunday, 12–5 P.M.
Built as the Chicago Public Library in 1897 at the cost of $2 million, most Chicagoans today have never been inside this masterpiece of marble, mosaic domes, majestic stairways, arched doorways, and tiffany lamps. After the 1893 World's Fair, the lush Beaux Arts style was reproduced in Preston Bradley Hall, where Italian Renaissance and Byzantine detailing is combined. Now that the library has a home of its own, the public spaces are entirely devoted to contemporary art: photography, painting, sculpture, and tough installations. Each year the curated and competitive "Chicago Show" hangs here.

Donors Forum
53 W. Jackson   431-0260
Hours: Monday–Thursday, 9 A.M.–4 P.M.
Chicago's only philanthropic research center. Find information on grants, foundations, and corporate giving: matching grants, getting emergency loan funds, preparing grants. Find state-indexed foundation directories—who gives what to whom and how to ask them. Shelves of corporate directories: by state and company, including foreign giving; Corporate 500 companies,

and Corporate Foundation Indexes. Learn about not-for-profit status, 990 tax forms, annual reports, guidelines, 501(c)(3) forms, and so on.

Gallery 400
University of Illinois
400 S. Peoria   996-6114
Hours: Monday–Friday, 9 A.M.–5 P.M.
Shows provocative temporary exhibitions of contemporary art, architecture and design.

State of Illinois Gallery
100 W. Randolph   814-5322
Hours: Monday–Friday, 9 A.M.–6 P.M.
In the Helmut Jahn building on the second floor, this gallery occasionally has very interesting displays of local and national talent.

SCULPTURE

Chicago is internationally recognized for the investment in public sculpture, and one is always pleasantly surprised walking through the city to encounter the sight and sound configurations. The best resource for the most current events in sculpture is **Sculpture Chicago** at 20 N. Michigan (456-7000).

The following is a brief list of some of Chicago's public sculpture:

Alexander Calder, "Flamingo" (1974), Federal Building Plaza

Harry Bertoia, "Sound Sculpture" (1975), Amoco Building

Marc Chagall, "The Four Seasons" (1974), location-specific mosaic, One First National Plaza

Jean DuBuffet, "Monument à la Bête Debout" (1984), State of Illinois Center

Joan Miro, "Miro's Chicago" (1982), across from Daley Plaza

Claus Oldenberg, "Bat Column" (1977), 600 W. Madison

AUCTIONS

Leslie Hindman
215 W. Ohio   670-0010; hot line: 282-8466
The only local year-round auction house, Hindman holds monthly auctions of furniture, jewelry, Old Master prints, 19th- and 20th-century drawings and prints, and an occasional painting auction (a recent Van Gogh brought many millions).

Christie's (787-2765) and **Sotheby's** (664-6800) conduct business (appraisals, research, referrals) but do not host sales in Chicago.

SUGGESTED READING

Artspeak: A Guide to Contemporary Ideas, Movements and Buzzwords by Robert Atkins

Chicago—Some Other Traditions by Dennis Adrian

Off the Wall and *The Bride and Her Bachelors* by Calvin Tomkins

Surfaces: Two Decades of Painting in Chicago by Judith Russi Kirshner

MAGAZINES

For a general overview: *New Art Examiner* and *Art in America*

For more specific contemporary art issues: *Artforum* and *Flash Art*

—Joelle Rabion, with Linda Bubon and Ann Christopherson contributing
"Women's Art Scene"

PERFORMANCE ART

You may find yourself at a club with someone at a microphone threatening to force yuppies to kiss the tires of their BMWs, or you may find yourself in a storefront theater watching a ballet of actions employing household appliances in an extremely unorthodox fashion, or you may find yourself stepping out of an art gallery around a makeshift scaffolding under the El train to witness a single person simulate his or her own hanging. Any one of these "events" would be considered Chicago performance art.

There is just as much performance art happening in Chicago as in any other city in the country. Like other cities, Chicago's current scene grew out of our local visual arts and experimental theater communities of the late sixties and early seventies. Events called "Happenings" were staged by sculptors and painters in parking lots, warehouses, and art galleries. And during the late-night hour in theaters, writers and actors performed plays that left the audience with no plot to savor or song to hum on the way home. What connected these events was a breaking from their own traditions and a borrowing from others. Dancers, musicians, actors, writers, sculptors, filmmakers, painters, photographers, and directors all stole inspiration from each other and themselves to create a new medium, performance.

The movement was national and international, but in Chicago it picked up its own flavor. Performance inherently resists classification, but even the eclectic medium couldn't escape the Midwest tradition of the story, the need to tell a story. From the writings of Studs Turkel to the paintings of Roger Brown and Second City's story theater, the tradition of storytelling can be seen in Chicago performance. You can find this connection in the internationally known local performance group Goat Island's piece "Can't Take Johnny to The Funeral," where story is embedded in a 30-minute section of vigorous athletic choreography and not one word is spoken. Or you can see it in the monologuist Paula Killen's "Music Kills a Memory," where backed up by two torch singers and a schmaltz piano, she weaves a bizarre tale of three woman who meet at Sex & Love Anonymous and tour the country as a singing trio to keep from falling off the wagon again. It is turned on its head, twisted and inverted, and told again, but it is still storytelling.

Another Chicago trait of performance art is the cabaret variety show. Starting in the mid-eighties, when performance wasn't finding a home in the regular runnings of local theaters though growing all the same, it found an audience open to the unexpected in the more offbeat nightclubs, coffeehouses, and theaters. The artists call them group shows, where you might find a poet performer, a monologuist, a puppeteer, a fire-eater, a musician, and a novelty act, none lasting more than 15 minutes, and hosted by another performance artist disguised as an MC. Bridget Murphy has for five years now performed as Milly, hosting her "Milly's Orchid Show" moving from the underground Club Lower Links to the more upscale Park West. Other Artist's curated group shows happen at art galleries and clubs, basing the shows around themes, such as sexuality, madness, contemporary puppetry, feminism. These shows will run the gamut from a transvestite lipsynching Sinatra to someone wrapped in tape from head to toe confessing having committed childhood incest. Some themes are set to create a dialogue for artists and audience, and some are just serious fun.

WHO DOES IT

Anyone could call him or herself a performance artist. Even you yourself could start reading the index of this book aloud in a public place, or private place for that matter, and call yourself a performance artist. But some people have been taking performance seriously as a medium for a while now, and local individuals and groups to be on the look out for include Jeff Abell, Anna Brown, Joan Dickenson, Fluid Measure, Goat Island, James Grigsby, Michael K. Meyers, Iris Moore, Bridgid Murphy, Kya Overstreet, Matthew Owens, Carmela Rago, Andy Soma, Lawrence Steger, and Ken Thompson.

Many have focuses in other disciplines but are also considered performance artists: Abiogenesis Movement Ensemble (movement), Joan Jett Black (cross dressing), Timothy Buckley (dance), Justin Hayford (critic), Jellyeye (theater/dance), Paula Killen (theater), Loofah Method (music/poetry), Anita Loomis (theater), Lauri Macklin (dance), Jenny Magnus (theater/music), Lou Mallozzi (sound), Heather McAdams (film/cartoons), Robyn Orlin (dance), Suzie Silver (video), Cheryl Trykv (poetry), Sock Monkeys (dance).

WHERE IT HAPPENS

Performance is an open field, and to find out what you're getting yourself into, look for clues in the title or the way the event is presented. There are no rules to make it safe or predictable because performance as a rule doesn't try to give an audience what it might expect. You don't have to necessarily wear a rubber suit, but be willing and open to be challenged.

Performance can be found at home in several different reliable venues. Cabaret-style nightclubs, experimental theaters, art galleries, and dance spaces all regularly program performance art events in their monthly and yearly calendars. Here's a list:

Beacon Street Gallery
4520 N. Beacon   528-4526

Beacon Street Gallery at the School Street
1225 W. School   528-4526
With the full-fledged theater space at the Gallery and a new experimental space at the School Street, Beacon Street offers 30–50 different performance art events a year. It strives for a multicultural audience and programming and presents mostly visually based performance both locally and nationally. Running September–June, with an average ticket price of $6.

Chicago Filmmakers
1229 W. Belmont   281-8788
While presenting mostly experimental and documentary films, Filmmakers also offers performance through their Spoken Word Cafe and PerforMedia Events programming. Drawing from local artists, they are either single-evening events or extended runs by performance groups.

Cheryl Trykv.

Club Lower Links
954 W. Newport 248-5238
Lower Links is probably the most active venue in town with 4–10 different performance art events each month, usually one-night stands but sometimes once weekly for up to four weeks. Lower Links is *the* underground club of Chicago with a lot of cabaret, great new music, and occasional theater. Tickets are $3–$10.

The Dance Center of Columbia College
4730 N. Sheridan 271-7928
As part of Columbia College, the Dance Center presents contemporary dance where you are likely to see dancers telling stories moving in unusual costumes with slide projections as well as dance troupes that are developing a new vocabulary for dance. Up to three weekends a month, September–July, it presents work at either its own space or other theaters, gyms, or centers in Chicago. It brings in a lot of national, international, and local performers offering lecture demonstrations, workshops, performance previews, artists' discussions, and classes—all open to the public.

Gallery 2
1040 W. Huron 226-1449
This space is a wing of the School of the Art Institute of Chicago and open to the public. Between September and July it offers about 30 presentations of video, film, exhibition, and performance from graduate students to visiting artists with the School of the Art Institute. Many of the performances are free or at the most cost $5.

International Performance Studio
1517 W. Fullerton 821-4114
Housed with Facets Multimedia video and film center, IPS is a studio theater space that offers a limited series of 4 to 6 international artists and companies for 2- to 4-week runs. Most of the work is experimental theater but often leans heavily toward performance. Tickets around $12.

Links Hall Studio
3435 N. Sheffield 281-4114
Primarily a dance performance space, Links Hall also schedules movement-based performance with contemporary dance. Their regular programming offers 15–20 different local artists throughout the year, as well as the occasional short-term workshops or residencies by a visiting artist. Tickets are almost all $7.

N.A.M.E. Gallery
700 N. Carpenter 226-0671
As the oldest art gallery presenting performance in Chicago, N.A.M.E. presents about two weekends a month September–June. The programming includes video screenings, literary readings, and performance from local and national artists.

Randolph Street Gallery
756 N. Milwaukee 666-7737
The first art gallery in town to have a space purely for performance, they have performances almost every weekend September–July. Randolph Street calls

its programming Time Arts to include experimental film, sound, video, and performance.

WHERE TO FIND OUT ABOUT IT

The Reader
You can pick it up free starting every Thursday at public places all over the North Side. They have a "Performance Review" section, though the performance listings are sectioned under the "Theater" section.

NewCity
Free every week, coming out on Wednesday with reviews that are short quick reads, but better yet because it offers a separate "Performance Listings" section.

P-Form
A quarterly journal devoted to performance art that is published out of Randolph Street Gallery. It offers reviews, interviews, and features on mostly Chicago work, but with its recent change to a large-scale format, P-Form is also covering work in other cities and countries. You can get it at Randolph Street Gallery and local bookstores.

—Blair Thomas

PHOTOGRAPHY

NATIONAL EVENTS

Photography is often used to capture the essence of the times, so it is not surprising that the recent most controversial art events were those concerning photo exhibitions. In the spring of 1990 the Cincinnati Contemporary Art Center faced a $10,000 fine in obscenity charges in the first prosecution of an art museum in U.S. history. The museum director, Dennis Barrie, was to pay $2,000 and undergo a one-year prison term for the pandering of obscenity and illegal use of minors and for displaying sexually explicit materials: photographs by Robert Mapplethorpe in "The Perfect Moment," a traveling 175-piece retrospective. After a 10-day trial and the museum's loss of $300,000 in legal fees and additional expenses, Barrie was acquitted. The Mapplethorpe show was organized in 1988, a year before the artist died from AIDS. Before the Cincinnati showing, this exhibition was brought to the Museum of Contemporary Art in Chicago (1989), and with it came the highest attendance in the museum's history.

A year prior, in an exhibition at the Southeastern Center for Contemporary Art in Winston-Salem, there appeared a cibachrome photograph of a wooden crucifix submerged in an amber liquid: Andres Serrano's "Piss Christ" (1987). It is a beautiful and compelling work, without the title. The American Family Association caught news of this entry and issued a public statement charging Serrano with blasphemy, and it requested that the federal National Endowment for the Arts (NEA) support be withdrawn from the museum. Ironically, Serrano's photo represents an attack on the commercialization of religion and the multimillion-dollar evangelist industry. With preachers being caught in sex scandals, evading taxes, and making shady real estate deals, Serrano questions the exploitation of spiritual beliefs and the debasement of human values.

In response to these two shows, outspoken anti-arts Senator Jesse Helms (R–NC) requested that Congress cut the NEA visual arts program by $400,000 and ban for five years all money to the institutions sponsoring the exhibitions. The museums were subsequently placed on probation for one year, and the NEA budget was cut by $45,000, the exact amount of grant money given for the Mapplethorpe and Serrano shows. (See the "Arts" chapter for more on NEA funding.)

The obscenity obsession swept the country, and by the summer of 1991, museum directors were practicing censorship on their own turf. Elizabeth Broun, at Washington's Smithsonian Museum, had the Sol LeWitt's "Muybridge I" (1964) removed from the "Motion and Document—Sequence and Time" exhibition. The LeWitt work is an arrangement of 10 identical boxes lighted from inside, each having its own aperture. Within each box, one can observe a photograph of a naked woman, advancing toward the viewer, until the last box where only her navel is visible. The artist's purpose was to show the potential of any image of female nudity becoming subject to an erotic gaze, and the reality of a sexual interpretation. Broun found the piece "a degrading pornographic experience" and "offensive to women." After the organizers stated they would close the show entirely without this work, it was reinstalled—framed by warning signs with a book nearby for viewer comments. Broun perceived her act as a gesture toward the protection of women rather than one of censorship.

PHOTOGRAPHY IN CHICAGO

There is an abundance of photo resources in Chicago, including a major center for photography at the Museum of Contemporary Photography, many galleries, schools, and alternative places to investigate in pursuit of photo fulfillment.

Museums

Museum of Contemporary Photography
600 S. Michigan   663-5554
Hours: Monday–Friday, 10 A.M.–5 P.M.; Saturday, 12–5 P.M.; closed Sunday. Call during summer months for scheduling. Free admission.
This is the only museum in the Midwest dedicated exclusively to the medium of photography. As a development of the Chicago Center for Contemporary Photography, Columbia College founded the museum in 1984 to provide the public with exceptional programs in photographic instruction and exhibition. Although it has served primarily as a resource for the students of Columbia College, the museum's innovative and diverse exhibitions have created an international public following. Its mission is to promote the appreciation and understanding of contemporary photography and to further explore photography's relationships with art and culture. The permanent collection began in 1980 with an emphasis on American photography, and it is continuously being expanded with challenging current work. Other programs include special exhibits organized in collaboration with outside art institutions, a Print Study Room sponsoring midwestern photographers, lectures and panel discussions, traveling exhibitions, and publications. All shows are free.

Art Institute of Chicago
Michigan Avenue at Adams Street   443-3600
Hours: Monday, Wednesday–Friday, 10:30 A.M.–4:30 P.M.;
Tuesday, 10:30 A.M.–8 P.M.; Saturday, 10 A.M.–5 P.M.;
Sunday and holidays, 12–5 P.M..
$6 suggested donation, $3 for senior citizens, students, children 6–14, free for kids 5 and under; Tuesday, free to all.
Already by 1900, the Art Institute had mounted its first photography exhibition, and a permanent collection was initiated in 1949 with the donation of a major portion of the Alfred Stieglitz Collection by Georgia O'Keefe. Today the Institute's collection is the most considerable in the Midwest (15,000 works), holding both contemporary and historical photographs, with the Modern Master collection estimated as one of the strongest in the world. Acquisitions include early purchases of Paul Strand, Eugene Atget, and Andre Kertesz; the Julien Levy Collection, a gift of more than 200 photographs including Edward Weston; and most recently, the Ruttenberg donation, a diverse group of works ranging from street photography to obscure conceptual pieces.

For those interested in becoming more involved, the Institute's Photographic Society is a membership organization committed to sharing and increasing the knowledge of the art and history of photography and to learning about personal collecting, as well as raising funds for the museum collection. The group hosts private exhibitions and previews, lectures and symposiums, exclusive tours of private collections, and it offers opportunities for workshops through the Department of Photography.

Galleries

The photo galleries in Chicago each have a unique vision of photography's importance today. All are most definitely worth visiting.

Ehlers Caudill Gallery
750 N. Orleans   642-8611
Opened to the public in 1989, the two women operating this gallery have been in the photo business since the mid-1980s. Their primary focus is on the experimental and postmodern contemporary; however, the gallery also has a broad collection of 1920s and 1930s European vintage photographs. The dealers go twice a year to the auctions to stay on top of the market, as, unlike most contemporary art, vintage photography has maintained a steady market. Of the photo galleries in Chicago, this one follows the *aucourant*, including Holly Roberts, Sally Skoglin, and Helen Chadwick.

Catherine Edelman
300 W. Superior   266-2350
Committed to photographers working today, Edelman has had her contemporary gallery for 4½ years. Showing explorations of the traditional to the avant-garde in photography, she exhibits a variety of regional and national names, including Barbara Crane, Michael Kenna, Richard Misrach, and David Cloud.

Edwynn Houk
200 W. Superior   943-0698
When Houk recently formed a New York partnership, much of his well-known vintage left for New York. Now one finds great-quality contemporary photography, including Annie Leibovitz and Sally Mann, and modern Andre Kertesz. Houk also produces exquisite exhibition catalogs and represents many photography estates. Call for details.

Other Galleries That Often Show Photography

Chicago Cultural Center
78 E. Washington   744-6640
Thoughtful, provocative exhibitions of local and national photographers, changing every six to eight weeks. Galleries are on the first and fourth floors.

Columbia College Art Gallery
72 E. 11th   663-1600, ext. 104
Affiliated with Columbia College, this gallery alternates student and alumni exhibitions and has undergraduate and master's photo shows each year.

Jacques Baruch Gallery, Ltd.
40 E. Delaware 944-3377
Private dealer Anne Baruch shows fine prints, photos, and drawings primarily from Czechoslovakia and Hungary.

Kelmscott Gallery
4611 N. Lincoln 784-2559
Shows architectural photography and exhibitions of a sociopolitical nature. The gallery is away from downtown but worth the trip.

Nancy Lurie
1632 N. LaSalle 337-2883
Often exhibits contemporary American photographers.

Photo Events

Chicago Photograph & Print Fair
Held each September with a changing location; watch the papers for the listing. Most of the Chicago photo galleries do not participate directly in the annual International Art Exposition but do benefit from the traffic generated at this important event.

Press

In Chicago, photography receives more press than most other art forms. The critics are extremely devoted to providing a thorough and up-to-date portrayal of what's where, when, and why. Check the "Friday" section in the *Chicago Tribune* for exhibition openings and listings and other photography-related matters. Chicago also has an abundance of camera clubs, photo contests, workshops, and seminars year-round.

Education

If you are considering schooling, all of the following should be researched; Chicago has a vast selection of schools and approaches to teaching photography.

Columbia College
600 S. Michigan 663-1600
Columbia offers both undergraduate and master's programs in photography. A solid technical foundation in the bachelor's program can become more individualized in the graduate classes, which include experimental and architectural photography, as well as history and criticism courses. This school produces many commercial photographers.

School of the Art Institute of Chicago
Columbus Drive at Jackson Boulevard 443-3783
For a more academic approach to photography, the B.F.A. program includes basic photo classes. At a graduate level, the students directly apply their knowledge; work is strictly in the studio and critiqued by a faculty member, creating a personalized tutorial.

IIT, Institute of Design
3300 S. Federal   567-3250
The Institute of Design offers an intensive liberal arts undergraduate degree
and more specialized master's of design in photography, with an emphasis
on social documentary and computer imaging.

University of Illinois–Chicago (UIC)
601 S. Morgan   996-3337
Photography classes here are both practical and theoretical and are given at
undergraduate and graduate levels. The M.F.A. program includes a four-
semester series of "contemporary seminars" with an emphasis on theory and
is completed by an independent study where one is critiqued by a panel of
outside professionals.

University of Chicago Midway Studios
6016 S. Ingleside   753-4821
The U of C provides a most rigorous approach to education and holds great
respect nationwide; however, a specific program in photography is not offered. Photography courses are incorporated in the general B.F.A. and M.F.A.
programs, with theory and history emphasized.

Photo Labs

Chroma Color
1001 W. Adams   243-2500
Will process the film of all photographer's assistants at a nominal fee. Great
color processors.

Gamma
314 W. Superior   337-0022
A very seriously staffed photo operation. High-quality film processing, a little
less expensive than Ross-Ehlert.

Pallas
319 W. Erie   787-4600
Former Gamma people. The prices are competitive, and the staff is very
service oriented.

Ron Gordon
714 S. Dearborn   663-9447
An architectural photographer himself, Ron does an amazing job of fine art
black and white film printing, all hand-done with archival formatting.

Ross Ehlert
225 W. Illinois   644-0244
Everybody's favorite—a great-quality, professional lab with excellent service.

Equipment and Film

Calumet
520 W. Erie   440-4920
The professional photographer's store. Despite the "hard sell," sometimes
sexist behavior of the staff, here one finds a great inventory of rental equipment: cameras, videos, projectors, lighting, with sane rental policies.

Central Camera
230 S. Wabash   427-5580
Great place to buy a camera, however simple or complex. They do a fabulous job on color film processing. All for a good price.

Darkroom Aids
3449 N. Lincoln   248-4301
Good for general supplies.

Helix
310 S. Racine   421-6000
Excellent place for well-priced equipment—ignore the occasional staff superiority complex.

Lion Photo
66 E. Madison   346-2288
For the nonprofessional. Offers cameras, accessories, and film processing. Locations outside the downtown area also.

—Joelle Rabion

LITERARY LIFE

According to common wisdom, Chicago has never really thought of itself as a literary town. A newspaper town, sure, but that's quite a different image. There's a definite reverse snobbism at work here. Chicagoans prefer to think of themselves as blue collar, or entrepreneurial, or anything but bookish and "cultured," right?

OK, then who are all those people sitting around in all those coffeehouses with their noses buried in what could only be called, well, books? The truth is, Chicago is a city of subcultures, and the literary subculture runs pretty strong and always has. How else do you explain Harriet Monroe and *Poetry*, the little magazine that launched a national literary movement in the 1910s? And how do you account for Theodore Dreiser, Saul Bellow, Paul Carroll, or the hundreds of other creative writers who have lived and worked here over the years?

Today, literary life in Chicago encompasses a variety of forms, from small, specialized bookstores to popular, crowded poetry readings; from established literary journals to upstart, activist presses. In this chapter I've tried to capture all facets of the literary scene—everything from the chain bookstores in the Loop to the latest alternative literary journals.

BOOKSTORES

General Bookstores

Chicago is home to a plethora of chain stores as well as many independent booksellers. Most of the stores pride themselves on their knowledgeable, friendly service and a wide selection of books ranging from best-sellers to classics, encompassing all kinds of fiction and nonfiction. Their palpable love of books makes them great places to browse and buy. Many bookstores hold readings, book parties, and other events and serve as cultural centers as well as excellent places to find great books.

Barnes & Noble
659 W. Diversey   871-9004

Barnes & Noble
1701 N. Sherman, Evanston   (708) 328-0883

Stuart Brent Books
670 N. Michigan   337-6357
Pleasantly overcrowded; a Michigan Avenue fixture.

Chandler's
630 Davis, Evanston   (708) 475-7200

Coopersmith's
900 N. Michigan   337-0330

Doubleday Bookshops, Inc.
435 E. Illinois   222-2524
In North Pier.

57th Street Books
1301 E. 57th 684-1300
Part of the Seminary Co-op (see below), 57th Street excels in literature, film, children's books, music, mysteries, science fiction, and just about everything else.

Great Expectations Book Store
911 Foster, Evanston (708) 864-3881
Particularly strong in fiction, literary criticism, and philosophy.

Guild Books
2456 N. Lincoln 525-3667
Focuses on politics, literature, and the arts. Its longtime commitment to social change has made it a leader in Chicago's cultural scene.

Left Bank Bookstall
104 S. Oak Park, Oak Park (708) 383-4700

Lincoln Park Bookshop
2423 N. Clark 477-7087

Modern Bookstore
3118 S. Halsted 225-7911
Small general bookstore featuring modern literature, history, and social thought.

Platypus Bookshop
606 Dempster, Evanston (708) 866-8040
Contemporary American, Native American, African-American, and foreign literature, as well as women's studies, spirituality, psychology, children's books. Stocks many interesting books from small presses.

Rizzoli International Bookstore & Gallery
Water Tower Place 642-3500
Definitely not the place to spill a cup of coffee. Beautiful collection of art, architecture, design, and foreign language books. Plush carpeting, classical music—a browser's delight.

Sandmeyer's Bookstore
714 S. Dearborn 922-2104
Literature, children's books, travel, cards.

Seminary Co-op Bookstore
5757 S. University 752-4381
Internationally known, the Seminary Co-op stocks more than 100,000 titles and has one of the best selections of academic books in the country. Anyone can join the cooperative; members receive a discount.

Unabridged Bookstore
3251 N. Broadway 883-9119
Excellent fiction and film-theater collections, plus a huge gay-lesbian section. Helpful, knowledgeable staff.

Chain Bookstores

Chicago has two excellent local chains, the venerable **Kroch's & Brentano's** and the upstart **Barbara's Bookstore**. Both hold readings, book signings, and other events regularly; cited here are Chicago, Evanston, and Oak Park locations.

Barbara's Bookstore
1350 N. Wells   642-5044
3130 N. Broadway   477-0411
1800 N. Clybourn   664-1113
1100 Lake, Oak Park   (708) 848-9140
Barbara's Bestsellers, 2 N. Riverside   258-8007
Barbara's offers a superb collection of classic and current literature. Browsing is encouraged, there's a fine selection of magazines and periodicals, and the staff is very helpful.

Kroch's & Brentano's
29 S. Wabash   332-7500
230 S. Clark   553-0171
516 S. Michigan   321-0989
30 N. LaSalle   704-0287
2070 N. Clybourn   528-2800
Water Tower Place   943-2452
1530 E. 53rd   288-0145
1711 Sherman, Evanston   (708) 328-7220
1028 Lake, Oak Park   (708) 848-9003
At Kroch's, "the full-service bookstore," you'll find a wide selection of books plus gifts, cards, and calendars at many of its outlets. Its flagship at 29 S. Wabash is still a great—if chaotic—store, with a large magazine section, an especially strong crop of technical and business books, and bargain books galore.

Three national chains offer Loop and shopping mall pedestrians convenient locations, the latest best-sellers, and various specialties.

Crown Books
24 N. Wabash   782-7667
201 W. Jackson   341-0505
309 W. Washington   346-8677
1660 N. Wells   642-3950
2711 N. Clark   327-1551
4842 W. Irving Park   736-0886
Discounted best-sellers and other books, as well as a nice selection of inexpensive remaindered books.

Waldenbooks
Brickyard Shopping Center   745-8660
Ford City Shopping Center   581-4833
Sears Tower   876-0308
616 W. Diversey   549-3792
127 W. Madison   236-8446
Particularly strong on self-help, do-it-yourself, cooking, and current events books.

B. Dalton Bookseller
175 W. Jackson   922-5219
645 N. Michigan   944-3702
129 N. Wabash   236-7615
222 Merchandise Mart Plaza   329-1881
Their Wabash store has one of the largest computer book and software departments in the city.

Specialty Bookstores

Chicago's many ethnic groups and subcultures support a variety of specialty bookstores with important, enlightening, fascinating, and sometimes very odd collections. But don't take my word for it—see for yourself.

Minority, Women, Gay-Lesbian Studies

African-American Book Centers
7524 S. Cottage Grove   651-9191
1801 E. 71st   752-2275
Diverse collection of fiction, social issues, history, psychology, African history and culture, mysticism, religion, art, theater, children's books. Book parties, readings, and discussions are frequent. Children's storytelling and annual children's book fair.

Afrocentric Bookstore
234 S. Wabash   939-1956

Freedom Found Books/The Underground
5206 S. Harper   288-2837
1727 E. 87th   768-8869
General bookstore specializing in African-American culture.

21st Century Books
607 E. Muddy Waters (43rd St.)   538-2188
A self-described Radical and Third World Literature Distribution Center open Thursday–Saturday, serving the African-American community. The diverse collection includes African, American, and Caribbean works. Also operates a small publishing house.

West Side Books & Afrocentric Boutique
5937 W. North   622-0052
16 S. Pulaski   722-0723

NAES College Bookstore
2838 W. Peterson   761-5000
Chicago's Native American college offers a wide selection of American Indian books.

People Like Us Books
3321 N. Clark   248-6363
The city's only exclusively gay and lesbian bookstore.

Women & Children First Bookstore
5233 N. Clark   769-9299
A key feminist institution and gathering place. Literature by and for women, children's books, gay-lesbian books, women's music, posters, and jewelry. A monthly calendar lists readings, discussions, workshops. Children's storytelling and monthly Women's Book Discussion.

Ethnic and Foreign Language

Europa Bookstore
54 E. Walton   335-9677
824 Foster, Evanston   (708) 866-6262
Large selection of foreign language books and dictionaries; some periodicals.

Scholars Bookstore
1379 E. 53rd   288-6565
Specializes in Asian studies. Books in Japanese, Chinese, Korean, Vietnamese, and other languages, as well as Asian studies books in English.

Rosenblum's Hebrew Book Store
2906 W. Devon   262-1700

Chicago Hebrew Bookstore
2942 W. Devon   973-6636

Japan Books & Records
3450 W. Peterson   463-7755

Korean Books
5800 N. Lincoln   769-1010

Polonia Bookstore & Publishing Company
2886 N. Milwaukee   489-2554

Russian-American Bookstore
2746 W. Devon   761-3233

Spanish Speaking Bookstore
5127 N. Clark   878-2117

Tres Americas Books
3532 W. Irving Park   509-9090
Large selection of fiction, children's books, dictionaries, and reference books in Spanish.

Ukrainian Bookstore
2315 W. Chicago   276-6373

New Age

Aurum Solis
5142 N. Clark   334-2120
Occult, metaphysical, and theosophical books and supplies.

Healing Earth Resources
2570 N. Lincoln   327-8459

Isis Rising
1129 Emerson, Evanston   (708) 570-0055

The New Moon
1016 North, Oak Park   (708) 386-0085
Metaphysics, women and men's spirituality, philosophy, and personal growth.

Occult Bookstore
1561 N. Milwaukee   292-0995
Witchcraft, magic, ESP, the occult, parapsychology.

Vedanta Book Store
5423 S. Hyde Park   363-0027

Travel

Ed and Fred
1007 W. Webster   477-6220
Ed and Fred own and operate this inviting travel store, which has a particularly good selection of books on environmentally sound, anti-touristy, and adventure travel. There's a plush armchair and free coffee, and help yourself to the candy jar!

Grand Tour World Bookstore
3229 N. Clark   929-1836
Comprehensive travel store featuring guidebooks, dictionaries, maps, foreign language novels, and children's books.

Kopi, A Traveler's Cafe
5317 N. Clark   989-5674

Rand McNally Map & Travel Store
444 N. Michigan   321-1751
150 S. Wacker   332-2009

The Savvy Traveler
50 E. Washington, 2nd floor   263-2100
Transport yourself from the bustling all-too-familiar streets of the Loop to distant lands by taking the elevator up to the second floor of 50 E. Washington and browsing through books devoted to every corner of the earth.

Theater, Plays, Film, and Television

Act I
2632 N. Halsted   348-6757
The largest collection of theater books and plays, new and used, in the city. Also theater magazines.

Metro Golden Memories
5425 W. Addison   736-4133
Film, TV, and old-time radio books. Tapes and records of old radio shows and big bands, posters, cards.

Scenes Coffeehouse & Dramatist Bookstore
3168 N. Clark   525-1007
An extensive stock of plays and theater and film books in a casual, relaxed coffeehouse.

The Wayback Machine
5725 N. Central   594-1214
Books and memorabilia on movies, TV, film stars; poster art and collectibles.

Mystery, Science Fiction, Fantasy, and Horror

Aleph Bookshop
831 Main, Evanston   (708) 869-6410
Used and rare science fiction, fantasy, and horror. Shares space with Chicago Historical Bookworks.

I Love a Mystery
55 E. Washington   236-1338

Mystery Loves Company Bookstore
3338 N. Southport   935-1000

Stars Our Destination
2942 N. Clark   871-2722
Science fiction, fantasy, and horror books and art.

Comics

Comic Relief
69 E. Madison   332-0043
219 W. Jackson   431-1515
1601 Sherman, Evanston   (708) 869-3888
DC Comics.

Larry's Comic Book Store
1219A W. Devon   274-1832
New and back issues.

Variety Comic Book Store
4602 N. Western   334-2550

Miscellaneous

Quimby's
1328 N. Damen   342-0910
Specializes in small press and underground books, magazines, and comics.

New World Resource Center
1476 W. Irving Park   348-3370
An independent left bookstore. Progressive titles, international newspapers and periodicals, posters, cassettes. Holds discussion sessions and classes.

Revolution Books
3449 N. Sheffield   528-5353
Offers "books on the burning questions of the day!" Progressive, radical, and revolutionary books. Philosophy, politics, economics, international books, novels, and women's and black studies. Literature of the Revolutionary Communist Party.

C. G. Jung Institute Bookstore
550 Callan, Evanston   (708) 475-4848
Psychology, dreams, mythology, fairy tales, women's and men's studies, art and creativity, spirituality.

Psychology Bookstore
220 S. State, 6th floor   341-3480
Specializes in clinical psychology.

Abraham Lincoln Bookshop
357 W. Chicago   944-3085
Regional history, the Civil War, Abraham Lincoln. Rare books and first editions.

Chicago Architecture Foundation Shop & Tour Center
224 S. Michigan   922-3432
Local and general architecture and design books, gifts, cards.

Chicago Historical Bookworks
831 Main, Evanston   (708) 869-6410
Chicago, Illinois, and Midwest history, books by Chicago authors, Civil War, WPA publications. Also a publishing house specializing in regional history, biographies, and WPA guides. Shares space with Aleph Bookshop.

Prairie Avenue Bookshop
711 S. Dearborn   922-8311
Architecture, design, science.

N. Fagin Books
1039 W. Grand   829-5252
Natural history and anthropology.

The Children's Bookstore
2465 N. Lincoln   248-2665

Books Off Berwyn
5220 N. Clark   878-9800
Specializes in Dover books.

Season to Taste
911 W. School   327-0210
Large selection of cooking and wine books.

Note: Museum bookstores often contain excellent collections of books in their particular fields. Check out the Art Institute, Chicago Academy of Science, Chicago Historical Society, the DuSable Museum of African-American History, and the Museum of Contemporary Art.

Used Books

Aspidistra Bookshop
2630 N. Clark   549-3129
Dusty, musty, lots of books.

Back Alley Books
6920 N. Glenwood   465-4610

Bookman's Alley
1712 Sherman, Evanston   (708) 869-6999
Many comfortable rooms filled with used books, rare books, first editions, artifacts. Homey atmosphere.

Bookman's Corner
2959 N. Clark   929-8298

Booksellers Row
2445 N. Lincoln   348-1170
408 S. Michigan   427-4242
Especially good fiction selection at the Lincoln Avenue location.

Bookworks
3444 N. Clark   871-5318

Fiery Clockface
5311 N. Clark   728-4227

Officer Bob's Paperbacks
4340 N. Milwaukee   736-9522

O'Gara & Wilson's Bookstore
1311 E. 57th   363-0993
Huge selection—you could get lost in here.

Powell's Bookstore
1501 E. 57th   955-7780
2850 N. Lincoln   248-1444
Another massive selection.

Shake, Rattle & Read
4812 N. Broadway   334-5311
A small space crammed with books from top to bottom.

University Bookstores

Beck's Bookstore (serving Loyola University and Truman College)
6435 N. Sheridan   743-2281 (and other locations)

Columbia College Bookstore
624 S. Wabash   427-4860
Specializes in books on photography, film, video, and other creative arts.

Epicenter Bookshop
University of Illinois at Chicago, Circle Center
750 S. Halsted, #210   413-5540
Mainstream and academic publishing, including history, fiction, poetry, philosophy, women's and black studies.

University of Chicago Bookstore
970 E. 58th   702-8729
Academic and general interest, medical and scientific.

DePaul University Bookstore
2324 N. Seminary   362-8423
Primarily arts and sciences.

DePaul Loop Bookstore
25 E. Jackson   362-6225
Business and law, trade and textbooks.

Northwestern University Norris Center Store
1999 N. Sheridan, Evanston   (708) 491-3991
Trade and textbooks.

Roosevelt University Bookstore
431 S. Wabash   341-3592
Academic and general interest.

LIBRARIES

Hooray! After decades of civic inaction and political wrangling, Chicago finally has a real central library—and it's proved a hit (entering the library, you'll be surprised at how many people still do seem to read). We're so happy about this turn of events we've included the library as one of the *"other* top 10 sights" in Chicago; see that chapter for details. But for the record, it's the **Harold Washington Public Library** (400 S. State, 747-4300; Monday–Thursday, 9 A.M.–7 P.M.; Friday–Saturday, 9 A.M.–5 P.M.). Chicago's two regional public libraries contain extensive collections, comfortable reading rooms, and helpful staff. Both offer GED classes, English as a Second Language, children's programming, and other events. (Hours for both: Monday–Thursday, 9 A.M.–9 P.M.; Friday–Saturday, 9 A.M.–5 P.M.). The Chicago Public Library system also operates more than 80 branch libraries, located throughout the city and listed in the "Government" section in the front of the phone book.

Conrad Sulzer Library
4455 N. Lincoln   744-7616
Housed in an attractive, modern facility, the North Side's library includes an excellent children's section and all the periodicals you could ever want to read.

Carter G. Woodson Library
9525 S. Halsted   747-6900
The South Side branch houses the Vivian G. Harsh Collection of Afro-American History and Literature.

But your library options are not limited to public facilities. The city also has independent and university libraries containing both general and specialized collections. Call ahead to find out about regulations and hours.

Independent Libraries

Newberry Library
60 W. Walton   943-9090
The Newberry is an independent research and reference library specializing in history and the humanities. Free and open to the public, the library offers an extensive noncirculating collection of rare books, maps, and manuscripts from Europe and the Americas dating from the late Middle Ages to the 20th century. Its internationally known collection attracts scholars from across the country. If you're exploring your roots, its excellent genealogy collection might help you out. The library also sponsors an intriguing array of classes, concerts, tours, and other educational programs. Free tours are given on Thursdays at 3 P.M. and Saturdays at 10:30 A.M.

Art Institute Library
Michigan Avenue and Adams Street   443-3666
You guessed it—an excellent collection of books on art, art history, and architecture.

Chicago Historical Society Library
Clark Street and North Avenue   642-4600
This is the place to research Chicago and Midwestern history, as well as 19th-century American history (particularly the Civil War).

Midwest Women's Center Library
53 W. Jackson   922-8530
This library offers a noncirculating collection of books and periodicals on women's issues. It's particularly strong in employment (especially blue-collar skilled trade) and culture. It also keeps extensive files on women's groups, including brochures, newsletters, and other materials.

Municipal Reference Library
City Hall, # 1002, 121 N. LaSalle   744-4992
An excellent resource for information about the city, the Municipal Reference Library contains reports written by city agencies, building and tax code information, ordinances and regulations, statistics, and newspaper clippings.

University Libraries

The regulations for using university libraries vary from school to school. Since most are open on Sundays while Chicago's public libraries are not, they may be your best bet for a quiet Sunday place to study or do research.

University of Illinois at Chicago
801 S. Morgan   996-2726
Roomy and well stocked.

Regenstein Library
1100 E. 57th   702-7874
The University of Chicago's library is one of the best in the country but almost impossible for ordinary folks to enter.

Northwestern University Library
1935 Sheridan, Evanston   (708) 491-7658
More accessible to the public, like those at Loyola and DePaul.

Loyola University Library
6525 N. Sheridan   274-3000

DePaul University Library
2323 N. Seminary   341-8085
DePaul also has a good business library at its downtown campus (25 E. Jackson, 341-8432).

READINGS

Readings are all the rage nowadays at bookstores, coffeehouses, bars, and various cultural gathering places around the city—so much so that it's impossible to include here all the spots to catch the latest in word slinging. Three free, widely distributed publications—*NewCity*, the *Reader*, and *Letter eX*—carry listings of who, when, and where. Also, the *Chicago Tribune's* Sunday book section contains a calendar of literary events. But here's a list of some of the more interesting venues for readings and discussions.

Bookstores

African-American Book Centers

Barbara's Bookstore
(various locations)

Kroch's & Brentano's
(various locations)

Fiery Clockface

57th Street Books
(the Hyde Park Poetry Series)

Guild Books

Left Bank Bookstall

New World Resource Center

Unabridged Bookstore

Women & Children First Bookstore

Cultural Centers and Performance Spots

Chicago Cultural Center
78 E. Washington   744-6630
The former library still offers a plethora of readings, lectures, discussions, and storytelling sessions. It issues a monthly calendar.

Guild Complex at the Hot House
1565 N. Milwaukee   278-2210
This center of alternative culture holds a variety of events, including the NEA Poetry/Fiction Series, roundtable discussions, performance art, and poetry and fiction readings.

Harold Washington Library
400 S. State   747-4300
Check out its crowded monthly calendar.

Links Hall
3435 N. Sheffield   281-0824
A longtime alternative cultural mecca.

The Poetry Center of the School of the Art Institute
Columbus Drive and Jackson Boulevard   477-3287
Often features guest poets of national stature.

Bars and Coffeehouses

The Bop Shop
1807 W. Division   235-3232
"The New, New, Upbeat Dancing Poets" open-mike poetry on Monday nights.

Cafe Voltaire
3231 N. Clark   528-3136
Holds poetry workshops with performance and readings of songs and poems composed during the session.

DeJoie's Bistro
230 W. Kinzie   528-8723
Tuesdays are Poets Night Too, featuring open-mike poetry, prose, and verse of African-American writers.

Dreamerz
1516 N. Milwaukee   252-1155
Offers the Dreamerz' Fiction Series.

Estelle's
2013 W. North   486-8760
Home of the Wicker Park Poetry Project.

Fitzgerald's
6615 W. Roosevelt, Berwyn   (708) 788-2118
West Side Poetry Slam, Tuesdays.

Green Mill
4802 N. Broadway   878-5552
Home of the Uptown Poetry Slam, the grandfather of poetry slams. (Trust Chicagoans to turn a poetry reading into something resembling a sports event.) Sunday night open-mike performance and competition, featuring wildly cheering audiences.

No Exit
6970 N. Glenwood   743-3355
Sponsors "In One Ear," an open-mike poetry series.

Spices Jazz Bar
812 N. Franklin   664-6222
Monday night is Poets Nite, open-mike poetry with guest hosts. Crowded but intimate atmosphere, African-American poetry and jazz.

GETTING PUBLISHED

Whether you're a poet, an investigative reporter or some other form of word-monger, Chicago offers opportunities for getting published. The city supports a variety of newspapers, magazines, literary journals, book publishers, and other outlets for the written word. The two largest free weeklies, the *Reader* and *NewCity*, welcome freelance writers, as does the *Heartland Journal*, a free paper that appears every month or so. The neighborhood Lerner newspapers frequently use stringers to cover local events. Even the *Tribune* and *Sun-Times* publish freelance articles, although they're pretty hard to crack—it's best to call first and discuss your idea with the appropriate editor. A diverse array of magazines—local and national, specialized and general—are published here.

Some resources for finding both local and national publishing outlets are the *Writer's Guide to Chicago Area Publishers*, the *Writer's Market*, the *Writer's Handbook*, the *International Directory of Little Magazines and Small Presses*, the *Gale Directory* (a guide to magazines), and *Writer's Digest*. The Chicago Public Library carries all these guides. It also carries periodicals and literary journals from around the country.

To get you started, here are some listings of local publications.

Literary Journals

Another Chicago Magazine
P.O. Box 11223, Chicago, 60611
Contemporary poetry, essays, and fiction, published by Another Chicago Press.

Black Books Bulletin
7524 S. Cottage Grove, Chicago, 60619
Reviews and essays published bimonthly, plus a more extensive annual edition with fiction, poetry, and criticism. Published by the Institute of Positive Education, an umbrella organization for several African-American cultural institutions.

Chicago Review
5801 S. Kenwood, Chicago, 60637
Well-established quarterly that publishes poetry, fiction, and essays. Published chapters of Burroughs's *Naked Lunch* in the fifties. Still known for printing experimental works.

Letter eX
1608 N. Milwaukee, Chicago, 60647
Free, widely distributed monthly poetry newsletter publishes reviews, essays, interviews, and news about the poetry scene. Contains an extensive calendar of readings and other events.

Libido: The Journal of Sex and Sensibility
Libido Inc., P.O. Box 146721, Chicago, 60614
Carries fiction, poetry, essays, photography, and cartoons. The title pretty much says it all.

Literary Xpress
P.O. Box 438583, Chicago, 60643
Poetry, essays, reviews, drawings, and photographs by women of color. Published quarterly by the Literary Exchange (see below).

New American Writing
2920 W. Pratt, Chicago, 60645
The latest poetry, fiction, and essays, published by Oink Press.

NOMMO
P.O. Box 438488, Chicago, 60643-8488
An annual anthology of African-American poetry, fiction, and essays, published by OBAhouse Press. Solicits material from all over the country, including work developed through the OBAC Writers' Workshop (see below).

other voices
University of Illinois at Chicago, Department of English (M/C 162), Box 4348, Chicago, 60680
Dedicated to fresh, original, diverse stories and novel excerpts. Published twice a year.

Poetry
60 W. Walton, Chicago, 60610
Now housed at the Newberry Library, this venerable literary journal (founded in 1912) introduced the world to the likes of T. S. Eliot, Ezra Pound, Marianne Moore, and William Carlos Williams. Published monthly by the Modern Poetry Association.

Primavera
700 E. 61st, P.O. Box 377547, Chicago, 60637
Founded by a University of Chicago feminist organization in 1975 as a vehicle for women artists and writers who could not find a voice in the mainstream press. Publishes both male and female writers with a feminist outlook.

Review of Contemporary Fiction
236 S. Washington, Naperville, 60540
Features criticism of contemporary novelists.

Rhino
8403 W. Normal, Niles, 60648
Poetry and short prose; published annually.

Triquarterly
2020 Ridge, Evanston, 60201
Nationally known literary magazine publishing fiction, poetry, and essays by Americans and Europeans. Affiliated with Northwestern University.

Whitewalls
P.O. Box 8204, Chicago, 60680
Focuses on writings by visual artists, including journals, essays, fiction, and poetry.

Wire
Eye of the Comet Press, 2696 Summit, Highland Park, 60035
A relatively new journal that publishes fiction, poetry, and criticism, with an emphasis on the experimental. Has a growing readership.

Book Publishers

Publishing is actually big business in Chicago, although the area's publishing industry lacks the glamour and visibility of New York City's. That's because most of our publishers specialize in business and law, textbooks, reference books, medical books, and other meat-and-potatoes subjects. You don't see too many best-sellers published here, but you will find lots of people working in the publishing industry. Also, Chicago's publishers are spread throughout the city and suburbs, so there's not a real cohesive publishing community. But the diversity and number of area publishers may surprise you.

Trade Publishers

Academy Chicago, Ltd.
213 W. Institute, Chicago, 60610   751-7300
Publishes well-designed fiction, mysteries, feminist novels, biographies, books of local interest.

Another Chicago Press
P.O. Box 11223, Chicago, 60611
Poetry, fiction, drama, often of the more experimental variety.

Bonus Books Inc.
160 E. Illinois, Chicago, 60611   467-0580
Publishes trade nonfiction.

Chicago Review Press
814 N. Franklin, Chicago, 60610   337-0747
Specializes in trade nonfiction and books of local interest (like the one you've got in your hands).

Contemporary Books
180 N. Michigan, Chicago, 60601   782-9181
Chicago's largest trade publisher by far, Contemporary concentrates on popular nonfiction such as cookbooks, sports books, health and fitness, nutrition, how-to books, popular culture.

Noble Press
213 W. Institute, Chicago, 60610   642-1168
A young, activist-oriented publisher of books on social, ecological, and environmental issues.

Third Side Press
2250 W. Farragut   271-3029
Founded in 1991, Third Side publishes feminist books with a focus on lesbian fiction and women's nonfiction. Publisher Midge Stocker is always on the lookout for new manuscripts.

Third World Press
7524 S. Cottage Grove, Chicago, 60619   651-0700
The longest-running African-American publisher in the country (founded in 1967), and one of the largest. Publishes fiction and nonfiction in all genres, attracting writers from around the country and internationally, including Gwendolyn Brooks, Sonia Sanchez, Chancellor Williams, and Keorapetse Kgositsile.

Triumph Books
644 S. Clark   939-3330

University Presses

Loyola University Press
3441 N. Ashland, Chicago, 60657   281-1818

Northwestern University Press
625 Colfax, Evanston, 60201   (708) 491-5313

University of Chicago Press
5801 S. Ellis, Chicago, 60637   702-7700

Other Publishers

The city's largest book publisher is **Encyclopaedia Britannica; World Book** is here too. Textbook and educational publishing is big—**Scott-Foresman & Co.; Holt, Rinehart & Winston; the National Textbook Co.; McDougall, Littell & Co.;** and **Ligature Inc.,** an innovative development house, head the list. Business publishers include **Probus Publishing Co., Financial Sourcebooks, Dearborn Trade, Business One Irwin.** For a more complete list of Chicago-area publishers (of both books and periodicals), see *A Writer's Guide to Chicago-Area Publishers*, edited by Jerold L. Kellman (1985).

Resources/Organizations

Chicago Book Clinic
111 E. Wacker, #200, Chicago, 60601   946-1700
Open to anyone involved in or interested in all facets of publishing, with a special emphasis on book production. Holds an annual book show for book designers and a biannual publishing trade show, PubTech. Sponsors educational programs and monthly meetings on a wide range of topics.

Chicago Dramatists Workshop
1105 W. Chicago, Chicago, 60622 633-0630
A nonprofit theater organization whose mission is to develop original works and writers for the stage. Offers play readings, panel discussions, and playwriting and screenwriting classes. Provides a supportive environment for playwrights to develop their craft. Also operates a theater where new works are produced and issues a quarterly newsletter.

Chicago Women in Publishing
2 N. Riverside Plaza, #2400, Chicago, 60606 641-6311
Networking and support services for women involved or interested in any area of publishing. Educational monthly meetings feature guest speakers and panels. Other services include a support group for freelance editors, a job referral service, a monthly newsletter, and an annual all-day career workshop.

Feminist Writers Guild
P.O. Box 25477, Chicago, 60625 784-6725
Offers workshops on fiction, playwriting, poetry, and nonfiction writing, book discussion groups, a newsletter, and calendar of events.

Independent Writers of Chicago
7855 Gross Point Road, Skokie, 60077 (708) 676-3784
A resource for professional freelance writers, IWOC holds monthly meetings and educational seminars on writing and on operating a freelance business. Helps members connect with potential clients and expand their client base. Produces a biannual rate survey and an annual directory of freelance writers. Operates the Writers' Line, a job referral service. Holds an annual freelance writing trade show to introduce potential clients to area freelancers.

The Literary Exchange
P.O. Box 438583, Chicago, 60643 509-6881
Writers' support network and membership organization for women of color. Holds book discussion sessions and other events. Publishes the *Literary Xpress* (see above), which includes a quarterly calendar and news of interest to the community.

Organization of Black American Culture (OBAC) Writers' Workshop
P.O. Box 438488, Chicago, 60643-8488
On every first and third Wednesday of the month, black writers gather to read and critique works in progress at the South Side Community Art Center (3831 S. Michigan, 373-1026). More than 25 years old, the OBAC Writers' Workshop also runs OBAhouse Press, which publishes NOMMO (see above) and other anthologies of African-American writing.

—*Deborah R. Weiner*

ARCHITECTURE

THE CHICAGO SCHOOL

1871 is the ideal time to begin a brief history of Chicago architecture. That year the core of the city was razed by a fire reputed to have been started by a cow. It's only fair, therefore, to give Mrs. O'Leary's bovine a substantial portion of the credit for the high quality of Chicago's architecture. Fortunately, the push to fill the void left by the fire was concurrent with two major technological developments: new lightweight iron and steel framing systems, which freed architects and engineers from the solid masonry bearing walls that had restricted both the size of window openings and the overall height of buildings, and the elevator, which freed them from the constraints of keeping rentable space an easy climb from street level. The architecture that followed is now often referred to as the "Chicago school."

Rookery Building
209 S. LaSalle
Burnham and Root, 1888
Restored in 1991 by the McClier Corporation and Hasbrouck Peterson Associates, from 1872 to 1884 the Rookery served as Chicago's city hall and got its name because of its reputation for attracting a multitude of pigeons. Unlike the Manhattan Building, the exterior walls of the Rookery are solid masonry bearing walls. Only the interior walls are framed in iron. The lobby and atrium were designed by Frank Lloyd Wright in 1905.

Manhattan Building
431 S. Dearborn
William Le Baron Jenney, 1890
The first building in the world framed entirely with iron and steel (and the tallest building in the world at the time it was built).

Reliance Building
32 N. State
Burnham and Root, 1890
Originally designed to be 5 stories, Burnham added an additional 10 stories after Root's death, a testament to the structural flexibility of the steel frame. Its filigree of terra cotta, once as beautiful as could be found, is now the victim of neglect.

The Monadnock Building
53 W. Jackson
North half: Burnham and Root, 1891
South half: Holabird and Roche, 1893
This building provides a case study in the evolution of structure in late 19th-century Chicago. The north half is of traditional brick bearing wall construction, which requires the walls to be six feet thick at the base to support the weight of the brick piled above. In contrast, the south half has a skeletal steel frame from which the bricks, acting as a skin for the building, are hung.

Marquette Building
140 S. Dearborn
Holabird and Roche, 1895
Enter the lobby for full appreciation of this landmark treasure. J. A. Holzer's mosaics around the balcony depict the life of French priest and explorer Père Marquette. Reinforcing the quirkiness of the building is the column centered in the lobby.

Fisher Building
343 S. Dearborn
D. H. Burnham and Co., 1896
North addition: Peter J. Weber, 1907
Note the use of intricate terra cotta into which were cast eagles, salamanders, and various fish—pun intended. The Gothic arches reflect Burnham's eclectic vision.

CLASSICISM, 1893, AND THE WORLD'S COLUMBIAN EXPOSITION

The simple form of the steel skeleton naturally carried through to the facade of the new Chicago school buildings, which gave them a rather spare and austere look. Later, architects of the European avant-garde idealized this look as a rejection of traditional classical systems of design organization. At the time, however, Chicago architects created these simple forms as a necessary consequence of the economic and social conditions in place, not a radical protest against them. A colleague once said of William Le Baron Jenney, one of the pioneers of steel skeletal design, that "while he felt he was contributing to the making of new architectural forms, that was not his motive. His main purpose was to create structural features which increased the effective floor areas and made it possible to secure more daylight within the building." In fact, when it came time to design the World's Columbian Exposition of 1893, the early individualistic efforts of the Chicago school were regarded as lacking a central organizing principle and not dignified enough to host a world party. Daniel Burnham, the most prominent of the Chicago architects commissioned for the Exhibition, was easily persuaded by the East Coast architects who were also involved to switch to the Classical style for its easy adaptability to the scope of the project. The sole survivor of the fair's classical grandeur, though in greatly altered form, is the Museum of Science and Industry. The tremendous popularity of the Exposition brought classicism to the forefront of Chicago architectural fashion, which thus influenced many Chicago architects to follow.

Museum of Science and Industry
E. 57th Street and Lake Shore Drive
D. H. Burnham and Co., 1891
Graham, Anderson, Probst, and White, 1929
Originally designed as the temporary brick and plaster Palace of Fine Arts for the Columbian Exposition, the architects borrowed Greek revival elements from the acropolis in Athens to derive its classical form.

Art Institute of Chicago
Michigan Avenue at Adams Street
Shepley, Rutan, and Coolidge, 1892
Numerous additions since by various architects

Cultural Center
Michigan Avenue between Randolph and Washington Streets
Shepley, Rutan, and Coolidge, 1897
Restored by Holabird and Root, 1977
This Boston firm also designed the Art Institute. Note the Tiffany stained glass dome on the third floor.

Northern Trust Company
50 S. LaSalle
Frost and Granger, 1905 and 1930

City Hall–County Building
Clark, Randolph, LaSalle, and Washington Streets
Holabird and Roche, 1911
The massive Corinthian columns around the perimeter suggest strength, stability, and power—everything a government building is intended to convey for those times when its contents don't live up to the ideal.

Federal Reserve Bank
230 S. LaSalle
Graham, Anderson, Probst, and White, 1922

Soldier Field
425 E. McFetridge
Holabird and Roche, 1922–26
Originally built as a war memorial, this is currently the home of the Chicago Bears. Now that the battles are within, nothing's changed but the price of admission.

Continental Illinois Bank
231 S. LaSalle
Graham, Anderson, Probst, and White, 1924

Union Station
210 S. Canal
Graham Burnham and Co., 1924
The monumental waiting room is one of a few of its kind left.

Tribune Tower
435 N. Michigan
Hood and Howells, 1925
The Tribune Tower is the product of an international design competition held by *Tribune* publisher Robert McCormick in 1922. The neo-Gothic result is a quirky yet endearing landmark for the city. Pillaged from across the globe are fragments of other famous landmarks embedded into the facade along the base of the tower.

SULLIVAN AND WRIGHT

Though Louis Sullivan's now-demolished Transportation Building was made part of the 1893 Columbian Exhibition, he and Frank Lloyd Wright resisted the trend toward classicism and continued to work in their exceptional individual styles. Examples include the Charnley House on Astor Street, one of Wright's last projects as an employee of Adler and Sullivan; Sullivan's ornate decorative work for the Carson Pirie Scott store; and the original Chicago Stock Exchange, now demolished but visible in pieces at the Art Institute. On his own, Wright began his long and fertile career with the residential projects that dot Chicago and the suburbs, particularly Oak Park and River Forest. Truly shocking in their day, Wright's Prairie houses are marked by long, low profiles and open, flowing interior spaces.

Auditorium Theater
430 S. Michigan
Adler and Sullivan, 1889
The Auditorium was home to the Chicago Opera Company until 1929, when it moved into the newly constructed Civic Opera House in spite of the reputedly perfect acoustics of the Auditorium. The theater went bankrupt during the Depression, but fortunately Roosevelt University bought the building in 1946. It was restored in 1967 by Harry Weese.

Charnley House
1365 N. Astor
Adler and Sullivan, 1892
The house was rendered asymmetrical by a later addition to the south. The building has been recently restored and currently houses an architectural think tank.

Frank Lloyd Wright Home and Studio
931 Chicago, Oak Park
Frank Lloyd Wright, 1889–1909
Tours available: (708) 848-1976
Continually remodeled by Wright as his architectural ideas developed, the buildings have been restored to appear as they did in 1909, the year Wright left his family to be with the wife of a client. Information on walking tours of Oak Park and River Forest also is available.

Gage Building
18 S. Michigan
Facade: Louis Sullivan
Holabird and Roche, 1898

Carson, Pirie, Scott and Co.
1 S. State
Adler and Sullivan, 1899–1904
The ornate entrance is the epitome of Sullivan's decorative style and contrasts brilliantly with the spare elongated "Chicago windows" along State Street.

Unity Temple
875 Lake, Oak Park
Frank Lloyd Wright, 1906
Tours available: (708) 848-6225
The simple geometric masses of this Unitarian-Universalist Church are
rendered in reinforced concrete—quite radical for both neighborhood and
function at the turn of the century. Though the building appears rather
massive from the street, the interior is airy and filled with light.

Robie House
5757 S. Woodlawn
Frank Lloyd Wright, 1909
Tours available: 702-8374
Built as a private home, this house was donated to the University of Chicago
and is currently the office of the alumni association. It embodies the Prairie
style as well as any of Wright's houses.

ART DECO IN CHICAGO

Chicago never became a center for the American Art Deco movement—New
York has that honor—yet there are several noteworthy individual buildings
from the years surrounding the Century of Progress exposition in 1933. The
more subtle examples of this style are buildings whose basically classical
details and materials have been streamlined and flattened, as at the 333 N.
Michigan building, the Chicago Motor Club, the Adler Planetarium, and the
Merchandise Mart. The images used in decorative panels, sculpture, and
murals are often works of art in their own right. Crowning the Chicago Board
of Trade is the sleek 1930 statue of Ceres, the goddess of grain, by John Storrs.
Perhaps she still figures in the prayers of options traders. For a closer look,
see the study for the statue on display at the Art Institute.

333 N. Michigan
Holabird and Roche, 1928
The first of the Art Deco skyscrapers in Chicago, this building is a knockoff of
Eliel Saarinen's second-place entry to the Tribune Tower competition. The
figures sculpted on the elevator doors are by Edgar Miller, whose work can be
seen on Art Deco buildings across the city.

Carbide and Carbon Building
230 N. Michigan
Burnham Brothers, 1929
Designed by the sons of Daniel Burnham, this tower has a gilt terra cotta top
and terrific brass work in the lobby.

Chicago Motor Club Building
66 E. South Water
Holabird and Root, 1929
The lobby is worth a peek, especially to see the giant road map of the United
States by muralist John Norton.

Chicago Board of Trade
141 W. Jackson
Holabird and Root, 1929–30
1980 addition: Helmut Jahn
Don't miss the lobby designed by Gilbert Hall.

Civic Opera House
20 N. Wacker
Graham, Anderson, Probst, and White, 1929
The mass of the building developed by Samuel Insull resembles a chair, hence
the original nickname, "Insull's Throne."

Commonwealth Edison Substation
Dearborn Street between Randolph and Washington Streets
Holabird and Root, 1929
The relief sculpture on the facade is by Sylvia Shaw Judson, the daughter of
architect Howard Van Doren Shaw.

Merchandise Mart
Merchandise Mart Plaza (350 N. Wells)
Graham, Anderson, Probst, and White, 1930
Restored by Graham, Anderson, Probst, and White, 1986–88
The Mart has a commanding presence on the north side of the Chicago River,
between Wells and Orleans streets. It also has four million square feet of floor
space.

Palmolive Building
919 N. Michigan
(formerly known as the Playboy Building)
Holabird and Root, 1930

Adler Planetarium and Astronomical Museum
1300 S. Lake Shore Drive
Ernest A. Grunsfeld, Jr., 1931
This was the first planetarium to open in the United States.

Frank Fisher Apartments
1209 N. Parkway
Andrew Rebori, 1936–37

MIES AND HIS DISCIPLES

Aside from Mrs. O'Leary's cow, there may be no one more influential in the
development of Chicago architecture as it appears today than Mies van der
Rohe. Having already developed a reputation in Europe, Mies came to
Chicago in 1938 and began to build on a larger scale. Like many of his
contemporaries in Europe, Mies saw Chicago architecture as embodying his
own desire to reject Old World historical baggage. Here Mies perfected his
signature high rise with its open collonaded space around a solid shaft. The
glass-and-steel skin of a high rise like the IBM Building is carefully detailed to
represent the steel structure within. Mies spent hours developing these
minute details to perfection, often deliberating for months over fractions of
inches to achieve the right proportions, play of light, and simplicity.

In Chicago, Mies had the opportunity to manipulate space on an urban scale; his campus plan for the Illinois Institute of Technology, his trio of buildings at the Federal Center, and a pair of residential high rises at 860 and 880 N. Lake Shore Drive each tread the line between containing a plaza's space and letting it flow through the seams between buildings. Mies' influence on Chicago's architecture extends far beyond the buildings he himself designed. As head of the architecture department at IIT, the curriculum developed around his ideas was very influential and has only recently been challenged by the faculty. Mies' students, colleagues, and protégés built many "Miesian" buildings in Chicago and indeed throughout the world, although only a handful can hold a candle to those of the master.

Illinois Institute of Technology
State Street between 31st and 35th Streets
Mies van der Rohe, 1940–58
Crown Hall houses the school of architecture and is an excellent example of Mies' work.

Federal Center Complex
Dearborn Street between Jackson Boulevard and Adams Street
Mies van der Rohe, 1964–75
Alexander Calder's red "Flamingo Stabile" may periodically cause Mies to roll over in his grave. One overlooked gem among the assemblage is the brick power station, which can be seen behind the Dirksen Building at the north end of the axis of Plymouth Court. The brick work is particularly well crafted.

IBM Building
330 N. Wabash
Mies van der Rohe, 1971
A bust of Mies is in the lobby of this 52-story tower, the last office building he designed.

MIESIAN DISSEMINATION

Two firms became the first followers of Mies: Skidmore, Owings, and Merrill (SOM) and C. F. Murphy. SOM crystallized Miesian form in the Inland Steel building and the Daley Center. And as the expression of the clean box of office space was perfected, Chicago's architects and engineers, aided as always by Chicago's developers, moved on to greater feats. They developed an engineer-based architecture of structural expression. Architect Bruce Graham and engineer Fazlur Khan of SOM designed two of the tallest buildings in the world: the John Hancock Tower and Sears Tower. Both facades express the building's ability to resist gravity and wind load. SOM and C. F. Murphy became the primary big shoulders firms of Chicago architecture—firms whose stature as Chicagoans led to huge success internationally.

Inland Steel
30 W. Monroe
Skidmore, Owings, and Merrill, 1957
SOM crystallized Miesian form in this building, pushing its elevator and service elements to the rear and the columns to the exterior, which leaves the office floors pristinely uninterrupted. Its green glass and stainless steel cur-

tain wall expanded Mies' basic black color scheme, becoming a vivid symbol of the client's business.

Marina City and Towers
300 N. State
Bertrand Goldberg, 1964
Always difficult to categorize, this version of modernist structural expression is brilliantly executed in concrete rather than steel. Unfortunately, the twin corn cobs are showing their age and could use some restoration.

Richard J. Daley Center
Dearborn and Randolph Streets
C. F. Murphy and Associates; Loebl Schlossman and Bennett; Skidmore, Owings, and Merrill, 1964
The architects used huge floor spans and Cor-Ten steel to express the raw muscularity of the new aesthetic.

Lake Point Tower
505 N. Lake Shore Drive
Schipporeit-Heinrich Associates, 1968
This high rise was based on an idea developed for Berlin by Mies prior to his arrival in the United States.

John Hancock Tower
875 N. Michigan
Skidmore, Owings, and Merrill, 1969
Crisscrossed by diagonal bracing, Hancock Tower is a tapered form, vertically cantilevered into the sky.

Amoco Building
200 E. Randolph
E. D. Stone; Perkins and Will, 1974
New white granite cladding replaced a Carrara marble skin, which could not withstand the wind and temperature extremes of Chicago. Eighty stories tall, this is the third tallest building in Chicago, behind the Sears Tower and the John Hancock Tower.

The Sears Tower
233 S. Wacker
Skidmore, Owings, and Merrill, 1974
Sears Tower is a set of nine square tubes, bundled together to give strength to the whole. The gradual dropping away of tubes as the building ascends reinforces the independence of the nine elements.

POST-MIES

As interest in structural expressionism deepened into exhibitionism, a new tolerance for flamboyance developed. Previously taboo, architects again felt comfortable including purely decorative elements, yet the forms they used for decoration were distinctly modern. In a sense, these architects were practicing mannerist modernism in buildings like the Brunswick Building, which uses its concrete frame to echo the sweep of the Monadnock Building down the street; the Seventeenth Church of Christ, Scientist, with its round auditorium clearly marking a bend in the Chicago River; and the Xerox, with its sensual curved screen at the top. These buildings are clearly based on the modern idiom but strive to be more figurative and less abstract in their structural character.

Brunswick Building
69 W. Washington
Skidmore, Owings, and Merrill, 1964

Seventeenth Church of Christ, Scientist, Chicago
55 E. Wacker
Harry Weese and Associates, 1968

Metropolitan Correctional Center
71 W. Van Buren
Harry Weese and Associates, 1975
There are no bars on the exterior of this prison. The windows are five inches wide, the maximum allowed by law.

Xerox Centre
55 W. Monroe
C. F. Murphy Associates, 1980

The Associates Center
150 N. Michigan
A. Epstein and Sons, 1983
A product of the era of sliced roofs, this one resembles a cloven hoof and dominates Michigan Avenue from the south.

State of Illinois Building
Clark and Randolph Streets
Murphy/Jahn; Lester B. Knight and Associates, 1985
Best seen from the inside, the renowned architecture critic Vincent Scully said of the atrium, "It's the only time I've experienced vertigo looking up."

United Airlines Terminal
O'Hare International Airport
Murphy/Jahn, 1986
This high-tech futurist vision of travel, complete with moving sidewalks, will make you feel like a member of the Jetson family. It's well worth a visit and the round-trip CTA fare, even if you aren't flying anywhere.

NBC Tower
200 E. Illinois
Skidmore, Owings, and Merrill, 1989
Art Deco meets the Tribune Tower at this limestone and granite-clad monument to broadcasting.

CULT OF THE STRANGER

After decades of dominance by native Chicagoans, the 1980s saw the opening of the Chicago architectural market to non-Chicagoans. The 1980s were a boom time in speculative office development, and local developers turned to superstar names to give an aura of added importance to their buildings. With their striking building at 333 W. Wacker, New Yorkers Kohn, Pedersen, Fox et al. quickly became the most popular out-of-town firm to build in this city.

Soon came other New York names such as Philip Johnson, Kevin Roche, and Cesar Pelli. International stars are the most recent arrivals, such as Kenzo Tange from Japan and Ricardo Bofill from Spain.

333 W. Wacker
Kohn, Pedersen, Fox; Perkins and Will, 1983
Arguably the most elegant of recent buildings in Chicago, 333's curved facade reflects the Chicago River in both shape and color, while its southeast corner conforms to the square intersection of Franklin and Lake streets.

190 S. LaSalle
John Burgee Architects with Philip Johnson, 1986
Here Philip Johnson attempts to honor John Wellborn Root, the architect of the Rookery across the street. The copper roof is a quotation from Chicago's now-demolished Masonic Temple Building.

Leo Burnett Building
35 W. Wacker
Kevin Roche-John Dinkeloo and Associates, 1989
A takeoff on Adolph Loos' 1922 entry to the Tribune Tower competition, the Leo Burnett Building is a gigantic column supported on a five-story arcade of pillars.

225 W. Wacker
Kohn, Pedersen, Fox, 1989

American Medical Association Building
515 N. State
Kenzo Tange with Shaw and Associates, 1990
Elegant and simple in its massing and detailing, this is the first Chicago building to have an intentional hole in it.

Sporting Club
211 N. Stetson
Kisho Kurokawa, 1990

181 W. Madison
Cesar Pelli and Associates, 1990

311 S. Wacker
Kohn, Pedersen, Fox with Harwood K. Smith and Partners, 1990
To be joined in the future by two similar towers, the world's tallest reinforced concrete office building is an urban disaster, from the vast surface parking lots surrounding it to the "members only" Winter Garden, to the 1,852 fluorescent tubes overwhelming the nighttime skyline in a cross between a White Castle and Close Encounters of the Third Kind.

R. R. Donnelley Center
77 W. Wacker
Ricardo Bofill Arquitectura/Taller USA with DeStefano/Goettsch Ltd., 1992
A pastiche of classical ornament taped over a glass tube topped by a pedimentary hat.

HERE AND NOW

Architecture in Chicago today lacks a common voice. Great pleasure (or great remorse, depending on your bent) can be found in the extreme diversity of the recent buildings, which are a tribute to individual expression, although very few of the new structures exhibit any connection to their surroundings. From Ralph Johnson's reinterpretation of Russian Constructivism in the Morton International Building, to Tom Beeby's take on classicism at the Harold Washington Library Center. Chicago is alive with reworking, recycling, and in some cases regurgitating architectural forms.

Commonwealth Edison Substation
Southwest corner of Dearborn and Ontario Streets
Tigerman McCurry, 1989
One would never know from outside that behind the neogeorgian facade of English cross-bonded brick and limestone are four giant electrical transformers.

Chicago Bar Association
321 S. Plymouth
Tigerman McCurry, 1990
This building has a sort of Art Deco/Gothic derivation. Could this be the last historically based building from Tigerman?

Crate and Barrel Store
646 N. Michigan
Solomon Cordwell Buenz and Associates, 1990
Both the building and its contents attract crowds. Be sure to step out on the balcony for a view up and down the avenue.

Morton International Building
Chicago River between Randolph and Washington Streets
Perkins and Will, 1990
For the public this complex offers a long arcade along the river. The structural system ingeniously solves a problematic site by cantelevering over the railroad tracks below.

Two Prudential Plaza
Southwest corner of Stetson and Lake Streets
Loebl Scholossman and Hackl, 1990
New York's Chrysler Building appears to have inspired this tower via work in Texas and Philadelphia by Helmut Jahn. Unfortunately, by the time this third-generation design arrived in Chicago, it lost its sparkle, as well as any sense of context.

Banana Republic
744 N. Michigan
Robert A. M. Stern Architects, 1991
This is the best island hut on the Magnificent Mile, hands down.

Harold Washington Library Center
State Street at Congress Parkway
Hammond, Beeby, Babka, 1991
This is the winning entry from a competition also featuring the work of
Murphy/Jahn, Lohan and Associates, and Skidmore, Owings, and Merrill. Its
monumental massing is the scale of the City Hall–County Building. The new
library provides Chicago with a sorely needed central facility. Check out the
winter garden on the top floor, as a place to rest feet, read a book, or enjoy the
view.

NEIGHBORHOODS

Chicago's neighborhoods are an often-overlooked mine of architectural
treasures. Major buildings outside of the central business district have been
mentioned elsewhere, but many other areas are worth wandering for their
texture and architectural clues to the history of their residents. Moving clock-
wise from the south, with the Loop at the center:

Pullman (on the far South Side) is a model town, planned by George
Pullman and S. S. Beman for the railway car manufacturer's employees in the
1880s. The town was to be a self-contained and controllable environment for
all levels of management and labor, so it included housing for all strata,
schools, a hotel, church, and market square.

The streets of **Hyde Park** and **Kenwood** are lined with mansions from their
heyday as fashionable neighborhoods. Woodlawn Avenue running south
from 49th to the Midway Plaisance is a fine example. Along the Midway, the
University of Chicago's collegiate Gothic quadrangles date primarily from
1900 to 1920. At the west termination of the Midway lies sculptor Laredo
Taft's "Fountain of Time" from 1922. Jackson Park, the site of the Columbian
Exposition, still shows the remnants of Frederic Law Olmsted's plan and
some artifacts of the fair. The Palace of Fine Arts is now rebuilt as the
Museum of Science and Industry, the Midway itself is the former site of
everything from the ferris wheel to the Moorish Palace, and a 1918 gilt replica
of "Republic" from the French pavilion stands at Richards Drive and Hayes
Avenue.

Riverside is a suburb planned in 1989 by Frederick Law Olmsted, designer
of New York's Central Park, with varying density and lot size, curving
streets, central parkland, and a couple Frank Lloyd Wright homes. Fellow
suburbs **Oak Park** and **River Forest** are notable for their Frank Lloyd Wright
buildings and many Victorian homes.

Wicker Park and **Bucktown** are recently fashionable neighborhoods for
the artist crowd. Centered around the Flat Iron building at Milwaukee and
North avenues, the neighborhood is full of late 1800 masonry homes, many
appearing to have settled a full story below ground. In reality, the houses
have stayed put—the streets were raised to install the sewer system.

Logan Square is the starting point for a drive down Logan Boulevard. Part
of Olmsted and Burnham's "Plan for Chicago," the center parkway is flanked
by stately mansions and apartment buildings from the early 1900s. Today the
area is a mix of decay and gentrification.

Ravenswood and **Lincoln Square** are noteworthy for creative commercial
architecture, such as the Louis Sullivan–designed terra cotta storefront at 4711

N. Lincoln. Down the street is Tom Beeby's Sulzer Regional Library from 1984.

The **North Shore's** wealth of mansions can be seen in a drive along Sheridan Road, from Evanston at the south; past Northwestern University; Wilmette's Baha'i Temple; and on to Lake Forest, an exclusive suburb as early as the 1850s, with its Market Square by Howard Van Doren Shaw.

Back in the city, the **Lakeview** neighborhood surrounds Wrigley Field, Chicago's jewel of an urban ballpark. Around the corner is Alta Vista Terrace, a quiet block of two-story rowhouses, where the west side of the street is the mirrored reverse of the east side. A few blocks north is Graceland Cemetery, where the elaborate mausoleums and grave markers record the names of Chicago's most prominent families.

Lincoln Park and **Old Town** are crowded with interesting residential architecture, from Chalmers Place on the DePaul campus to recent houses by local architects (Krueck and Olsen, etc.).

ADDITIONAL INFORMATION

The **Archi Center** (782-1776) and the **Chicago Architecture Foundation** (922-3432), both located at 224 S. Michigan Avenue, offer walking, bus, boat, and chartered CTA El tours of Chicago and Chicago-area architectural highlights. (They have yet to introduce a Rollerblade tour of Chicago architecture.) They also have a bookshop and host special events. Call for hours and tour information.

SUGGESTED READING

Chicago on Foot by Ira Bach and Susan Wolfson.

Wild Onions: A Brief Guide to Landmarks and Lesser-Known Structures in Chicago's Loop, edited by Deborah Slaton.

—*Anthony Hurtig and D'Andre Willis*

MUSEUMS

There's at least one Chicago museum for every taste—for high art or low, the refined or the macabre, the multicultural or the chauvinist, the practical or the ethereal. Here's a quick review of the city's major museums, plus a sampling of some of the more interesting smaller ones.

Prices listed are for adult admission. Call the museum for information on discounts for children, students, and seniors. For information on children-oriented museums, exhibits, and programs, see the "Kids" chapter.

THE BIGGIES

Adler Planetarium
1300 S. Lake Shore Drive   322-0300
Hours: Monday–Thursday, 9:30 A.M.–4:30 P.M.; Friday, 9:30 A.M.–9 P.M.;
Saturday, Sunday, and holidays, 9:30 A.M.–5 P.M.
Free admission; Sky Show, $3
The first planetarium in the Western Hemisphere features exhibits on astronomy and space exploration. Learn about our place in the universe (a humbling experience), the Big Bang theory, how to use a telescope, the history and current state-of-the-art of space exploration. A one-hour multimedia Sky Show changes every few months. After the Friday evening Sky Show, views from the observatory's 20-inch telescope are projected onto the Sky Theater dome. Classes and lectures are frequently offered. Check out the great view of Chicago's skyline behind the building.

Art Institute of Chicago
Michigan Avenue at Adams Street   443-3600
Hours: Monday, Wednesday–Friday, 10:30 A.M.–4:30 P.M.;
Tuesday, 10:30 A.M.–8 P.M.; Saturday, 10 A.M.–5 P.M.;
Sunday and holidays, 12–5 P.M.
$6 suggested admission, free on Tuesday
One of the world's leading art museums, best known for its unparalleled collection of Impressionist and post-Impressionist paintings. It also has an excellent collection of 20th-century European and American art, outstanding early European paintings, and extensive exhibits on art of Asia, Africa, and the Americas. There's sculpture, photographs, prints and drawings, decorative arts, architectural drawings—even arms and armor. Frequent large-scale special exhibitions are mounted. A monthly calendar of events lists daily gallery talks, lectures, tours, films, concerts, and special programs. The museum store includes a good selection of books on art and architecture.

Chicago Historical Society
Clark Street at North Avenue   642-4600
Hours: Monday–Saturday, 9:30 A.M.–4:30 P.M.; Sunday, 12–5 P.M.
$3 admission, free on Monday
Both Chicago and American history are on display at this recently remodeled museum. Chicago's growth is traced from pioneer days to emergence as a modern metropolis. The multimedia exhibit "A House Divided: America in the Age of Lincoln" is a must-see for anyone interested in the Civil War era.

251

Other exhibits explore the founding of the nation and Illinois frontier life. Innovative special exhibits cover everything from sports to fashion to more typical museum topics like art and architecture. Lectures, films, and special events are offered. An extensive research collection is available for study.

Field Museum of Natural History
Roosevelt Road at S. Lake Shore Drive   922-9410
Hours: Daily, 9 A.M.–5 P.M.
$4 admission, free on Thursday
From a full-scale replica of a traditional Pawnee earth lodge to huge dinosaur skeletons, the Field Museum has a wide range of exhibits on zoology, geology, botany, and anthropology. Undergoing an eight-year renovation, it now offers a "journey" through the Pacific Islands and lifelike renderings of animals in their native habitats. Old standbys include the "Inside Ancient Egypt" exhibit, complete with mummies, entered through a "pharaoh's tomb." The American Indian exhibits have been updated somewhat in response to concerns of modern Native Americans. An extensive educational program includes lectures, classes, concerts, and the Webber Resource Center library.

Museum of Science and Industry
57th Street and Lake Shore Drive   684-1414
(24 hours a day from a touch-tone phone)
Hours: Monday–Friday, 9:30 A.M.–4 P.M.;
Saturday, Sunday, and holidays, 9:30 A.M.–5:30 P.M.;
Crown Space Center open Friday and Saturday to 9 P.M.
Call for Omnimax Theatre showtimes and ticket availability. $5 admission (with Omnimax Theatre, $8); free on Thursday (with Omnimax Theatre, $5)
Chicago's most popular tourist attraction contains more than 2,000 displays demonstrating the impact of science and technology on modern life. If you can ignore blatant corporate propagandizing, the museum can be a lot of fun, with hands-on exhibits that you don't have to be a kid to enjoy (although you'll see plenty of them running around). Some highlights: a full-size mock-up of a NASA space shuttle, a coal mine, a German sub, chicks hatching, a walk-through heart, and a hand-carved circus. The Omnimax Theatre features spectacular films on a five-story domed screen. A broad-based educational program includes science demonstrations, classes, laboratories, lectures, and a library.

Shedd Aquarium
1200 S. Lake Shore Drive   939-2438
Hours: Daily, 9 A.M.–6 P.M.
$3 admission (with Oceanarium, $7), free on Thursday (with Oceanarium, $4)
The world's largest aquarium. Its Oceanarium, which opened in 1991 with much fanfare, features whales, dolphins, sea otters, seals, and penguins in a naturalistic setting with good old Lake Michigan as a backdrop. Presentations are held there daily. The highlight of the main aquarium is the 90,000-gallon "Coral Reef" tank, best viewed during feeding times when the diver hands out nourishment to sharks, barracudas, eels, and other assorted creatures. An educational program offers science courses and excursions.

ART MUSEUMS

Museum of Contemporary Art
237 E. Ontario   280-5161
Hours: Tuesday–Saturday, 10 A.M.–5 P.M.; Sunday, 12–5 P.M.
$4 admission, free on Tuesday
Art on the cutting edge. Installations, photography, painting, video, performance art, sculpture, computer graphics—contemporary art in every medium is shown here, from Christo's first U.S. wrap to Mapplethorpe's photographs, to challenging works by local artists. The museum focuses on special exhibitions, although its growing permanent collection will necessitate a move to a much larger facility in 1995. Free gallery talks are held on weekends and Tuesdays. Check out the excellent museum store and basement cafe/bookstore.

Museum of Contemporary Photography
600 S. Michigan   663-1600
Hours: Monday–Friday, 10 A.M.–5 P.M.; Saturday, 12–5 P.M.;
open June–July until 4 P.M.; closed in August
Free admission
Based in Columbia College, this is the only museum in the Midwest devoted exclusively to collecting, exhibiting, and promoting contemporary photography. Special exhibits showcase local, national, and international photographers. A Print Study Room enables curators, dealers, and the public to see photographs on loan from leading midwestern photographers (call for an appointment).

Museum of Holography
1134 W. Washington   226-1007
Hours: Wednesday–Sunday, 12:30–5 P.M.
$2.50 admission
Artists are doing some truly astonishing things with holography, and this is the place to discover them. The museum, dedicated to promoting holography (three-dimensional laser-produced images) as an art form, mounts unique special exhibits and displays works from its permanent collection. You can also find some unusual gifts here.

David and Alfred Smart Museum of Art
5550 S. Greenwood   702-0200
Hours: Tuesday–Friday, 10 A.M.–4:30 P.M.; Saturday and Sunday, 12–6 P.M.
Free admission
The University of Chicago's fine arts museum. Its collection is wide ranging: ancient Greek vases and Chinese bronzes, old-master prints, Frank Lloyd Wright furniture, sculpture of modern masters, Walker Evans photographs, German expressionist watercolors, and modern Japanese ceramics share the gallery. Special exhibits have covered such varied topics as Sigmund Freud and art, 19th-century Russian painting, and black American art during the civil rights era. Lectures, gallery talks, films, and other programs accompany exhibits.

Terra Museum of American Art
666 N. Michigan   664-3939
Hours: Tuesday, 12–8 P.M.; Wednesday–Saturday, 10 A.M.–5 P.M.;
Sunday, 12–5 P.M.
$4 admission
One of the few museums in the country devoted exclusively to American art. Its permanent collection, which spans just about every period and style over the past 200 years, is particularly strong on American Impressionism and naive art. Sargent, Chase, Cassatt, Homer, Whistler, and Wyeth are among the artists who are well represented. Key works are on display, and special exhibitions are mounted regularly. The museum offers lectures, classes, and daily public tours.

Ukrainian Institute of Modern Art
2320 W. Chicago   227-5522
Hours: Tuesday–Sunday, 12–4 P.M.
$2 suggested donation
This small art museum has an excellent collection of modern works by North American artists of Ukrainian descent. It also mounts special exhibitions of art by both Ukrainians and non-Ukrainians. The staff is friendly, knowledge-able, and glad to show you around. While you're in the neighborhood, stop by the **Ukrainian National Museum** down the block (2453 W. Chicago) to see its folk art collection and exhibits on the people of the Ukraine.

ETHNIC MUSEUMS

Balzekas Museum of Lithuanian Culture
6500 S. Pulaski   582-6500
Hours: Daily, 10 A.M.–4 P.M.; Friday until 8 P.M.
$4 admission
Balzekas celebrates Lithuanian culture with exhibits on the art, history, and customs of the Balkan state. Items on display include folk art, antique armor and weapons, native costumes, and one of the world's largest collections of amber jewelry outside Lithuania. Immigrant history and modern Lithuanian artists are also featured.

DuSable Museum of African-American History
740 E. 56th Pl.   947-0600
Hours: Monday–Friday, 9 A.M.–5 P.M.; Saturday and Sunday, 12–5 P.M.
$2 admission
Since it began in 1961 in the home of founder Margaret Burroughs, this museum (named for Chicago's first settler, black Haitian trader Jean Baptiste Pointe duSable) has been a cultural beacon for the African-American com-munity. Now housed in a handsome Washington Park facility, the museum documents the experience and achievements of black America. Artifacts and artwork related to African heritage, slavery, blacks in Illinois, and outstand-ing African-Americans are displayed. Frequent lectures, performances and other events are offered; a research library is available for students and scholars.

Mexican Fine Arts Museum
1852 W. 19th   738-1503
Hours: Tuesday–Sunday, 10 A.M.–5 P.M.
Free admission
The largest Mexican cultural center/museum in the nation, created to show-case the wealth and breadth of Mexican culture. It exhibits the work of contemporary Mexican artists and displays a growing permanent collection of Mexican art. Rotating exhibits have focused on textiles, mural art, toys, sculpture, and papier mâché. A special highlight is the annual Dia de Los Muertes exhibit. A large performance space features dance, theater, music, and poetry. The museum offers art classes and other educational programs.

Polish Museum of America
984 N. Milwaukee   384-3352
Hours: Daily, 12–5 P.M.
Free admission
One of the oldest and largest ethnic museums in the country, with exhibits on Polish history and culture, immigration to America, and Chicago's Polish community, which happens to be the largest concentration of Poles outside of Warsaw. A substantial collection of Polish-American art is displayed, along with folk art, native costumes, military memorabilia, and much more. Find out who Pulaski was and why he's got such a long street named after him. Don't miss the 13- by 27-foot stained glass window *Poland Reborn*. The museum offers educational activities and an extensive research library.

Maurice Spertus Museum of Judaica
618 S. Michigan   922-9012
Hours: Sunday–Thursday, 10 A.M.–5 P.M.; Friday, 10 A.M.–3 P.M.
$3.50 admission
Contains nearly 3,000 works spanning 3,500 years of Jewish history, religion, and culture. The permanent collection features Jewish decorative arts and ceremonial objects. The powerful Holocaust Memorial documents the rise of Nazism, the destruction of European Jewry, and the struggles of individuals facing extreme adversity. Special exhibits range far and wide and have in-cluded Biblical prints by Chagall, a history of the Sephardic Jews, and portraits of famous modern Jews.

MUSEUMS OF HISTORY, SCIENCE, CULTURE

Jane Addams's Hull House Museum
800 S. Halsted   413-5353
Hours: Monday–Friday, 10 A.M.–4 P.M.; Sunday (summer only), 12–5 P.M.
Free admission
Jane Addams chose the Hull mansion as the site of her famous settlement house in 1889 because it stood in the midst of the Near West Side, the teeming "port of entry" neighborhood for Chicago's immigrants. In 1963 the neigh-borhood and Hull House complex were destroyed to make way for the University of Illinois, but the original Hull House (built in 1856) and an adjoining building were spared. The University now operates them as a museum/historic site. Exhibits focus on the influential work of Addams and

her colleagues, life at Hull House, and the historic surrounding multiethnic neighborhood.

Chicago Academy of Sciences
2001 N. Clark   871-2668
$1 admission, free on Monday; call for fees and hours of special exhibits.
The oldest science museum in the Midwest (founded in 1857) offers exhibits on natural history, with an emphasis on the geology and ecology of the Great Lakes region. You can walk through a coal forest that was Chicago 300 million years ago and explore a model of Starved Rock canyon. Large display windows and lifelike dioramas re-create the area's natural habitats. Each year the Academy sponsors a major special exhibit; recent focus has been on dinosaurs. Field trips, lectures, and other educational programs are offered.

Chicago Cultural Center
Randolph Street and Michigan Avenue   346-3278
Hours: Monday–Thursday, 9 A.M.–7 P.M.; Friday, 9 A.M.–6 P.M.;
Saturday, 9 A.M.–5 P.M.
Free admission
The former site of the Chicago Public Library is evolving into a multifaceted cultural facility run by the city's Department of Cultural Affairs. A sometimes bewildering array of free programs, lectures, concerts, and films are offered, usually related to a particular theme such as Black History Month or Chinese New Year. Art shows are often on display in the four gallery spaces. The building itself is a showcase, featuring a Tiffany-domed rotunda, a grand staircase, and lots of marble. The Peace Museum and the Museum of Broadcast Communications are currently housed here (see below).

International Museum of Surgical Science
1524 N. Lake Shore Drive   642-6502
Hours: Tuesday–Saturday, 10 A.M.–4 P.M.; Sunday, 11 A.M.–4 P.M.
$2 suggested donation
Did you know the first human surgery involved boring holes in peoples' skulls to release the evil spirits? This museum's got the skulls to prove it. You can learn fascinating things here about the history of surgery around the world and medical advances that turned it from a brutal practice to a healing art. Highlights include a re-created turn-of-the-century American drugstore, an iron lung, a collection of surgical tools dating from ancient Rome, and some truly shocking paintings depicting surgical procedures of the past. The museum, founded in 1953, is housed in an elegant Lakefront mansion.

Museum of Broadcast Communications
Washington Street and Michigan Avenue   629-6000
Hours: Monday–Saturday, 10 A.M.–4:30 P.M.; Sunday, 12–5 P.M.
$3 suggested donation
From Charlie McCarthy to CNN, this museum celebrates radio and TV history. Exhibits focus on Chicago's pioneering TV days, commercials, old radio, and more. You can even make your own newscast. The museum's archives contain thousands of radio and TV programs and commercials available for viewing. Its video theater shows vintage primetime TV and special retrospectives.

Oriental Institute Museum
1155 E. 58th   702-9520
Hours: Tuesday, Thursday–Saturday, 10 A.M.–4 P.M.;
Wednesday, 10 A.M.–8:30 P.M.; Sunday, 12–4 P.M.
Free admission
The University of Chicago's Oriental Institute holds one of the world's major collections of ancient Near Eastern artifacts, many excavated by the Institute's own field expeditions. Its museum showcases the history, art, and archaeology of the ancient Near East civilizations of Egypt, Anatolia, Persia, Mesopotamia, and Syria/Palestine. Treasures include a 40-ton human-headed winged bull from Assyria and a colossal statue of Tutankhamun. The Institute offers tours, lectures, classes, workshops, and free Sunday afternoon films.

Peace Museum
Chicago Cultural Center
Randolph Street and Michigan Avenue   541-1474
Free admission
The only museum in the country dedicated to promoting the art of peace through exhibits and educational programs. Exhibits have focused on issues of war and peace as interpreted by famous musicians, artwork from survivors of Hiroshima and Nagasaki, toys that promote peace instead of war, Martin Luther King, Jr.'s role as peacemaker, and more. The museum has attracted attention nationally, and its exhibits frequently travel around the country. The Museum lost its gallery space in 1991; at press time it is located at the Chicago Cultural Center. Call for hours and times as well as current exhibitions.

—Deborah R. Weiner

Recreation

OUTDOORS
SPORTS
FITNESS

OUTDOORS

Chicagoans are fortunate to live in a region that has been shaped by the last Ice Age. The receding glaciers left in their wake a unique ecosystem of hills, ravines, ridges, meadows, lakes, marshes, and bogs that are home to several varieties of plant and animal life. Just outside the city are several forest preserves and nature centers where one can enjoy, explore, or study nature—or just get away from it all.

In the city itself are several gardens, parks, and beaches that also host an abundance of plant and animal life. Lincoln Park has a conservatory as well as a zoo, and, like several areas in and around Chicago, it lies along the route of migratory birds. Several other parks are a profusion of flowers in spring and summer and offer a variety of activities around the year.

Most preserves have interpretive centers that offer displays, tours, talks, and classes on a wide range of topics. The preserves also contain several miles of hiking and bicycle trails, picnic areas, and campsites.

For the more adventurous, there are several organizations that sponsor outdoor activities such as hiking, backpacking, skiing, and canoeing. Most trips are led by experienced outdoor enthusiasts and are either free or relatively inexpensive. If you plan to hit the trails, wear comfortable clothes and sturdy shoes. Carry water and a snack, especially if you plan to hike in wilderness areas. Stay on marked trails. Littering and collecting specimens are prohibited. Pets are not allowed in most parks, as they disturb the wildlife.

NATURE CENTERS AND FOREST PRESERVES

Most of the locations listed here have restrooms and water fountains. However, because of budget cuts, it's advisable to call ahead for information about hours and facilities. For information and maps of the forest preserves and nature centers in the counties adjoining Chicago, contact the offices listed below.

Cook County Forest Preserve District
801 N. River Road, Mount Prospect   (708) 824-1900

DuPage County Forest Preserve District
P.O. Box 2339, Glen Ellyn, 60138   (708) 790-4900

Illinois Department of Conservation
Office of Public Information, 524 S. 2nd, Springfield, 62701-1787
(217) 782-7454

Lake County Forest Preserve District
2000 N. Milwaukee, Libertyville, 60048   (708) 367- 6640

Chain O'Lakes State Park
729 E. State Park, Spring Grove, 60081   (708) 587- 5512
A network of 10 connected lakes fed by the Fox River, this park contains the largest concentration of lakes in Illinois. The parkland consists of peat deposits covered by freshwater bog and contains an abundance of wildlife, including deer, mink, fox, raccoons, as well as migrating birds and songbirds.

The abundance and variety of trees makes for a spectacular display of colors in fall. Not to be missed are the lotus flowers on Grass Lake, near the eastern end of the park. Recreational facilities include hiking, horseback riding, boating, canoeing, and picnicking. In addition, there are facilities for skiing, sledding, and ice skating in winter. Contact the park superintendent for information about camping.

Crabtree Nature Center
On Palatine Road, 1 mile west of Barrington Road   (708) 381-6592
(contact the Cook County Forest Preserve District for more information)
A wilderness preserve containing 1,100 acres of rolling terrain, intended for nature study and education. The Nature Center contains exhibits on the glacial history of Illinois and its prairies. The Center has one of the most attractive prairie restoration projects. The marshes and ponds are home to a variety of birds and animals and also attract migratory birds in spring and fall. Picnicking is not allowed.

Des Plaines River Trail
Follows west bank of the river in Lake County for most of its course until it reaches Sterling Lake, near the Wisconsin border.
The trail is wooded along most of its length and is accessible to hikers and bikers at several points along the way. A good place for bird-watching, as the trail lies on a migration route. For information and maps, contact the Lake County Forest Preserve District.

Green Bay Trail
Starts at Shorewood Park in Wilmette, Elmwood Street and Green Bay Road
Pleasant wooded and paved trail winding through the northern suburbs. This is a great route to Ravinia in Highland Park.

Grosse Point Lighthouse Park
2600 Sheridan, Evanston, 60201   (708) 864-5181
Tours of the 1873 lighthouse are given on weekends in summer, from late April to October. The lighthouse is surrounded by a wooded area with gardens, a wildflower walk (at its best in April and May), sand dunes, a small museum, and an experimental greenhouse. Walk down some steps to the beach below (admission to all Evanston beaches: adults $4, children $2).

Illinois Beach State Park
Along Lake Michigan between Waukegan and the Wisconsin border
(contact the Superintendent, Illinois Beach State Park, Zion, 60099
(708) 662-4811)
The park has two units with hiking and cross-country skiing trails, beach access, picnicking, and camping facilities. It attracts a variety of birds as it lies on a migration route. The southern unit has an interpretive center that offers talks and guided walks. An unusual feature of this park is the Dead River, a slow stream obstructed by a sandbar. For most of the year, the river is actually a long pond. During heavy rains, though, the excess water flows through the sandbar into the lake.

Indiana Dunes National Lakeshore
Visitor Center, 3 miles east of Indiana 49 on U.S. 12 on Kemil Road;
100 N. Mineral Springs, Porter, IN 46304   (219) 926-7561
This area has 13,000 acres of an unusual ecosystem of plants, animals, and dunes and is constantly changing as a result of the winds blowing from Lake Michigan. The dunes inland have been stabilized by vegetation, but the foredunes (those closer to the shore) are constantly shifting with the wind and the sand deposits. The ponds, marshes, and bogs that dot the area are reminders of the Ice Age. The varied topography supports a wide variety of plant life not common to the area, such as southern dogwood, artic bearberry, plains flowers, and cactus. Wildlife, including migratory birds, can be seen here. Recreational facilities include swimming, hiking, dune climbing, camping, boating, picnicking, horseback riding, cross- country skiing, snowshoeing, and environmental programs. Park rangers are very helpful.

Indiana Dunes State Park
At 1600 N. 25 East, Chesterton, IN 46304   (219) 926-4520
Offers group and family camping facilities and a naturalist program; special fees and regulations apply.

Kettle Moraine State Park
In Wisconsin, about 20 miles north of Lake Geneva, on County Road H,
1.5 miles north of the intersection with Route 12   (414) 626-2116
A long drive (about 2.5 hours from the Loop), but worth the effort. A beautiful park, with hilly terrain and large craterlike hollows ("kettles") fashioned by the receding glaciers. Entrance fee per car.

Moraine Hills State Park
914 S. River, McHenry, 60050   (815) 385-1624
The forested hills and ridges, swamplands, and bogs of this park are characteristic of moraines. The park supports a variety of plant and animal life. Wildflowers abound in spring, and the fall colors are brilliant, especially in the rear part of the park. Lake Defiance is one of the few relatively undisturbed glacial lakes in Illinois. A network of trails for hiking, biking, and cross-country skiing is here, as well as some nature trails.

Palos and Sag Valley Forest Preserve Divisions
Contact Palos Division Headquarters, Cook County Forest Preserve
District, 9900 S. Willow Springs (104th Avenue), Willow Springs, 60480
(708) 839-5617
Located just southwest of Chicago, these two adjoining divisions cover more than 10,000 acres of hills, woodlands, marshlands, lakes, ponds, sloughs, and swamps. Evidence of the retreating glaciers can be seen in the varied terrain. Plenty of wildlife, wildflowers, and vegetation. Facilities include excellent hiking and biking trails, riding, boating, and picnicking. The Sag Valley division has six toboggan slides and a warming shelter. Both divisions have facilities for sledding and cross-country skiing in winter. The Little Red Schoolhouse Nature Center is located approximately in the middle of the preserve and on top of the Valparaiso moraine.

Ryerson Conservation Area
21950 Riverwoods, Deerfield   (708) 948-7750
Located between Lincolnshire and Riverwoods in Lake County, this area is primarily a conservation area with a nature center, library, and a working farm. Wildflowers grow in abundance in spring and this preserve is the best site in Lake County for viewing fall foliage. There are about 10 miles of trails for hiking and cross-country skiing. Picnicking, riding, and biking are not allowed.

Starved Rock State Park
About 115 miles from the Loop, 1 mile south of Utica, 4 miles south off I-80 on SR 178   (815) 667-4726
Located along the Illinois River, this beautiful park covers 2,630 acres of wooded bluffland, with canyons, overhangs, cliffs, and waterfalls. The park is best known for its unusual sandstone rock formations. The porous sandstone supports lush vegetation, which in turn supports an abundance of wildlife. There are well-marked hiking trails as well as facilities for boating, horseback riding, cross-country skiing, picnicking, and camping. Maps for the park as well as for the nearby **Matthiessen State Park** can be picked up at the park headquarters or by writing to Starved Rock State Park, Box 116, Utica, IL 61373.

Volo Bog State Natural Area
28478 W. Brandenburg, Ingleside, 60041   (815) 344-1294
Another relic of the Ice Age, Volo is the state's only remaining open-water bog exhibiting all stages of the natural succession of a bog. Facilities include a visitor's center and an interpretive trail. Because of the fragility of the ecosystem, hiking and skiing are not allowed.

Waterfall Glen Forest Preserve
On Cass Avenue, off I-55
The largest preserve in DuPage County, Waterfall Glen has one of the most diverse ecosystems and covers over 2,400 acres of hills, prairies, savannah, oak-maple woodlands, ponds, and marshes. Wildlife is abundant; signs of beavers are evident from the trees cut down. This is also an excellent place for bird-watching. The preserve is unusual in that it is shaped like a doughnut; it surrounds Argonne National Laboratory. Because of the rugged terrain, hiking is strenuous. Well-marked hiking and riding trails wind through ravines, meadows, and woods. For more information, contact the DuPage County Forest Preserve District.

GARDENS AND ARBORETA

To enjoy the wilderness in a more formal setting, visit one of the places listed below.

Chicago Botanic Garden
Located just east of U.S. 41 on Lake Cook Road, Glencoe   (708) 835-5440
Three hundred acres of landscaped hills, lakes, and islands, interspersed with prairies, nature trails, demonstration gardens, and a Japanese garden. Narrated tram tours take visitors around the garden. Fee for parking and the tram tours.

Fabyan Forest Preserve
On IL 25, one mile south of the intersection of IL 38 and IL 25 near Geneva
(708) 232-1242
This preserve covers about 260 acres on both sides of the Fox River. The main
house, designed by Frank Lloyd Wright, houses a museum exhibiting the
varied interests of Colonel Fabyan. The extensive grounds contain a Japanese
garden with reflecting pools, dense woodlands, and an authentic Dutch
windmill. Free.

Garfield Park Conservatory
300 N. Central Park   533-1281
Considered to be the world's largest conservatory under one roof, it houses
more than 5,000 varieties of plants. Four major annual flower shows are held
at the Horticultural Hall: azalea and chrysanthemum shows in early spring
and fall, respectively, and Easter and Christmas shows. Among the attractions is a garden for the blind, where visitors are encouraged to touch and
smell specially selected plants.

Ladd Arboretum
2024 McCormick, Evanston   (708) 864-5181
Twenty-three acres of labeled trees and shrubs along the North Shore Channel of the Chicago River. Also contains a prairie restoration area and hiking
and biking trails. The Arboretum houses the Ecology Center, home of the
Evanston Environmental Association.

Morton Arboretum
Located just north of the intersection of SR 53 and the East-West Tollway
(708) 968-0074
This renowned arboretum houses about 5,000 species of plants, shrubs, and
trees on 1,500 acres of land. Not to be missed are the spectacular display of
flowers in May and the fall foliage in October. Trees and shrubs are labeled for
identification. Picnicking is not allowed. Fee per car and for the bus tours.

PARKS AND BEACHES

The Chicago Park District manages the city's parks and beaches. For information about the hours and activities, call the Information Office at 294-2493.

Grant Park
Located between the Loop and Lake Shore Drive, Grant Park has formal
gardens, trees, paths, and Buckingham Fountain. The shady trees attract both
native and migrating birds.

Lincoln Park
Chicago's largest park, Lincoln Park covers 1,212 acres of greenery and
lakefront. In addition to several beaches, lagoons, gardens, and playgrounds,
the park is home to a bird sanctuary and also has several miles of running and
biking trails. Recreational facilities are available for archery, tennis, golf,
miniature golf, swimming, baseball/softball, basketball, and football. Its
location, along Lake Shore Drive between North and Hollywood avenues,
makes it one of the most accessible and used parks in the city. The **Lincoln
Park Conservatory** (294-4770) houses rare orchids, ferns, palm trees, and
other exotic plants. Just outside the building are several colorfully laid-out

gardens, water lily ponds, and a fountain. The **Lincoln Park Zoo** (294-4660) is home to about 2,500 wild animals and birds. Popular exhibits are a petting zoo for children, a zoo nursery, and the farm-in-the-zoo, a replica of a working farm.

Promontory Point
On the South Shore, at 55th Street and the lakefront, is a favorite place for sunbathing, fishing, and picnicking. Although the park is located on the waterfront, there is no beach here, only lots of grass. An underground tunnel leads to the park from the east end of 55th Street. Walk or bike along the lakeshore all the way to the northern end of the city. Tends to get crowded in summer with barbecuers and Frisbee players. Great views of downtown Chicago, especially at night.

OUTDOOR ACTIVITIES

For those who would like to explore with a group, there are several organizations that sponsor local outdoor activities. Additional listings can sometimes be found in the "Friday" section of the *Chicago Tribune*.

American Youth Hostels (AYH)
3712 N. Clark, Chicago, 60613   327-8114
Bicycling, camping, hiking, and skiing trips; also offers instruction and inexpensive accommodations.

Forest Trails Hiking Club   (708) 475-4223
Sponsors day hikes every weekend. Locations include urban and wilderness areas in Illinois, Wisconsin, Indiana, and Michigan. Call for schedule.

Lakeshore Walking Club, Evanston   (708) 869-5745
Sponsors 3- to 10-mile walks every Sunday. Meets at the northwest corner of Dempster Street and the lakefront in Evanston at 2 P.M., near the tennis courts.

Sierra Club
Sponsors hiking, biking, skiing, and canoeing trips. Find out more about trips and other programs on the third Wednesday of every month at Beaumont's, 2020 N. Halsted, at 6:30 P.M.

CONSERVATION/ENVIRONMENTAL ORGANIZATIONS

Several organizations are dedicated to protect, preserve, and enhance the wilderness areas for the enjoyment and edification of present and future generations. They are always in need of volunteers.

Audubon Illinois Society
34W269 White Thorn, Wayne, IL 60184   (708) 584-6290
For avid bird-watchers.

The Nature Conservancy
79 W. Monroe, #708   346-8166
Sponsors several projects in Illinois, especially prairie restoration.

Sierra Club
506 S. Wabash   431-0158

One final note: this is not the only chapter in this book for nature lovers. For information on what Chicago is (and isn't) doing to protect the outdoors you so enjoy, as well as listings of recycling centers, please see the "Environment" chapter.

—Prathima Christdas

SPORTS

Chicago is quite possibly the most sports-crazy town in the nation, as the length of this chapter will attest. In fact, the fine art of spectating alone can keep you almost too busy to participate. But, just in case, I've compiled a little of a lot of what Chicago has to offer in both areas.

Chicago's pro teams are steeped in so much tradition and folklore that some have taken on an almost legendary status. Take the White Sox, whose one-time owner, Bill Veeck, used to attract fans the old-fashioned way—by pulling stunts like giving away free beer, sending a midget to bat (to shorten the pitcher's strike zone), and shooting off fireworks from the scoreboard. Today's Sox owners, unfortunately, are a little less creative and a lot more revenue conscious and so try more corporate ways to bring in the fans—like building a spiffy new taxpayer-subsidized stadium (with lots of skyboxes) and buying an overpriced shooting star like Bo Jackson. Although the Sox could only manage a second place in the AL West in 1991, there's always the hope that a noninjured George Bell could keep things interesting.

And then there's the Cubs, whose dismal World Series record (they haven't won since 1908) makes them ripe for excuses and reasons why. My personal favorite being the one about Sam Sianis, original owner of the Billy Goat Tavern, putting a hex on the Cubs for barring his and his lucky pet goat's entrance into the 1945 World Series, after allowing them in all season. And even though the hex was supposedly removed by a relative of Sianis, the best the Cubs have done since 1945 is to twice come up short in the National League championship.

You can't overlook the (da) Bears who acquired their "junkyard dog" mystique stemming from a history of attracting tough characters like Dick Butkus, Bulldog Turner, George Blanda, Jim McMahon, Dan Hampton, Buddy Ryan, and Mike Ditka. It keeps the games interesting and the fans loyal even if they have only won the Superbowl once (1985).

When it comes to basketball, the Bulls' greatest legend—(Michael Jordan)—is more recent. Since Rookie of the Year in 1984, Michael has spent his entire professional career astounding fans and helping to build up a championship team in Chicago. And it finally paid off in 1990 with the Bulls' first NBA title in 16 years, then back-to-back world championships in 1991 and 1992.

But Chicago's real basketball heroes were the Harlem Globetrotters, who started when a group of five outstanding black basketball players from Chicago's Phillips High School got together to play against the mostly all-white teams of the day. It wasn't until the 1950s that they switched to clowning antics to pay the bills.

PROFESSIONAL SPORTS

Tickets can usually be purchased by calling the team's ticket office numbers or Ticketron or Ticketmaster outlets, although it is advised to call as far in advance as possible (like before opening day). Or you can try your luck hanging around outside the gates in hopes some gracious soul will "give" away extra tickets (I've seen it happen). As a last resort you could try one of the area's wildly expensive ticket brokers.

Baseball

Chicago Cubs
Wrigley Field
1060 W. Addison (Howard El, Addison stop; Clark Street bus 22)
404-CUBS
Wrigley Field's vine-covered wall and fan-friendly confines and neighborhood make it one of the nation's most revered ballparks, especially on a sunny, cold beer–inspiring day. Some night games available, although they're not as much fun (even in the bleachers).

Chicago White Sox
Comiskey Park
333 W. 35th (Dan Ryan El, 35th Street stop)   924-1000
Well, the new base"mall" stadium is now in its second year, looking as bright and colorful as ever, but there's still no sign of baseball's greatest tavern: McCuddy's (evicted when the new stadium was built). Warning: the upper-deck seats are not for those prone to nosebleeds or height phobias.

Basketball

Chicago Bulls
Chicago Stadium
1800 W. Madison (Madison Street bus 20)   943-5800
Always a sell-out crowd and a great show no matter what the standings (the Bulls brothers, the Bulls blimp, and the Bullettes make sure of that). Try downtown restaurants, like the Como Inn and Red Kerr's, who offer free bus shuttles if the idea of parking around the stadium scares you.

Hockey

Chicago Blackhawks
Chicago Stadium
1800 W. Madison (Madison Street bus 20)   733-5300
Loud, gregarious fans like to watch the Blackhawks mix it up on the ice as much as they like to mix it up in the stands. Best organ music selection in town. Free downtown bus shuttles available for Blackhawks games, too.

Soccer

Chicago Power
Rosemont Horizon
6920 Mannheim (you're on your own for this one), Rosemont
(708) 299-9000
Chicago's outdoor soccer team, the Sting, never quite made it, so a faster, indoor version is now giving it a try.

Football

Chicago Bears
Soldier Field
425 E. McFetridge (12th Street and Lake Shore Drive)   663-5408
Catch a game at intimate, open-air Soldier Field before owner Michael Mc-Caskey sells out to the suburbs for more skybox revenue. Free bus shuttles from Grant Park and neighborhood restaurants like Ranalli's and Southport City Saloon, or take Clark Street bus 22 to the end of the line (at Blackie's Tavern) and walk over.

Horse Racing

Arlington International Racecourse, Ltd.
N. Wilke Road and Euclid Avenue
Arlington Heights (CNW Train to Arlington)   (708) 255-4300
From out of the ashes of the old Arlington Park Race Track (burned down in 1985) has grown a bigger and better thoroughbred racing/entertainment center. Even the new name sounds more spectacular. Catch a band at the picnic area on Friday and lots of fun things for the kids on Sunday.

Balmoral Park Race Track
Route 1 and Elms Court Lane, Crete   (708) 568-5700
Harness racing only.

Hawthorne Race Course
3501 S. Laramie, Cicero   (708) 780-3700
Harness and thoroughbred racing.

Maywood Park Trotting Association
North Avenue and 5th Street, Maywood   626-4816 or (708) 343-4800
Trotters and pacers.

Sportsman's Park
3301 S. Laramie (next to Hawthorne), Cicero   (708) 780-3700
Thoroughbred and harness racing.

The Winner's Circle
177 N. State   419-8787
223 W. Jackson   427-2300
Downtown, off-track betting for those allergic to real animals and mud.

Gambler's Anonymous
30 W. Washington   346-1588
When they start missing you at work. . . .

Polo

Polo and Equestrian Club
700 Oak Brook, Oakbrook   (708) 990-7656
Keeping a 70-year polo tradition alive in Oakbrook, after the Oakbrook Polo Club (and Michael Butler) went bankrupt a few years back. The season runs May–October with spectator matches every Sunday at 1 P.M. and 3 P.M.. Practice matches can be fun, too; call for details.

Sports Car Racing

Santa Fe Speedway
9100 S. Wolf, Hinsdale   (708) 839-1050
What's a nice quiet suburb like Hinsdale doing with a clay stock car track?

Notable Events

The Chicago Marathon   744-3315
Held the last Sunday in October, it's the biggest running event of the year and attracts a lot of big names.

The Mackinac Sailboat Race   861-7877
It's the oldest sanctioned race in America and covers 333 miles from Belmont Harbor to Mackinac Island in Michigan. Sponsored by the Chicago Yacht Club.

The Virginia Slims Tennis Tournament   413-5700
Attracts tennis biggies like McEnroe and Navratilova to the UIC Pavilion every year, usually in February.

The Western Open   (708) 257-5872
In early July, top pros descend upon Cog Hill Golf Course for the biggest Chicago golfing event of the season.

College Sports

Because Chicago is blessed with so many colleges of all sizes and shapes, only major universities and their primary spectator sports are listed below. You may want to check your local colleges for some fine, inexpensive sports entertainment, too.

DePaul University
Lincoln and Fullerton avenues   341-8010
Joey Meyer, son of beloved basketball folk hero Ray Meyer, is doing a pretty good job of keeping DePaul's great basketball heritage alive. Games are played at the parking lot–encased Rosemont Horizon, 6920 Mannheim in suburban Rosemont. DePaul claims no football teams but does tout its men's soccer and women's volleyball and softball teams.

Northwestern University
Evanston   (708) 491-7070
Chicago's only Division 1 conference (Big 10) football/basketball representatives. Trying hard to downplay their egghead reputation and win some games, the Wildcats have had some success over the last few years (they beat the U of I in football in 1991). They play football at Dyche Stadium, and basketball at McGaw Hall on their Evanston campus.

University of Illinois–Chicago
Halsted Street and the Eisenhower Expressway   966- 5880
For a good time at a nice, uncrowded stadium, try a Mid-Continent Conference basketball or hockey game at the UIC Pavilion.

University of Chicago
Hyde Park   702-7681
Yes, University of Chicago. Would you believe they were once stars of the Big 10 and even claim to have spawned the first Heisman Trophy winner? But, alas, sports were determined to be at odds with the school's educational mission in the early 1940s and hence their current Division III standing. However, they do still have football and basketball games as well as wrestling, tennis, and track to watch that costs nothing (or next to nada) to attend.

Loyola University
6525 N. Sheridan   274-1211
For some big basketball games on an intimate, friendly court, catch Loyola (1963 NCAA champs) at the UIC Pavilion.

PARTICIPANT SPORTS

Having so few nice days for spontaneous outside activities has perhaps made Chicago overcompensate with clubs, events, and leagues in virtually every sports-related area you can imagine. If you still can't find exactly what you're looking to do here, try the *Chicago Tribune* Friday "Weekend" section, *Windy City Sports* (a free bimonthly magazine) or *The Amateur Athlete* (available at some local book and sports stores.)

Major Resources

Chicago Park District   294-4607
The only bad thing about having the world's largest park district is that it may take a little longer to get an answer to your question over the phone. The good part is that you have access to everything from archery to zoos at little or no cost. Some of their more impressive statistics include

- **561** parks with almost **7,500** acres to play in,

- **720** tennis courts,

- **285** softball diamonds,

- **110** ice skating areas,

- **90** swimming pools, and

- **6** golf courses (and one miniature golf area at Diversy Harbor).

   To find out which parks have what, call for your copy of "Table of Parks and Park Facilities," or ask for specific information on your area of interest.

Chicago Area Women's Sports Association (CAWSA)   235-1913
CAWSA is an all-volunteer, nonprofit advocacy group for women's and girl's sports. A broad-based, networking organization, they have a speakers' bureau and act as a clearinghouse for information on all sports. Occasionally they have provided grants for individual sportswomen. CAWSA's Outings Club for Women plans year-round outdoor activities, including skiing, cycling, and hiking trips and workshops.

Chicago Forest Preserves (708) 771-1330, TDD (708) 771- 1190
Another phenomenal recreational facility that offers some of the best scenery Chicagoland has to offer and includes 36 fishing lakes, 157 miles of multipurpose trails (hiking, jogging, biking, horse), 10 golf courses, 2,700 picnic sites, ice fishing, tobogganing, and 67,000 acres available for hiking or cross-country skiing. Call for a "Recreational Facilities Map."

Hosteling International 327-8114
It's neither a terrorist organization or even just a student travel network anymore. Its a travel, recreational, and educational not-for-profit federation that offers classes and trips in backpacking, biking, canoeing, sailing, skiing, and even spelunking. Call for more details.

Chicago YMCAs 280-3450
This area's 24 chartered YMCAs are well known for their swimming and basketball facilities and lessons. Many offer volleyball and football clinics and leagues as well as classes in a wide variety of other athletic activities. Membership fees or per-activity rates are very reasonable; and if you can show that you're economically disadvantaged (according to Illinois guidelines), you are eligible for a fee waiver—kind of like a YMCA scholarship. Call the Y nearest you for a specific rundown on its facility, as they will vary.

Chicago Social Club (CSC) 883-9596
In 1990, a group of young urban Lincoln Park professionals (YULPPIES) put together a football league for their busy friends. It was so popular that it was expanded to year-round sports leagues and opened up to everyone. Team rates are not cheap but comparable to alternative leagues for the most part. (Try getting your favorite tavern to sponsor you in return for on-the-field advertising and in-their-bar eating and drinking).

The general season line-up includes

- **Winter:** Indoor volleyball—Oz Park

- **Spring:** Indoor volleyball, touch football—Lincoln and Oz parks

- **Summer:** Beach volleyball—North Avenue Beach; softball—Lincoln Park

- **Fall:** Touch football—Lincoln and Oz parks; basketball—Oz Park

Colleges

University of Illinois–Chicago (996-2695), the **University of Chicago** (753-4680), and **Northwestern University** (491-7070) all offer classes to the public in a variety of the sports activities listed later. Sorry, DePaul and Loyola are for students and affiliates only, but try some of your local community colleges as well.

Special Adult Education Network

Several Lincoln Park organizations have compiled a variety of special interest classes to the busy city person. You can sign up for everything from fencing, martial arts, and boxing to belly dancing, stunt fighting, and even airplane flying. You can even find such mundane things as swimming, volleyball, and tennis through the following groups:

The Discovery Center   348-8120

The Latin School Live & Learn Center   664-8760

Francis Parker Evening Classes   535-3375

ACTIVITIES

Archery

Try the Park District's (294-2309) archery ranges, four indoor, four out-door, or call **Archery Sales and Service** (588-2077) for even more ranges and instruction.

Badminton

Start with the Badminton Association of Chicago (736-1072) for the lowdown on best places to play, tournaments, and so on.

Baseball

The Park District (294-2309) has 353 junior diamonds and 176 senior diamonds. Call for the ones nearest you.

Basketball

Once again the Park District comes through with over 1,000 backboards, leagues, and lessons, too (294-2309). Other good bets are your area YMCA (280-3450) and the Chicago Social Club (883-9596); many churches sponsor teams as well.

Beaches

You can't miss running into a beach if you walk east from most parts of the city. The Park District runs 31 for free, and many North Shore suburbs have nice ones, too (for a fee). If you're feeling the need to get a little farther away, try the Illinois Beach State Park straight north in Zion, or for a little more scenery, try the Indiana or Michigan Dunes, only a few hours away by train or car. And now you can try out New Buffalo's beach via ferry, which shuttles back and forth from Navy Pier.

Biking

The Park District (294-2309) offers 19 different bike paths in 19 different parks, and the Forest Preserve ([708] 771-1330) maintains 8 Class 1 trails (paved for 2 lanes) in addition to 157 miles of multipurpose trails. Ask for maps. Additionally, Hosteling International (327-8114) puts together a lot of trips, and there are lots of club and charity rides throughout the spring and summer. Try the groups below for more information:

Illinois Cycling Association (708) 251-6021

Chicagoland Bicycle Federation
42-PEDAL, its 24-hour biking event and information hot line

Billiards

Pool, like many throwbacks to the fifties, is experiencing a resurgence, and so you no longer have to play in a smoky dimly lit club (unless you want to). Some good bets are

The Corner Pocket
2610 N. Halsted   281-0050
New and trendy.

The Cue Club
2833 N. Sheffield   477-3661
Also new and trendy.

St. Paul Billiards
1415 W. Fullerton   472-9494
In the movie *Color of Money*, and really is smoky and dimly lit.

The Gingerman
3740 N. Clark   549-2050
Also claims a credit in *The Color of Money* and has a great selection of beers.

And for tournament information try the **Illinois Billiards Club** (737-6655).

Bowling

Chicago has always been a bonanza for bowling, with lots of typical 1970s schtick lanes, and a few more interesting versions, too. A few worth trying:

Rock 'N' Bowl
2211 W. Diversey   227-5800
6432 W. North   637-1400
Open all night and 'til 5 A.M. on weekends.

Southport Lanes
3325 N. Southport   472-1601
If you thought real live pinboys were a thing of the past, you're in store for a treat. Not as authentic and friendly as when Leo and Ella owned it, but still fun, and the lanes are always available for open bowling.

Spencer's Marina City Bowling
300 N. State   527-0747
Your only good bet for bowling downtown.

Timberlanes
185 W. Irving Park   549-9770
Perfect for parties, eight lanes with a bar about five steps back. Call a couple of months ahead. Some open bowling.

Boxing

For those who enjoy being knocked about the head, or just enjoy watching.

Lincoln Park Boxing Program   294-4750

Degerberg Academy of Martial Arts and Physical Fitness, Inc.   728-5300

Bungie Jumping

Drastic Elastic Bungie Jumping   642-9696
If strapping a large rubber band to your body and free- falling hundreds of feet sounds like a good time, call this place—they have three different sites in the Chicago area, including one downtown. Their "season" runs every weekend May–August, with jumps at other times during the year scheduled on a week-by-week basis.

Canoeing

Yes, canoeing can be done in Chicago, just ask the Forest Preserve about their Illinois and Michigan Canal and Chicago Portage routes. Or call Hosteling International (327-8114) to find out about trips they're planning (even down the Chicago River).

Cricket

Although the Park District no longer has an official pitch (field), any of their 69 outdoor soccer fields can be used for this purpose. Call the Park Supervisor at Washington Park (294-2200) for more information on clubs and tournaments.

Darts

Before pool and bowling came back in style, dart leagues were just about the only sanctioned bar sport. To track down the best tavern clubs, ask **Windy City Darters** (286-3848). They're a clearinghouse for dart clubs and can send you a list of taverns with dart leagues in your area, if you ask nicely.

Fencing

Even though Errol Flynn hasn't made a movie in years, there's still quite a good following for his art in Chicagoland. Several YMCAs (286-3450) and the Adult Ed Networks all offer lessons. Or call the **Great Lakes Fencing Association** in Hanover Park ([708] 213-7287) for instructions and/or practice.

Fishing

The Forest Preserve ([708] 771-1330) has 36 water areas for a total of 2,000 acres of fishing waters (including ice fishing when there's at least 4 inches of ice). Or for the citified version, join fishermen at lakefront harbors and lagoons. (I once saw a huge [live] salmon pulled right out of Diversey Harbor). Don't forget to get a license!

Football

The Chicago Social Club (883-9596) probably has the biggest and the best run touch football league, but you can also try the Park District (294-2309) and the YMCA (296-3450) for league info.

Golf

The Park District (294-2272) has 6 public courses, 5 9-hole and 1 18-hole, and the Forest Preserve ([708] 771-1300) has 10, plus 4 driving ranges. And there are many more expensive courses throughout the suburbs from which to choose, some requiring membership, some not.

Gymnastics

A group called the American Turners (*turner* literally means gymnast) has a great reputation for gymnastics classes and in fact has trained several Olympic contenders. Find out more from their city branch, the **Lincoln Park Turners** (248-1682). Or try the Park District (294-2309), YMCAs, and fitness clubs in your area.

Handball

Check with the **Chicago Team Handball Club** ([708] 662-6548) for the ins and outs (and backs and forths) of this sport.

Hang Gliding

The **Chicago Hang Gliding Organization** (281-3338) say they've really taken off in the last few years (watch the attempts as you're catching some rays at Michigan dunes).

Hiking

There's lots of trails in the near vicinity, try the **Forest Trails Hiking Club** ([708] 475-4223), Hosteling International (327-8114), or our old standbys, the Park District and the Forest Preserve.

Hockey

Check the Park District's McFetridge Center (478-1210) for league times and locations.

Horseback Riding

The Forest Preserve has over 200 miles of scenic trails, many starting points are near rental stables. And for riding in the city, try the indoor arena at **Coach Horse Equestrian Center** (266-7878).

Kayaking

Hosteling International (327-8114) and the **Chicago Area Sea Kayak Association** ([708] 766-3773) can steer you in the right direction.

Labocci (Bocci Ball)

Yes, the Park District (294-2309) has this, too (10 courts, no less).

Lacrosse

Appears to be on the upswing in Chicago, as there are quite a few clubs in the area. A few to start with:

Chicago Chapter of the Lacrosse Foundation   (708) 446- 6694

Chicago Lacrosse Club   348-0846

Chicago Lacrosse Association   621-4195

Lawn Bowling

Bowling outside? What a concept! Find out more from the Lakeside Lawn Bowling Club, 684-9799.

Martial Arts

Karate, tae kwon do, kung fu, judo, jujitsu, and aikido are all Asian arts emphasizing meditation, breathing, and concentration for sports and self-defense. Lots of private facilities in the yellow pages, or try the YMCA (286-3450), the Adult Ed Networks, and colleges.

Orienteering

Or, "How to make a sport out of getting lost." Find your way to the **Chicago Orienteering Club** ([708] 359-7355).

Racquetball

This is the health club territory (see the "Fitness" chapter), so try your local health clubs. The Park District (294-2309) also has 10 courts, and many of the colleges and other Adult Ed Networks offer classes.

Rafting

You may be surprised at the amount of whitewater within a few hours of Chicago. Try the **Chicago Whitewater Association** in Arlington Heights, or Hosteling International (327-8114).

Rowing

Who says the East Coast is privy to all the finer things in life? Get stroking at the **Chicago River Aquatic Center** (616-0056) or the **Lincoln Park Boat Club** (278-5539).

Rugby

A popular sport in this rough-and-tumble town.

Chicago Griffins Rugby Football Club   588-0350

Chicago Lions Rugby Club   621-1137

Lakeshore 7's Women's Rugby Club   792-9202

Southside Irish Rugby Club   422-8065

Sailing

The Park District (294-2272) offers classes at their various harbors, as do most of the yacht clubs. You can also try Hosteling International (327-8114) and the **Chicago Sailing School** (871-2628).

Scuba Diving

You might not see a lot of exotic fish around here, but you can get certified for your next trip to the Caribbean through many colleges and Adult Ed Networks or through

Illinois Institute of Diving   929-0500

Underwater Safaris Scuba Center   337-9265

Skating

You can ice skate outdoors at the Daley Centennial Building, across from Marshall Field's, or at the Park District's Grant Park facility, or any of the lagoons or harbors as long as the ice is at least four inches thick. You can also skate on any of the Forest Preserve's waters, abiding by the four-inch thick rule. A good indoor facility is the Park District's **McFetridge Center** (478-0210).

Roller skating has taken on a new meaning with the advent of in- line skating, and a good place for renting and lessons is **Londo Mondo** (751-1446). **Latin School** (664-8760) also offers lessons; and if you're still interested in the old-fashioned indoor versions, give **United Skates of America** a call (271-5668). Even if you're not an Olympic hopeful, you may want to try your feet at speedskating. Glen Ellyn's **AAA Speedskating Club** ([708] 469- 6713) can help.

Skiing

Cross-country skiing can and is done all over the parks when snow conditions permit. The Forest Preserve ([708] 771-1330) also has 8 developed trails and encourages skiing throughout all of its 67,000 acres. Rentals available through the Forest Preserve and many sports stores (M. C. Mages [337-6151] and Erewhon [644-4411] to name a few).

Downhill is best done when you have enough money and time to go out west, or at least Michigan's Upper Peninsula, although skiing is available at Alpine Valley and Devil's Head in Wisconsin. Hosteling International (327-8114) arranges a lot of ski trips, as do many of the hundreds of ski clubs in the area. Check with the **Chicago Metropolitan Ski Council** (346-1268) or the Friday *Tribune*, "Weekend" section.

Sky Diving

It's not allowed in the Chicago metropolitan area because air space is too dense, but there are some facilities nearby.

Hinckley Parachute Center
Hinckley, IL   (815) 285-9230

Wisconsin Skydiver's Parachute Club
Milwaukee, WI   (414) 252-3434

Parachutes and Assoc.
Frankfort, IN   (317) 654-6188

Snowboarding

Try the **Midwest Snowboard Association** ([513] 376-1970) for more information on this cold-weather version of surfing.

Soccer

The Park District (294-2309) has some excellent leagues, and you can also try the **Illinois Soccer Association** (463-0653).

Softball

The Park District runs numerous leagues, many hard to get into, but call anyway (294-2309) or check with your closest park. Also try the Chicago Social Club (883-9596), which is just getting the ball rolling this year.

Squash

Many health clubs have courts available, and you can also check with the **Illinois Squash Rackets Association**.

Swimming

The Park District (294-2309) is great in aquatics, with 58 outdoor pools, 32 indoor pools, and 2 swimming lagoons, but if there isn't a facility near you, try a YMCA, a branch of the American Turners, or a neighborhood health club.

Tennis

The Park District (294-2309) has 726 courts, most of them outside, but at least 6 at their McFetridge Center facility (478-0210). Small fees are charged most places, and reservations may be required, although many use the early "rack-up" system. Lessons and tournaments available here and through many colleges, and Adult Ed Networks, some YMCAs, and many health clubs. Or try the **Chicago District Tennis Association** ([708] 803-CDTA).

Tobogganing

Simple sledding wasn't good enough for the Forest Preserve, so they elected 14 slides that can be used when conditions are right (4 inches of snow and below 20 degrees). The five locations (complete with toboggan rentals) are open from 10 A.M.–10 P.M..

Bemis Woods Ogden Avenue west of Wolf Road, Western Springs

Dan Ryan Woods 87th Street and Western Avenue, Chicago

Deer Grove 5 Quinten Road, north of Dundee Road, Palatine

Jensen Slides Devon and Milwaukee avenues, Chicago

Swallow Cliff Rte. 83, west of Mannheim Road (Rte. 45), Palos Park

Track and Field

The 24-mile jogging course along the lakefront from Bryn Mawr to 71st Street on the South Side is great for uninterrupted running and lots of interesting scenery, both people and nature. And the **Chicago Area Runners Association** (CARA) is a great source for races, events, clubs, you name it. Call 666-9836 and/or check out their newsmagazine, *The Chicago Runner*.

Triathlon

The *Chicago Sun Times* ([708] 328-3678) sponsors the world's biggest version of this grueling event at the end of August. You'd better start training now:

Chicago Triathlon Club 549-1661

U of I–Chicago's class in triathelete training 996-2695

Windsurfing

Classes are available through Adult Ed Networks and Northwestern University (491-7070), which teaches right off the shoreline of their Evanston campus. Also try **Windward Sports Windsurfing Shop** (472-6868).

—Pat Ladd

FITNESS

The fitness boom of the eighties has not left Chicago unscathed; just thumb through the vast yellow pages section on "Health Clubs." We owe thanks for this great selection to the aerobics craze popularized by Dr. Kenneth Cooper. It was he who heavily promoted the fact that stimulating heart and lung activity could bring about many health benefits (that is, if you do it for at least a half hour, 3 times a week). But, alas, since surveys indicate that still over 80 percent of us don't get enough exercise, herewith are some good just go-ahead-and-get-it-over-with strategies.

FACILITIES

Chicago Park District 294-2309
These people make it easy to get active, with 19 different bicycle paths; 24 miles of jogging, biking, walking paths along the lakefront; 4 obstacle/fitness courses (2 in Lincoln Park); 14 fitness centers with all the latest in cardiovascular equipment and weight machines; and 90 swimming pools.

The Forest Preserves (708) 771-1330
The place for hundreds of miles of biking, hiking, cross-country skiing, and horseback riding, not to mention skating, swimming, golf, and canoeing. The experts say you end up in better shape (and prevent boredom) if you vary your exercise, so now there's no excuse.

FITNESS ACTIVITIES

Biking, Running, and Swimming

Chicago is a great place to do all three either individually or with a crowd; see the "Sports" chapter for more details on facilities, clubs, and events.

Dancing

Try the Park District (294-2309), your local YMCA (286-3450), and the Adult Ed Networks for a wide variety of contemporary lessons (ballroom, salsa, belly, etc.). For a real good ol' time try the **Chicago Barn Dance Co.** (342-5474) for square dancing, two-stepping, cajun, y'all name it. And for some real fun check out the **Baby Doll Polka Club** (582-9706). If you're interested in more traditional dance lessons and performances (ballet, jazz, tap), the best source to start with is the **Chicago Dance Coalition** (419-8384), the service organization for Chicago's dance community.

Walking

The perfect sport for Chicago (it definitely beats the El) as both the Park District and the forest preserves have miles upon miles to explore. Make up your own rules and routes or try **Hosteling International** (327-8114) or the **Chicago Walker's Club** (424-3546) for info on more organized endeavors.

Yoga

Try it for the best stretching and strengthening exercises you'll ever find (for body and soul). The New City YMCA has some great classes, and there are lots of independent operators around, like the **Wild Onion Yoga** (868-0400) and the **Yoga Circle** (645-0750).

Fitness Centers and Clubs

The more traditional citified way to squeeze in exercise is through a nearby health club. While the best idea is to check in the yellow pages for a place near you, we've provided a rundown of some of the more popular ones to give you an idea of the range of facilities and costs.

The key to facilities:

A=Aerobics,
C/V=Cardiovascular equipment,
R=Racquetball, S=Swimming,
T=Tennis, Tr=Track,
W=Weights

The key to annual costs:

Cheap $	Under $300
Not bad $$	$300–$700
Getting up there $$$	$800–$1,100
Bad news $$$$	$1,200–$1,600
Ouch $$$$$	$1,600+

While the ranges listed are "normal" rates, it is wise to wait for the club you've selected to have a special (almost all do at least once per year, often in the spring), as it can save you up to 50 percent.

	Facilities	Specialties	Cost
U of I/Chicago Halsted and the Eisenhower 996-2695	A,C/V,W,S,R,T	Wallyball, dance, scuba, martial arts	$
U of Chicago Hyde Park 753-4680	A,C/V,W,R,T,S	Pick-up B-ball	$$
Chicago YMCAs 286-3450	S,A,C/V,W	Yoga, basketball, dance, martial arts, supercircuit	$
Bally's Chicago Health Club	R,A,S,C/V,W	Locations throughout the city	$$
Women's Workout World 664-2106	A,C/V,W	No-frills, all women	$
Downtown Sports Club 441 N. Wabash, 644-4800	T,R,S,W,Tr,A,C/V	Squash courts, jacuzzi, steam room, juice bar	$$$

	Facilities	Specialties	Cost
East Bank Club 500 N. Kingsbury 527-5800	T,A,R,C/V,S,W,Tr	Driving range, outdoor pool	$$$$$
Galter Life Center Swedish Covenant Hospital 878-9936	S,A,C/V,W	Physical therapists, cardiac rehab, personal trainers	$$
Jamnastics 2727 N. Lincoln 477-8400	A,W	Ranked top 25 gyms by *Self* magazine	$$
Lakeshore Athletic 1320 W. Fullerton 477-9888	T,A,C/V,W,Tr,R	Tanning, outdoor grill and bar	$$$$
Lehman Sports Center 2700 N. Lehman 871-8300	A,C/V, Tr	B-ball, V-ball, fireplace lounge	$$$
Midtown Tennis Club 2020 W. Fullerton 235-2300	T, C/V	18 courts, tourneys, whirlpool, sauna	$$$
The Sporting Club 616-9000	A,W,S,C/V	Rock-climbing wall, squash	$$$

ENVIRONMENTALLY SOUND FITNESS ACTIVITIES

Feel like doing something good for the community as well as yourself? Try one of these for a more creative workout.

Field Museum   322-8854
For ecology field trips.

Lincoln Park Zoo   294-4649
For gardening, animal care, and grooming volunteer work.

Sierra Club/Illinois   431-0158
For volunteer prairie restoration activities.

Friends of the Park   922-3307
For hands-on outdoor Park projects.

FITNESS FOR SPECIAL NEEDS

With the Americans with Disabilities Act in full effect now, the Park District is doing quite a bit of innovation to help people with disabilities take full advantage of park facilities. Several beaches are equipped with mats that allow wheelchairs and strollers to be rolled right down to the water. And a "surf wheelchair" will be available for the first time at some locations. They include umbrellas, carrying bags, water bottles, and are good for land and water. The Park District (294-4768, TDD 986-0726) can also tell you about interpreted nature trails, special day camps, swimming lessons, and sites for Special Olympics training. Try these groups for other ideas: **Rehabilitation Institute of Chicago** (908-4292) and **Special Olympics of Illinois** ((309) 888-2551).

FOOD FOR THOUGHT (AND BODY)

As we all know, exercise alone won't give us that great healthy glow, so here are a few places for eating healthy, too:

Foodworks
1002 W. Diversey   348-7800

Sherwyn's Superstore
645 W. Diversey   477-1934

New City Market
1811 N. Halsted   280-7600

Nok-Yong Market
3519 W. Lawrence   588-4636

And for eating-out healthy:

Blind Faith Cafe
525 Dempster, Evanston   (708) 328-6875

The Bread Shop
3400 N. Halsted   528-8108

The Chicago Diner
3411 N. Halsted   935-6696

Heartland Cafe, Buffalo Bar, and General Store
7000 N. Glenwood   465-8005

The Lo-cal Zone
912 N. Rush   943-9060

Sunshine's Health Food & Juice Bar & Cafe
67 E. 75th   994-8235

—Pat Ladd

Miguel del Valle (left), state senator for the fifth district, talking to channel 44 anchor Augusto Torres.

Media

LOCAL PRESS
RADIO

LOCAL PRESS

What other city so reveres the press community that it names a city bridge after a newspaper columnist? (That's the Irv Kupcinet Bridge crossing the Chicago River at Wabash.) Walking north across the river on Michigan Avenue takes you right onto the 50-yard line of the Chicago press community, as rival media giants face off across Michigan Avenue. To your right is the *Tribune* empire, an impressive building and headquarters of print and broadcast operations. A little farther on the right is the NBC Tower, while behind the Wrigley Building stands the home of the *Sun-Times*.

An easy afternoon stroll allows you to observe WMAQ putting the evening news together through a glass panel located in the NBC Tower lobby, view WGN radio operations from Michigan Avenue, and walk through the public gallery at the *Sun-Times* building to watch the giant presses roll every afternoon. Actual tours are listed below. Complete your tour with a trip to the Billy Goat Tavern on lower Michigan, a traditional watering hole for press and press groupies made famous by Mike Royko and the "Saturday Night Live" ("Cheeseburger, cheeseburger") routine.

TOURS

WMAQ
Monday–Friday, 10 A.M., 2 P.M., or by group reservation   836-5555

Chicago Tribune
Monday–Friday, 9:30 A.M.–3:30 P.M. (reservations required)   222-2116

Chicago Sun-Times
Tuesday–Thursday, 10:30 A.M.   321-2032

THE PRESS

Chicago press style grew out of the fiercely competitive world of several dailies, multiple editions fighting for exclusives in a city with big bosses and big industry. Big names ran the presses: Medill, McCormick, Fields, Murdoch. Chicago was a place to learn your craft, hone your skills, and enter the national arena.

The television era led to reduced demand for newsprint. Megamergers changed the structure of the industry. Budget cuts depleted staffs. Where there were once four dailies, Chicago is now served by only two major papers: The *Tribune* and the *Sun-Times*. The *Trib* staked out the suburbs, while the *Sun-Times* became the best-selling city paper.

Meanwhile, the television stations compete for viewers during evening news hours; public television and cable programs, narrowly targeting special issues, are taking over debate formats; and radio generates headlines, traffic, and talk.

Today, the majors are perplexed about how to present news to a fractured mass audience. More than ever, reading just one paper or using just one media format will not keep you sufficiently versed on important city issues, political debates, neighborhood concerns, or individual interests. Hence, search out those newsletters, monthlies, neighborhood papers, cable programs, and alternative papers to satisfy your news appetite.

The Dailies

Chicago Tribune
435 N. Michigan, Chicago, 60611   222-3232
The *Chicago Tribune* is the oldest city paper and a part of the Tribune Company, a powerful media conglomerate. The *Trib* supported Abraham Lincoln in his first run for office, opposed the New Deal, supports business, and generally endorses Republican candidates.

Long on the lookout for new technologies, the *Trib* pioneered using early telegraph lines to Washington and radio lines to Europe and started its own radio station (WGN—"World's Greatest Newspaper") in 1924. Today the *Trib* is heavily zoning the papers, with separate news bureaus in various suburban communities. For instance, readers no longer see the same "Chicagoland" section issue in DuPage County and the city.

The *Tribune* provides the best national and international coverage of the city papers. Its readership is largely middle- to upper-class, college educated, and often suburban. Stories outside the Loop are gradually moving out of the crime and victim genre, but they're doing so more slowly for coverage of the South and West sides.

The *Tribune* does have a wealth of talented columnists and critics with a loyal following: Mike Royko writes a tough, sarcastic political commentary with a unique, gruff style that epitomizes old Chicago. Bob Greene follows social trends and human issues, commenting on life in the nineties. Ann Landers is *Chicago Tribune* based. Critics Dave Kehr and Gene Siskel (movies), Richard Christiansen (entertainment), Alan Artner (art), and John Von Rhein (classical music) keep a watchful eye on this cultural mecca.

Chicago Sun-Times
401 N. Wabash, Chicago, 60611   321-3000
The *Sun-Times* is better known for covering Chicago city stories. It's easier to find (and more widely read) in many South and West side neighborhoods. The *Sun-Times* has good investigative reporters, though less fully staffed than in the past, who still go after important issues (most recently the juvenile court system).

The *Sun-Times* has weathered the Rupert Murdoch era, the loss of Mike Royko, and the continuous clamor that it won't survive. But it does. Its strengths remain good local coverage and sports. Other notable writers include Roger Ebert, Michael Sneed, and investigative reporter Deborah Nelson.

Weeklies and Monthlies

Entertainment, city issues, and more in-depth features are the main fare of Chicago's many weekly and monthly publications. *The Reader* is a well-written liberal weekly with lengthy, in-depth reports on stories the dailies miss (e.g, a good look at Carol Moseley Braun before the 1992 primary). But there are no particular news beats or "hard" news reporting, just good writing motivated by an interest in getting behind the scene.

The Reader
11 E. Illinois, Chicago, 60611 828-0350
The Reader gives excellent coverage of what's happening in entertainment. This is your best guide to the week's concerts, club dates, plays, and movies. Its also a great place for connections—finding an apartment, lecture, book club; the rugby, lacrosse, or hiking organizations; or for meeting an interesting person. *The Reader* is free and distributed to bookstores, bars, and retail outlets in great stacks on Thursday afternoons and quickly disappears. Most stacks are found on the North Side, Loop, Hyde Park, Evanston, and Oak Park.

And then came the followers:

NewCity
711 S. Dearborn, #807, Chicago, 60605 663-4685
Free weekly dated Thursday, usually available Wednesday afternoon. *The Reader* proved you could assemble good writers for a free publication and succeed. *NewCity* targets a younger audience but provides some good stories and a smaller entertainment guide. You can find it in the same places you pick up *The Reader*: stores, bars, restaurants.

Heartland Journal
7000 N. Glenwood, Chicago, 60626 465-8005
This bimonthly features a variety of articles and book reviews on environmental, Native American, and multicultural topics.

Crain's Chicago Business
740 N. Rush, Chicago, 60611 649-5200
Crain's Chicago Business, a weekly available by subscription or from newsstands, provides excellent coverage of the Chicago-area business community. This is a must read if you do business in Chicago, and it's certainly well read by upper management. *Crain's* ranks companies within industries on an annual basis in banking, health care, and advertising.

Restaurant news is best covered by the following two glossy tomes. Both offer comprehensive guides to what's happening each month in their target region, but their real strengths are following the restaurants and their style stories.

Chicago Magazine
414 N. Orleans, Chicago, 60601 222-8999
Monthly—available by subscription or from newsstands, bookstores, and supermarkets.

North Shore Magazine
874 Green Bay, Winnetka, 60093
Monthly—available by subscription or from north suburban newsstands, bookstores, and supermarkets.

Issue-oriented newspaper/newsletters are invaluable for taking a serious look at important issues. *Chicago Enterprise, Chicago Reporter,* and *Neighborhood Works* are highly recommended. It's worth the effort to track them down.

Chicago Enterprise
One First National Plaza, Chicago, 60603   853-1203
Monthly—available by subscription only.

Chicago Reporter
332 S. Michigan, #500, Chicago, 60603   427-4830
Monthly—available by subscription or from larger newsstands and bookstores.

Neighborhood Works
207 S. Wabash, 8th floor, Chicago, 60604   278-4800
Bimonthly by subscription or from larger newsstands and bookstores.

African-American

Aside from uneven coverage in the mass media, Chicago's African-American communities, representing 41 percent of the population, cull their news from a variety of sources. No single publication serves this diverse community completely, in part because of the community's very diversity. Between the major papers, the *Sun-Times* provides better coverage; however, you still won't read much beyond crime and victim's reports. Radio may be the best source for news and analysis related to African-American interests.

Print

Chicago Defender
2400 S. Michigan, Chicago, 60616   225-2400
The *Chicago Defender*, founded in 1905, was once the leading voice of the black community. In the early days the paper reached Mississippi and other southern states, attracting thousands from farms to a new urban life in the North. Today this daily paper suffers from dwindling circulation and targets primarily blue-collar readers.

The *Chicago Reporter* (see listing, above) is a newsletter monthly that covers race relations with significant depth. The stories it covers frequently get retold by the dailies or broadcast press in Chicago and beyond. In the past year it has reported on correlated factors to black students' retention, sexually transmitted diseases, education, and public utility issues in minority communities.

The neighborhood papers cover issues, events, and businesses in individual communities. Given the demographic skewing still present in Chicago, the neighborhood papers offer a valid perspective for evaluating alternative views and finding local events and businesses.

Austin Voice
5309 W. North, Chicago, 60639   921-5505

Austin Weekly News
5634 W. Chicago, Chicago, 60651   237-9351

Chicago Shoreland News
11740 S. Elizabeth, Chicago, 60643   568-7091

Chicago South Shore Scene
7426 S. Constance, Chicago, 60649   363-0441

Citizen Newspapers
412 E. 87th, Chicago, 60619   487-7700

N'Digo
54 W. Hubbard, #400, Chicago, 60610   527-5757

New Crusader
6429 S. King, Chicago, 60637   752-2500

New Metro News
3437 S. Indiana, Chicago, 60616   791-0880

Tri-City Journal
8 S. Michigan, Chicago, 60603   346-8123

Westside Journal
16618 S. Hermitage, Markham, 60426   (708) 333-2210

Windy City Word
5090 W. Harrison, Chicago, 60644   378-0261

Several monthlies are directed to the black lifestyle.

Ebony, EM, Jet **Magazine**
820 S. Michigan, Chicago, 60605   322-9200
John Johnson built a publishing empire on meeting an unfilled need: serving
the black community with high-quality publications reporting on issues and
celebrities, society, lifestyle, and fashions. *Ebony* debuted in 1945, a forerun-
ner to *People*. The glossy magazine covers fashion, entertainment, and news.
Jet magazine is news and issues oriented with limited entertainment features
(i.e., Top 10 lists); it's been a popular supermarket magazine since 1951. *EM*
(Ebony Male) focuses on fashions and features for black men. All three
publications are nationally distributed. Linda Johnson Rice oversees the
publishing businesses today from the Johnson Publishing building overlook-
ing Grant Park.

Dollars & Sense
7853 S. Stony Island, Chicago, 60649   375-6800
Corporate bimonthly addresses the black business community as well as
cultural and political affairs.

Black Enterprise
130 Fifth, New York, NY, 10011   (212) 242-8000
Not based in Chicago, obviously, but a good glossy monthly for the business
professional featuring news you can use—investment, management articles,
and travel and leisure features.

Broadcast

WVAZ 103 FM
Provides news information as well as personalities and programs such as Richard Steele, John Davis, Donald Palmer's current affairs program, and "Today's Black Woman" features (targeted at a 25- to 55-year-old age group).

WGCI 107.5 FM
This stations reaches a considerably younger audience with its urban contemporary format, which impacts its news and talk segments.

Latino

Although diverse, the Latino community is well served by a focused press corps committed to representing their audience. Reporters do a good job of holding politicians accountable for the policies they support. If you want to understand the impact of a bill, education reform, immigration policy, or other grass-roots issues on a minority community, this is a good place to start reading or listening. Increasingly, the Latino community is becoming an important voice in the city.

Print

El Heraldo de Chicago
300 N. Michigan, #220, 60601   732-0988
Weekly published on Thursday, available in West and North side communities.

El Mañana Daily News
2700 S. Harding, Chicago, 60623   521-9137
Free Monday–Friday paper covering city and international news. Available in food stores and retail outlets.

Extra **Publications**
3918 W. North, Chicago, 60647   252-3534
Bilingual weekly with great coverage of local issues. Available in Latino neighborhoods as well in newsboxes on Michigan Avenue at Ontario Street. Excellent way to improve your Spanish while learning about the local community.

La Raza
3909 N. Ashland, Chicago, 60613   525-9400
Serves metro Chicago and 20 suburbs. Published on Friday, *Raza* covers Central and South American political events as well as city and community issues.

Broadcast

WCIU-TV Channel 26
Talk show: "Aydua," Sunday, 10:30 P.M.

WFLD-TV Channel 32
Talk show: "Esta Semana," Saturday, 6–7 A.M.

WSNS-TV Channel 44
Talk show: "Mesa Redonda," Sunday, 12–12:30 P.M.; "Linea Abierta," Saturday, 9:30 P.M.

WOJO 105.1 FM
Targets upscale Latinos.

WIND AM 560 AM
Directed to recent immigrants. Talk show: "La Voz del Pueblo," Sunday, 11–noon.

WGN 720 AM
Talk show: "Hispanic Happenings," Saturday, 11:05–11:30 A.M.

WCRW AM 1240 AM
WCRW public affairs program; schedule varies.

WCEV AM 1450 AM
Talk show: "Mosaic" (in English), Thursday and Sunday evening.

Other Ethnic Press

Czech

Hlas Naroda
2340 S. 61st, Cicero, 60650   (708) 656-1050
Catholic Czech weekly. Primarily in Czech language, available in Austin, Oak Park (south of the city).

Denni Hlasatel
6426 Cermak, Berwyn, 60402   (708) 749-1891
Since 1891, now twice-weekly. International emphasis in Czech language.

Danish

Den Danske Pioneer
Bertelsen Publishing Co.
1582 Glen Lake, Hoffman Estates, 60195   (708) 882-2552
English and Danish weekly.

German

Wochenpost (*Abendpost*)
Troy, MI   (313) 528-2810
One of the oldest German/English-language papers in the United States, now merged and managed in Michigan. Chicago edition includes the *Abendpost* with local news.

Amerikawoche
4732 N. Lincoln, Chicago, 60625   275-5054
German-American weekly published in Chicago.

Eintracht
9456 N. Lawlor, Skokie, 60077   (708) 677-9456

Greek

The Greek Star
4710 N. Lincoln, Chicago, 60625   878-7331

Indian

India Abroad
2323 W. Devon, Chicago, 60659   338-1118
Weekly publication with reports from around the United States.

India Tribune
2702 W. Peterson, Chicago, 60659
English-language weekly focusing on city news.

Irish

The Irish American News
2142 W. Greystone, Hoffman Estates, 60195   (708) 882- 4410
Monthly serving city, suburbs, and nation.

Korean

Joong Ang Daily News
4546 N. Kedzie, Chicago, 60625   583-2770
Satellite-transmitted daily; available in Lawrence area.

Hankook Ilbo (Korean Times)
4447 N. Kedzie, Chicago, 66025   463-1050
Daily Korean paper.

Lithuanian

Draugas
4545 W. 63rd, Chicago, 60629
Daily paper targeted to post-WWII immigrants, with a conservative tone.
Published by the Lithuanian Catholic Church.

Polish

Polish Daily News
55 E. Jackson, Chicago, 60604   368-4855
Polish-language paper, 125 years-old, covering politics in Poland and the
United States (formerly *Zgoda*).

Ukrainian

New Star Ukrainian Catholic Weekly
2208 W. Chicago, Chicago, 60622   772-1919
Ukrainian-English language weekly serving the city and suburban Ukrainian
communities with local and national news.

Neighborhood Papers

The neighborhood papers are an excellent source for local issues, crime reports, news affecting schools and commercial districts, and aldermanic responsiveness. These are also the best sources of classified ads for apartments, garage sales, cars, and local services. Papers are available at newsstands, local stores, and by subscription. Aside from these presses, local news can also be found by block club and community organization publications.

Chicago Post
P.O. Box 478369, Chicago, 60647   772-3300
Serves 61 neighborhoods on the North and Northwest sides, zoned into five regions to better target local interest. Fairly thin, though.

Citizen Newspapers
412 E. 87th, Chicago, 60619   487-7700
Publishes award-winning papers (i.e., *Chatham Citizen*) in south, southeast city and south suburban neighborhoods such as Chatham, Harvey, Markham, and Robbins.

Hyde Park Herald
5240 S. Harper, Chicago, 60615   643-8533

Lerner Newspapers
1115 W. Belmont, 60657   281-7500 or (800) 244-7100
Published as the *Skyline, Booster, New-Star, Life,* and *Times,* the Lerner papers cover the north and northwest city area including Lakeview, Lincoln Park, Rogers Park, Harlem-Foster, Harwood Heights, Elmwood Park, River Grove, Morton Grove, and Skokie.

Nadig Newspapers
4941 N. Milwaukee, Chicago, 60630   286-6100
Papers for the Northwest Side and north suburban areas. City coverage includes Jefferson Park, Edison Park, Mayfair, Albany Park, and Edgebrook. Suburban coverage also includes Park Ridge, Niles, Skokie, and Des Plaines.

Pioneer Press
1232 Central, Wilmette, 60091   (708) 251-4300
This suburban chain publishes 38 papers in North Shore, far north, and northwest communities including Barrington, Palatine, Hoffman Estates, Libertyville, Highland Park, Deerfield, Wilmette, and Evanston.

Southtown Economist
5959 S. Harlem, Chicago, 60638   586-8800
One of the best neighborhood papers, this thick daily serves the Southwest Side and surrounding suburbs and is frequently cited by the broadcast press.

Southwest News Herald
6225 S. Kedzie, Chicago, 60629   476-4800

Wednesday Journal of Oak Park and River Forest
141 S. Oak Park, Oak Park, 60302   (708) 524-8300
A free weekly covering Oak Park and River Forest. Same organization publishes the *Forest Park Review.*

The Lincoln Park, River North, Gold Coast areas are swamped with numerous small papers and magazines trying to reach their well-educated, upwardly mobile, active community members. An occasional sampling of papers will keep you up to date on what's happening.

Lifestyle, Specialty Press, Alternative Papers

Some are free, some are not. The success of *The Reader* proved that narrow-casting papers targeted to a specific market for specific interest are viable vehicles for ideas, writers, and advertisers. Numerous weeklies and monthlies are available throughout the city.

Arts

New Art Examiner
1255 S. Wabash, Chicago, 60605   786-0200
A nationally distributed magazine covering painting, sculpture, video art, and performing arts.

Audition News
6114 W. North   637-4695

Catholic

The Chicago Catholic Newspaper
1144 W. Jackson, Chicago, 60606   243-1300

Education

Catalyst, Voices of Chicago School Reform
322 S. Michigan, Chicago, 60604   427-4830
A free monthly newsletter published by the Community Renewal Society reports on overcrowding, teachers' surveys, skill building.

Environmental

Resources, EarthDayChicago
28 E. Jackson, Chicago, 60604   408-0444
Articles, listings for recycling news.

Family

Chicago Parent **Magazine**
141 S. Oak Park, Oak Park, 60302   (708) 524-8300
New publication targeting professional parents, available free in newsboxes around the city. Articles and advertisements keep parents informed on health matters, trends, and local services.

Gay and Lesbian

Windy City Times
Sentury Publications, Inc.
3225 N. Sheffield, Chicago, 60657   935-1790
Free weekly that covers local, national, and international news for the gay and lesbian community. Complete listing of organizations, merchants, bars, and restaurants. Easily available in bookstores, restaurants, and bars on the North Side, particularly in New Town, and Hyde Park.

Chicago Outlines
3059 N. Southport, Chicago, 60657   871-7610
Provides a weekly entertainment and nightlife guide and monthly news magazine covering local, regional, and national news. Also has listings of organizations, bars, and restaurants. Available in bookstores, bars, and other locations.

Law

Chicago Daily Law Bulletin
415 N. State, Chicago, 60611   644-7800

Music

CAMM
180 W. Park, #105, Elmhurst, 60126   (708) 941-2030
A hard rock publication found in music stores around the city.

Down Beat
180 W. Park, #105, Elmhurst, 60126   (708) 941-2030
Monthly magazine with a national reputation for covering jazz. Also does a good job reporting blues, country music, and other forms.

Illinois Entertainer
2250 E. Devon, #150, Des Plaines, 60018   (708) 298-9333
The suburban version of *The Reader* for comprehensive coverage of entertainment, particularly local rock. This free magazine covers popular entertainment and performing arts around Illinois.

Politics

In These Times
1300 W. Belmont, Chicago, 60657   772-0100
Well-written, independent socialist weekly.

Sports

Illinois Sports News
906 S. Wabash, Chicago, 60605   939-5900
Daily racing news.

Windy City Sports **Magazine**
1450 W. Randolph, Chicago, 60607   421-1551
Windy City is the free amateur sports magazine listing all the upcoming events, clubs, and meets. Found in sports/health stores.

Women

Today's Chicago Woman
233 E. Ontario, Chicago, 60611   951-7600
Free monthly available in newsboxes, features a prominent woman each month and reports on promotions, new businesses, and upcoming meetings of interest to professional women.

Writing

Strong Coffee
Found in coffee shops, it's an eclectic mixture of writing, poetry, and art, spinning from idea to idea like a coffeehouse conversation.

WHERE TO FIND THAT PAPER

A city ordinance in early 1992 eliminated many traditional newsstands around the city. The best place to find the paper you want depends on the information you are looking for. Major papers and business press can be found at lobby newsstands in large Loop/River North office buildings or near public transportation. Community and ethnic newspapers are found in specific communities at newsstands, retail stores, or by subscription.

Chicago Main Newsstand
Chicago Avenue and Main Street, Evanston   (708) 864-2727
Best place to find that *Washington Post, Dallas Herald*, or other out-of-town/international papers.

SPECIALTY PRESS

Specialty press—alternative freebies—are best found in high rises, retail outlets, bars, coffeehouses, and bookstores frequented by clientele interested in that subject, particularly in the River North area or North Side. Visit the four spots below for starters. If you are interested in galleries or tourist-type activities, remember hotel concierges and the Illinois Department of Tourism can answer questions or provide brochures.

Dearborn Station
47 W. Polk   554-4400

Illinois Tourist Information Center
310 S. Michigan   793-2094

Potash Bros Supermarket
875 N. State   266-4200

Rienzi Plaza
600 W. Diversey (Concierge Chicago racks)

GETTING INVOLVED IN THE PRESS

Chicago remains the kind of city where you can make things happen. With declining budgets and reduced staffs, news organizations rely on press releases to identify stories or events. Getting your issues covered is sometimes a matter of promoting good stories or creditable sources.

Community Media Workshop
Malcolm X College   942-0909, ext. 617
Community Media Workshop offers training workshops and media-skills courses to community-based organizations and individuals. CMW's mission is to empower neighborhood organizations to claim our public airwaves for important public debate. The basic course covers strategic media planning, understanding different media (print, radio, TV), and how to present your story to the press.

—Patricia M. Ruch

RADIO

Chicago's radio, like its counterpart in nearly any other American town, has its share of the ordinary and generic, but at least some of the 33 AM and 42 FM offerings pay tribute to the city's undeniable musical heritage. Some jazz is available; ethnic programming can be found; and you can listen to classical, country and western, and gospel, but, unfortunately, the same cannot be said for some other styles. Sadly, authentic blues is nearly absent from the airwaves, and this failure to regularly present in a meaningful way one of the city's distinguishing musical styles is Chicago radio's most unforgivable shortcoming. For folk programs, see the radio section in the "Folk Music" chapter.

ROCK

This is by far the style with the greatest selection of programs and stations from which to choose. In fact, there's probably too much selection. Do you like adult rock (**WABT,** 103.9 FM) or adult contemporary (**WZSR,** 105.5 FM) and (**WJPC,** 106.3 FM), or do you prefer pop adult (**WKQX,** 101.1 FM)? Is it Top 40 (**WBBM,** 96.3 FM) you want, or just plain rock (**WLUP,** 97.9 FM), and (**WWBZ,** 103.5 FM)? What about progressive rock (**WCBR,** 92.7 FM) or (**WXRT,** 93.1 FM)? Or pure rock (**WONC,** 89.1 FM)? Or classic rock (**WCKG,** 105.9 FM)? Probably no typical person knows what really distinguishes most of these stations.

The consensus is probably that the city's dominant rock station is WXRT. As Chicago's musically correct radio, its playlist is more likely than some others to contain newer, lesser known rockers. It can be the most interesting of the rock stations because it doesn't play just the hits, and the disc jockeys are excellent.

Northwestern University's campus is home to **WNUR** (89.3 FM), the city's super-eclectic station. There is a variety of programming, the format changing throughout the day. Don't miss the ska show at 9 P.M. Sunday. The DJs are evidently unpolished college students so the announcing may be a little uneven, but the station is a treasure.

JAZZ

Regrettably, there is no 24-hour jazz station in Chicago. Jazz is difficult to get on Chicago radio. There is a fine AM jazz station: **WKDC** (1530 AM) way on the right of the dial, broadcasting from suburban Elmhurst. The signal may be weak, however, and the reception poor in many parts of the city. **WNUR** (89.3 FM) has a 5 A.M.–1 P.M. jazz show weekdays, but its playlist can sometimes lean too heavily on the avant-garde sound.

By far, Chicago radio's best jazz can be found on **WBEZ** (91.5 FM) with Dick Buckley's "Archives of Jazz" (Monday–Thursday 8–9 P.M. and 3–4 A.M., Sunday 1:30–4 P.M.). It is simply one of the best jazz shows you'll ever hear, brought to you by someone with firsthand knowledge of the music and its performers. Neil Tesser's excellent Monday and Wednesday night "Jazz Forum" 9–11 P.M. features straight-ahead jazz (also hosted by Chris Heim Tuesday and Thursday 9–11 P.M. and by Larry Smith Monday–Thursday

Stuart Rosenberg, host of "The Earth Club" on WBEZ.

11 P.M.–3 A.M., Friday 11 P.M.–5 A.M.). For jazz-loving insomniacs, WBEZ also offers some shows 4–5 A.M.: "Jazz Set" on Monday, "River Walk" on Tuesday, "Worldwide Jazz" on Wednesday, and "Four Queens Jazz" on Thursday.

BLUES

Pitifully little here, so don't blink. Only a few stations can be commended for making time for the blues. **WXRT** (93.1 FM) offers "Blues Breakers" Monday at 10 P.M.. **WGCI** (1390 AM) has a Saturday blues program, but only from 5–9 P.M. **WNUR** has a strong Sunday show, also only from 5–9 P.M. For more one can then go on to **WPNA** (1490 AM) for its blues show beginning at midnight on Sunday. Blues can more regularly be heard on **WVON** (1450 AM). Here Pervis Spann hosts "The Bluesman Show" Monday–Saturday, but only from midnight–4 A.M. Arlington Heights's **WCBR** (92.7 FM) is said to play some blues, but its signal is so weak as to be practically inaudible in all but the northern suburbs.

ETHNIC

With the exception of **WVVX** (103.1 FM) (see "Miscellaneous"), this format is pretty much in the province of AM. If you want to get your mornings off to the start they really deserve, then try Chet Gulinski's "Morning Drive Time Polka Time," 7 A.M. weekdays on **WPNA** (1490 AM). The Polish-owned and-operated **WCEV** (1450 AM), whose call letters stand for "We're Chicagoland's Ethnic Voice," broadcasts in various languages: Polish, Lithuanian, Croatian, Ukrainian, Czechoslovak, Serbian, Slovenian, and even has Gaelic and Haitian programs. The station broadcasts seven days a week, weekdays from 1–10 P.M. Three Spanish-language stations can be heard clearly throughout Chicago: **WIND** (560 AM), **WOPA** (1200 AM), and **WOJO** (105.1 FM).

CLASSICAL

Chicago has two classical stations: **WFMT** (98.6 FM) and **WNIB** (97.1 FM). Both stations broadcast 24 hours a day.

COUNTRY AND WESTERN

There's only a single country station currently broadcasting in Chicago, but it's a fine one—the 10-year-old **WUSN** (99.5 FM).

GOSPEL

If you're an early riser, you can start your day with Effie Rolfe's gospel show weekdays 4–6 A.M. on **WGCI** (1390 AM). There is another broadcast beginning at 10 P.M. Sunday and continuing through until Monday morning. **WCEV** (1450 AM) has Marilyn Frizzle's afternoon show on weekdays at 1:05 P.M. **WPNA** (1490 AM) begins a Sunday evening of gospel music at 5 P.M.

URBAN/DANCE

WGCI (107.5 FM) used to dominate here, but now **WBBM** (96.3 FM), whose "B-96" bumper sticker one sees all over the place, is at or near the top; it is exclusively a dance/hip hop format. Loyola University's **WLUW** (88.7 FM) is another all-dance format. On Saturday its midnight "Pipeline" show features the latest in rap. A softer, more mellow sound can be heard on **WJPC** (950 AM, 106.3 FM); the FM reception may be poor, however.

NEWS/TALK

On National Public Radio's **WBEZ** (91.5 FM) one can hear both "Morning Edition" (Monday–Friday 5–9) and "Weekend Edition"(Saturday and Sunday 8–10 A.M.) as well as "All Things Considered" (Monday–Friday 4–6 P.M., Saturday and Sunday 4–5 P.M.). It also presents the Garrison Keillor show on Saturday evening 5–7 P.M. (repeated Sunday morning 10 A.M.–noon) and the very funny "What'ya Know?" with Michael Feldman on Saturday at 10 A.M.–noon. On **WVON** (1450 AM) one can hear Chicago's only black talk radio. **WLS** (890 AM) and **WGN** (720 AM) are Chicago's famous (but traditional) call-in, talk radio stations. WGN also broadcasts Cubs and Bears games. **WMAQ** (670 AM), a 24-hour news station, broadcasts Sox and Bulls games. Like sports? There's an all-sports station, **WSCR** (820 AM).

MISCELLANEOUS

The Dr. Jekyll–Mr. Hyde award goes without question to **WVVX** (103.1 FM). You're not going to believe this, but here's an ethnic station that broadcasts in over 20 languages and then at night switches to heavy metal! That's right, Pastor Cho's nightly "Korean Christian Broadcast" is followed immediately by "Real Precious Metal," offering the very best in heavy metal. Then at 1 A.M. comes "Night People," a program featuring only local bands and musicians.

By sending a recording, name, and brief biography to **WVVX**, local musicians have a chance to be heard over the air.

Weekday programming on **WGCI** (1390 AM) is such that it's basically a black oldies station. The playlist includes all the Motown artists, James Brown, Jackie Wilson, Aretha, etc. The "New Age" sound is programmed on **WNUA** (95.5 FM); this is also advertised as "Smooth Jazz," but its format bears little resemblance to the music played on the stations listed in the jazz category.

If this summary is intended to do anything, it's meant to allow you to at least begin your own radio survey. No brief description like this one can be complete, but I hope it's representative of the variety and uniqueness of Chicago radio—and a helpful starting point.

—Michael C. Armijo

People

KIDS
SENIORS
LESBIANS
GAY MEN

KIDS

You think you know everything there is to know about Chicago—and then you have a kid. There's no better, faster way to get an all-new perspective on what the city offers!

KID MUSEUMS

Most of Chicago's major museums have special programs for children. For information about activities and workshops for kids, contact the educational department of the museums listed here.

The Field Museum of Natural History
South Lake Shore Drive and Roosevelt Road 922-9410
The Field Museum is one of the best kid museums in town. Ancient mummies, gigantic dinosaur fossils, detailed animal habitat dioramas, and a splendid North American Indian collection are just a few of its top attractions. Special weekend sleep-overs let grade-school children explore the museum's silent halls by flashlight. "The Place for Wonder" lets younger children handle rocks, fossils, botanical samples, and other artifacts.

It's three floors of fun for all ages—and when you're all tuckered out, stop and refresh at McDonald's or Starbucks, both conveniently located in the basement.

Museum of Science and Industry
57th Street and Lake Shore Drive 684-1414
This famous museum takes a scientific view of things. Perennial favorites like the coal mine, the U-505 submarine, the enormous Santa Fe Railway installation, and the annual "Christmas around the World" tree display are supplemented by enjoyable educational exhibits that demonstrate how the heart works, how sound travels, what happens when a toilet flushes, and other fascinating scientific and technical phenomena. "The Curiosity Place" and the Fairy Castle are both sure-fire stops for the under-six set.

Don't miss the **Henry Crown Space Center** and its **Omnimax Theater**, whose five-story screen will immerse your children in Antarctica, space, the habitat of beavers, and other marvelous environments. Admission to the Space Center and theater are separate. Fortunately for parents of overscheduled children, both are open late on weekend evenings.

Oceanarium of the John G. Shedd Aquarium
1200 S. Lake Shore Drive 939-2438
The Oceanarium is home to a wide variety of marine life, including beluga whales, harbor seals, and Magellanic penguins. The largest indoor marine mammal exhibit in the world, it lets children examine marine life of the Pacific Northwest from viewing galleries above and below water level.

Since it opened, the Oceanarium has somewhat overshadowed the other galleries of the Aquarium. But 800 different kinds of aquatic animals still dwell in the Aquarium's galleries, and the Coral Reef Exhibit is still a must-see.

Tickets should be purchased in advance of your visit, especially if you plan a weekend excursion.

Adler Planetarium
1300 S. Lake Shore Drive   332-0300
This is where to go for a sky show! They are presented daily in the **Kroc Universe Theater** and the **Sky Theater**. Special shows for children under six are held several times a week. Check with the Planetarium's education staff for information on special workshops and classes on celestial topics.

Art Institute of Chicago
Michigan Avenue and Adams Street   433-3680
The Art Institute has a Junior Museum that offers a wide assortment of workshops, demonstrations, tours, and other activities for children and families.

The David and Alfred Smart Museum of Art
The University of Chicago
5550 S. Greenwood   702-0200
Older children will have an interesting art excursion at the Smart Museum, which has a collection that spans 4,000 years.

Rosenbaum Children's ARTiFACT Center at the Spertus Museum
618 S. Michigan   922-9012
Even school-age children can become archaeologists here, where ancient Middle Eastern history comes alive. The Center's tell is no sandbox—it's a replica of an archaeological dig site. Children learn about the tools, practices, and purposes of archaeology before they are set loose in the 10-foot-tall site. As they dig, they log their discoveries in field notebooks. When they have finished, they can discover the age and the history of each artifact they have collected. Parents are encouraged to participate. According to the staff, few can resist.

While their older siblings are digging in the tell, preschoolers and kindergartners can explore family life in the Israelite House, a model of a 3,000-year-old Israeli home.

The Mitchell Indian Museum
Kendall College
2408 Orrington, Evanston   (708) 866-1395
Although it is not geared specifically to children, the Mitchell Indian Museum welcomes families interested in learning more about the Woodlands, Plains, Pueblo, and Navajo Indians. It's a favorite resource of local YMCA Indian Guides and Indian Princesses, elementary schools, and older children interested in Native American culture.

The DuSable Museum of African-American History
740 E. 56th   947-0600
The DuSable Museum celebrates African culture and African-American history in exhibits that encourage parent-child participation. Special workshops on mask and costume making and holidays like Kwanzaa dramatize the richness of African-American culture. Groups of 10 or more can arrange a special children's tour.

The Chicago Historical Society
Clark Street at North Avenue 642-4600
The Society brings Chicago's past to life in vivid exhibits and installations that children will enjoy. The **Discovery Corner** gives children a tactile experience with the past, allowing them to handle familiar artifacts and period toys. But children will respond to almost every one of the displays, since all of them deal with a place children know well: their own city.

The Chicago Academy of Sciences
2001 N. Clark 549-0600
Although it has been around since 1857, the Academy is making a few changes. To carry out its mission to promote science literacy, it is adding entertaining, interactive, educational teaching exhibits and workshops for children, parents, and teachers.

In the third-floor **Children's Gallery** (549-0775), kids can handle small animals and numerous educational puzzles, displays, and games. On the same floor is the **Celestial Sphere**, the oldest planetarium in Chicago. The second-floor **Touch Cart** gives kids a chance to explore, play, or experiment with specimens on a particular topic.

The museum's Knee-High Naturalist program offers many classes for children ages five through eight. Family workshops and field trips, nature walks, and overnights also are available.

THE TWO TOP KID MUSEUMS IN TOWN

Kohl Children's Museum
165 Green Bay, Wilmette (708) 256-6056
The best romper room in town! Under the Kohl Museum's roof is a fantastic array of activities for children ages 2–10. Parents may find the noise level a little painful, but kids won't run out of things to do. From the miniature Jewel/Osco to the tabletops filled with Legos, the trays of bubble fluid, the do-it-yourself video stage, and the second- floor computer games, it's hard to think of a better way to spend a morning.

During winter and spring school vacations, it's best to arrive early. When attendance surges, the Kohl controls its crowd by selling entrance tickets for 10:00 A.M., 11:00 A.M., and 1:00 P.M.

If you have to wait or if hunger pangs strike your children, walk next door and eat at **Walker Brothers Pancake House** (153 Green Bay, [708] 251-6000). Its friendly staff can efficiently handle parties of any size, and they are perfectly willing to handle complicated kid requests like seconds on hot chocolate, chocolate chip pancakes, or pigs-in-blankets.

The Chicago Children's Museum
North Pier
435 E. Illinois 527-1000
In the summer of 1994, the Chicago Children's Museum will move to Navy Pier. Its permanent installations include Amazing Chicago, a kid-sized collection of Chicago institutions that introduces kids to Chicago architecture; Touchy Business, a miniature kitchen, tactile tunnels, and a fantasy vehicle designed especially for toddlers and preschoolers; and NEWSbrief!, a fully

operational TV studio and press bureau that introduces kids to the basics of broadcast and print journalism.

Admission to the museum is complimentary on Free Family Night, every Thursday from 5:00 P.M. to 8:00 P.M.. With the money you save on admission, you can treat your kids to supper in the basement food court of North Pier. During the summer months, you can eat al fresco along Ogden Slip, where boats of all sizes are docked.

KID PLAYS, PUPPETS, AND PERFORMANCES

There's always plenty of children's theater happening in Chicago. And some of it is even free.

Good Day Saturday
Inside the 1800 N. Clybourn complex

Hosts a different musician, magician, or performer every Saturday at 11:00 A.M. There's no charge—simply show up and enjoy the show.

Funstuff
The Chicago Improv
504 N. Wells   527-2500

Every Saturday afternoon during the school year, Funstuff offers a fast-paced, hour-long variety show of kid music, magic, and comedy. The admission price includes free popcorn and soda and a half-hour of cartoons before the show. In the summer, it's best to phone first; the Funstuff players take their vacations then.

The Cookie Crumb Club
Organic Theatre
3319 N. Clark   327-5588

This ever-changing collection of silly songs for children ages two to seven is cowritten and coperformed by Chicago folk singer Jim Post and his wife Kathleen. Everyone who attends receives a membership card good for reduced admissions to this ongoing "club," which meets Saturday and has an open run.

Lifeline Theatre Kid Series
6912 N. Glenwood   761-4477

When it comes to full-length children's plays, Lifeline has a distinctly literary bent. It specializes in adaptations of childhood classics like *Mr. Popper's Penguins* and *Bunnicula*. The intimate children's theater allows kids to sit on mats close to the stage; adults are banished to chairs in the rear. In addition to its two children's productions, Lifeline produces one slightly longer family show each year. *A Wrinkle in Time* is a recent and very successful example.

Marriott's Lincolnshire Theatre for Young Audiences
10 Marriott, Lincolnshire   (708) 634-5909

At the conclusion of their children's productions, the crew opens a question-and-answer session. Kids are encouraged to ask actors about behind-the-scenes costumes, lighting, and special effects that they notice during the show.

Chicago Children's Theatre
310 Green Bay, Wilmette (708) 491-0643
The theater plans to move to Chicago just as soon as it can find a kid-friendly venue, but for now it mounts two productions a year in Wilmette. Production staff lead onstage tours of the set, lighting, and special effects, and actors are available after the show to greet children and answer questions. Chicago Children's Theatre also offers workshops on design, acting, improvisation, and storytelling.

Drury Lane Children's Theatre
2500 W. 95th, Evergreen Park (708) 422-0404

Centre East Family Theatre
7701 Lincoln, Skokie (708) 673-6300
Two additional sources for children's theater. In all, Centre East sponsors a dozen shows a year, mixing theater with acrobatics, musical productions, and other live performances.

Pitt Players
Beverly Arts Center
2153 W. 111th 445-3838
Kids who want to see other kids act should watch for productions of this troupe, a group of actors from ages 7 to 16.

AnimArt
3901 N. Kedzie 267-1209

Hystopolis Puppet Theater
441 W. North 787-7387

The Puppet Parlor
1922 W. Montrose 989-0308
These three venues allow kids to see puppets in action. The Puppet Parlor also sponsors workshops on the art of puppetry for children over 12.

KID MUSIC

Ravinia (708) 433-8800
On six summer Saturdays, Ravinia offers special music, dance, puppet, and storytelling events at 11:00 A.M. Families are welcome to stay and picnic when the show is over. During the holiday season, Ravinia sponsors Winter Wonderland, an indoor-outdoor family festival featuring children's music, caroling, clowns, and jugglers. Admission to this benefit is a can of food; all donations are passed along to local food closets.

Grant Park Concert Society 819-0614
This group is serious about introducing children to classical music. Its morning summer Picnic Performances, held at 10:00 A.M. in Grant Park's Petrillo Music Shell, expose summer school students and day campers to a variety of formats, including symphonic, operatic, ballet, and choral music. Your children are welcome to attend. Selected Sunday evening performances of the Grant Park Symphony begin at 5:00 P.M. instead of 7:30 P.M., so children and their families can enjoy a full-length symphonic performance and still get to

bed on time. Check the newspaper for program information, or call the Society for details.

Lincoln Opera 549-3249
If there's a budding young opera lover in your family, call the Lincoln Opera. Its Sunday afternoon productions, held in the cozy auditorium at Loyola University, are a fine way to introduce children to opera. In fact, bringing opera to children is Lincoln Opera's mandate: 57 Chicago-area elementary schools attend its special school performances, which condense a full production into a 50-minute cut. Individual families are welcome to attend these Tuesday morning performances. On occasion, the Lincoln produces operas specifically for children—like "Chip & His Dog," a short, sweet Menotti opera written for and sung by kids. And stage moms, take note: the Lincoln Opera lets kids appear on stage in singing and nonsinging roles whenever a libretto gives an excuse for it.

KID FILM

Except for the occasional Disney flick, it's hard to find good films for children.

Omnimax Theater at the Museum of Science and Industry 684-1414
Its features don't change very often, but the Omnimax offers consistently high-quality films on topics that appeal to adults and children. You can try to purchase tickets immediately before the show, but it's better to buy them in advance through Ticketron.

Facets Multimedia
1517 W. Fullerton 281-9075
The collection of children's videos here is the largest around. Busy parents can even rent videos by mail—especially convenient if you don't live in the Facets neighborhood. Each October, Facets also sponsors the **Chicago International Children's Film Festival**, a 10-day festival of movies for children by directors from around the world. For less than the cost of a standard first-run shoot-'em-up movie, your kids can sample fine animated shorts and full-length features written, acted, and produced specifically for children.

KID FINE ARTS

Beverly Arts Center
2153 W. 111th 445-3838
Instruction in ballet, jazz, tap dance, drawing, painting, cartooning, creative story writing, and drama, as well as guitar, piano, and violin.

Kids and Clay
4905 N. Damen 878-5821
Classes on the North side in pottery, wheel throwing, drawing, photography, piano, puppetry performance, and puppetry construction. Classes are primarily geared to children seven years of age and older, although pottery workshops are available for three- to six-year-olds.

The Old Town School of Folk Music
909 W. Armitage   525-7793
When it comes to learning music, there's no better source than the Old Town School. Even a six-month-old baby can enjoy the Wiggleworms program, a parent-child music and motion class geared to the very youngest children. (Check out Wiggleworm Family Night, an evening of songs, finger play, and dances for the whole family offered every other month.) Older children can choose between song and movement-based classes like Glowworms or Orff Schulwerk, or more structured group or private instruction in the Suzuki method.

The Old Town School Children's Chorus gives 6- to 14-year-olds an opportunity to practice and perform a variety of song styles and arrangements. And in addition to classes, the Old Town School sponsors numerous folk, blues, and ethnic music performances that the whole family can enjoy. Call them for a complete schedule of children's classes and special concerts.

People's Music School
4750 N. Sheridan   784-7032
This school has been bringing music to the masses since 1976. There is no hourly fee for these half-hour private lessons; only a modest $10 registration fee and a two-hour-a-month volunteer commitment are required. (Students must borrow or purchase their own instrument.) Children five years of age and older may study piano, violin, cello, percussion instruments, guitar, flute, recorder, saxophone, clarinet, or trumpet. Students of the school may also participate in the Children's Choir, which practices weekly and performs around Chicago. People's Music School holds regular student and faculty recitals in its Uptown facilities.

KIDDIE LIT: BOOKSTORES AND LIBRARIES

Chicago abounds in bookstores catering to children and their parents.

Children's Bookstore
2465 N. Lincoln   248-BOOK
You'll find a wonderful collection of children's books, including a terrific selection of science books and toys, multicultural materials, books on parenting and child care, and a basement entirely devoted to books for 8- to 15-year-olds. No registration is required for the Story Hour held at 10:30 A.M. every weekday. Note: You can park your minivan in the lot behind the store, accessible from Altgeld Street.

Women & Children First
5233 N. Clark   769-9299
In addition to stocking quality literature for children (and adults) of all ages, this store makes a special point of stocking books on contemporary issues like adoption, disabilities, gay-lesbian parenting, and divorce, as well as old standbys like potty training and new sibling arrival. Storyteller-owner Linda Bubon reads to two- to five-year-olds every Wednesday morning at 10:30 A.M..

Magic Tree Bookstore
141 N. Oak Park, Oak Park   (708) 848-0770
An extensive selection of children's literature. Story hour is at 10:00 A.M. Tuesday and Thursday.

Bookworm Children's Books & Records
1722 Central, Evanston   (708) 328-4660
A nice selection of cassettes, CDs, and videos along with books.

Chicago Public Library
With 80 branches throughout the city, the Chicago Public Library sponsors many children's story hours and reading programs. Check with your local or regional library for specific program dates and times.

Thomas Hughes Children's Library
400 S. State   747-4200
Occupying 18,000 square feet at the new Harold Washington Library Center, this library's collection and the diversity of its programs, directed at children from preschool to eighth grade, have grown as much as its size. You can receive a monthly schedule of events if you call and put your name on the library's mailing list.

KIDS CUT LOOSE! OR, RECREATION

Looking for new ways to let your kid run amok, safely and constructively? Try these worthwhile outlets for intensely physical activity.

Roller Skating

Rainbo Roller Rink
4836 N. Clark   271-6200

Fleetwood Roller Rink
7231 S. Archer, Summit   (708) 458-0300
You and your kids can skate to the beat of high-volume hip-hop. A pulsing light show, great music, tasty pizza, and Cokes—roller skating doesn't get much better than this. And during the afternoon family sessions, you can still do the hokey-pokey. A smaller, separate rink for beginners is a nice feature of this family-oriented rink, which is a great treat after school or during school vacations. Call for a schedule of sessions for younger skaters. The Fleetwood is the Rainbo's South Side counterpart.

Bumper Bowling

To make bowling enjoyable for kids of all ages, many bowling alleys cover the gutters with inflatable "bumpers" that make it easy to knock pins over every time. Blah. Ask the alley nearest you for its bumper bowling schedule, and you'll thrill to your highest bowling score ever.

Miniature Golf

ArtGolf
1800 N. Clybourn   ART-GOLF
The artist-designed course features conceptual delights like "the hole in the ozone layer."

City Golf
In North Pier
455 E. Illinois   836-5936
Here you can sink a birdie among scaled-down Chicago landmarks like the Sears Tower.

Novelty Golf
3640 W. Devon, Lincolnwood   (708) 679-9434
An outdoor course open in the spring and summer.

Chicago Park District

Never mind its scandalous past and rumors of its shady practices. We Chicagoans are fortunate to have an abundance of recreational opportunities at our door. From indoor and outdoor ice skating to gymnastics and swimming classes, inexpensive year-round toddler programs and summer day camp programs, supervised public beaches and playgrounds, and organized athletic teams, the Chicago Park District offers so many programs for kids that it deserves a guidebook of its own.

Most of the 600 Park District facilities in Chicago publish a printed schedule of programs and activities. To find out about programs in your area, check with the parks closest to you. If your local park doesn't offer what you are looking for, chances are good its employees can tell you how to find it. But if you're completely at a loss, go to the top. The Park District's Communication Department (294-2493) will do its best to match you with the right program.

Playgrounds

As Chicagoans, your children have an almost limitless choice of safe, secure playgrounds and pocket parks where they can play to their hearts' content. Most of them are in pretty good shape, thanks to the Park District's recent renovation efforts.

Oz Park
2021 N. Burling

Indian Boundary Playground
2500 W. Lunt
These two playgrounds are worth going out of your way to visit. The signature castle turrets and towers of playground designer Robert Leathers dominate. The fantastic combinations of nooks, crannies, tunnels, ladders, and bridges will occupy kids for hours.

KID FOOD

Skip the fettucine and the arugula, and head straight for these famous purveyors of hot dogs, hamburgers, french fries, pizza, and ice cream.

Two Chicago hot dog institutions go out of their way to accommodate children:

Fluky's
6821 N. Western   274-3652
Fun to visit any time, but the ornate Hannukah and Christmas displays make the winter holidays a special time to visit.

Byron's
6016 N. Clark   973-5000
An outerspace wonderland bursting with colorful three-dimensional space rockets and space creatures that are even more spectacular than the hotdogs.

SuperDawgs Drive-In
6363 N. Milwaukee at Devon   763-0660
Remember when drive-ins, not drive-throughs, stood on every corner of suburban America? Give your kids a taste of the good old days by visiting SuperDawgs. You can eat in your car at this bona-fide Chicago landmark, a replica of the Midway Airport Control Tower. Carhops attach a tray of hot dogs and onion rings to your car window, so you can savor your food and the panoramic view of Milwaukee Avenue at the same time. When you're done, let your kids switch on the red light. Presto! Your carhop will return to sweep away the debris and collect a tip. To grownups over 30, it's a pretty sentimental experience. To kids, it's way cool.

The Choo Choo Restaurant
600 Lee, Des Plaines   (708) 298-5949

Snackville Junction
11016 S. Western   233-1313
Both spots feature a model train traveling around the counter delivering sandwiches and fries to delighted little eaters.

Chuck E. Cheese
5030 S. Kedzie   476-0500
(and half a dozen locations in the suburbs—check your phone book)

Little Caesar's Family Fun Pizzeria
7300 W. Foster   774-7330
Perennial pizza favorites, both offer vast, noisy rooms filled with rides, video and computer games, and play equipment that children can use to their hearts' content.

Home Run Inn Pizza
4254 W. 31st   247-9696
A South Side favorite that also serves video games on the side.

For sinful ice cream creations at family-friendly prices:

Zephyr Ice Cream Parlor
1777 W. Wilson   728-6070
The neon blue art deco interior pulses with energy on the weekends, when Ravenswood teenagers make it "date central."

Petersen's Ice Cream
1100 Chicago, Oak Park   (708) 306-6131

Gertie's Ice Cream Parlor
5858 S. Kedzie   737-7634
Gertie's old-fashioned interior and homemade treats have been a Chicago institution since it opened in 1920.

Leona's
(Five locations—check the phone book.)
For a nice mix of kid food and grown-up comestibles, try Leona's. Each one offers great family food in a noisy, friendly atmosphere that takes kids in stride. Crayons and paper and wall-mounted television sets keep the kids busy while you eat.

CIRCUSES, MAGIC SHOWS, AND OTHER SPECIAL EVENTS

Shriners Circus
600 N. Wabash   266-5000
Every spring the Shriners roll into the big top at the Medinah Temple. A bonus of this three-ring extravaganza is its accessibility: Shriners volunteers will go out of their way to help disabled kids get in and out and use the Temple's facilities.

Cirque de Soleil and **The Moscow Circus**
Both are splendid circuses that amaze adults and children alike. The Canadian Cirque de Soleil—the "rock and roll circus," to my son—approaches the circus as a total performance piece, commissioning haunting original music and lavish costumes for its beautiful production. Since it is comprised strictly of human beings clowning around and performing dazzling acrobatics, it's the circus of choice for animal-rights activists. When it's in town, you can find its yellow and blue tent at North Pier. The Moscow Circus's breathtaking aerial acrobats and daredevil animal handlers mount their show at the UIC Pavilion.

IBM Ring 43 Annual Magic Show
If your kids love magic, watch for this show, conjured up each fall at Mather High School on Lincoln Avenue. Ring 43, the local chapter of the International Brotherhood of Magicians, showcases eight different professional magicians in each year's show. Because it's only presented once in a smallish auditorium, tickets for this festival of sleight-of-hand are hard to come by. Limited numbers are available at **Magic, Inc.** (5028 N. Lincoln, 334-2855). It's worth noting that in addition to selling tricks and accessories, Chicago's premier magic store acts as a clearinghouse for Chicago magicians, whose performances are posted on the Magic, Inc., bulletin board.

The Magic Masters
South Side magic lovers should watch for this annual spring dinner and show. At this family-oriented event, magicians perform table tricks during dinner and mount a platform show afterward. You can try tracking them down through Magic, Inc., too.

American Indian Center of Chicago Pow Wow
Any child intrigued with Native American culture will be impressed by this event, held annually in the fall. Hundreds of Native Americans from tribes all over the country participate, with Native American foods, crafts, and competitive dancing, drumming, and singing. A dazzling grand march of all participants kicks off each evening's program. It's a unique opportunity to learn about tribal costumes, purchase Native American crafts, and sample fry bread and corn soup. Contact the **American Indian Center** (1630 W. Wilson, 275-5871) for details on the dates and location of this and its other seasonal special events.

KIDS, ANIMALS, AND THE OUTDOORS

The Lincoln Park Zoo
2200 N. Cannon   294-4660
For a free day outdoors, visit this great urban zoo. Every single day, the Children's Zoo offers spur-of-the-moment presentations on zoo babies, animal diets, and animal senses, along with ample opportunities for kids to get their hands on various fuzzy, furry, friendly beasts. If you're planning a visit, call the **Children's Zoo** first (295-7846) to find out what's scheduled. Activities tend to be more frequent during summer months.

Kids Corner: A Discovery Place is a multimedia resource/exploration center where families with children under 12 can drop by and touch artifacts, play with educational games, watch videos, do crafts activities—all on zoo-related themes.

More structured family workshops are offered by the zoo's Education Department (294-4649). Its Urban Safaris visit hard-to-get-into spots like water reclamation facilities and the deep tunnel project—all for the purpose of enhancing our awareness of Chicago's natural resources and their impact on our lives.

During the dog days of summer, enroll your kids in Zoo Camps, held early July through mid-August for children ages 5–12. These week-long sessions immerse kids in topics like animal habitat and animal adaptation. Subjects change every summer, so budding zoologists can attend year after year after year and never hear the same thing twice.

Brookfield Zoo
First Avenue and 31st Street, Brookfield   (708) 485-0263
Also hosts special events in its Children's Zoo. From Memorial Day through Labor Day, the Seabury Arena is the site of Animals in Action shows that highlight different zoo animals. An elephant birthday party, the teddy bear picnic, and the Zoo Thanksgiving Day feast are supplemented by various educational programs offered throughout the year. (You'll have to call the Zoo for information.)

All of these programs take place amid a wealth of innovative, naturalistic, mixed-species exhibits that reveal how a wide variety of living organisms depend on their environments and on one another for survival. The Zoo's Tropic World, for example, represents the rain forest regions of South America, Asia, and Africa. The Fragile Kingdom re-creates the exotic deserts and rocky ledge environments of Africa and Asia.

Indian Boundary Zoo
Indian Boundary Park, 2500 W. Lunt
It doesn't offer any programs or special activities, but this zoo lets children get close to smaller animals like goats, llamas, and raccoons. It's a low-key, low-density place that has the great advantage of sitting right next to the spectacular Indian Boundary playground, which makes it perfect for a picnic day in the park.

North Park Village Nature Center
5801 N. Pulaski   744-5472
On the grounds of an old tuberculosis sanitarium, the Center offers outdoor family activities like bird walks, star watches, and weekend hikes. Seasonal activities include the Maple Syrup Festival in March; the very spooky Haunted Trail, held at Halloween; and the Winter Solstice Party, where children and their families can toast marshmallows, make edible ornaments for bird, and enjoy winter in the woods. Most programs are free or require a minimal materials fee.

RESOURCES FOR PARENTS

Of course, raising children in Chicago isn't always food, field trips, and fun. Fortunately, there is no shortage of resources for parents who need help with all manner of minor and major family crises.

Northside Parents Network   929-2507
This co-op of 160 families has been flourishing for almost 15 years. Run by volunteers, it offers seminars for new mothers, play groups for toddlers, and three babysitting co-ops, as well as special family events and a regular newsletter. Membership is $20 a year.

Parent's Resource Network
A not-for-profit group that facilitates lectures on topics of interest to parents and sponsors a "Warm Line" parents can call for support and nonmedical advice on parenting questions. To date its programs have focused on pre-school children, but the Network is expanding its programs and services to reach parents of school-age children as well.

Parentheses Parent/Child Center
405 S. Euclid, Oak Park   (708) 848-2227
A family support center that combines peer support with professional advice in a warm, friendly environment. In addition to its morning drop-in program, it offers programs for working families, teen parents, single parents, and parents of premature infants. Its annual preschool fair is a great way to find out about area preschools.

Day Care Action Council
4753 N. Broadway   561-8000
For a sliding-scale fee, the Council will provide lists of licensed child care providers for any location in Cook County. If you're in the market for a new caregiver, give them your zip code, and you'll receive a list of qualified caregivers in zip codes adjacent to your home.

SUGGESTED READING

Chicago Parent
The monthly guide to activities for children in Chicago. Available wherever parents gather (day-care centers, schools, children's resale shops, etc.), it provides an excellent roundup of resources for kids, along with thought-provoking articles on parenting topics. If you're looking for a hospital, camp, afterschool program, school, or babysitter, start here.

Chicago with Kids: Places to Go and Things to Do by Sheribel Rothenburg and Ellen Dick.
An encyclopedia of great things to do with kids in Sweet Home Chicago. Its chapter on behind-the-scenes tours of Chicago institutions is particularly good.

Somewhere over the Dan Ryan: Day and Weekend Outings for Chicago-Area Families by Joanne Y. Cleaver.
Lots of things to do indoors and out, all within a few hours of Chicago.

—Anne Basye

SENIORS

Chicago is a good place for retirees. Finally you have the time for all the activities the city has to offer. Besides, several organizations offer discounts for seniors. This chapter is an introduction to services that are specifically designed for the needs of the senior community. Several of the organizations listed here cannot only provide information but will also help find an exercise class, a new activity, a support group, or assistance with filling forms or filing a complaint.

INFORMATION AND REFERRAL

Many government agencies and private businesses have toll-free (800) numbers. Call toll-free information (1-800-555-1212) to see if the agency you are trying to reach has a toll- free number.

GOVERNMENT AGENCIES

Chicago Department on Aging and Disability (DAD)
510 N. Peshtigo, Chicago, 60611   744-4016, TDD: 744-6777
Provides a wide range of services and can answer any question relating to seniors. Services include, but are not limited to, health care, legal aid, recreation, transportation, employment assistance, meal programs, and case management. Other offices located at this center are

DAD Library   744-7304

Foster Grandparents   744-3221

Job Training and Placement Service   744-4407

The DAD has five regional centers that offer services ranging from social activities to help with filling out forms:

Central/West Center
2102 W. Ogden, Chicago, 60612   226-2525, TDD: 744-0319

Northeast Center (Levy)
2019 W. Lawrence, Chicago, 60625   878-3564, TDD: 744-0320

Northwest Center (Copernicus)
3160 N. Milwaukee, Chicago, 60618   744-6681, TDD: 744-0321

Southeast Center (Atlas)
1767 E. 79th, Chicago, 60649   731-5523, TDD: 744-0322

Southwest Center
6117 S. Kedzie, Chicago, 60629   476-8700, TDD: 744-0323

HEALTH AND MEDICINE

Information and Referral

Chicago Department of Public Health
Office of Public Information and Communication
50 W. Washington, Chicago, 60602   744-4278
Call for information about neighborhood clinics.

Nutrition

Meals on Wheels   431-0022

Evanston Meals at Home   (708) 251-6827 (call before 1 P.M.)
Volunteers deliver hot meals to the homebound; payment is on a sliding
scale. New volunteers are always welcome.

Community and Economic Development Association of Cook County
600 S. Michigan, Chicago, 60605   207-5444
A community action program administering nutrition services in Cook
County.

Illinois Department of Public Aid, Cook County Office
624 S. Michigan, Chicago, 60605   793-4706
Provides assistance to residents of Cook County and administers the Food
Stamp program.

Day Care

The following organizations provide day care for adults with physical limitations. Call the centers for information about the services offered.

Council for the Jewish Elderly
1015 Howard, Evanston, 60202   (708) 492-1400

Holy Cross Hospital
2701 W. 68th, Chicago, 60629   471-7300

Hyde Park Neighborhood Club
5480 S. Kenwood, Chicago, 60615   643-4062

Japanese American Service Committee
4427 N. Clark, Chicago, 60640   275-7512

Warren Barr Pavilion of Illinois Masonic Medical Center
66 W. Oak, Chicago, 60610   337-5400

The following organizations provide day care at home.

Catholic Charities Senior Community Services
126 N. Des Plaines, Chicago, 60606   236-5172
Homemaker and other housekeeper services; reduced cost for eligible
families.

Family Care Services Homemaker and Respite Program
234 S. Wabash, Chicago, 60604   427-8790
Trained workers provide homemaker and housekeeping services to assist families and individuals following illness. Fees are based on a sliding scale.

Seniors Action Service, Inc. (SASI)
1610 Maple, Evanston, 60201   (708) 864-7274
Provides services to individuals who need assistance at home, for a fee.

Support Services

These organizations provide much-needed support not only to those with health limitations but also to their families and caregivers.

Alcoholics Anonymous
205 W. Wacker, Chicago, 60606   346-1475
Provides general information and directs callers to local groups in their communities.

Alzheimer's Association (ADRDA)
Chicago Area Chapter
845 Chicago, Evanston, 60202   (708) 864-0045
Provides information and support for families and friends of persons with Alzheimer's.

Alzheimer's Disease Clinical Center
1715 W. Harrison, #1030, Chicago, 60612   226-1491
Services include evaluation, psychosocial support, and long-term follow-up for Alzheimer's patients who are ambulatory.

American Cancer Society
37 S. Wabash, Chicago, 60603   372-0471
Provides educational programs and materials on cancer. With a physician's reference, patients can participate in rehabilitation/support programs. Also arranges for loans of hospital beds and wheelchairs.

American Foundation for the Blind
203 N. Wabash, #1302, Chicago, 60611   269-0095
Provides information and educational programs for the blind.

Arthritis Foundation
79 W. Monroe, #1120, Chicago, 60603   782-1367
Services include speakers, health fairs, conferences, and forums on arthritis; also provides a self-help course.

Chicago Hearing Society
10 W. Jackson, Chicago, 60603   939-6888
Services include education, information, and support.

Chicago Heart Association
20 N. Wacker, Chicago, 60606   346-4675
Literature on heart disease and its prevention.

EDUCATION AND RECREATION

Several senior citizens clubs have ongoing educational and recreational activities. The **Chicago Park District** (294-2309) has over 114 senior citizens clubs throughout the city. Activities include but are not limited to field trips, swimming, yoga, dancing, arts and crafts, choral singing, drama, and holiday parties. Call for the location of a club in your neighborhood.

American Association of Retired Persons (AARP)
2720 Des Plaines, #113, Des Plaines, 60018   (708) 298-2852
Informational and educational programs, consumer advocacy. Membership benefits include subscription to *Modern Maturity* and newsletters related to aging.

Education Network for Older Adults
36 S. Wabash, #624, Chicago, 60603   782-8967
Clearinghouse for educational opportunities in a wide range of subjects; no fees.

Levy Senior Citizen Recreation Club
1700 Maple, Evanston, 60201   (708) 869-0727
Provides a variety of programs including exercise classes, arts and crafts classes, educational programs, trips, and volunteer opportunities.

White Crane Tai Chi Club
906 W. Belmont, Chicago, 60657   883-7151
Tai Chi classes for the elderly.

EMPLOYMENT

Several nonprofit organizations offer part- or full-time employment to seniors.

City of Chicago, Department of Human Resources
345 W. Chicago, 5th floor, Chicago, 60610   744-5994
Gives information about part-time jobs under the Title V program for seniors.

Jewish Vocational Service
1 S. Franklin, Chicago, 60606   346-6700
Counseling and referral; open to all faiths.

Operation ABLE
36 S. Wabash, Chicago, 60602   782-7700
Provides job-seeking programs, including support groups led by trained counselors.

National Caucus and Center on Black Aged, Inc.
2100 S. Indiana, Chicago, 60601   225-2500
Hires older workers in Cook county.

ADVOCACY AND LEGAL AID

Cook County Assessor's Office
Senior Citizens' Exemption Department
118 N. Clark, 3rd floor, Chicago, 60602   443-6151
Helps eligible senior homeowners to register for property tax exemptions.

Cook County Legal Assistance Foundation, Inc.
828 Davis, #201, Evanston, 60201   (708) 475-3703
Provides free legal aid to low-income individuals. Services include help with disability benefits and Medicare and Medicaid claim assistance.

Cook County State's Attorney
Nursing Home Advocacy
Richard J. Daley Center, #519, Chicago, 60602   443-4377
Investigates nursing home complaints; helps with filing suits against nursing homes.

Illinois Office of Attorney General
Senior Citizen Advocacy Division
100 W. Randolph, 13th floor, Chicago, 60601   917-3382
Assists consumers with queries and complaints regarding senior services, health insurance, tax programs, and more.

Illinois Department of Revenue
100 W. Randolph, C-300, Chicago, 60659   (800) 732-8866
Taxpayer assistance.

Illinois Guardianship and Advocacy Commission
1735 W. Taylor, Chicago, 60612   996-1650
Provides legal and guardianship counseling; also serves as guardian if none is available; investigates complaints of abuse or neglect against nursing homes and state facilities. Employment opportunities for older workers.

RESIDENTIAL/HOUSING SERVICES

Illinois Citizens for Better Care
220 S. State, #800, Chicago, 60604   663-5120
A watchdog group that monitors nursing homes; provides help with nursing home selection, complaints, and rights. Supported by consumers and foundations, this is a good place to begin your search for a nursing home. Spend some time in the home before signing the contract.

Lieberman Geriatric Health Care Center for the Council for Jewish Elderly
9700 Gross Point, Skokie, 60076   (708) 674-7210

St. Francis Extended Care Center
500 Asbury, Evanston, 60202   (708) 492-3320
A long-term care facility that provides intermediate and skilled nursing care. An affiliate of St. Francis Hospital.

Warren Barr Pavilion of Illinois Masonic Medical Center
66 W. Oak, Chicago, 60610   337-5400

Westshire Retirement and Healthcare Center
5825 W. Cermak, Chicago, 60650   656-9120
Affiliate of the University of Illinois–Chicago's medical Center.

CONSUMER PROTECTION

Organizations

Attorney General of Illinois Consumer Fraud and Protection Division
100 W. Randolph, Chicago, 60602   814-3381

Better Business Bureau
211 W. Wacker, Chicago, 60601   444-1188

Chicago Department of Consumer Sales
121 N. LaSalle, Chicago, 60602   744-9400

Consumer Product Safety Commission
230 S. Dearborn, Chicago, 60604   353-8260

Council for Disability Rights
343 S. Dearborn, #1501, Chicago, 60604   922-1093, TDD: 922-1092

Gray Panthers
343 S. Dearborn, #1421, Chicago, 60604   663-9093
A social action group that fights age discrimination.

Jane Addams Center Senior Caucus
3212 N. Broadway, Chicago, 60657
Active in health issues, tenants' rights, and peace issues.

Legacy: An Association for Lesbian and Gay Seniors
P.O. Box 148444, Chicago, 60614   327-2734

Lieutenant Governor's Office   (800) 252-8652
Citizen's advocate program offering information and assistance with the state government.

Metropolitan Seniors in Action
220 S. State, #706, Chicago, 60604   427-6262

HOTLINES

Attorney General   (800) 252-2518

Commerce and Community Affairs   (800) 252-8643
Energy hot line provides information on utility assistance to low-income families.

DHHH Inspector General   (800) 368-5779
Handles complaints regarding fraud, waste, and abuse of government funds, including Medicare and Medicaid; assists people who have been overbilled or billed for services not rendered.

PRODUCT SAFETY

Consumer Product Safety Commission (800) 638-2772,
TDD: (800) 638-8270

PUBLIC AID

Public Assistance Inquiries (800) 793-4706

—Prathima Christdas

LESBIANS

Think of the urban lesbian, and visions of San Francisco and Greenwich Village are certain to come to mind. Think of Chicago and you're more likely to think of meatpacking, the Mob, and the Bulls.

The large and diverse lesbian social scene is one of the Midwest's best-kept secrets. Who would guess that Chicago has more to offer for lesbians socially than either San Francisco, New York City, or Los Angeles? The incredible, wonderful truth is that it does, and I will describe to you just a few of the options available to you as I take you on a tour of wild lesbo-Chicago.

CHICAGO IS LESBO-CHIC-A-GO-GO!

Lesbo-Chicago is a great place to be. We provide a large array of possibilities to anyone who wants a way to hook in, connect, and find community. Whether your interests are nightlife, politics, athletics, religious affinity, recovery, business networking, or any other possibility, the resources are here and at your disposal. All of these wide-ranging special interest groups are collected and served through the clearinghouses of local bookstores and the gay press. All it takes to get involved is your initiative.

Here's a suggestion of ways to spend your lesbian Chicago weekend.

The Andersonville Stroll

Andersonville is a largely Swedish shopping district located on North Clark Street, around Foster Avenue, that has recently become a mecca of cool, woman-owned businesses. It's a perfect place to spend a Saturday afternoon Chicago lesbian-style.

First off, there is mandatory breakfast at **Ann Sather's** (5207 N. Clark), a very popular woman-owned Swedish restaurant that serves complimentary cinnamon rolls that are to die for, followed by a visit to **Women & Children First Bookstore** (5233 N. Clark), one of the largest feminist bookstores in the world. Be prepared to spend at least an hour here, and be sure to ask the staff about current social happenings—they're well informed and can be very helpful. Then, hop over to **WomanWild** (5237 N. Clark), a unique gallery of women-made arts and crafts. Head north for a truly unique vintage shopping experience; take in the area's two metaphysical book and herb shops, **Aurum Solis** (5142 N. Clark) and **Bell, Book, and Candle** (5246 N. Clark); and finally, lunch at one of the many fine restaurants that cater to carnivores and vegetarians equally well. Of these, I would strongly recommend the gay-owned **Dellwood Pickle** (1475 W. Balmoral), which is just east of Clark on Balmoral; **Maya** (2130 W. Cermak), a warm and wonderful Central American restaurant; **Andie's** (2535 N. Clark), which is a Middle Eastern restaurant that serves up the best falafel sandwiches in town; or the **Kopi Cafe** (5317 N. Clark) for a luscious dessert and coffee.

Sundays in New Town

New Town is a hip, fun, and diverse area around the vicinity of Clark and Belmont. It is also one of the biggest per-capita gay neighborhood's in Chitown. It's a perfect place to do a lot of footwork on a temperate afternoon.

Brunch at one of the many gay-friendly restaurants in the neighborhood. I'd recommend **Buddie's** (3301 N. Clark), a gay bar-slash-restaurant, or **Moti Mahal** (2525 W. Devon), which has an awesome East Indian weekend brunch special (all-you-can-eat buffet), followed by day-after bloody mary's at **The Closet** (3325 N. Broadway), a mixed gay bar with a largely lesbian clientele. On the way to The Closet, be sure to make a detour to visit **People Like Us** (3321 N. Clark), Chicago's exclusively gay and lesbian bookstore, and **We're Everywhere** (3434 N. Halsted), which features entirely gay- and lesbian-oriented clothes and other assorted doodads.

In the summer, I'd recommend that this be followed by a walk to the lake (just a block or two east), where you can either scope the scene at the gay hang-out, the Belmont Rocks, or head north to Addison and be a spectator to an afternoon of dyke softball. Other New Town summer highlights are the **Halsted Street Market Days** in early August (major crowd watching) and the **Chicago Lesbian and Gay Pride Parade** at the end of June, which boasted 100,000 participants in 1991.

Marathon O' Nightlife

Bar-time socializing isn't for everyone, but it happens to be my forte, and I relish in providing tips and details to the Chicago bar-hopping novice. If you're just going to be in town for the weekend and want to get in as much as you can, have I got a road map for you! At first glance, it may seem an overwhelming night of adventure, but I know from experience that it can be done. For your own safety, however, I'd recommend cabbing it.

I suggest starting out your evening of adventure at **Paris Dance** (1122 W. Montrose). Paris is Chicago's premiere lesbian-owned women's dance bar. Cover charge on weekends is $5, but free if you get there before 10 P.M.. There you can dance to DJ-spun music or, if you prefer, sit at the bar in the next room, play darts, or grab a cappuccino or sandwich at the adjoining **Luna Park Cafe** (1122 W. Montrose). Saturdays are the bar's busiest night, when women from all over cram in for a night of dancing and cruising.

When you've had your share of Paris, hop in a taxi and go around the corner to **Augie and CK's** (3726 N. Broadway). A little looser and rowdier than Paris, CK's also offers great DJ-spun dance music, as well as two pool tables for billiards aficionados. Worn out your dancing shoes, but still feel like partying? Well, you're a trooper, so time to jump into yet another cab, and go south to **The Closet** (3325 N. Broadway). A mixed gay and lesbian bar, The Closet has a large majority lesbian clientele. Often loud and crowded on weekends, the bar has five video monitors, with a great mix of progressive and dance music videos. The Closet is open 'til 5 A.M. on Saturday, but its a great place to hang out any night of the week.

If you have more than a weekend of exploring time at hand, check out some of the other nightlife attractions. Women's Obsession Night at **Berlin** (954 W. Belmont) is a must-go event that occurs on every first and third

Wednesday of the month, and there's always some other roving alternative dyke night. **Mountain Moving Coffeehouse** (1545 W. Morse) is one of the nation's oldest women's coffehouses, a chem-free space that features top music performers and entertainment, open every Saturday night.

There are also other great lesbian bars to visit, and a host of other community events occur regularly throughout the year, one notable one being the **Chicago International Gay and Lesbian Film Festival**, which occurs in November. The local media is a great source of information on current happenings.

GENERAL RESOURCES

Retail/Boutiques

WomanWild
5237 N. Clark   878-0300
A unique women's arts and craft gallery.

Jan Dee Jewelers
1425 W. Diversey   871-2222
Custom jeweler specializing in commitment rings.

People Like Us
3321 N. Clark   248-6363
Chicago's exclusive gay and lesbian bookstore. Features regular programs and book signings, as well as a great selection of gay and lesbian books and magazines.

We're Everywhere
3434 N. Halsted   404-0590
Gay- and lesbian-oriented T-shirts, sweatshirts, and more.

Women & Children First Bookstore
5233 N. Clark   769-9299
Women & Children First is, in my biased eyes, *the* feminist bookstore of the Midwest. Regular programs and author appearances, great selection of women's music and videos, magazines, buttons, posters, and, of course, books.

Health/Fitness

Chicago Women's Seido Karate/Thousand Waves Spa
1212 W. Belmont   549-0700
Offers classes in self-defense and martial arts, as well as full spa facilities.

Chicago Women's Health Center
3435 N. Sheffield   935-6126
Women's health services include gynecological exams and counsel.

Lesbian Physicians of Chicago   404-8950

Chimera Self-Defense for Women
59 E. Van Buren, #714, Chicago, 60604

Newtown Alano Clubs
4403-7 N. Clark   271-6822
Twelve-step programs, Alanon, NA, CA, OA, ACOA—all geared to the gay and lesbian community.

Lesbian Community Cancer Project   549-GRAY
Provides support services for lesbians battling cancer.

Sports/Recreation

Out Spok'n
1400 W. Belmont   404-2919
Bicycles, bike-related merchandise, and full services.

Frontrunners-Frontwalkers Chicago
P.O. Box 148313, Chicago, 60614
Gays and lesbians run and walk together twice a week, on Tuesday at 6:30 P.M. and Saturday at 10 A.M. Meet at the totem pole at Addison and Lake Shore Drive.

Local Media

Gay Chicago Magazine
3121 N. Broadway, Chicago, 60657
A weekly glossy mag aimed at the gay male audience.

HOT WIRE magazine
5210 N. Wayne, Chicago, 60640
A national magazine of women's music and culture, based in Chicago.

Literary Xpress Journal
P.O. Box 438583, Chicago, 60643
An African-American women's literary magazine.

Nightlines Weekly
3059 N. Southport, Chicago, 60657
A weekly guide to arts and entertainment for the Chicago area.

Outlines Newsmagazine
3059 N. Southport, Chicago, 60657
A monthly paper of world news, arts and entertainment, gossip, and more, for the gay and lesbian community.

Windy City Times
970 W. Montana, Chicago, 60614
A weekly gay and lesbian newspaper, includes nightlife and local and world news.

Culture

Artimis Singers
P.O. Box 578296, Chicago, 60657   764-4465
Chicago's very own lesbian-feminist chorus plays frequently around town.

Great Lakes Freedom Band
Rodde Center
4753 N. Broadway, #1200   474-6966
Gay and lesbian concert band.

Literary Exchange
P.O. Box 438583, Chicago, 60643   509-6881
A literary discussion group for African-American women.

Lesbian Book Discussion Group
Gerber-Hart Library
3352 N. Paulina   327-7431
Gerber-Hart Library is the Chicago area's les/gay library. Monthly book discussions of lesbian novels are held there.

Social Resources

Chicago 35   271-5909
Social group for lesbians over 35.

Daisy   784-1360
Social group for lesbians of color.

Lavender Bouquet
P.O. Box 3955, Oak Park, 60303   (708) 848-8369
West suburban social group for lesbians.

Lesbians in Leather/Chicago
P.O. Box 138342, Chicago, 60613

Lesbians Latinas en Nuestro Ambiente
P.O. Box 107, 1955 W. Cermak, Chicago, 60608   227-3881
Social and political organization for Latina lesbians.

P/A/Ls Networking—Chicago
P.O. Box 317, 1340 W. Irving Park, Chicago, 60613   929-7360
Pacifica/Asian lesbians.

Nightlife

Augie & CK's
3726 N. Broadway   975-0449
Open Tuesday–Sunday; dance bar, pool.

Berlin
954 W. Belmont   348-4975
Women's Obsession Night every first and third Wednesday.

The Closet
3325 N. Broadway   477-8533
Mixed bar, mostly women; videos.

His 'N' Hers
5820 N. Broadway   769-1616
Mixed bar, mostly women; neighborhoody.

Intrigue
528 Stateline, Calumet City (708) 868-5240
Open seven days; dance bar.

Lost & Found
3058 Irving Park 463-9617
Neighborhoody; pool, two-stepping Tuesdays.

Pangea
3209 N. Halsted 296-6471
Female Thang every Wednesday; dancing, videos.

Paris Dance
1122 W. Montrose 769-0602
Open seven days; dance bar, cafe.

Temptations
10235 W. Grand, Franklin Park (708) 455-0008
Open seven days; dance bar, entertainment, videos, sports.

Visions
3432 W. Irving Park 539-5229
Sports bar; wide-screen TV, dancing.

Vortex
3631 N. Halsted 975-6622
Thursday nights are "Girlbar"; dancing, videos.

—Kathie Bergquist

GAY MEN

There's so much gay life in Chicago one could easily make his sexual orientation a full-time occupation. Whether this would be advisable is open to debate. There are hundreds of gay-identified businesses, clubs, organizations, bars, churches, cruising areas, activist groups, restaurants, and everything in between. If one were so inclined, he could boycott mainstream society and still have a full-spectrum social, professional, political, and artistic life completely within the gay subculture. We call this creature "a professional homosexual"—it's not really a compliment. But the fact is, over the past 22 years homophobia forced construction of a near-complete gay city within the city. There are, after all, more homosexuals in Chicago than there are people in Des Moines.

A number of generalizations can be made about Chicago's gay community. It is friendlier than New York's, folks claim. It is less closeted than Washington, D.C.'s, some say. It is less fanatically political than San Francisco's, and also somewhat less ghettoized and stereotype-laden. More uptight than New Orleans's, more active than Los Angeles's, less earthy than Seattle's, less apathetic than Miami's.

Unlike San Francisco or perhaps New Orleans, not as many Chicago gays moved to Chicago specifically to *be* gay. More commonly, people who happen to be gay are here to live their lives in the larger city.

All that said, I must confess that my favorite gay activity is Lake Michigan. The gayest locale is "the Belmont Rocks," a stretch of grass south of Belmont Harbor and just north of the closed gun club. When the mercury rises above 70, gay men flock to the Rocks—hundreds on steamy days. But, in fact, the entire lakeshore from Oak Street (1000 North) to Hollywood Avenue (5700 North) is gay stomping ground. Gays, like nongays, bike, walk pooches, jog, play volleyball, and soak up rays. Nongays don't know who's who, but God gave gays "gaydar." It allows us to identify each other within five seconds anywhere on Earth.

The lake gaydar scene is a testament to Chicago's world-class status. Gay ratings of major European cities are not based on their bar and club life but on how many men stroll about the city's most beautiful outdoor areas and how easy it is to meet them. Paris, not San Francisco, is probably the world's gayest city.

An old gay-lib slogan went "Out of the closets and into the streets!" Now that gay lib has succeeded (yes, we won, they lost), the slogan seems to be "Out of the bars into the sun!" You doubt that we won? Where are you reading this essay? In a mainstream book for hip yuppies.

FOOD, DRINK, AND HOW TO FIND THEM

Bars and Clubs

OK, some days the sun don't shine in Chicago. So maybe you want to access the massive gay infrastructure (not to be confused with wet Loop tunnels). Where to start? For my money, **Sidetrack**, (3349 N. Halsted). The kind of man who would buy this book would find at Sidetrack other men who bought this book. Also directly across the street is **Roscoe's** bar and cafe.

Why Sidetrack? The owners of this video bar have put a great deal of effort into making it special and have been rewarded with SRO crowds seven nights a week. Mondays there are show tunes on the big video screen. Two hundred homosexuals trance out before the likes of Judy, Barbara, Bette, Mae et al., and before the Divine Entity Itself, Metro Goldwyn Mayer Studios. Tuesday there's video country and western dancing. Showtune queens are replaced by swaggering cowboys. Woof. Wednesday it's the music of the fifties, sixties, and seventies. Where else can you see a clip of the Partridge Family singing "I Think I Love You"? Or a high-fidelity recording of the opening to "The Brady Bunch"? Not to mention nice Mama Cass and Sonny & Cher collections. Thursday is comedy night, and video connoisseur Pepin Pena has built an amazing library of queer tape.

There are about 75 gay bars in the metro area, so we can only note a few.

AA Meat Market 2933 N. Lincoln
Leathermen do it at AA Meat Market. The back room sizzles on weekends.

Deeks 3401 N. Sheffield
Good dancing.

Manhole 3458 N. Halsted

Chronic cruisers might hit these clubs:

Little Jim's 3501 N. Halsted

The Loading Dock 3702 N. Halsted

Manhandler 1948 N. Halsted

Young dancers might be happy here:

Vortex 3631 N. Halsted

Trendoids should check out these:

Berlin 954 W. Belmont

Cairo (Sunday only) 720 N. Wells

Drag queens (there are still a few) will feel at home here:

Baton Show Lounge 436 N. Clark

Chit-chat bars include these two:

Buddies 3301 N. Clark

The North End 3722 N. Halsted

Professionals over 35 meet here:

Gentry 712 N. Rush

There are go-go boys at:

The Lucky Horseshoe Lounge 3169 N. Halsted

Gay Press

Three of Chicago's four gay publications print bar guides each week, complete with a detailed code system to lead you to just what you *have* to have. Pick up *Nightlines*, *The Windy City Times*, or *Gay Chicago* at the above bars or hundreds of other North Side businesses.

Nightlines is a nightlife and entertainment guide, but it also covers breaking local news. *Gay Chicago* is the oldest of the publications. It dwells heavily on the nightlife scene but also includes columns on taxes, health, coming out, and other matters, along with personal advice and reflections. It runs national news from the AP wire. *Windy City Times* and *Outlines*, the fourth publication, are serious newspapers. *Outlines* is noted for international coverage, in-depth local reporting, and wide-ranging features. *Windy City Times* covers local politics thoroughly. Few U.S. cities are so well served by gay media.

Restaurants

The newspapers can also lead you to restaurants frequented by gays; a few are listed below.

Ann Sather's   929 W. Belmont

Cornelia's   748 W. Cornelia

The Melrose   930 W. Belmont and 3233 N. Broadway

Nookies Tree   3334 N. Halsted

OTHER RESOURCES

But sometimes you're full, not in a bar mood, and have already digested the week's gay press. Fear not. There are, all exaggeration aside, hundreds of options. Two gay sports associations, the **Metropolitan Sports Association** and the **Windy City Athletic Association**, offer year-round team activities from bowling to volleyball to baseball. There are also two gay swim clubs, **Aqua Fags & Aqua Dykes** and **Chicago Smelts**; a square-dance club, **Chi-Town Squares**; a running club, **Frontrunners**; and a motorcycle club, **Open Road Riders of Chicagoland**, for starters.

The city has numerous gay religious organizations, including several parishes of the gay-founded **Metropolitan Community Church** (the largest gay organization in the world; see the "Religion" chapter) and gay groups attached to every major religion. Gay Catholics have an intriguing choice. There's **Dignity**, which Cardinal Joseph Bernardin banned from church property because members refused to concede that the Catholic Church is correct in labeling gay sex "intrinsically evil" and gays "objectively disordered." The Cardinal later felt guilty, apparently, and formed **Archdiocesan Gay and Lesbian Outreach**, which holds Sunday evening mass at a Catholic parish. The gay religious groups, and their meeting times and places, are listed in the gay press.

Another educated guess we can make is that readers of this book will feel comfortable with **Chicago Professional Networking Association** (296-CPNA), a low-profile organization of 500 gay businessmen. The group holds huge monthly meetings and smaller social activities throughout the month.

Recent speakers at the monthly gatherings were Mayor Richard Daley, psychic Irene Hughes, and Dick Sargeant, the "Bewitched" Darrin who came out of the closet. Members claim the determinedly nonpolitical group is an excellent place to find a husband.

But perhaps you are politically inclined. Rowdy radicals should check out **ACT UP** (509-6802), which stands for the AIDS Coalition to Unleash Power. If your idea of a fun afternoon is chasing Daley or Bush around the city shouting about AIDS funding, if being thrown out of City Council by a burly policeman trips your trigger, ACT UP is home.

If, on the other hand, you'd groove on making a splashy public spectacle of your queerness, check out **Queer Nation**. The sometimes political, sometimes merely *faaabulous* group adds a queer element to mainstream public events and is heavily involved in a lengthy fight to force County Board President Richard Phelan to push through a county gay-rights law like the one Chicago passed in 1990. Yes, it's illegal in the city of Chicago to discriminate based on sexual orientation in employment, housing, and so-called public accommodations (restaurants, taxis, zoos, etc.). One recent lawsuit of note led to a sizeable monetary settlement for two men who were kicked out of a Division Street straight pick-up bar for dancing together. Low on cash? Go dance at Rush and Division!

If you're neither aggressively *faaabulous* nor radical, there are numerous other political options. The **Illinois Gay and Lesbian Task Force** lobbies the state legislature, which sooner or later will join Connecticut, Hawaii, Massachusetts, New Jersey, Vermont, and Wisconsin in protecting gays statewide. The **Chicago Area Republican Gay Organization** is self-explanatory. Critics insist that "gay Republican" is an oxymoron, but, in fact, the majority of gay men (unlike lesbians) are likely no more "liberal" than Americans in general. **Citizens for Gay Action** works for the legalization of same-sex marriage, quite unsuccessfully to date. (Gay marriage is legal nowhere in the world but Denmark.) **IMPACT** is the state's gay political action committee. It raises money and hands it out in hopes of influencing politicians. This tends to work in Chicago.

Other activist groups are not overtly political. The **Pink Angels** patrol gay neighborhoods to thwart gay bashings. Every university in the area has a gay student group. On the social, self-help, and special-interest front are such resources as gay **Alcoholics Anonymous, Asians and Friends,** the **Association of Latino Men for Action,** the **Bisexual Political Action Coalition,** the **Chicago Faerie Circle** (use your imagination), **Gay & Lesbian Physicians of Chicago,** the **Lambda Car Club** (gay grease monkeys?), **Leather United,** the **Lesbian and Gay Bar Association** (gays in corporate drag), **Men of All Colors Together,** the **Metropolitan Business Association,** and on and on. And on.

Chicago has a gay library, the **Gerber-Hart Library**; a gay community center, the **Rodde Center**; a gay social service agency, **Horizons Community Services** (929-HELP, 6 P.M.–10 P.M. daily); and two highly regarded gay choruses, the **Chicago Gay Men's Chorus** and the **Windy City Gay Chorus**.

All the above groups, organizations, and agencies (and much more) are listed in the gay media, along with details on special events.

LET'S BE FRANK: AIDS AND SEX

AIDS organizations exist for every conceivable angle to the epidemic you can imagine—from "zapping" politicians to delivering hot meals to shut-ins, from tracking experimental underground therapies to handing out clean needles. Again, pick up any of the gay papers, or check out the "Physical Health" chapter.

Chicago is not as hard hit by AIDS as the coasts, but estimates are that 25 to 30 percent of the city's gay men are HIV-positive (compared with 50 percent in San Francisco and New York). HIV arrived here a little later than on the coasts, which means most HIV-positives have not progressed to AIDS, given the average 10-year lag between HIV infection and development of the disease. The city has seen a little under 5,000 AIDS cases to date, 72 percent of them among what the city calls "men who have sex with men." Unfortunately, we are going to see more of our friends fall ill in the coming five years.

Well, there's no easy transition out of that paragraph but to zing directly from death to frivolity. . . .

My editors said it was not only OK but desirable for this essay to stray into the realm of the funky, so I'm pleased to provide some info on, shall we say, *specialized* gay cruising, which, naturally, attracts a lot of men who don't consider themselves gay. (This phenomenon, which is why the city uses the phraseology it does, is another essay altogether.) One cruises for SAFE SEX only, of course. It might be going too far to list interesting restrooms at major department stores, high-rise malls, and public transportation terminals (hint, hint), but we can point out such areas as the lake-access road (Simmons Drive) between Montrose and Foster avenues; intriguing forest preserves, such as Groves 9–12 of Schiller Woods far out on Irving Park Boulevard (forest preserves are not completely safe, from either fag bashers or police trappers—sex in the open air is, for some reason, illegal); and institutions such as the Bijou Theater (1349 N. Wells) and the Ram Bookstore (3511 N. Halsted). All "adult" bookstores are noteworthy.

Of course, safe sex is an issue of *what* you do, not where you do it or how many people you do it with. "On me, not in me" is a good rule of thumb. Condoms are mandatory for intercourse. Use a water-based lubricant, such as KY Jelly. Oil-based lubricants, such as Vaseline or hand cream, dissolve rubbers. Ten years into the epidemic, oral sex seems to be proving low risk, especially if your partner pulls out before climax and you don't have any small abrasions in your mouth or dental problems.

As major U.S. cities go, Chicago is clearly one of the top four or five places to be gay. The community's political clout has skyrocketed in the past five years. The resources available are greater in number than, and of equal quality to, anywhere. And the men are said to be relatively sexy. Something about those Midwest farm boys who end up in the Big City.

Enjoy.

And play safe.

—*Rex Wockner*

Day-To-Day

TRANSPORTATION
EMPLOYMENT
PHYSICAL HEALTH
MENTAL HEALTH
CRISIS INTERVENTION
LEGAL SERVICES
RELIGION

Chicago Street Number Map

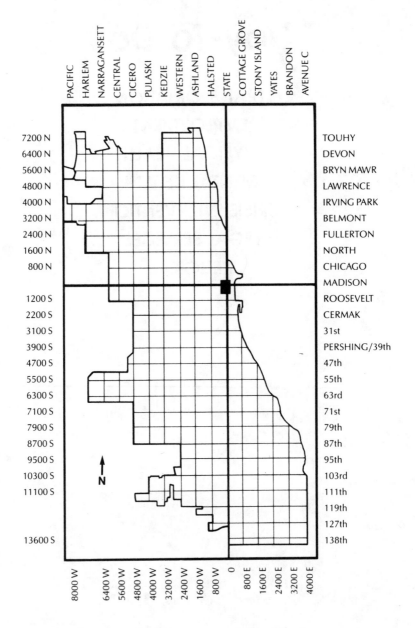

Corresponding street names appear in opposite border.

TRANSPORTATION

You've read about the Chicago sights to see, the beaten paths to take or ignore, the North Shore shoppers to avoid. But how goeth thee? Whether by foot, wheels, track, or flight, you can get from point A to point B without straining your brain, your boots, or your budget.

Unlike those other major cities, owning a car in Chicago is practical but not necessary. Though parking can become a hair-pulling experience downtown and in the Lakefront neighborhoods, there is inevitably a space to be had around the corner or down the street from your residence. And parking garages downtown, though somewhat expensive, rarely run full and are found every other block. Many high-rise apartments, and certainly condominiums, also offer underground parking for a reasonable increase in rent/mortgage.

If monthly car payments are not at the top of your priority list, however, you can find a ride to just about anywhere you'd care to go. Chicago boasts a transportation system that rivals any major metropolitan area this side of Tokyo. Buses, trains, and taxis are a dime a dozen in Chicago, and all are relatively inexpensive. There are transportation alternatives for the disabled and elderly as well.

LAY OF THE LAND

Before discussing the various transportation choices, it may behoove a first-time Windy City traveler to get a feel for the lay of the land. The greater Chicago area sprawls across 275 communities and six counties. Chicago proper is made up of many vastly different neighborhoods—from the quaint brownstones of Old Town to the rural areas only miles outside of the city. Instead of the congested burroughs of New York, Chicago offers a splendid inner city of skyscrapers and lights in the Loop and Magnificent Mile, only to transform into a small community literally blocks away. (For a lengthy and informative discussion of Chicago's many communities, see the "Neighborhoods" chapter and, well, this entire book.)

The city nestles closely to the shores of Lake Michigan, or simply "the Lake," which lies to the east. If ever completely at a loss for direction, this is about the easiest landmark to locate. (Hence the common phrase "the Lake is always east.") Drive toward Chicago from any direction, and you'll notice first the impressive buildings rising up from the horizon like books of varying heights and shapes. The John Hancock Building stands as a northern bookend; to the south and west stands the world's tallest building, the Sears Tower. Between these two Chicago landmarks is the heart of Chicago.

The Loop

The Loop is the nucleus of Chicago's business district, named for the elevated trains that have channeled into the city and looped around its center since the 1890s. Today, the Chicago Transit Authority's elevated trains, known affectionately by commuters as the "El," circle the Loop's five- by seven-block area. Though certainly not Chicago's only business section, it is in the Loop

DAY-TO-DAY

where the majority of the city's skyscrapers loom and where much of the city's inner workings take place.

Finding your way around the Loop is a systematic and simple procedure. Think of State Street (running north-south) and Madison Avenue (running east-west) as the "zero" intersection. Whenever you move away from this intersection in any direction, the addresses increase 100 per block. Thus, north-south street addresses get higher as they move away in either direction from Madison Avenue. East-west street addresses get higher as they move away in either direction from State Street.

As an example, if you are looking for a building at 5 S. Wabash, you can assume that building is within the first block south of Madison Avenue on Wabash. And if you're searching for the address of 305 E. Wacker, you'll find it three blocks east of State Street on Wacker Drive. Wacker Drive, that wacky little street, can be the one confusing street to follow in the Loop. It runs north-south, then hits the Chicago River and curves around to continue east-west. Don't be fooled by the city planner's idea of a good joke—Wacker Drive addresses still follow the State Street/Madison Avenue "zero block" guidelines.

The Magnificent Mile

Running adjacent to the Lake, the Magnificent Mile of Michigan Avenue represents the northeast end of the metropolis. Shopping heaven, you can find almost anything you need to purchase on the Magnificent Mile for the most ridiculous prices. Buy a futon for the price it takes to make it in gold. Hey, make it in gold! And why not, this is the mecca of fur coats and obscene displays of wealth. So take a stroll around Water Tower Place or Gucci's near Superior. But be sure to dress accordingly. And please don't insult the sales staff of Gucci's by asking for assistance. *Très* gauche.

Michigan Avenue runs north straight into Lake Shore Drive, which consists of the "Inner Drive" and the "Outer Drive." Take the Outer Drive along the Lake for an express ride south of the city all the way to the Chicago Skyway, or north to Loyola University where it connects to Sheridan Road. Take the Inner Drive for those frequent local stops downtown. Lake Shore Drive is an alternative to the freeway, which often becomes terribly congested during rush hours and is difficult to access from locales east in the city.

Over the River

Over the river and through the Merchandise Mart, and you're in "River North" heading for "Near North." With art galleries, trendy loft offices, and theaters sprouting up like poppy seeds, the area just west of the Magnificent Mile and north of the Loop provides an alternative setting to the power ties and congestion of the Loop. Further north you'll find yourself smack in the middle of Yuppiedom—the Gold Coast, Old Town, and Lincoln Park districts: clean, beautiful, a veritable mecca of BMWs. To the northwest of River North is the Cabrini Green housing project.

Onward

Go northward, and you'll hit the DePaul University (or "Sheffield Neighbors") district, which is fast emerging as an impressive arts community. To the west is Bucktown, Old Wicker Park, Ukrainian Village, and, appropriately, West Town. Moving south you'll travel through the South Loop, Pilsen, Bridgeport, and the Prairie Shores. And surrounding Chicago proper are dozens of suburbs stretching up to the Wisconsin border and down to good old Gary, Indiana. Got the general layout? Now, how to get there. . . .

THE CTA (CHICAGO TRANSIT AUTHORITY)

The El

The El, or elevated trains, take you as far south as Lake Calumet, north to Wilmette, and to Rosemont and O'Hare Airport to the west. The El is a convenient transit line for traveling within the city, is relatively fast and inexpensive, and offers six transit routes. Don't be confused by a Chicagoan's liberal use of the term "subway"—two of the elevated train lines submerge underground for part of their routes through the Loop.

All six routes—the Evanston Express, Howard/Englewood/Jackson Park (north-south route), Lake/Dan Ryan (west-south), O'Hare/Congress/Douglas (west-northwest), Ravenswood, and Skokie Swift—channel into the Loop. Most routes also have "A" and "B" trains, with different station stops for each (during rush hours). For a detailed map or information regarding Rapid Transit routes and schedules, contact the **RTA Travel Information Center** at 1 N. Dearborn, 11th floor (836-7000 or 1-800-972-7000) or the **CTA Office** at the Merchandise Mart, seventh floor.

Rates for travel on the El are subject to change but these days cost $1.50 plus $.30 for a transfer ticket (good for two hours after time of purchase). Ten tokens can be purchased for $12 at currency exchanges, Jewel stores, Dominick's, and some other grocery stores. (Unfortunately, tokens are not sold at El stations.) Senior citizens, the disabled, and children ages 7–11 pay a fare of $.65 with $.15 for a transfer. Children under seven ride free.

The CTA, the parent company of the El and PACE buslines, has long littered headlines for poor service, lack of decent security, labor-management troubles, and its long-term financial condition. All this, and taxpayers shoulder the privilege of dishing out a bundle annually to keep the CTA afloat. There are two sides to this coin: the CTA might have difficulties, but they maintain that this city's transit cost-recovery ratio is enviable compared to the majority of transit authorities nationwide. Difficult to explain that to the wheelchair-ridden individuals whose tax dollars contribute to the CTA but who are not provided a means of access to El platforms in most stations.

Additional observations about the El: during the winter, the train cars are stuffy and overheated. During the summer, the train cars are stuffy and overheated. Most lines become sardine-packed well before entering or exiting the Loop. And coy individuals must quickly overcome their shyness, as every one of their major body parts will inevitably rub against those of a neighbor. It can also be an exercise in acrobatics to keep your footing on the El.

Chicagoans have long suspected El conductors to be either pranksters looking for a chuckle or former acid-droppers braking at shadows. Whatever the explanation, the El is definitely an El-ride, so be prepared to step on some toes, and leave your pretensions of grace back at the platform.

CTA Buses

The CTA runs buses along the major streets. Some run on "Owl Service," while others shut down during the late-night hours. Bus fares are as follows: $1.20 during non–rush hours and $1.50 during rush hours (6–9 A.M. and 3–6 P.M.). A transfer costs $.30. Children 7–11, senior citizens, and disabled citizens ride for $.55 and pay $.15 for a transfer. (Transfers are your ticket when you switch from one El or bus line to another.) Of course, there are frustrations: it isn't uncommon to stand on a corner, unable to cross the street against a red light, and watch not one but two Halsted 8 buses (or any of numerous other varieties) sweep through the intersection. Then the light changes, and you cross to the bus stop and wait 20 minutes for another bus. (Karma *must* be a factor.)

The CTA sells monthly passes for $45 and week-day passes (not good on weekends) for $12. With these passes, you also must pay an additional $.25 every time you use it.

METRA

There's another way to commute to the city from areas farther away from the Loop and immediate region. Metra is the commuter rail service provided to over 225 stations throughout a six-county area. Metra offers 11 commuter routes and can transport passengers from Wisconsin to Indiana, and as far west as Harvard in McHenry County.

Rates for Metra trains vary based upon travel distance, but monthly, 10-ride, and weekly passes are available at discounted rates. Reduced fares are also available for senior citizens, the disabled, students, children, and military personnel.

The upside to traveling Metra is comfort, plain and simple. There's ample seating, clean cars, and effective climate control on every Metra line. Conductors are courteous and exceptionally efficient.

Comfort, unfortunately, costs. A one-way ride from close-proximity stations such as Rogers Park or Kedzie to downtown costs $1.75. And commuters coming from the distant burbs can bet on spending up to $172.80 for a monthly pass. That's over $2,000 each year, for those of you without calculators.

Yet, Metra proves cost-efficient when compared to the alternatives. The cost of gas and parking to drive daily to the city far exceeds Metra's highest-zone fares. Carpooling is an option, but do we really need another car on the road? Let's face it, Metra has a good thing going, and it's worth the price. What's more, it's a dependable mode of travel when time is of the essence. Metra Rail Service boasts a 97 percent on-time performance record.

For detailed information regarding Metra schedules, routes, and fares, call 322-6777 weekdays from 8 A.M.–5 P.M., or 836-7000 evenings and weekends. From the suburbs, call toll-free 1-800-972-7000. Hearing impaired can dial TDD 836- 4949. For ticket-by-mail ordering information or Metra timetables, write Metra, Marketing Department, 547 W. Jackson, Chicago, 60660-6840. Or visit one of the four Metra stations downtown:

NorthWestern Station
500 W. Madison

Randolph Street Station
151 E. Randolph

LaSalle Street Station
414 S. LaSalle

Union Station
210 S. Canal

AMTRAK

Union Station is also the home of Chicago's Amtrak. Just as Chicago's O'Hare airport is the hub of connecting flights, so Chicago's Amtrak station links East Coast travelers to the West, and vice versa. Fares are relatively inexpensive, though travel cross-country by track can be somewhat tedious. Travelers to Milwaukee, Madison, and Indianapolis, however, may be surprised by Amtrak's efficiency, comfort, and value. For more information regarding Amtrak schedules, call 1- 800-USA-RAIL.

PACE BUSES

You can see them lumbering down most major thoroughfares in Chicago— the PACE buses. Always crowded, somewhat slow, PACE bus lines are also cheap and, most of all, just darned convenient. Anywhere Metra or the El doesn't go, PACE usually does. Often, commuters coming from neighbor- hoods without train service will ride the bus to the closest El station, since transfer tickets can be interchanged between PACE buses and the El. And, if you take Metra into town but need a quick ride to the office, Metra ticket holders are offered a reduced monthly ticket on PACE through the Metra ticket-by-mail program mentioned in the Metra section.

PACE assures riders that busy PACE drivers will "stop to pick you up at any safe intersection along the route. Just wave." Unless this is your first visit to the big city, you know better. Best to wait directly under the blue and white PACE bus stop signs at most major intersections.

Exact fare is required on all PACE buses and will vary depending upon the route and time of day traveled. PACE also offers senior citizens, persons with disabilities, and students reduced fares with the Special User's Card pro- gram. Again, call the RTA Travel Information Center (836-7000) for more information on obtaining the Special User's Card and bus route information in your area. In some communities, PACE offers door-to-door transportation for senior and disabled citizens. Check the RTA Travel Information line for these communities.

BEHIND THE WHEEL

Now, for you car owners, a little guidance. Chicago is a manageable city from behind the wheel. Sure, there's traffic, but come on, you're in this country's third largest city. And OK, you may come across a pothole or two that some foreign car models can't quite traverse. But overall, the streets are laid out as straightforwardly as the local news vendor.

Most streets run north-south and east-west in a grid pattern. Clark Street and Lincoln Avenue are exceptions: wayward avenues that travel northwest and provide some fairly hairy three-street intersections just above North Avenue. You'll suddenly be using phrases like "take a hard left" or "soft right" as maneuvering tools upon approaching these six-way stops. Other exceptions include Milwaukee, Elston, Clybourn, Ogden, and Archer. The diagonal streets can be disconcerting to the newcomer, but many Chicagoans find them essential shortcuts that slice through the most colorful sections of the city.

Again, parking can be a nightmare in the congested neighborhoods near the Lake (Lincoln Park, Gold Coast) and downward toward the Loop. Downtown, parking is available at one of Chicago's many parking garages, but rates run as high as $11–$15 per day. Many garages offer monthly parking rates, but you're not saving much, and with car insurance, car payments, and maintenance, who needs the added monthly expense? If driving into the Loop is a necessity, try a parking garage on the city's fringes—the farther you move away from the Loop's nucleus, the lower the rates drop. There are garages near the NorthWestern and Union Metra stations that offer all-day parking for rates as low as $5. But bring your walking shoes.

Highways and Byways

What makes Chicago a city that can "shoulder" the steady growth in population is its exceptional, ever-expanding infrastructure. Yes, "ever-expanding" is synonymous with "ever-under-construction" in this case, and you may find yourself cursing this book when caught in a rush-hour traffic nightmare. All things considered, however, the highways and byways that feed into this fine city are far more accommodating than those found in most metropolitan areas.

There are four major expressways that channel into the Loop and surrounding regions from every direction. The following will give you some idea of the highway layout and recommended routes.

Kennedy Expressway (Interstate 90)

The Kennedy is your direct route to O'Hare Airport, running east-west and merging in with Interstates 290 and 94 near the city. Interstate 90 is a slow-paced expressway during the sluggish rush hour, however, and it's best to avoid I-90 during peak travel times. I-90 becomes the Chicago Skyway south of the Loop, melting into the Indiana Skyway farther on—a limited-access toll road.

Dan Ryan Expressway (Interstate 94)

The Dan Ryan is the main expressway for entering and exiting the city. Running parallel to downtown, it is the major expressway used for access to Chicago. I-94 claims an east-west layout, but it basically runs north-south. About 25 miles north of the city, I-94 breaks off to become the Tri-State Tollway, with Illinois 41 continuing as a highway north. The Dan Ryan is the

North Shore's link to the city and a direct line to Milwaukee. South of the city, I-94 continues as the Calumet Expressway, with Interstate 57 feeding into it from Will County.

Stevenson Expressway (Interstate 55)

The Stevenson Expressway runs into the City from the southwest, connecting Chicago to the booming areas of Joliet, Lockport, Bolingbrook, and Romeoville.

Eisenhower Expressway (Interstate 290)

I-290 is another east-west route that passes through the suburbs of Elmhurst, Maywood, and Forest Park. The Eisenhower is also a link to other major interstate systems, namely the Tri-State Tollway (I-294 west of the city) and the East-West Tollway (I-88).

Clearly, there's more to Chicago's infrastructure than can be described in this section. An excellent map to check out is the *Chicago Tribune* and Rand McNally's "Chicagoland Map," available at most bookstores. Another map that gives exceptional detail and street numbers for downtown locations is Rand McNally's "Chicago Visitors Guide & Map" published by Peirson Graphics Corporation. If a nearby bookstore is out of stock, call the Chicago Association of Commerce and Industry (580-6900) or the Chicago Convention and Tourism Bureau (567-8500).

Taxicabs

Taxis are everywhere, and rarely is it necessary to order a taxi by phone when traveling within Chicago proper. A quick jaunt out-of-doors and a sharp whistle should do the trick.

Lines of taxis can also be found at most transportation centers, such as airports or Metra stations. However, if no cab is in sight, check a nearby yellow pages listing for a company you trust. Rates are consistent from company to company. And because the city is somewhat compact, riding taxis to and from work or play won't bust your budget too badly.

BY FLIGHT

Chicago has often been referred to as the "hub of the nation," a resting point between the beaches of Los Angeles and the chaos of New York. It's the Midwest's largest link to the rest of the country and has been cultivated as a distribution and shipping center. It is also the most widely used location for connecting domestic flights, a trait that makes Chicago's O'Hare Airport easily the "busiest in the world."

O'Hare

Nearly 170,000 travelers pass through O'Hare International Airport every day on one of the facility's 50 airlines. Lying approximately 35 miles northwest of downtown, O'Hare is easy to access by way of car or El. There's plenty of parking at O'Hare, too, with rates only $6 for each 24-hour period in the remote/long-term parking lots. Short-term parking runs approximately $2 per hour, up to $12 for each 24- hour period.

A faster, hassle-free alternative to fighting traffic to the airport is the subway. The El's subway can take you from the Loop to inside the airport in under 25 minutes, and you won't have to remember in which color-coded parking lot you left your vehicle.

Once there, O'Hare's many terminals might seem intimidating. In fact, inside, you'll find this airport under constant construction in a never-ending expansion program. The O'Hare Development Program (ODP) was established in 1982 to meet the needs of O'Hare's exponential growth. With impressive new concourses for Delta, United, and American airlines jutting from the airport's main entrance, as well as an expanded international terminal next door, ODP has actually succeeded in accomplishing its goal: to serve a heavier volume of passengers with improved and comfortable facilities. And O'Hare boasts complete self-sufficiency in that no local tax dollars are used for operations or improvements to the airport.

The general airport information phone number at O'Hare is 686-2200.

Midway

Chicago's other airport is Midway—not as accessible as O'Hare and a whole lot smaller. Really, Midway serves as an afterthought to O'Hare, especially since the demise of Midway Airlines in the fall of 1991. The airport continues its long effort to expand its domestic business.

What may eventually aid Midway in its expansion is a new El connection to the airport. Located 10 miles southwest of Chicago, Midway Airport sprouts up like a bad neighbor amid the working-class community of Cicero. The Stevenson Expressway has been the only route available to Midway Airport from downtown, off of which one must then drive down the scenic Cicero Avenue a few miles before finally arriving at the airport. Ground was broken in 1987 for the new CTA station and moving sidewalk that will connect the station to Midway's terminal building. The project is slated for an October 1992 unveiling, and it may just be the kick in the pants needed to siphon in some of O'Hare's passenger traffic.

To call Midway for general information, dial 838-4500.

Meigs Field

Not an airport worth too much mention—really, it's just a hiccup in the great scheme of domestic air traffic. But Merrill C. Meigs Field does offer one domestic carrier, Britt Airways, with service to Springfield, Illinois. Got an urge to visit the state's capital? Call Britt Airways at 341-9125. For general information regarding Meigs Field and private flight information, call 744-4787.

Another Airport?

City officials, their staff, and the Chicago media spent much of 1991 and 1992 talking about a third airport. State and local officials, fueled by sunny economic development estimates and somewhat optimistic future air traffic forecasts, insisted a third airport was necessary. Mayor Daley, in his ongoing and dogged pursuit of more jobs for Chicago, argued tirelessly for building the new airport, with Lake Calumet as his preferred location. Meanwhile, neighborhood groups threatened by the prospect of a major airport in their backyards denounced the third airport plan as superfluous. Environmentally aware Chicagoans wondered (often and aloud) how much damage another airport the size of nearly 15,000 football fields would do to good old Mother Earth and her air. The idea started to die. Springfield, it turned out, wasn't *really* behind the idea. Daley then went on to talk up a rail link between O'Hare and Midway. So instead of a third airport we might soon have just one one mega-airport. Stay tuned.

JUMP ON A BOAT

Here's an alternative to those poorly ventilated El trains and expensive cab rides! You can get from West Madison Avenue to the Wrigley Building on Michigan Avenue via blue-green waters! Wendella Commuter Boats cost only $1, and give you a relaxing seven-minute ride up the Chicago River and out of the Loop. The boats depart every 10 minutes during the morning and evening rush hours from a commuter dock located just north of Madison Avenue, or from the Wendella dock just south of Michigan Avenue and below the Wrigley Building. For longer excursions through the Chicago River Lock and onto Lake Michigan, Wendella also offers guided lake and river cruises at 2-hour, 1½-hour, and 1-hour rates. Seniors and children under age 11 enjoy reduced prices.

However you traverse Chicago, however you choose to exit and enter, no matter what happens to its many systems of transportation, keep the old, ever-true saying in mind: the Lake is *always* east.

—*Kelly O'Rourke*

EMPLOYMENT

CHICAGO'S JOB MARKET

International events over the past few years have left some economic experts struggling to forecast employment trends. In a down economy, Chicago has the potential to fare better than other metropolitan areas because of its diverse economic makeup and less dependence on federal funding. However, the nineties recession has resulted in many companies playing it safe; they're maintaining smaller staffs and giving those employees more responsibility (in other words, fewer people working harder). Meanwhile industry is shifting its focus to the international market, weeding out many businesses that cannot stay globally competitive and affecting Chicago's economy.

Jobs once plentiful in the Chicago area, such as those in manufacturing, are diminishing as companies move production to labor-intensive Mexico, for example, or to nations experiencing the economic explosion of democracy and capitalism.

And with technological advancement, the work force is also changing. The unskilled labor sector is rapidly disappearing as industries today utilize more and more complicated operating systems. Secretaries not only must know how to type but must also be computer savvy. Even fast-food establishments require that their employees attend demanding training programs before they may peddle fries and shakes—at minimum wage.

Amid so much change, it is difficult to project specific employment outlooks, although recent employment projections from the Illinois Department of Employment Security (IDES) may give us insight to Chicago's long-term employment shifts.

Growth in the services area (at a projected 1.7 percent) should come as no surprise, as analysts have been predicting this at national levels for some time. As I said earlier, however, a decrease in manufacturing jobs is expected to occur as a result of labor-saving management and production techniques. Growth is expected to occur in our region in construction (1.7 percent annual rate) and in trade (1.5 percent annual rate), adding more than 220,000 people to payrolls by the year 2000.

So the overall projections show a healthy rate of employment increase through the year 2000. And whatever your career objective, Chicago clearly offers an array of opportunities for those willing to spend some time in their job search. The question is, how can you guarantee you will be one of those employed?

JOB-HUNTING TECHNIQUES

Not surprisingly, the majority of self-help books on finding a job turn their noses up at relying on the classifieds or employment agencies. Though some suggest using all the resources available, the prevailing advice is to concentrate on one specific and effective job search technique: direct contact.

Yes, there are other strategies. You can wait for the *Chicago Tribune* or *Chicago Sun-Times* every Sunday morning and check the classifieds. Then mail one or two résumés to employers already receiving hundreds for the same ad. You can send out hundreds of résumés in a blanket sweep of vaguely acceptable employers, only to discover that employers are not interested in trite cover letters and general résumés. You can set up appointments with countless employment agencies hoping that maybe they know something that you don't know. Sometimes, they do. Usually, they don't.

Direct Contact

The direct contact technique is advisable for two reasons: it forces you to focus on specific job objectives, and it gives you some direction. Rather than wasting valuable time swimming from possibility to possibility, you'll whittle down your job position choices. Chicago is a very large city, and to someone looking for a job it can seem like a very large black hole. Direct contact is based on the strategy that a well-directed letter to the right person for the right position will provide the best results.

With direct contact, first you must decide exactly what position you desire. Next, research the companies in Chicago that offer the position you have chosen. Then, choose the companies that provide a career path, benefits, and atmosphere that are acceptable to you. Find out the correct person to contact in the organization, and send a cover letter and résumé to that hiring executive. And finally, follow up with a phone call. With direct contact, you are selecting the companies that you believe would fulfill your needs and those with whom you are interested in working. Also, many businesses do not bother with the classifieds or employment agencies to fill positions that become available. With a bit of luck, your letter and résumé will fall into the right hands, at the right time.

Choosing a Career Path

I won't go into much detail here about choosing a career. "Finding yourself" and the career that's perfect for you is the subject of countless books. Check out the nearest library, and pay special attention to these excellent choices:

What Color Is Your Parachute? by Richard Nelson Bolles
Also an excellent guide to job hunting, this annually updated guide is well written, offering sound advice to the career changer.

Encyclopedia of Careers and Vocational Guidance by William E. Hopke
Four volumes of listings, from industry profiles to general and special careers.

Joyce L. Kennedy's Career Book by Joyce L. Kennedy
Geared toward the younger set, but relevant to the older, this is a comprehensive guide to making career choices.

The American Almanac of Jobs and Salaries by John W. Right
Provides statistical information on job descriptions, salary ranges, and advancement changes for all sorts of professions.

The Jobs Rated Almanac by Les Krantz
Ranks the best and the worst jobs by more than a dozen vital criteria, including salary, stress, benefits, and travel.

Career Counseling

If you attended college and prefer the guidance of a professional career planner, you may consider contacting your alma mater. Most universities provide career counseling and placement programs for undergraduates and graduates, even those who could no longer be considered a "recent" grad. No alma mater? No matter. Career counseling services are offered through a number of organizations, some of which are listed in Camden and Schwartz's How to Get a Job in Chicago (listed in the following section). Be careful and do some comparison shopping. A few counseling centers can get very pricey and may hard-sell services you simply do not need—anything from vocational testing to interview techniques. Check with the Better Business Bureau before putting down your money.

The Career Consulting Association   346-5835
Career counselors can also be helpful to those interested in changing careers. The Career Consulting Association, a professional association of career development specialists, can help you select a career consultant.

One last comment about choosing a career path: don't panic. If you don't have all the answers, dive into a job you're curious about and check it out for a while. You'll be bringing home a paycheck while getting a better feel for your individual career preferences. The bottom line is this: Accepting a job, any job, is not a life sentence. In this age of mergers, lay-offs, and diminishing job security, employees, too, must reserve the right to change their minds.

Research

If you know the position you desire, now's the time to find out exactly what companies and organizations offer that position.

Chicago's Public Library's Business Information Center
400 S. State   747-4300
Again, the public library is a wonderful source, with updated employer information and a plethora of books on the local job bank. Three exceptional guides are available at the library or in bookstores and offer more comprehensive listings than we can fit in this chapter:

How to Get a Job in Chicago by Thomas Camden and Susan Schwartz
This is an "Insider's Guide" series that offers tips to researching the area job market as well as naming more than 1,500 major employers, the people to contact at each, addresses, and phone numbers.

The Greater Chicago Job Bank published by Bob Adams, Inc.
An excellent sourcebook to Chicago employers, as well as employment agencies, executive search firms, and professional and trade associations.

Doing Business in Chicago by Jeffrey P. Levine
Unfortunately difficult to find, Levine's "Yearbook of Business for the Chicago Area" is the most comprehensive guide to major area employers, offering corporate profiles of the top 246 public and 750 private and subsidiary Chicago companies. Try ordering it through a bookstore if the library cannot locate a copy (published by Dow Jones–Irwin).

There are government and private agencies as well that can provide up-to-date employer listing and detailed employment information.

The Chicago Association of Commerce and Industry 580-6900
This association publishes the Metropolitan Chicago Major Employers Directory annually.

The City's Department of Economic Development 744-CITY
This office can also provide statistical information.

Résumés and Cover Letters

You've whittled down your list of prospective employers and have the names and addresses of the correct contacts at each. It's time to sit down and draft a cover letter and résumé to introduce yourself to those contacts.

This process can produce panic in even the most stouthearted job seekers. How can you possibly convey your qualifications, sincerity, and enthusiasm in a one-page letter to someone you have probably never met? How can you convincingly translate in a résumé that your three years of experience as a gas station attendant makes you an exceptional candidate in sales?

Again, refer to the guidebooks suggested in the "Research" and "Career Counseling" sections for some helpful advice on crafting a résumé and cover letter. The following books are excellent sources, too:

The Complete Resume Guide by Marian Faux

Dynamic Cover Letters by Katharine Hansen

Effective Resumes for Executives and Specialized Personnel by J. L. Angel

Entering the Job Market by Marian Faux

The Perfect Cover Letter by Richard H. Beatty

The Resume Kit by Richard H. Beatty

The Resume Writer's Handbook by Michael Holley Smith

There are résumé-writing services as well that will write and print your résumé for a flat fee. Though seemingly an easy "out," this technique usually results in a flat, generic résumé. Only you can effectively convey your individual strengths and experience and create a quality résumé for yourself.

Persistence

After you've sent your cover letter and résumé, don't assume no news is goods news when you receive no reply. The direct contact technique is just that: directly contacting the hiring executive in preferred companies. Give them a week, then give them a call. Selling yourself may not come naturally, but persistence is essential in the competitive job-hunt arena.

And you don't have to be pushy to be effective. Be polite, concise, and yourself. Ask the contact if they have received your résumé and if you can set up a meeting to discuss possible job opportunities in the company. If they have "no positions currently open," ask that they keep you in mind when one does present itself. Then call back a few weeks later. Many experts also suggest calling the prospective employer prior to sending your résumé as an introductory step. Though this may seem like overkill, it is a good way to get your name once again in front of your contacts.

Networking

Although it is no longer considered the divine search technique once lauded by the power-lunching, hand-pumping "me" generation, networking remains an essential job- hunting technique. Based on the premise "It's not what you know, it's who you know," networking involves the meeting of people in your chosen profession and cultivating those relationships as possible leads.

As Julius Scheffers of the Human Resources firm Paul Bomrad & Associates states, "Most people want to help others, and will if asked." To network, seek out organizations, clubs, and associations that cater to the profession you have chosen. Attend meetings and social events that people in your field are likely to attend. Keep in touch with those whom you've met and express your interest in finding a job. Often people not even in hiring positions will know those who are and can lead you to an interview. As Scheffers says, "Networking allows you to be at the right place at the right time through others. It's a snowball effect—one contact leads to three, which leads to six, and so on. The results are really overwhelming."

The following professional and trade organizations represent just a few of the many in the Chicago area. Again, research the resources previously mentioned to find the organization that represents your interests. Or look up one of these specialized networks:

AFTRA

Agate Club of Chicago

Alliance of American Insurers

American Association of
  Hospital Dentists
  Individual Investors
  School Librarians
  Senior Physicians
  Women Dentists

America
  Bar Association
  Board of Medical Specialties
  College of Surgeons
  Dairy Association
  Dental Assistants Association
  Dental Association
  Dietetic Association
  Farm Bureau Federation
  Film and Video Association
  Group of CPA Firms
  Hospital Association
  Institute of Banking

American (cont.)
  Library Association
  Marketing Association
  Medical Association
  Nuclear Society
  Organization of Nurse Executives
  Rental Association

American Society
  for Healthcare Risk Management
  for Hospital Marketing and
    Public Relations
  of Women Accountants

Veterinary Medical Association

Women's Society of Certified
  Public Accountants

Association for School, College and
  University Staffing

Association of
  Cosmetologists and Hairdressers
  Free Community Papers
  Legal Administrators

Association of (cont.)
Mental Health Administrators
Rehabilitation Nurses

Broadcast Advertising
Club of Chicago

Builders Association of Chicago

Chicago
Advertising Club
Association of Commerce and
Industry
Association of Savings Banks
Computer Society
Council on Fine Arts
Finance Exchange
Jewelers

Commercial-Investment
Real Estate Council

Council of Logistics Management

Defense Research Institute

Dietary Managers Association

Electronic
Industries Association
Representatives Association

Engine Manufacturers Association

Financial Managers Society

Foundation for Savings
Institutions

Healthcare Information and
Management Systems Society

Human Resources Management
Association

Ice Skating Institute of America

Illinois
Arts Council
Bankers Association
CPA Society

Independent
Cosmetic Manufacturers and
Distributors
Writers of Chicago

Institute of Environmental
Sciences

International
Association
for Hospital Security
for Orthodontics
of Business Communicators
of Defense Counsel
of Electrical Inspectors
Customer Service Association
Electronic Packaging Society
Formalwear Association
Society of Appraisers

League of Chicago Theaters

Library Administration and
Management Association

Marine Retailers
Association of America

Marketing
Agents for Food Service Industry
Research Association

Material Handling Equipment
Distributors Association

Medical-Dental-Hospital
Bureaus of America

Medical Library Association

Municipal Women of Chicago

National
Academy of Television Arts and
Sciences
American Wholesale Lumber
Association
Association of
Architectural Metal
Manufacturers
Bank Women
Bar Executives
Boat Manufacturers
Bond Lawyers
Concessionaires
Food Equipment Manufacturers
Futures Trading Advisors
General Merchandise
Representatives
Hispanic Publications
Medical Staff Services
Printers and Lithographers
Realtors

National
  Association of (cont.)
    Retail Dealers of America
    Service Managers
    Service Merchandising
    Sporting Goods Wholesalers
    Women Business Owners
  Black MBA Association
  Council of State Boards of
    Nursing
  Dairy Council
  Employee Services and
    Recreation Association
  Eye Research Foundation
  Family Business Council
  Federation of
    Paralegal Associations
    Priests' Councils
  Food Distributors Association
  Insurance Association
  PTA
  Safety Council
  Society for
    Fund-Raising Executives
    the Study of Education
  Sound and Communications
    Association
  Sporting Goods Association
  Wine Distribution Association
  Wood Window and Door
    Association
North American Wildlife Foundation
Pharmaceutical Advertising
  Council
Preferred Hotels Association
Professional Career Counselors
  Network

Profit Sharing Council of America
Public
  Library Association
  Relations Society of America
  Works Historical Society
Realtors Land Institute
Retail Advertising Conference
Safety Equipment Distributors
  Association
Society for
  Information Management
Society of
  American Registered Architects
  Architectural Administrators
  Professional
    Business Consultants
  Journalists, Sigma Delta Chi
  Research Administrators
  Women Engineers
Sporting Goods Agents Association
Suburban Newspapers of America
Telecommunications Industry Association
Underground Contractors Association
Water Quality Association
Women in
  Communications
  Design/Chicago
  Publishing
Women's
  Advertising Club of Chicago
  Council of Realtors

The Classifieds

Quite simply, the classified ads are a numbers game. One classified ad very often produces 200 to 300 responses, and out of those, only a handful are even asked to interview. That's not to say that answering classified ads in the *Chicago Tribune, Chicago Sun-Times, The Reader,* or trade publications should be completely discounted. There is a position to fill, and you may be the lucky one hired. But spend a small proportion of your time responding to classified ads. It's a passive, ineffective approach to job hunting at best.

Employment Agencies and Executive Search Firms

Employment agencies are usually paid by the employer and act as the middle person in placing prospective employees. There are countless employment agencies representing a multitude of fields in the Chicago area. Camden and Schwartz's book cited earlier lists many private employment agencies of substance. Be sure to read the fine print before signing on with any employment agency, however. Often, applications are contracts.

Executive search firms deal primarily with high-level job placements and prefer to find you, rather than be found. Again, they are paid by the hiring company—usually a percentage of the hired employee's first-year salary.

Reputable employment agencies and executive search firms are listed in the yellow pages or any classified ad section of the *Chicago Tribune, Chicago Sun-Times,* or *The Reader.* Don't hesitate to ask pertinent questions. Who pays the finder's fee? In what fields does the agency specialize?

The reason many self-help guides to job hunting refuse to condone employment agencies is twofold. First, no one can sell you better than you. And second, an agency has its best interests at heart. Even if you do get placed through an employment service, which is a feat in itself, chances are it won't be the right "fit" for you. Remember, agencies want to fill positions and pad their pockets—whether the hiring company is your ideal place of employment is not their priority.

Executive search firms, on the other hand, build their reputations on matching qualified candidates with the companies they represent. If you're qualified for a management or top-level executive position, a search firm, or "headhunter," might be helpful. But they're hard to come by. Headhunters usually recruit their own job candidates and rarely keep unsolicited résumés. Try to get a personal referral to an executive search firm if you want to be taken seriously.

TEMPORARY AND PART-TIME EMPLOYMENT

Again, you can contact the myriad of temporary agencies available in the Chicago area for placement in temporary or part-time positions. Camden and Schwartz's book lists quite a few agencies from which to choose, or try one of the many listed in the local classified ads.

Temporary and part-time employment enables individuals to earn money while maintaining a more flexible schedule. Those raising children, in school, or simply in need of additional income often turn to temporary work. And as Chicago's art scene grows exponentially, budding actors, writers, filmmakers, and artists may also consider the freedom temporary employment allows them to practice their crafts.

Temporary employment agencies usually specialize in certain areas; one may specialize in the placement of legal secretaries, for instance, while another might strictly place word processors. Make sure you are signing on with an agency that specializes in the type of work you enjoy.

When visiting temporary agencies, be prepared for tests. Many agencies require some indication of your qualifications and skills. Secretaries, for example, commonly undergo typing, spelling, and word processing tests.

Temporary agencies sign you on as an "employee," usually pay you directly (and weekly), and take out the necessary taxes.

Need a better hourly wage than temporary agencies offer? Try independent contracting. Seek out companies that may be in need of your services on a temporary (often long-term temporary) basis. You'll receive the extra wage the temporary agency would otherwise pocket and can negotiate the length of employment. With so many companies downsizing these days, there's a huge market for "outsourcing" (hiring part-time specialists in place of once full-time positions). The catch: you'll owe Uncle Sam big come April, so put aside the correct percentage of your income for taxes (about a third).

SERVICES AND AGENCIES

The following resources may help you get started in your job hunt.

Illinois Job Service
35 S. 19th, Maywood, 60153   450-5900
This government agency provides a computerized listing of job openings in many fields throughout the state. To get this list, you need to fill out the job service form at your nearest branch office. Call their headquarters at the above location for more information.

Mayor's Office of Employment and Training
510 N. Peshtigo, #2A, Chicago, 60611   744-8787
Training and placement for jobs in the private sector. Clients must meet low-income guidelines to qualify for most services. Subcontracts with many community agencies to provide employment services throughout the city.

Women

Chicago Women in Publishing
2 N. Riverside, #2400, Chicago, 60606   641-3611
This group is directed to women in both editorial and production positions in publishing. It sponsors career programs and runs a networking registry for job hunters.

Chicago Women in the Trades
37 S. Ashland   942-1444
This support and advocacy group is for carpenters, plumbers, electricians, and so forth. It provides counseling, preapprenticeship training, advocacy, and job placement.

Midwest Women's Center
828 S. Wabash, #200, Chicago, 60605   922-8530
One of Chicago's oldest women's organizations, this not-for-profit group helps women achieve economic self-sufficiency and economic parity. It offers job training and placement, literacy education, and general referral services. It also works to influence public policy in the city on a range of women's issues.

National Association of Women's Health Professionals
1007 Church, #307, Evanston, 60201 (708) 869-0195
NAWHP is a national professional organization serving multidisciplinary women's health professionals through education, training, information services, conferences, and publications.

Women Employed
22 W. Monroe 782-3902
Women Employed is a nonprofit membership organization of working women. The organization offers career planning and job-hunting programs, including low-cost seminars, networking events, and career counseling. It also conducts research, education, and advocacy programs on issues relating to equal employment opportunity.

Minorities/Ethnic

American Indian Business Association
4753 N. Broadway, Chicago, 60640 784-2434
Provides job readiness training and placement for all who can certify that they have Native American heritage no matter how far removed.

Chicago Urban League
Employment Counseling and Training Dept.
4500 S. Michigan, Chicago, 60653 285-1253
Counseling and job placement for all regardless of race, creed, and religious preference.

Minority Economic Resource Corporation
1565 Ellinwood, Des Plaines, 60016 (708) 297-4705
Attention: Rev. Clyde H. Brooks
Helps minorities find jobs in the city and northwest suburbs. Places teens in job readiness and skill-teaching programs. Adults are placed immediately if they're job ready and a position is available. Training in word processing, typing, and 10-key calculator.

Spanish Coalition for Jobs
2011 W. Pershing, Chicago, 60609 247-0707
1737 W. 18th, Chicago, 60608 243-3032
Training in word processing, typing, and electronics, followed by placement. Services open to all, including young people (18 and over, but must possess high school or GED diploma). Clients must meet low-income requirements.

Veterans

Chicago Heights Veteran Center
1600 Halsted, Chicago Heights, 60411 (708) 754-0340
Counselors available on Wednesdays for vocational guidance and placement.

Chicago Veteran's Center
565 Howard, Evanston, 60202 (708) 332-1019
A readjustment center serving all Vietnam-era vets and all post-Vietnam combat zone vets. Employment services include job clubs, job-seeking techniques, skills assessment, and job placement. Illinois Job Service counselors available on Tuesday, Wednesday, and Friday mornings.

Oak Park Veteran Center
155 S. Oak Park, Oak Park, 60302   (708) 383-3225
Illinois Job Service counselors available two or three days a week for employee placement programs and five days per week for vocational counseling. Welcomes appointments.

Veteran Resource Center
5505 S. Harper, Chicago, 60637   684-5500
Make appointments for job placement services, training, and vocational guidance.

Youth

Chicago Commons
4100 W. Belmont, Chicago, 60641   685-1010
Operates five job training programs for 17-year-olds and older, aimed at helping high school dropouts, although others may also join the program. Programs offered in automatic screw machine set-up, plastic injection molding, package machine and mechanics, and industrial mechanical inspection. Has a 94 percent placement rate and an excellent reputation.

Jobs for Youth
67 E. Madison, #1900, Chicago, 60603   782-2086
Serves economically disadvantaged youths 16 to 21 years of age, both high school graduates and dropouts. Programs include preemployment training (interviewing skills, résumé writing), job placement, and GED classes. Has an excellent reputation.

Mayor's Office of Employment and Training
See Services and Agencies listing above.

Older Workers

Operation ABLE
180 N. Wabash, #802, Chicago, 60601   782-3335
Network of community-based agencies providing employment services primarily for people over 55 years of age, regardless of income (some programs are open to people 40 and over).

Workers with Disabilities

State of Illinois
Department of Rehabilitation Services
9730 S. Western, #804, Chicago, 60642   (708) 857-2380
Services provided for all persons with physical, emotional, or mental disabilities. Services for the blind provided by the Bureau of Blind Services; call for information. Provides individual vocational rehabilitation, counseling, diagnostic vocational evaluation, instruction and training, and placement, as well as books, materials, and equipment for persons interested in self-employment.

Ex-Offenders

Safer Foundation
Operation DARE
571 W. Jackson, Chicago, 60661-5701   922-2200
Job search assistance, referral, placement, and GED classes for ex-offenders.

Dislocated Workers

Dislocated workers—people who have lost their jobs because of lay-offs or plant relocation—are eligible for programs designed to counsel, retrain, and place them in new jobs. Call the **Mayor's Office of Employment and Training,** 510 Peshtigo (744-8787) to find out about these programs. Union members should note that your union may also provide such services.

UNEMPLOYMENT

If you have been laid off, you are entitled to unemployment compensation provided your employer has paid the unemployment tax.

Illinois Department of Employment Security   793-5280
Find the closest unemployment office nearest you by calling the Illinois Department of Employment Security. When you file for benefits, bring your social security number and two pieces of identification. Benefits should begin arriving in two weeks.

All Illinois residents receiving unemployment benefits must register with the Illinois Job Service, listed in the "Services and Agencies" section of this chapter. In Illinois, persons receiving unemployment benefits may continue to receive full benefits while enrolled full-time in a state-approved retraining program. Ask at your local unemployment office for a list of these retraining programs.

RIGHTS ON THE JOB

Equal Employment Opportunity Commission
Public Information and Assistance
536 S. Clark, #930, Chicago, 60605   353-2713
If you feel you have been discriminated against, contact the EEOC.

Illinois Department of Human Rights
State of Illinois Center
100 W. Randolph, #10-100, Chicago, 60601   814-6200
Also handles discrimination charges, including employment discrimination because of disability, marital status, and sexual harassment.

Chicago Area Committee on Occupational Safety and Health
506 S. Wabash, Chicago, 60605   666-1611
For employee complaints about safety and health.

STARTING YOUR OWN BUSINESS

If you're ready to take the leap into financial independence, Chicago's got the climate to do so. At the state level, small business establishments (500 employees or less) make up 88.5 percent of all businesses in Illinois. That's 48 percent of the state's employee population. Statistics for Chicago proper are difficult to come by, but most of your questions can be answered by one of the following organizations. The following is a short list of services available to budding entrepreneurs.

Chicago Association of Neighborhood Development Organizations
939-7171
Business plan development, marketing assistance, and individual and group consulting.

Chicago Business Development Center 444-9884
Marketing, business plan, and loan consulting for both for-profit and not-for-profit companies.

Cosmopolitan Chamber of Commerce 786-0212
Consulting, classes, and seminars.

Department of Commerce and Community Affairs
Small Business Hot Line: (800) 252-2923
Equity investments, loans, grants, and management assistance.

Department of Economic Development 408-7400
Loans and equity investments.

Economic Development Commission 744-9550
Consulting advice from transitional to new technologies.

Entrepreneur Development Division of the Neighborhood Institute
933-2021
Marketing and licensing advice, accounting assistance, and general consulting.

Small Business Administration 353-4528 (Chicago office)
Management and loan assistance.

Women's Business Development Center 853-3477
Business consulting, legal counseling, and entrepreneurial training.

VOLUNTEER WORK

Probably one of the fastest growth areas in contemporary employment is voluntarism. A once self-absorbed generation has grown up to become socially aware, and the increase in involvement of not-for-profit organizations reflects this awakening of social consciousness. There is invariably an opportunity to volunteer for just about any cause imaginable, from literacy programs to abuse counseling, environmental advocacy to emergency shelter organizations.

And while you're volunteering your time and energy to helping others, you're doing a great deal to help yourself. Yes, the education and fulfillment you will experience in any volunteer program is priceless. And it may also prove invaluable to your eventual job search. What you gain is knowledge and experience, two assets to add to any résumé. And most not-for-profit organizations also need full-time employees, so a volunteer situation could lead to a paid position. For the most part, we're not talking high-paying here. But, if your priority is social betterment, any pay may be pay enough.

Turn to the "Volunteering" chapter in this book for a host of relevant resources. Also check the *Directory of Voluntarism* or the Association of Volunteers' *Voluntarism* in your local library for additional listings. Another interesting volunteer guide is *Volunteer Vacations* by Bill McMillon. It might sound opportunistic, but it is actually a great guide to volunteer opportunities in the United States and abroad.

—Kelly O'Rourke

PHYSICAL HEALTH

By now terms like *cholesterol, SPF, saturated fat,* and *fiber* have so inundated popular American culture that most people have a pretty good idea of what constitutes a healthful lifestyle. Getting enough sleep, eating three low-fat (preferably vegetarian) meals a day, exercising 20 minutes three times a week, not smoking, avoiding excessive periods in the sun, and getting regular medical and dental check-ups are vital. Any symptom that's unusual for you is worth a prompt exam. Cancer's seven warning signs, for example, can be remembered with **C-A-U-T-I-O-N:**

Change in bowel or bladder habits

A sore that doesn't heal

Unusual bleeding and discharge

Thickening or lump in breast or elsewhere

Indigestion or difficulty in swallowing

Obvious change in wart or mole

Nagging cough or hoarseness

Chicago has hundreds of clinics and hospitals, including some top university hospitals, and an equally large number of advocacy and educational agencies. Some of the latter are cited here, but for a thorough listing try *The Human Care Services Directory of Metropolitan Chicago* ($32.50) or *The Directory of Self-help Mutual Aid Groups* ($29.75). Both are in most public libraries or can be purchased through the publications department of **United Way/Crusade of Mercy Community Information and Referral Services** (560 W. Lake, Chicago, 60661, 876-0010).

REFERRAL AND ADVOCACY OFFICES AND CLINICS

Access Living
310 S. Peoria, #201, Chicago, 60607   226-5900; TDD: 226-1687
The purpose of Access Living is to help people with disabilities create independent lives and participate fully in all aspects of life. They do this through advocacy, public education, and direct services. In addition to referrals, Access Living provides in-depth assistance in everything from hiring a personal assistant or overcoming housing discrimination to dealing with domestic violence, a problem to which women with disabilities are particularly vulnerable. They strive for equal rights of access to public transportation and facilities, to education and housing, and for the employment opportunities and the same social services available to the nondisabled.

American Cancer Society
77 E. Monroe, #1200   372-0471
Hours: Monday–Friday, 9 A.M.–5 P.M.
ACS has a wealth of information at its fingertips on all types of cancer and related topics via its computerized Cancer Response System. Say you're worried about radon or the quality of your mammogram, or your father's just been diagnosed with colon cancer. You can ask about dangers, accredita-

tion, dietary precautions, stages of cancer from beginning to end, all treatments, survival rates, and so forth, and have an easy-to-understand print-out sent to you. The system's tumor registry lists how many cancer surgeries and what type have been done at various Chicago hospitals. For the most current or very specific information, you'll be referred to the National Cancer Institute in Maryland. The ACS office here updates its data base monthly, but its purposes are more general, in public and professional education, service, and rehabilitation. Its Reach to Recovery program is led by breast cancer survivors to help women who have recently undergone mastectomies; they offer temporary prostheses, advice, and support. ACS has available, free, all sorts of materials, from wigs for people in chemotherapy to materials for laryngectomy patients. Home medical equipment, however, is not free, but Medicare or health insurance will usually cover this cost as long as it's been prescribed by a physician.

Chicago Area Committee on Occupational Safety and Health
37 S. Ashland   666-1611
The first such group formed in the United States, CACOSH has provided educational, medical, technical, and legal information to workers since 1972 via workshops, seminars, and its booklet *Injured on the Job* ($5; also available in Spanish).

Chicago Department of Health
50 W. Washington (business office)   744-8500
What a lot of people call the "Board of Health" is actually the Department of Health, the largest single provider of outpatient care in Chicago. Services are either free or at very low cost. It offers testing (for the HIV virus—this is free and anonymous—sexually transmitted diseases, diabetes, etc.) and counseling at 18 physical health and 18 mental health clinics all over the city. Call the business office to find the one nearest you or best suited to your needs. The Department of Health provides prenatal care to about 25 percent of all pregnant women in the city, and 75 public health nurses are available to make home visits and assist young parents. The department is also the place to request a copy of your birth certificate if you were born here after 1955 ($5; call 744-3790).

Chicago Easter Seal Society
220 S. State, #312   939-5115
This group has dental and optometry programs for both children and adults with disabilities; people with no insurance or public aid may have their costs covered with an ESS grant. For kids, ESS also offers a free orthopedic clinic, outpatient rehabilitation centers (physical, occupational, and speech therapy), summer camps, aquatic therapy, and wheelchair evaluation. (National ESS headquarters are based in Chicago at 70 E. Lake, 726-6200.)

Chicago Medical Society
515 N. Dearborn   670-2550
CMS will refer you to three physicians from its data base of about 10,000, with details on fees and the doctor's background and practice.

Chicago Runaway Switchboard   1-800-621-3230
This 24-hour switchboard serves 11- to 18-year-old teens in crisis, and its Metro Help division will make referrals to health and social services available for young people. Outside Illinois call the **National Runaway Switchboard** (1-800-621-4000).

Chimera, Self-Defense for Women
59 E. Van Buren, #714, Chicago, 60605   939-5341
The Chimera style of self-defense was developed by women who wanted effective skills that are easy to learn and remember and that do not rely on pure physical strength. Since a woman's most effective response to a situation may be psychological or physical or contain elements of both, Chimera students learn how to block, kick, and strike effectively to break holds; they also learn the warning signals of an impending attack and the typical rhythms, plans, and tactics of an attacker. The emphasis is on practical, effective solutions whether the situation is an all-out attack or a more subtle form of sexual harassment. Classes are offered at various locations around the city.

Gay and Lesbian Physicians of Chicago
P.O. Box 14864, Chicago, 60603   281-3639
You can either leave a message or write for confidential referrals to gay and lesbian doctors in the city.

Howard Brown Memorial Clinic
945 W. George   871-5777
Howard Brown serves the general community, with additional services for gay and lesbian patients. Founded in 1974, this clinic has become Chicago's largest provider of anonymous HIV/AIDS testing and support services. Its anonymous HIV testing ($60, by appointment) includes sessions with a counselor, both at the time of the test and one week later, when the results are in. Howard Brown also offers STD testing on a drop-in basis on Tuesday and Thursday, 7–9 P.M. and Sunday 2–4 P.M. (base cost, $35). Thorough AIDS programs include aerosolized tentamidine treatment, housing assistance, a staff nutritionist, financial and legal aid, and support groups for not only AIDS patients but also their family and friends and people who are HIV-positive but asymptomatic. All social services are free to those with AIDS and ARC (AIDS-related complex), and Spanish is spoken.

Illinois Citizens for Better Care
53 W. Jackson   663-5120
This organization monitors nursing homes to ensure quality care and can advise you on how to select a reputable nursing home.

Midwest Association for Sickle Cell Anemia
65 E. Wacker Pl., #2200   663-5700
One in 10 African-Americans carries the sickle cell trait in his or her genes, but it's also found in people of Mediterranean, Asian, Indian, and Puerto Rican descent. The MASCA recommends all people of child-bearing age in these groups get tested for the trait. The trait can develop into sickle cell anemia with symptoms including severe chest pain, swollen and hot feet and hands, jaundice, and sores around the ankles that won't heal. Besides general

information, the MASCA also provides counseling, referrals, emergency grants, college scholarships, and a summer camp.

Physicians for Social Responsibility
220 S. State, #1330 663-1777
PSR works to inform the public about the medical effects of nuclear war, through its speakers bureau and workshops.

Visiting Nurses Association
322 S. Green 738-8622
With over 100 nurses, aides, and physical therapists on staff, this group can send a nurse to your home for all medical care. The cost is usually covered by health insurance.

AIDS PROGRAMS

The National Center of Disease Control reported at the end of 1991 that there were then 206,392 fully diagnosed cases of AIDS in the country, 5,272 in Chicago (the city's rate per 100,000 was 21.2). Preventive measures like using condoms and not sharing hypodermic needles are the wisest steps to take to avoid contracting the HIV virus. For testing, see the previous sections on the Chicago Department of Health and the Howard Brown Memorial Clinic.

Persons with AIDS or ARC (AIDS-related complex) have 50–70 support agencies in Chicago to turn to; a handful are described here. Also, the state of Illinois has a general information hot line at 1-800-AID-AIDS from 10 A.M.–10 P.M. daily.

AIDS Foundation of Chicago
1332 N. Halsted, #303, 60622 642-5454 (general information) or
642-3763 (information and Dept. of Rehabilitation Services referrals)
Hours: Monday–Thursday, 9 A.M.–1 P.M.;
Friday, 1–5 P.M. for information and referrals
The AIDS Foundation was set up in 1985 as a fund-raising organization that now also administers federal funds to educational and prevention programs, services for HIV-infected persons, and public advocacy and legal groups. Since 1988 it has awarded $3.3 million in federal funds plus more than $1.2 million in other grants to local agencies, which makes it the top philanthropic group, financially speaking, in Chicago. Its Information and Referral Service can provide detailed information about more than 300 advocacy and educational agencies and doctors in the Chicago area specializing in AIDS treatment, as well as data on national groups and agencies out of state.

Chicago House and Social Service Agency
3150 N. Lincoln, #2S, 60657 248-5200
This agency provides communal-type apartment living for up to 30 people with AIDS and ARC. Rent is 25 percent of the person's income. To get on the agency's waiting list, contact program director Mary Ellen Krems.

Chicago Women's AIDS Project
5249 N. Kenmore 271-2070
CWAP categorizes its services into education/prevention and client services, for all HIV-positive women. The Girls' Night Out program, for adults and teens, deals with issues outside of AIDS per se, such as negotiation, abuse,

and power within relationships. "We talk about taking care of yourself," explained Director Cathy Christeller, "and what that means more fully. It might involve evaluating the relationship you're in." The peer leadership program trains women to lead community seminars on safe sex. Client services include phone counseling and referrals (all services the group will suggest are free), patient advocacy, financial assistance with car fare or bus passes, free weekly massages, stress management courses, and, most importantly, a very strong support network. The "come and ventilate" group that meets every Saturday, for example, is very family oriented, said Christeller. Lunch and child care are provided, and any diagnosed patient can participate; just call ahead of time to let the staff know you'll be there.

Stop AIDS
909 W. Belmont, Chicago, 60657   871-3300
2154 E. 71st, Chicago, 60649   752-STOP
The mission at Stop AIDS is education and prevention. Its South Side office on Jeffery Avenue (in the South Shore Methodist Church) is designed for the African-American community; the North Side branch on Belmont Avenue serves primarily the general population and gay and bisexual men. Staff will refer you to service agencies or invite you to participate in a small-group educational meeting depending on your needs. These are one-time sessions lasting about 3 hours that can take place in private homes, schools, or community centers. Groups are kept to no more than 15 people and are arranged separately for African-Americans, Latinos, women, gay and bisexual men, the hearing impaired, and others. The hope is to empower people to volunteer as AIDS educators.

Test Positive Aware Network
1340 W. Irving Park, #259   404-8726 (404-TPAN)
TPA Network is a good starting place to learn more about AIDS services in Chicago. The organization has peer-led self-help support groups covering dozens of topics for all people infected or strongly affected by the HIV virus, including married couples, women, and people not tested but wanting more information. Fifteen sessions are held every week, including two daytime meetings. TPA Network also holds various other activities such as stress-reduction sessions, book study groups, and social events. Its monthly journal *Positively Aware* costs $25/year and is distributed nationally to 60 cities.

ALTERNATIVE MEDICINE

The Chicago yellow pages lists dozens of health care facilities for people interested in drugless treatments; a few are cited here.

Chicago National College of Naprapathy
3330 N. Milwaukee   282-2686
The emphasis in naprapathy is on nutritional counseling and an extremely gentle system of joint manipulation to restore vascular and lymphatic circulation. It differs from chiropracty in focusing less on spinal alignment and stressing proper diet. Naprapathy is not yet a licensed area of medicine; to practice a person must hold a medical, osteopathic, or chiropractic license in addition to a naprapathy degree. There are about 100 naprapaths in the

country, with the most in Chicago. The number one ailment treated at the national college here, according to Dr. Edward Koziol, is lower-back pain. First-time patients have a thorough back exam and fill out a questionnaire about their diet.

Midwest Center for the Study of Oriental Medicine
4334 N. Hazel, #206   975-1295

Acupuncture has become the catchword for all Oriental medicine, including herbs, nutrition, and medical exercise like qi-gung. This center is both a clinic (including acupuncture, shiatsu, chiropracty, and conventional care) and the only accredited school of acupuncture in the Midwest, with 95 full-time students and 35 faculty members (there is a Racine, Wisconsin, branch campus as well). This is where doctors and nonprofessionals alike come for instruction. According to President William Dunbar, "The issue isn't whether acupuncture works. The AMA now refers people to acupuncturists. Most acupuncturists are more interested in being complementary to regular doctors." He reminds patients to ask whether the practitioner is board certified and uses disposable needles.

Myo Inc.
4601 N. Malden   463-2220

Myotherapy uses pressure techniques and a prescribed exercise program (versus the nutritional therapy common to naprapathy) to relieve such conditions as bursitis, whiplash, back pain, headache, and repetitive-motion syndrome. The procedure was developed about 20 years ago by a group of people including Dr. Janet Travell, Pres. John F. Kennedy's personal physician. Sharon Sauer at Myo Inc. says she has helped people who could hardly walk into her office because of an acute injury in 15–45 minutes. And if you're an out-of-towner who can't even walk into her office, she is happy to come to your hotel to treat you. To avoid a recurrence of the problem, Sauer teaches a patient and his or her partner exercise and massage techniques, in person and then with follow-up audio or videocassettes.

Natural Health Family Practice
1342 W. Belmont   549-6518

This clinic offers naprapathy, chiropracty, acupuncture, ultrasound, heat and cold therapy, Chinese herbal therapy, and homeopathic remedies (for which there is no regulation in Illinois).

The Temple of Kriya Yoga
2414 N. Kedzie   342-4600

Offered here are classes in hatha and kriya yoga (emphasizing physical and spiritual aspects, respectively), astrology, palmistry, tarot, and philosophy. On Sunday at 10:30 A.M. and 1:15 P.M. there are hour-long drop-in sessions for $5 to introduce beginners to the gentle stretching and physical postures of hatha yoga. Also on Sunday, at noon, the temple holds meditation services with no yoga, just an uplifting message presented by a different priest of the temple every week.

DENTISTRY

Chicago Dental Society
401 N. Michigan, #300   836-7300; 726-4321 for 24-hour emergency referral
This office is mainly for member dentists, but it will refer you to three dentists in your neighborhood.

Northwestern University Dental School
240 E. Huron   908-5950
Dental school clinics offer lower-cost treatment done by students under the supervision of dentist-teachers. At Northwestern's office, you can drop in at 8:30 A.M. or 1:30 P.M.; from the time you register to your exam is usually about 2–2½ hours, on a first-come, first-served basis. If you need an emergency filling, though, you'll be taken care of right away. For kids the registration and examination fee is $5; for adults the cost is $49, which includes registration, X rays, and a study model of your mouth. Then a cleaning and a general exam costs $27 and up.

University of Illinois at Chicago Dental Clinic
801 S. Paulina   996-7555
Adult registration at the UI clinic starts at 8 A.M. weekdays, at 9 A.M. for children. No appointment is necessary. All new adult patients must have a $10 screening exam before they can go on for either emergency treatment or a general complete exam with X rays. This latter treatment costs $52; other services are extra. The wait between registration and your assignment to a dental student for treatment depends on the kind of exam you need and the time of year. You must pay at the time of your visit, even if you have dental insurance (your insurance company will reimburse you later). Public aid may cover some of the charges.

SUBSTANCE ABUSE

Most hospitals operate clinics to help people overcome alcoholism or drug abuse, in addition to hundreds of independently run programs in the Chicago area. For additional resources for substance abusers and their families, see the following chapter, "Mental Health."

Alcoholics Anonymous
205 W. Wacker   346-1475 (24 hours)
Besides this general office, there are Spanish-speaking AA offices at 3612 W. North (278-6251) and 8842 S. Houston (978-1181) and the **Al-Anon Alateen Center of Information** at 4259 S. Archer (890-1141). Check out the **Adult Children of Alcoholics Bookstore** at 4011 N. Damen (525-2171).

Gateway Foundation
2855 N. Sheffield   929-1865
Established in 1968, Gateway is one of the oldest substance abuse programs in Illinois. It offers intensive outpatient treatment stressing behavior modification. Groups meet for 10 weeks either Monday–Thursday or Tuesday–Friday for 4 hours a day, then move to "aftercare" sessions for 2 ½ hours once a week. Gateway also has individual counseling and drug testing available. Fees are on a sliding scale, and Medicaid is accepted.

Interventions Counterpoint Youth Clinic
2043 N. Sheffield 549-8388
In a renovated three-flat in Lincoln Park, Interventions is a long-term residential program for about 30 chemical-dependent men aged 18–24. It also offers outpatient services. "It's a behavior modification place," said counselor Steve Fiorito. "We concentrate on changing behavior first, then attitudes and thinking. We tear down old personalities that don't work and build new ones that do." Residents can move into the Step Down program, which is for men ready to reintegrate themselves into the community. They get vocational counseling and help finding work and a place to live.

Women's Chemical Dependence Program
2520 N. Lakeview 883-8200 (24 hours)
Affiliated with Columbus Hospital, this program has both inpatient detoxification and rehabilitation and intensive outpatient treatments. The latter is available either days or evenings, with free child care for evening participants. Also free are Project Hope, designed for women with children from birth to age 3, and a sibling project for mothers with older kids; both of these are for the perinatal, primal, and postpartum drug user.

WOMEN'S HEALTH AND FAMILY PLANNING

Women's health and reproductive concerns have become stars on the political stage, with abortion being one of the most hotly contested topics all over the country. Since *Roe v. Wade* legalized abortion in 1973, pro-life groups have been working diligently to undermine its availability. An increasingly conservative Supreme Court implies that some day *Roe* will likely be overturned, and several lawsuits have already imposed severe restrictions. Three cases in particular have left their mark on reproductive health care nationwide, including many Chicago area clinics and hospitals:

- The 1989 *Webster v. Reproductive Health Services* decision, which states that any medical facility that receives federal funds via Title X may not perform abortions.

- The 1991 *Rust v. Sullivan* decision, which prohibits health care professionals from discussing abortion in any way to patients inquiring about pregnancy options—the "gag rule." In November 1991 Pres. George Bush vetoed legislation to overturn the gag rule completely, but the administration revised its position in March 1992 to permit physicians *only* to discuss abortion as a pregnancy option. Formal implementation of the gag rule, however, is off until Congress votes on reauthorizing Title X and reversing the gag rule, sometime in fall 1992.

- The 1992 *Planned Parenthood of Southeastern Pennsylvania v. Casey* suit, the most damaging decision to abortion rights because it downgrades their constitutional protection to that of "liberty interests" (a new standard) rather than Fundamental rights. Now more responsibility has been transferred from the federal government to the states, which can restrict access to abortion services as much as they want, as long as these obstacles don't place a so-called "undue burden" on women. What constitutes an undue burden is up in the air, but in the *Casey* ruling, the Supreme Court let pass into law a 24-hour "cooling-off period" before women can receive their scheduled abortion, the most restrictive minor's access law in the country (a parent must review state-biased information on abortion at the clinic *and* give consent), and a publicly available list of the names and addresses of abortion patients. Needless to say, if these restrictions aren't regarded as undue burdens, almost anything goes. *Roe v. Wade* has been effectively squashed as a result.

Outside the legislative realm, groups like Operation Rescue and Lambs of Christ block entrance to clinics and harass patients by holding prayer vigils (i.e., demonstrations) or sometimes taking their protest a step further by doing such things as gluing door frames shut or locking themselves to the steering wheels of their cars, parked to block the road. Most engage in passive resistance as they are arrested. Bogus clinics have sprouted up: anti-choice zealots lure women in by posing as medical practitioners offering pregnancy testing, etc., and then try to sway women away from opting for abortion.

In Chicago all news is not bad news, however. The **National Abortion Rights Action League** (100 E. Ohio, 644-0972) and the **National Organization for Women** (53 W. Jackson, 922-0025) lobby legislators and educate the community on reproductive issues. Current concerns include these:

- Publicizing the benefits of the French drug RU 486. This pill allows women to terminate a pregnancy up to the eighth week; a safe, nonsurgical method with a 93 percent success rate. RU 486 may also prove beneficial in treating breast cancer, endometriosis, glaucoma, ulcers, and Cushing's syndrome and in reducing the number of cesarians by inducing labor. Currently, however, the Food and Drug Administration has RU 486 on its list of restricted drugs: it cannot be imported into the United States, even for private use.

- Garnering support for the Freedom of Choice Act, cosponsored by Illinois Sen. Paul Simon. The act basically paraphrases *Roe v. Wade* to guarantee women's right to an abortion up to 24 weeks. State-imposed restrictions would be allowed during the third trimester, unless they put a woman's health or life in danger.

- Lobbying for the Reproductive Health Equity Act, which would restore state funding for abortions.

- Supporting Cook County Board Pres. Richard Phelan, who issued an executive order in September 1992 to lift a 12-year ban on abortions at Cook County Hospital, extending full reproductive choice once again to the low-income patients the hospital serves. Pro-life groups continue to file appeals.

In addition, pro-life demonstrations in the Chicago area are strongly counter-resisted by volunteers trained in clinic escort by the **Illinois Pro-Choice Alliance** (office at the ACLU, 203 N. LaSalle, 201-9740) so that patients can be assured to receive their scheduled abortions. In September 1992, State Representative Jeff Schoenberg of Wilmette took things a step further by introducing the Safe Choice Zone bill, which would allow groups to demonstrate peacefully outside abortion clinics while at the same time impose harsher penalties on people who verbally or physically harass patients or damage property. The IPCA also evaluates local abortion clinics and uses a guide put out by the Chicago Abortion Fund in fall 1991.

Listed below are several groups and clinics catering to women's health. All the clinics cited here are *not* affected by the gag rule; that is, they either perform abortions or openly discuss all pregnancy options with their patients.

American College of Certified Nurse Midwives (local chapter)
712 Carpenter, Oak Park   (708) 848-6556

Midwifery is an increasingly popular specialty within nursing. At one time it was common only among low-income women, but now it's chosen among other mothers-to-be as well. Midwives tend to spend much more time than a traditional physician with the patient, before and during labor. Betty Schlater, coordinator of the midwifery program at the University of Illinois at Chicago, said that a study done in Texas recently showed that patients with support people during labor had significantly fewer cesarians. Midwifery also proves more cost-effective than conventional delivery because fewer cesarians are done, fewer tests are performed, and patients are discharged earlier. Quick discharge is possible because of midwives' willingness to accede to the patient's desire and because they offer follow-up care at home. In Chicago and the surrounding areas there are about 100 practicing midwives, and the local chapter here can refer you to one. Medicare and Medicaid cover midwifery costs.

Chicago Women's Health Center
3435 N. Sheffield   935-6126

This clinic supplies care regardless of a woman's ability to pay. For the Well Women program, which includes Pap smears, infection checks, birth control, and pregnancy testing, the patient is simply handed an envelope and asked to put in what she can afford. Four obstetrician/gynecologists plus several health workers are available, but the clinic emphasizes self-help. It receives no federal funds; it operates on the monies from its direct services and some grants. For example, the Chicago Community Trust gave the center money to establish a counseling program for incest survivors and rape victims, carried out by clinical social workers. Abortions are not done on-site, but patients will be referred to reputable clinics if they request one. The "morning after" pill, which must be taken within 72 hours of unprotected intercourse, is available here. The clinic's hours include Tuesday and Wednesday evenings and Saturday mornings; call the office to schedule an appointment.

Family Planning Associates Medical Group
5086 N. Elston   725-0200
659 W. Washington   707-8988

This is a private facility that offers abortions, plus tubal ligation and general gynecological exams with a Pap smear at affordable rates. At the Elston branch the cost of such an exam is $55; at Washington it's $35. Both offices offer birth control options as well; pills, for example, are $10/month at Elston and $5/month at Washington.

Homefirst Family Practice Unlimited
6122 N. Lincoln   539-0808
Home births are this clinic's specialty, and the founder of the practice in 1974,
Dr. Mayer Eisenstein, gets requests around the country to open similar offices
elsewhere. Besides this Lincoln Avenue location, there are four suburban
Homefirst clinics. Doctors on staff in Chicago include obste-
trician/gynecologists, a pediatrician, a family practitioner, and a derma-
tologist. They perform no ultrasounds (because they supply unnecessary
radiation) and no amniocentesis (because it can damage the amniotic sac).
Patients aren't cleared for a home birth until the 36th week of pregnancy, then
deliveries are done with a doctor and nurse. Homefirst routinely performs
natural deliveries for women who have had C sections previously. Dr.
Eisenstein also hosts a call-in radio show on family practice on WILL 106.7
FM, Saturday at 10 A.M.

Planned Parenthood
Administrative Office: 14 E. Jackson, 10th floor, Chicago, 60604   427-2276
Information/Education Hot Line: 427-2275 (427-2ASK)
Clinics:

Austin Center: 5634 W. Chicago   287-2020

Harris Center: 14 E. Jackson, 10th floor   427-2270

Midwest Center: 1201 N. Clark, #301   266-1033

Northside Center: 6353 N. Broadway   973-3393

Roseland Center: 9520 S. Halsted   233-3131

Planned Parenthood is committed to high-quality, low-cost care. About 10
percent of the Chicago operation's budget comes from federal funds, and the
state office is still working on implementation guidelines for all its clinics
regarding response to the gag rule. (The bulk of Planned Parenthood is
financed through private donations and patient fees.) For now the Chicago
branches will voluntarily give up federal funding, amounting to about
$400,000, if necessary to continue to provide full-options counseling—on
adoption, prenatal care, and abortion—for pregnant women. Thus far the
Austin and Roseland centers have retained a sliding-fee scale. The Midwest
Center is the only Chicago Planned Parenthood clinic where abortions are
performed; women seeking abortions elsewhere are referred only to area
clinics that have been screened by an independent health care provider. All
Chicago branches offer the "morning after" pill ($45 for Planned Parenthood
patients, $70 otherwise). For a $50 first-time visit, you are registered as a
patient (and can then transfer to any Planned Parenthood clinic in the
country) and receive a thorough gynecological and physical exam, plus advice on choosing a contraceptive. Birth control pills are $10/month, and you
are asked to return then for a weight and blood pressure check every 6
months for $10. IUDs cost $190, complete diaphragm fitting and supplies are
$42, foam and condoms cost $6–$8, and the matchstick-sized Norplant inserts
providing 5 years' protection are available for $600. Costs are lower at the
Teen Clubs at the Austin and Roseland clinics; there the first exam is $15 and
oral contraceptives are $1/pack. Planned Parenthood's hot line (Monday–
Friday, 9 A.M.–5 P.M.) answers questions about everything from the proper use

of condoms to where to get a vasectomy. Its volunteers are busy lobbying legislators and motivating the community to keep abreast of all reproductive health issues.

Women's Health Resources
7331 N. Sheridan   262-7331
1003 W. Wellington   525-1177
Established in 1982 with a half-time internist and a resource library, Women's Health Resources was the first hospital-based women's health center in the country, being affiliated with Illinois Masonic Hospital. Its all-women staff offers a full range of physical and mental health services. First visits, which include a Pap smear, cost $45 with a nurse-practitioner; follow-up visits are $35. With an internist, the cost is $65 the first visit, $45 thereafter. The Sheridan clinic offers mammograms for $60. Psychotherapists provide individual, couple, and group therapy, including sessions for alcoholics, survivors of incest, and women trying to quit smoking. The clinics regularly hold workshops on topics like stress management and self-esteem, and their speakers make community presentations. Women's Health Resources is funded by the Illinois Masonic Hospital and is not affected by the gag rule; all family planning options are discussed, and staff can refer patients to abortion clinics if necessary.

SUGGESTED READING

Anatomy of an Illness and *Head First: The Biology of Hope* by Norman Cousins. Both books present medical evidence supporting the author's claim that a strong positive attitude and rapport with your doctor combine for strong healing power to lessen pain and increase your chances for overcoming serious illness.

The Complete Drug Reference, a Consumer Reports Book by U.S. Pharmacopeia. Easy-to-understand, detailed descriptions by an independent evaluator of over 5,500 prescription and over-the-counter drugs—their uses, side effects, precautions, etc.

The Food Pharmacy Guide to Good Eating by Jean Carper. Over 200 recipes using foods with therapeutic or preventive benefits.

The Hospice Movement by Sandol Stoddard. The new revised edition presents humane advice on how to care for the dying, with a special section on AIDS and an appendix on how to handle symptoms of various terminal diseases.

Our Bodies, Ourselves by the Boston Women's Health Collective. A comprehensive self-help book covering physical and mental conditions.

—*Laura E. Larson*

MENTAL HEALTH

The chances are good that sooner or later a mental health problem will touch you or someone close to you. Fortunately, Chicago offers a large number and wide variety of mental health professionals—the listings in this chapter are just a sampling. So, whether you are debilitated by a severe mental illness or are coping fine but want to know yourself better, help is available.

It's available at community mental health centers, teaching institutions, not-for-profit clinics, and private practices. And it's available from psychiatrists (medical doctors who have received special training in psychiatry), clinical psychologists (who have doctorates in psychology), and nurse clinicians, social workers, and marriage and family counselors (most of whom have master's degrees). Some therapists specialize in solo, couple, family, or group therapy; some focus on specific segments of society, such as women, gays and lesbians, specific ethnic groups, or specific age groups. With so many choices available, the task of finding the right mental health care may seem overwhelming. Indeed, choosing a therapist requires energy, courage, and perseverance, but the rewards of finding one who is right for you are worth the effort.

When seeking a therapist, you must first consider the severity of the problem. If the problem is severe and acute—that is, you are in danger of physically harming yourself or someone else—either go to a hospital emergency room or call 911 or one of the hot lines listed in this chapter and in the following chapter, "Crisis Intervention."

If the situation is not acute, more choices are available. One of the primary considerations is your financial limitations. When thinking about what you can afford, first check with your insurance company: What education or certification must a therapist have in order to be covered? How much of the cost of each visit is covered? Is there a limit to the number of visits? How much of the cost of medications is covered? Unfortunately, although mental and physical health factors are often indistinguishable from one another, insurance companies usually separate them and pay fewer benefits for services relating to mental health.

Most private practitioners charge a flat fee, with psychiatrists tending to be the highest (up to $180 a session) and social workers the lowest (more like $70 a session). Not-for-profit clinics, however, usually have a sliding-fee scale based on the patient's income. Many mental health facilities accept Medicaid and Medicare as well as private insurance payments, and some accept public aid.

Once you have figured out what you can afford, look for a therapist in your price range. A referral from your physician might be your best bet, but your minister, priest, or rabbi and your personal friends will also have recommendations. In addition, many organizations and associations offer referral services, some of which are listed in this chapter.

Don't hesitate to check a therapist's credentials by calling the professional association to which he or she belongs or to check the credentials of a hospital, mental health center, or substance abuse program by calling the

Joint Commission on Accreditation of Healthcare Organizations ([708] 916-5600).

Once you've located a competent therapist, it's important to make sure that he or she is compatible with you. Give him or her a try while keeping in mind that you are not locked in and that you are the paying customer. During your first visit, interview the therapist as you would anyone you were hiring for a job. Ask questions: What are your qualifications? What will happen in therapy? What is the rationale for what will take place? What is the effectiveness of this service I'm paying for? How long can I expect to be in therapy? What can I realistically expect the results to be?

While a good therapist is flexible enough to tailor his or her treatment to the patient, a therapist or institution is often oriented toward or expert in a specific approach to psychotherapy. Ask the therapist about his or her leanings and discuss frankly whether or not he or she can provide what you want from therapy.

There are dozens of modes of psychotherapy, and the more knowledgeable you are about them, the more able you'll be to make the right choice for you (see the bibliography at the end of this chapter).

Psychodynamic psychotherapy, also called "insight-oriented" psychotherapy, is a blend of approaches but emphasizes examining a person's past in order to make changes in the present. This approach takes insight on the part of the client and may take more time than he or she is willing to spend—or cost more than an insurance company is willing to pay.

Thus "short-term" or "brief" psychotherapy has become more common. Sometimes referred to as a "problem-solving" approach, it can be approached in many ways (cognitive and behavioral therapy are usually short-term, for example), but the aim is to deal with the here and now, for a limited time, and for quick results.

For more serious mental illnesses, schizophrenia and severe depression in particular, medication (often in combination with talk therapy) is likely to be warranted. While only a psychiatrist can prescribe drugs, you can hold down therapy fees by seeing a psychologist, nurse, or social worker who has a collaborative relationship with a psychiatrist.

A personal affinity with your therapist is as important as a compatible therapeutic approach. Beware of one who tries to intimidate you or bully you into staying. If you dislike him or her, try someone else. Incompatible or incompetent therapy can be worse than no therapy at all.

As a patient, you have the right to confidentiality. If you have any questions about your rights as a patient or feel that your rights have been violated by a therapist, treatment center, or insurance company, call the **Legal Assistance Foundation, Mental Health Project** (341-1070). Fees are on a sliding scale.

Instead of, or in addition to, a traditional mental health care professional, you may wish to try a practitioner of an alternative type of health care—homeopathy, nutrition therapy, massage therapy, relaxation therapy, yoga, meditation, biofeedback therapy, or hypnosis, to name only a few. Exercise consumer caution here: get personal recommendations, ask practitioners about their qualifications, and check their credentials when possible. (For example, a hypnotherapist should be a member of the American Society of

Clinic Hypnosis, and a biofeedback therapist should belong to the Biofeedback Society of America.) *Conscious Choice*, a free publication available at health food stores and bookstores, is a useful source for such alternative health care providers.

Whatever therapy you choose, remember that it cannot be a cure-all. It will make you neither perfect nor eternally blissful. Rather, it can help you cope with life's ups and downs, become more self-accepting, and improve your relationships with others. If a therapist offers to work miracles, he or she is not to be trusted and is a potential menace to your mental health.

CRISIS SITUATIONS

If you're desperate and need immediate help, you have the choice of calling a hot line or going to a hospital emergency room. More emergency resources—including those that offer emergency housing and those that provide help for victims of sexual assault or domestic violence—are listed in the following chapter, "Crisis Intervention." Some church-run shelters are listed in the "Religion" chapter.

Hot Lines

24-Hour Hot Lines

Alcohol Abuse 332-5309
Action help line and treatment.

Contact Chicago 644-4357; TDD: 644-5510
Trained volunteers provide active listening, crisis intervention, and information and referral services.

Evanston Hospital
Crisis Intervention and Referral Service (708) 570-2500
For the Chicago area.

Helpline of DuPage County (708) 293-4357
Confidential telephone counseling, crisis intervention, and suicide prevention, plus information and referral for DuPage County.

Parental Stress Services Hot Line 372-7368 or 427-6644
A crisis line and referral service for parents who are too stressed out to interact constructively with their children.

Ravenswood Hospital
 Community Mental Health Center 769-6200; TDD: 728-3737
Crisis intervention hot line staffed by hospital personnel who provide referrals to and services at the clinic.

Talkline/Kids Line

These three lines provide 24-hour crisis intervention, emotional support, problem-solving help, and information and referrals for the Chicago suburban area, although the volunteers will talk to anyone:

Kids Line (708) 228-5437
This children's help line provides latch-key kids with information, referral, guidance, and comfort from a trained adult.

Talkline for Adults (708) 228-6400

Teen Line (708) 228-8335
Professionally trained peer counselors are available 6 P.M.–9 P.M. daily.

Other Hot Lines

AIDS Hot Line 1-800-AID-AIDS (243-2437); TDD: 1-800-782-0423
Hours: Daily, 10 A.M.–10 P.M.
Information on AIDS and referrals to education, medical, and support services throughout Illinois. For information on specific AIDS programs, see the preceding chapter, "Physical Health."

Horizons Community Services, Inc., Lesbian and Gay Helpline
929-HELP (929-4357) or 472-6469; TDD: 327-4357
Hours: Daily, 6 P.M.–10 P.M.
Information and referral and intake for other programs of this gay and lesbian social service agency.

In Touch Hot Line
University of Illinois at Chicago 996-5535
Hours: Daily, 6 P.M.–3 A.M.
Student volunteers provide crisis intervention, telephone counseling, and referrals in all areas of human concern and is an information and referral service for the metropolitan area.

Teen Contact
Contact Chicago 644-2211
Hours: Daily, 5 P.M.–9 P.M.
Adult and teen volunteers provide active listening, suicide prevention, and information and referral services.

Hospital Emergency Rooms

If you feel you may physically harm yourself or someone else, or if you have been raped or been a victim of domestic or other violence, go to a hospital emergency room. Northwestern, Ravenswood, and Michael Reese hospitals' emergency rooms are among those with good reputations. Some of the hospitals with outpatient mental health clinics are listed below, under "Outpatient Clinics with Sliding Scales." See also the following chapter, "Crisis Intervention," for information about a service called Rape Victim Advocates, which serves 10 area hospitals.

INFORMATION AND REFERRALS

The following organizations can direct you, and some can provide services themselves.

Alliance for the Mentally Ill of Greater Chicago
833 N. Orleans, Chicago, 60610   642-3338; TDD: 642-8457
This group is dedicated to improving the quality of life for the severely mentally ill and their families. Among the group's offerings are crisis and routine information and referrals, informational meetings, speakers, a newsletter, a journal, a circulating library, and support groups in English and Spanish.

Community Information and Referral Service   876-0010 or 1-800-564-5733
Hours: Monday–Friday, 8:30 A.M.–5 P.M.
Trained social work consultants will link you with qualified service providers in the seven-county Chicago area. After-hours and weekend calls are taken by Contact Chicago (see above, under "Hot Lines"). Supported by the United Way/Crusade of Mercy, this bilingual and confidential service deals with problems ranging from substance abuse, aging, and infertility to legal aid, domestic violence, and emergency food and shelter.

Depression after Delivery National Hot Line   (215) 295-3994
Hours: Tuesday, Thursday, and Friday mornings
Refers women suffering from postpartum distress to self-help groups and mental health professionals who are part of this support network.

EZRA Support Line   1-800-248-1818
Hours: Daily, 24 hours
This information and referral service has a large file of both emergency and long-term resources, including hospitals, substance abuse programs, self-help groups, and counseling agencies for individuals, couples, families, and children. It's operated by the Jewish Children's Bureau of Chicago, but you don't have to be Jewish to use the help line's services.

Illinois Psychiatric Society
20 N. Michigan, Chicago, 60602   263-7391
The district branch of the American Psychiatric Association, its personnel refer callers to members of the society, all of whom are board-certified psychiatrists.

Illinois Psychological Association
203 N. Wabash, Chicago, 60601   327-7610
This organization, which is affiliated with the American Psychological Association, offers consumer information and refers callers to members of the association, all of whom are licensed clinical psychologists.

Institute for Psychoanalysis
180 N. Michigan, #2300, Chicago, 60601   726-6300
Hours: Monday–Friday, 9 A.M.–5 P.M.
This organization, which offers graduate and postgraduate education in psychoanalysis, also provides an information and referral service as well as psychoanalytic therapy for children, adolescents, and adults for fees lower

than most psychoanalysts'. Psychoanalysis is a long-term treatment that aims to resolve underlying causes of present problems.

Mental Health Association of Greater Chicago
104 S. Michigan, Chicago, 60603   781-7791 (information and referral)
This organization provides public education, public policy advocacy, and the comprehensive *Mental Health and Substance Abuse Services Directory for Illinois*. Association personnel will refer you to public and private services in your area.

National Association of Anorexia Nervosa
and Associated Disorders National Resource Hot Line   (708) 831-3438
Hours: Monday–Friday, 9 A.M.–5 P.M.
This Highland Park–based organization has a referral list of programs and therapists for people with eating disorders and sponsors free self-help groups across the nation.

National Association of Social Workers (NASW)
180 N. Michigan, #400, Chicago, 60601   236-8308
This is the Illinois chapter of a national organization whose members must meet professional qualifications for training and experience (a master's degree, two years' clinical experience, a national exam, and ongoing educational requirements). Its personnel will refer you to a licensed clinical social worker whose services, under Illinois law, must be covered by insurance.

GOVERNMENT FACILITIES

Because there is no single source of funding for mental health care in Illinois, there is no mental health "system"; rather, Illinois is a hodgepodge of state facilities and local programs that vary in quality. These public programs can turn nobody away because of inability to pay, but they may have long waiting lists.

The major state agency responsible for the care of the mentally ill is the **Illinois Department of Mental Health and Developmental Disabilities** (100 W. Randolph; call 814-2735 for general and consumer health protection information). It is responsible for serving "the sickest and the poorest," the seriously mentally ill and developmentally disabled who don't have access to privately funded services and would otherwise go unserved. There are critical staff shortages in the Chicago area, and most state facilities provide barely adequate care.

In Chicago, the **Chicago Department of Health's Bureau of Mental Health** (50 W. Washington, 744-8033) directs and coordinates 18 city-funded community mental health centers for outpatient care. Services vary from center to center but may include individual, group, and family therapy, crisis intervention, aftercare for patients discharged from state hospitals, aid for the homeless, and emergency housing. Each center serves a "catchment area," and you are supposed to go to the one in your neighborhood, but exceptions are made. Fees begin at $1 a visit and are on a sliding scale. Call the Bureau to find the center in your area, but be prepared for the often frustrating experience of dealing with a city employee.

OUTPATIENT CLINICS WITH SLIDING SCALES

Chicago Osteopathic Hospital and Medical Center
Mental Health Clinic
5200 S. Ellis, Chicago, 60615   947-4870
Hours: Tuesday, Wednesday, and Friday, 8:30 A.M.–5 P.M.;
Monday and Thursday, 8:30 A.M.–9 P.M.
Not-for-profit hospital with a sliding scale provides individual psychotherapy, group and family therapy, substance abuse programs, and crisis stabilization. An adult day program (947-3048) provides support and rehab for those with chronic mental illness.

Community Mental Health Council
8704 S. Constance, Chicago, 60617   734-4033
Hours: Monday, Tuesday, and Thursday, 9 A.M.–9 P.M.; Wednesday and Friday, 9 A.M.–5 P.M.; and 24-hour crisis line at above number
Mental health center for residents living and working in the South Shore, Chatham, Avalon, Burnside, and Greater Grand Crossing neighborhoods. It provides, among other services, screening and referrals, crisis intervention (including rape and sexual assault), outpatient care for children, adolescents, adults, and seniors, and community residential services for adults with no drug- or alcohol-related diagnoses.

DePaul University Community Mental Health Center
2219 N. Kenmore, Chicago, 60614   341-8292
Hours: Monday–Friday, 9 A.M.–5 P.M. and evenings by appointment
This counseling center for DePaul faculty, staff, and students is also a training facility for clinical psychologists and a community health center that specializes in treating children and adolescents. It offers crisis intervention, diagnostic testing and interviewing, individual psychotherapy, and family therapy for Loop, Near North, and Lincoln Park residents. Fees are very reasonable, ranging from free to $45 a session.

Edgewater Uptown Community Mental Health Center
4740 N. Clark, Chicago, 60640   769-0205
This state- and federally funded comprehensive mental health center serves Edgewater and Uptown; its bilingual services are open to all Chicago residents. Preventive, outpatient, rehabilitation, outpatient counseling, aftercare, and emergency services (including a rape crisis service) are available at this location and several branches.

The Family Institute
680 N. Lake Shore Drive, #1306, Chicago, 60611   908-7285
Hours: Monday–Thursday, 8:30 A.M.–9 P.M.; Friday, 8:30 A.M.–5 P.M.;
Saturday, 8:30 A.M.–4:30 P.M.
A postgraduate training facility and independent affiliate of Northwestern University, the Family Institute provides counseling and therapy services for families, couples, individuals, children, and adolescents. The therapists are clinical psychologists and social workers, and the emphasis is on short-term, problem-centered therapy. Fees range from free to over $100 a session. Several suburban locations.

Illinois Masonic Medical Center
Katharine Wright Psychiatric Clinic
836 W. Nelson, 2nd floor, Chicago, 60657 296-7065
Hours: Monday, Tuesday, and Thursday, 9 A.M.–9 P.M.; Wednesday and
Friday, 9 A.M.–5 P.M.
This clinic, affiliated with the Illinois Masonic Medical Center, has outpatient
programs for adults and children. It offers individual, group, couples, and
family therapy as well as medication management, learning disabilities
evaluation and remediation, and counseling and social support for AIDS
patients and their significant others. The sliding scale begins at $30 for a
session of individual psychotherapy.

Michael Reese Hospital and Medical Center
Wexler Psychiatric Clinic
2960 S. Lake Park, Chicago, 60616 791-3900
This clinic offers psychiatric evaluation and treatment for children, adolescents, adults, and families. Therapy tends to be psychodynamically oriented
and long-term. Fees range from $20 to $60 a session, and public aid is
accepted.

Northwestern Memorial Hospital
Superior Street and Fairbanks Court, Chicago, 60601   908-2000
24-hour emergency program: 908-8100
Northwestern Hospital offers a wide variety of mental health services. As a
community mental health center, **Northwestern's Institute of Psychiatry**
(908-8055) provides care on a sliding scale to residents of the area east of the
river and between Roosevelt Road and Diversey Parkway. The services of the
Northwestern Medical Faculty Foundation (908-9400) are available to all
Chicago area residents on a flat-fee basis. These include general psychiatric
services as well as programs for older adults, adolescents, sex therapy, and
eating and sleep anxiety disorders.

Ravenswood Hospital Community Mental Health Center
4055 N. Western, Building B, Chicago, 60618 463-7000
Hours: Monday–Thursday, 8:30 A.M.–9 P.M.; Friday, 8:30 A.M.–6 P.M.
Offers a full range of psychiatric services for adults, including sex therapy, to
individuals, couples, families, and groups. Fees range from $5 to $70 a session. Sponsors a variety of self-help groups and courses on topics ranging
from compulsive eating to spirituality to codependency.

Southwest Women Working Together
3201 W. 63rd, Chicago, 60629 436-0550
For women and their families from the Southwest Side and nearby suburbs.
Provides individual and family counseling, an information and referral service, and support groups for women, single parents, and survivors of incest,
sexual assault, domestic violence, and child abuse.

University of Chicago Hospitals and Clinics
Department of Psychiatry
5841 S. Maryland, Chicago, 60637 702-1000
This educational and research center extends many free services to the surrounding communities and offers inpatient and outpatient psychiatric ser-

vices on a fee basis without geographic restrictions. Includes outpatient clinics for sleep, eating, anxiety, and affective disorders. The diagnostic assessment is $250; follow-up psychotherapy sessions range from $70 to $120.

University of Illinois Hospitals and Clinics
Department of Psychiatry
912 S. Wood, Chicago, 60612   996-7362
This teaching and research center offers an inpatient psychiatric unit and several outpatient clinics aimed at specific problems, from psychosomatic illnesses to sleep disorders to depression. The patient undergoes a full range of diagnostic assessments as well as stabilization and follow-up care (which may include medication, psychotherapy, or both). Fees are based on a sliding scale ranging from $50 to $120 per therapy session.

FAMILY SERVICE AGENCIES

Family service agencies provide a wide variety of services for free or for a low fee, including family, marital, and individual counseling (usually by social workers) and information and referrals. The major family service agencies in Chicago have centers throughout the area.

Catholic Charities Chicago   236-5172
Serves all Cook and Lake county residents, regardless of religious affiliation.

Jewish Federation of Metropolitan Chicago   346-6700
Hours: Monday–Friday, 8:30 A.M.–5 P.M.
A federation of Jewish welfare, education, and medical agencies and services aimed at the Jewish community primarily but also the general community.

Lutheran Social Services of Illinois   (708) 635-4600
Offers counseling, referrals, and a wide variety of social services for people of all faiths all over the Chicago area.

Salvation Army   725-1100
Nondenominational organization with community centers all over the city and suburbs.

United Charities   986-4000
Family, individual, and group counseling, assessment and referral, consumer credit counseling service, and other services all over the Chicago area.

SUBSTANCE ABUSE TREATMENT

For severe addictions, sometimes a protective environment is the right choice. Substance abuse treatment programs have proliferated in the past decade, and there are many options. Choose a program with care. It should be accredited by the **Joint Commission on Accreditation of Healthcare Organizations** ([708] 916-5600) and offer comprehensive services—inpatient, outpatient, and follow-up care. (See the "Physical Health" chapter for additional services for substance abusers.)

Chicago Lakeshore Hospital
4840 N. Marine, Chicago, 60640   878-9700 or 1-800-888-0560
This for-profit hospital offers inpatient and outpatient programs for adults and adolescents with alcohol, drug, and other addictive problems. Fees are at a flat rate, but health insurance and Medicare are accepted.

Grant Hospital Chemical Dependence Program
550 W. Webster, Chicago, 60614   883-3898
Offers inpatient and outpatient care, detoxification, family program, ongoing 12-step groups. First consultation is free. Outpatient fees are on a sliding scale.

Jackson Park Hospital Center for Chemical Dependency
7531 S. Stony Island, Chicago, 60649   947-7500
Substance abuse and psychiatric services: 947-7900
Inpatient substance abuse rehab: 947-2400
A comprehensive substance abuse rehab, medical detox, and aftercare center. The first consultation is free.

Lutheran Social Services of Illinois
Alcoholism-Drug Dependence Program   282-7800
Ten locations throughout the Chicago area offer counseling and referrals for persons addicted to alcohol or drugs. Alcoholics Anonymous groups, educational programs, and individual, family, and group therapy are also available.

Northwestern Memorial Hospital Chemical Dependence Program
24-hour hot line: 908-2255
Offers individualized, flexible inpatient and outpatient programs.

Parkside Medical Services   1-800-PARKSIDE (1-800-727-5743)
Lutheran General Healthcare is the parent company of this privately funded, nonprofit recovery facility with a good reputation. Seven inpatient and out-patient programs are available in five locations in the Chicago area, including Lutheran General Hospital in Park Ridge.

St. Elizabeth's Hospital
Comprehensive Alcoholic Rehabilitation Environment Unit (CARE)
1431 N. Claremont, Chicago, 60622   278-5015
This West Side hospital offers individualized inpatient and outpatient programs in English, Spanish, and Polish.

St. Francis Hospital of Evanston
355 Ridge, Evanston, 60202   (708) 492-6385
Outpatient alcohol and drug abuse treatment program for Chicago and the northern suburbs. Fees are on a sliding scale, and Medicaid and public aid are accepted.

SELF-HELP GROUPS

Self-help groups consist of people with common problems who support and help each other. Many groups are open- ended and many are free of charge. Often no professional health care worker is in attendance. The Chicago area seems to have something for everyone, and the **Self-Help Center** ([708] 328-0470), located in Evanston, is a clearinghouse for hundreds of support groups that will help you find one that fills your needs.

Al-Anon/Alateen (708) 848-2707
Support and education for families and friends of alcoholics. Al-Anon is for adults, Alateen for 12- to 20-year olds.

Alcoholics Anonymous 346-1475 (24 hours); Spanish: 278- 6251
Support and education for people who want to stop drinking.

Cocaine Anonymous 202-8898
For people recovering from cocaine addiction.

Depression after Delivery
Chicago Support Group 625-3196 (Tina)
This volunteer support network sponsors self-help groups in Oak Park, Glen Ellyn, and Lisle as well as in the city.

Family AIDS Support Network 404-1038 (Betty)
Sponsors Circle of Care Support Group. Free and confidential. (For other AIDS-related programs, see the preceding chapter, "Physical Health".)

Gamblers Anonymous 346-1588
Help for compulsive gamblers. Also groups for family members.

Howard Brown Memorial Clinic
945 W. George, Chicago, 60657   871-5777
Hours: Monday–Friday, 9 A.M.–5 P.M.
This clinic's many HIV/AIDS support services include support groups for people who are HIV-positive but asymptomatic as well as for AIDS patients and their family and friends. (For more AIDS- related programs, see the preceding chapter, "Physical Health".)

Narcotics Anonymous (708) 848-4884
Support for individuals recovering from drugs and alcohol.

**National Association of Anorexia Nervosa and
Associated Disorders** (708) 831-3438
Support and education for people with eating disorders. Local groups meet all over the Chicago area; phone the Chicago group at 361-6134.

National Depressive and Manic Depressive Association
730 N. Franklin, Chicago, 60610   642-0049
Support for people with unipolar or bipolar depression and their families. Phone the Chicago group at 993-0066 or 275- 6513.

Overeaters Anonymous 992-7676
For compulsive eaters.

Parents Anonymous 372-7368
Sponsored by Parental Stress Services, for overwhelmed or frustrated parents. For Chicago residents only.

Single Moms Support Group
DePaul University Community Mental Health Center 341-8292
A closed, 10-week group that's offered in the fall, winter, and summer, free of charge.

Vietnam Vet Centers
These publicly funded centers are located at 5505 S. Harper (684-5500), and in Oak Park ([708] 383-3225), Evanston ([708] 332-1019), and Chicago Heights ([708] 754-0340). They offer support groups for vets who served active duty between August 6, 1964, and May 7, 1975. Individual, group, and family therapy are also available.

Weight Watchers of Chicago (708) 573-8700
Group support for men and women who want to control their eating. Many locations throughout the city and suburbs.

SUGGESTED READING

This selection of books and directories will get you started on your way to being an informed consumer of mental health care services. Books on this topic are shelved on the north end of the fourth floor of the Harold Washington Library (400 S. State).

Books

The Consumer's Guide to Psychotherapy by Jack Engler, Ph.D., and Daniel Goleman, Ph.D. Comprehensive guide for making informed choices.

Darkness Visible: A Memoir of Madness by William Styron. A gripping personal account of the nearly suicidal depression of the well-known American writer.

The Feeling Good Handbook by David D. Burns, M.D. Follow-up to *Feeling Good*: more up-to-date (1989) self-help book based on cognitive therapy.

Feeling Good: The New Mood Therapy by David D. Burns, M.D. A good introduction to cognitive therapy and a commonsense approach to dealing with depression.

How to Cope with Depression: A Complete Guide for You and Your Family by Raymond J. DePaulo Jr., M.D., and Keith Russell Ablow, M.D. A readable, useful guide.

The Psychotherapy Maze: A Consumer's Guide to Getting in and Out of Therapy by Otto Ehrenberg, Ph.D., and Miriam Ehrenberg, Ph.D. Basic, helpful information.

Public Policy and Mental Illness in Illinois. Describes Illinois public policy on mental illness and its implementation. Costs $4.50 plus $1.50 postage and handling; order by calling 939-5935.

The Recovery Resource Book by Barbara Yoder. Comprehensive national guide to resources—books, magazines, organizations, self-help groups—that aim at recovery from addictions.

Trusting Ourselves by Karen Johnson, M.D. A guide to the complete emotional well-being of women.

What You Need to Know about Psychiatric Drugs by Stuart Yudofsky, M.D., Robert E. Hales, M.D., and Tom Ferguson, M.D. Comprehensive, consumer-oriented guide to all kinds of drugs used for treating psychiatric illnesses.

When You Don't Know Where to Turn: A Self-Diagnosing Guide to Counseling and Therapy by Steven J. Bartlett, Ph.D. A clear and comprehensive introduction to various kinds of therapies and to finding the right therapy for your specific personality and needs.

Directories

A Directory of Mental Health Services Available to the Residents of DuPage County, 1988. A listing of crisis, hospital, and alcohol treatment services, counseling agencies, self-help groups, and township and transportation services. Free by sending a self-addressed, stamped envelope to Mental Health Association in DuPage, 408 E. Devon, #200, Elk Grove Village, 60007.

A Profile of Community Services for the Mentally Ill in Illinois. Includes the results of a statewide survey of community-based services for the mentally ill as well as recommendations for policy changes. Costs $5 plus $1.50 postage and handling; order by calling 939-5935.

1991–92 Mental Health and Substance Abuse Services Directory. Listings include hospital psychiatric services, mental health centers and clinics, emergency and intermediate housing, self-help groups, and specialized services for children, the elderly, alcohol and drug abuse, rehab, and more. Costs $50 plus $4 postage and handling; order by calling 781-7780.

1991–1992 Human Care Services Directory of Metropolitan Chicago. Published by the United Way/Crusade of Mercy, this comprehensive listing cites human service organizations in the six-county area, including hundreds of mental health care providers. Order by calling 876-0010 or by sending a check for $32.50 to United Way, 560 W. Lake, Chicago, 60661, Attn: HCSD.

—*Katherine Willhoite*

CRISIS INTERVENTION

In times of crisis, shelter, food, clothing, counseling, and other help are available. For more resources that can provide help in an emergency, including hot lines, mental health centers, and social service organizations, see the preceding chapter, "Mental Health."

If faced with an emergency, call 911 or contact the **Chicago Department of Human Services** at one of these numbers:

General Emergency 744-5829

Hearing Impaired (TDD) 744-6189

Sexual Assault Hot Line 744-8418

Energy Assistance 744-7617

Emergency Shelter 1-800-654-8595

Besides administering dozens of social programs at centers throughout the city, this city department provides direct services in crisis situations. Its 24-hour communication center is linked to the police and fire departments and dispatches emergency social service teams to provide immediate on-the-spot assistance.

The **Community Information and Referral Service** (876-0010 or 1-800-564-5733, 24 hours)—which is bilingual, confidential, and free—is a link to health and human services of all kinds. Trained social work consultants deal with problems ranging from emergency food and shelter and domestic violence to substance abuse and child care. They will connect you with qualified providers in the seven-county Chicago area.

RESOURCES FOR VICTIMS OF RAPE AND SEXUAL ASSAULT

Crisis intervention for women is often a response to violence against women. Rape and other forms of sexual assault and/or physical battery against women or their children can occur in the home, in the workplace, or on the street. It is estimated that one in four women will be the victim or rape or attempted rape during their lifetime.

In the Chicago area, both immediate assistance and longer-term counseling are available free of charge to victims of rape or attempted rape. Even if a rape survivor decides not to go to the hospital or the police at the time of the rape, she may still seek help at a later date.

Chicago Department of Human Services
Sexual Assault Hot Line 744-8418

Community Mental Health Council
8704 S. Constance, Chicago, 60617 734-4033
This South Side mental health center operates a 24-hour phone crisis line and provides crisis intervention and psychiatric aftercare.

Edgewater Uptown Community Mental Health Center
Rape Crisis Service
4740 N. Clark, Chicago, 60640   769-0205
This mental health center provides 24-hour emergency services as well as outpatient and aftercare services.

Rape Victim Advocates   733-6954
Ten area hospitals offer a service called Rape Victim Advocates, whose trained volunteers are on call from hospital emergency rooms 24 hours a day. When paged by the hospital, a Rape Victim Advocate comes to the hospital within 20 minutes and stays with the victim through the physical examinations and discussions with police, attorneys, family members, and friends. The advocate also can provide emergency clothing, housing, food, and lock repair as well as follow-up telephone contact. Spanish- and German-speaking staff is available. The organization also provides public education and training.

The hospitals affiliated with Rape Victims Advocates are Chicago Osteopathic, Edgewater, Grant, Illinois Masonic, Northwestern, Norwegian American, St. Francis of Evanston, Swedish Covenant, University of Illinois, and Weiss Memorial.

SHELTERS

Some shelters in Chicago are aimed at homeless individuals, while others serve as safe houses for victims of domestic violence. Some shelters are for men only and some for women only; some take children and others do not.

A selection of various types of shelters and shelter hot lines is listed here, and some church-run shelters are mentioned in the "Religion" chapter. If you or someone you know is in need of emergency overnight shelter, however, the best way to find it is to call the Chicago Department of Human Services' 24-hour hot line (1-800-654-8595). The department acts as a clearinghouse for information on bed availability in emergency shelters throughout Chicago.

Shelters for Homeless Persons

The Ark
2341 W. Devon, Chicago, 60659   973-6046
Hours: Monday–Thursday, 9 A.M.–5 P.M.; Friday, 9 A.M.–2 P.M.
This organization operates an emergency shelter program for homeless and economically disadvantaged Jews referred by a social worker. Yiddish, Hebrew, and Russian are spoken.

Lake View Overnight Shelter
835 W. Addison, Chicago, 60657   528-6657
November 1–April 30: 10:30 P.M.–6:30 A.M.
This is an emergency overnight shelter for up to 20 men. It also operates a daytime drop-in center (327-1389) and other programs.

Pacific Garden Mission
646 S. State, Chicago, 60605   922-1462 (24 hours)
This large overnight shelter for men, women, and children offers a medical and dental clinic and employment counseling services, all free of charge. The

mission's Christian Servicemen's Center is "a home away from home" for GIs. Staff members speak Polish, German, Spanish, Italian, Yugoslavian, and French.

REST(Residents for Emergency Shelter)
5253 N. Kenmore, Chicago, 60640   784-0909
Hours: Monday–Friday, 9 A.M.–5 P.M.
This organization, aimed at single men and women in Edgewater and Uptown, provides counseling and is designed to aid a transition from the street to suitable housing. It runs a temporary overnight shelter for men November 1–May 1 at 941 W. Lawrence (989-9882) and one for women October 1–June 1 at 1011 W. Wilson (728-1458). Children are not permitted to stay at these shelters.

Salvation Army
Emergency Lodge
800 W. Lawrence, Chicago, 60640   275-9383
Temporary lodging and meals for families or for women and children. Counseling services related to housing and short- term needs are available.

Unity Shelter
7953 S. Escanaba, Chicago, 60617   374-5481 (24 hours)
This is a transitional living center (up to 120 days) for homeless males ages 18–25. Clothing, meals, counseling, education, job placement, medical, and other services are provided.

West Town Emergency Shelter Team
1866 N. Milwaukee, Chicago, 60647   489-5960
This shelter for homeless men and women that additional social services. It will accept people with drug dependence problems if they are willing to participate in a treatment program. Spanish-speaking staff is available.

Shelters and Hot Lines for Victims of Domestic Violence

Domestic violence, which 97 percent of the time involves a man beating a woman, is part of American family life. The U.S. Department of Justice estimates a woman is beaten every 15 seconds, in families of all races, at all income and education levels. While this shocks no one today, just 15 years ago domestic violence was a hidden problem. Feminists organized a grassroots movement to create shelters and safe houses for women and children who were victims. The actual locations of Chicago's shelters are ofteh kept confidential to protect the victims of domestic violence.

Apna Ghar   334-4663 (334-HOME)
Offers shelter and counseling for Asian women victims of domestic violence.

Chicago Abused Women Coalition/Greenhouse Shelter
P.O. Box 477916   278-4566 (24 hours)
Women and children who are the victims of domestic violence may find shelter at Greenhouse Shelter or be referred to other shelters, counseling services, support groups, and legal advocacy assistance. Spanish, Polish, and German are spoken.

Family Rescue
P.O. Box 17528, Chicago, 60617   375-8400 (24 hours)
This shelter and support service for battered women and their children offers individual counseling and support groups, children's play therapy groups, and legal and public aid advocacy. Spanish-speaking staff is available.

Family Violence Program Helpline   94-ABUSE (942-2873)
Over-the-phone counseling, information and referrals, and telephone follow-up service to victims and witnesses of domestic violence are offered via this 24-hour hot line based in the emergency room of Rush-Presbyterian-St. Luke's Medical Center.

A Friend's Place
P.O. Box 5185, Evanston, 60204   274-HELP ([312] 274- 4357)
Hours: Monday–Friday, 9 A.M.–9 P.M.; answering machine on at all times
A Friend's Place is a shelter in Rogers Park for women and children victims of domestic violence. It offers a crisis line, individual and group counseling, referrals, education, and financial assistance for women fleeing abusive situations.

Lifespan
P.O. Box 445, Des Plaines, 60016   (708) 824-4454 (24 hours)
Aimed at women and their children in crisis situations, this organization provides information and referrals for physical, psychological, and sexual abuse as well as support programs, individual counseling, and legal advocacy.

Rainbow House/Arco Iris   762-6611, TDD: 762-6802
Hot line for this shelter for battered women and their children. The shelter offers an information and referral service, a children's play therapy program, and counseling and support groups to abused women on the Southwest Side. Spanish-speaking staff is available.

Sarah's Circle
4455 N. Broadway, Chicago, 60640   728-1991
Hours: Monday–Thursday, 1–9 P.M.; Friday, 1–5 P.M.; Sunday, 1:30–4:30 P.M.
Not an overnight shelter but a drop-in center for women of all ages that distributes food and clothing and provides a referral service for victims of rape and sexual abuse and those in need of legal aid or emergency housing. Showers and bathroom facilities, as well as a fixed mailing address, are available.

Sarah's Inn   (708) 386-3306; 24-hour hot line: (708) 386-4225
This shelter, located in Oak Park, is for women and their children who are victims of physical or emotional abuse and residents of West Side and west suburban Cook County. Group and individual counseling are offered, as is a group treatment program for Men Who Batter.

Shalva   583-4673 (583-HOPE)
Hours: Monday–Friday, 9 A.M.–5 P.M.
This Rogers Park organization offers a 24-hour emergency hot line, shelter, medical care, legal advocacy, counseling, and other services for Jewish women who are victims of domestic violence.

South Suburban Family Shelter
P.O. Box 937, Homewood, 60430   (708) 335-4125
Emergency shelter for battered women and their children in the south suburbs. Provides counseling for women and men and a men's program for abusers.

OTHER RESOURCES

Association House of Chicago
2150 W. North, Chicago, 60647   276-0084
This organization provides crisis intervention for neglected or abused children and emergency food and clothing services, among many other programs.

Inspiration Cafe
1325 W. Wilson, Chicago, 60640   878-0981
This Uptown agency feeds the homeless with dignity. Breakfast every day and dinner on weekends are free to clients, but the Inspiration Cafe is not a soup kitchen; it looks and acts like a restaurant.

MOV (Men Overcoming Violence)
835 W. Addison, Chicago, 60657   327-0036
This center offers weekly group discussions of problems with anger related to divorce, marriage, relationships, and parental stress. A $10 donation is requested.

Mujeres Latinas en Acción
1823 W. 17th, Chicago, 60608   226-1544
Hours: Monday–Friday, 9 A.M.–5 P.M.
Latin Women in Action provides free social services, including crisis intervention, support groups, counseling, drug and alcohol prevention, information and referrals, and educational programs on domestic violence in Spanish and English. The agency serves Pilsen and the Little Village areas but takes referrals from the rest of the city.

National Runaway Switchboard   1-800-621-3230
Twenty-four-hour referral, information, and crisis intervention switchboard that acts as a clearinghouse for information about youth services in the metropolitan area. Outside Illinois call 1-800-621-4000.

Salvation Army
Front Line Feeding Program
1515 W. Monroe, Chicago, 60607   738-3333
Free meals are distributed at 12 locations Monday–Friday.

Travelers and Immigrants Aid of Chicago
327 S. LaSalle, #150, Chicago, 60604   435-4500; after-hours answering service: 222-0265
Hours: Monday–Friday, 8:30 A.M.–5 P.M.
This not-for-profit group provides a wide variety of services, including emergency aid, individual and family counseling, and information and referrals at the Greyhound Bus Station and O'Hare Airport. At other locations it offers immigration counseling and legal assistance, refugee resettlement and social services, and referrals for persons seeking political asylum.

The organization's **Women's Program** at 1950 W. Pershing (847-5602, 24 hours) offers emergency services, counseling and legal information, parenting instruction, and support groups.

The group also provides health care for the homeless at 3355 N. Clark (281-6689). This includes health care screening and basic treatment, mental health services, substance abuse counseling, and client advocacy as well as emergency services.

YWCA—Metro Chicago (Loop)
180 N. Wabash, 3rd floor, Chicago, 60601   372-6600
The most comprehensive source of aid to women, the Loop Y's women's services include a crisis line for directing emergencies, assessing domestic violence cases, and referring women to shelters in specific locations. Staff members can help women with medical emergencies, housing, employment, and both individual and group counseling.

YWCA—Harriet M. Harris Center
6200 S. Drexel, Chicago, 60637   955-3100
Primarily serving women on the South Side, the Harris Y offers counseling for rape victims and their families, rape prevention programs, child and senior day care, and other services similar to those of the Loop YWCA.

—Katherine Willhoite, Linda Bubon, and Ann Christopherson

LEGAL SERVICES

In Chicago the legal system has usually been more about politics than about justice. Judges are elected, and voters usually have no idea who they are voting for. Traditionally a judge's main qualification might be an Irish name or loyal service in a ward organization. A judgeship has traditionally been viewed as a way for a politician to ease into a cushy job. Lawyers have often been more prized for who they know rather than what they know. Payoffs in minor cases, and some not so minor, have not been uncommon. But in the last decade undercover federal investigations have put many crooked judges and lawyers in jail. More and more women, African-Americans, and Latinos have become judges and lawyers, which makes the legal community in Chicago more representative of the city's diversity. When you go to court, you are likely to receive a fair hearing on the merits of your case (if for no other reason than judges are never quite sure who might be listening in). So you would be wise to look for a competent lawyer rather than merely a well-connected one. For relatively minor disputes, mediation is an attractive alternative to costly and lengthy litigation.

WHEN TO HIRE A LAWYER

You know you really need a lawyer when

- you have been charged with a crime.
- you are being sued over a civil matter.
- you are drafting your will (to ensure that all statutory requirements have been satisfied).
- you have been arrested for DUI (driving under the influence of alcohol or drugs).
- you need to file for bankruptcy.
- you are buying or selling real estate. An attorney can make certain the title is good and that all documents have been checked and are in order.
- you are getting a divorce and have children or property.
- your driving record is poor and you have gotten another speeding ticket.
- you have been fired without just cause.
- you are a victim of sexual harassment.
- you have been subject to discrimination on the basis of race, creed, sex, or sexual orientation.

You may not really need a lawyer when

- you are sued for a small amount of money.
- you are getting a divorce and have no children or property.
- you sue someone for a modest amount of money and want to avoid legal fees. In this case you may want to take your case to *pro se* court.
  Pro se court, a division of the Cook County Circuit Court, handles small claims (up to $1,000) for people not represented by lawyers. You can

represent yourself in other courts too, but it is not usually a very good idea. (Defendants may have attorneys in *pro se* if they wish.)

HOW TO FIND A LAWYER

There are various ways to find a lawyer. You could look in the yellow pages, but that's not a very good idea. Talk to friends and relatives to see whether they know of a lawyer who handled a similar matter. Bar associations make referrals, but they usually won't give you an evaluation of the lawyer's ability. Attorneys can now advertise the fields in which they practice, their experience, and the fees they charge. Some run newspaper adds. As with all advertising, be skeptical.

Before you hire a lawyer, be sure to find out the fee you will be charged. It's difficult to list even ballpark estimates of legal fees because they vary so widely. However, here are a few rough estimates of fees: simple divorce with few property issues, $500–$1,500; residential real estate closing, $400–$500; DUI defense, $1,500 and up. The fee will depend on the nature and complexity of the case. Fees can be a fixed rate for a case, an hourly rate, a contingent fee (the attorney gets paid a portion, usually 33 percent of the judgment, if you win the case—primarily used in personal injury cases), or a combination of these. Some attorneys will give you a free initial consultation; others will charge you for this service. Find out before you make an appointment. If you lack the money to hire a lawyer, there are some organizations (see below) that provide legal services at reduced or no cost.

If you want some basic legal information before seeing a lawyer, you might try **Dial-Law** (747-4304), free tape-recorded messages on about 75 general interest legal questions. Dial-Law is sponsored jointly by the Chicago Public Library and the Chicago Bar Association. Areas covered and sample topics include real estate law (home mortgages), landlord-tenant law (eviction, security deposits), immigration law (permanent visas, work permits), family law (divorce, adoption), bankruptcy, employment rights, and many others. To hear the messages and get a complete list of topics, call during the following hours: Monday–Thursday, 9 A.M.–7 P.M.; Friday and Saturday, 9 A.M.–5 P.M.

Another good source of legal information is **Call a Lawyer** (554-2001), sponsored by the Chicago Bar Association. Volunteer attorneys answer questions on civil and criminal matters over the phone. Call from 9 A.M. until noon on the third Saturday of each month.

COURTS AND GOVERNMENT BUILDINGS

City Hall/County Building
LaSalle and Randolph Streets
Connected by an underground tunnel to the Daley Center. Located here are the mayor's office, City Council chambers, and various city and county agencies.

Criminal Courts Building
26th Street and California Avenue
Most criminal felony trials are held here. If you want a heavy dose of reality, this is the place to go. It can be grim. Adjacent is the Cook County Jail.

Dirksen Federal Building
219 S. Dearborn
The Dirksen Building and the adjacent Kluczynski Building together make up Chicago's Federal Center. Federal cases are held in the Dirksen Building. Usually there is a newsworthy trial going on somewhere in the building. Federal agencies are housed in both the Dirksen and Kluczynski buildings.

Richard J. Daley Civic Center
Clark and Randolph Streets
State civil cases are heard here. Leave your knives and guns at home or risk activating lobby metal detectors.

State of Illinois Center
100 W. Randolph
The Helmut Jahn atrium is an amusing place to visit. Perhaps the first state building to combine a shopping mall with offices for state agencies.

Traffic Court Building
321 N. LaSalle
If you get a traffic ticket in Chicago and want to contest it, this is where you go. Always crowded with lost people trying to find their courtrooms and overeager attorneys looking for clients.

BAR ASSOCIATIONS

Most of these organizations have a referral system and can assist you in finding an attorney.

Chicago Bar Association
321 S. Plymouth, Chicago, 60604   554-2000
554-2001 (lawyer referral service)
Most lawyers in Chicago belong to this association. They have an extensive referral system—$20 for an initial evaluation; after that, the fee is set by the attorney. The attorneys they refer you to have been prescreened by a panel to determine their qualifications in particular areas of the law.

Chicago Council of Lawyers
220 S. State, #800, Chicago, 60604   427-0710
The second largest and most activist of the major bar associations in Chicago. Offers the most critical recommendations of judges up for the election. Does not refer lawyers.

Decalogue Society of Lawyers
179 W. Washington, Chicago, 60602   263-6493
Bar association of Jewish attorneys. The largest ethnic bar association in the country.

National Lawyers Guild
Contact Ora Schub (chapter president)   226-5900
The Legal Left. Members have worked in the antiwar, antiracism, pro-choice, lesbian-gay rights, and disabled rights movements.

Women's Bar Association of Illinois
309 W. Washington, #900, Chicago, 60606 541-0048
Referral system available to general public but refers only to female attorneys. Initial 30-minute consultation costs $25.

CIVIL RIGHTS ORGANIZATIONS

American Civil Liberties Union (ACLU)
20 E. Jackson, #1600, Chicago, 60604 427-7330
This organization chooses its cases carefully and generally limits itself to cases involving important issues of civil liberties and constitutional rights.

Chicago Lawyers Committee for Civil Rights under the Law
185 N. Wabash, Chicago, 60601 630-9744
Founded in 1969 as a cooperative. Five full-time staff attorneys and volunteers from 42 top Chicago law firms provide free legal services in civil rights. It is less interested in constitutional law principles and more interested in representing the poor, minorities, and community groups.

Equal Employment Opportunity Commission (EEOC)
536 S. Clark, Chicago, 60605 353-2713
Federal agency that polices job discrimination.

Illinois Department of Human Rights
100 W. Randolph, Chicago, 60610 814-6200
This state agency is the starting point for discrimination claims.

CONSUMER PROTECTION AGENCIES

Attorney General of Illinois, Consumer Fraud Division
100 W. Randolph 814-3580

City of Chicago, Consumer Protection Division
121 N. LaSalle (City Hall) 744-8656

OTHER LEGAL ORGANIZATIONS

Attorney Registration and Disciplinary Commission (ARDC)
203 N. Wabash, #1900, Chicago, 60601-2474 346-0690 or 1-800-826-8625
If you want to complain about an attorney's services or conduct, this is the place to contact.

Business and Professional People for the Public Interest
17 E. Monroe, #212, Chicago, 60603 641-5570
Has sponsored environmental lawsuits and challenged lax utility regulation. Works on major issues; usually does not take individual cases.

Lawyers Committee for Better Housing
1263 W. Loyola, Chicago, 60626 274-1111
Does exactly what its name says. (See also the "Housing Law" section later.)

Lawyers for the Creative Arts
213 W. Institute, #411, Chicago, 60610 944-2787
Legal referrals for low-income artists and not-for-profit artistic organizations.

Leadership Council for Metropolitan Open Communities
401 S. State, #860, Chicago, 60605   341-1470;
1-800-659-OPEN for housing discrimination complaints;
Legal Action Program, 341-1531; Fair Housing Center, 450-0070
Works toward eliminating racial discrimination and housing segregation in
Chicago and its suburbs.

FREE LEGAL HELP

Chicago Volunteer Legal Services Foundation
205 W. Randolph, #510, Chicago, 60606   332-1624
Free legal aid by volunteer lawyers, many from the most blue-blooded law
firms in the city. Maintains offices throughout the city, but most are open
limited hours, usually some nights and weekends. Call the central office for a
referral and to make appointments.

Cook County Legal Assistance Foundation
Civil legal aid in the suburbs.
828 Davis, Evanston, 60201   (708) 475-3703
1146 Westgate, Oak Park, 60302   (708) 524-2600
15325 Page, Harvey, 60426   (708) 339-5550
Civil legal aid in the suburbs.

Illinois Guardianship and Advocacy Commission
527 S. Wells, #300, Chicago, 60607   793-5908
A state agency that protects the rights of the disabled. Helps those with
mental, physical, and emotional disabilities.

Chicago Regional Office
1735 W. Taylor   996-1650

Legal Aid Bureau
14 E. Jackson, Chicago, 60604   922-5625
Privately funded legal aid for needy people. Civil cases only.

Legal Assistance Foundation of Chicago
343 S. Dearborn, Chicago, 60604   341-1070
Free legal services in civil law matters to individuals and not-for-profit organizations unable to afford legal counsel. Strict eligibility requirements. As
of this writing a single person cannot earn more than $8,275 per year. The
downtown office offers a variety of projects, including the **Divorce and
Family Law Project** (341-1046), legal assistance for migrant workers
provided by a staff fluent in Spanish (341-9180), and help for the disabled,
mentally ill, and homeless.

This foundation also conducts the **Women's Law Project**, which has a
guide to free and low-cost legal services for women in the Chicago area
(entitled *Yes, She Can Afford a Lawyer*) as well as *A Handbook for Battered
Women*.

Neighborhood offices:

18th Street Office
1661 S. Blue Island   421-1900

Englewood Office
852 W. 63rd   651-3100

Mid-South Office
4655 S. Michigan   538-0733

Northwest Office
1212 N. Ashland   489-6800

Uptown Office
4753 N. Broadway   769-1015

Westside Office
911 S. Kedzie   638-2343

Legal Clinic for the Disabled
448 E. Ontario, 6th floor, Chicago, 60611   908-4463
Free civil legal services to low-income, disabled Cook County residents. Offers referrals to area attorneys doing pro bono work for the disabled. You must make an appointment.

Pro Bono Advocates
165 N. Canal, #1020, Chicago, 60606   906-8010
Pro Bono Advocates provides free legal assistance to women victims of domestic violence. Occasionally they will handle women's sexual harassment and employment discrimination cases. Their staff is composed of lawyers and volunteers (for volunteer information, call 906-8013).

Public Defender of Cook County
200 W. Adams, Chicago, 60606   609-2040
Free criminal defense for indigent people. Judges appoint public defenders for those charged with a crime who cannot afford a private attorney. Public defenders range from idealistic young law school graduates to embittered hacks. Some are excellent lawyers; others couldn't get hired anywhere else and are just marking time. Public defenders are assigned to various courtrooms throughout the city and suburbs; most are overworked. The quality of the office has improved markedly in recent years. There is a concerted effort under the new chief public defender, an African-American woman, to hire more minorities. Call to get the location of the office nearest you.

Neighborhood offices:

Public Defender
13th Street and Michigan Avenue   341-2730

Criminal Court
26th Street and California Avenue   890-3217

Juvenile Division
2240 W. Ogden   738-4630

Juvenile Court
1100 S. Hamilton   738-7047

Additional Projects

Crime Victims' Assistance Project
911 S. Kedzie, Chicago, 60612   638-4111

Legal Center for Immigrants
1661 S. Blue Island, Chicago, 60608   226-0173

State's Attorney's Child Support Enforcement Unit
32 W. Randolph, Chicago, 60601   580-3257
Unit will represent free of charge any parent seeking to have a father or mother declared as such and will seek to institute child support payments. There is no indigency requirement.

Supplementary Security Income Advocacy Project
407 S. Dearborn, #350, Chicago, 60605   427-5200

Mediation

Center for Conflict Resolution
28 E. Jackson, #1700, Chicago, 60604   939-7383
Provides mediation services as an alternative to going to court, at no charge. Mediators are volunteers who come from all walks of life and are trained by the Center. Faster and cheaper than going to court, and an ideal way to solve minor problems.

LAW SCHOOL LEGAL CLINICS

Legal clinics are staffed by second- and third-year law students under the supervision of faculty members. With the exception of Chicago-Kent, these clinics provide services only in certain areas of the law and serve only those with financial need. The Chicago-Kent clinic has no restrictions on who may use its services and operates like a full-service law firm handling all sorts of legal problems. Its fees are generally lower than what private schools charge.

DePaul University Law Clinic
23 E. Jackson, #950, Chicago, 60604   362-8294
Civil cases only. Specializes in family law (divorce, child support), personal bankruptcy (Chapter 7), landlord-tenant, and social security disability.

IIT–Chicago Kent College of Law
Law Offices
565 W. Adams, #600, Chicago, 60661   906-5050
Fee is determined by a sliding scale.

Loyola University Law Clinic
721 N. LaSalle, 5th floor, Chicago, 60610   266-0573
Specializes in four areas: Social Security (especially disability), landlord-tenant, family law, and general consumer law (fraud).

Northwestern University School of Law
Legal Assistance Clinic
357 E. Chicago, Chicago, 60611   503-8574
Handles landlord-tenant, family law, unemployment compensation, special education, and juvenile delinquency cases.

University of Chicago Law School
Mandel Legal Aid Clinic
6020 S. University, Chicago, 60637   702-9611
Affiliated with the Legal Aid Bureau.

HOUSING LAW

Tenants' Rights Ordinance

The Chicago Tenants' Rights Ordinance, officially known as "Residential Landlord and Tenant Ordinance," was first enacted in 1986 after years of struggle by tenants and housing organizations. The ordinance was amended in 1991 and is now considered one of the strongest and most comprehensive tenant's rights organizations in the country. The ordinance applies to tenants who live in all rental units with written or oral leases, except owner-occupied buildings containing six units or less. A summary of the ordinance must be attached to all leases.

The ordinance establishes a balance between the rights of tenants and landlords and defines in detail the obligations each has toward the other. Most importantly, it sets out specific actions that a tenant may take if the landlord does not properly maintain the property in compliance with the rental agreement and the provisions of the Chicago Building Code. If a necessary repair is not made, the tenant has several options:

- If the noncompliance by the landlord renders the "premises not reasonably fit and habitable," the tenant can request in writing that the landlord make repairs in 14 days or can terminate the lease.

- The tenant can request in writing that the landlord make repairs in 14 days, or the tenant can reduce his or her rent by an amount that reasonably reflects the reduced value of the unit.

- The tenant can request in writing that the landlord make repairs in 14 days, or the tenant may have the repairs made and deduct up to $500 or half the rent, whichever is more. The repairs must be "done in a workmanlike manner and in compliance with existing law and building regulations." The tenant must supply the landlord with a receipt for the repairs and deduct no more from the rent than the cost of repairs.

- The tenant can file suit against the landlord to recover damages or obtain injunctive relief (an order requiring the landlord to make repairs).

- The tenant may *not* exercise any of the above remedies if damage is the fault of the tenant, tenant's family, or guests.

The ordinance also addresses other areas such as tenant's responsibilities, landlord responsibilities, loss of essential service (gas, electricity, water, heat, hot water, plumbing), security deposits (on which interest must be paid), subleases, lockouts, and eviction. You can pick up a summary of the ordinance at the **Chicago Department of Housing** (318 S. Michigan, 747-2755) or buy a copy from the **Office of the City Clerk** (City Hall, Room 107, 121 N. LaSalle, Chicago, 60602, 744-4000). A copy is also available at the **Municipal Reference Library** in Room 1002 of City Hall.

Landlord Responsibilities

Landlords are responsible for supplying adequate heat from September 15 to June 1, hot water, ventilation, plumbing, security (doors that lock), extermination of pests, general maintenance, and a number of other services. To obtain a complete listing of landlord responsibilities, get a copy of the *Tenant-Landlord Handbook* from the Legal Assistance Foundation (341-1070) for $9.95. If these responsibilities are not being met, you should first call the owner, janitor, or management company. If nothing happens in a reasonable amount of time, send your landlord notice that you will start reducing your rent, or exercise one of the other options available to you under the Tenants' Rights Ordinance (see description above). At the same time, contact your local tenant union, community organization, or one of the legal or other resources listed in this chapter.

If matters are really serious, you can call to request that a city building inspector come out and inspect the problem. Call the 24-hour number for the **Mayor's Office of Inquiry and Information** at 744-5000. Or you can sue your landlord in *pro se* court. The **Chicago Urban League** (285-5800) publishes an excellent free handbook for tenants and community groups on how to make your way through housing court called the "Housing Court Handbook." An almost encyclopedic source of information about housing in Chicago is *Chicago's Tenants' Handbook* by Ed Sacks.

Tenants' Organizations

Chicago is unique for the number of tenants' organizations it has. Tenants' organizations organize tenants (as you might have guessed), give advice to tenants with problems, work alongside lawyers they know and trust to help resolve problems, and will often accompany tenants to court. If you don't know if your area has a tenants' organization, call the **Metropolitan Tenants Organization** (549-1631) and ask them for advice and referrals. Some of the larger tenants' and community organizations are listed below.

Action Coalition of Englewood
6001 S. Justine, Chicago, 60644   287-4570

Illinois Tenants Union
4616 N. Drake, Chicago, 60625   478-1133
A nonprofit corporation that can help tenants in Chicago, Evanston, and Mount Prospect break leases, get rent reductions, handle eviction disputes, and get security deposits returned. There's a low fee for an initial office consultation; and if your case looks sure to win in court, a lawyer will be provided free.

Kenwood/Oakland Community Organization (KOCO)
1236-38 E. 46th, Chicago, 60653   548-7500

Lakeview Tenants Organization
3212 N. Broadway, Chicago, 60657   549-1631
Housing hot line, 549-1986, Monday, Tuesday, and Thursday 6 P.M.–8 P.M.

Metropolitan Tenants Organization
3212 N. Broadway, Chicago, 60657 549-1631
A coalition of tenants' organizations. They give advice over the phone, make referrals, work on Housing Court reform issues, and handle complaints from those with children who face discrimination from landlords. They also conduct workshops for local groups about the tenants' rights ordinance.

North River Commission
4745 N. Kedzie, Chicago, 60625 478-0202

Rogers Park Community Action Network
1545 W. Morse, Chicago, 60626 973-7888
Housing hot line at above telephone number Monday–Thursday, 6 P.M.–8 P.M.; Friday, 12 P.M.–2 P.M.

South Austin Coalition Community Council
5112 W. Washington, Chicago, 60644 287-4570

South Shore Tenants Organization
2555 E. 73rd, Chicago, 60649 734-7507

Southwest Community Congress
2832 W. 63rd, Chicago, 60629 436-6150

Woodlawn East Community and Neighbors (WECAN)
1541 E. 65th, Chicago, 60637 288-3000

Other Groups That Help

Chicago Council of Lawyers
220 S. State, #800, Chicago, 60604 427-0710
A public interest bar association. A standard lease fair to both landlords and tenants is free. Just call.

Chicago Department of Housing
318 S. Michigan, Chicago, 60604 747-2755

Lawyer's Committee for Better Housing
1263 W. Loyola, Chicago, 60626 274-1111
Primarily serves the Rogers Park, Edgewater, and Uptown communities. Provides legal advice to both tenants and landlords on building conditions. They don't represent people in court, but they will offer advice on landlord-tenant problems and intervene to a degree. Especially interested in discrimination against families. Does not focus on defense against eviction.

Legal Assistance Foundation
343 S. Dearborn, Chicago, 60604 341-1070
Free legal help for low-income residents, including assistance with tenant-landlord problems. Distributes the *Tenant-Landlord Handbook* ($9.95 by mail). See listings earlier in this chapter for addresses of neighborhood locations.

Mayor's Office of Inquiry and Information
24-hour number, 744-5000
The place to call when you want to request an inspection from a city housing inspector. Can also give you other information and put you in touch with the right parts of the city bureaucracy. To find out who your alderman is, and

how to contact him or her, call 269-7900. Since aldermen depend on keeping their constituents happy for their political survival, they can often be quite helpful. Also, look in the blue pages in the white-pages phone book under City of Chicago, Consumer Services, Streets and Sanitation, and the Health Department for more city numbers to call for help.

Neighborhood Housing Services of Chicago, Inc.
747 N. May, Chicago, 60622   738-2227
Focuses on helping lower-income people buy and maintain homes. Has a lease-to-purchase program that helps lower-income people go from renting to owning. Buys and resells vacant and foreclosed houses. Helps buyers get loans and homeowners obtain home improvement loans. Has nine neighborhood offices; call for locations.

—Bob Skolnik

RELIGION

In the kaleidoscope that is Chicago, one vivid pattern that continues to emerge strongly is the city's rich religious culture. The dozens of ethnic groups here have brought a dizzying array of religious faiths with them. Whether you're a Spanish-speaking Mormon, a Catholic from Vietnam, or simply a curious onlooker, you can find the church that's right for you among the 4,000 congregations in Chicago. The denominational offices listed later can help you pinpoint the church best suited to your spiritual, cultural, and altruistic needs.

SELECTING A CHURCH

Your first step in choosing a church should be to promise yourself you'll visit at least 10 different churches before making a final decision. Congregations usually are extremely friendly toward visitors, and you don't want this warm welcome alone to influence you. Next, identify what's important to you: Ministry to the poor? Overseas missions? Development of your own spirituality? Authority of the Scriptures? Style of worship, including music? A look at a church's budget and governmental structure can help you learn where its priorities lay. Keep in mind, too, that research shows that most people focus on the pastor when they first visit a church, but it's the friendships they develop or not after joining that determine whether they will remain as members. Many churches have small-group kinship meetings or Bible studies to facilitate making friends. Finally, don't let your past experiences with a particular denomination or church sway your opinion. Especially in a city as diverse as Chicago, there is bound to be a congregation you'll like.

A CHURCH SAMPLER

Most churches operate community outreach and social service programs in addition to meeting their community's religious needs. Below are listed only a few local churches, with brief descriptions of some of their services and, in some cases, other noteworthy qualities. This small sampling is by no means either an endorsement of any particular faith or church or a full depiction of the huge variety of spiritual outlets available to the people of Chicago. If you're interested in historical or architectural details of a particular church, try calling Neil Vogel of **Inspired Partnerships** (294-0077), which works to preserve area churches, or Vince Michael of the **Landmarks Preservation Council** (922-1742), which publishes the booklet *Spires in the Streets*.

Baptist

First Baptist Congregational Church
1613 W. Washington   243-8047
Services: Sunday, 11 A.M.
Prayer Services: Weekdays, 6 A.M.; Monday, noon;
 Wednesday, noon and 7:30 P.M.; Friday, 5:30 A.M., noon; Sunday, 8 A.M.
With about 2,000 members, this church has the people power for six outstanding choirs, including the Inspirational Choir, which performs old
gospel; the Gospel Chorus, which sings contemporary gospel; and youth and
children's choirs as well. First Baptist conducts a Sunday school (9:15 A.M.)
and an additional service at the Henry Horner Homes housing project.

North Shore Baptist Church
5244 N. Lakewood   728-4200
Services:
English—Sunday, 11 A.M.; Wednesday, 7 P.M.
Japanese—Sunday, 11 A.M.
Spanish—Sunday, 12:30 P.M.; Latino Bible study: Wednesday, 7 P.M.
Famous for the gorgeous Jade Window in its chapel, North Shore Baptist is a
large American Baptist church with about 50 Latino and 25 Japanese mem-
bers in its congregation. They donate regularly to the food pantry at Care for
Real on Broadway Avenue.

Uptown Baptist Church
1011 W. Wilson   784-2922
Service: Sunday, 11 A.M.
This Southern Baptist church offers religious services in English, Spanish,
Vietnamese, Cambodian, Korean, and Russian. A Filipino congregation meets
at a different building. Monday nights it cooks a free meal for the homeless
and gives clothes away another day a week from its clothing room. It also
serves as a distributor of government surplus food once a month. The Program for Women in Crisis provides counseling to help women find a job, for
example, or go back to school. From October 1 to April 30, Uptown Baptist
also operates an overnight shelter for single homeless women.

Catholic

Holy Family Roman Catholic Church
1080 W. Roosevelt   243-7207
Services: Sunday, 8:30 A.M., 9:45 A.M. (with gospel choir); 11 A.M. (in Spanish)
The second oldest church in Chicago, having been built by Irish immigrants
in 1857 and completed in 1860, Holy Family illustrates better than most social
organizations the indomitable power of faith and perseverance. In 1985 the
Gothic church was closed because of water damage to the roof that was
causing plaster to fall. Now that it served only about 300 people,
predominantly African-Americans, rather than 20,000 as it once had, its Jesuit
owners proposed tearing down the church in 1988 and replacing it with a
smaller, more functional building. Parishioners and others protested, stressing Holy Family's historical significance (it's one of only five public buildings
to have survived the 1871 Chicago Fire) and its architectural beauty, with

vaulted ceilings, carvings, and 226-foot bell tower—Chicago's original "tall-est building." The Jesuits compromised by giving the church a December 31, 1990, deadline to raise $1 million toward a goal of $4 million for restoration costs. Under the Rev. George Lane's battle cry of "Say prayers and send money," the church had raised all but $65,000 on the Sunday before its deadline. Then 3,000 visitors toured the church and made donations, and Oprah Winfrey pitched in $50,000 specifically to renovate the community center, which has a food pantry, thrift store, child care, and other services. Donations from around the country ranged from pennies wrapped in tin foil to $15,000 checks. When counted on January 1, 1991, Father Lane happily announced that the church had raised about $2.1 million. Work began imme-diately to replace the slate roof and copper gutters, tuckpoint the whole building, and repair the bell tower's chimes and clock. Once the exterior restoration is complete, the focus will shift to renovating the interior. "It will be a real historical, cultural, and religious centerpiece," said Father Lane. He added that the goal was met with "people, prayers, and publicity" and hopes contributions will continue to be made.

Holy Name Cathedral
735 N. State   787-8040
Services: Sunday, 7, 8:15, 9:30, 11 A.M., 12:30 and 5:15 P.M., plus at
10:15 A.M. at North Pier, mezzanine level; Saturday, 5:15 and 7:30 P.M.;
plus weekdays, 6, 7, 8 A.M., 12:10 and 5:15 P.M.
Holy Name is the cathedral for the Chicago archdiocese and the site for much glorious music, including world-famous guest organists. The church has five choirs and several other ministry groups, and it also provides televised service for shut-ins on TV channel 66, Sunday at 8 A.M.

Old St. Patrick's Church
718 W. Adams   782-6171
Services: Sunday, 7, 8:30, 9:45, 11:15 A.M. and 5 P.M.; Saturday, 12:10P.M.;
weekdays, 7 and 8 A.M., 12:10 P.M.
Built in 1856, Old St. Patrick's is the oldest church building in Chicago and one of only a few structures to have survived the 1871 Chicago Fire. As distinguished as its brick and limestone exterior are the church's lovely stained glass windows. They were designed, made, and installed by famous Chicago artist Thomas O'Shaughnessy, the last person allowed to sketch from the eighth-century Irish Book of Kells. The windows' design reflects this rich Celtic heritage, and they were made from the old technique of melting minerals in the glass itself for a spectacular effect.

Old St. Patrick's mismatched steeples—one Romanesque, the other East-ern—symbolize the meeting of the East and West and inspired the church's title as "Crossroads Center for Faith and Work." "We minister to the workplace because we're near the Loop," explained Director of Communica-tions Ellen Placey. The church places strong emphasis on adult spirituality and good liturgy, and this combination has increased its membership from four in 1983 to 1,400 today, plus another 9,000 affiliate members. Its com-munity outreach programs include tutoring kids in housing projects and adults in literacy, playing sports with Latino youths, and counseling victims of political oppression. It also hosts the largest block party in the world the last weekend in July; in 1991 more than 20,000 people showed up. Old St. Patrick's opened the first school in the archdiocese in 20 years in 1989, from preschool through second grade with plans to open a grade a year. "It's a socioeconomically and culturally diverse school," Placey said, "with 50 percent white, 30 percent black, and 20 percent Hispanic. Thirty percent of the students are on scholarship, so they come from all economic backgrounds."

Jewish Reformed

Emanuel Congregation
5959 N. Sheridan   561-5173
Services: Friday, 8 P.M.; Saturday, 11 A.M.
A Jewish Reformed Congregation of 750 members located on the North Side, Emanuel has a library and several musical and educational programs. There is a scholars-in-residence program held over three-day weekends, the Melton Minischool meets Monday evenings to discuss subjects relevant to Jewish living, and traditional Jewish religious classes are offered also. The congregation's Young Parents Association engages in several activities.

Methodist

Chicago Temple—First United Methodist Church
77 W. Washington   236-4548
Services: Sunday, 8:30 and 11 A.M.; Wednesday, 12:10 P.M.; Saturday, 5 P.M.
Noted by *Chicago* magazine as a place to visit and by the *Guinness Book of World Records* as the tallest church in the world, Chicago Temple is famous for its spectacular Sky Chapel. Donated by the Walgreen family, the recently refurbished chapel is 568 feet from the ground and holds about 60 people. Its circular glass viewing area and 16 stained glass windows make it a popular choice for weddings. Free tours are given every day at 2 P.M. plus Sunday after worship. The church also houses the corporate headquarters for the Northern Illinois Association of the United Methodist Church.

Presbyterian

Fourth Presbyterian Church
126 E. Chestnut   787-4570
Services: Sunday, 8:30 and 11 A.M., 6 P.M.
This 5,200-member church is located between Rush Street and the Water Tower. It splits its outreach services into three main centers: (1) The Lorene Replogle Counseling Center is in itself a full-service counseling center; (2) the Center for Older Adults is for people aged 65 and older who may attend, for instance, workshops on medical consulting and tax tips; and (3) the Social Service Center operates through the church and provides clothes, food, even bus tokens for homeless people, plus childcare. Fourth Presbyterian offers its members several active groups for singles and young couples.

Second Presbyterian Church
1936 S. Michigan   225-4951
Service: Sunday, 11 A.M.
Founded in 1842, Second Presbyterian was rebuilt in 1874 in the 15th-century English Gothic style after the Chicago Fire destroyed the original neo-Gothic structure. Now it ranks as a city, state, and national landmark, regarded as "the crown jewel of the Arts and Crafts movement in Chicago," with beautiful murals, Tiffany stained glass windows, and a hand-carved limestone baptismal font from 19th-century Italy. Tours may be arranged by contacting Lois Chubb at 922-4533.

United Church of Christ

St. Luke's (San Lucas) United Church of Christ
2914 W. North   227-5747
Service (bilingual): Sunday, 11 A.M.
This predominantly Puerto Rican congregation has a variety of community programs. As a member of the Anti-Hunger Network it runs a food pantry and serves hot meals. It holds workshops in Humboldt Park for the Infant Mortality Project, offering nutritional counseling as well as milk and cereal under dire circumstances to young mothers on public aid. As part of its Youth Service Project, St. Luke's sponsors the groups Parents Too Soon and Teens Adapting to Parenting. It will also help people find housing and pay their gas and electric bills in emergencies.

St. Pauls United Church of Christ
2334 N. Orchard   348-3829
Services: Sunday, 11 A.M.; in German, first Sunday of each month, 9 A.M.
In honor of its founding by German immigrants, St. Pauls has retained its name's authentic German spelling. It engages in outreach programs beyond its location just east of Children's Memorial Hospital. The church does a lot of hands-on work such as building a school for a Native American community in North Dakota and houses in Chicago neighborhoods as part of the Habitat for Humanity program. Rotating with Lincoln Park Presbyterian Church and St. Clement's Catholic Church, St. Pauls helps run the Lincoln Park Community Shelter November 1–March 31 by providing breakfast, dinner, and overnight accommodations.

Its congregation has an excellent musical program, with several members being professional musicians and vocalists with the Chicago Symphony Chorus. Children and adults also put on the Bible Story Theatre about once a year.

Trinity United Church of Christ
532 W. 95th   962-5650
Services: Sunday, 8 and 11 A.M., 6 P.M.
"Unashamedly black, unapologetically Christian" is how a Trinity United representative described her church. This is an afrocentric congregation that continually highlights the presence of blacks in the Bible. With about 4,800 members, it is also one of the biggest, fastest-growing churches in the country. The Winter 1992 issue of *Spirit Matters* adds that this is a "congregation amid double-digit unemployment, rich and poor, college-educated and

illiterate, professionals and welfare mothers." As diverse as Trinity United's membership is its variety of musical, social, and educational programs. In addition to childcare, Head Start, and food basket services, the church has a special ministry for men and boys called Isuthu that instructs in areas of African-American history.

University Church (Church of Christ/Disciples of Christ)
5655 S. University 363-8142
Service: Sunday, 10 A.M.

"This is an open and affirmatory congregation," according to Karen Fields, church secretary. The 150 or so members include a "core of regulars" plus students and faculty of the nearby University of Chicago for a great mix. Worship features a range of music plus the 10–12 members of a dance group that performs in various styles to correspond to different religious seasons. The church has existed since 1894, but it became particularly well known via the old Blue Gargoyle coffeehouse in the sixties. That local hangout metamorphosed into the Youth Services Center, which today offers counseling, job training, a homework club, and an "alternative high school" for people 16–21 "who should be in school but aren't, for whatever reason," Fields said. The church has literacy and GED programs for adults, too, and its United Campus Ministry has informal dinners Sunday at 5:30 P.M. for fellowship and ecumenical meetings with other groups and speakers. University Church is a nuclear weapon–free zone, and its Sanctuary Committee is currently sponsoring a refugee family from Guatemala. Fields added that the church operates a network of volunteers and can direct people to a group or agency in Chicago that interests them.

Wellington Avenue United Church of Christ
615 W. Wellington 935-0642
Service: Sunday, 11 A.M. (10 A.M. in summer)

Wellington Avenue is another sanctuary congregation and nuclear weapon–free zone. It is active with about 25 groups covering many social causes, including women's shelters, aid to immigrants, and teen and youth homeless. Its Outreach Committee deals with international issues like the political and cultural scenes in the Middle East, Haiti, and Central America. The church is equally proud of its musical program; the pastor's wife sings with the Chicago Symphony Chorus, and other members perform with the folk-singing group Voices.

Other

Baha'i House of Worship
Sheridan Road at Linden Avenue, Wilmette 256-4400
Services: Daily, 12:15 P.M.

Listed on the National Register of Historic Places, the Baha'i House of Worship is the only such temple in North America of the seven in the world. It is also the oldest one in existence now; the Baha'i temple in Ashkabad, Turkmenia (in the former U.S.S.R.), was demolished after being damaged in an earthquake. Construction using ground quartz and portland cement was started in Wilmette in 1912 and completed in 1953. The temple's lovely design features a lacy-looking dome and nine sides—nine symbolizing the unity of religions and also the numerical equivalent to the Persian and Arabic word

from which is derived the name of the religion's 19th-century founder,

Now the second most widely spread faith in the world, after

Christianity, Baha'i teaches that humanity is one, men and women are equal,

and a universal language should be created or adopted as an auxiliary to

other languages for truly universal communication. Services are very simple,

with no sermons, but do feature readings from all world religions and an a

cappella choir on Sunday. All Baha'i temples are considered by its members

as a "gift to humanity, not to exclude anyone," and people are welcome to

visit any time. Tours can be arranged, and the Visitors Center opens at 10 A.M.

and closes at 5 P.M. in fall and winter, 10 P.M. in spring and summer.

57th Street Friends Meeting House

5615 S. Woodlawn   288-3066

Service: Sunday, 10:30 A.M. (hymn singing at 10 A.M.)

This Quaker group of about 50 members has met at 57th Street since 1950. It

has a Wednesday evening study group, with dinner at 6:30, worship at 7:30,

and reading of assorted religious works—Scripture, Quaker commentary,

Catholic writer Dorothy Day, and so forth—at 8 P.M. The 57th Street Meeting

House also is the site for the Quaker House Residential Community, current-

ly the home for 11 adults and two infants. The group looks for new residents

from time to time, people interested in Quakerism but not necessarily ex-

pected to attend services. Residents are usually in transition—that is, recently

graduated, new to Chicago, or between jobs. They can live at the Community

for up to three years.

First Unitarian Church

5650 S. Woodlawn   324-4100

Service: Sunday, 10 A.M.

First Unitarian sponsors several community activities, including community

meetings for Fifth Ward Alderman Larry Bloom, Emotions Anonymous, the

Hyde Park Academy Preschool, Prologue Theater rehearsals, and classes of

the Chicago School of Ballet. Its Social Justice Committee organizes social

events at Cabrini Green, raises money for charities with a walk-a-thon and

flea markets, and gives seminars on topics such as aging and environmental

awareness (a local environmental task force has designated First Unitarian as

a "model church"). The church's food pantry specializes in collecting and

distributing peanut butter, and its members serve a soup-and-salad lunch

four days a week at another facility.

Good Shepherd Parish Metropolitan Community Church

615 W. Wellington   472-8708

Service: Sunday, 7 P.M.

The United Fellowship of Metropolitan Community Churches was created in

1968 by the Rev. Troy Perry in California when his fundamentalist congrega-

tion learned that he was gay and asked him to leave. Today, Good Shepherd

Parish, along with Wellington Avenue United Church of Christ (housed in the

same building), offers affirmatory outreach to the gay and lesbian com-

munity. The church holds an additional Sunday service at 11 A.M. at the

Illinois Masonic Hospital, where some of its 100 members also pay social

visits (pastoral visits on request) to patients in the AIDS ward. The church's phone number serves as a 24-hour information line for other area MCC churches and referrals for counseling.

LaSalle Street Church
1136 N. LaSalle   787-3756
Services: Sunday, 9:15 and 11 A.M.
LaSalle Street Church boasts such lovely architecture and interior design, dating from the 1880s, that even many nonmembers choose it for their wedding services. WTTW-TV called its choir one of the four best in the Chicago area, and worship services feature a great variety of music—classical, gospel, rock, and so on. LaSalle Street engages in many social services, most of which focus on Cabrini Green residents. Its CYCLE program, for example, employs 80 people and a $1.6 million budget (funded by individual donors, United Way, and community groups) to tutor adults and youths. The church also offers summer camps, a legal aid clinic, a Young Life Program, and sliding-scale counseling services.

To overcome the fact that 80 percent of international students never enter an American home, LaSalle Street works with city colleges to befriend foreign students via social visits or holiday meals.

DENOMINATIONAL OFFICES

African Methodist Episcopal Zion Church
6930 S. Cottage Grove   493-8624

American Baptist Churches of Metro Chicago
28 E. Jackson, #210   341-1266

American Friends Service Committee (Quakers)
59 E. Van Buren   427-2533

American Jewish Congress
22 W. Monroe, #1900   332-7355

Baha'i Chicago Center
1233 Central, Evanston   (708) 869-9039

Charismatic Renewal Office (Roman Catholic archdiocese)
12905 Division, Blue Island   (708) 371-2727

Chicago Board of Rabbis
(Conservative, Reformed, Traditional, and Reconstructionist)
1 S. Franklin   444-2896

Chicago Rabbinical Council
(Orthodox)
3525 W. Peterson   588-1600

Chicago Disciples Union (Disciples of Christ)
634 N. Austin, Oak Park   (708) 383-3113

Christian Science Church
72 W. Adams   782-8181

Church of the Brethren
1451 Dundee, Elgin   (708) 742-5100

Church of Jesus Christ of Latter Day Saints (Mormons)
1319 Butterfield, Downers Grove   (708) 969-2145

Episcopal Diocese of Chicago
65 E. Huron   787-6410

Evangelical Covenant Church
5101 N. Francisco   784-3000

Evangelical Free Church
5249 N. Ashland   561-7544

Evangelical Lutheran Church in America
8765 W. Higgins   380-2700

Greek Orthodox Church
40 E. Burton   337-4130

Hindu Temple of Greater Chicago
12S701 Lemont, Lemont   (708) 972-0300

Islamic Center of Chicago
4380 N. Elston   725-9047

Lutheran Church—Missouri Synod
2301 S. Wolf, Hillside   (708) 449-3020

Midwest Buddhist Temple
435 W. Menomonee   943-7801

Muslim Community Center
24 N. Pulaski   533-9558

Northern Illinois Conference of the United Methodist Church
77 W. Washington, #1806   346-8752

Presbyterian Church, U.S.A.
100 S. Morgan   243-8300

Roman Catholic Church
155 E. Superior   751-8200

Southern Baptist Convention
329 Madison, Oak Park   (708) 848-9120

Unitarian Universalist Association
114 S. Marion, Oak Park   (708) 383-4344

United Church of Christ
332 S. Michigan   939-5918

Universal Fellowship of Metropolitan Community Churches
615 W. Wellington   472-8708

Vineyard Christian Fellowship
2145 N. Maplewood   276-7286

Vivekananda Vendata Society
5423 S. Hyde Park   363-0027

Zen Buddhist Temple
608 Dempster, Evanston   (708) 869-0554

SPECIAL MINISTRIES

Agape House
University of Illinois at Chicago
1046 W. Polk, Chicago, 60607   666-2676
Agape is an interdenominational Protestant group with two full-time campus
ministers and another working with area churches in their relationships with
students. It likes to think of itself as a "house of hospitality" for a wide array
of social, religious, and ethnic groups. Currently it hosts two Korean student
groups, a discussion group focused on issues of racism, and meetings of
Alcoholics Anonymous. Agape participates in Habitat for Humanity about
twice a month by building or rehabilitating houses in the area, and a recent
student outing was a trip to the National Civil Rights Museum in Memphis,
site of Dr. Martin Luther King's assassination. In addition, the center offers
problem-solving, crisis, and vocational counseling, and occasionally it makes
available bare-bones accommodations (i.e., no beds, no showers) for out-of-
town students.

Chicago Catholic Women
5249 N. Kenmore, Chicago, 60640   561-5668
Chicago Catholic Women's goal is to "work toward structural change within
church and society in order to promote the full giftedness and personhood of
women and a world of justice for all." They do this by providing a number of
programs, including liturgical, educational, advocacy and solidarity, networking, and direct services. The center on Kenmore Avenue is open to
people of all faiths. Its members guarantee you will meet some great people,
use your volunteer time well, and assist people who need your help.

Chicago Christian Industrial League
123 S. Green, Chicago, 60607   421-0588
Begun 83 years ago by a Scottish minister, CCIL is a nondenominational
social service agency for the homeless, occupying nine buildings on the
corner of Halsted Avenue and Monroe Street. It houses 250 people regularly,
with 170 more beds made available in winter, under three Transitional Living
Programs, one each for men, women, and families. According to Lisa
Gnidovic, communications director, participants "need to be sober and not
using any substances; otherwise, they just must have the will and be committed to getting back on their feet and restructuring their lives." She added
that CCIL is the first shelter in Chicago to cater to homeless families. "Forty
percent of the homeless are part of intact families," she said, "usually women
with kids. We'll house them, give them family counseling and job training."
There's also a daytime drop-in center for women, with medical assessments,
laundry facilities, and social activities available. Residents can partake in job
training, adult literacy, and meals at the soup kitchen. Men may move on to
CCIL's special low-cost housing option, in which a small rent covers a
"roomette" plus three daily meals. Attendance at the agency's 8 A.M. Wednes-

day service or Bible studies is by no means obligatory. "We find that most of our clients are people probably going through the worst time of their lives," Gnidovic said. "They look to a higher power, and they can define that themselves."

Community Renewal Society
332 S. Michigan, #500, Chicago, 60604   427-4830

Sponsored by the United Church of Christ, Community Renewal Society is a richly diverse group that likes to foster work between suburban and city people of varying ethnic backgrounds. Its musical programs reflect this variety; its children's and adult choirs perform classical, pop, and ethnic music all around Chicago. In 1991, for example, the Society performed "Porgy and Bess" at Orchestra Hall with the Chicago Sinfonietta. CRS offers technical assistance to community-based groups including churches and social agencies—everything from hands-on help to tips on how to write grant proposals or create boards. Its Paternal Involvement Program is geared for helping 18- to 35-year-old fathers get more involved with their kids, including retreats at the Pleasant Valley Outdoor Center. The farm there also serves as the site for a summer camp and environmental center. CRS publishes two journals of note: *Chicago Reporter*, a critically praised alternative, investigative journal, and *Catalyst*, a publication discussing school reform issues in layperson's terms.

Hillel Foundation of B'nai Brith
1 S. Franklin, Chicago 60606   346-6700

Hillel holds cultural, social, educational, and religious activities primarily for university students, faculty, and staff. Visiting professors are often guest speakers on issues pertaining to Israeli life. Its social projects run the gamut from food pantries to summer softball leagues. Friday night and Saturday religious services are also held. Call Hillel's downtown office (see above) for branches at campuses other than those listed here:

Loyola University
1132 W. Loyola   508-2193

Northwestern University
1935 Sherman, Evanston   (708) 328-0650

University of Chicago
5715 S. Woodlawn   752-1127

University of Illinois at Chicago
924 S. Morgan   829-1595

John Paul II Catholic Student Center
University of Illinois at Chicago
700 S. Morgan, Chicago, 60607   226-1880

Geared primarily for UIC students, this center holds religious services Monday through Friday at noon, plus at 5 P.M. Sunday at Notre Dame Church (1336 W. Harrison). Its other programs include communion services for patients at the University of Illinois Hospital, work at the local soup kitchen, personal skill-building summer camps in Colorado, Bible study, and a popular $2 lunch on Monday–Thursday open to everyone.

Limina
P.O. 4092, Oak Park, 60303-4092   (708) 386-8522
A nonprofit organization, Limina works to restore the feminine aspect of the divine to living awareness, particularly through a deeper connection to nature and the seasons, and to reconcile masculine and feminine realities in the life of the individual, culture, and our endangered planet. Limina offers participatory educational experiences in which women celebrate their life passages and affirm their unique creative power.

Night Ministry
835 W. Addison   935-3366
Night Ministry focuses on youth homeless, with pastoral and crisis counseling 24 hours a day, several youth shelters, and Mobile Health Outreach, which offers free health screening and medical testing for young people.

Women's American ORT   973-6243
Women's American ORT, an organization with over 1,000 chapters nationwide, has been in the vanguard of social and humanitarian action for 65 years, building schools and training students in Jewish communities around the world.

BOOKSTORES

Chicago is a haven for bibliophiles. Many of the large retail bookstores have departments devoted to religious materials, but here is a listing of bookstores that specialize in the field.

Chicago Baptist Institute Bookstore
5120 S. King   268-2253
Hours: Monday–Friday, 9 A.M.–5 P.M.; Saturday, 9 A.M.–3 P.M.
Carries books on all religions except Catholicism.

Chicago Hebrew Bookstore
2942 W. Devon   973-6636
Hours: Monday–Wednesday, 9 A.M.–6 P.M.; Thursday, 9 A.M.–7 P.M.;
Friday, 9 A.M.–2 P.M.; Sunday, 10 A.M.–4 P.M.
Has an entire line of Judaica, perhaps the largest selection of menorahs in Chicago.

Covenant Press
3200 W. Foster   478-4676
Hours: Monday–Friday, 9 A.M.–5 P.M.; Saturday, 9 A.M.–3 P.M.
Affiliated with the Swedish Covenant Church; also carries gifts and communion items.

Logos Book Store
101 N. Oak Park, Oak Park   (708) 848-6644
Hours: Monday and Thursday, 10 A.M.–8 P.M.; Tuesday, Wednesday, and Friday, 10 A.M.–6 P.M.; Saturday, 9:30 A.M.–5 P.M.
Books on psychology and sociology besides religion, plus gifts and greeting cards.

Moody Bible Institute Book Store
150 W. Chicago   329-4352
Hours: Monday, Tuesday, and Thursday, 8:45 A.M.–7 P.M.;
Wednesday, Friday, and Saturday, 9:45 A.M.–5 P.M.
Complete Christian bookstore plus clothes with the Institute logo, music, videos, and children's section.

Mustard Seed Christian Bookstore
1139 W. Sheridan   973-7055
Hours: Monday–Saturday, 9:30 A.M.–6:30 P.M.
Full Christian collection plus counseling and psychology books to serve the local college market.

Rosenblum's World of Judaica
2906 W. Devon   262-1700 or 1-800-626-6536
Hours: Monday–Wednesday, 9 A.M.–6 P.M.; Thursday, 9 A.M.–7 P.M.;
Friday, 9 A.M.–3 P.M.; Sunday, 10 A.M.–4 P.M.
The Midwest's oldest Jewish bookstore and "the largest selection of Jewish religious articles between New York and Los Angeles," according to its owner.

St. Paul Catholic Book and Media Center
172 N. Michigan   346-4228
Hours: Monday–Friday, 9:30 A.M.–5:30 P.M.; Saturday, 9:30 A.M.–5 P.M.
Catholic works available in every medium.

Seminary Cooperative Bookstore
5757 S. University   752-4381
Hours: Monday–Friday, 8:30 A.M.–9 P.M.; Saturday, 10 A.M.–6 P.M.;
Sunday, noon–6 P.M.
In a full-range inventory of a couple hundred thousand books, about 10 percent are religious titles. The store only rents space from one of the seminaries at the University of Chicago; if it doesn't have what you're looking for, one of the other nearby bookstores likely will.

SUGGESTED READING

Chicago Churches and Synagogues by George Lane and Algimantas Kezys. Richly illustrated book by a priest at Holy Family in Chicago detailing 125 historically and architecturally significant places of worship.

Essential Sacred Writings from Around the World by Mircea Eliade. Features all major non-Western religions, including Native American, Aborigine, and African oral accounts and excerpts from the Book of the Dead and the Quran.

Mere Christianity by C. S. Lewis. A classic, written for the non-Christian skeptic, that serves as an excellent introduction to major Christian denominations.

No Compromise by Melody Green. A biography of the author's husband that provides a good snapshot of the late-1960s counterculture and the Jesus People movement of that era.

To Be a Jew by Rabbi Hayim Halevy Donin. Comprehensive, practical information on Jewish philosophy and law. The same author has written *To Pray as a Jew* and *To Raise a Jewish Child.*

Zen and the Art of Motorcycle Maintenance: An Inquiry into Values by Robert M. Pirsig. This book is not about orthodox Zen Buddhism or motorcycles per se; it is, as the author says, a "culture-bearing book . . . that challenges value assumptions" and provides "an expansion of the meaning of 'success.'"

—*Laura E. Larson*

Real City Causes

THE ENVIROMENT/RECYCLING
VOLUNTEERING
ACTIVISM

THE ENVIRONMENT/RECYCLING

The quality of life enjoyed by Chicagoans continues to be threatened by pollution of our air and water, misuse of open lands, and the destruction of wetlands. In fact, less than 3⁄10 of 1 percent of the native Illinois landscape survives today. The implementation of environmental law at all levels of government will have a positive effect on Chicago during the next 10 years, but it is realistic to say that our natural resources will continue to be challenged well into the next century.

Environmental law is passed by the U.S. Congress, respective state legislatures, and local city councils, and it is enforced largely by the U.S. Environmental Protection Agency (U.S. EPA) and the Illinois EPA (IEPA). The jurisdiction of each agency is determined by the scope of the law (federal vs. state law) and resource designation (waters, lands, and air that cross interstate boundaries). Typically, the U.S. EPA sets regulations for a law, such as the Clean Air Act, that the state EPA must then implement. However, both agencies have implementation and enforcement power.

Chicago has persistent environmental threats. The amount of traffic in the city, and other factors, present an urban smog problem. Smog consists largely of ground-level ozone that is formed when nitric acid (from coal-burning sources) and hydrocarbons (from burning fossil fuels, mainly gasoline) combine in the presence of sunlight. At ground level, ozone is a respiratory irritant that is especially harmful to children, pregnant women, elderly citizens, and those who suffer from respiratory disease.

The implementation of the Clean Air Act Amendment of 1990 may have a dramatic effect on reducing ground-level ozone largely through its impact on vehicle emissions and the contents and type of gasoline used. A few provisions of the act that will make this possible are

- issuing tighter tailpipe emission standards,
- mandating the use of alternative fuels,
- improving the on-board pollution control devices for cars, and
- requiring a higher percentage of oxygen in gasoline.

A second area of concern for Chicago's air quality is air toxics. Not only are these hazardous to fish and wildlife, but they account for more than 50 percent of Lake Michigan's pollution as well. Such pollutants as polychlorinated biphenyls (PCPs), dioxins, furans, and heavy metals come from a variety of industrial sources and end up in Lake Michigan. Some main sources of these toxics are waste incinerators, chemical factories, coke ovens (used in the steel industry), electroplating processes, dry cleaners, and coal-burning utility plants. These substances affect fetal development and have a negative impact on the pulmonary, nervous, reproductive, and immune systems of the body. The Clean Air Act now lists more than 100 of these substances as being toxic and thus requiring emission controls. It also regulates a greater number of sources and has provisions for accidental release of the most poisonous of these chemicals.

428 REAL CITY CAUSES

Disposal of solid waste currently poses a major problem to Chicago officials and citizens. The majority of the nearly four million tons of trash annually thrown away by Chicagoans is currently disposed of in landfills that are rapidly filling. There is currently a moratorium on building any new landfills within the city of Chicago, and public opposition makes it increasingly difficult to find sites for new landfills. The public opposition is well founded given the potential health and pollution problems that result from landfills. Even using current technology, all landfills will eventually leak, and the leakage causes groundwater contamination.

Incineration has been considered as an alternative to landfills. Incinerators, however, do not eliminate the need for landfills. Twenty to 25 percent of the garbage burned ends up as ash that then needs to be disposed of. Incineration also presents environmental risks (by contributing to the air-toxics problem). Also the ash created through incineration may contain concentrated levels of toxic metals such as lead and cadmium. When landfilled the toxic ash threatens groundwater supplies.

In 1988 the Illinois legislature passed the Solid Waste Planning and Recycling Act, which requires the largest Illinois counties, including Cook County, to develop and implement plans for the management of waste over the next 20 years. The plans are required to include methods that will achieve the recycling of at least 25 percent of the waste. In response to this act, the City of Chicago passed a Solid Waste Management Plan for handling Chicago's trash. Unfortunately, in the plan presented, the city has shown that it intends to maintain its current course of using landfills and incinerators as the main methods of handling waste. For the recycling of Chicago's waste the city has proposed an inadequate blue bag program: Chicagoans will place all household recyclables (which at this point include paper, glass, cans, and plastic) in a special blue bag that will then be collected and compacted with all other trash. Then the trash will be delivered to Material Recovery and Recycling Centers, where the blue bags will be retrieved and the recyclables separated.

The proposed blue bag program, slated to begin by the end of 1993, has brought harsh criticism from Chicago's environmental organizations. The following problems have come up with the blue bag program:

- Bag breakage, which causes the materials enclosed to become part of the regular trash that is landfilled or incinerated.

- Compacting the bags with other trash causes glass breakage. This makes it impossible to separate the glass by color, which significantly reduces its market value.

- Mixing all recyclables together contaminates the paper and reduces the amount that can be recycled.

- A program such as this has never been successfully implemented in a major city.

Environmental organizations have unsuccessfully submitted alternative proposals for a comprehensive waste reduction and recycling program, and the blue bag program will be implemented in Chicago despite environmentalists' opposition.

In addition to concerns about air and solid waste, Chicago must plan for the utilization and protection of its open lands, lakefront, and forest preserve districts. While the logging industry is not a threat to Chicago's local environment, a constantly increasing urban population is. Lakefront management is critical for halting shoreline erosion and the disruption of the natural movement of sand on the lake bottom.

The potential weakening of federal wetlands protection laws can have a devastating impact on outlying Cook County and the Lake Calumet areas. As a new airport has been discussed for Lake Calumet, the city's capacity to mitigate the damage to the valuable wetlands in this area is seriously threatened. Wetlands serve not only as habitats and sources of nourishment for numerous animal, plant, and bird species but also as filter systems for the Great Lakes Basin.

ENVIRONMENTAL ORGANIZATIONS

Numerous organizations in Chicago work to improve the quality of Chicago's air, water, land, and animal life. Many of these organizations depend heavily on volunteers and offer the opportunity for Chicagoans to influence, firsthand, the quality of their environment. If volunteering is not an option for you, memberships are usually available and will probably offer the benefit of receiving current environmental literature. Different organizations tend to focus on different environmental issues, and a few deal with a wide range of issues. For a more complete list of enviromental organizations, see the *EarthDay Chicago Resource Directory*.

Chicago Lung Association
1440 W. Washington Blvd., Chicago, 60605   243-2000
The Chicago Lung Association's environmental involvement relates to indoor air quality and the associated health problems.

Chicago Recycling Coalition
2125 W. North, Chicago, 60647   278-4800
The Chicago Recycling Coalition is comprised of community-based environmental and civic organizations along with recycling businesses (both for-profit and not-for-profit) that work to promote recycling and reduction of sources of waste in Chicago. The Chicago Recycling Coalition uses volunteers for a variety of projects.

Citizens for a Better Environment
407 S. Dearborn, #1775, Chicago, 60605   939-1530
Citizens for a Better Environment (CBE) was founded in Chicago in 1971. It currently has offices in Illinois, Minnesota, and Wisconsin. CBE works to protect the public's health from toxic pollution. In order to achieve this, the organization has a full-time staff of policy analysts and technical experts who work to influence and shape environmental policies. These professionals research pollution problems in order to recommend solutions to government decision makers and the public. CBE has a continuous need for volunteers to do office work and an occasional need for volunteers to work at special events.

EarthDay Chicago
28 E. Jackson, Chicago, 60604   629-1995
EarthDay Chicago was set up in 1989 to help coordinate events for the April 20, 1990, 20th anniversary of the first Earth Day. The organization positions itself between consumers and other environmental organizations and corporations in order to facilitate the dissemination of environmental information. EarthDay Chicago assists other environmental organizations by increasing public awareness and encouraging participation in environmental issues. The group also assists businesses by spreading the word on the positive environmental steps the businesses have taken. EarthDay Chicago distributes a quarterly publication, *EarthDay Chicago Resource Directory*, that offers, among other things, current updates on Chicago's environmental issues, a calendar of local events, and information on recycling and recycling centers. EarthDay Chicago has recently opened a retail store, **EarthDay The Store**, and office at 10 S. State. This location sells environmental products and disseminates environmental information.

Friends of the Chicago River
407 S. Dearborn, #1580, Chicago, 60605   939-0490
Friends of the Chicago River is an advocacy group with the goal of protecting and improving the Chicago River. The organization works to increase access to the river; sponsors riverbank cleanups; and promotes a balanced use of the river by industry, government, community, and recreation groups. It offers to the public inexpensive and informative walking and biking river tours and also conducts one-day canoe trips. Friends of the Chicago River offers a number of volunteer opportunities through the following committees: Rivertrail Docents, Office Help, Rivertrail Maps, Planning and Design, Communications, and Special Events.

Friends of Lincoln Park
4753 N. Broadway, #918, Chicago, 60640   907-2186
This organization was founded in 1984 with the purpose of preserving and improving the Lincoln Park assets through funding and special projects. Friends of Lincoln Park is an all-volunteer citizens organization that sponsors numerous activities for the public, such as a winter lecture series, free concerts, and summer activities for children and adults. The Friends also benefits Lincoln Park by monitoring the Park District; restoring monuments; managing Lincoln Gardens, a perennial garden located at 50 W. North; working to protect the park's environment; and planning for the future of the park. Any amount of volunteer time is welcome for everything from helping with special events to sitting on the Board of Directors.

Friends of the Parks
407 S. Dearborn, #1590, Chicago, 60605   922-3307
Friends of the Parks is an advocacy group for Chicago's parks. They work to preserve, protect, and improve the parks. Friends of the Parks uses volunteers for outdoor park projects, an Adopt-a-Park program, office work, and environmental education programs. They also hold a number of special fund-raising events throughout the year such as theater outings, a black-tie party, a boat trip, and a midnight bike ride. Both volunteers and participants are needed for these special events.

Greenpeace
1017 W. Jackson, Chicago, 60607 666-3305
Greenpeace is a national organization that concentrates on worldwide issues such as protecting ocean ecosystems; ending the production, use, and export of toxic wastes and pesticides; protecting the rain forests; calling for disarmament; and promoting renewable energy sources. Greenpeace advocates humans creating a sustainable balance with nature. The local group is involved mainly with toxics in the Great Lakes, fighting incineration, and global warming.

Illinois Environmental Council
407 S. Dearborn, #1775, Chicago, 60605 554-0086
The IEC is the state's grass-roots lobby for conservation and environmental issues. Formed in 1975, the council represents more than 70 Illinois organizations, including the Audobon Council of Illinois, Citizens for a Better Environment, the Chicago Lung Association, Sierra Club, and the Nature Conservancy. The Chicago office hosts regular events aimed at educating Chicagoans about environmental issues and the legislative process.

Lake Michigan Federation
59 E. Van Buren, Chicago, 60605 939-0838
This organization concerns itself with issues facing Lake Michigan. It is headquartered in Chicago and also has offices in Wisconsin and Michigan. Lake Michigan Federation's main objectives include improving and maintaining water quality in Lake Michigan, its tributaries, and its surrounding environment; promoting sound plans for shoreline management; and using public and school-based education to increase the appreciation of Lake Michigan. Lake Michigan Federation offers unpaid environmental internships for qualified individuals. The Federation uses volunteers on a regular basis. It has recently begun a Shorekeepers program where volunteers adopt a stretch of shoreline to monitor. Volunteers are also needed for special events such as beach cleanups.

The Nature Conservancy
79 W. Monroe, #708, Chicago, 60603 346-8166
The main goal of The Nature Conservancy is to protect rare plants and animals by protecting the land on which they live. This is a national organization and is responsible for the largest system of privately owned nature preserves in the world. One role of The Nature Conservancy is to act as real estate brokers for the environment. Often they will sell or lease land to government or educational institutions with the agreement that the buyer or lessor will preserve it and allow public access. The Nature Conservancy has a volunteer network of stewards and also uses volunteers for fieldwork.

North Branch Prairie Project
The Nature Conservancy
79 W. Monroe, #708, Chicago, 60603 346-8166
This organization assists the Forest Preserve District of Cook County and other agencies in protecting and restoring native Illinois ecosystems. Volunteers meet on Saturdays and Sundays throughout the year to perform restoration work at nine natural areas along the North Branch of the Chicago River

in Chicago and several northern suburbs. They also gather during the week for other activities, such as controlled burns and seed-mixing parties.

Openlands Project
220 S. State, #1880, Chicago, 60604   427-4256
Openlands Project works to increase and protect land open to the public for conservation, recreation, and aesthetic appreciation. The organization's geographic focus is northeastern Illinois, and since its inception in 1963, it has protected over 19,000 acres of park land, nature preserves, and trails. To achieve its goals, Openlands Project educates the public to gain support for open space issues, provides technical training and advisory services to community groups and government on land acquisition and preservation, and acts as an advocate for open space with government. Openlands Project has a volunteer network called Treekeepers who, after receiving special training, help preserve Chicago's urban forest.

Sierra Club—Illinois Chapter
506 S. Wabash, #505, Chicago, 60605   431-0158
The Sierra Club is a grass-roots environmental organization whose members "explore, enjoy and protect . . . wild places." It is a nationwide organization with local chapters in every state. (Call the above number for information on the Illinois Chapter closest to you.) The Sierra Club has some paid staff, but the local chapters are volunteer run. There is room for volunteer involvement on the local, state, or national level in both environmental activism and outdoor recreation. The Chicago Group of the Sierra Club is involved in a full range of topics such as wetlands, air, solid waste, and Alaska issues. Involvement includes lobbying and other political activities, environmental education, and conservation. The Chicago Group also has an outings program (Sierran Outdoors) and an urban outreach group (Inner-City Outings).

RECYCLING

As discussed earlier, solid waste is a continuing problem in Chicago and the surrounding area. The best way you can help mitigate the solid waste problem is to reduce the amount of trash you create. A few ideas for accomplishing this include these:

- Do not purchase products that are overpackaged.
- Use reusable cloth or string bags when shopping.
- Use cloth, rather than disposable diapers.
- Use nondisposable razors and shaving cream in a tube.

The general message is to be creative. Look at everything you throw away and consider alternatives that would create less waste.

After considering how you can reduce the volume of waste you create in your household, recycle as much of the remaining waste as possible. The common materials households might have that can be recycled include newspaper, aluminum, steel cans, glass, plastics, organic waste, and car batteries. The store or service station where you bought your battery (half of which is lead) may accept it for recycling. Or, for a battery take-back center near you, see the list of recycling centers below or contact Battery Council

International, Attn. Larry Fleischman, 401 N. Michigan, Chicago, 60611 (1-800-658-1200). The Enviromental Defense Funds reminds do-it-yourself car mechanics to recycle their motor oil; the equivalent of 11 Exxon *Valdez* oil spills winds up in the ground or sewer every year. Many other items can also be recycled:

- Appliances may contain recyclable materials such as pipe, copper, and lead.
- Old clothing can be taken to thrift stores.
- Corrugated cardboard can be recycled into more cardboard.
- High-grade paper such as typing, computer, and copier paper can also be recycled.
- Keep your car's tires properly inflated and rotated (low tire pressure alone wastes more than 2 million gallons of gas a *day* in the U.S.), then find a dealer who'll handle their disposal properly by recycling them into a variety of products, from retreads to tugboat bumpers. Write for the *Directory of Scrap Tire Processors by State*, Scrap Tire Management Council, Attn. Connie Gilmore, 1400 K Street NW, Washington, D.C., 20005 ([202] 408-7784).

The market for the different materials will vary depending on the current demand for them. As an incentive, keep in mind that the same amount of energy is required to produce an aluminum can from raw materials as is required to produce 20 cans from recycled aluminum, and 25 percent less energy is used in producing glass from recycled glass rather than raw materials.

Below is a list of places in Chicago that accept materials for recycling. Following each location is a guide to the materials they will accept. Materials accepted might change, however, depending on the market for the materials, so call first to verify the materials they currently accept. You will also want to ask if any special preparation of the recyclables is expected. For example, newspapers may need to be bundled or glass may need to be separated by color. Of course, you should also verify that their address has not changed. The market for the materials will also determine if the places will pay for the materials and how much they will pay.

Some of the places listed are just drop-off locations. Others are attended recycling centers whose purpose is to collect the more common household recyclables. Many places listed here, however, are actually in the junk or salvage business and purchase recyclables (usually aluminum, other metals, and auto batteries) as part of their day-to-day business. Because of the wide variety of businesses in the recycling market, if you find dropping your recyclables at one location to be an unpleasurable experience, then try others until you find one that fits your needs and expectations.

The following list is by no means all-inclusive. A more complete list is available from the Chicago Recycling Coalition.

Northeast Side

Elston Metal & Salvage, Inc.
2320 N. Elston   278-7060
Aluminum and other metal, auto batteries.

Lakewood Recycling Center
1305 W. Belmont   472-4800
Aluminum, auto batteries.

Lincoln Park Cultural Center
2045 N. Lincoln Park West   294-4750
Plastic.

Lincoln Park Cultural Center
4921 N. Marine   294-4750
Plastic.

Loop Recycling
1800 W. Balmoral   989-1168
Aluminum and other metal, glass, auto batteries.

J. Sandman & Sons, Inc.
1500 W. Webster   549-3151
Aluminum cans.

Rockwell Scrap Co.
3046 N. Elston   478-3108
Aluminum and other metal, auto batteries.

S. Edelman & Son
2960 W. Lawrence   463-3545
Aluminum and other metal, auto batteries.

Serlin Iron and Metal
2501 N. Bosworth   348-4432
Aluminum and other metal.

Uptown Recycling Station, Inc.
4716 N. Sheridan   769-4488
Aluminum and other metal, glass, newspaper.

Wrightwood Neighbors
Lincoln/Sheffield/Wrightwood
(7-Eleven Parking Lot)   787-7078
Aluminum and other metal, glass, newspaper.

Northwest Side

AAA Alloys Scrap Iron and Metal
4630 W. Armitage   237-8585
Aluminum and other metal, auto batteries.

American National Can Recycling Division
8770 W. Bryn Mawr   399-3493
Aluminum cans.

Global Recycling
1800 N. St. Louis   276-0730
Aluminum and other metal, glass, batteries.

Grand Aluminum
4555 W. Grand   252-5633
Aluminum and other metal, batteries.

North Park Village
5801 N. Pulaski   744-1252
Aluminum and steel cans, glass, paper, plastic.

West Side

AAA Mid-City Recycling Co.
820 W. Cermak   226-3825
Aluminum and other metal, glass, auto batteries.

American Metals
2420 W. Cermak   927-0060
Aluminum and other metal, glass, auto batteries.

Barry's Metal Shop
1818 S. Federal   842-1215
Aluminum and other metal.

Bethel Recycling
831 N. Cicero   261-8340
Aluminum and other metal, glass.

Biltmore Metals, Inc.
813 W. Cermak   829-2066
Aluminum and other metal, auto batteries.

BLM Rebuilders
2100 S. Sawyer   522-4545
Aluminum and other metal.

Chicago Paperboard Corporation
949 N. Elston   997-3131
Cardboard boxes, corrugated paper, newspaper.

Fillmore Junk Shop
4536 W. Grenshaw   826-4223
Aluminum and other metal.

Illinois Scrap
2048 W. Hubbard   421-0549
Aluminum and other metal.

Loop Recycling
1956 W. 17th   942-0042
Aluminum and other metal, glass, batteries.

Maxworks Cooperative
717 W. Maxwell   226-3248
Aluminum and other metal, glass, newspaper, cardboard, books, lumber.

North Avenue Metals
1917 W. North   278-4370
Aluminum and other metal.

Reynolds Recycling   1-800-228-2525
Call for location nearest you.
Aluminum and other metal.

West Side Recycling
1020 S. Cicero   378-0551
Aluminum and other metal, auto batteries, auto parts.

Southwest Side

A. Archway
4619 S. Knox   585-3030
Aluminum and other metal.

Abco Metals
1020 W. 94th   723-1975
Aluminum and other metal, batteries.

Advance Cullet Corp.
3717 S. Albany   523-2200
Aluminum and other metal, glass.

Courtesy Metal
3711 S. California   847-3330
Aluminum and other metal.

Curbside Collection & Recycling Company
3120 W. 37th Pl.   376-6363
Aluminum and other metal, glass.

Dobb's Recycling Service Co.
901 W. 115th   568-0700
Aluminum and other metal, glass, paper, plastic, batteries.

Edco Recycling Company
8224 S. Vincennes   873-1600
Aluminum and other metal, clear and brown glass, auto parts.

Empire Iron & Steel
1515 W. 122nd   928-0400
Aluminum and other metal.

Loop Recycling, Inc.
2401 S. Laflin   942-0042
Aluminum and other metal, batteries.

On State Recycling
5825 S. State   667-8283
Aluminum and other metal, glass, newspaper, plastic, batteries.

T & B Recycling
6301 S. Bell   776-5616
Aluminum and other metal, batteries.

West Pullman Iron & Metal Co.
11954 S. Peoria   785-0534
Aluminum and other metal.

Wolf Mill Supply Co., Inc.
6901 S. Bell   436-4546
Aluminum and other metal, glass.

Southeast Side

B. L. Nicholson Iron & Metal
8501 S. Baltimore   375-0874
Aluminum and other metal, batteries.

M & G Recyclers
815 E. 93rd   783-0771
Aluminum and other metal, batteries.

Railroad Recycling Station
7070 S. Dorchester   493-1470
Aluminum and other metal, glass, newspaper, plastic.

The Resource Center
222 E. 135th Pl.   821-1351
Aluminum and other metal, glass, newspaper.

The city of Chicago's current recycling program consists of a drop-off location in each of the 50 wards. Materials accepted at these drop-off locations include newspaper, glass, all metal cans, and plastic coded with a 1 or 2. (The number is a guide to the materials used in manufacturing the plastic. A 1 indicates polyethylene terephthalate, which usually includes soda bottles, microwave food trays, and frozen boil-in-bag pouches. A 2 indicates high-density polyethylene, which usually includes milk jugs, detergent and bleach bottles, trash bags, and aspirin bottles.) To get the address of the recycling drop-off location in your ward and other city recycling programs, call 744-SORT (744-7678).

Remember, the success of recycling depends not only on your delivering your materials for recycling but also heavily on your demanding products made from recycled materials.

Illinois state law prohibits the disposing of yard waste in landfills. Yard waste includes grass clippings, edging, leaves, branches, prunings, potted flowers and plants, garden waste, and so forth. Yard waste must be placed in special 30-gallon biodegradable paper bags that can be purchased at a variety of retail stores. The bags should be placed next to your regular garbage to be picked up and recycled by the city. Alternatives to disposing of your yard waste include mulching or composting your yard waste and mowing your lawn often and leaving the clippings on the lawn. For information on home composting, call the **State Department of Energy and Natural Resources** (1-800-252-8955).

The city of Chicago also has a tire disposal program for Chicago residents. Up to 15 tires can be dropped off at the following locations:

- 4014 W. Fullerton

- 2505 W. Grand

- 1400 W. Pershing

- 10301 S. Doty

Be prepared to show proof that you are a Chicago resident. For more information, call 744-SORT. The city is currently investigating recycling possibilities for the tires.

ENVIRONMENTAL PROTECTION AGENCY

U.S. EPA, Region 5
Office of Public Affairs
77 W. Jackson, Chicago, 60626   353-2072
The U.S. EPA is divided into 10 regions. Illinois is included in Region 5, along with Indiana, Michigan, Minnesota, Ohio, and Wisconsin. The Office of Public Affairs receives thousands of calls weekly from citizens with information requests. Region 5 also has a toll-free hot line for environmental questions, assistance, and problems: 1-800-621-8431. Other U.S. EPA toll-free numbers are:

Chemical Emergency Preparedness   1-800-535-0202
Community Right-to-Know.

Pesticide Hot Line   1-800-858-PEST

RCRA/Superfund Hot Line   1-800-424-9346

Safe Drinking Water Hot Line   1-800-426-4791

Stratospheric Ozone Hot Line   1-800-296-1996

Whistle Blowers Hot Line   1-800-424-4000
Office of the Inspector General hot line for reporting fraud, waste, and abuse within the EPA programs or operations.

The 12th floor of the U.S. EPA's office in Chicago has a visitor information center. On display here is a sampling of informational materials published by the EPA and available to the public. Other publications can be received by calling the Office of Public Affairs. Informational topics include general publications and regulations, air, pesticides and toxic substances, waste management, and water. Located behind the information center is a library, also open to the public.

The central phone number for the U.S. EPA's Public Information Center is (202) 260-2080.

Illinois EPA
Public Affairs Office
2200 Churchill, Springfield, 62706   (217) 782-5562
General questions about Illinois' environment and requests for printed material and monthly newsletters should be directed to the public affairs office in Springfield. IEPA has a Cook County regional office at 1500

Maybrook, Maywood, 60153 ([708] 865-6165). However, questions and complaints concerning toxic spills and other violations of the law in Chicago should be referred to the City of Chicago Environmental Services, 121 N. LaSalle, Chicago, 60602 (744-9514).

The State of Illinois' 24-hour emergency number for reporting pollution problems, accidents, or spills in Illinois is (217) 782-3637.

—Julie Delong

VOLUNTEERING

Why volunteer?

A few years ago *Time* magazine devoted a cover story to the rise of volunteerism across the nation. It seems that baby boomers, reluctant to jettison the good vibes and freedom of the sixties, were trying to clean up the debacle of post-Reagan America, dig in and, like some of the characters on the now-defunct "Thirtysomething" television show, do something for others.

In Chicago, however, no one particular generation has ever cornered the market of volunteering time, energy, and service hours to improve conditions or share passions. If this is "the city that works," it's because many Chicagoans are trying to improve this urban sprawl: parks, museums, neighborhoods, apartment complexes, art, theater, and the daily lives of the disenfranchised.

Frankly, the bleak pictures painted on the nightly news and printed in the daily papers seem to tell us that we're going from bad to worse: funding for the arts is shrinking (funding for anything, period, is shrinking), the numbers of AIDS victims are growing, more and more families are becoming homeless. Most people know volunteering says "We're in this together," and the numerous opportunities the city offers enable you truly to contribute to the welfare of the community. Be creative, and think about it this way: if you have a skill, are motivated by a concern, or can provide service as a professional or an individual, give it freely. That's all it takes to be a volunteer.

If you'll be here a while, settling into a new community, or visiting for an undetermined time, volunteering is a great way to meet the small-town, midwestern soul of Chicago. (Hey, after all, we are the city that rose from the O'Leary's lantern-induced ruins.) If you are new to Chicago, you can call the clearinghouse, or "network," organizations listed below, which handle referrals based on your interests and the kind of work you'd like to do. Their information is extensive and thorough; they are happy to link new volunteers to programs. You also may ask if the organizations have intern programs: if you know where you want to work, don't be shy about getting your foot in the door.

Following the list of network organizations are community-oriented groups with various neighborhood branches followed by several umbrella organizations. These groups need people to lend a neighborly hand by doing "general volunteer work," which includes a wide variety of tasks, from cooking and delivering meals to tutoring GED students and caring for infants.

After the list of organizations that need all kinds of help for all kinds of efforts is a section called "Specific Causes," where you'll find numbers to call if you know you want to work with Chicago's youth or raise money for AIDS patients. Keep in mind, however, that this chapter intends to be social, not political. For more potently political work, see the "Activism" chapter.

The "Religion" chapter also lists numerous organizations that will welcome your volunteer time, and both "Theater" and "Museums" provide phone numbers you can call if you're interested in being a volunteer usher or tour guide. Area schools such as DePaul, Columbia, Loyola, Roosevelt, the city colleges, Northeastern, and St. Xavier's offer worthy programs, too, sometimes in conjunction with community groups.

Happy volunteering!

NETWORK ORGANIZATIONS

The following organizations will match your talents and concerns with organizations that need you.

Chicago Commons
915 N. Wolcott, Chicago, 60622   342-5330
Helps needy people, senior citizens, and recent migrants with comprehensive programs, including emergency aid, job training, counseling, and GED (high school equivalency) and English language classes. Outposts all over the city.

Travelers & Immigrants Aid
327 S. LaSalle, Chicago, 60604   435-4500
Well established throughout the city; works with many community organizations on programs related to housing, shelter, women's programs, and child welfare, to name a few.

The Volunteer Center
United Way/Crusade of Mercy
560 W. Lake, Chicago, 60661   906-2245
Recruits, refers, and places volunteers in not-for-profit civic, welfare, and health organizations. Offers consultations to agencies and corporations that want to start volunteer programs. Also does specialized placements of managers and executives on boards of directors of not-for-profit agencies.

Volunteer Network
300 W. Washington, #1414, Chicago, 60606   606-8240
Placed more than 1,000 volunteers with several hundred nonprofits in 1991, and continues working both with nonprofits and volunteers to determine needs and long-range projects.

Women's Switchboard
828 S. Wabash, Chicago, 60605   663-4163
Refers callers interested in helping out women's organizations.

COMMUNITY WORK/GENERAL VOLUNTEERING

Community

Because Chicago is a city of neighborhoods, there are as many ways as there are residents to get involved. Check with community parks, churches, schools, tenants or homeowners organizations as well as ward offices for programs in your area. Here are some groups that do good work in community support and advocate for safe, strong neighborhoods.

Acorn Community Organization
410 S. Michigan, Chicago, 60605   939-7488
The nation's largest nonprofit grass-roots community organization. Runs an internship program rather than maintaining a volunteer staff; call to apply.

Interns assist in fund raising and grant writing, with some phone and office work.

Ada S. McKinley Community Services
725 S. Wells, Chicago, 60610   554-0600
(headquarters for citywide organization)

Afro-American Cultural Center
1509 W. Victoria, Chicago, 60660   878-7101

Austin People's Action Center
5719 W. North, Chicago, 60639   804-0166

Back of the Yards Neighborhood Council
1950 W. 51st, Chicago, 60609   434-8080

Beverly Area Planning Association
Housing Center
10233 S. Wood, Chicago, 60643   445-1919

Brainerd Community Development Corporation
9453 S. Ashland, Chicago, 60620   238-6699

Cambodian Association of Illinois
1105 W. Lawrence, Chicago, 60640   878-7090

Chicago Roseland Coalition for Community Control
11015 S. Michigan, Chicago, 60628   264-3500

Chinese Mutual Aid Association
1100 W. Argyle, Chicago, 60640   784-2900

Community Renewal Society
332 S. Michigan, Chicago, 60604   427-4830

Council for Jewish Elderly
Neighborhood Services
1522 W. Morse, Chicago, 60626   973-6065

Englewood Grassroots Organization
6040 S. May, Chicago, 60621   925-8010

Ethiopian Association of Chicago
4750 N. Sheridan, Chicago, 60640   728-0303

Ezra Jewish Helpline   1-800-248-1818
Offers 24-hour information and crisis help.

Friends of Downtown
17 N. State, Chicago, 60602   977-0098

Friends of Refugees of Eastern Europe
6335 N. California, Chicago, 60659   274-5123

Greek American Community Services
3940 N. Pulaski, Chicago, 60641   545-0303

Guardian Angels
6928 N. Wayne, Chicago, 60626   761-2676

Historic North Pullman Organization Chicago
10432 S. Maryland, Chicago, 60628   928-6300

Horizons Community Services
961 W. Montana, Chicago, 60614   871-2273 (antiviolence project);
929-4357 (helpline)
Serves Chicago's gay and lesbian community.

Hull House Association
118 N. Clinton, Chicago, 60606   726-1526
After-school programs:
910 W. Sheridan, Chicago, 60613   528-8885
3212 N. Broadway, Chicago, 60657   549-1631
Jane Addams defined hands-on social work from her Hull House on Chicago's Near West Side by working with immigrant communities, trying to provide burgeoning areas with centers where they could feel comfortable and get basic needs met, questions answered. Volunteers are needed to help offer a great variety of services such as day care, family and group counseling, tutoring and adult education classes, employment counseling, arts and crafts, theater, photo and dance classes, shelter and counseling for abused women, and services for the elderly. Check your neighborhood to see if a Hull House extension exists there.

Hyde Park Neighborhood Club
5480 S. Kenwood, Chicago, 60615   643-4062

Kenwood Oakland Community Organization
1238 E. 46th, Chicago, 60653   548-7500

Indo-American Center
2643 W. Devon, Chicago, 60659   973-4444

Iranian American Society
3224 W. Bryn Mawr, Chicago, 60659   588-8055

Irish American Heritage Center
4626 N. Knox, Chicago, 60630   282-7035

Japanese Mutual Aid Society of Chicago
1740 W. Balmoral, Chicago, 60640   769-2226

Muslim Community Center
4380 N. Elston, Chicago, 60641   725-9047

Pilsen Little Village Habitat for Humanity
1909 N. Ashland, Chicago, 60622   226-6966

Uptown People's Community Service Center
4409 N. Broadway, Chicago, 60640   769-2085

Voice of the People
4554 N. Broadway, Chicago, 60640   769-2442

General Volunteering

Catholic Charities
126 N. Des Plaines, Chicago, 60606   236-5172
This huge umbrella organization serves people of all ethnic and religious backgrounds. Offers information and makes referrals to other programs and community resources. Among services provided are a refugee resettlement program, schooling and counseling for pregnant girls, adoption services, addiction prevention services, shelters for the homeless, a Latin American youth center, legal services to the poor, and help for the elderly.

Executive Services Corps of Chicago
25 E. Washington, #801, Chicago, 60602   580-1840
ESC needs volunteers who are presently or are soon to be retired from a business, management, or professional career to consult with nonprofit organizations in areas such as fiscal management, marketing, public relations, personnel, facilities, management, and other services.

Friendship House
1746 W. Division, Chicago, 60622   227-5065
A center for nonviolent social action with programs for raising the public's awareness of social problems and for making lasting change. Most of their clients, according to the House, "fall between the cracks of organized social services."

Jewish Community Centers of Chicago
1 S. Franklin, Chicago, 60606   346-6700
Comprehensive community centers located mostly at North Side locations, but with one center in Hyde Park on the South Side. Primarily for Jewish residents, but open to the general public. Services vary according to location, but many include gymnasiums, recreational and educational programs, day care and nursery schools, and programs for the elderly.

Lieutenant Governor's Office of Volunteer and Senior Services
100 W. Randolph, #15-200, Chicago, 60601   814-2789
Maintains a statewide resource center on programs for voluntary action and citizen participation in Illinois.

Operation PUSH (People United to Serve Humanity)
930 E. 50th, Chicago, 60615   373-3366
Founded by Reverend Jesse Jackson, PUSH is a large organization with a broad base of popular support, especially within the African-American community. PUSH offers educational programs and classes, and social activities, as well as a clearinghouse for referrals to other agencies, services, and individuals for legal and other forms of assistance.

Travelers & Immigrants Aid of Chicago
327 S. LaSalle, #1500, Chicago, 60604   435-4500
Centers at Union Station, Greyhound Bus Station, and O'Hare Airport provide emergency services as well as information and referral services to travelers, women, immigrants, refugees, and people who are homeless.

United Charities of Chicago
14 E. Jackson, Chicago, 60604   461-0800
Centers all over the city for family, individual, and group counseling, family financial services, and services to older adults.

Volunteers of America
224 N. Des Plaines, Chicago, 60661   707-8707
Foster care and adoption agency, often recruiting tutors to cover basic subjects.

YMCA
755 W. North, Chicago, 60610   280-3400
Centers all over the city provide a great variety of services to men, women, and children, including counseling for individuals, families, and groups, day care and day camps, emergency services, employment and training, physical fitness classes and centers, programs for senior citizens, and residences for men and women.

YWCA
180 N. Wabash, #301, Chicago, 60601   372-6600
Centers throughout the city provide comprehensive programs primarily for women and girls, including counseling (for employment, legal issues, domestic violence, rape), hot lines, classes and seminars, child care and day care, employment services, day care for senior citizens, and physical education and athletics.

SPECIFIC CAUSES

AIDS

AIDS Foundation of Chicago
1332 N. Halsted, #303, Chicago, 60622   642-5454 (general office); 642-3763 (information and referrals)

AIDS Legal Council of Chicago
220 S. State, #1330, Chicago, 60604   427-8990

AIDS Outreach Projects–UIC
1509 N. Milwaukee, Chicago, 60622   252-4422
4650 S. King, Chicago, 60653   536-4509

AIDS Walk Chicago
4753 N. Broadway, Chicago, 60640   334-0448

Chicago House and Social Service Agency
3150 N. Lincoln, #2S, Chicago, 60657   248-5200
Chicago House is a residential program for persons with AIDS or AIDS-related conditions. It needs volunteers to be "buddies," who provide practical and emotional support for residents, and "groupies," who are assigned to a residence. Groupies are involved in preparing group meals, outings, and cleanup. Chicago House also needs volunteers to do fund raising and clerical work.

Stop AIDS Chicago
909 W. Belmont, Chicago, 60657   871-3300
2154 E. 71st, Chicago, 60649   752-STOP

Test Positive Awareness Network
1340 W. Irving Park, #259, Chicago, 60613   404-8726 (404-TPAN)
Largest nonprofit support and information network for those affected by the HIV virus.

Animals

Animals Rights Mobilization
617 W. Fulton, Chicago, 60661   993-1181
A multi-issue animal rights organization providing educational programs on all forms of animal abuse and exploitation.

Concerned Citizens for Ethical Research   792-7117

Arts

Business Volunteers for the Arts
55 E. Monroe, #3705, Chicago, 60603   372-1876
People with business experience are linked up with arts organizations needing skills such as legal, marketing, public relations, accounting, and fund raising. Also runs training sessions in arts management.

Lawyers for the Creative Arts
213 W. Institute, #411, Chicago, 60610   944-2787
Pro bono legal work for arts organizations. Supplies referrals.

Cancer

American Cancer Society
77 E. Monroe, Chicago, 60603   641-6150
An all-volunteer organization, ACS provides public education, patient services, lobbying efforts, professional education, and research/grant writing. Volunteers can use their professional skills, or equally important, be on hand to drive patients to and from treatments.

Children/Youth

Better Boys Foundation
Family Center/Community Services
1512 S. Pulaski, Chicago, 60651   277-9582
Family Services Program
541 W. Roosevelt, Chicago, 60607   829-0246

Big Brothers–Big Sisters of Metropolitan Chicago
542 S. Dearborn, Chicago, 60605   427-0637
A mentoring program that entails spending time as a surrogate big brother or big sister with a child in need of guidance.

Big Buddies Youth Services
7145 S. South Chicago, Chicago, 60619   288-6258

Boy Scouts of America
730 W. Lake, Chicago, 60606 559-0990

Build, Inc. (Broader Urban Involvement in Leadership Development)
1223 N. Milwaukee, 2nd floor, Chicago, 60622 227-2880
A gang prevention program that works with elementary schools on gang prevention and remediation of gang members.

Center for Counseling and Tutoring Services
102 W. 100th Pl., Chicago, 60627 264-2838

Chicago Youth Center
951 E. 132nd Pl., Chicago, 60627 785-5043

Girl Scouts of Chicago
55 E. Jackson, Chicago, 60604 435-5500

Misericordia/Hearts of Mercy
6300 N. Ridge, Chicago, 60660 973-6300
Provides educational and training programs for mentally retarded children. Children and young adults also live at Misericordia.

RIF (Reading Is Fundamental)
1330 W. 43rd, Chicago, 60609 507-3947
This 20-year-old national organization accepts parent volunteers and book and financial donations, all for the sake of encouraging youngsters to read.

Environment

Citizens for a Better Environment
407 S. Dearborn, Chicago, 60605 939-1530
Environmental advocacy group that works with citizens throughout Illinois to fight toxic pollution problems.

Friends of Conservation
1520 Kensington, Oak Brook, 60521 (708) 954-3388
Works through programs of direct action and education to halt the threat on habitat and wildlife. Works mainly in East Africa, but provides educational programs in the United States and United Kingdom.

Lake Michigan Federation
59 E. Van Buren, #2215, Chicago, 60605 939-0838
An independent civic organization working to protect Lake Michigan and its tributaries. Houses resource centers on pollution and wetlands management technologies.

Openlands Project
220 S. State, #1880, Chicago, 60604 427-4256
Civic organization that negotiates and coordinates public education for expanding public lands acquisition for conservation and recreational purposes. Also works to improve the quality of existing open public space.

Sierra Club
506 S. Wabash, #505, Chicago, 60605 431-0158
Volunteer organization working on a full range of environmental issues.

Family

Association House of Chicago
2150 W. North, Chicago, 60647 276-0084 (main office/information)

Bi-Racial Family Network
P.O. Box 489, Chicago, 60653 288-3644

Casa Aztlan
1831 S. Racine, Chicago, 60608 666-5508
This comprehensive organization offers adult education, GED/ESL, youth intervention program, counseling, tutoring, after-school programs (K–7), arts and crafts program for youths and adults, parent-child reading circle, family literacy, amnesty classes, information and referral, and emergency food.

Central Baptist Family Services
546 W. Washington, Chicago, 60606 930-9375
201 N. Wells, Chicago, 60606 782-0874
2831 S. Michigan, Chicago, 60616 326-3361

Child Abuse Prevention Services
600 S. Federal, Chicago, 60605 427-1161
A counseling service and hot line for the prevention of child abuse.

Heart Disease

American Heart Association of Metropolitan Chicago
20 N. Wacker, Chicago, 60606 346-4675

Homelessness and Hunger

Center for Street People
4455 N. Broadway, Chicago, 60640 728-0727

Chicago Coalition for the Homeless
1325 S. Wabash, Chicago, 60605 435-4548
A privately funded advocacy organization that works on systemic problems of the homeless. This is not a crisis center.

Clothing and Food for the Needy, Inc.
2708 W. Division, Chicago, 60622 276-6722

Chicago Anti-Hunger Federation
2380 S. Halsted, Chicago, 60614 850-3700
Works to provide food to shelters' kitchens.

The Common Pantry
3744 N. Damen, Chicago, 60618 327-0553

Community Emergency Shelter Organization
1337 W. Ohio, Chicago, 60622 633-0881

Crusaders of America
1217 W. Wilson, Chicago, 60640 275-5949
Organize to pick up clothing, furniture, and other items.

Deborah's Place
1110 N. Noble, Chicago, 60622   292-0304
Needs volunteers to work in daytime program (weekdays) and a 24-hour transitional living program for women who are homeless.

Diversey Emergency Food Pantry
2803 N. Leavitt, Chicago, 60618   327-1515

Greater Chicago Food Depository
4529 S. Tripp, Chicago, 60630   247-3663

House of Good Shepherd   935-3434

Lakeview Pantry
3212 N. Broadway, Chicago, 60657   525-1777
Collects food for shelters and the homeless; works out of the Hull House community center and has been a major contributor for years.

Pacific Garden Mission
646 S. State, Chicago, 60605   922-1462
This familiar site in the south Loop has been serving people almost as long as Chicago's been in existence, 112 years.

Literacy

Chicago Literacy Hot Line   939-8600

Illinois Literacy Hot Line   1-800-321-9511

Literacy Volunteers of Chicago
9 W. Washington, Chicago, 60602   236-0341
Matches reading tutors with students; provides referrals to related agencies. Also offers assistance to businesses or other groups needing adult tutoring programs in reading or English as a second language. Needs translators in all languages.

Literacy Council of Chicago
77 W. Washington, #1124, Chicago, 60602   372-3446
Concentrates on one-on-one classroom instruction in basic reading. Tutor-training workshops are offered monthly.

People with Disabilities

Access Living of Metropolitan Chicago
Services to Disabled and Hearing Impaired
310 S. Peoria, Chicago, 60607   226-5900; TDD: 226-1687
Offers a range of human services, from counseling domestic violence survivors to relocating homeless.

Chicago Lighthouse for the Blind
1850 W. Roosevelt, Chicago, 60608   666-1331
Job counseling, training, employment and placement, low-vision services, and recreational activities.

Blind Service Association
22 W. Monroe, 11th floor, Chicago, 60603   236-0808
Relies on volunteers who service blind and visually impaired persons by one-to-one readings and/or tape recordings, primarily textbooks and work materials.

Chicago Association for Retarded Citizens
8 S. Michigan, Chicago, 60603   346-6230

Home Deliver Meals of Mt. Greenwood
10517 S. Whipple, Chicago, 60655   238-4571

Seniors

Little Brothers Friends of the Elderly
1658 W. Belmont, Chicago, 60657   477-7702
Needs volunteers to make friendly visits to senior citizens in their homes, deliver meals, and in general help in any way possible.

Operation ABLE
180 N. Wabash, #802, Chicago, 60601   782-3335
Works to help older workers find employment, cosponsors an annual job fair for older workers, and tries to educate the public and encourage hiring of older workers.

Service Core of Retired Executives (SCORE)
500 W. Madison, #1250, Chicago, 60661   353-7723
Sponsored by the Small Business Administration. SCORE needs volunteers with business backgrounds to provide one-on-one counseling with small business entrepreneurs in all areas of business management, including accounting, marketing, financing, manufacturing, merchandising, and engineering.

Voter Registration

Chicago Voter Registration Coalition
431 S. Dearborn, Chicago, 60610   427-6220
Help get out the vote!

Women

Clara's House Shelter
1650 W. 62nd, Chicago, 60636   778-8861
A shelter for homeless and battered women.

Chicago Abused Women Coalition   278-4110

Chicago Sexual Assault Service Network
2730 W. 15th Pl., Chicago, 60608   277-6080

Deborah's Place
1110 N. Noble, Chicago, 60622   292-0304
Needs volunteers to work in a daytime program (weekdays) and a 24-hour transitional living program for women who are homeless.

Korean American Women in Need (KAN-WIN)
P.O. Box 25139, Chicago, 60625   583-0880

Mujeres Latinas en Acción
1823 W. 17th, Chicago, 60608   226-1544

Southwest Women Working Together
3201 W. 63rd, Chicago, 60629   436-0550

—Genevieve Sedlack and Kate Hinely

ACTIVISM

Several years ago, an insurance company met with a group of community activists. One bewildered executive asked, "What do you people want?"

"We want a decent, affordable place to live, a safe neighborhood, and a good school for our kids," said a veteran community organizer.

The executive just looked at the group, shaking his head. "Yeah, but what do you *really* want?"

In many cases, no matter what the issue is, community activists in Chicago have always stuck to the basics of how to improve their neighborhoods— even when a local government official or business hasn't understood that. Typically, communities in Chicago do not have a specifically liberal or conservative agenda. They just want to have control over their communities and build a better future.

Chicago remains a center for community action, with people all around the city getting involved in community groups focusing on issues that hit home. The real neighborhood activists in Chicago are our neighbors. Community groups bring them together with others in the community to push for solutions on neighborhood issues and involve us in their cause.

The legacy of Saul Alinsky, often called the father of community organizing, permeates today's community organizations in Chicago. They still develop leaders within the community. And they are still willing to use confrontation to get what they want.

"If City Hall doesn't pick up your garbage, bring your garbage to City Hall," said one community leader, explaining Alinsky's philosophy. If letters, phone calls, and meetings fail, community groups in Chicago have found creative and effective ways to reach—and rattle—their opponents. When the Chicago Bears tried to build a stadium on the Near West Side, members of one community group bused out to the owner's house in the suburbs and played football on his lawn. The press loved it, the Bears' owner was embarrassed, and the team eventually abandoned the idea of moving to the Near West Side.

While community groups may work on several issues at one time, their agenda is not cast in stone. Activism in Chicago is a movement of people. In a few years, it's very likely that the people who make up the organizations listed here will still be active, although some of their issues will have changed.

At the same time, some community-based groups have become more professionalized, offering more services to the community, developing housing, and spending more time and resources on community-based planning. Sometimes the lines get blurred between social services, housing and business development, and the traditional tactics of community action. But what community activists in Chicago have in common is their struggle for better neighborhoods—a struggle in which people in Chicago are making the difference.

Many activist organizations in Chicago are not listed in this directory, although you can find most of them through the groups listed under "Resources." In addition to community-based organizations and coalitions, we have included many national and local organizations focusing on a specific issue or constituency.

Countless community residents have emerged from the many activist organizations that fill this city to lead their neighborhoods on important issues. Together, they have put Chicago at the forefront of community activism.

NATIONAL ORGANIZATIONS' CHICAGO OFFICES

American Civil Liberties Union (ACLU)
203 N. LaSalle, #1405, Chicago, 60601   201-9740
Advocates of individual rights on many issues, including abortion and freedom of expression.

American Friends Service Committee
59 E. Van Buren, Chicago, 60605   427-2533
Quaker-based peace and justice organization that currently works with Guatemalans in Chicago, African-American youth, Latina women on legal rights issues. Also working for Middle East peace and on free trade issues.

Greenpeace
1017 W. Jackson, Chicago, 60607   666-3305
Great Lakes regional office for the international environmental group whose current campaigns include pulp and paper, atmosphere and energy, toxics, Great Lakes.

Illinois ACORN
410 S. Michigan, Chicago, 60605   939-7488
ACORN (Association of Community Organizations for Reform Now) organizes in low-income neighborhoods; very active in Englewood.

League of Women Voters of Chicago
332 S. Michigan, Chicago, 60604   939-5935
Advocacy on targeted social issues. Recent campaigns include push for better education in Illinois, more equitable city and state tax system.

National Abortion Rights Action League (NARAL)
100 E. Ohio, #426, Chicago, 60611   644-0972
Illinois affiliate of the political arm of the pro-choice movement, dedicated to keeping abortion safe, legal, and accessible for all women in Illinois.

National Association for the Advancement of Colored People (NAACP)
3346 W. Jackson, Chicago, 60624   826-4311
7 E. 63rd, Chicago, 60637   363-8600
Local branch of old civil rights organization that handles complaints of racial discrimination.

National Organization for Women (NOW)
53 W. Jackson, Chicago, 60604   922-0025
Advocacy on many causes, including abortion rights and job discrimination against women.

National People's Action
810 N. Milwaukee, Chicago, 60622   243-3038
Chicago-based national coalition of community groups that meets in Washington each year to disrupt key government agencies with demonstrations and lobby on issues.

National Writers Union
Chicago Local 12
P.O. Box 3454, Chicago, 60654   348-1300
Chicago local of a growing union pushing for improved pay and working conditions for writers.

Planned Parenthood
14 E. Jackson, Chicago, 60604   427-2276
Reproductive rights advocacy, education, and services.

COMMUNITY-BASED GROUPS AND COALITIONS

Arts

Greater Chicago Citizens for the Arts
1150 Lake Shore Drive, #13D, Chicago, 60611   280-1025
Membership group of artists and arts workers that endorses candidates who support the arts and free expression.

Children's Issues

Maternal & Child Health Coalition
3411 W. Diversey, #5, Chicago, 60647   384-8828
Policy and advocacy group with 60 member organizations throughout the state. Issues vary but have included substance abuse and the role of women and children's needs within a national health care plan.

Network for Youth Services
3600 W. Fullerton, Chicago, 60647   227-0416
West Side coalition targeting youth issues including education, employment, gangs.

Voices for Illinois Children
208 S. LaSalle, Chicago, 60604   456-0600
Advocacy on child and family welfare issues.

Crime

Broader Urban Involvement and Leadership Development (BUILD)
1223 N. Milwaukee, Chicago, 60622   227-2880
Works to reform young gang members and potential recruits through on-the-street intervention. Also provides prevention programs in schools and organizes neighborhood adults.

Chicago Alliance for Neighborhood Safety (CANS)
28 E. Jackson, #1215, Chicago, 60604   461-0444
Leads the charge for community policing in Chicago and formed the Leadership Institute for Neighborhood Policing to develop a core of leaders on the issue.

Citizen Alert
407 S. Dearborn, Chicago, 60605   663-5392
Police watchdog group, active on police brutality long before the Rodney King incident in Los Angeles.

John Howard Association
67 E. Madison, #1416, Chicago, 60611   263-1901
Advocacy for prison reform.

Project to Combat Bias Violence
c/o Chicago Lawyers' Committee for Civil Rights under Law, Inc.
185 N. Wabash, #2110, Chicago, 60601   630-9744
Works with police to ensure that charges are levied; provides legal services to victims and community outreach and education.

Task Force to Confront Police Brutality
c/o People's Law Office
1180 N. Milwaukee, Chicago, 60622   235-0070
Targets specific cases; pushes for reform on the police brutality issue.

Safer Foundation
571 W. Jackson, Chicago, 60606   922-2200
Provides services for ex-offenders, including substance abuse counseling, literacy training, and employment counseling.

Disabled Rights

Access Living
310 S. Peoria, #201, Chicago, 60607   226-5900
Independent living center and advocate for people with disabilities.

Council for Disability Rights
208 S. LaSalle, #1330, Chicago, 60604   444-9484
Information and referral center on disability rights, often used by job seekers and employers.

Economic Development

Back of the Yards Neighborhood Council
1751 W. 47th, Chicago, 60609   523-4416
Organization that community organizer Saul Alinsky helped found now making its mark in economic development.

Chicago Association of Neighborhood Development Organizations (CANDO)
343 S. Dearborn, #910, Chicago, 60604   939-7171
The nation's largest citywide coalition of neighborhood development organizations. Promotes neighborhood revitalization and also packages loans

for commercial and mixed-use real estate as well as business and industrial expansion.

Community Workshop on Economic Development
100 S. Morgan, Chicago, 60607   243-0249
Coalition of community and citywide organizations and technical assistance providers that promotes economic development in Chicago's low-income neighborhoods.

Fifth City Industrial Promotions
212 S. Kedzie, Chicago, 60624   489-3425
Pushes for new industry on the West Side and greater community input on development issues.

Greater Englewood Local Development Corporation
1249 W. 63rd, Chicago, 60636   925-5332
Commercial, industrial, and housing development in Englewood.

Greater North Pulaski Development Corporation
4054 W. North, Chicago, 60639   384-7074
Industrial and real estate development, exporting assistance, and community development in Humboldt Park, Austin, and Logan Square.

Greater Southwest Development Corporation
2601 W. 63rd, Chicago, 60629   436-1000
Leading economic development group working to spur development on the Southwest Side. Also pushing for a transit line to connect the Loop and the Southwest Side.

Industrial Council of Northwest Chicago
2023 W. Carroll, Chicago, 60612   421-3941
Works for retention and development of businesses on the Northwest Side.

Lawrence Avenue Development Corporation (LADCOR)
4745 N. Kedzie, Chicago, 60625   478-0202
Works with businesses and neighborhoods to preserve and develop communities on the Northwest Side.

LEED Council
1333 N. Kingsbury, Chicago, 60622   266-5401
Employment and economic development organization that helped lead a successful effort to bring planned manufacturing districts (PMDs) to help the North Side retain and attract industry.

Chicago Local Initiatives Support Corporation (LISC)
547 W. Jackson, Chicago, 60661   697-6100
Technical assistance to community development corporations for housing, industrial, and commercial development.

Education

Chicago Panel on Public Schools
Policy and Finance, 220 S. State, #1212, Chicago, 60604 939-2202
Played a major role in school reform movement; initiated "Monitoring School Reform in Chicago" to "assess and report upon changes in student achievement as they occur."

Citizens' Schools Committee
36 S. Wabash, #1202, Chicago, 60603 726-4678
Oldest school reform group in Chicago, started in 1933, that offers advocacy, a citizens' resource center, and training for local school councils.

Citywide Coalition for School Reform
228 S. Wabash, 6th floor, Chicago, 60604 592-6105
Diverse coalition of parents and community activists working with local school councils toward school reform.

Designs for Change
220 S. State, #1900, Chicago, 60604 922-0317
Children's research and advocacy group that plays a major role in the school reform movement.

Parents United for Responsible Education
1145 W. Wilson, #2424, Chicago, 60640 989-6225
Parent advocate group that pushed for the School Reform Act and continues to work for improvements in Chicago public schools.

Environment

Bethel New Life Material Recycling Facility
4746 W. Rice, Chicago, 60651 533-8180
The first material recovery center developed by a nonprofit organization in Chicago.

Chicago Recycling Coalition
c/o Center for Neighborhood Technology
2125 W. North, Chicago, 60647 278-4800
Pushes for reform in city recycling policy and calls for neighborhood-based collecting and processing and economic incentives for waste disposal.

Citizens for a Better Environment
407 S. Dearborn, #1775, Chicago, 60605 939-1530
Fights environmental health threats through research, advocacy, and education; provides technical assistance to community groups.

Community Land Use Network
343 S. Dearborn, #910, Chicago, 60604 285-6606 or 939-7171
Promotes neighborhood control of open-space projects, economic development, housing.

Openlands Project
220 S. State, #1880, Chicago, 60604 427-4256
Membership organization dedicated to protecting open space in northeastern Illinois (public parks, forest preserves, bike trails, etc.).

People for Community Recovery
13116 S. Ellis, Chicago, 60627 468-1645
Well known for work on environmental issues—toxics, hazardous waste—that affect its South Side neighborhood.

The Resource Center
222 E. 135th, Chicago, 60627 821-1351
Nonprofit recycling center with two buyback centers, curbside pickup in several neighborhoods, and two drop-off centers.

South Cook County Environmental Action Coalition
P.O. Box 428317, Evergreen Park, 60647 238-8925
Technical assistance and research for community groups on environmental issues; also educates the community and businesses on alternative waste options.

Uptown Recycling, Inc.
4716 N. Sheridan, Chicago, 60640 769-4488
Community-based recycling on the North Side.

Gay Rights

ACT UP/Chicago 509-6802
Direct-action AIDS advocacy.
(ACT UP stands for the AIDS Coalition to Unleash Power.)

Impact
909 W. Belmont, #201, Chicago, 60657 528-5868
Gay and lesbian advocacy.

Health Care

AIDS Foundation of Chicago
1332 N. Halsted, Chicago, 60622 642-5454 (general information) or 642-3763 (information and Dept. of Rehabilitation Services referrals)
Fund-raising, public policy, and case management.

Health & Medicine Policy Research Group
332 S. Michigan, Chicago, 60604 922-8057
Develops policies and advocates on public health issues.

Lead Elimination Action Drive
1545 W. Morse, Chicago, 60626 973-7888
Coalition of community groups working for prevention, treatment, and reform on lead poisoning issue.

West Side Health Authority
5437 W. Division, Chicago, 60651 378-0233
Coalition spawned from a growing concern about public health issues and the need for national health insurance.

Housing

Chicago Coalition for the Homeless
1325 S. Wabash, Chicago, 60605   435-4548
Feisty coalition that works for housing, jobs, and representation for the more than 50,000 homeless people in Chicago.

Chicago Rehab Network
53 W. Jackson, #742, Chicago, 60604   663-3936
Provides advocacy, technical assistance, support to community-based organizations on low-income housing development issues; also packages multifamily housing loans.

Community Investment Corporation
600 S. Federal, Chicago, 60605   341-0070
Chicago's leading lender in multifamily rehabilitation financing.

18th Street Development Corporation
1839 S. Carpenter, Chicago, 60608   733-2287
Develops townhouses for low-income residents of Pilsen.

Housing Resource Center
4520 N. Beacon, Chicago, 60640   561-3500
Manages scattered-site housing on the North Side, with an emphasis on tenant involvement.

Lakefront SRO Corporation
4946 N. Sheridan, Chicago, 60640   561-0900
Affordable housing for the homeless of Lakeview, Uptown, and Edgewater.

Latin United Community Housing Association
2750 W. North, Chicago, 60647   276-5338
Chicago's only Puerto Rican community housing group, currently in the process of building the first new construction SRO in Chicago in 50 years.

Metropolitan Tenants Organization
3212 N. Broadway, Chicago, 60657   549-1631
Tenants' rights advocates for low-and moderate-income communities.

Neighborhood Housing Services
747 N. May, Chicago, 60622   738-2227
City's largest neighborhood revitalization organization. Rehabs and lends for low-and moderate-income properties.

People's Housing
1607 W. Howard, #207, Chicago, 60626   262-5900
Low-income housing developer in Rogers Park of almost 400 units in 22 buildings; also active on community issues. Has established a unique model for a shared-equity cooperative.

People's Reinvestment and Development Effort (PRIDE)
342 S. Laramie, Chicago, 60644   379-4412
Purchases, rehabs, and manages apartments on the West Side.

Property Management Resource Center
53 W. Jackson, Chicago, 60604   939-7766
Technical assistance, training, and information for managers of low- and moderate-income properties.

Voice of the People
4927 N. Kenmore, Chicago, 60640   769-2442
Community-based, nonprofit developer of affordable housing for families in Uptown and the surrounding area, involving community residents in housing development.

Woodstock Institute
417 S. Dearborn, #400, Chicago, 60605   427-8070
Researches housing issues; very active in fight for reinvestment in low-income communities.

Infrastructure

Neighborhood Capital Budget Group
343 S. Dearborn, #910, Chicago, 60604   939-7171
Coalition of business and community organizations working to change the city's capital spending policies and bring public works improvements to city neighborhoods.

Jobs

Chicago Jobs Council
6 N. Michigan, #1308, Chicago, 60602   782-3803
Only citywide, community-based advocacy organization focusing on employment issues, from the effectiveness of city job programs to the impact of national legislation.

Midwest Center for Labor Research
3411 W. Diversey, #14, Chicago, 60647   278-5418
Research and consulting group that works for unions, community and development organizations, and others on jobs issues.

Latino Groups

Comité Latino
5137 N. Clark, Chicago, 60640   878-8886
Works with other community groups on immigration issues (with an emphasis on labor), education, housing, leadership development.

United Neighborhood Organization of Chicago
125 N. Halsted, Chicago, 60661   441-1300
Primarily Latino group that played a key role in the movement for school reform; also works on naturalization issues. The UNO organizes in southeast Chicago, Back of the Yards, Pilsen/Little Village, and Bucktown/Westtown.

Law Offices

Chicago Lawyers' Committee for Civil Rights under Law, Inc.
185 N. Wabash, #2110, Chicago, 60601   630-9744
Cooperative effort of law firms providing free legal assistance to the poor and
minorities on housing, education, and employment issues.

Community Economic Development Law Project
220 S. State, #300, Chicago, 60604   939-3638
Provides legal counsel and technical assistance to community-based
developers.

Lawyers' Committee for Better Housing
1263 W. Loyola, Chicago, 60626   274-1111
Works closely with community-based groups on a wide range of housing
issues.

Legal Assistance Foundation of Chicago
343 S. Dearborn, Chicago, 60604   341-1070
Still provides services to low-income Chicagoans despite huge cuts in legal
services in the 1980s.

People's Law Office
1180 N. Milwaukee, Chicago, 60622   235-0070

South Chicago Legal Clinic
2938 E. 91st, Chicago, 60617   731-1762
Counsels many community-based organizations on environmental issues.

Neighborhoods

North Side

Concerned Allied Neighbors
2507 N. Greenview, Chicago, 60614   472-1083
Present issues include gangs, housing, community planning, and development.

Edgewater Community Council
1112 W. Bryn Mawr, Chicago, 60660   334-5609
Currently has three key program areas: organizing on crime, housing, and an
emergency food and clothing pantry.

Heart of Uptown Coalition
4409 N. Broadway, Chicago, 60640   769-2087
Coalition working on low-income neighborhood issues in Uptown.

Lakeview Citizens' Council
3245 N. Sheffield, Chicago, 60657   472-4050
Community group that frequently targets issues related to the impact of
Chicago Cubs and Wrigley Field on neighborhood residents and businesses.

The Northwest Community Organization
1109 N. Ashland, Chicago, 60622   276-0211
Assistance in organizing neighborhood groups on local issues, including
housing, crime, community development, energy.

Northwest Neighborhood Federation
4959 W. Belmont, Chicago, 60641   545-9300
Serves eight Northwest Side neighborhoods totaling 25,000 people on neighborhood issues including housing and crime.

Organization of the NorthEast
5121 N. Clark, Chicago, 60640   769-3232
Diverse community organization with expanded goals and constituency through community planning process to form a "multiethnic mixed economic community."

Rogers Park Community Action Network
1545 W. Morse, Chicago, 60626   973-7888
Community group active on housing, crime, and drug issues; formerly the Rogers Park Tenants Committee.

Rogers Park Community Council
1637 W. Morse, Chicago, 60626   764-4326
Older, membership-based community group, working on victim advocacy, housing, youth development.

South Side

Action Coalition of Englewood
6001 S. Justine, Chicago, 60636   471-0080
Provides summer programs for children; works on low-income energy, drug, and housing issues.

Centers for New Horizons
4150 S. King, Chicago, 60653   373-5700
"Human development" agency that provides "womb to the tomb" services at 14 sites for high-risk populations on the South Side. Concerns range from infant mortality and youth services, to family crises and senior outreach.

Chicago Roseland Coalition for Community Control
11015 S. Michigan, Chicago, 60628   264-3500
Community group instrumental in forming the South Side Banking Alliance, a partnership of banks designed to spur on area business; also pushed for reinvestment in low-income housing.

Developing Communities Project
139 E. Kensington, Chicago, 60628   928-2500
Church-based community organization on the far South Side working on education, job training, housing, child welfare, and other issues.

Greater Grand Crossing Organizing Committee
213 E. 79th, Chicago, 60619   846-5552
Currently a West Side community-based group. Recent projects include a voter registration drive, plus work on education, health care, and jobs issues.

Interfaith Community Organization
1641 S. Allport, Chicago, 60608   666-1323
Organizing for improved housing, policing, family issues. Develops housing through a nonprofit development arm, the Pilsen Resurrection Project.

Kenwood-Oakland Community Organization
1238 E. 46th, Chicago, 60653   548-7500
Longtime group that currently emphasizes voter registration, GED program, jobs program, and placement for youth.

The Neighborhood Institute
1750 E. 71st, Chicago, 60649   684-4610
Grass-roots group that is also a community-development corporation (CDC); develops both "human and physical capital" working on neighborhood issues and developing low-income housing.

Pilsen Neighbors Community Council
2026 S. Blue Island, Chicago, 60608   666-2663
Community group working on housing, development of industry, education, senior citizens center, youth issues.

South Chicago Community Committee
9000 S. Buffalo, Chicago, 60617   734-1129
Emphasis on youth issues: crime, drugs, gangs, education.

Southwest Community Congress
2832 W. 63rd, Chicago, 60629   436-6150
Organizes on housing, crime and drugs, education, other community issues.

Southwest Parish and Neighborhood Federation
3302 W. 63rd, Chicago, 60629   776-9522
Anticrime efforts include removing graffiti and working to eliminate drug houses; provides senior citizens with an escort service.

The Woodlawn Organization (TWO)
6040 S. Harper, Chicago, 60637   288-5840
Community group working on crime prevention, education, housing, employment, and other neighborhood issues.

West Side

Bethel New Life, Inc.
367 N. Karlov, Chicago, 60624   826-5540
Multifaceted community-based organization on the West Side that develops housing and offers programs for families and seniors, including employment services.

Interfaith Organizing Project
1617 W. Washington Blvd., Chicago, 60617   243-3328
Near West Side community group that won a breakthrough agreement with the Bulls and Blackhawks to reinvest in the community when a new stadium is built.

Logan Square Neighborhood Association
3321 W. Wrightwood, Chicago, 60647   384-4370
Works to preserve community in a gentrifying neighborhood through efforts on housing, crime, drug, and education issues.

Midwest Community Council
301 N. Kedzie, Chicago, 60612 826-2244
Well-known group that targets key neighborhood issues—infant mortality, housing, health, education, crime.

Northeast Austin Organization
5057 W. North, Chicago, 60639 745-0294
Active community group that works with many others on the West Side; focus includes community policing and neighborhood patrol, youth issues, job readiness and placement, housing, energy programs, health care.

Northwest Austin Council
5758 W. Potomac, Chicago, 60651 379-7822
Works on neighborhood issues, including housing, jobs, crime, and drugs (especially efforts to shut down drug houses).

South Austin Coalition Community Council
5112 W. Washington Blvd., Chicago, 60644 287-4556
Active in many West Side coalitions of community groups; also works on local housing, energy, crime, and drug issues.

West Side Survival Initiative
5323 W. Lake, Chicago, 60644 921-7501
Works for job training programs and opportunities, public welfare.

Organizing

The Gamaliel Foundation
220 S. State, #2026, Chicago, 60604 427-4616
Brings community organizing training to neighborhoods through workshops, leadership development, organizational development.

Midwest Academy
225 W. Ohio, #250, Chicago, 60610 645-6010
Activist training center to teach people to organize for social, political, and economic justice.

National Training and Information Center (NTIC)
810 N. Milwaukee, Chicago, 60622 243-3035
Training and technical assistance for community groups. The NTIC also led the movement for community reinvestment.

Parks

Friends of the Parks
407 S. Dearborn, #1590, Chicago, 60605 922-3307
Parks advocacy group that works with citizen advisory councils in each park district.

Public Interest

Better Government Association
230 N. Michigan, Chicago, 60601 641-1181
Watchdog group that investigates and exposes corruption and inefficiency in government and pushes for reform.

Business and Professional People for the Public Interest
17 E. Monroe, #212, Chicago, 60603 641-5570
Public interest law and policy center that counsels "underrepresented groups" on a variety of issues, including housing, energy, school reform, the environment, children, and family services.

CPAs for the Public Interest
222 S. Riverside Plaza, Chicago, 60606 993-0393
Works to strengthen nonprofit organizations through technical assistance, providing public issue analysis, and short-term accounting assistance.

Illinois Public Action
220 S. State, Chicago, 60604 431-1600
The state's largest public interest organization, working on a wide range of consumer, environmental, and health care issues.

Resources

Center for Neighborhood Technology
2125 W. North, Chicago, 60647 278-4800
Nonprofit technical assistance corporation that works with community groups on issues including energy use, housing development, waste management. Publishes a bimonthly magazine, *The Neighborhood Works*.

Citizens' Information Service
332 S. Michigan, #1142, Chicago, 60604 939-4636
Nonpartisan civic group that encourages citizen participation through information, training, and education.

Community Media Workshop
Malcolm X College
1900 W. Van Buren, Chicago, 60612 942-0909
Assists Chicago community organizations in better communicating their issues and programs in their neighborhood, to both the press and the general public.

Community Renewal Society
332 S. Michigan, #500, Chicago, 60604 427-4830
Urban mission agency dedicated to addressing issues of poverty and racial discrimination. Publications include *The Chicago Reporter* (11 times a year), on race and poverty issues, and *Catalyst* (9 times a year), on Chicago school reform.

Donors Forum of Chicago
53 W. Jackson, #430, Chicago, 60604 431-0260
Information on Chicago's nonprofit organizations, including a library that's open to the public.

Institute of Urban Life
1 E. Superior, Chicago, 60611 787-7525
Researches urban issues; many published works include books on housing, neighborhood revitalization, schools.

Voorhees Center for Urban Economic Development
University of Illinois at Chicago
P.O. Box 4348, Chicago, 60607 996-6671
Research and technical assistance for neighborhoods from the University of
Illinois.

Seniors' Issues

Illinois Alliance for Aging
327 S. LaSalle, #920, Chicago, 60604 922-5890
Membership organization working on issues affecting older adults.

Metro Seniors in Action
220 S. State, Chicago, 60604 341-4733
Coalition of seniors' groups fighting for seniors' rights on transportation,
health care, and more.

Urban Issues

Chicago Urban League
4510 S. Michigan, Chicago, 60653 285-5800
City's oldest and largest race relations agency. Provides "direct service, advocacy, and research activities in areas such as education, employment and
empowerment."

Clergy and Laity Concerned (CALC)
166 W. Washington, #300, Chicago, 60602 899-1800
Well known in the 1960s for its work against the Vietnam War. Now focuses
on issues related to racism, especially institutional racism.

Jewish Council on Urban Affairs (JCUA)
220 S. State, #1910, 60604 663-0960
Educates and mobilizes the Jewish constituency on urban issues and curriculum for religious schools. Also involved in low-income housing development and outreach on social and economic justice issues.

Operation PUSH
930 E. 50th, Chicago, 60615 373-3366
Civil rights organization.
(PUSH stands for People United to Save Humanity.)

Utilities

Citizens Utility Board (CUB)
208 S. LaSalle, Chicago, 60601 263-4282
Works for better utility company policies and rates, more citizen input.

Labor Coalition on Public Utilities
204 S. Ashland, Chicago, 60607 243-7172
Union-based coalition that advocates against Com Ed rate hikes, nuclear
reactor construction, safety issues, and more.

Voting

Project LEAP Educational & Research Fund
22 W. Monroe, Chicago, 60603 726-3954
Election reform and monitoring group.
(LEAP stands for Legal Elections in All Precincts.)

Project VOTE Illinois
332 S. Michigan, 5th floor, Chicago, 60604 986-8229
Voter registration in low-income and minority communities.

Welfare Issues

Public Welfare Coalition
100 S. Morgan, Chicago, 60607 829-5568
Policy analysis, advocacy, and public education on public aid issues.

Women's Issues

Chicago Foundation for Women
230 W. Superior, 4th floor, Chicago, 60610 266-1176
Largest and most comprehensive philanthropic women's organization in Chicago.

Chicago Women in Trades
37 S. Ashland, Chicago, 60607 942-1444
Support and advocacy for women wanting to get into and remain in non-traditional jobs. Programs target leadership development and preapprenticeship training. Offers a job hot line.

Midwest Women's Center
828 S. Wabash, #200, Chicago, 60605 922-8530
Recruitment, assessment, and training of women for the workplace.

Women United for a Better Chicago
1325 S. Wabash, #305, Chicago, 60605 939-3636
Multiracial coalition advocating for women in areas of health, housing, and leadership development.

Women's Self-Employment Project
166 W. Washington, #730, Chicago, 60602 606-8255
Programs to encourage and develop innovative, entrepreneurial businesses owned and managed by women.

SUGGESTED READING

Chicago: City of Neighborhoods, Histories, and Tours by Dominic Pacyga and Ellen Skerrett.

Cold Anger by Mary Larkin.

Corrective Capitalism: The Rise of America's Community Development Corporations by Neil R. Peirce and Carol F. Steinbach.

The Dynamics of Organizing by Shel Trapp (available through the National Training and Information Center).

Let Them Call Me Rebel: Saul Alinsky, His Life and Legacy by Sanford Horwitt.

The Local Community Fact Book by William Erbe, Project Director (published by the University of Illinois at Chicago).

Organizing for Change: A Manual for Activists in the 1990s by Kim Bobo, Jackie Kendall, and Steve Max.

A People's History of the United States by Howard Zinn.

Reveille for Radicals, and *Rules for Radicals* by Saul Alinsky.

Savage Inequalities by Jonathan Kozol.

There Are No Children Here by Alex Kotlowitz.

Who Will Tell the People? by William Greider.

—Dan Baron

CONTRIBUTORS

Michael C. Armijo (Radio) is a recent arrival to Chicago and is still learning about it. He's a physical chemist by training and enjoys stained glass, farming, theology, beer, and baseball.

Dan Baron (Activism) is a writer specializing in community issues. While working in the fast-paced world of public relations, he ran out of positive things to say about kitty litter, dental implants, and other marketable products. He has been writing about community issues ever since.

Anne Basye (Kids) is a writer and editor who has lived in Chicago for nine years, five of them with her son Alexander. In Chicago, she has found the city, the neighborhood, and the good friends she only dreamed of when she was growing up in California's Central Valley. She would like to thank Peggy, Roman, Chloe, and Gwen Zabicki for sharing their favorite South Side kid spots with readers of *Sweet Home Chicago*.

Kathie Bergquist (Lesbians) is a semi-professional socializer who supports her social habits by working at Women and Children First Bookstore and writing the column "Kathie Klub" for *Chicago Nightlines*, as well as other freelance writing work. She has three ambitions in life: to make a living off of writing, to become an expatriate living in Amsterdam, and to be the all-time video champion of "America's Funniest Home Videos." Kathie dedicates her contribution in this book to her mom, Chance, and Jenny, her faithful dog.

Ann Boyd (Dance) has choreographed and danced in Chicago for the past four years. She was a member of Mordine and Company for two years and is currently a member of the Organic Theater Greenhouse Collective.

Linda Bubon (Crisis Intervention, general contributor) spends her time promoting, performing, and selling the best in women's and children's literature and raising her six-year-old son. She has been active in the women's community in Chicago for the past 15 years and is the co-owner of Women and Children First bookstore.

Prathima Christdas (Outdoors, Seniors) moved to Chicago in 1990 from Santa Cruz, California, and was pleasantly surprised to find hills and forests within driving distance of Chicago, instead of the unbroken vista of cornfields that her friends had told her to expect. When she's not hiking or checking out places to hike in the wilderness, she is a linguist. She has written a book on the sound system of Tamil, a language spoken in India and Ceylon.

As co-owner of Women and Children First bookstore and member of WRAGE, her women's book group, **Ann Christopherson** (Crisis Intervention, general contributor) spends much of her time reading and talking about books. Most of the rest of it goes to cavorting with friends and loved ones, playing basketball, and supporting feminist and lesbian/gay political and cultural work.

Julie DeLong (The Environment/Recycling) is an environmental activist who lives to hike and camp. She would like to thank her information sources: Chicago Recycling Coalition, City of Chicago, Earth Day Chicago, Karyn Roggatz, U.S. Environmental Protection Agency, and all the environmental organizations that sent her literature regarding their work.

Cynthia Gordon (Neighborhoods, Country Music) has lived everywhere in Chicago. She is a number cruncher by day and spends her evenings at blues and jazz clubs. She enjoys all the good things in life: cooking, traveling, and playing the sax.

Mark Guncheon (Film) is the owner and president of All My Features, Inc., an information services company he founded in 1983 which, among other features, produces movie reviews heard in more than 65 cities in the U.S. A freelance writer and author, Guncheon fulfilled his boyhood dream by managing the Parkway Theatre in Chicago and the Varsity Theatre in Evanston, showing classic films on a daily and three-times weekly basis. He is married to Blair, and they are the parents of two great little boys, Cooper and Norris. Guncheon has been a Cubs fan since 1953.

Anthony Hurtig (Architecture, Restaurants and Cafes) is a freelance architect in Chicago and cofounder of the Asymptote Design Group. Although he has a master's degree in architecture and a bachelor's degree in philosophy, he has recently realized that in order to live in the manner to which he is willing to become accustomed (which includes frequenting the establishments listed in the restaurant chapter), he may have to go back to school to get yet another degree in a more lucrative field.

Michael Hush (Nightlife) is that guy you always see out at bars and parties, and have no doubt admired from a distance. His writing career, which began with such glittering promise, has lately seen him penning chewing gum commercials at a large advertising agency. In order to write the "Nightlife" chapter, Michael spent long stretches in drinking establishments, an activity that he later described to his accountant as "research."

Hugh Iglarsh (Theater) has been reviewing plays for *NewCity*, a local weekly, for several years. He is an ex-English major who in real life edits *The Ragan Report*, a weekly newsletter on organizational communication. He'd like to acknowledge his wife Lisa, who has been a boon companion during many of those risky moments known as opening night.

Julie Johnson (Neighborhoods) is a Chicago writer, part-time housewife, all-the-time mother of one, and urban activist.

Pat Ladd (Sports, Fitness) is a die-hard Cubs fan and amateur sports aficionado when not in training to become a special education teacher.

Laura E. Larson (Religion, Physical Health), a card-carrying member of the Cubs die-Hard Fan Club, runs Nik's Great Leap for Words from her home in Evanston. Religious experiences occur regularly for her in the form of long runs, Coffee Heath Bar Crunch ice cream, and cross-country car trips. Loving thanks to her Zen mechanic and favorite brother Larry for his help with "Religion," among other things.

Jim Alexander Newberry (photographer) is a freelance photographer who regularly contributes to *The Reader* and *NewCity*. He has also been published in the *Chicago Tribune, Sun-Times, Musician* magazine, and *Hot Bike*.

Mark Noble (Neighborhoods) is a Freudian existentialist who likes cooking and critical theory though practices neither as an ideology. He recently completed his master's thesis on the subject of reification, but he can't decide what to call it. His thanks to Anne Pearson for her expertise on Hyde Park and its environs.

Kelly O'Rourke (Transportation, Employment) is a native of Chicago and the former editor of the executive business monthly, *Commerce* magazine. Her work has appeared in *Cosmopolitan,* the *Chicago Tribune, Central Florida Magazine, Stagebill,* and internationally for *Cosmopolitan* in Greece and in Spain. Kelly has also written for television and the big screen in Los Angeles, but she says "Chicago is a *real* city. L.A. is a warped suburb."

Judith A. Ponticell (Chicago Schools) was a professor at the College of Education at the University of Illinois at Chicago and was active in Chicago's education reform movement until her recent move to work in education in Texas.

Seven-year Chicago resident and promoter, **Joelle Rabion** (Art, Photography) is an avid arts enthusiast and advocate, free-lance writer, translator, art dealer, and cat lover.

Patricia M. Ruch (Local Press) arrived in Chicago on a "Today" show assignment one January and vowed to find a way to return. She is a freelance writer working in the marketing, advertising, and public relations community.

June Skinner Sawyers (Folk Music) is an editor and freelance writer. She is the author of *Chicago Portraits: Biographies of 250 Famous Chicagoans* and with Sue Telingator the coauthor of *The Chicago Arts Guide.*

Genevieve Sedlack (Late Night and All Night, Secondhand Shopping, Volunteering), 24, is a struggling freelance writer this time around. She has a passion for passion, black-and-white movies, and the saxophone; thinks life's best teacher is experience and laughter is humankind's best medicine; and believes Yeats had the right idea: history is a spiraling mess and we're all in it together. She is grateful to her friends and fellow adventurers scattered around the globe and plans to live in Buenos Aires someday.

Bob Skolnick (Legal Services) is a freelance writer who while taking a year off from law school decided it was more interesting to write about the law than to study it.

When not scouring Chicago's better bars and clubs for that perfect vodka tonic or that perfect man, **Ellen Snook** (Nightlife) spends most of her time writing press releases about America's number two coffee liqueur and beef carcasses for a "food-focused" advertising agency. In her spare time, she tutors a Polish immigrant in English, rides her bike along the lakefront, and avoids Cubs fans like the plague.

Lee Swets (Rock) has lived and played music in Chicago for 12 years. He wanted to do the "Eating" chapter (his first Chicago love), but the editor politely declined the offer.

Blair Thomas (Performance Art) is a puppeteer and director with Redmoon Theater. He also teaches in the Time Arts Department at the School of the Art Institute of Chicago.

Deborah R. Weiner (The Other Top Ten Sights, Literary Life, Museums) is a freelance writer and editor who works primarily with community-based organizations. Her peripatetic career as organizer, writer, and editor has taken her all the way from Chicago to Joliet and back. She really did take a canoe trip down the Chicago River and nearly got tossed overboard at Monroe Street when a curious Wendella boat came a little too close.

Ray Wilding-White (Classical Music, Jazz, Blues and the Avant-Garde, Gospel, Ethnic, and More), a pupil of Aaron Copland, is a composer, writer, and photographer. He has over a 150 musical works to his name and in 1991 had his violin concerto premiered in Grant Park. Earlier this year, he prepared a 14-part series of one-hour programs focusing on music in Chicago. Formerly a jazz pianist, arranger, and teacher, he now writes articles, toils on his first book, and most recently, presented a memoriam to John Cage on WFMT-FM.

Katherine Willhoite (Mental Health, Crisis Intervention), managing editor for Contemporary Books, Inc., has lived in Chicago since 1981.

D'Andre Willis (Architecture) is an architect practicing in Chicago with Nagle, Hartray, and Associates and is a cofounder of the Asymptote Design Group. She is an ardent urbanist whose interests also include furniture design and construction, painting, and baseball. In a past life she played blues guitar, yet she doesn't regret being born a Hoosier in this one. Her favorite space in Chicago is the plaza of the Federal Center followed closely by the end of the couch with her cats, Lilly and Detroit.

Rex Wockner (Gay Men) is a staff reporter for *Outlines* and *Nightlines*. He also writes a weekly *Nightlines* column, "Boys Town." His news reports are syndicated to 40 gay newspapers across the United States and in 10 other countries.

Rodd Zolkos (Chicago Politics) is a Chicago journalist who reports on government and public policy issues across the country. He's been known to claim Chicago is the greatest city in the world, usually following a weekend lakefront stroll with his weimaraners, Clancy and Jiggs.

INDEX